December 2009

Dear Cara —

For our favorite actor!

Hope to see you in a play
sometime soon.

Love,

Aunt Connie, Uncle Rick
+ Tom

THEATRE
FOR
CHILDREN

THEATRE FOR CHILDREN

Fifteen Classic Plays

Coleman A. Jennings,
Editor

St. Martin's Press ⚄ New York

www.stmartins.com

ISBN 0-312-33639-X
EAN 978-0-312-33639-4

First Edition: June 2005

10 9 8 7 6 5 4 3 2 1

Dedicated to the memory of Lowell Swortzell
1930–2004
professor, playwright, colleague, and friend

Grateful Acknowledgment Is Made To:

Lola H. Jennings, my wife

The Houston Endowment, Inc., for support from the Jesse H. Jones Professorship in Fine Arts, Department of Theatre and Dance, The University of Texas at Austin.

Anchorage Press Plays for permission to reprint *Bless Cricket, Crest Toothpaste and Tommy Tune* by Linda Daugherty; *Ezigbo, The Spirit Child* by Max Bush and Adaora Nzelibe Schmiedl and *The Wolf and Its Shadows* by Sandra Fenichel Asher.

Casarotto Ramsay Associates Limited and Samuel French for permission to reprint *The Witches* by David Wood.

The Children's Theatre Company (Minneapolis) for permission to reprint *Dr. Seuss' How the Grinch Stole Christmas* by Timothy Mason and Mel Marvin.

Dramatic Publishing for permission to reprint *Braille: The Early Life of Louis Braille* by Lola H. and Coleman A. Jennings; *Country Mouse and the Missing Lunch Mystery* by Sandra Fenichel Asher; *Mississippi Pinocchio* by Mary Hall Surface and David Maddox; *Two Donuts* by José Cruz González; and *A Village Fable* by James Still.

Faber and Faber and Samuel French, Inc. for permission to reprint *Ernie's Incredible Illucinations* by Alan Ayckbourn.

Houghton Mifflin and The Joyce Ketay Agency for permission to reprint *The Witch of Blackbird Pond* by Y York.

Little House Heritage Trust, Noel L. Silverman and Laurie Brooks for permission to reprint *A Laura Ingalls Wilder Christmas* by Laurie Brooks.

Playwrights Canada Press for permission to reprint *Inuk and the Sun* by Henry Beissel.

Samuel French, Inc. for permission to reprint *The Great Gilly Hopkins* by David Paterson and Steve Liebman.

Contents

Foreword

A Conversation Between Peter Brosius
and Coleman A. Jennings

The foreword to this anthology is based on an extensive conversation about children and theatre between Peter Brosius, artistic director of the Children's Theatre Company in Minneapolis, and the editor in May 2004. The editor's comments and Brosius's reactions were transcribed from a voice recorder and edited for clarity.

The Children's Theatre Company (CTC) is recognized as one of the leading theatres for young people and families in North America as well as a major cultural and artistic resource in Minneapolis. Founded in 1965, CTC has set a standard for excellence in theatre for young people, the development of new works, and arts education. In 1997, Peter C. Brosius joined CTC as the theatre's third artistic director, and Managing Director Teresa Eyring joined the theatre in 1999. Together they have led the CTC staff and board in redefining the role of the theatre and its work.

CTC is located on a campus in south Minneapolis along with the Minneapolis Institute of Arts and the Minneapolis College of Art and Design. It operates in a 60,000-square-foot facility built in 1974 and has a 746-seat performance space. During its thirty-year existence over six million children and adults have seen CTC productions. Nearly two-thirds of the public performances are sold out. Typically, more than 283,000 people attend over 390 performances each year.

CTC raised $20.5 million, including $5 million in state bonding funds, for its expansion and renovation project. Highlights of the expansion include a new 288-seat theatre, which is designed specifically for teens and preschool children, as well as a classroom and rehearsal space. The expansion and renovation was the first for the CTC facility since it was built in 1974. CTC no longer has to turn away hundreds of children from education programs due to lack of adequate space. The expansion also allowed CTC to increase its focus on education and its reach into the greater Minnesota community, both of which are fundamental priorities.

The operating budget for 2004 was $8.3 million, with 55 percent from ticket sales and earned revenue. The remainder came from gifts, grants and endowments. National supporters include the Shubert Foundation, AT&T, the Rockefeller Foundation, the Pew Charitable Trusts and the National Endowment for the Arts.

Stephen Kinzer, national correspondent for *The New York Times*, has written that the Children's Theatre Company is "one of those cultural nuggets you come upon in unexpected parts of the country."

At CTC Brosius has directed *Mississippi Panorama*, *Green Eggs and Ham*, *The Old Man Who Loved Cheese*, *A Village Fable*, *Whale*, *Afternoon of the Elves*, *Boundless Grace*, *Dragonwings*, *The Snow Queen*, *Amber Waves* and *The Magic Mrs. Piggle Wiggle*. Previously, he was the artistic director of the Honolulu Theatre for Youth (HTY). During his tenure at HTY the theatre was invited to the Kennedy Center's New Voices/New Visions Festival and Robert Red-ford's Utah Sundance Playwrights Laboratory and was the first professional U.S. theatre company to perform in the Marshall Islands with support from the Rockefeller Foundation. He directed world premier productions by James Still and Velina Hasu Houston as well as the American professional premiers of Dockteatern Tittu of Stockholm. He also produced American premiers of celebrated theatre artists C. P. Taylor, Volker Ludwig and others.

Before his work at HTY Brosius was the Artistic Director of the Improvisational Theatre Project of the Mark Taper Forum in Los Angeles where he commissioned and directed numerous world premiers by authors such as Lisa Loomer, Erin Cressida Wilson and Peter Mattei as well as the U.S. premiers of *One Thousand Cranes* by Colin Thomas, *Stamping, Shouting and Singing Home* by Lisa Evans, and *Robinson and Crusoe* by Teatro Dell Angollo. At the Taper he also directed numerous productions for the Taper's New Work Festival and for its main stage.

In addition Brosius has directed at theatres across the country including South Coast Repertory, Arizona Theatre Company, South Street Theatre on Theatre Row, the Kennedy Center for the Performing Arts and Off-Broadway for Pan Asian Repertory. He has also spent many years as a director-in-residence at the Sundance Playwrights Laboratory.

For almost thirty years Broadway has acknowledged that great theatre happens nationwide, not just in New York, by giving an annual Regional Theatre Tony Award. In 2003, the Children's Theatre Company received a Tony Award for sustained artistic excellence and contributions to the field nationally—one of the best professional regional theatres in the United States. It was the first Tony ever awarded to a children's theatre. By coincidence the same year, the production of *A Year with Frog and Toad* moved from CTC to Broadway where it received three Tony nominations, including one for best musical. Although not developed through CTC's established production process, the musical, having been first staged at CTC, raised the national prominence of the Children's Theatre Company.

Peter, who is married to playwright Rosanna Staffa and is the father of daughter Daria and son Gabriel, is also the recipient of numerous other awards including Theatre Communications Group's Alan Schneider Directors' Award and honors from the Los Angeles Drama Critic's Circle Awards, Dramalogue and the Children's Theatre Foundation of America.

While visiting with him during the run of his production of *The Magic Mrs. Piggle Wiggle,* the editor discovered an exuberant, passionate Brosius who spoke both as a theatre professional and parent.

How did you become involved in theatre for young audiences?

I grew up as a theatre person and always felt so lucky to be part of this field. The people who have inspired me most in the field of theatre for young people were those artists in Europe who broke such new ground with their work for young people, challenging them, engaging them and respecting them so much. I was so fortunate to see the work of artists like Volker Ludwig, Ad de Bont, C.P. Taylor, Teatro members of *Dell Angollo* and others. They believe tremendously in the power of the theatre. They make work that is theatrical, on the side of young people, and beautifully done.

What is a highlight of your experience as an undergraduate at Hampshire College in Amherst, Massachusetts?

I had a great time at Hampshire. There were three highlights—one was my introduction to the amazing new work for young people happening in Germany by Jack Zipes, who was a colleague of one of my professors. I was able to read his translations of work hot off the press and direct U.S. premiers of this new work by the GRIPS Theatre. I also got to learn about the history of political theatre in the U.S. through a grant from the college which allowed me funds to do research at the Library of the Performing Arts at Lincoln Center, and then, turn that research into a course and a film/lecture series on political theatre, both contemporary and historical. What was really great about the college was that it was cross-disciplinary. I started doing dance, and regularly the dancers, the sculptors and the-atre people all worked together. Those things that can be so problematic in some institutions—dancers in one place, sculptor's studio in another, theatre people in other spaces weren't that way when I was at Hamp-shire.

And a memorable event during your graduate work at New York University?

The opening night of my thesis project, after three long and grueling years in the MFA Directing Program. I had directed Dario Fo's *Accidental Death of an Anarchist*, and as it sometimes happens, it seemed to come to-gether. The audience responded and at the end, I was celebrating and be-ing congratulated by fellow students, audience members and actors. Out of the corner of my eye I saw the Chair of the Department, Carl Weber, gesturing to me to come over. I did. He leaned in to me and said "Peter, don't always believe the audience." Now after three intense years and one billion dollars of debt, I thought I would explode on this seemingly grand opening night of my final show. But as harsh as it was to hear that night, it was an incredible gift: don't always believe the audience when they love it; don't always believe the audience when they loathe it; make sure that you are the toughest critic, the harshest judge of your own work. It is a lesson I never forgot.

How has the mission statement of CTC evolved since your becoming Artistic Director?

Recently we went through a major revisiting of the theatre's mission. We spent a lot of time with the entire board and the entire staff in articulating values that we feel challenged by every day. Ones we should live by every day, a vision of ourselves that I think is important. The mission statement is quite different than it used to be. Today, it states the following:

MISSION, VISION, AND VALUES

Mission

The Children's Theatre Company exists to create extraordinary theatre experiences that educate, challenge and inspire young people.

Vision

The Children's Theatre Company seeks to be an international model for excellence in theatre. We strive to lead in the creation of new work for young people, in theatre training and in generating initiatives for using theatre in education and community development.

The Children's Theatre Company will create an urban cultural center for young people and families, where theatre is the centerpiece, out of which emerge programs and activities celebrating diverse art forms, ideas and cultures. We will utilize the power of theatre to open discussion, touch hearts and question accepted notions.

Values: We believe

Young people embody complex realities, imagination and possibility, and their concerns must be central to our programming choices.

Young people have the power to know the world and transform it.

The mentoring of young people is a key responsibility of the Children's Theatre Company.

We are part of a larger world, and our theatre has a responsibility to illuminate connections, build bridges and celebrate diverse cultures.

Theatre must encourage the power of imagination and critical thinking.

Artists must be valued and provided with the tools to achieve excellence and realize their vision.

We do our best work when all are involved as collaborators in the pursuit of the artistic vision.

We must be attentive stewards of our resources.

We must embrace the fundamental attributes of young people: curiosity, risk taking, candor and imagination.

Education is certainly important, but I assume that your first goal is not to educate, but to entertain in the true sense of the word, "To gain and hold attention."

We do not see ourselves as curriculum or pedagogically driven. We see ourselves driven by the needs and challenges of young people and the vision and imagination of artists. This is a complex balancing act because sometimes these two come together gorgeously, and other times it is an extraordinary struggle to create work that inhabits fully both of these passions. We also hope and encourage artists who work with us to find their own incredible joy and excitement in creating work for this audience—to be of generous spirit and an ally of young people.

For me, plays that have education as their primary goal seldom exemplify good dramatic literature.

If you don't have a great story with great characters, you don't have a great play.

How then is CTC involved in education?

We are dedicated to education and community partnerships and building relationships with teachers, schools and our community. The power of theatre is used to develop critical thinking and self-confidence as well as to engage the imagination. CTC's Neighborhood Bridges program is perhaps the clearest example of our philosophy in action. Developed by Jack Zipes and now in seventeen classrooms year round it is an in-depth residency program dedicated to creating critical literacy. It places the intelligence and imagination of the child at the center of the work. It uses storytelling as a leaping off place for young people to think critically and then, create their stories that get turned into plays, into books and into an understanding, an experience in which you can take ownership of the narrative of your life. In addition CTC's Theatre Arts Training (TAT) Program provides extraordinary, in-depth training that is not necessarily geared to train future actors but to develop confident people who understand the power of working together to achieve success. Each year 800 students, ages eight to eighteen, take part in this training. Fully-staged productions for students in the TAT intensive included *Cabaret, A Streetcar Named Desire, One Flew Over the Cuckoo's Nest* and *Chicago*. This work is built through an intensive process of deep understanding of the stakes of these characters and the given circumstances of the world of the play, as well as through improvisations specifically geared to letting these student actors connect viscerally to the issues and ideas of the text. Advanced students also have the opportunity to participate in all aspects of mounting a production—from lights, to sound, to stage management, etc.

We offer other opportunities for teens as well. We have developed the idea of The Collective which has been created as a laboratory for ensemble-created work. We have brought in nationally renowned hip hop artist Will Power to work with young people on creating new work in a hip hop aesthetic. We have worked with dancers and spoken word artists like Toki Wright and Leah Nelson to have students create their own spoken word pieces. We have created a Council where teen artists read scripts we are considering. They advise us on our education programs, help design graphics for our teen shows, challenge and inspire us.

In addition we also have an extraordinary program for young people ages eight to twelve as well. This work is dedicated to young people creating their own work inspired by a theme, a period, an issue. We have done everything from the Ballet Russe, to child labor, the Leadbelly and the blues to the folktales from the Weimar Republic and the music of Eisler. Recently CTC's junior conservatory participated in the Eleventh Symposium of the International Brecht Society as the only American theatre and only children's theatre selected. They performed an original theatre piece at the GRIPS Theater in Berlin. Additionally, 75,000 children attend special matinees each year, and we conduct free teacher workshops. Each year we select a number of schools in Minneapolis and St. Paul to be part of our School Partnership Program that provides free tickets, free buses, free workshops and study materials for several shows a year.

One of our favorite partnerships is with our local elementary school, the Whittier Community School for the Arts. It is a neighborhood school and one with a largely new immigrant population. Each year we partner with the school to have the students see our plays, and then, we choose one in particular for a special Whittier Night. First, the children see the play, then they create art pieces and writing in response to the play, and we turn our lobby into an art gallery. We invite the families of the children and the staff to be our guests, so that they not only see the play but also are welcomed to the theatre by their young artists and a beautiful display of the students' art filling the lobby.

Have you always cast age appropriate actors in the roles of children and young people?

No. In directing in New York, Los Angeles and Hawaii I used only adults for the young characters, so casting age appropriate young people in the children's roles was new to me. Once I started here at CTC, I didn't make it a rule one way or the other—we leave the casting decisions entirely up to the director. If the character is written as seven, a ten- or eleven-year-old child might play it. The playwright's designation of age seven does not in casting equal seven, for us seven equals young person. We are talking about playable age.

I have found that something quite extraordinary, something rather magical can happen in mixed casts of adults and young people. The mentoring by the adult actors, the respect for discipline, and the professional preparation they bring to their work can be truly inspiring for the young actors. The energy, enthusiasm and dedication of the student actors is equally bracing for the adults. There is a moment in *The Magic Mrs. Piggle Wiggle*, a tiny moment in the choreography of one number in which the group of children are frustrated by constant rain. In searching through improvisations for the best way to express the frustration of the young people, the choreographer had all of the cast, both students and professionals, take a pillow and use it as a tool to express their frustration. The students were throwing the pillow and whacking the ground when suddenly, one of our adult actors who is playing one of the children took the pillow, threw it on the ground, and then leapt insanely high into the air to come crashing down upon and crushing that pillow on the floor. We thought he was going to break every bone in his body. The whole room went, "Whoa." I thought this is a teaching moment for these students—a moment of a startling actor commitment in which his brave gesture expressed extraordinary character frustration. It's not a huge moment, but for the young actors in the room it was a tiny moment of seeing the depth of commitment, the risk, the daring to create a startling stage image that expressed that frustration indelibly. It was just mentoring by example.

Again, casting young people is not a requirement of our theatre. However, one of my most moving stories is when I did *Dragonwings* here with an older professional cast. Adults played all the leads, but because we are also a teaching institution, I wanted a chorus of young people, actors who enhanced the story through Chinese water dances, flag dances—all elements of Beijing Opera. Our designers and choreographer explained every aspect of the production, from research of Chinese art, Chinese culture, to the racism that many Chinese immigrants encounter when they first came to America. The children, including a number of Asian-Americans, were learning from some of the major Asian-American actors in this country as they discussed the differences in acting in film, television and theatre, as well as what it is like to be an Asian-American actor working in the profession. Encounters of type casting and racist attitudes were also explored. This sharing by the adult professionals about their lives and experiences was their idea. I set up the design presentations, but the actors did the rest. Their generosity was an incredible gift for the kids. From mentors who love the theatre, they learned some of the realities of theatre and of life from their unique and critical perspective.

When Tazewell Thompson came to direct *Stamping, Shouting & Singing Home*, a story of segregation in the Deep South that includes a policeman's offstage shooting of a little girl, we had a very fascinating experience. He said, "I know you sometimes cast young people, but this material is extremely emotional—like Antigone. I think it is perhaps just too powerful for young actors."

"Fine," I said, "but do me a favor. I have two young women I want you to see. You don't have to use them, but I very much want you to see them."

The two young women, ages twelve and fourteen, were truly extraordinary actors. I was not in the audition room, but I was there when Tazewell came out and said that there was something so vulnerable and real and powerful about these words coming out of the mouths of these young people. He said he couldn't see it with any other actors. He cast those two student actors and created a truly powerful piece of theatre.

Within the profession there is disparity of opinions concerning child actors.

True.

What do you think?

We are looking for, talking about children who are really talented. Not the stereotyped child actor who has been well trained, technically, but has no honesty. There are kids who are professional and others who are "child actor" charmers. Rather than charm we look for authenticity, realness, for truth.

It's interesting that in children's dramatic literature the majority of the protagonists are not young children, but adolescents or older.

We have produced plays with kids of many different ages. In *Amber Waves*, the story of a farm family trying to keep their financial troubles from their two children, the daughter is twelve and the son, sixteen. *Snapshot Silhouette*, about the tensions between African-American and Somali immigrant children in our own neighborhood, has a wide mix of ages. Many of our pieces feature characters of substantially different age groups.

Older actors play the younger characters. In your production of Lilly's Purple Plastic Purse, *how did the audiences respond to them?*

What I find is that there really is no problem whatsoever with older actors playing younger characters. If the actor is alive and vital and present, the audience will respond and follow him or her anywhere regardless of the actor's age.

The suspension of disbelief is unmistakable in an audience of children.

Yes, indeed. One of my favorite stories. We had an actor who weighed at least 190 pounds and was over six feet tall playing Benjamin, the very young protagonist of *The Yellow Boat*. After a performance, this child came up to the actor and looked at his shoes, size twelve, and said: "You have really big feet for a third grader." "Yes, I do, but I am thirty years old." The child was not dissuaded. As he had known him onstage as Benjamin, he still couldn't accept that Benjamin's feet could be that big.

If the characters are truthfully portrayed, why should he believe otherwise?

That's right. Isn't that fantastic? That's why this theatre is so much fun.

In our production of Yankee Doodle *at the University of Texas there was a moment when the actors' opening of red fans represented the burgeoning of apples. For the children they were not fans but apples. Some of the adults were not certain.*

The children thrill to such creativity—which is why theatre is such a fantastic form. They love it. That is what they do all the time—they take a cup and change it into a spyglass, a hat, a shoe, a tower. They are happily involved with transformation, in metaphor, in play daily. It is an essential part of who they are and how they make and remake their world.

Once in the theatre how long can we hold the children's attention?

We don't have time limits at CTC. We have produced plays that lasted fifty minutes to ones that were two-and-a-half hours long. Frankly, if it's good work, the playing time is immaterial.

Yet, the majority of the published scripts have a playing time of an hour to an hour-ten-or-fifteen.

Playing times have nothing to do with the reality of children's attention spans or their ability to comprehend. Time limits have repeatedly been determined by school and bus company schedules.

Some playwrights write specifically to fit into the school time frame, while others state that sixty minutes, more or less, is exactly what they needed to tell the story.

My hope is that the professional children's theatres, the Children's Theatre Company, Seattle Children's Theatre, the Coterie, the Dallas Children's Theatre, Child's Play, and many, many others, will, hopefully lead the way in changing the thinking and to allow us all, playwrights and producers, to tell the story that needs to be told in whatever time it takes to tell it. I don't think any playwright wants to create the Haiku or abridged version of their story.

We do have many remarkable plays, all created within time limits.

You can do good work in that time, but it's harder—it's a trickier equation. Some plays need only fifty minutes. *Lilly's Purple Plastic Purse* works in that time frame. There are other pieces that simply take longer. I continue to hope that playwrights, directors, producers and school administrators will all fight to tell the tale that needs to be told, specific to that piece of theatre.

What about intermissions?

For the longer productions we have intermissions.

And for the daytime school performances?

Since our schools, administrators and teachers don't require that the children be back at a certain time, we have intermissions as needed. We share the specifics of the play with the schools and tell them the length of the production. There is never a question about when the children have to return. We are lucky that this is a long established operating procedure of this organization. Everyone, first and foremost, asserts the value of the theatrical experience.

How do you promote and advertise your productions to school staff and teachers?

A great thing about CTC is the fact that the theatre has been in existence so long. People know the work. We have so many who simply sign up regardless of what we are producing. They come back because of the consistent quality of the work. We generally do not have a problem in marketing either to the public or the schools. Of course, there are many who choose very specific titles and base their selection only on what the titles are that we are offering.

Every year we send a season's brochure and postcards describing each production directly to the schools. Reservations begin arriving soon after.

How do you help the teachers and children prepare for attending the production?

Like most of our colleagues we do extensive study guides. We work very closely with a very talented education writer and a group of teacher/advisors to make our materials dynamic, imaginative and useful. However, it is important to note that theatre going is a very established part of life here in Minnesota. We never do curtain speeches describing how we expect children to behave in the theatre. We see that as the work of the play. It is simply our job to create theatre that is vivid and captivating. If the audience talks or is disconnected, it is not their fault, it is ours. Whenever we have student actors in age appropriate roles in our productions, we invite their teachers to a technical or final dress rehearsal as a thank you and as a way for them to understand our educational goals while seeing the play. With a large cast we might have fifty teachers involved. In this age of standardized testing and school attendance requirements there are difficult challenges in getting the students excused from their classes to perform in our productions. We make certain that the local principals and classroom teachers understand the educational benefits of their students being cast. From rehearsals to performances they learn a whole set of skills that are extraordinary.

What types of pre-show or classroom activities do you have for the children?

For the schools we haven't chosen to do major pre-show work. We have wrestled mightily. Well, not mightily. We wrestled a bit. I wish that we had wrestled mightily in trying to meet the challenge. We haven't the staff to conduct such a major undertaking.

But you do have study guides, that is teacher/parent resource packets?

Certainly. Study Guides—Family Guides—are available for each production. These include a full synopsis, a bibliography, a videography, exercises, games, tools to inspire discussion pre- and post-show. Suggestions of other organizations for the school or parent to explore for further depth, and further connection to the subjects explored in the play. I also believe that we are the only theatre in the country to offer family guides— guides designed specifically for families to let them deepen and extend their theatre experience. It offers many of the same things as the study guide and is sent to subscribers and all who ask and are on our Web site.

And what about after the production, the post-show activities?

My problem with post-show question-and-answer sessions began in the adult theatre. There was always the not terribly enlightened guy who dominated the entire session. I was always upset by the fact that the audience left the theatre not thinking about the production and its ideas but the comments of one or two audience members.

When I arrived at CTC, one of my first orders of business was to try to kill the post-show activities. I wanted the audience to leave with the theatrical experience, not "How long did it take to learn your lines?" "How much money do you make?" "How did the fire come out of the well?" For me something contrary happens when you go from the spiritual, aesthetic experience of the production and story to questions of "How did you do it?" So I tried a variety of different things.

The first year we created a series of questions for the actors to ask the audience. Unfortunately, they were not trained as classroom leaders—we had actors, good ones, but we underestimated the difficulty of facilitating such work. It was not our best gig in the schools or after the public performances. So I said, "Stop, no more post-show activities." After that, we got some of the angriest letters I have ever received from people demanding to know why we were denying the children the chance to ask questions about the production. So have we solved the problem? No. Is there a better way to do it? Yes, I have always wanted to have facilitators who could conduct small group discussions in the schools several days after the shows to let the experience rumble around in the child's head. We just have never had the resources to afford such a staff of facilitators. Hopefully the teachers, with the aid of our Study Guides, will do some of this important work.

What is the "around series"?

For our public audience, not the schools, we have activities pertinent to the play: music performances, discussions, art shows, dance performances, poetry events and of course, food, either before or after the performance in our lobby. The idea of this series is to deepen the context of the piece and connect our audience to other fantastic local artists, thinkers and organizations. We do a series of events for each production and publicize these through ads, postcards and postings on the Web site.

So basically they are pre- and post-show drama exercises?

It's enhancement of the theatre experience. The activities vary depending upon the particular script with everything taking place in the lobby. When Nilo Cruz's *A Very Old Man With Enormous Wings* was produced, we shared Spanish folktales along with discussions of poverty in Latin America, Spanish language lessons and a program on the various paintings, drawings and sculpture of angels present in the collection of the Minneapolis Institute of the Arts with whom we share the building.

In *Korczak's Children,* a play about orphans in the Warsaw ghetto during World War II and the incredible visionary Janusch Korczak who led the orphanage as a fighter for children's rights, we created a very significant set of events for the Around Series. We had a presentation by a Holocaust survivor, who in addition to being a very significant physician, had also created a remarkable body of painting as a way of healing himself. We had evenings of Jewish culture with everything from Klezmer bands to blintzes. We also hosted a gathering of religious leaders from various faith traditions who brought their congregations to have an Interfaith Dialogue inspired by the production.

During *Stamping, Shouting & Singing Home* we arranged for the contemporary gospel choirs of the Twin Cities to assemble in the lobby near the end of the play. As the audience came into the lobby, the singing began a glorious celebration for audiences, the choir, the company, for everyone. It welcomed many of these choirs and congregations to our theatre, and it connected our audience to the beautiful choirs performing in our community today.

When we produced *Dragonwings,* the story of the hardships and discrimination faced by Chinese immigrants in San Francisco during the early part of the twentieth century and the story of the first Chinese to build and fly an airplane in the United States, we had Chinese immigrants telling their stories. Kite making workshops, calligraphy workshops, Chinese musicians and Chinese dance performers were all happening in the lobby, most were free.

We want the children to wrestle with the questions of the play, with its meaning, with the characters' dilemmas. Such enriching, educational endeavors have so far been limited to the public performances. School day schedules don't allow for the additional time needed for such deepening experiences.

What is the public's response to lesser-known plays and original scripts?

We do a tremendous amount of new material. Our audience has welcomed the new work, whether it is culturally specific work, or work that springs out of a unique historical situation or an investigation of our region. We have had them journey into the mind of Galileo, travel the length of the Mississippi with John Banvard a painter who popularized the Panorama form with his three-mile-long canvas of the river, consider contemporary tensions between the African American and Somali communities in the Twin Cities. We know that these audiences will not be the same size as for adaptations of popular children's titles. Attendance is always less for these productions even with great shows, great casts, great reviews. So you adjust your planning and budget for that fact. I believe that we face challenges to this innovation from many sources. One is that our culture seems so driven by fear, particularly in the way electronic media preys upon our concerns and insecurities. We often seek comfort in the security of the known title. Of course, like all parents I also want to introduce children to the stories I have known and loved. So for the lesser-known titles we have to work a little harder to help the audiences see why we are doing the play, and why they should attend.

New play development is a priority for CTC and involves an in-depth, long-range commitment to developing original work for our audiences. Leading playwrights who have worked here include Nilo Cruz, Jeffrey Hatcher and Kia Corthron. We seek out funding locally and nationally to support the new work and regularly partner with other organizations in creating and developing that work, from New Dramatists in New York City, to the Playwrights Center, Intermedia Arts, the Guthrie and others.

What's the response from the schools when you produced original, unknown titles?

There's little variation for any of our weekday performances. We generally sell out our school matinees. Is there more work involved with new work? You bet. We work extremely hard to make the new work dynamic, inventive, clear, compelling and exceptional theatre. We want them to be delighted and surprised and rewarded for taking the risk to see something new.

What's your approach in reviving classic productions? Are the plays mounted exactly as originally presented by CTC?

With each revival of the best-selling titles we ask ourselves, "How can we give this the urgency and vitality of when this work was first imagined?" We are a theatre not a museum. As we bring extraordinary artists to the table, we strive to understand what made the original production so successful, why it was so alive and vital. There are no rules to do it exactly as it was done before—only how do you take this opportunity to make extraordinary theatre. With remounts of shows from the repertoire of CTC we have done things so many different ways: from keeping the script and creating an entirely new production; keeping the set and costumes but transforming the choreography; and the moment to moment acting work. We do not do very many revivals, but each time it is a new adventure.

Then there is censorship and the related issues of political correctness.

Oh, sure. One knows that one will get letters about whatever one does. It comes with the territory. The number of complaints are a small portion of our audience responses, infinitesimal, but they get a tremendous amount of attention inside the staff. I try to call every single person back who writes or sends an e-mail of complaint. The good thing about our parents and teachers is that they believe, as we do, that we are all part of a community—that we care.

There are people who are of the fundamental belief that they are in the theatre just to have a good time and not have issues raised, such as crisis of the family in *Amber Waves*; tough questions linked to the refugees from Somalia [*Snapshot Silhouette*]; even Lilly's initial treatment of her baby brother [*Lilly's Purple Plastic Purse*]. Our hope is that parents and teachers see the complex moments in a tale as teachable moments—moments that will spur conversation and allow them to see just how rich and thick the lives of their children are. In explaining the choices in our production I always start with what the artists were trying to do, what they are striving to accomplish. Maybe it worked, maybe it didn't, but let's talk about it. There have been times when their comments have caused me to reexamine a moment or two in a production.

Changes are made after the production has opened?

Yep. Things that escaped our attention, changing a line reading, changing business—changing an action. Not all the time, but I am grateful to know when something in the staging is being seriously misread.

Have you sought changes in what some adults might consider inappropriate dialogue in children's theatre?

I am keenly conscious of language, any inappropriate language. For me I tend to err on the side of the bigger challenges of the script. I know that for a percentage of the audience certain words can stop them cold. They stop listening. They become totally disengaged in the story. I want the audiences to embrace the bigger issues, the aesthetic challenges of the production.

In studying the child audience during my more than forty years I have found that they basically behave in the theatre the same today as they always have.

I don't quite have your years of tenure. I don't know. Still when the lights go down in a theatre, there is the power of being in a special place, the power of the theatre space, an environment that is for YOU. It can be an extraordinary moment. Even with our tremendous diversity of cultures, in a transforming nation with children from so many different lands, I believe they will still find their way to the work in the same ways. I don't know if I disagree. I don't know if I see a profound difference in the behavior when the work is good.

If it's not a successful production, they tend to misbehave.

So true. Even in good productions, if there is a boring moment, they check out. But they come back. They are so forgiving that their generosity is truly moving.

Fortunately, today we have more good scripts and excellent productions than ever.

There is work out there that is terminally clever, condescending, but more and more that is great theatre. If it is not there, you create it. There are people who haven't worked in theatre for young people, and one of my joys is to introduce them to this field. As more artists cross over to children's theatre and have a great time, they become missionaries. Soon you find people willing to turn down other work to be in the field.

In addition to the professional children's theatres, more adult regional theatres than ever are offering excellent family programs. This is a remarkable, historic time, for children's theatre. There has been nothing less than a sea change in the field, all for the better. As a result I am an extraordinary optimist about the profession with so many fine playwrights, great scripts and superior productions created by major theatre artists. And it's occurring nationally.

Keeping the target audience in mind the whole time.

Yes, remember that we are creating work for people who are generations younger than the artists are. Our audiences are complex; they are quick and smart, yet they can be manipulated, cheated, by second-rate, shoddy productions. One must continually challenge yourself to see children, as they really are, in their contradictions and sophistication. The perpetual challenge is to be truly honest, to respect, to understand children as they are, not as you might want them to be.

As a theatre professional and parent what most do you want your children to remember about their theatre experiences?

The theatre is a place of possibility, of hope, of transformation. It is a home for your imagination. I hope that the theatre becomes a launching pad for their dreams and plans, ideas and arguments. The theatre is that great place where you get to collaborate with others to make a kind of magic that brings people together; that lets them see themselves anew and breathe in the bigness of what it means to be human in all its mad complexity. It is simply a model of how we should live as people. We come together with others to make something of beauty that matters to the world and makes it a more humane and creative place.

Selecting scripts for an anthology of children's plays is challenging and complicated. As you know, the original plan for this collection was to include only new works that premiered at CTC and other regional children's theatres. Unfortunately the rights to include dramatizations of well-known novels were denied for a variety of reasons: the licensing of the story by film companies; the unwillingness of publishers of the original book to allow the script to be published in any form; imprecise instructions in the will of the author of the original book; etc. Knowing that it is often impossible to get the publication rights to great novels, how have you obtained the stage rights to such literature?

The answer to how we have received the rights for adaptation is, in short, persistence. It has taken detective work to find out who holds the rights and an immense amount of energy to contact the correct individual who can potentially release the rights, and sometimes endless work to convince them that it is in their interests to allow us to adapt the work. In our most extreme example of the lengths we have had to go, playwright Nilo Cruz personally went to Madrid to talk to the agent for Gabriel Garcia Marquez to finally get the rights to *A Very Old Man With Enormous Wings*. This happened after literally months and months of work trying to find a way to bring this matter to the attention of the agent and get an answer. Luckily Nilo was going to Spain anyway and scheduled an additional trip to Madrid to attempt to secure the rights. Nilo is, of course, quite charming, and I am sure that didn't hurt our case. For every time we have been given the rights, there are numerous other examples of our hard work resulting in rejection when we have been told that the rights have been pulled or bought out by a studio or production company in Hollywood. Often we have been told to come back in five or so years. We wait and then go back. One simply cannot give up.

So true. Of the following fifteen scripts only four are dramatizations of well-known books that premiered at a major regional children's theatre. Four others were only recently published. In juxtaposing the new works with recently and previously published scripts this collection is comprised of plays that are suggested primarily for lower and upper elementary school students. Although categorizing plays in terms of those appropriate for specific age groups can be shown to be imperfect, these scripts, nevertheless, do appeal primarily to either younger or older audiences. In this anthology plays for younger children appear first followed by those more appropriate for older youth.

Country Mouse and the Missing Lunch Mystery by Sandra Fenichel Asher

Ernie's Incredible Illucinations by Alan Ayckbourn

Two Donuts by José Cruz González

Dr. Seuss' How the Grinch Stole Christmas by Timothy Mason and Mel Marvin

A Laura Ingalls Wilder Christmas by Laurie Brooks

Braille: The Early Life of Louis Braille by Lola H. and Coleman A. Jennings

Bless Cricket, Crest Toothpaste, and Tommy Tune by Linda Daugherty

The Great Gilly Hopkins by David Paterson and Steve Liebman

The Witches by David Wood

Mississippi Pinocchio by Mary Hall Surface and David Maddox

The Wolf and Its Shadows by Sandra Fenichel Asher

Ezigbo, The Spirit Child by Max Bush and Adaora Nzelibe Schmiedl

Inuk and the Sun by Henry Beissel

A Village Fable by James Still

The Witch of Blackbird Pond by Y York

Directors and producers are reminded that any group that produces a play for an audience, whether for paid admission or not, is required by copyright law to purchase from the publisher enough copies of the script for the entire production company and to pay a prescribed royalty fee for each performance in advance. Information for purchasing scripts and for paying the royalty fee precedes each play in the anthology.

THEATRE
FOR
CHILDREN

COUNTRY MOUSE AND THE MISSING LUNCH MYSTERY

(from *Blackbirds and Dragons, Mermaids and Mice*)

by
Sandra Fenichel Asher

COUNTRY MOUSE AND THE MISSING LUNCH MYSTERY

CHARACTERS

Country Mouse
City Mouse
First Little Kitten
Second Little Kitten
Third Little Kitten
Bus Driver
Mouse Patrol
Bus Riders and Deputy Mice (optional)*

TIME

Just before lunch . . .

SETTING

COUNTRY MOUSE's kitchen is R. CITY MOUSE's kitchen is L. Each has a small table or counter with a telephone on it, and perhaps a stove or refrigerator. They "share" a long table and chairs at C, with tablecloths and chairs showing their different styles on either side of an imaginary line down the center of the table. At times, downstage serves as a country road and a city street. A signpost indicates CITY to the left; COUNTRY, to the right.

PLAYING TIME

About 30 minutes

---

*Note: BUS DRIVER and MOUSE PATROL may be doublecast for a cast of 6 actors, or MOUSE PATROL may be played by more than one actor—a MOUSE CHIEF and extras as DEPUTY MICE. If extras are used, they may also be seen as additional riders on the bus. These extras may be chosen ahead of time from the audience, in which case two groups of children will be assigned roles as either bus riders or deputies. While female and male here, characters may be of either gender, with pronouns changed accordingly. KITTENS are larger than MICE, but should still be fun, not frightening.

(AT RISE: *A plate of cheese sits on* COUNTRY MOUSE's *side of the table. Meows, giggles and "shushings" are heard offstage left. MUSIC plays.* THREE LITTLE KIT- TENS *sneak onto stage from UL, motion audience to "hush," tiptoe over to* COUNTRY MOUSE's *side of table.* ALL *wiggle their noses, searching for food. MUSIC fades under dialogue.*)

FIRST KITTEN: He's gone for now!

SECOND KITTEN: Hurry!

THIRD KITTEN: Hush!

SECOND KITTEN: Quick! Before he hears us!

FIRST KITTEN: Shhhhhhh! *(Follows nose to cheese.)* There it is!

THIRD KITTEN: *(Also zeroing in on cheese.)* A plate of cheese!

SECOND KITTEN: Cheese! My favorite!

THIRD KITTEN: Meow-meow-meee-yummy!

COUNTRY MOUSE: *(Offstage R, singing.)* Old MacDonald had a farm, E-I-E-I-O . . .

FIRST KITTEN: He's coming back!

SECOND KITTEN: Hurry!

THIRD KITTEN: Sshhhhhhhhh!

(KITTENS *grab cheese, leaving empty plate, and dash off UL.* COUNTRY MOUSE *enters DR with two baskets, one filled with eggs, the other with fruit and vegetables. Still singing:*)

COUNTRY MOUSE: And on that farm he had some eggs, E-I-E-I-O. With a—*(He looks around, puzzled.)* SQUEEEK! Something's not right here. *(He puts down baskets, gets himself more and more worked up as he tries to calm himself down.)* It must be me. I'm just too nervous, that's all. I've got to calm down. Just because my cousin City Mouse is coming for lunch is no reason to get myself in a tizzy. Just because my cousin City Mouse is a gourmet cook and the fussiest eater in the entire mouse world is no reason to get myself all in a dither. Just because my cousin City Mouse has never once entirely approved of anything I've served her to eat is no reason to get myself turned inside out and upside down! *(In a tizzy, in a dither, and totally turned.)* SQUEEEEEEEK! Squeak-squeak-squeaksqueaksqueak!

(CITY MOUSE *appears, L, a figment of his overheated imagination, much more stiff and formal than she will appear in real life,* COUNTRY MOUSE *mimes fetching and offering food, but to audience, not directly to her. She reacts with very formal politeness, but to audience, not directly to him.*)

COUNTRY MOUSE: The first time she came to visit, I offered her cheese, and she said—

CITY MOUSE: *(Pleasant, well-mannered, but confused by the lack of variety.)* Cheese! *(Mimes tasting a bit.)* Very nice. But is this all?

COUNTRY MOUSE: What more do we need?

CITY MOUSE: A slice of bread, perhaps?

COUNTRY MOUSE: So the next time she came to visit—(CITY MOUSE *spins in place, "arrives" again.)* I offered her bread, and she said—

CITY MOUSE: Bread! *(Mimes tasting, as before.)* Very nice. But is this all?

COUNTRY MOUSE: What more do we need?

CITY MOUSE: An egg, perhaps?

COUNTRY MOUSE: So the next time she came to visit—(CITY MOUSE *"reenters" as above.*) I offered her a *dozen* eggs, and she said—

CITY MOUSE: A *dozen* eggs. Very . . . generous. (*Mimes tasting, as above.*) But is this all?

COUNTRY MOUSE: *What more do we need?*

CITY MOUSE: Veggies, perhaps? A piece of fruit?

COUNTRY MOUSE: So the next time she came to visit—(CITY MOUSE *"reenters" as above.*) I offered her a whole basketful of apples, and she wanted—

COUNTRY MOUSE & CITY MOUSE: (*He's exasperated; she's matter-of-fact.*) CHEESE!

COUNTRY MOUSE: (*As* CITY MOUSE *moves away and begins fussing, realistically now, around the kitchen on her side of stage.*) I didn't realize until I finally ventured into the city and had lunch at *her* house that she meant she enjoyed a little of everything, all at once, instead of one treat at a time! Why didn't she just *say* so? Too polite, I suppose. Well, I've got it all straight this time. (*Checks baskets, breadbox.*) Eggs *and* fruit *and* vegetables *and* bread *and* cheese *and*—(*Checks table.*) Oh, no! Where is my cheese? There *was* cheese! On a plate. On this table. A moment ago. I know I had cheese! SQUEEEK!

(*He dashes off R, squeaking. MUSIC.* KITTENS *tiptoe in L, sniffing for treats.*)

FIRST KITTEN: Look! A basket of eggs.

SECOND KITTEN: Eggs! My *best* favorite!

THIRD KITTEN: Meow-meow-meee-yummy!

(KITTENS *pass eggs to one another, then exit, leaving empty basket as* COUNTRY MOUSE *reenters, in a tizzy. MUSIC ends.*)

COUNTRY MOUSE: SQUEEEK! Squeak-squeak-squeak-squeaksqueak! No cheese, anywhere! What am I to do? My cousin City Mouse will be so disappointed. I better call her and let her know ahead of time so she can prepare herself to be disappointed . . . again. (*He dials; phone rings in* CITY MOUSE'S *kitchen.*)

CITY MOUSE: (*Answers phone.*) City Mouse here.

COUNTRY MOUSE: Oh, Cousin City Mouse, I have terrible news for you.

CITY MOUSE: (*Always calm and somewhat formal, but not cold.*) Terrible news?

COUNTRY MOUSE: Yes. It seems that all my cheese—has disappeared.

CITY MOUSE: Disappeared, you say?

COUNTRY MOUSE: Vanished. Evaporated. Poof! All gone.

CITY MOUSE: That is very strange.

COUNTRY MOUSE: Isn't it though? (*Begins to sniffle.*) And I did so want to serve you *all* of your favorites, all at once, just the way you like them.

CITY MOUSE: (*Genuinely kind, far kinder than he expected.*) Never mind, Cousin Country Mouse. I've plenty of cheese here. I'll bring some along for our luncheon.

COUNTRY MOUSE: Oh, will you? Oh, that's wonderful! Oh, thank you, Cousin City Mouse!

CITY MOUSE: No trouble at all. See you soon! (*She hangs up; goes to prepare cheese and places it in a small basket.*)

COUNTRY MOUSE: (*Hangs up.*) Well, isn't she a dear! Even if she is a fussy eater! (*Bustling about kitchen.*) So, we'll have some nice cheese after all. And bread. And fruit and veggies. And eggs and . . . (*Looks in egg basket.*) Where are the eggs? What's going on here? First the cheese disappears, now the eggs are gone! Could the chickens have taken them back? SQUEAK! Squeak-squeak-squeaksqueaksqueak!

(*He runs off. MUSIC.* KITTENS *reenter, find fruit and vegetables, as before.*)

FIRST KITTEN: Look! Fruit and veggies!

SECOND KITTEN: Fruit and veggies! My *super-duper best* favorites!

THIRD KITTEN: Meow-meow-me-double-yummy-wow!

(KITTENS *pass out fruit and vegetables until* COUNTRY MOUSE *enters and they run off. MUSIC ends.*)

COUNTRY MOUSE: (*Quietly desperate now.*) No luck. No eggs. Nowhere. (*Goes to phone and dials.*) Wait 'til my Cousin City Mouse hears about this!

(*Phone rings in* CITY MOUSE's *kitchen.*)

CITY MOUSE: (*Answers phone.*) City Mouse here.

COUNTRY MOUSE: Hello. It's me again.

CITY MOUSE: Oh, hello. I've got the cheese all packed. I was just about to leave—

COUNTRY MOUSE: There's something I need to tell you first.

CITY MOUSE: Yes?

COUNTRY MOUSE: It's about the eggs.

CITY MOUSE: Yes? What about the eggs?

COUNTRY MOUSE: (*With great difficulty, great regret.*) They're . . . all . . . oh . . . nothing.

CITY MOUSE: You've called to tell me nothing about the eggs?

COUNTRY MOUSE: No. I've called to tell you the eggs *are* nothing. No way. No how. No where.

CITY MOUSE: You mean—the eggs are gone? As is the cheese?

COUNTRY MOUSE: I'm afraid so. (*Begins to sob now, more and more loudly.*)

CITY MOUSE: My goodness!

COUNTRY MOUSE: (*Blows his nose.*) Oh, I knew you'd be upset. And I so wanted to serve you all your favorites, all at once, just the way you like them.

CITY MOUSE: Now-now, this is only a minor setback. I've plenty of eggs. I'll just pack them in with the cheese and be on my way.

COUNTRY MOUSE: Oh, thank you, Cousin City Mouse.

CITY MOUSE: Think nothing of it. (*She hangs up the phone; takes the cheese out of the small basket and repacks it in a larger basket, with eggs.*)

COUNTRY MOUSE: (*Hanging up the phone.*) What a nice mouse! (*Checks on his goods.*) So—we shall have eggs and cheese after all. And bread and fruit and—*(Realizes basket of fruit and vegetables is gone.)* SQUEEEEEEK! My beautiful fruit and veggies are gone! Who is doing this? And *why?* Oh, there's no time to worry about that now. I must gather more food!

(He runs off. MUSIC. KITTENS *enter, as before.)*

FIRST KITTEN: Look! Freshly baked bread!

SECOND KITTEN: Bread! My *other* super-duper best favorite!

THIRD KITTEN: Meow-meow-me-*triple*-yummy-wow!

(They load up with bread and run off as COUNTRY MOUSE *reenters and MUSIC ends.)*

COUNTRY MOUSE: *(Angry now.)* Too late! It's market day. Everything ripe has been picked clean off the vine, clear off the tree. There's not a bean left to boil! *(Dials phone.)* How can I tell my Cousin City Mouse? *(As phone rings in* CITY MOUSE's *kitchen.)* What will she think? What will she say? What will she do?

CITY MOUSE: *(Answering phone.)* City Mouse here. *(*COUNTRY MOUSE *tries to speak, but all that comes out is a series of inarticulate SQUEAKS.)* Hello? Is anyone there? Cousin Country Mouse, is that you? *(She SQUEAKS and nods, trying to say, "Yes, it's me.")* Have you lost something else? *(He SQUEAKS something like, "Yes, the fruit and the veggies and there's nothing left to pick and I don't know what to do . . ." but* CITY MOUSE *can't really understand him. She takes a guess.)* The fruit, perhaps? *(He nods vigorously, whimpering and squeaking in fury. As he squeaks,* CITY MOUSE *gets out an even bigger basket and transfers the cheese and eggs.)* And the vegetables? *(More nods and whimpering. An even* bigger *basket, but before she begins to fill it,* CITY MOUSE *pauses to ask:)* And the bread? *(*COUNTRY MOUSE *whimpers "no," then glances around, notices bread is missing and squeaks a frantic affirmative.)* Now-now, Cousin Country Mouse, calm down. I have cheese. I have eggs. I have fruit. I have vegetables. I have bread. *(*COUNTRY MOUSE *is still inarticulate, but calming down.)* The only problem is, I can't carry them all. *(*COUNTRY MOUSE's *happier squeaks falter and fall.)* So why don't you just pull yourself together, get on the bus, and come *here* for lunch? After all, this is where lunch seems to be.

COUNTRY MOUSE: *(Pulling himself together.)* Oh, Cousin City Mouse, you are so kind!

CITY MOUSE: Think nothing of it. Hurry along!

(She hangs up and gets to work unpacking basket, creating a sumptuous feast, setting the table, etc. COUNTRY MOUSE *gathers his things: hat, scarf, gloves.* KITTENS *watch him from UL.)*

COUNTRY MOUSE: Lunch in the city is always such a treat. This day is already taking a turn for the better. Oops, here comes the bus. Better hurry.

(He exits R. MUSIC plays as KITTENS *enter fully, putting on their hats, scarves and mittens.)*

FIRST KITTEN: Lunch in the city!

SECOND KITTEN: My *all-time, super-duper-whooper best* favorite!

THIRD KITTEN: Meeeeeeeeeeeeeeee—*(Pauses, out of breath and possibilities.)* too!

(KITTENS *hurry off R. MUSIC segues into TRAVEL MUSIC as* BUS DRIVER *chugs and shuffles on from L, driving "bus" and making all relevant sounds: brakes, horn, etc. If extras are used, they play* RIDERS *and may assist in making the appropriate travel sounds.* COUNTRY MOUSE *hurries on.* BUS DRIVER *stops bus for him. TRAVEL MUSIC stops.)*

BUS DRIVER: Cow-to-Concrete Connections. All aboard.

COUNTRY MOUSE: *(Boards "bus" and pays fare.)* One for the city, please.

BUS DRIVER: *(Taking his fare.)* One for the city. Thank you very much.

(COUNTRY MOUSE *"takes a seat" in bus. If there are other* RIDERS, *each says "Good morning" in a unique voice as he passes down the aisle to a "seat" in the back, and he nods in response to each.* KITTENS *rush on from R and repeat his actions.)*

FIRST KITTEN: Three for the city, please.

BUS DRIVER: Three for the city. Thank you very much. (KITTENS *"take their seats" on bus, to the same series of "Good mornings.")* Everybody ready? *(ALL ad lib "Yes! SQUEAK! Ready! MEOW!" etc.)* Thank you very much. Here we go! *(TRAVEL MUSIC. All shuffle behind* BUS DRIVER *as bus circles stage and ends up DL. TRAVEL MUSIC ends.)* Four for the city, this is your stop. Watch your step, please. We appreciate your choosing Cow-to-Concrete Connections and look forward to serving you again soon. *(As* COUNTRY MOUSE *moves up the aisle toward the* BUS DRIVER, *extra* RIDERS *ad lib "Good day" in their various voices.* COUNTRY MOUSE *nods as he goes and ad libs. "Thank you, goodbye," to* BUS DRIVER, *and gets off of bus. A beat, and then* KITTENS *do the same, exiting the bus soon after him.)* Cow-to-Concrete Connections. All aboard.

(TRAVEL MUSIC. BUS DRIVER *and extra* RIDERS *circle stage, chugging, honking, etc., and exit, as* COUNTRY MOUSE *and* KITTENS *watch and wave. TRAVEL MUSIC ends.)*

COUNTRY MOUSE: *(To audience.)* What a pleasant bus driver! (KITTENS *meow in agreement.* COUNTRY MOUSE *goes about his business, unaware that* KITTENS *are following him. He finds* CITY MOUSE'S *house and knocks on "door.")* Seven-oh-three Grand Avenue. Ah, here it is. Cousin City Mouse? It's me! Squeak-squeak-squeak.

CITY MOUSE: Oh, Cousin Country Mouse, I am glad to see you. Come in, come in. Lunch is almost ready. *(Gathering food from here and there and setting it all on table.)* See? I've made you a lovely soufflé.

COUNTRY MOUSE: *(Puzzled.)* A Sue Fly?

CITY MOUSE: *Soufflé.* Eggs and cheese, baked to perfection.

COUNTRY MOUSE: *(Rubbing his tummy in anticipation.)* Ooooh, squeaksqueak-squeaksqueaksqueak!

CITY MOUSE: And here, we have a fine ratatouille.

COUNTRY MOUSE: *(Shocked.)* Rat-a-tooey?

CITY MOUSE: *Ratatouille.* Veggies. Lots of veggies. Nothing but veggies, I assure you.

COUNTRY MOUSE: *(Sniffs at the dish, shows his approval.)* Ahhhhhhhhhhhhhh, squeaksqueaksqueaksqueaksqueak!

CITY MOUSE: Then we have our freshly baked croissants.

COUNTRY MOUSE: You've baked our cross aunts?

CITY MOUSE: *Croissants.* Rolls. *Bread.* See?

COUNTRY MOUSE: Oooooooooooooo, squeeksqueeksqueeksqueeksqueek!

CITY MOUSE: And for dessert, berries and cream.

COUNTRY MOUSE: *(He knows this one.)* Ah, berries and cream! *(Looks around expectantly.)* Where?

CITY MOUSE: In the refrigerator. We'll leave them there while we wash up.

COUNTRY MOUSE: *(Following him off L.)* Good idea. I've had a long trip.

CITY MOUSE: Right this way.

(They exit. MUSIC plays as KITTENS creep on and descend upon food. Completely overwhelmed, they try to taste everything at once—first with their mittens on, then they fling their mittens aside. MUSIC grows louder and faster.)

FIRST KITTEN: Soufflé! Ratatouille! Croissants!

SECOND KITTEN: My *all-new, all-time, super-duper-whooper best* favorites!

THIRD KITTEN: Mee-yum, mee-yum, mee-yip-yip-yip-yip-yip-yip-yip-yip-yow!

FIRST KITTEN: *(As they gobble with one hand and pack up more with the other.)* Here.

SECOND KITTEN: There.

THIRD KITTEN: What?

SECOND KITTEN: Where?

FIRST KITTEN: Take this.

THIRD KITTEN: Hold that.

SECOND KITTEN: Take that.

THIRD KITTEN: Hold this.

FIRST KITTEN: Hurry!

SECOND KITTEN: Hush!

THIRD KITTEN: They'll hear us!

FIRST KITTEN: They'll see us!

SECOND KITTEN: That's it!

THIRD KITTEN: We've got it!

SECOND KITTEN: *(At refrigerator.)* There's more!

THIRD KITTEN: That's enough!

SECOND KITTEN: Just one?

FIRST KITTEN: Maybe two—

THIRD KITTEN: Let's go!

(Stuffing their faces as they exit, they carry all the food off, except the berries and cream, as COUNTRY MOUSE and CITY MOUSE enter. MUSIC fades.)

CITY MOUSE: *(To COUNTRY MOUSE, as they enter.)* Well, *someone* is obviously taking all your food. But *who* could it be?

COUNTRY MOUSE: Someone very hungry, I suppose.

CITY MOUSE: As soon as you get home, you must call your sheriff and report the problem.

COUNTRY MOUSE: I will. I would have done it before I left, but I didn't want to miss the bus—or lunch.

CITY MOUSE: Ah, yes. Shall we dine—? (*Both see food is missing.*)

CITY MOUSE & COUNTRY MOUSE: Ahhhhhhhhhh! SQUEAKsqueaksqueak-squeaksqueak!

CITY MOUSE: It's gone. Our entire meal is gone!

COUNTRY MOUSE: I must have brought my bad luck with me.

CITY MOUSE: (*Dialing phone.*) Luck has nothing to do with it.

(*Phone rings offstage.*)

MOUSE PATROL: (*Enters R, answering phone.*) Mouse Patrol here.

CITY MOUSE: City Mouse here. I want to report a great deal of missing food.

MOUSE PATROL: What sort of missing food?

CITY MOUSE: Well, let's see, we had a lovely soufflé.

MOUSE PATROL: A Sue Fly?

CITY MOUSE: No, a *soufflé*. Oh, what difference does it make? It's not here any-more!

MOUSE PATROL: I'll be right over.

CITY MOUSE: Good. We'll be waiting for you.

(*PATROL MUSIC as* MOUSE PATROL, *with or without extra* DEPUTIES, *crosses stage in "police car," making appropriate noises: siren, etc. He arrives at* CITY MOUSE's *house and "knocks" at "door."* CITY MOUSE *hangs up phone, nods at* COUNTRY MOUSE *confidently, and answers door. MUSIC fades.* MOUSE PATROL *lines may be divided among* DEPUTY MICE *if a larger cast is used.*)

MOUSE PATROL: Mouse Patrol, at your service. What seems to be the trouble here?

COUNTRY MOUSE: It's our food.

MOUSE PATROL: You're having trouble with your food?

CITY MOUSE: No. We're having trouble *without* our food.

MOUSE PATROL: I beg your pardon?

COUNTRY MOUSE: It's all gone.

MOUSE PATROL: Your food is gone?

COUNTRY MOUSE: Yes! Every bit!

MOUSE PATROL: Have you eaten it?

CITY MOUSE: No!

MOUSE PATROL: Have you lost it, then?

COUNTRY MOUSE: Not exactly.

MOUSE PATROL: Someone took it?

CITY MOUSE & COUNTRY MOUSE: Yes!

MOUSE PATROL: Ah! We must search for clues.

CITY MOUSE: Clues?

COUNTRY MOUSE: Clues?

CITY MOUSE: Where?

COUNTRY MOUSE: How?

MOUSE PATROL: We must *search* for them. (*Whips out a magnifying glass and demonstrates.*)

CITY MOUSE & COUNTRY MOUSE: Oh! (*Look at one another, shrug, plunge in willingly.*) Clues!

(*MUSIC plays as ALL begin to search, exiting in different directions, possibly through audience. In a ballet of entrances and exits—KITTEN MUSIC and PATROL MUSIC might alternate—*COUNTRY MOUSE, CITY MOUSE *and* MOUSE PATROL *each discover one pair of mittens, exclaim "Ah, ha!" and hurry off, just missing* KITTENS, *who stagger on and off stage one at a time, stuffed to bursting, and moaning in pain. After last* KITTEN *exits,* MICE *and* MOUSE PATROL *finally bump into each other at C. Each holds up a pair of mittens.*)

COUNTRY MOUSE: Clues!

CITY MOUSE: Clues!

MOUSE PATROL: And more clues!

(*As each pair of mittens is examined, sniffed and tasted, a corresponding* KITTEN *enters, reaches toward mittens, moans, and collapses, clutching his or her aching tummy.*)

CITY MOUSE: Soufflé!

FIRST KITTEN: Oooooh!

COUNTRY MOUSE: Ratatouille!

SECOND KITTEN: Ahhhhhhh!

MOUSE PATROL: Croissants!

THIRD KITTEN: Uhhhhhhhh!

COUNTRY MOUSE: (*Noticing sick* KITTENS.) My goodness!

CITY MOUSE: Could these be the culprits!

MOUSE PATROL: (*Rounding up* KITTENS *and bringing them* C.) Quite possibly! Returning to the scene of the crime!

FIRST KITTEN: We ate too fast!

SECOND KITTEN: We ate too many!

THIRD KITTEN: We ate too much!

(KITTENS *continue to mew sadly, then become more and more distraught as dialogue continues until they are weeping and wailing up a storm.*)

MOUSE PATROL: (*To* MICE.) Do you know these kittens?

COUNTRY MOUSE & CITY MOUSE: No, we don't.

MOUSE PATROL: Hmmmmm. (*To* KITTENS.) Do you know these mittens?

KITTENS: Yes, we do.

MOUSE PATROL: Ah, ha! Case solved.

FIRST KITTEN: Are you going to give back our mittens?

CITY MOUSE: Are you going to give back our food?

SECOND KITTEN: We can't!

CITY MOUSE: Then we can't give back your mittens.

THIRD KITTEN: But we mustn't go home without them!

FIRST KITTEN: Mama will say we're soooooo naughty!

CITY MOUSE: You *are* naughty!

COUNTRY MOUSE: You took our lunch—twice!

SECOND KITTEN: We didn't mean any harm.

THIRD KITTEN: We were just hungry.

FIRST KITTEN: And it was just . . . *there.*

SECOND KITTEN: *(Very sadly.)* All my favorites!

FIRST KITTEN: It seemed like a game.

THIRD KITTEN: Hide and seek.

SECOND KITTEN: With refreshments! *(Their weeping breaks the others' hearts.)*

COUNTRY MOUSE: Oh, well, what could be hungrier than a growing kitten?

CITY MOUSE: *Three* growing kittens, I suppose.

MOUSE PATROL: Care to press charges?

(KITTENS *mew in alarm.* COUNTRY MOUSE *and* CITY MOUSE *exchange a glance.*)

CITY MOUSE: No. We'll handle this ourselves. (KITTENS *rub up against him, purring gratefully, nearly knocking him over.*) Oh! Sit! SIT! SIT! *(They don't.)*

COUNTRY MOUSE: Very well, then, I'll just take them back to the country with me and let their mother know what they've been up to. (KITTENS *quickly sit.*) Unless, of course, they're willing to help me gather more eggs—(KITTENS *mew and nod enthusiastically.*) And pick fruit and veggies—(KITTENS *mew, less enthusiastically.*) And make cheese—(KITTENS *nod, even less enthusiastically.*) And bake bread—*(Mews and nods give way to moans of exhaustion.)* So I can serve a proper lunch to my cousin City Mouse very soon.

MOUSE PATROL: *(To* KITTENS*)* Agreed? (KITTENS *nod and mew, wearily.*) Better wash and dry your mittens, too, before your mother gets a look at them. (KITTENS *mew and collapse to the floor, sound asleep against one another and snoring gently.* OTHERS *place mittens gently beside them.*) Guess my work is finished here. I'll be on my way.

CITY MOUSE: No, wait! We still have berries and cream. Won't you have some with us?

MOUSE PATROL: Mmmmmm. Don't mind if I do!

(MOUSE PATROL *follows* CITY MOUSE *to table.* CITY MOUSE *serves berries and cream.* COUNTRY MOUSE *speaks to* KITTENS.)

COUNTRY MOUSE: Kittens? Would you like to join us? (KITTENS *snore loudly.*) Perhaps not just now.

MOUSE PATROL: Hurry!

CITY MOUSE: Hush!

COUNTRY MOUSE: Quick! Before they hear us!

ALL *(To audience.)* Shhhhhhh!

(MUSIC. COUNTRY MOUSE *scampers to table.*)

CURTAIN

ERNIE'S INCREDIBLE ILLUCINATIONS

by
Alan Ayckbourn

ERNIE'S INCREDIBLE ILLUCINATIONS

CHARACTERS

Ernie
Mum
Dad
Receptionist
Doctor
Officer
Auntie May
First Barker
Second Barker
Third Barker
Fourth Barker
Referee
Timekeeper
Man
Woman
Kid Saracen
Second Man
Lady
Library Attendant
Girl Librarian
Lady Librarian
A Tramp
Patients, Soldiers, Crowds, Boxers, etc.

SETTING

The action takes place in a doctor's waiting-room and surgery—and elsewhere

TIME

The present

(At one side of the stage is a doctor's waiting-room. It is filled with an assortment of miserable-looking patients, coughing, wheezing, sneezing and moaning. Amongst them sit Mr. and Mrs. Fraser and their son, ERNIE.)

ERNIE: *(To the Audience, after a second.)* If you ever want to feel ill—just go and spend a happy half-hour in a doctor's waiting-room. If you're not ill when you get there, you will be when you leave.

(A man enters, having seen the doctor. He is moaning. He crosses the waiting-room and goes out. The other patients look at him and sorrowfully shake their heads. The RECEPTIONIST enters.)

RECEPTIONIST: Mr. and Mrs. Fraser . . . (MUM *and* DAD *rise.*) Doctor will see you now.

MUM: Thank you. Come on, Ernie. (MUM *and* DAD *and* ERNIE *follow the* RECEPTIONIST *across the stage to the* DOCTOR *who sits behind a table.*) 'Morning, Doctor. *(The* RECEPTIONIST *leaves.)*

DOCTOR: Ah. Ah. Mr. and Mrs. Fraser. Is that it?

MUM: That's right. I'm Mrs. Fraser—and this is my husband, Mr. Fraser—and this is our son—Ernie.

DOCTOR: Ah yes. Ernie. I've been hearing all sorts of things about you, young Ernie. Now, what have you been up to, eh?

DAD: Illucinations.

DOCTOR: I beg your pardon?

DAD: Illucinations.

DOCTOR: Oh, yes, illuci—quite, yes.

MUM: What my husband means, Doctor, is that Ernie has been creating these illusions.

DOCTOR: Ah.

MUM: Well, they're more than illusions, really.

DAD: I'll say.

DOCTOR: Beg pardon?

DAD: I'll say.

MUM: He's been causing that much trouble. At school, at home, everywhere he goes. I mean we can't go on like this. His dad's not as strong as he was, are you, Albert?

DAD: No.

DOCTOR: What?

DAD: No.

DOCTOR: Perhaps it would be better if you told me a little more about it. When did you first notice this . . . ?

MUM: Ah well . . .

DAD: Ah.

MUM: Now then . . .

DAD: Now . . .

MUM: He'd have been . . . well, it'd have been about . . . near enough . . . er . . .

DOCTOR: Go on.

(ERNIE *steps forward. During his speech* MUM *and* DAD *remain seated. The* DOC-TOR *moves to the side of the stage, produces a notebook and makes notes on what follows.*)

ERNIE: It started with these daydreams. You know, the sort everybody gets. Where you suddenly score a hat trick in the last five minutes of the Cup Final, or you bowl out the West Indies for ten runs—or saving your granny from a blazing helicopter, all that sort of rubbish. It was one wet Saturday afternoon and me and my mum and my dad were all sitting about in the happy home having one of those exciting afternoon rave-ups we usually have in our house.

(ERNIE *sits at the table in the* DOCTOR's *chair and starts to read a book.* MUM *has started knitting and* DAD *just sits, gazing ahead of him. There is a long silence.*)

ERNIE: It was all go in our house.

(Pause.)

MUM: I thought you'd be at the match today, Albert.

DAD: Not today.

MUM: Not often you miss a game.

DAD: They're playing away.

MUM: Oh.

DAD: In Birmingham. I'm damned if I'm going to Birmingham. Even for United.

ERNIE: Meanwhile—while this exciting discussion was in progress, I was reading this book about the French wartime resistance workers and of the dangers they faced—often arrested in their homes. I started wondering what would happen if a squad of soldiers turned up at our front door, having been tipped off about the secret radio transmitter hidden in our cistern—when suddenly . . .

(*The tramp of feet, and a squad of soldiers comes marching on and up to their front door.*)

OFFICER: Halte! *(He bangs on the door.)*

(Pause.)

DAD: That the door?

MUM: What?

DAD: The door.

MUM: Was it?

OFFICER: Open zis door. Open the door! *(He knocks again.)*

MUM: Oh, that'll be the milkman wanting his money. He always comes round about now. Albert, have you got ten bob . . . ?

DAD: *(Fumbling in his pockets.)* Ah . . .

OFFICER: *(Shouting.)* Open zis door immediately. Or I shall order my men to break it down! *(He bangs on the door again.)*

MUM: Just a minute. Coming.

DAD: Should have one somewhere . . .

OFFICER: We know you're in there, English spy! Come out with your hands up . . . !

MUM: What's he shouting about? Oh, I'd better ask him for three pints next week, if Auntie May's coming . . .

OFFICER: Zis is your last chance . . . *(He knocks again.)*

MUM: Oh shut up . . . *(The Officer signals his men. Two of them step back, brace their shoulders and prepare to charge the door.)* I'm coming—I'm coming.

ERNIE: I shouldn't go out there, Mum . . .

MUM: What?

ERNIE: I said don't go out there.

MUM: What . . . ?

ERNIE: It's not the milkman. It's a squad of enemy soldiers.

MUM: Who?

ERNIE: They've come for me . . .

MUM: Who has?

ERNIE: The soldiers. They've found out about the radio transmitter.

MUM: What radio?

DAD: Hey, here, that's a point. Have you paid our telly licence yet, Ethel? It might be the detector van.

MUM: Oh, sit down, Albert. Stop worrying. It's just Ernie. Shut up, Ernie.

ERNIE: But Mum . . .

DAD: I think I'll take the telly upstairs. Just in case . . .

(The Soldiers charge at the door. A loud crash.)

ERNIE: Don't go out, Mum.

MUM: Shut up!

DAD: *(Picking up the television, struggling with it.)* Just take it upstairs.

ERNIE: *(To Mum.)* Don't go!

MUM: I can't leave him out there. The way he's going he'll have the door off its hinges in a minute . . . *(She moves to the door.)*

DAD: Mind your backs. Out of my way . . .

ERNIE: Mum . . .

(MUM opens the door just as the two Soldiers are charging for the second time. They shoot past her, straight into the hall, collide with DAD and land in a heap with him. DAD manages to hold the television above his head and save it from breaking.)

MUM: Hey . . .

DAD: Oy!

(The OFFICER and the other Soldiers enter. ERNIE crouches behind the table.)

OFFICER: Ah-ha! The house is surrounded.

MUM: Who are you?

OFFICER: Put up your hands. My men will search the house.

DAD: *(Feebly)* Hey . . .

OFFICER: *(Shouting up the stairs.)* We know you're hiding in here, you can't get away . . .

DAD: Hey—*hey*—HEY!

OFFICER: Ah-ha. What have we here?

DAD: Oh. It's the telly. The neighbour's telly. Not mine.

OFFICER: Ah-ha.

DAD: Just fixing it for him, you see . . .

OFFICER: Outside.

DAD: Eh?

OFFICER: You will come with me.

DAD: What, in this? I'm not going out in this rain.

OFFICER: Outside or I shoot.

DAD: Here . . .

MUM: Albert . . .

ERNIE: Hold it! Drop those guns!

OFFICER: Ah, so . . . *(He raises his gun.)*

ERNIE: Da-da-da-da-da-da-da-da-da-da-da.

(The Soldiers collapse and are strewn all over the hall. MUM screams. Then there is a silence.)

MUM: Oh, Ernie. What have you done?

ERNIE: Sorry, Mum.

DAD: Oh, lad . . .

MUM: Are they—dead?

DAD: Yes. *(MUM screams again.)* Steady, steady. This needs thinking about.

MUM: What about the neighbours?

DAD: Could create a bit of gossip, this could.

MUM: What about the carpet? Look at it.

DAD: Hasn't done that much good.

MUM: What'll we do with them?

DAD: Needs a bit of thinking about.

(ERNIE steps forward. As he speaks and during the next section, DAD and MUM carry off the bodies.)

ERNIE: Well, Mum and Dad decided that the best thing to do was to pretend it hadn't happened. That was usually the way they coped with all emergencies . . .

(The DOCTOR steps forward.)

MUM: (*Struggling with a body.*) We waited till it got dark, you see . . .

DOCTOR: Yes? And then . . . ?

DAD: We dumped 'em.

DOCTOR: I beg your pardon?

DAD: We dumped 'em. Took 'em out and dumped 'em.

DOCTOR: Dumped them? Where, for heaven's sake?

DAD: Oh—bus shelters—park benches . . .

MUM: Corporation car-park.

DAD: Left one in the all-night cafeteria.

MUM: And one in the Garden of Rest.

DAD: Caused a bit of a rumpus.

DOCTOR: I'm not surprised.

MUM: We had the police round our way for days—trying to sort it out . . .

DAD: They never did get to the bottom of it, though.

DOCTOR: Extraordinary. And then?

ERNIE: (*Stepping forward.*) And then—Auntie May arrived to stay. I liked my Auntie May. (AUNTIE MAY *enters. The* DOCTOR *steps back again.*)

AUNTIE: 'Ullo, Ernie lad. Have a sweetie.

ERNIE: Ta, Auntie. And Auntie May took me to the fair.

(*The stage is filled with jostling people, barkers and fairground music. The* BARKERS *speak simultaneously.*)

FIRST BARKER: Yes, indeed, the world's tallest man! He's so tall, madam, his breakfast is still sliding down him at tea time. Come along now, sir. Come inside now . . .

SECOND BARKER: Ladies and gentlemen. I am prepared to guarantee that you will never again, during your lifetimes, see anything as unbelievably amazing as the Incredible Porcupine Woman. See her quills and get your thrills. Direct from the unexplored South American Jungle . . .

THIRD BARKER: Try your luck—come along, madam—leave your husband there, dear, he'll still be there when you come back—tell you what—if he isn't I can sell you a replacement—five shots for sixpence—knock 'em all down and pick up what you like . . .

ERNIE: Can I have a go on that, Auntie?

AUNTIE: Not now, Ernie.

ERNIE: Oh go on, Auntie May.

AUNTIE: I want a cup of tea.

ERNIE: Have an ice-cream.

AUNTIE: I've had three. I can't have any more. It'll bring on my condition . . .

ERNIE: What condition, Auntie?

AUNTIE: Never you mind what. But I should never have had that candy floss as well. I'll suffer for it.

FOURTH BARKER: Just about to start, ladies and gentlemen. A heavyweight boxing bout, featuring the one and only unofficial challenger for the heavyweight championship of the world—Kid Saracen. The Kid will be fighting this afternoon, for the very first time, a demonstration contest against the new sensation from Tyneside, Eddie "Grinder" Edwards. In addition, ladies and gentlemen, the Kid is offering fifty pounds—yes, fifty pounds—to any challenger who manages to last three three-minute rounds . . .

ERNIE: Oh, come on, Auntie. Let's go in and watch.

AUNTIE: What is it?

ERNIE: Boxing.

AUNTIE: Boxing? I'm not watching any boxing. I don't mind wrestling but I'm not watching boxing. It's bloodthirsty.

ERNIE: Auntie . . .

AUNTIE: Nasty stuff, boxing . . .

FOURTH BARKER: Come along, lady. Bring in the young gentleman. Let him see the action . . .

AUNTIE: Oh no . . .

FOURTH BARKER: Come along. Two is it?

ERNIE: Yes please. Two.

FOURTH BARKER: Thank you, son.

AUNTIE: Eh?

ERNIE: This way, Auntie.

(Before AUNTIE MAY can protest, she and Ernie are inside the boxing-booth. The Crowd have formed a square around the ring in which stand Kid Saracen, Eddie Edwards and the REFEREE.)

REFEREE: Ladies and gentlemen, introducing on my right, the ex-unofficial challenger for the World Heavyweight Championship—KID SARACEN . . . (Boos from the Crowd.) And on my left, the challenger from Newcastle upon Tyne—EDDIE EDWARDS . . . (The Crowd cheers.)
    (To the boxers.) Right, I want a good, clean fight, lads. No low blows and when I say "break"—stop boxing right away. Good luck.

TIMEKEEPER: Seconds out.

(The bell rings. The Crowd cheers as the boxers size each other up. They mostly cheer on Edwards—"Come on, Eddie," "Murder him, Eddie," etc. The boxers swap a few punches.)

AUNTIE: Oooh. I can't look.

(The man next to her starts cheering.)

MAN: Flatten him, Eddie!

(Auntie peers out from behind her hands in time to see the Kid clout Eddie fairly hard.)

AUNTIE: Hey, you stop that!

MAN: Get at him, Eddie . . . !

AUNTIE: Yes, that's right, get at him!

MAN: Hit him!

AUNTIE: Knock him down!

MAN: Smash him!

AUNTIE: Batter him! *(She starts to wave her arms about in support of* EDDIE, *throwing punches at the air.)*

MAN: That's it, missis. You show 'em.

AUNTIE: I would, I would.

MAN: Give 'em a run for their money, would you?

AUNTIE: I'm not that old . . .

MAN: Eddie!

AUNTIE: Come on, Eddie!

ERNIE: Eddie!

(In the ring the KID *throws a terrific blow which brings* EDDIE *to his knees.)*

REFEREE: One—two—three—

MAN: Get up, Eddie . . .

AUNTIE: Get up . . . get up . . .

REFEREE:—four . . .

*(*EDDIE *rises and blunders round the ring. The* KID *knocks him clean out. The* REFEREE *counts him out. The* CROWD *boos wildly. The* KID *walks smugly round the ring, his hands raised above his head in triumph.)*

AUNTIE: You brute.

MAN: Boo. Dirty fight . . .

AUNTIE: Bully . . .

REFEREE: *(Quietening the* CROWD.*)* And now, ladies and gentlemen, the Kid wishes to issue a challenge to any person here who would like to try his skill at lasting three rounds—any person here. Come along now—anybody care to try . . .

(Muttering from the CROWD.*)*

AUNTIE: *(To the Man.)* Go on then.

MAN: Who, me?

AUNTIE: What are you frightened of, then?

MAN: I'm frightened of him . . .

REFEREE: Come along now. We're not asking you to do it for nothing. We're offering fifty pounds—fifty pounds, gentlemen . . .

AUNTIE: Go on. Fifty quid.

MAN: I'd need that to pay the hospital bill . . .

AUNTIE: Go on . . .

MAN: It's all right for you, lady—just standing there telling other people to go and get their noses broken.

AUNTIE: All right, then. I'll go in myself. Excuse me . . . *(She starts to push through the* CROWD *towards the ring.)*

MAN: Hey . . .

ERNIE: Auntie, where are you going?

AUNTIE: Out of my way . . .

MAN: Hey, stop her—she's off her nut . . .

ERNIE: Auntie!

AUNTIE: *(Hailing the* REFEREE.*)* Hey, you . . .

REFEREE: Hallo, lady, what can we do for you? Come to challenge him, have you?

(Laughter from the CROWD.*)*

AUNTIE: That's right. Help me in.

REFEREE: Just a minute, lady, you've come the wrong way for the jumble sale, this is a boxing-ring . . .

AUNTIE: I know what it is. Wipe that silly smile off your face. Come on then, rings out of your seconds . . .

(The CROWD *cheers.)*

REFEREE: Just a minute. Just a minute. What do you think you're playing at . . . ?

AUNTIE: You said anyone could have a go, didn't you?

WOMAN: That's right. Give her a go, then.

REFEREE: *(Getting worried.)* Now, listen . . .

KID SARACEN: Go home. There's a nice old lady . . .

(The CROWD *boos.)*

AUNTIE: You cheeky ha'porth.

SECOND MAN: Hit him, Grandma.

(The CROWD *shouts agreement.)*

REFEREE: Tell you what, folks. Let's give the old lady fifty pence for being a good sport . . .

AUNTIE: I don't want your fifty pence . . . Come on.

WOMAN: Get the gloves on, Granny.

AUNTIE: I don't need gloves. My hands have seen hard work. I was scrubbing floors before he was thought of . . .

WOMAN: That's right, love.

ERNIE: *(Stepping forward.)* And then suddenly I got this idea. Maybe Auntie May could be the new heavyweight champion of the world . . .

(The bell rings. AUNTIE MAY *comes bouncing out of her corner flinging punches at the* KID, *who looks startled. The* CROWD *cheers.)*

AUNTIE: Let's have you.

KID SARACEN: Hey, come off it!

(The REFEREE *tries vainly to pull* AUNTIE MAY *back but she dances out of reach.)*

KID SARACEN: Somebody chuck her out.

(The KID *turns to appeal to the* CROWD. AUNTIE MAY *punches him in the back.)*

AUNTIE: Gotcher!

KID SARACEN: Ow!

*(*AUNTIE MAY *bombards the* KID *with punches.)*

ERNIE: *(Commentator style.)* And Auntie May moves in again and catches the Kid with a left and a right to the body and there's a right-cross to the head—and that really hurt him—and it looks from here as if the champ is in real trouble . . . as this amazing sixty-eight-year-old challenger follows up with a series of sharp left-jabs—one, two, three, four jabs . . . *(The* KID *is reeling back.)* And then, bang, a right-hook and he's down . . . !

(The KID *goes down on his knees. The* CROWD *cheers.)*

AUNTIE: *(To the* REFEREE.*)* Go on. Start counting.

CROWD: One—two—three—four—five—six . . .

(The KID *gets up again.)*

ERNIE: And the Kid's on his feet but he's no idea where he is—and there's that tremendous right uppercut—and he's down again . . . ! *(The* CROWD *counts him out.* AUNTIE MAY *dances round the ring with glee. The* CROWD *bursts into the ring and* AUNTIE MAY *is lifted onto their shoulders.)*

(The CROWD *goes out with* AUNTIE MAY, *singing "For She's a Jolly Good Fellow." The* REFEREE *and the* KID *are left.)*

REFEREE: Come on. Get up—Champ.

KID SARACEN: Ooooh. *(He staggers to his feet.)*

(The KID *goes out, supported by the* REFEREE. ERNIE, DAD, MUM *and the* DOCTOR *are left.)*

DOCTOR: *(Still writing, excitedly.)* Absolutely incredible!

MUM: Terrible it was. It took it out of her, you know. She was laid up all Sunday.

DAD: And we had all those fellows round from the Amateur Boxing Association trying to sign her up to fight for the Combined Services.

MUM: So I told his dad on the Monday, seeing as it was half-term, "Take him somewhere where he won't get into trouble," I said. "Take him somewhere quiet."

DAD: So I took him down to the library. *(The* DOCTOR *retires to the side of the stage again.* DAD, MUM *and* ERNIE *exit.)*

(The scene becomes the Public Library. It is very quiet. Various people tip-toe about. At one end sits an intellectual-looking LADY *with glasses, reading; at the other, an old* TRAMP *eating his sandwiches from a piece of newspaper. One or two others. A uniformed* ATTENDANT *walks up and down importantly. The* LADY *with glasses looks up at the lights. She frowns.)*

LADY: Excuse me . . .

ATTENDANT: Sssshhh!

LADY: Sorry. *(Mouthing silently.)* The light's gone.

ATTENDANT: *(Mouthing.)* What?

LADY: *(Whispering.)* I said the light's gone over here.

ATTENDANT: *(Whispering.)* What?

LADY: New bulb. *(The* ATTENDANT *shakes his head, still not understanding.)* *(Loudly.)* Up there! You need a new bulb—it's gone. I can't see!

PEOPLE: Sssshhhh!

ATTENDANT: *(Whispering.)* Right.

LADY: *(Whispering.)* Thank you.

(The ATTENDANT *tip-toes out as* DAD *and* ERNIE *tip-toe in.)*

DAD: *(To Ernie.)* Sssshhhh!

*(*ERNIE *nods. They tip-toe and sit.)*

ERNIE: *(To the Audience.)* I didn't really think much of this idea of my mum's . . .

PEOPLE: Ssssshhhh!

ERNIE: *(Whispering.)* I didn't really think much of this idea of my mum's. It was a bit like sitting in a graveyard only not as exciting. The trouble is, in library reading-rooms some bloke's pinched all the best magazines already and you're left with dynamic things like *The Pig Breeder's Monthly Gazette* and suchlike. I'd got stuck with *The Bell Ringer's Quarterly.* Which wasn't one of my hobbies. Nobody else seemed to be enjoying themselves either. Except the bloke eating his sandwiches in the corner. I reckoned he wasn't a tramp at all, but a secret agent heavily disguised, waiting to pass on some secret documents to his contact who he was to meet in the library and who was at this very moment lying dead in the Reference Section, a knife in his ribs. Realizing this, the tramp decides to pick on the most trustworthy-looking party in the room—my dad!

(The TRAMP *gets up stealthily and moves over to* DAD. *As he passes him he knocks his magazine out of his hand.)*

DAD: Hey!

TRAMP: Beg pardon, mister. *(He bends to pick up the magazine and hands it back to* DAD. *As he does so he thrusts his newspaper parcel into* DAD's *hands.)* Sssshhhh. Take this. Quickly! They're watching me. Guard it with your life.

DAD: Eh? *(The* TRAMP *hurries away. A sinister man in a mackintosh gets up and follows him out.)* Who the heck was that?

ERNIE: Dunno, Dad.

DAD: *(Examining the parcel.)* What's all this, then?

ERNIE: Dunno.

DAD: I don't want his sandwiches. Spoil my dinner. *(As he unwraps the parcel.)* Hey!

ERNIE: What is it?

DAD: Looks like a lot of old blue-prints and things. Funny. This anything to do with you?

ERNIE: *(Innocently.)* No, Dad.

(The ATTENDANT *enters with a step-ladder. He places it under the light. A* GIRL LIBRARIAN *who has entered with him steadies the step-ladder. The* ATTENDANT *produces a bulb from his pocket and starts to climb the step-ladder. Watching the* ATTENDANT.*)* And now, as Captain Williams nears the summit of this, the third highest mountain in the world, never before climbed by man . . . *(Wind noises start.)* He pauses for a moment through sheer exhaustion . . . *(The* ATTENDANT, *feeling the effects of the wind, clings to the step-ladder for dear life. It sways slightly.)*

ATTENDANT: *(Shouting down to the* LIBRARIAN.*)* More slack. I need more slack on the rope . . . !

LIBRARIAN: *(Shouting up to him.)* More slack. Are you all right?

ATTENDANT: I—think—I can—make it.

LIBRARIAN: Be careful. The rock looks treacherous just above you.

ATTENDANT: It's all right. It's—quite safe—if I—just aaaaaahhh! *(He slips and holds on with one hand.)*

LADY: Captain! What's happened?

ATTENDANT: Damn it. I think I've broken my leg . . .

LADY: Oh, no.

LIBRARIAN: How are we going to get him down? *(*DAD *rises.)*

ERNIE: And here comes Major Fraser, ace daredevil mountaineer, to the rescue.

DAD: Give me a number three clambering-iron and a hydraulic drill-lever, will you? I'm going up.

LIBRARIAN: Oh no, Major.

DAD: It's the only way.

LADY: Don't be a fool, Major.

DAD: Someone's got to go. Give me plenty of line . . . *(He starts to climb.)*

LIBRARIAN: Good luck.

LADY: Good luck.

(A sequence in which DAD *clambers up the ladder, buffeted by the wind.)*

DAD: Can you hold on?

ATTENDANT: Not—much—longer.

DAD: Try, man, try. Not much longer . . .

LADY: Keep going, man.

*(*DAD *reaches the* ATTENDANT. *People cheer. The two men slowly descend the ladder.)*

ERNIE: And here comes the gallant Major Fraser, bringing the injured Captain Williams to safety . . .

*(*DAD *and the* ATTENDANT *reach the floor. More cheers and applause from the onlookers. The* ATTENDANT *is still supported by Dad with one arm round his neck. There is a general shaking of hands. The wind noise stops.)*

ATTENDANT: *(Coming back to reality, suddenly.)* Hey, hey! What's going on here? *(To Dad.)* What do you think you're doing?

DAD: Oh.

ATTENDANT: Let go of me.

DAD: Sorry, I . . .

ATTENDANT: Never known anything like it. This is a public building, you know . . .

DAD: Ernie . . .

ERNIE: Yes, Dad?

DAD: Did you start this?

ERNIE: *(Innocently.)* Me, Dad?

DAD: Now listen, lad . . .

(A SECOND LIBRARIAN *enters, screaming.)*

SECOND LIBRARIAN: Oh, Mr. Oats, Mr. Oats . . .

ATTENDANT: What's the matter, girl? What's the matter?

SECOND LIBRARIAN: There's a man in the Reference Section.

ATTENDANT: Well?

SECOND LIBRARIAN: He's dead.

LADY: Dead?

SECOND LIBRARIAN: Yes. I think he's been killed. There's a knife sticking in his ribs . . . *(The* FIRST LIBRARIAN *screams. The* ATTENDANT *hurries out, followed by the others.* ERNIE *and* DAD *are left.)*

DAD: Ernie!

ERNIE: Sorry, Dad.

(The DOCTOR *moves in.* MUM *joins them.)*

DOCTOR: Incredible.

DAD: Embarrassing.

DOCTOR: Yes, yes.

(The scene is now back to where it was at the beginning, with the four in the DOCTOR's *room on one side and the waiting-room full of patients on the other.)*

MUM: Can you do anything, Doctor?

DOCTOR: Mmmm. Not much, I'm afraid.

MUM: No?

DOCTOR: You see, it's not really up to me at all. It's up to you. An interesting case. Very. In my twenty years as a general practitioner I've never heard anything quite like it. You see, this is a classic example of group hallucinations . . .

DAD: Illucinations, yes.

DOCTOR: Starting with your son and finishing with you all being affected . . .

MUM: All?

DOCTOR: All of you. You must understand that all this has happened only in your minds.

DAD: Just a minute. Are you suggesting we're all off our onions?

DOCTOR: Off your . . . ?

DAD: You know. Round the thing. Up the whatsit.

DOCTOR: No . . .

DAD: My missis as well?

DOCTOR: No. No.

DAD: Then watch it.

DOCTOR: I was just explaining . . .

DAD: You don't need. It's Ernie here, that's all. He imagines things and they happen.

DOCTOR: Oh, come now. I can't really accept that.

DAD: Why not?

DOCTOR: It's—impossible. He may *imagine* things . . .

DAD: He does.

DOCTOR: But they don't *really* happen. They *appear* to, that's all.

DAD: Is that so?

DOCTOR: Of course.

(*A slight pause.*)

DAD: Ernie.

ERNIE: Yes, Dad.

DAD: Imagine something. We'll see who's nutty.

ERNIE: What, Dad?

DAD: Anything, son, anything. Just to show the doctor.

MUM: Nothing nasty, Ernie. Something peaceful . . .

DAD: How about a brass band? I like brass bands.

MUM: Oh dear. Couldn't it be something quieter? Like—a mountain stream or something . . .

DAD: Don't be daft, Ethel. The doctor doesn't want a waterfall pouring through his surgery. Go on, lad. A brass band.

ERNIE: Right, Dad. (*He concentrates.*)

(*A pause.*)

DOCTOR: Well?

DAD: Give him a chance.

(*A pause.*)

MUM: Come on, Ernie. (*Pause.*) He's usually very good at it, Doctor.

DAD: Come on, lad.

ERNIE: It's difficult, Dad, I can't picture them.

DOCTOR: Yes, well I'm afraid I can't afford any more time just now, Mr. and Mrs. Fraser. I do have a surgery full of people waiting to see me—(*He calls.*)—Miss Bates!—so you will understand I really must get on.

(*The RECEPTIONIST enters.*)

RECEPTIONIST: Yes, Doctor?

DOCTOR: The next patient, please, Miss Bates.

RECEPTIONIST: *(Going.)* Yes, Doctor. *(The* RECEPTIONIST *exits.)*

DOCTOR: *(Getting up and pacing up and down as he speaks.)* What I suggest we do is, I'll arrange an appointment with a specialist and—he'll be able to give you a better diagnosis—*(His steps become more and more march-like.)*—than I will. I'm quite sure—that—a—few—sessions—with a trained—psychiatrist—will—be—quite—sufficient—to—put—everything—right—right—left—right—left—left—left—right—left . . . *(The* DOCTOR *marches to the door of his room, does a smart about-turn and marches round his desk. The* PATIENTS *from the waiting-room enter and follow him, some limping, some marching and all playing, or as if playing, brass instruments.)* L-e-e-e-ft . . . Wheel . . . *(After a triumphal circuit of the room everyone marches out following the* DOCTOR, *who has assumed the rôle of drum major.)*

ERNIE: *(Just before he leaves.)* It looks as though the Doctor suffers from illucinations as well. I hope you don't get 'em. Ta-ta.

*(*ERNIE *marches out jauntily, following the band, as—)*

CURTAIN

TWO DONUTS

by
José Cruz González

TWO DONUTS

CHARACTERS

Pepito is a small boy. He has dark curly hair and loves eating donuts.
Abuela Pepito's grandmother. She loves to sing and tell stories.
Panadero is our storyteller and local barrio baker. He wears a mustache,
a baker's hat, and apron.
Madre Pepito's mom. She looks a lot like Abuela but only younger.
Modesto & Ridiculo. Two Guatemalan Worry Dolls dressed in Armani suits
and ties.
Little Girl Footsteps. A girl with the gift to transform into a coconut
and rock or just about anything by holding her breath. She is a
super agent spy and protector of the last flower in Cuate-Malo.
Commandante Boots is the evil dictator of Cuate-Malo. He wears
sunglasses, military uniform, boots and lots of medals.
Sergeant Botas is an army sergeant. He is Commandante Boots' sidekick.
Tirado is a single tire. That is all that is left of him. He is a very
nervous type.
The Great Sea Tortuga is a wise, giant sea turtle. She leads the resistance
against Commandante Boots.
Arm, Eye, Nose, Bi-Plane Pair of Shoes, Baby Manatee, Luna,
Bumble Zapper, other characters seen throughout the play.

PRODUCTION NOTE

The play can be presented several ways with 3 actor-puppeteers (2 male and
1 female) or with a larger cast up to 12 actors with some double casting (7
males and 5 females).

Where do the tears of children go?

Where do the tears of children go?
Are they wiped away by a mother's loving hand?

Do they become absorbed in a father's shirtsleeve?
Or do they evaporate in the warm sunlight of day?

Maybe the tears of children fall on earth
Turning into little water streams capturing light
Or maybe they become great rivers flowing towards the open sea

Into an ocean of tears, maybe?

Palabras en Español
(Words in Spanish)

Abuela—grandmother

Amigo—friend

Arco iris—rainbow

Ayúdame—help me

Barrio—neighborhood

Bonito—pretty

Buenos días—good morning

Cafecito—a little cup of coffee

Commandante—commander

Corazón—heart

Cuentos—stories

Dos donas—two donuts

El sol—the sun

Escuela—school

Español—Spanish

Estúpido—stupid

Excellente—excellent

Familia—family

Flores—flowers

Gracias—thank you

Grito—a shout, scream

Guatemala—a Latin American country in Central America

Hola—hello

Idiota—idiot

La luna—the moon

La noche—the night

La playa—the beach

Leche—milk

Mambo—a dance from Latin America

Masa—dough

Monstruo Botas—monster boots

Muchacho—boy

Muy bien—well done or very good

Panadería—bakery

Pan dulce—sweet bread

Por favor—please

Quihubo—an informal greeting, something like "Hello!"

Regalo—gift

Tirado—dirt cheap or something thrown away

Tortilla—a thin flat round Mexican bread made from corn meal or wheat flour

Tortuga—turtle

Trabajo—work

Triste—sad

Vámonos—let's go

(A bakery in the heart of the barrio. At rise Mambo music plays as PANADERO, *the local barrio baker appears. He wears a big mustache, a baker's hat and apron. He balances a stack of pink donut boxes.)*

PANADERO: *Quihubo!* I'm *Panadero,* the local baker. Each morning before the sun rises, I'm busy baking *pan dulce.* That's sweet bread. My customers have got to have their *pan dulce* with their *leche* or *cafecito* at breakfast. When I bake I listen to the radio in *Español.* I love to sing loudly, and sometimes even the neighborhood dogs join in. Every now and then I even dance the *mambo!* I can't help it. It starts at my feet and everything else follows. *Mambo!*

*(*PANADERO *presents an old wooden house with porch and steps. The house sits in the old part of town. A tire hangs from a tree, and an old bucket rests in the garden, while a used pair of shoes, newly shined, rest nearby.)*

PANADERO: I have a story to tell you. It's about a little boy named *Pepito. Pepito* loved eating donuts. My delicious donuts baked fresh, the scent would reach him next door where he lived and he would instantly arrive at my bakery.

*(*PEPITO *appears. He is a boy.)*

PEPITO: *Hola, Señor Panadero!*

PANADERO: *Buenos días, Pepito!* He was a small boy with black curly hair and eyes as dark as a moon's eclipse. He would always order—

PEPITO: *Dos donas, por favor!*

PANADERO: Two donuts.

PEPITO: *Gracias!*

PANADERO: *De nada!* One for him and the other for his *Abuela.*

*(*ABUELA, PEPITO's *grandmother appears.)*

ABUELA: *Pepito, qué me trajieste hoy?* (What did you bring to me today?)

PEPITO: What else *Abuela?*

ABUELA: Oh, yummy, *una dona!*

PANADERO: *Pepito* and *Abuela* would sit on their porch steps and delight in my sweet creations. *(Admiring the garden.)* Oh, what a lovely garden *Abuela* has.

PEPITO: Mmm, good!

ABUELA: *Mmm, muy buena!*

PANADERO: His *Abuela* would tell him stories of the old country where jaguars roamed, eagles soared and rivers flowed endless like a poet's imagination. They shared a language all their own.

ABUELA: *Pepito,* there's a tale about how *la luna* came to be. Have you heard it?

PEPITO: No, *Abuela.*

ABUELA: Then I'll tell it to you. Long ago there was a God of Lightning who became very hungry.

(The GOD OF LIGHTNING *appears. He may be played by* PANADERO.*)*

ABUELA: His stomach rumbled like the earth when it shakes. He searched the heavens for something to eat, but found only—

GOD OF LIGHTNING: *Masa!*

PEPITO: That's dough!

ABUELA: *Muy bien!* The God of Lightning wasn't sure what do with the *masa.* So he rolled it into a ball, but it accidentally fell.

GOD OF LIGHTNING: Oh-oh.

ABUELA: So he spread it flat like a pancake using a giant redwood tree—

PEPITO: —*Abuela,* a redwood tree so big?

ABUELA: And threw it onto *el sol* to cook! Soon the *masa* began to bake.

GOD OF LIGHTNING: *Masa, masa, masa!*

ABUELA: The smell was so delicious. The hungry god couldn't wait so he reached for it, but he burned his hand instead yelling a great *grito.*

GOD OF LIGHTNING: Aaaghhh!

ABUELA: He threw the *tortilla* high into the sky where it stuck.

PEPITO: No way!

ABUELA: And that's how *la luna* came to be. But every now and then, that God of Lightning still gets hungry, and takes a giant bite out of that big *tortilla* moon. That's why you sometimes see it half eaten!

PEPITO: *Abuela,* is your story true?

ABUELA: *Tú qué crees?* (What do you think?)

PEPITO: I think eating *donas* is always fun with you!

PEPITO & ABUELA: Breakfast of *campeónes!* (Champions!)

(PEPITO *burps.*)

ABUELA: *Ese es mí nietecito!* (That's my grandson!)

PANADERO: *Pepito* loved his *Abuela* very much.

(ABUELA *crosses into an empty lot. She picks up garbage and an old boot throwing it into the trashcan.*)

ABUELA: Oh, look at this neighborhood. *Necesita mucho amor.* (It needs a lot of love.)

PEPITO: *Abuela,* don't start. We've got enough work to do all ready.

ABUELA: Once we've fixed up our *casita,* I bet we could make the whole neighborhood *bonito* with a little paint and *flores.*

PEPITO: *Abuela,* our street has got too many potholes. Most of the houses are boarded up, and the people living here are all strangers. What's the use of fixing things up if they're only going to get wrecked anyway?

ABUELA: This is our new home. *Debemos estar muy orgullosos.* (We should take pride in it.)

PEPITO: Don't say the "T" word, *Abuela.*

ABUELA: *Bueno,* moving into an old *casa* does take a lot of *trabajo.*

PEPITO: You said the "T" word! *Trabajo,* work, yuck!

ABUELA: A little *trabajo* doesn't hurt anyone.

PEPITO: But a lot of *trabajo* does. It's not good for little kids to work so much.

ABUELA: *Es verano y no hay escuela.* (It's summer and there's no school.)

PEPITO: But by the time I start third grade, I'll be all used up! No good for *nada!* An empty shell.

ABUELA: *Trabajo* makes you an *hombre!*

PEPITO: *Trabajo* makes you an old *hombre!*

ABUELA: *Quizás, tienes razón.* (Maybe you're right.) Maybe I have been working you a little—

PEPITO: —too much? *Abuela,* I think it's time we went to the beach.

ABUELA: *La playa?*

PEPITO: Please just say "yes"! *Por favor!*

ABUELA: *Bueno pues,* okay! (Oh, all right!)

PEPITO: You really mean it?

ABUELA: *Es una promesa!* (It's a promise!)

PEPITO: Hurray, *Abuela!* Maybe I'll even get to see my little *tortuga* turtle swimming in the sea!

ABUELA: I'm glad you and your *Papá* let her go free.

PEPITO: I bet she's all grown up. Well, I'm ready!

ABUELA: *Pepito, tenemos mucho trabajo que hacer. Las flores necesitan agua.* (Pepito, we've got a little work to do first. The flowers in the garden need watering.)

PEPITO: Okay. *Flores.* Water.

(PEPITO *waters the garden with an old bucket, while* ABUELA *gathers flowers.*)

ABUELA: I brought two things with me when I left my beloved homeland.

PEPITO: Memories of your country . . .

ABUELA & PEPITO: ". . . And a pocketful of seeds."

PEPITO: *Abuela,* did you feel sad leaving *Guatemala?*

ABUELA: Oh, *sí.* When I was a little girl I could run barefoot everywhere and pick flowers whenever I wanted but then *soldados con armas y botas* came and took everything away.

PEPITO: Soldiers with guns and boots?

ABUELA: I never looked at their faces just their shiny new *botas.* I was always hiding from them. They stole my country and they broke my heart.

PEPITO: I would have fought them.

ABUELA: Many of our people tried, but the soldiers made them disappear.

PEPITO: Did they use magic?

ABUELA: No. They used the cover of *la noche* (the night) to come into people's homes and take them away.

PEPITO: I would've run out of there as fast as I could.

ABUELA: *Eso lo que yo hice.* (That's what I did.) I listened to my heart and I came here so our *familia* would have a better future. That's why it's important you water these sweet *flores.* They remind me of the good things we brought with us. Always remember, *Pepito* to trust what's inside your heart.

PEPITO: I'm all done watering!

ABUELA: *Andale.* (Go on.) Go get your shorties and towel and I'll pack us a *lunche.*

PEPITO: I'm going to build the biggest sandcastle ever!

(PEPITO *rushes into the house.* ABUELA *sweeps the porch steps and sings a lively song in Spanish.* ABUELA *stops sweeping.*)

ABUELA: Oh, my . . . (*She sits on the porch to catch her breath.*)

PANADERO: *Pepito* and *Abuela* never did get to the beach that day. You see, *Abuela* became very ill. (PANADERO *covers over* ABUELA *with a piece of fabric.*) And soon she didn't even get out of bed. Days passed and nights came and *Abuela* died. She left behind a very sad, *triste Pepito.*

(ABUELA *and* PANADERO *exit.* PEPITO *enters in a white shirt and clip-on tie. He holds one of* ABUELA's *flowers. He sits on the porch steps and covers his face. A silhouette of* PEPITO's MADRE *appears in the doorway.*)

MADRE: *Pepito?*

PEPITO: . . .

MADRE: *Pepito* where are you?

PEPITO: I'm out here *'Amá.*

MADRE: Come inside the house.

PANADERO: *Pepito's* mother and father were away at work most of the time. *Abuela* had always looked after him since he was a baby. Now, he would have to take care of himself.

MADRE: *Pepito*, it isn't safe out there.

PANADERO: *Abuela* would always give him a dollar on Friday mornings and send him to my bakery to buy two donuts but now that would change too. (*To* PEPITO.) *Buenos días, Pepito.*

PEPITO: Hi, *Panadero.*

PANADERO: I'm sorry about *Abuela.*

PEPITO: . . .

PANADERO: Her garden still looks beautiful.

PEPITO: . . .

PANADERO: I brought you two donuts. I thought you might want to share one with your *mamá.* I bet she'd love to hear one of your *Abuela's* stories.

PEPITO: (*To himself.*) My *'amá* and *papá* are too busy for stories.

(PANADERO *places the donut bag near* PEPITO.)

PANADERO: Well, I—

PEPITO: *Panadero,* when you die, where do you go?

PANADERO: That's difficult to answer. Some people believe you go to heaven.

PEPITO: Is that where my *Abuela* went?

PANADERO: Isn't that where you want her to be?

PEPITO: No. No, I want her here with me.

PANADERO: Well, maybe she is.

PEPITO: (*Sarcastically.*) I don't see her anywhere.

PANADERO: That's because she's inside you in your *corazón.* You've got so many good memories of her. And you have her *cuentos,* too.

PEPITO: Her stories?

PANADERO: Her stories are like seeds. They'll grow in your heart and bloom. And when you share them with others it will be like *Abuela* is sitting on the porch steps right beside you listening.

PEPITO: She shouldn't have left me.

PANADERO: She didn't have a choice.

PEPITO: She was going to take me to the beach.

PANADERO: I bet she would have if she could.

PEPITO: But she never did. She lied. She broke her promise!

PANADERO: Well, I better go. I've got tomorrow's bread to bake. Goodbye *Pepito*. Over the next few days, *Pepito* kept to himself. You could see a dark cloud forming over his head. Thunder and lightning too.

MADRE: *Pepito*, if you're staying outside then water *Abuela's* garden.

PEPITO: . . .

MADRE: Answer me young man!

PEPITO: Okay! (PEPITO *kicks a bucket. He then picks it up and begins to water the garden. A bumblebee buzzes by circling and annoying* PEPITO.) Get out of here you dumb bumblebee! Get! (PEPITO *gets stung.*) Ouch! You stung me you dumb bug! What's the use of watering this stupid old garden! She's not even here to see it! Everything in this garden is *estúpido!* This neighborhood is *estúpido!* These flowers are *estúpido! Estúpido!* (PEPITO *stomps on the garden flowers crushing them. He runs into the house.*)

PANADERO: That night, *Pepito* sat on the couch all by himself reading a book and watching TV before bedtime.

(*The glow of a television appears illuminating* PEPITO's *face. He looks at a book with the picture of a manatee on the cover. The sound of sirens and gunfire is heard.*)

MADRE: (*Offstage.*) Pepito, turn off the TV!

PEPITO: Okay, 'Amá! (PEPITO *turns the television off but the sound of gunfire and sirens continues.*)

MADRE: Didn't I tell you to turn that thing off?

PEPITO: But I did!

MADRE: *Ay, Dios mio!* Pepito, get down! Get down now! (PEPITO *sits on the floor.*)

PANADERO: *Pepito* sat in the darkness as the sound of gunfire and sirens grew louder. Most nights in the neighborhood are peaceful and calm, but on occasion violence can strike deadly like a rattlesnake's bite. *Pepito* and his family turn out the lights and TV and sit in the darkness waiting until it is safe. That night *Pepito* went to sleep with a troubled heart.

PEPITO: *Estúpido* neighborhood! (PEPITO *falls asleep on the couch. The television fades up as* ABUELA *appears on its screen.*)

ABUELA: *Pepito* . . . (PEPITO *turns over in his sleep.*)

PEPITO: *Masa* . . .

ABUELA: *Pepito* . . . (PEPITO *turns over again and snores.*)

ABUELA: *Pepito.* (PEPITO *releases a little gas.*)

ABUELA: *Ese es mí nietecito!* (Ah, that's my little grandson!)

PEPITO: *Abuela!* What are you doing in the TV?

ABUELA: I've come to give you something.

(A small Guatemalan pouch magically appears in PEPITO's *hand.)*

PEPITO: Wow! What is it?

ABUELA: *Un regalo.* A gift. Now, come give me a kiss.

PEPITO: I don't want to. (PEPITO *opens the pouch removing two small figurines.)*

PEPITO: What are they?

ABUELA: They're Guatemalan Worry Dolls. They're supposed to help you when you're worried about something.

PEPITO: I'm not worried about anything.

ABUELA: You place them under your pillow before you go to sleep and in the morning all your worries will be gone.

PEPITO: Can they bring you back to life?

ABUELA: No.

PEPITO: Then what good are they?

ABUELA: Make a wish and you'll see.

(The television fades out. PEPITO *throws the* WORRY DOLLS *to the floor, a moment later he places them under his pillow. He goes back to sleep, talking to himself and snoring. Music. The* MOON *appears over the house. From under* PEPITO's *pillow appears a* WORRY DOLL *named* RIDICULO. *He wears a Guatemalan Armani suit and tie. New Yorker type.)*

RIDICULO: Free at last! Yo, Modesto, hurry up! (PEPITO *turns over in his sleep smashing* MODESTO.)

MODESTO: I'm right behind— Agghhh! *Ridiculo,* get this kid off of me!

RIDICULO: I got your back! (RIDICULO *pulls* PEPITO's *hair.)*

PEPITO: Ouch! *Abuela?*

(RIDICULO, MODESTO's brother appears from the other side. He also wears a Guatemalan Armani suit and tie.)

MODESTO: Do we look like your *Abuela?*

RIDICULO: Yeah, do we?

PEPITO: Who are you?

RIDICULO: I'm *Ridiculo.*

MODESTO: I'm *Modesto.*

MODESTO & RIDICULO: And we're the Worry Doll Brothers! *(They hi-five each other.)*

RIDICULO: Oh, yeah!

MODESTO: Lookin' good!

PEPITO: So?

RIDICULO: So?!

MODESTO: So?!

RIDICULO: Are you's for real, Kid?

MODESTO: You's ain't playing with a full deck, are you's?

PEPITO: What are you talking about?

RIDICULO: Spell it out for him, *Modesto.*

MODESTO: Okay, Kid, this is how it works. You make a wish and we make the worry go away. No questions asked.

RIDICULO: Nobody gets hurt.

MODESTO: Nobody sees nothing. Capiche!

PEPITO: Capiche?

RIDICULO: So what's your first wish gonna be?

PEPITO: You mean I have more than one?

RIDICULO: You got three.

MODESTO: So you's want somebody rubbed out?

PEPITO: Rubbed out?

RIDICULO: You's want somebody to sleep with the fishes?

PEPITO: Sleep with the—

MODESTO: Kid, we ain't got all day!

RIDICULO: Time is money!

PEPITO: I . . . I . . . I wish to go to *Guatemala*!

RIDICULO & MODESTO: Guatemala?

PEPITO: That's right, *Guatemala.*

RIDICULO: You ever heard of it, *Modesto*?

MODESTO: Not on your life, *Ridiculo.*

PEPITO: I'd rather go there than stay in this crummy old neighborhood.

MODESTO: Let me explain this to you, Kid.

RIDICULO: It's real simple—

MODESTO & RIDICULO: We don't go to Guatemala!

PEPITO: But aren't you Guatemalan Worry Dolls?

RIDICULO: Wow, hold on there, Pisano!

MODESTO: Who says we're from Guatemala?

PEPITO: Well aren't you?

RIDICULO: We may look like we're from Guatemala.

MODESTO & RIDICULO: But we're from New York. (MODESTO's *cell phone rings.*)

MODESTO: Hold it there cowboy. Hello?

RIDICULO: Who is it?

MODESTO: The Boss. (MODESTO *and* RIDICULO *listen to the phone together.*)

RIDICULO: He's right here.

MODESTO: You want him to—

RIDICULO: Right now?

MODESTO: But he's got three—

RIDICULO: Consider it done.

MODESTO & RIDICULO: No problemo. (MODESTO *puts his cell phone away.*)

MODESTO: So we're on a mission, Kid.

PEPITO: A mission?

RIDICULO: We gotta take you to *Cuate-Malo*.

PEPITO: *Cuate-Malo?* I don't want to go to there.

MODESTO: It's just like Guatemala. Right, *Ridiculo?*

RIDICULO: Oh, yeah, you's could say that. They're like identical twin countries.

MODESTO: Yeah, tropical and stuff.

RIDICULO: Coconuts and grass skirts.

PEPITO: But doesn't *Cuate-Malo* mean "the bad twin"?

MODESTO: Look Kid, you gotta save a country.

PEPITO: Me?

RIDICULO: Except, you're gonna have to be real careful.

PEPITO: Careful?

RIDICULO: 'Cause it's risky.

PEPITO: Risky?

MODESTO: And dangerous.

PEPITO: Dangerous?

MODESTO: Get ready, Kid.

PEPITO: But I don't want to go to *Cuate-Malo!*

RIDICULO: Don't forget your donuts!

(Thunder and lightning. PEPITO, MODESTO, RIDICULO *are sucked into the television set. It sprouts wings and flies away.)*

PANADERO: *Pepito* was swept up into the sky on a chariot with wings heading towards a mysterious land called *Cuate-Malo*, The Bad Twin! He didn't know what he'd find. He didn't know what they wanted from him. He didn't even know how dangerous it would be.

(The television set crash lands. PEPITO *stands in a tropical jungle. Behind him is a volcanic mountain, which occasionally releases rings of smoke and a little gas.)*

PEPITO: *Modesto? Ridiculo?* Where am I?

*(*LITTLE GIRL FOOTSTEPS' *face appears in a coconut hanging from a palm tree.)*

LITTLE GIRL FOOTSTEPS: Be quiet you!

PEPITO: Who said that?

*(*LITTLE GIRL FOOTSTEPS' *face appears on a rock.)*

LITTLE GIRL FOOTSTEPS: Shhh!

PEPITO: How do you do that?

(Her face disappears. PEPITO *lifts up a rock. A flower springs up instantly.)*

PEPITO: Wow!

*(*LITTLE GIRL FOOTSTEPS' *face reappears in the coconut. She holds out an old bucket and starts to water the flower.)*

LITTLE GIRL FOOTSTEPS: I'll tell you my secret but you can't tell anyone. I hold my breath and disappear!

PEPITO: Yeah, right!

LITTLE GIRL FOOTSTEPS: That way they won't find me.

PEPITO: Who?

LITTLE GIRL FOOTSTEPS: Put that rock back this instant!

PEPITO: Not until you tell me what I'm doing here!

(The sounds of boots marching are heard off in the distance.)

COMMANDANTE BOOTS & SERGEANT BOTAS: Your left. Your left. That's why your mother packed up and left. Your left. Your left.

LITTLE GIRL FOOTSTEPS: Oh, no, they know you're here!

PEPITO: Who cares!

LITTLE GIRL FOOTSTEPS: You better hide!

PEPITO: I'm not moving 'til you start talking!

LITTLE GIRL FOOTSTEPS: Oh, you're a stubborn *muchacho! The Great Sea Tortuga* made a big mistake choosing you! How are you going to save *Cuate-Malo!*

PEPITO: I'm not saving *Cuate-Malo!*

LITTLE GIRL FOOTSTEPS: Hide! They're here!

(LITTLE GIRL FOOTSTEPS places the rock back covering the flower. She disappears.)

PEPITO: Wait! Come back you! Oh-oh!

(PEPITO hides. Fanfare. COMMANDANTE BOOTS wears sunglasses, military uniform, large boots and lots of medals; and SERGEANT BOTAS, who wears a large pair of army boots, march in together.)

COMMANDANTE BOOTS: Halt!

SERGEANT BOTAS: Attention!

COMMANDANTE BOOTS: Sound off!

SERGEANT BOTAS: One! *Commandante* Boots, I'm ready and accounted for, Sir!

COMMANDANTE BOOTS: Good! Where is the boy, Sergeant *Botas?*

SERGEANT BOTAS: Boy, *Commandante?*

COMMANDANTE BOOTS: Our mortal enemy, *idiota!* Go find him now you!

SERGEANT BOTAS: Yes, sir! Hut! Hut! Hut! *(SERGEANT BOTAS marches out. PEPITO pops out his head. COMMANDANTE BOOTS sniffs the air.)*

COMMANDANTE BOOTS: I smell boy. Boy?

PEPITO: . . . *(PEPITO quickly hides somewhere else as COMMANDANTE BOOTS searches for him.)*

COMMANDANTE BOOTS: Boy?

PEPITO: . . .

COMMANDANTE BOOTS: Come out; come out wherever you are! *(COMMANDANTE BOOTS finds nothing.)* I know you're hiding somewhere! Why must you play this silly game? It's only a matter of time, you know? I'll find you, and when I do, you'll wish you wished you had never come to *Cuate-Malo!* Boy? *(COMMANDANTE BOOTS kicks the rock. The beautiful flower springs up.*

COMMANDANTE BOOTS *has a panic attack.)* Oh, no! A flower! Sergeant *Botas!* Sergeant *Botas! (*COMMANDANTE BOOTS *walks around in a daze almost kicking the old water bucket.)* I almost kicked the bucket!

*(*SERGEANT BOTAS *runs in.)*

SERGEANT BOTAS: What is it *Commandante* Boots?

COMMANDANTE BOOTS: It's a— It's a—

SERGEANT BOTAS: Oh, a flower! It's so beautiful!

COMMANDANTE BOOTS: *Exactamente!* Step on it, *idiota!*

SERGEANT BOTAS: *A sus ordenes, Commandante! Estúpido! (*SERGEANT BOTAS *quickly stomps on the flower crushing it.)*

COMMANDANTE BOOTS: *(To himself.)* This boy is cleverer than I thought. He must have planted that flower to trick me. Leaving that bucket for me to kick! *(To* SERGEANT BOTAS*.)* I want this whole field swept for buckets and seeds!

SERGEANT BOTAS: Seeds, *mí Commandante?*

COMMANDANTE BOTAS: *Sí*, seeds!

SERGEANT BOTAS: *Sí, mí Commandante!*

COMMANDANTE BOOTS: Double the patrols, triple the defense budget; ask for more foreign aid! I want this boy captured immediately!

SERGEANT BOTAS: More patrols are on their way, Sir!

COMMANDANTE BOOTS & SERGEANT BOTAS: Your left. Your left. That's why your mother packed up and left. Your left. Your left—

(They march off together. LITTLE GIRL FOOTSTEPS *appears as a rock.)*

PEPITO: That guy's messed up. Who is he?

*(*LITTLE GIRL FOOTSTEPS *appears as a coconut.)*

LITTLE GIRL FOOTSTEPS: A very bad pair of boots. He hates everything that's beautiful. Like white clouds against a blue sky, magnificent spider webs and flowers. Especially flowers. *(*LITTLE GIRL FOOTSTEPS *appears as a rock.)* Oh, this one's stomped to bits, which means there's only one left in the whole country. Thanks to you! *The Great Sea Tortuga* shouldn't have picked you!

*(*LITTLE GIRL FOOTSTEPS *appears as a coconut.)*

PEPITO: Hey you, stop that! You're making dizzy! Who are you anyway?

LITTLE GIRL FOOTSTEPS: I'm Little Girl Footsteps, Protector of the Last Flower in *Cuate-Malo* and Super Agent Spy!

PEPITO: You're on my complaint list, Footsteps Girl!

LITTLE GIRL FOOTSTEPS: Oh, I'm scared! *(*LITTLE GIRL FOOTSTEPS *appears as a rock for a moment and then disappears.)*

PEPITO: Hey! Where'd you go? *(Shouting.)* I want to see this *Great Sea Tortuga* now! I got some things to say LIKE WHY AM I HERE?

*(*LITTLE GIRL FOOTSTEPS *appears as a coconut.)*

LITTLE GIRL FOOTSTEPS: You don't have to shout. *The Great Sea Tortuga* is hiding where *Commandante* Boots' navy can't find her. You've got a long and dangerous journey ahead of you. I hope you can swim real good.

(LITTLE GIRL FOOTSTEPS *appears as a rock.*)

PEPITO: Swim? Like in the sea?

LITTLE GIRL FOOTSTEPS: Yup.

PEPITO: I changed my mind. I'm not going. I want to go back home now.

LITTLE GIRL FOOTSTEPS: There's no time. *(She whistles.)*

LITTLE GIRL FOOTSTEPS: *Tirado,* our local taxi will take you to the Sea of Tears.

(A single black tire rolls in, screeching to a stop. The tire is TIRADO, *the local taxi. He's got lots of tire patches all over his body. Whenever* TIRADO *speaks he stutters.)*

TIRADO: Wh-wh-what honor!

PEPITO: What did he say?

LITTLE GIRL FOOTSTEPS: "What an honor."

TIRADO: T-t-to seat you!

LITTLE GIRL FOOTSTEPS: This is *Tirado.*

PEPITO: Is that all of him?

TIRADO: Th-th-that's it! Swizzle-stick!

LITTLE GIRL FOOTSTEPS: When *Commandante* Boots took power he imprisoned all those resisting him and sent them to Smoking Mountain Compound. *Tirado* was one of them. He came back that way.

TIRADO: Ha-ha-hop on son!

PEPITO: I don't think this is a good idea.

LITTLE GIRL FOOTSTEPS: For heaven's sake get in!

TIRADO: Si-si-sit! Lickety-split!

(Marching is heard.)

LITTLE GIRL FOOTSTEPS: Oh, no, the *Monstruo Botas!*

*(*PEPITO *climbs into* TIRADO.*)*

PEPITO: Aren't you coming?

LITTLE GIRL FOOTSTEPS: I can't! I've got to guard the last remaining flower in *Cuate-Malo.* It's hidden nearby. Get in! Don't fail us, *Pepito!*

TIRADO: To-to-to the sea! Pep-eee! *(*TIRADO *screeches off as* PEPITO *spins.)*

PEPITO: Aaagghhh!!! *(*PEPITO *and* TIRADO *journey across the countryside.)*

PANADERO: *Pepito* and *Tirado* traveled across *Cuate-Malo.* It was a tiny country with big mountains, deep valleys and bumpy roads.

PEPITO: Ouch!

PANADERO: *Pepito* saw what *Commandante* Boots had done to the country. He had transformed it into a land of fear and sorrow where even laughter was outlawed.

ARM: *Alto!*

(At a military checkpoint. A long ARM *appears with a sign that reads, "*ALTO.*"* TIRADO *screeches to a stop.* PEPITO *falls out.)*

PEPITO: Aaagghhh!

TIRADO: Shhh!

PEPITO: What is it now?

TIRADO: Ch-ch-check point! D-d-danger! Stranger!

(A large NOSE *appears sniffing everything in sight. It behaves like a bulldog barking occasionally. The* ARM *holds the* NOSE *by a leash* PEPITO *and* TIRADO *hide behind a fern.)*

PEPITO: We've got to get passed them, don't we?

TIRADO: Ay! Ay! Eye!

(A large single EYE *appears searching. It's like a searchlight.)*

PEPITO: We're sitting ducks! We've got to find a way!

(In silhouette ANIMAL REFUGEES *are seen leaving.* A BABY MANATEE *is left behind. The* NOSE *barks loudly at the* BABY MANATEE.*)*

BABY MANATEE: *(Terrified.) Mamí? Mamí?* (Mommy? Mommy?)

PEPITO: Look, it's a baby manatee!

BABY MANATEE: *Donde esta mí mamí?* (Where's my mommy?)

ARM: *Dámelo!* (Give it to me!)

(The ARM, NOSE *and* EYE *surround the* BABY MANATEE *confiscating her little book.)*

PEPITO: They're taking her picture book away!

(The NOSE *barks loudly at the* BABY MANATEE *scaring her away.)*

BABY MANATEE: *(Crying.) Mamí!*

PEPITO: They can't do that!

(The NOSE *goes sniffing towards* PEPITO *and* TIRADO.*)*

TIRADO: Hi-hi-hide! *(It begins to rain.* TIRADO *opens a small umbrella.)* Wh-wh-what sadness.

PEPITO: It's raining.

TIRADO: Ch-ch-children's tears.

PEPITO: *(Whispering.)* Why is *Commandante* Boots doing these horrible things?

TIRADO: Wh-wh-when *Commandante* was a small pair of baby boots he played rough and s-s-sometimes cheated—

PEPITO: That's awful.

TIRADO: —we never t-t-thought that he'd leap from a size four to a size twelve and become—

PEPITO: So evil?

TIRADO: Ye-ye-yes.

PEPITO: Somebody's got to stop him.

TIRADO: You, you, you.

PEPITO: No, no, no. I'm just a little kid. I wouldn't know what to do.

TIRADO: R-r-rain gone!

(The sun appears and a beautiful rainbow follows.)

PEPITO: *Mira, un arco iris!* (Look, it's a rainbow!)

(The EYE *screams and* NOSE *barks.)*

EYE: *Ay, ay, ay!*

PEPITO: I know their weakness!

TIRADO: Wha-what? Chowchow?

PEPITO: They can't look at beautiful things! This is our chance! *Vámonos!*

*(*TIRADO *picks up speed as the rainbow shines. Sirens and gunfire erupt. The large* ARM *tries to catch them but can't. The* NOSE *chases after them but gives up. And the* EYE *just watches. A beach shore is heard.)*

TIRADO: We-we-we made it! Se-Se-Sea of Tears, *Pepito!*

PEPITO: But where's *The Great Sea Tortuga?*

TIRADO: Ou-ou-out there.

PEPITO: But I can't swim too good!

TIRADO: F-f-find way! Me-me-me help Little Girl Fo-Fo-Footsteps.

PEPITO: *Tirado,* don't go! I don't want to be alone!

*(*TIRADO *exits screeching.)*

PEPITO: What can I do? How can I save a country when I can't even take care of myself? I bet *Abuela* would know what to do. (PEPITO *sits.* PEPITO *opens his donut bag and removes his two donuts. He bites into one.)* Ouch!

(He strikes both donuts and they chime. PANADERO *appears. He may also play* EL SOL.*)*

PANADERO: Poor *Pepito* sat there alone on the beach while *El Sol* baked him all day like *masa.*

PEPITO: *El Sol,* it's so hot today. I'm so thirsty. The sea looks like a big cool glass of water.

EL SOL: I wouldn't drink from there if I were you.

PEPITO: Why not?

EL SOL: Because it'll make you sad and then more sadder.

PEPITO: I don't care. Go away!

EL SOL: Very well.

*(*PEPITO *drinks from the Sea of Tears.* EL SOL *is replaced by* LA LUNA. LA LUNA *is the moon.* PEPITO *cries softly.)*

LUNA: *Pepito.*

PEPITO: Hello, *Luna.*

LUNA: You must be hungry?

PEPITO: Yes, I am. My tummy won't stop growling.

LUNA: How would you like to eat a *Tortilla* Moon?

PEPITO: Won't the God of Lightning be angry?

LUNA: Oh, no, he can always make another for himself.

PEPITO: I'll just take a bite.

(LUNA *descends toward* PEPITO. *He reaches up and tears a small piece.* LUNA *returns to the sky.*)

LUNA: Well?

PEPITO: It tastes good, but I'd rather have a donut instead.

LUNA: Rest your little eyes. Tomorrow is a new day.

A musical underscore. LUNA sings in Spanish.

PEPITO: *Abuela,* I miss your words in Spanish. I miss your soft hands when we'd cross a street. I miss your songs when I couldn't sleep. I miss your smile when you'd look at me. I miss everything about you and how life used to be. *Abuela?*

(PEPITO *lies down to sleep. A moment later he is softly snoring. The next day.* PEPITO *is sound asleep.* RIDICULO *and* MODESTO *pop out from behind him.*)

RIDICULO & MODESTO: Hey, Kid, wake up!

PEPITO: *Ridiculo, Modesto,* what are you doing here?

MODESTO: We go where you's go.

RIDICULO: We watch your back. Capiche?

MODESTO: What's on your mind, Kid?

PEPITO: I've got to find *The Great Sea Tortuga.* Since I don't swim so good I need something to float in like a boat or an ocean liner or even a battleship!

MODESTO & RIDICULO: A battleship?

PEPITO: Yeah.

RIDICULO: Time out. Conference. (MODESTO & RIDICULO *whisper to one another.* PEPITO *strikes the donuts repeatedly and they chime.*) Cut that out, Kid—

MODESTO: —we're trying to think here.

(PEPITO *continues to strike the donuts.* RIDICULO *and* MODESTO *suddenly look at each other.*)

RIDICULO: Wo!

MODESTO: Wo!

RIDICULO: *Modesto,* are you thinkin' what I'm thinkin'?

MODESTO: I'm thinkin' that!

RIDICULO: Okay, Kid, make your second wish.

PEPITO: What happened to my first?

MODESTO: We brought you's here.

PEPITO: But I wanted to go to *Guatemala!*

RIDICULO: Guatemala. *Cuate-Malo.* Same difference.

MODESTO: Make your wish, Kid!

PEPITO: I wish for a—

(*Thunder and lightning.* MODESTO *and* RIDICULO *disappear.* PEPITO *sits on a large donut floating in the middle of the sea.*)

PEPITO: Hey, what's this? A donut! *Modesto? Ridiculo?* This isn't fair!

(*A* BI-PLANE PAIR OF SHOES *enters flying.*)

PEPITO: It's a plane! I'm going to be rescued! Hello!

(*The* BI-PLANE PAIR OF SHOES *drops a* SHARK TORPEDO *into the sea.*)

PEPITO: Oh, no, it's one of *Commandante* Boots' planes! And a torpedo's coming right at me! Paddle!

(THE SHARK TORPEDO *circles* PEPITO *while he desperately tries to paddle away.* THE SHARK TORPEDO *takes a bite out of* PEPITO'S *donut deflating it.*)

PEPITO: Help! I'm sinking! *Ayúdame!*

(PEPITO *struggles to stay afloat, but he descends below the water. Suddenly out of nowhere* THE GREAT SEA TORTUGA *appears. She is a giant sea turtle. She brings* PEPITO *back to the surface on her shell.* THE GREAT SEA TORTUGA *has a magnificent voice.* PEPITO *awakens.*)

THE GREAT SEA TORTUGA: Hello, old friend.

PEPITO: (*Coughing.*) You saved my life.

THE GREAT SEA TORTUGA: I was afraid I had lost you.

PEPITO: You're the Great Sea *Tortuga!*

THE GREAT SEA TORTUGA: *Pepito,* you are so brave to come here. You don't recognize me, do you?

PEPITO: No.

THE GREAT SEA TORTUGA: Well, I was a lot smaller then.

PEPITO: Did your shell have a sandy beach, palm tree and a coconut painted on it?

THE GREAT SEA TORTUGA: Yes.

PEPITO: We used to play for hours together.

THE GREAT SEA TORTUGA: You do remember me!

PEPITO: Oh, I missed you my little *tortuga!* (*He tries to hug her shell.*)

THE GREAT SEA TORTUGA: And I you, *Pepito.*

PEPITO: Why am I here, *Tortuga?*

THE GREAT SEA TORTUGA: Because I need your help. We've tried to stop *Commandante* Boots but he has become too powerful and dangerous.

PEPITO: But I don't know what to do. I don't have an army of *Monstruo Botas.* I'm not even in the third grade yet.

THE GREAT SEA TORTUGA: You're our last hope. Trust your heart.

PEPITO: My heart?

THE GREAT SEA TORTUGA: Look to the beauty inside. We're here. *Adios amigo.*

PEPITO: Goodbye! (PEPITO *steps onto the beach.* THE GREAT SEA TORTUGA *disappears into the sea.*) What did she mean by the "beauty" inside? *Ridiculo! Modesto!* Anybody?

(RIDICULO *and* MODESTO *suddenly appear.*)

RIDICULO & MODESTO: What is it, Kid?

PEPITO: I need your help.

MODESTO: You's want us to take care of that no good *Commandante* Boots?

RIDICULO: Yeah, you's want us to fit him with a nice pair of concrete shoes?

MODESTO: Know what we mean?

PEPITO: That's not right. There's got to be a better way to defeat him. I just don't know what it is yet.

(MODESTO's *cell phone rings.*)

MODESTO: Hold it there cowboy. Hello? (MODESTO *and* RIDICULO *listen to the phone together.*)

RIDICULO: Kid, the news on the home front ain't good.

MODESTO: *Commandante* Boots' secret police found the last remaining flower in *Cuate-Malo.*

PEPITO: They did?

MODESTO: They arrested Little Girl Footsteps and *Tirado* too.

RIDICULO: They've been taken to *Commandante* Boots' Smoking Mountain Compound.

PEPITO: We've got to save them!

RIDICULO: What are you crazy?

MODESTO: The only way to get past *Commandante* Boots' army is to fly over them. Last time I checked I didn't have no aeroplane in my pocket, do you *Ridiculo?*

RIDICULO: No, I don't.

MODESTO: It's hopeless, Kid. We'll take you back home. Make your third wish.

PEPITO: I wish for a balloon made out of your suits!

(*Thunder and lightning.* RIDICULO *and* MODESTO *suits fly off. They wear only their ties and underwear. A colorful balloon instantly appears.*)

RIDICULO: Hey, look what you did to our fine suits!

MODESTO: Nobody said nothin' about slicin' or dicin'—

PEPITO: Boys, we're on a mission. Capiche? (PEPITO *climbs aboard. The balloon flies off.*)

MODESTO: Hey, Kid, where you going?

RIDICULO: Bring back our suits!

MODESTO: They cost us a bundle!

PEPITO: I can see everything from up here! There's the Sea of Tears! (*A gust of wind carries him higher.*) Wo! Guys, I don't feel so good. Guys?

RIDICULO: That's pretty low!

MODESTO: Ungrateful I say!

RIDICULO: What's a Worry Doll without his suit!

MODESTO: Exactly! Come on!

(*They exit.* PANADERO *appears.*)

PANADERO: A half-shaped moon appeared that night casting giant shadows across the Land of Sorrow and the Sea of Tears. *Pepito* flew over Tierra City; the once vibrant capital of *Cuate-Malo* now reduced to rubble and ash. And finally, there before him was Smoking Mountain. He was almost there.

(The balloon flies on towards Smoking Mountain Compound. A now visible LIT-TLE GIRL FOOTSTEPS *is held in a glass jar, while* TIRADO *hangs in the air.* SERGEANT BOTAS *stands near a bucket full of seeds.* COMMANDANTE BOOTS *looks on.)*

SERGEANT BOTAS: *Commandante Boots*, these are the last seeds we swept up. And the only flower left in *Cuate-Malo* is underneath that rock there.

COMMANDANTE BOOTS: *Excellente*, Sergeant *Botas*! Now, *Tirado*, where is the boy?

LITTLE GIRL FOOTSTEPS: He won't say a thing!

COMMANDANTE BOOTS: All I have to do is click my heels and orders are carried out. Things get done. Who here values their life?

SERGEANT BOTAS: I do!

COMMANDANTE BOOTS: Not you, *idiota!*

LITTLE GIRL FOOTSTEPS: We're not afraid of you!

COMMANDANTE BOOTS: But you should be. What do you say *Tirado*?

TIRADO: D-d-don't hurt me!

COMMANDANTE BOOTS: Ah, someone who understands their situation.

TIRADO: Wh-wh-what do to me?

COMMANDANTE BOOTS: Well, now, that depends on what you've got to tell.

TIRADO: N-n-nothing.

COMMANDANTE BOOTS: Sergeant *Botas*, what shall we do with *Tirado*?

SERGEANT BOTAS: String him up, Sir!

COMMANDANTE BOOTS: We've all ready done that, you *idiota!* No, we need something a little more persuasive. Sergeant *Botas* prepare the secret weapon!

SERGEANT BOTAS: Not the Bumble Zapper, Sir!

COMMANDANTE BOOTS: Yes, it's time we show him the power of my military.

SERGEANT BOTAS: But it's never been field-tested.

COMMANDANTE BOOTS: Go on!

*(*SERGEANT BOTAS *removes a box, which now and then rattles terribly.)*

SERGEANT BOTAS: Oh-oh . . .

COMMANDANTE BOOTS: *Tirado*, tell me where that confounded boy is to be found!

TIRADO: N-n-no Colombo!

COMMANDANTE BOOTS: Release the Bumble Zapper!

*(*SERGEANT BOTAS *releases the* BUMBLE ZAPPER. *It is a mechanical bumblebee with spiked hair, tattoos, and a bad attitude. He buzzes around madly.)*

BUMBLE ZAPPER: Buzz off! *(The* BUMBLE ZAPPER *fires a stinger missile striking* COMMANDANTE BOOTS *on his behind.)*

COMMANDANTE BOOTS: Ou-ou-ouchy!

SERGEANT BOTAS: Come here you! (SERGEANT BOTAS *grabs him putting him back in his box.*)

COMMANDANTE BOOTS: Medic!

(SERGEANT BOTAS *quickly reveals a medic insignia.*)

COMMANDANTE BOOTS: I need a band-aid!

SERGEANT BOTAS: But I don't have one, Sir!

COMMANDANTE BOOTS: In that case, I deserve a medal! A big one! (COMMANDANTE BOOTS *reveals a big shiny medal.*)

SERGEANT BOTAS: Oh, it's such a beautifully ugly medal, *Commandante Boots!*

COMMANDANTE BOOTS: It's *Generalismo* Boots! I just promoted myself. (*To* SERGEANT BOTAS.) Oh, get out of the way! Now, *Tirado,* shall I place the Bumble Zapper in Little Girl Footsteps' jar?

TIRADO: I— I— I—

COMMANDANTE BOOTS: Are you ready to tell me what I want to know?

LITTLE GIRL FOOTSTEPS: *Tirado,* don't say a thing!

TIRADO: *Sí-sí-sí!*

COMMANDANTE BOOTS: Did you say "sea"?

TIRADO: No-no-no!

COMMANDANTE BOOTS: Of course! The boy is with the Great Sea *Tortuga!* I'll send my warships there to destroy them! No one can stop me now!

(*Fanfare.* COMMANDANTE BOOTS *steps onto a soapbox.*)

COMMANDANTE BOOTS: At ease. Victory is ours! Ugly statues will be erected! Long and boring speeches will be written! Major motion pictures will be made! I decree that all things beautiful be deemed WRONG against the state. And if BEAUTY appears anywhere it will be STOMPED OUT by my legion of *Monstruo Botas!* Sergeant *Botas?*

SERGEANT BOTAS: *Sí, mí General?*

COMMANDANTE BOOTS: I will dispose of the last flower now.

SERGEANT BOTAS: But won't that harm you, *Mí General?*

COMMANDANTE BOOTS: I won't look! I'll let my boots do the talking! Remove the rock!

(SERGEANT BOTAS *lifts a rock and a flower instantly springs up.* COMMANDANTE BOOTS *steps on the flower crushing it.*)

COMMANDANTE BOTAS: Oh, that feels so good!

(*The balloon descends into the compound.*)

SERGEANT BOTAS: Look!

COMMANDANTE BOOTS: Don't interrupt me.

SERGEANT BOTAS: But . . . but . . .

LITTLE GIRL FOOTSTEPS: It's *Pepito!*

COMMANDANTE BOOTS: There you are boy! Finally, we meet!

PEPITO: Let my *amigos* go free, Boots!

COMMANDANTE BOOTS: Or you'll do what?

PEPITO: I got back up, See?

SERGEANT BOTAS: Yeah, you and whose army, Pal?

PEPITO: Me and— *Ridiculo? Modesto?* Guys? Oh, oh!

COMMANDANTE BOOTS: On guard!

LITTLE GIRL FOOTSTEPS: Watch out, *Pepito!*

(COMMANDANTE BOOTS *tries to stomp on* PEPITO. PEPITO *tries to avoid him but he is finally pinned to the ground.*)

LITTLE GIRL FOOTSTEPS: Oh, no!

SERGEANT BOTAS: Hurray, *Generalismo!*

COMMANDANTE BOOTS: The Great Sea *Tortuga* shouldn't have sent a boy to do a man's job!

PEPITO: I can't move!

COMMANDANTE BOOTS: You got anything to say before I finish you off boy?

LITTLE GIRL FOOTSTEPS: *(To* PEPITO.) Trust what's inside your heart, *Pepito!*

PEPITO: What did you say?

COMMANDANTE BOOTS: Nothing can stop me now!

LITTLE GIRL FOOTSTEPS: Beauty isn't dead yet!

COMMANDANTE BOOTS: I crushed the last flower and all that remains is that bucket of seeds!

PEPITO: Seeds?

COMMANDANTE BOOTS: *Sí*, seeds. And I'll stomp them out just like I will you boy!

LITTLE GIRL FOOTSTEPS: You can't destroy what's inside us!

PEPITO: Stories are like seeds!

LITTLE GIRL FOOTSTEPS: That's right, *Pepito!*

COMMANDANTE BOOTS: Victory will be mine!

PEPITO: They can flower in the heart!

LITTLE GIRL FOOTSTEPS: Go on!

PEPITO: And they'll grow beautiful like my *Abuela*'s stories!

(*The pounding of a drum is heard.* COMMANDANTE BOOTS *becomes disoriented.* PEPITO *is freed.*)

COMMANDANTE BOOTS: Stories? What stories?

PEPITO: The one's I got in my *corazón!*

(*Another drumbeat is heard.*)

COMMANDANTE BOOTS: I hate beautiful stories!

SERGEANT BOTAS: Oh-oh!

PEPITO: A God of Lightning once threw *masa* onto the sun to cook!

(*Another drumbeat.*)

COMMANDANTE BOOTS: Get away from me!

(LITTLE GIRL FOOTSTEPS *escapes from the jar.*)

LITTLE GIRL FOOTSTEPS: It's working *Pepito!*

PEPITO: It smelled so delicious he couldn't wait!

(*Another drumbeat.*)

COMMANDANTE BOOTS: What's happening to me?

PEPITO: He burned himself and yelled a great *grito—*

COMMANDANTE BOOTS: *Aagghhh!*

PEPITO: And that's how the *la luna* came to be!

(*The final drumbeat is heard.* COMMANDANTE BOOTS *literally kicks the bucket and drops to the ground.*)

SERGEANT BOTAS: *Dios mio,* he really did kick the bucket! Retreat!

LITTLE GIRL FOOTSTEPS: Freeze Soldier!

(SERGEANT BOTAS *freezes.*)

LITTLE GIRL FOOTSTEPS: *Pepito,* you defeated *Commandante* Boots and his army! You saved us! You saved our country!

(*A tiny pair of baby boots crawl out of* COMMANDANTE BOOTS' *boots. It runs around crying hysterically.*)

LITTLE GIRL FOOTSTEPS: Look, *Commandante* Boots isn't a general anymore! He's a pair of baby *botas!*

PEPITO: You've been very naughty!

(COMMANDANTE BABY *cries again.*)

LITTLE GIRL FOOTSTEPS: What are we going to do with him?

PEPITO: (*To* COMMANDANTE BABY.) As punishment, you and Sergeant *Botas* are going to plant every seed in this bucket all across *Cuate-Malo.* Not only that, you're going to water, weed and like it too!

(COMMANDANTE BABY *cries louder.*)

SERGEANT BOTAS: Oh, I like planting *flores.* Come on Baby *Botas!*

(SERGEANT BOTAS *and* COMMANDANTE BABY SHOES *exit with a bucket of seeds. Music. The crushed flower rises and blooms.*)

PEPITO: Look there! It's growing back!

LITTLE GIRL FOOTSTEPS: The last remaining flower in *Cuate-Malo* will now become our first. The whole country will transform into beauty once more. *Pepito,* I never have to be afraid or disappear again. I can run barefoot on the beach and play all I want.

PEPITO: This place is just like how *Abuela* described her homeland. She was right, you can make things better wherever you live.

LITTLE GIRL FOOTSTEPS: Thank you.

PEPITO: (*Embarrassed.*) Well, I better go.

TIRADO: *P-P-Pepito!*

PEPITO: What is it, *Tirado*?

TIRADO: T-t-take these seeds to-to-to remember us!

PEPITO: *Gracias, amigos.* (Thank you, friends.)

LITTLE GIRL FOOTSTEPS & TIRADO: Goodbye!

(LITTLE GIRL FOOTSTEPS *and* TIRADO *exit.*)

PEPITO: *Adios!* It's time for me to go home. My home. *Ridiculo? Modesto?*

(MODESTO *and* RIDICULO *appear in their underwear.*)

MODESTO & RIDICULO: We're ready to rumble, Kid.

PEPITO: It's all over.

RIDICULO: It looks like you didn't need our help after all.

PEPITO: But I still do. How will I find my way back?

MODESTO: The way we see it.

RIDICULO: We owe you's one good wish.

(*The balloon flies in.*)

PEPITO: My donut balloon! Then I'm ready! Thanks guys! *Vamonos!*

MODESTO: I tell you what my wish is, *Ridiculo.* I want my suit back. The dry cleaning is gonna cost me a bundle. Am I right?

RIDICULO: You sure are Modesto. Hey, is that kid leaving without us again?

MODESTO: After all we've done for him.

RIDICULO: I tell you's what, I'm going back to New York.

MODESTO: In your underwear? You're going to have to move to the Village!

(*They exit. A moment later,* PEPITO *lies sleeping on his couch.* MADRE *appears. She looks a lot like* ABUELA, *except younger.*)

MADRE: *Pepito.*

PEPITO: . . .

MADRE: *Pepito,* wake up!

PEPITO: *'Amá? (Recognizing her.) 'Amá!*

(PEPITO *hugs her.*)

MADRE: Oh, my, what's that for?

PEPITO: *'Amá,* you're not going to believe what happened to me!

MADRE: What?

PEPITO: I went to *Cuate-Malo* and there was this very bad pair of boots—

MADRE: Boots? *Pepito,* you're just like *Abuela.* Such an imagination.

PEPITO: He captured my *amigos* and I had to free them!

MADRE: I've got so much to do today.

PEPITO: Well, I've got such a story to tell you!

(*Beat.*)

MADRE: Why don't you go to *Panadero's* bakery and buy us two *donas!*

PEPITO: Really?

MADRE: Yes, really. The laundry and shopping can wait. I want to hear all about your adventure. What do you say?

PEPITO: Okay, *'Amá!*

(PEPITO *crosses to the garden. He looks in his pocket and finds three seeds out. It wasn't a dream!* PEPITO *looks up into the sky.*)

PEPITO: *Abuela,* these seeds are for your garden. Thank you for your beautiful stories. (PEPITO *kisses the seeds and plants them.* PANADERO *enters.*)

PEPITO: *Hola, Señor Panadero! Dos donas por favor!*

PANADERO: Two donuts coming right up! (PANADERO *hands* PEPITO *a small donut bag.* PEPITO *crosses to his* MADRE *who waits for him on the porch steps.*)

PEPITO: *'Amá,* I saved *Cuate-Malo!*

MADRE: Did you?

PEPITO: Ah huh, and I met all sorts of strange creatures like a taxi tire, a coconut-girl rock, a talking *tortuga*—

MADRE: A turtle?

(PANADERO *now holds a paintbrush and a bucket of paint.*)

PANADERO: *Buenos dias, Señora!*

MADRE: *Buenos dias, Panadero!* What a lovely morning it is.

PEPITO: Are you going to paint something?

PANADERO: I'm going to brighten up our little *barrio* with a mural on my bakery wall.

PEPITO: May I help, *Panadero?*

PANADERO: *Bueno, pues,* I can always use help!

PEPITO: Okay!

PANADERO: Well, *Pepito* came and helped me paint my mural. But first he had to tell his *'Amá* all about his adventure.

PEPITO: There was *Ridiculo* and *Modesto;* a television set with wings—

MADRE: Wings?

PEPITO: Yeah and—

PANADERO: They sat on their porch steps eating their two *donas.* And what a beautiful morning it was. The sun was shining, and the garden flowers were blooming, and the spiders were spinning their magnificent webs, while children laughed and played throughout the neighborhood. And for a brief moment it was paradise. Just like a distant country *Abuela* loved to remember.

CURTAIN

DR. SEUSS'
HOW THE GRINCH
STOLE CHRISTMAS

book and lyrics by
Timothy Mason

music by
Mel Marvin

ACT ONE

(We see the dark mouth of a massive cave, the size of the entire proscenium opening, hung with snow and icicles. We hear the echoing hoots of owls: WHOOO, WHOOO, WHOOO.)

(In an icy mist, there's a sudden vision: a GROUP OF CAROLERS *appears, singing.)*

DISTANT CHOIR:
>   The Holly And The Ivy, when they are both full grown . . .

(The CAROLERS *disappear. The sound of the voices is carried off with the wind.)*

(Suddenly we see a grizzled OLD DOG, *carrying a battered suitcase and wearing an old topcoat and muffler.* OLD MAX *is tall, slender and somehow elegant. He has graying hair and a little gray beard and thick black-rimmed glasses. With his urbane elegance, long-limbed grace and gently sardonic humor, he actually reminds me of* DR. SEUSS.*)*

OLD MAX: *(To us.)* Did you hear that? That's one I remember. I remember hearing that one each year in December. Listen!

(The CAROLERS *appear again, singing distantly.)*

DISTANT CHOIR:
>   Of all The Berrys in The Wood, The Holly Bears The Crown . . .

(The wind rises, the CHOIR *fades and vanishes.)*

OLD MAX: That's long ago now, I'm not the dog I used to be. But that hole in the mountain was once a home to me.

(A smaller version of the cave is lit. Icicles circle its mouth like gaping teeth.)

OLD MAX: *(continuing.)* You know who used to live up there, I'm sure you do. I lived there with him, I lived up there too. I'm on my way now, I'm leaving for good. But I wanted to see the old place once more if I could.

   See the old place, the mountain, and the Whos down below. I want to remember it all before I have to go. Now, every Who down in Who-Ville liked Christmas a lot . . .

(The sun rises quickly on the Who-Ville town-square. JP WHO *comes on pushing a wheelbarrow filled with wrapped Christmas presents and* LITTLE CINDY-LOU WHO. *She holds a mistletoe wreath twice her size, tied with a red ribbon as big as the wreath.)*

JP WHO: Who likes Christmas?

CINDY LOU: *Whos* like Christmas! *I* like Christmas!

JP & CINDY LOU: Whos like Christmas . . . a lot!

(Three strong WHOS *carry on the town-square Christmas tree. Suddenly the town is filled with* WHOS OF ALL SIZES AND SHAPES, *busily erecting the tree in the center of the square.)*

(Song: "Who Likes Christmas?")

WHOS:

> *Who likes Christmas?*
> *Whos like Christmas!*
> *Christmas future and present and past!*
>
> *We like Christmas*
> *Merry Christmas*
> *Present and future and past!*

INDIVIDUAL WHOS:

> *Whos like presents*
> *Whos like puddings*
> *Whos like pine-cones and snowflakes and jam*

WHO GROUP I:

> *Whos like parties*
> *Hale and hearties*
> *Parties with egg-nog and ham*

CHORUS:

> *Glo—o—o—o—o—rious!*
> *And the singing*
> *Voices ringing*
> *With the tenors all singing on key*

CHILDREN:

> *For a change*

ALL:

> *To remember*
> *In December*
> *To remember that first Christmas tree*

WHOS:

> *Who likes Christmas?*
> *Whos like Christmas!*
> *Christmas future and present and past!*
>
> *Whos like Christmas*
> *Merry Christmas*
> *Present and future and past!*

CHILDREN:

> *Give us presents*
> *Christmas presents*
> *Things that wind up and chatter and spin*
>
> *Give us dollies*
> *Sugar lollies*
> *And soldiers all made out of tin*
>
> *Deck the halls with sugar lollies*
> *Fa la la la la, la la la la!*

WOMEN:

> *And for dinner*
> *Christmas dinner*
> *We'll have roast-beast prepared under glass*

ALL:

> We love Christmas
> Merry Christmas!
> Christmas future and present and past!

WHO-EVER:

> Build a fire
> We won't tire
> Cause tomorrow will be Christmas Day
>
> As the fire
> Rises higher
> We're awaiting the sound of a sleigh!

ALL:

> The holly and the ivy
> When they are both full grown,
> Of all the berries in the wood
> The holly bears the crown

ALL:

> Who likes Christmas?
> Whos like Christmas!
> Christmas present and Christmas to be!
>
> Who likes Christmas?
> Merry Christmas!
> Very Christmas!
> Who likes Christmas?
> Meee!

(The WHOS *move off. Cross-fade to* OLD MAX.*)*

OLD MAX: Did I mention that the Who's down in Who-Ville liked Christmas a lot? But the Grinch, who lived just north of Who-Ville, did not.
The Grinch—he lived up there in the ice and the fog and I lived there with him. I'm Max, his old dog.

(A YOUNGER MAX *emerges from the cave. His fur isn't gray, and he has no beard, but he is tall and lanky and does wear thick black eyeglasses and a muffler and carries a cup of coffee. He stretches in the brisk morning light.)*

YOUNG MAX: Ahhhh.

OLD MAX: That's me when I was younger. Of course this was way back when I wasn't so gray, I was a *young* dog back then. Anyway, the Grinch *hated* Christmas, the whole Christmas *season.* Now please don't ask why—no one quite knows the reason.

YOUNG MAX: Well, Mister Grinch—it's beginning to feel a lot like Christmas.

(There's a terrible ominous chord from the ORCHESTRA.*)*

OLD MAX: Oh golly, I was young.

GRINCH: *(Thundering from off.)* What did you say?

(And the GRINCH *lurches out of his cave, his red eyes aflame and his sour mouth stretched down in a frown.)*

GRINCH: Maybe my hearing is going, or my head is broke, but it seemed to me, Max, it *seemed* you just spoke.

MAX: I only meant, sir, there's a brisk nip in the air and I'm not feeling so listless—I only meant, sir, it's beginning to feel a lot like . . .

GRINCH: Like what, Max?

MAX: Never mind, sir, it wasn't important.

GRINCH: I hate Christmas! The whole Christmas season!

MAX: Well, sir, I'm sure you must have a good reason . . .

GRINCH: I hate Christmas Eve! I hate Christmas Day! I hate it in every possible way! I hate Christmas trees and I hate every wreath, and I hate all the Whos down in Who-Ville beneath!

MAX: Well, sir, we all have our pet peeves. But sir—I was wondering *why*, if you please?

(Song: "I hate Christmas Eve!")

GRINCH:

> *I hate Christmas Eve! The whole Christmas season!*
> *I hate all the Whos, don't ask me the reason*
> *It could be their hearts are so full of mirth*
> *It could be the problem goes back to my birth*
> *Maybe peace on earth and good will just missed us.*
> *If I had my way, I'd cross out your Christmas!*

MAX:

> *He hates Christmas Eve! The whole Christmas season!*

GRINCH:

> *Don't ask me why!*

MAX:

> *I won't ask the reason!*

MAX:

> *It could be, perhaps, that your shoes are too tight . . .*
> *It could be your head's not screwed on just right . . .*

(The GRINCH goes after MAX, MAX dodges him.)

OLD MAX: But I think the most likely reason of all may have been that his heart was two sizes too small.

(Scrim burns through revealing the interior of the JP WHO FAMILY home, the entire family assembled, decorating their house for Christmas, hanging the stockings, wrapping presents, etc.)

CINDY-LOU: Mama, I'd like to make the old Grinch a gift. Don't you think that would give his spirits a lift?

MAMA WHO: You've never even seen the Grinch, Cindy-lou. Don't bother with him, we have enough to do.

CINDY-LOU: I've already made all the presents I'm giving—Just one for his cave? It must be a cold way of living.

MAMA WHO: You're a good little Who, Cindy.

PAPA WHO: And considerate, too.

MAMA WHO: Why don't you make something nice for your brother, Boo Hoo?

CINDY-LOU: Have you met the Grinch? Papa, have you?

JP WHO: Just twice.

CINDY-LOU: Well what is he like, Papa?

JP WHO: He's not very nice. He hates Christmas Eve! The whole Christmas season!

WHO CHILDREN: But *why?*

JP & MAMA WHO:
> *Children don't ask why, no one knows the reason.*
> *It could be his head's not screwed on just right*

ANNIE & DANNY WHO:
> *It could be, perhaps, that his shoes are too tight . . .*

GRANDPA SETH WHO:
> *No—I think the likeliest reason of all*
> *Must be that his heart is two sizes too small.*

MAMA WHO:
> *Whatever the reason, his heart or his shoes,*
> *He hates Christmas Eve and he hates all the Whos*

JP WHO:
> *He stares down from his cave with a mean* Grinchy *frown*
> *At the warm lighted windows down here in our town.*
> *For he knows every who here in Who-Ville beneath*
> *Is busy now, hanging a mistletoe wreath.*

GRINCH:
> *And I hate every who down in Who-Ville beneath*
> *Who's hanging a mis'rable mistletoe wreath!*

(Lights fade on the WHOS.*)*
> *And they're hanging their stockings! They're filled with good cheer!*
> *Tomorrow is Christmas! It's practically here!*

MAX:
> *You're scowling old Grinch, and your fingers are drumming!*

GRINCH:
> *There must be a way to keep Christmas from coming!*

MAX:
> *Keep Christmas from coming?*

GRINCH:
> *I must find a way to keep Christmas from coming!*
> *For tomorrow I know all the Who girls and boys*
> *Will wake bright and early. And race for their toys!*
> *I know it too well, I know just how it will be.*
> *Imagine it, Max—try to see what I see.*

(As the GRINCH *continues, the* GRINCH*-cave fills with a nightmarish vision of* WHO-CHILDREN *opening nightmarish presents: what the grinch imagines when he imagines Christmas.)*

(Song: "Why the Grinch Stole Christmas.")

GRINCH:

> *In they come tripping,*
> *It's simply too sweet.*
> *Sliding and slipping*
> *On little who feet.*
> *Acting Angelic*
> *Or so it would seem . . .*
> *So why do I have the*
> *Distinct urge to scream?*
>
> *Looking so pleasant,*
> *It's only an act.*
> *Give them a present*
> *And see them react!*

WHO KIDS:

> *Thumping and crumping a whatcha-ma-who!*
> *You got a whatcha-ma? I got it too!*
> *Wind up the whapper—see if it whaps!*

GRINCH:

> *Wind up my patience and see if it snaps.*

WHO KIDS:

> *Banging and binging a thing-a-ma ding!*
> *Bouncing a zippy new bounce-a-ma thing!*
> *Springing a sprocket up to the sky!*

GRINCH:

> *I want to stop it and you wonder why?*

WHO KIDS:

> *Love it when thing-a-mas zing out a tune!*
> *Like it when zing-a-dings shoot to the moon!*
> *Specially nice is the whatcha-ma fly!*

GRINCH: I want to stop all this—and you're honestly asking me why?

(The vision grows more nightmarish.)

WHO KIDS:

> *Give me a*
> *A bounce-a-ma*
> *Cutcha-ma-who*
> *Give me a cutcha-ma*
> *Cutcha-in-two!*

WHO KIDS:

> *Whapper snap*
> *Clapper dap*
> *Ratcheter zoo*
> *Give me a ratchet*
> *Give me a ratchet!*
> *Give me a ratchet!*
> *Give me a ratchet!*
> *I wanna ratchet!*

> *Give me a ratchet!*
> *And we'll ratchet you!*

GRINCH:

> *Shoo, shoo, shoo, shoo to you, too! Shoo!*

(The Nightmare WHO-*children vanish.)*

> *I want to stop it*
> *And you wonder why?!!*

(The GRINCH *is in agony.)*

GRINCH: Oh, the noise. Oh, the noise. Noise. Noise. Noise.

MAX: Those Who-girls and boys get some interesting toys.

GRINCH: You're a fool of a dog, Max—this time you're fired.

MAX: Pardon me, Mister Grinch, but—I wasn't hired.

GRINCH: And *then* the Whos, young and old, will sit down to a feast. And they'll feast! And they'll feast! And they'll *Feast! Feast! Feast! Feast!*

MAX: *(Interested.)* What'll they eat?

GRINCH: They'll feast on *Who*-pudding, and rare *Who*-roast-beast, which is something that I cannot stand in the least! And *then* they'll do something I like least of all! Every Who down in Who-Ville, the tall and the small, will stand close together, with Christmas bells ringing. I can hear it right now—it's carols they're singing!

(We see the entire WHO *community standing hand-in-hand on a miraculous horizon, singing. Perhaps it's a painted cut-out?)*

WHOS: *(Faintly, in the distance.)*

> *Good King Wenceslas looked out*
> *On the feast of Stephen*
> *When the snow lay round about*
> *Deep and crisp and even*
>
> *Brightly shone the moon that night*
> *Though the frost was cruel*
> *When a poor man came in sight*
> *Gath'ring winter fuel*

(The image fades, and with it, the carol. We're back with the GRINCH *and* MAX. MAX *is overcome, and wiping a tear from his eye with his long shaggy muffler.)*

MAX: I can't help it, I love these Christmas descriptions.

GRINCH: Put a cork in it, Max—they give me conniptions!

*(*OLD MAX *appears.)*

OLD MAX: And the more the Grinch thought of this *Who*-Christmas-Sing, the more the Grinch thought . . .

GRINCH: I must stop this whole thing! Why, for fifty-three years I've put up with it now! I must keep this Christmas from coming! . . . *But how?*

OLD MAX: Then he got an idea! AN AWFUL IDEA! The Grinch got a wonderful, awful idea!

(And the GRINCH looks right out at us, and his red eyes get wider, and the smile on his face grows suddenly snider.)

MAX: Oh, please, Mister Grinch—what *can* you be thinking? My heart's in my toes, that's how far down it's sinking.

GRINCH: Stop Christmas completely. Yes, stop it right now. Keep the whole thing from coming. And now I know how.

MAX: No, Mister Grinch—whatever it is, don't do it, I beg!

GRINCH: No Christmas for them! I'll take the Whos down a peg!

(And the GRINCH begins to laugh. It's not a pretty sound. MAX covers his ears.)

MAX: No, Grinch! No! No! No! No!

GRINCH:
> *I hate Christmas Eve! The whole Christmas season!*
> *I hate the Whos and there lies the reason*
> *Christmas, my dears, won't be coming this year!*
> *Christmas is banished and will not appear!*
> *I think I can promise because I'm so clever*
> *Christmas will vanish tomorrow forever!*

(The GRINCH grabs MAX in evil glee and dances and twirls him into the GRINCH cave. OLD MAX steps forward.)

OLD MAX: It was an awful idea. An awfully wonderfully rotten idea. I wanted to warn them, the Whos down beneath, but the Grinch kept me tied on a very short leash.

(Lights fade.)

ACT TWO

(Lights rise on downtown Who-Ville: a row of little Who-shaped shops and a couple of outdoor stalls with hanging signs—"TOYS," "MORE TOYS," "FRESH BEAST," "ALL TINSEL—HALF PRICE," "ANTIQUES," "THE WHO HISTORICAL SOCIETY.")

(WHOS come and go, in and out of the shops, pulling WHO-CHILDREN or being pulled by them. JP WHO and his family appear, everyone excited, CINDY-LOU carrying TINY WHO on her shoulders. MAMA WHO tries to line the whole clan into orderly lines.)

MAMA WHO: Children? Is everyone here? Oh, there are so many!

BETTY-LOU: Betty-Lou!

DANNY WHO: Danny Who!

CINDY-LOU: Cindy-Lou!

ANNIE WHO: And Annie!

MAMA WHO: *(Counting them off.)* There's Cindy-Lou and Annie Who and Brother Boo and Danny . . . There's you, my dear, and me, and Grandpa Seth and Granny . . .

GRANDPA SETH: *(To Grandma.)* I know what she's saying—that's you, Granny Who!

GRANDMA: That's right, my dear, and Grandpa Who is you!

MAMA WHO: Remember if you're lost and can't find each other, there's one brother per sister, one sister per brother.

GRANDPA SETH: What? I can't quite hear, is she still talking?

GRANDMA: We're shopping for presents to fill up your stocking!

GRANDPA SETH: Good. Wait a minute. You mean we're here shopping? Well for goodness sake, boys and girls—let's get hopping!

(Song: "Last Minute Shopping.")

WHOS:

> You've checked all the lists and you've checked them again
> You've tucked all the kids under covers and then
> You recall all the things you forgot to remember—
> It's why we look forward all year to December!
>
> You've bought all the presents, you've cooked all the food
> You've worked yourself into a turbulent mood
> And everyone's weary and bleary and dropping . . .
> And that's when you start to do last minute shopping!

(Orchestral Interlude, while the JP WHO family runs in and out of shops with the other WHOS in a scene of choreographed mayhem.)

WHOS:

> Pulling the kids or the kids pulling you
> Never once stopping, no not till you're through
> Cause shopping's more fun when there's pressure built in it
> You get it all done at the very last minute!

(Orchestral Interlude.)

WHOS:

> The kids are unruly and Grandpa's confused
> His temper is down to a very short fuse!
> It's starting to snow and the temperature's dropping . . .
> It's twenty below! It's a fine time for shopping!

(Orchestral Interlude.)

WHOS:

> The clerks are all giddy, the children can't wait—
> For last minute shopping it's never too late.
> We're dashing like crazy to get through the store—
> We've got all we need—we need to get more!
>
> The atmosphere's frigid, it cuts like a knife.
> I'm starting to question the meaning of life.
> But the holiday spirit, it runs through my veins,
> Cause the joy in the morning is worth all the pains!
>
> Watch this! We're shopping
> For Christmas,
> There's nothing like it for fun.

> *It's bliss, this shopping*
> *For Christmas*
> *When all the shopping is done!*
>
> *Shopping's more fun when there's pressure built in it—*
> *You get it all done at the very last minute!*

(Suddenly CINDY-LOU *shrieks and points, and there stands the* GRINCH *in the middle of Who-Ville.)*

CINDY-LOU: Eeek! Mama, what is it?

MAMA WHO: Don't say "it" Cindy-lou, in this case say "who."

JP WHO: Merry Christmas, Mister Grinch—how do you do?

GRINCH: You talking to me? What's it to you how I do?

JP WHO: It's simply a custom at this time of year to wish all of your neighbors health and good cheer.

GRINCH: Whatever for? What time of year is it?

JP WHO: It's Christmas!

GRINCH: I'll be darned—Christmas!—how could I miss it!

MAMA WHO: It's Christmas Eve, Mister Grinch—surely that's why you're here.

GRINCH: Oh. —Surely. *(To us.)* I decided to make merry this year.

GRANDMA WHO: And perhaps you'll do a little Yuletide shopping?

GRINCH: A little Yuletide shopping. That's it precisely. I'm shopping for *Christmas*, that's putting it nicely. That's why I trudged through the sleet and the snow—a gift for the Whos—because I love them so. *(To* BROTHER BOO.*)* Now here's a fine lad . . .

BROTHER BOO: —My name is Brother Boo!

GRINCH: De-lightful. I hope you get all that's coming to you!

JP WHO: Tomorrow, you know, we'll have our Christmas Who-sing, and our Christmas feast, if you like that sort of thing.

GRINCH: You know, that doesn't sound even halfway horrible. I just might drop by this sing-thing and warrible.

A FEW WHOS: Good king Wenceslas looked out on the feast of Steee . . .

(The GRINCH *freezes them with a glance.)*

CINDY-LOU: Mama? Papa? Do you think we could leave?

GRINCH: A little Who-girl! As I live and breathe!

*(*DANNY, ANNIE *and* BETTY-LOU WHO *come running out of a shop, bearing presents. They stop in their tracks when they see the* GRINCH.*)*

GRINCH: *(continuing.)* Tell me what you want for Christmas—you must be hoping? I'd hate to see you spend Christmas day moping.

*(*CINDY-LOU *hangs her head.)*

MAMA WHO: Cindy-Lou, don't be rude. She'll tell you, of course!

CINDY-LOU: Well. I wish Santy would bring me . . .

GRINCH: Yes?

CINDY-LOU: . . . a red rocking-horse.

GRINCH: A little red-rocking horse! That's no disgrace! I hope Santy brings you gifts . . . till you're blue in the face.

(The WHO-CHILDREN *recoil just a bit from the* GRINCH, *and the* GROWN-UPS *look uncomfortable.)*

GRINCH: *(Continuing.)* Say listen, I've just adored stopping with you, but now I've got *my* Yuletide shopping to do.

(JP WHO *gathers up his family and they leave, the* GRINCH *scurries among the shops, and* OLD MAX *steps out of one of the stores, a bundle of presents in his arms.)*

OLD MAX: From one store to the other the Grinch went shopping—He flew through Who-Ville, just now and then stopping.

(The GRINCH *stops at an outdoor clothing stall.)*

GRINCH: I want some red stuff, some bunting, for a little red jacket. Yes, that'll do nicely—now hurry and wrap it!

OLD MAX: The Grinch was rarely in town, from one year to the next. Now here he was shopping, and the Whos were perplexed.

GRINCH: Kindly give me a length of white cotton wool, and a strip of elastic, the kind you can pull.

OLD MAX: The Whos were amazed, they could *not* understand it—They didn't know this was how the Grinch planned it.

GRINCH: *(Singing.)*

> Giving's the reason for Christmas,
> Thinking of others—how nice.
> What shall I give them for Christmas?
> Something to make them think twice!

(And the GRINCH *takes off out of town with a horrible laugh.)*

OLD MAX: So the Grinch hurried on and the Whos went their way, the Whos never suspecting their danger that day. He scared all the clerks with his frightening frown, and he stole those old antlers on his way out of town.

(Who-Ville fades from view as OLD MAX *steps down toward us, his bags in his arms.)*

OLD MAX: What could he be planning? It all seemed fantastic. And what did he want with a strip of elastic?
   All the way up Mount Crumpit he laughed in his throat. And back in his cave he made a hat and a coat. And he called *me*, his dog Max, and with a length of red thread he tied those old horns on top of my head!

(The GRINCH *cave: a single bare lightbulb dangles from a wire. We glimpse, just outside the* GRINCH *cave, the front end of a huge ramshackle sleigh.* YOUNG MAX *disconsolately paws at the horns tied to his head.)*

MAX: Now ask yourself honestly, I'm begging you, *please!* Who'll take me for a Santy Claus reindeer in *these?*

(The GRINCH *enters in red coat and cap, and stands before a floor-length mirror, fixing the antlers on* YOUNG MAX's *head. The* GRINCH *adjusts his new red costume and gleefully snaps its elastic cotton wool trim.)*

GRINCH: Don't be a dimwit, it's a great Grinchy trick! And with this coat and this hat, I look just like Saint Nick! If anyone stops us, says where are you going? I'll say "It's Saint Nick, and I'm ho ho ho-ing."

MAX: Who's going to believe you, you're not Santy Claus! You hate Who-Ville and Christmas and children and dogs!

GRINCH: Yes I do, I'm a Grinch—that's what Grinches are for.

MAX: You said "Grinches," Mister Grinch—does that mean there's more?

GRINCH: No . . .

(Song: "One of a Kind.")

GRINCH:

> *I'm one of a kind,*
> *There's no one like me.*
> *One of a kind.*
> *Does that make me lonely,*
> *Being one of a kind?*
> *No, that makes me free.*
>
> *No kinfolk, no closeness*
> *No family, no friends*
> *No letters to open*
> *No letters to send*
>
> *I'm one of a kind.*
>
> *And that's hard to find.*
>
> *I don't mind.*
>
> *When you think of the fuss*
> *You get with an "us"*
> *You know it's much better*
> *With no one to trust.*
>
> *Trust?*
>
> *What a bust.*
>
> *I'm where it all starts,*
> *And where it all ends.*
> *No asking forgiveness,*
> *No making amends.*
>
> *Friends?*
>
> *Don't need 'em.*
>
> *When they finished with me*
> *They threw out the mold.*
> *I'm the one and onliest Grinch*
> *You'll ever behold.*
>
> *I'm cold.*
> *So cold.*
>
> *No dates to remember*

Appointments to keep
No phone calls to wake me
When I want to sleep

I'm one of a kind,
There's no one like me.
One of a kind.
Does that make me lonely,
Being one of a kind?
Don't make me laugh! Not me!

No pals to betray me
When I'm in a pinch
I'm all on my only
Because I'm the Grinch!

I'm one of a kind.

Do you mind?!

One of a kind.

Do you think I'm blind?

I love being one of a kind!

Get used to it!

BLACKOUT

(Lights rise on OLD MAX, *elsewhere.)*

OLD MAX: To be tied up like that—to be tied up and hitched—it was every dog's nightmare—and those antlers itched! I hated to watch the Grinch swagger and strut, but what could I do? I was just a young mutt. Well, the Grinch loaded some bags and some old empty sacks on a ramshackle sleigh for his "reindeer" named Max.

(Crossfade to a distant view of the mountain: we see a miniature version of the sleigh, and a proportionately smaller GRINCH *standing on it with reins in hand, and* YOUNG MAX *tied in front.)*

OLD MAX: *(Continuing.) (Voice-over)* And the Grinch said, "Giddap!" And the sleigh hurtled down toward the homes where the Whos Lay a-snooze in their town!

(From the Orchestra, *some sort of majestic Ride of the Valkeries strikes up. The* GRINCH *cracks his whip above* YOUNG MAX, *and the sleigh hurtles down the mountain toward the Whos.)*

BLACKOUT

ACT THREE

(We see OLD MAX *in the* GRINCH*-cave.)*

OLD MAX: It wasn't quite Christmas, but the night before when the Grinch cackled down from his cave with a roar. My back was blistered and my legs were aching, and under my fur my young heart was breaking.
    The village was quiet and the lights were turned low, and the streets

were all empty as they filled up with snow. But the children of Whoville were dreaming of toys, while the grown-ups tried hard not to make any noise.

(We see four DARK SHAPES, moving on tiptoe.)

GRANDMA WHO: Grandpa, these presents are heavy—can you please take them?

GRANDPA SETH: But we just got them to sleep—why should we wake them?

MAMA WHO: Shhhh!

GRANDMA WHO: No, *take* them! *Take* them!

JP WHO: Shhhh!

GRANDPA SETH: Take 'em where, I want to know, those children should sleep!

MAMA WHO: Grandpa, that's not what she said—never mind—it'll keep.

GRANDPA SETH: But I *know* the snow's deep, it's just billowing down.

JP WHO: Do you hear it? The silence all over the town?

(Interior, JP WHO's house. We see the fireplace hung with Who-socks, the Christmas tree trimmed with decorations, and wrapped presents covering the floor. Through a portal on the left, we see the five WHO CHILDREN asleep under the covers of a big bed. On the far right is another portal through which we can see a small portion of the kitchen and a big refrigerator.)

(The GROWNUPS move about making final preparations before bed, tiptoeing and hushing each other and now and then checking on the SLEEPING CHILDREN.)

(Song: "Now's the Time.")

JP WHO:
> Now the clock is all wound up
> Ticking off the hours.
> Now the gifts are all bound up
> Trimmed with Bows and Flowers.

MAMA WHO:
> Now the pie's set out to air
> Topped with nuts and cherries.

GRANDMA WHO:
> Now the pudding's all prepared
> Filled with plums and berries.

GRANDPA SETH:
> Shhh!

ALL:
> Now's the time we wait and pace
> Now's the time—here's the place
> One by one the hours chime
> Here's the place—now's the time

JP & MAMA WHO:
> All the gifts will come of course
> On a nighttime sleigh-ride
> Even Cindy's rocking horse
> For a Christmas hay-ride

GRANDPA SETH:

Now tomorrow morning's set
Everything is ready.
Look at that—it's snowing yet,
Falling soft and steady.

GRANDMA WHO:

Shhhh!

(GRANDMA *gently shoos* GRANDPA SETH *off to bed.*)

JP & MAMA WHO & GRANDMA:

Now the snow is drifting deep
All the expectation
All the children fast asleep
We're a tired nation

(GRANDMA *tiptoes off to bed.*)

JP & MAMA WHO:

Now's the time we wait and pace
Now's the time—here's the place
One by one the hours chime
Here's the place—now's the time

(JP *kisses* MAMA *and tiptoes off to bed.*)

MAMA WHO:

Now and then remembering
All our past Decembering
All we do we've done before
Is that Santa at the door?

WHO CHILDREN: *(In their sleep.)* Whoooo?

MAMA WHO: Shhhh!

(*Mama switches off the light and tiptoes out.*)

(*All is silent, but for the nocturnal hooting of owls somewhere. Perhaps a town bell tower tolls the hour.*)

(*Then, from the Orchestra, we hear an ominous "Jaws"-like theme: the universal marplot of Eden approaches. Suddenly we hear a scrambling scraping noise from above, and then furtive voices: "Ouch! This Way, Hurry! I'm Slipping!* MAX, *Let Go of My Leg!*)

MAX: *(From above)* Please go slowly, sir, it's a rather tight pinch.

GRINCH: Listen! If Santa can do it, then so can the Grinch!

(MAX *crashes down sootily into the fireplace. The sleeping* WHO CHILDREN *all murmur a soft "Whoooo" and turn over in their beds.*)

MAX: Oh, boy. (MAX *glances up.*) Oh, no, Mr. Grinch, please just give me a moment . . .

(*The* GRINCH *crashes down on top of* MAX. *The* WHO-CHILDREN *murmur and do another unison turn in their bed.*)

GRINCH: What a treat—to drop in for a Christmas visit! That's not something to be ashamed of—now is it? Oh, look! Little Who stockings all hung in a row. These dear little socks will be the first things to go!

MAX: I don't like this, Mr. Grinch . . .

GRINCH: *(Mimicing* MAX.*)* "I don't like this, Mr. Grinch"—No ifs, ands or maybes—What we're doing here MAX, is taking candy from babies!

*(*MAX *and the* GRINCH *disentangle themselves and tip-toe into the living room. As the* GRINCH *makes a survey of the house, we hear the* VOICE OF OLD MAX.*)*

VOICE OF OLD MAX: The Grinch slithered and slunk, with a smile most unpleasant, As he plotted his plot to take every present! Pop guns! And bicycles! Roller skates! Drums! Checkerboards! Tricycles! Popcorn! And plums!

(The GRINCH *opens the icebox.)*

MAX: MR. GRINCH, you wouldn't do that! Not the Whos' feast!

GRINCH: I'll take the Who-pudding, I'll take the roast beast! I'll clean out this icebox as quick as a flash!

MAX: Have you no shame! That's their last can of Who-hash!

GRINCH: And when everything's stolen, from the A to the Zee I'll end with a flourish and stuff up the tree!

(Song: "A Never Never Very Merry Christmas")

(As they sing, the GRINCH *and* MAX *stuff the toys in bags and cram them up the chimney.)*

GRINCH:

> Take the Happy Christmas Giggles,
> The kind that make me Gag,
> Take the Shiny Tinsel Wiggles
> And Stash 'em in a bag.
> Take the children's happy laughter,
> The kind that makes me Snore,
> And drag it quickly out the nearest door!
>
> Cause it's a never never very merry Christmas with me
> I'll Jingle all the bells and then I'll Hack the tree
> I'll rifle through the Christmas Gifts and stuff them up the Flue
> Till it's a never merry sad and scary Christmas for you!
>
> Take the glowing fireplaces
> That always make me cough
> Take the Bracing warm embraces
> And turn the power off!
> Take the Bulging Christmas stockings—
> They make me think of feet—
> We'll sweep their rotten Christmas off the street!

MAX:

> Cause it's a never never very Merry Christmas with him
> He'll pull up all the trees and hack them limb from limb
> He'll never stop he'll never rest until his task is through
> Till it's a never Merry sad and scary Christmas for you!

GRINCH & MAX:
> The joyful song
> The hopeful heart
> The happy throng

GRINCH:
> The giving part

GRINCH & MAX:
> The window panes
> A frosty chill
> The warmth inside—

GRINCH:
> It makes me ill.

GRINCH:
> Cause it's a never never very Merry Christmas with me

MAX:
> A never very Merry Christmas with him
> I'll jangle all the jingle bells and then I'll hack the tree

MAX:
> He'll pull the trees and hack them limb from limb
> I'll never stop I'll never rest until my task is through

GRINCH & MAX:
> Till it's a never merry sad and scary Christmas
> Totally unnecessary Christmas
> Never merry sad and scary Christmas—

GRINCH:
> For you! And you! And you!
> Boo!

(*The* GRINCH *has dragged the Christmas tree to the fireplace when suddenly he sees* CINDY-LOU WHO, *standing in the room, aghast.*)

CINDY-LOU: I can hardly believe it—Santy Claus, why, *why* are you taking our Christmas tree? *Why?*

GRINCH: Ummm . . .

CINDY-LOU: And why are you holding that fireplace log?

GRINCH: Ahhh . . .

CINDY-LOU: And why does your reindeer resemble a dog?

GRINCH: (*To* MAX.) Run along now, Prancer, do as you're told. (*To* CINDY-LOU.) He used to look fine, but he's getting old.

(MAX *slinks off into the kitchen.*)

Well, my sweet little tot, there's nothing to hide. There's a light on this tree that won't light on one side. So I'm taking it home to my workshop, my dear. I'll fix it up there. Then I'll bring it back here.

CINDY-LOU: All right. Be sure to return it by Christmas morning.

GRINCH: Of course. But why are you up when everyone's snoring?

(*She doesn't answer, but shivers a little and hangs her head.*)

Come on now, tell me—the minutes are flying—I've got work to do—
oh!—she's actually crying. Please, little Who, it can't be as bad as all
that—This is Santy Claus talking, as you can see by my hat.

(CINDY-LOU *continues to sniff.*)

Oh MAX?—Prancer! Come here on the double! The little Who-girl is in
some sort of trouble. (CINDY-LOU *throws herself into the* GRINCH'S *arms.*)

GRINCH: Oh this is really most terribly trying. I've never before seen a Who-
child crying. Suddenly something inside of me doesn't quite fit—Oh,
what can I say to convince her to quit!

CINDY-LOU: I had such a bad dream, and it gave me a fright—Do you think
you could stay here, just through the night?

GRINCH: But I'm Santa Claus, darling, and it's Christmas Eve! The things I
must do—well, you wouldn't believe.

CINDY-LOU: I understand. And when your long journey ends, you'll be going
back home, to your family and friends.

GRINCH: What?

CINDY-LOU: Your family. Your friends.

GRINCH: It depends. I suppose when I'm through with my work I'll go home.
Don't you see? Santa always spends Christmas alone.

CINDY-LOU: *(Singing.)* You're all alone?

GRINCH: I don't groan.

CINDY-LOU: All the time?

GRINCH: It's not a crime.

CINDY-LOU: There's no one there?

GRINCH: I don't care.

CINDY-LOU: But that's terrible, Santa—that's foolish, that's wrong! No matter
where you may be—you'll always belong.

GRINCH: Belong?

(Song: "Santa for a Day.")

(*Throughout the song, the lights on the Christmas tree slowly light and brighten
until they're blazing at the song's end.*)

CINDY-LOU:

> *Sometimes when you're all alone*
> *Christmas and there's no one home*
> *Seems like nothing's in your stocking*
> *No one knocking*
>
> *Please believe me when I say*
> *You're my Santa anyway*
> *I'll be in your Christmas stocking*
> *I'm the one who's knocking*
> *Christmas day*

CINDY-LOU:

> *Colored lights*
> *Starry nights*

> *Snowflakes glistening*
> *I'll be listening*
> *I'll be true*
>
> *Trim the tree*
> *Look at me*
> *Celebrating*
> *But I'm waiting*
> *For you*
>
> *Promise you'll remember me*
> *Doesn't matter where you'll be*
> *Specially when the snow is falling*
> *I'll be calling*
>
> *Even if we're far apart*
> *You've done something to my heart—so*
> *This is how you'll always stay*
> *My Santa for a day*
> *This will be our song*
> *You and I belong*
> *Heart to heart together*
> *Christmas day*

CINDY-LOU: Santa? What's wrong? Tell me—what's the matter with you?

GRINCH: Oh, it's nothing, my dear. You're a darling young Who. And look— look at this. What a strange thing to see. I seem to have fixed the light on this tree.

CINDY-LOU: I'm better, too, Santy—no more fears, no more fright. I'll be thinking of you, Santy Claus, all through the night.

GRINCH: You never did tell me, my Cindy-Lou Who—What *was* that nightmare that scarified you?

CINDY-LOU: I'd rather not say—I don't think that I should. Why talk about bad things when you've made it all good?

GRINCH: It's better to get all the scary stuff out. Then you can say, what was *that* all about!

CINDY-LOU: Well . . . There was someone with eyes that looked like a frog's . . .

GRINCH: Yes . . .

CINDY-LOU: And he hated Christmas and Who-Ville and children and dogs . . . (MAX *barks from the kitchen.*)
He was mean and unfriendly and terribly scary . . .
. . . and his arms and his face were horribly hairy.

GRINCH: *(Withdrawing his arms.)* I see.

CINDY-LOU: And I dreamed he was slinking along, inch by inch—
And then who did I see but that nasty old Grinch!

(The lights on the Christmas tree suddenly blink out.)

GRINCH: I see.

CINDY-LOU: Santy?

GRINCH: Go to bed now, little Who daughter. Go on, and I'll bring you a cup of cold water.

(CINDY-LOU *sleepily blows the* GRINCH *a kiss and stumbles off to bed.*)

(MAX *comes into the room, sniffling.*)

GRINCH: *(Continuing.)* Come here, Max. Stop sniveling. I'm warning you— Heel! We've still got the rest of their Christmas to steal!

(*With a roar, the* GRINCH *rips down a string of Christmas ornaments.*)

BLACKOUT

ACT FOUR

(*Lights rise on* OLD MAX *in another location.*)

OLD MAX: And when Cindy-Lou went to bed with her cup, he went to the chimney and stuffed the tree up! He tore through the town while I trotted behind, and he snatched and he grabbed every gift he could find. He ransacked their homes and emptied their fridges. He wrote Grinchy words on the sidewalks and bridges.

(*Lights rise on a bare, stripped room and a naked fireplace with a single log in it.*)

OLD MAX: *(Continuing.)* On their walls he left nothing but hooks and some wire, and the *last* thing he'd take was the log for their fire! (*The* GRINCH'S *red-clad arms reach down into the hearth, grab the log and vanish.*) And the one speck of food that he'd leave in the house was a crumb that was even too small for a mouse. (*A* MOUSE *puppet enters, checks out the crumb left by the fireplace, does a take to us, muttering to us in mouse-talk—"Oh, no!" Lights fade on* MOUSE.) And he did the *same* thing to *all* the Whos' houses, leaving crumbs much too small for the other Whos' mouses! He'd climb up their rooftops and then, very nimbly, he'd jiggle and wiggle his way down the chimbley!

(*We see the* GRINCH *in silhouette, standing on a Whoville rooftop, pulling a Christmas tree out of the chimney. Then the* GRINCH *shakes his fists at the heavens and the sleeping village. Lights fade.*)

OLD MAX: It was a quarter past dawn ... All the Whos, still a-bed, All the Whos, still a-snooze. When he packed up his sled, Packed it up with their presents! The ribbons! The wrappings! The tags! And the tinsel! The trimmings! The trappings! And cracking his cracker and whipping his whip he drove that old sleigh to the high mountain-tip!

(*We hear the crack of a whip and the jingle of sleigh bells, rising, rising.*)

OLD MAX: All through the night until dawn he rode up, and down in the valley the Whos all woke up.

(*Crossfade to* JP *and* MAMA *and* CINDY-LOU *isolated in a light.*)

JP WHO: There aren't any presents. There aren't any toys. I slept rather soundly—did *you* hear a noise?

MAMA WHO: There isn't a morsel of food in the house. There isn't a crumb that would interest a mouse!

JP WHO: I can't for the life of me think who would do it.

MAMA WHO: The house looks just like a tornado swept through it!

CINDY-LOU: Could it be? Mama, Papa—I know now who it was.

MAMA WHO: But Cindy-Lou—who?

CINDY-LOU: It was . . . a sort of Santy Claus.

MAMA WHO: What?

CINDY-LOU: He must be so lonely. No family, no friends, no presents to open, no presents to send . . .

JP WHO & MAMA WHO: Whoooo?

(The WHOS disappear. We hear a terrible cackling GRINCH laugh, and the crack of his whip.)

OLD MAX: Still riding, still driving, he roared through the night, up higher than high to a frightening height!

VOICE OF THE GRINCH: *(Voice-over.)* One thousand, two thousand, three thousand feet up! Up the side of Mt. Crumpit, Max! Up Max! Giddup!

OLD MAX: Three thousand feet high! To the crest of Mt. Crumpit, He rode with his load to the tiptop to dump it!

(Lights rise on the top of Mt. Crumpit. The light of dawn is just touching the top of the snowy mountain. The sled with its massive load teeters and creaks on the brink of the precipice, while the GRINCH gloats and MAX mopes.)

GRINCH: Pooh-Pooh to the Whos! that's the tune we're all humming. They're finding out now that no Christmas is coming! They're just waking up! I know *just* what they'll do! Their mouths will hang open a minute or two. Then the Whos down in Who-Ville will all cry Boo-Hoo!

MAX: *(Crying for real.)* Boo—H—H—H—Hoo!

GRINCH: Shut up, Max, do shut up—put your paw to your ear. There's a noise coming, Max, that I simply must hear! The Whos will cry buckets! That's *just* what they'll do! Get set, Max, get set for a Who-Ville Boo-Hoo!

(And from far below, faintly at first, we hear the WHOS singing.)

(Reprise: "Who Likes Christmas?")

WHOS:
(From far below.)

> *Who likes Christmas?*
> *Whos like Christmas!*
> *Christmas future and present and past!*
>
> *We like Christmas*
> *Merry Christmas*
> *Present and future and past!*

GRINCH: But this sound isn't sad! Why, this sound sounds merry! It just can't be so! But it is merry! Very!

WHOS:

> *Who likes Christmas?*
> *Whos like Christmas!*
> *Christmas future and present and past!*

> *We like Christmas*
> *Merry Christmas*
> *Present and future and past!*

(Music under.)

GRINCH: Do you see what I see? I'm popping my eyes! In fifty-three years I've not had such a surprise! Every Who down in Who-Ville, the tall and the small, Is singing! Without any presents at all!

MAX: Oh, joy.

GRINCH: It came! It came without ribbons! It came without tags!

MAX: It came without packages, boxes or bags! Puzzle on *that*, Mister Grinch! Then puzzle some more! I hope that you puzzle till your puzzler is sore!

WHOS:

> *Whos Love Christmas*
> *Cherish Christmas!*
> *Cherish family and friends to the last . . .*

GRINCH: I didn't stop Christmas! It came anyway! It came without presents— It's still Christmas Day!

MAX: Yessir. It's still Christmas Day.

GRINCH: Maybe Christmas—maybe it doesn't come from a store.
Maybe Christmas . . . perhaps . . .

MAX: Means a little bit more?

GRINCH: What is it, this "Christmas?" And what is a Who?
How *can* they be happy? How *can* it be true?

MAX: Don't ask me, how should I know? I'm just an old stray. You found me and bound me and tied me to a sleigh.

GRINCH: I'm cold.

(Reprise: "One of a kind.")

MAX:

> *You're one of a kind*
> *There's no one like you*
> *One of a kind*
> *And that makes you special*
> *Being one of a kind*

GRINCH: Of course it does!

MAX:

> *Yes that makes you free!*
> *You're free to be lonely*
> *You're free to be mean*

GRINCH:

> *The most one and only*
> *The world's ever seen!*

MAX: Well you can have it, Mr. Grinch! You can have it forever!

CINDY-LOU:

> *Promise you'll remember me*
> *Doesn't matter where you'll be*
> *Specially when the snow is falling*
> *I'll be calling . . .*

GRINCH:

> *She's singing to me?*
> *What could explain it?*
> *I stole her tree.*
> *That Cindy-Lou Who-girl,*
> *She still thinks of me?*
>
> *I don't understand.*

MAX:

> *They still have their Christmas*
> *They know how to share!*

GRINCH:

> *I took all her presents*

MAX:

> *And she doesn't care!*

CINDY-LOU:

> *Even if we're far apart*
> *You've done something to my heart . . .*

GRINCH:

> *There's something not right here*
> *There's something I've missed*
> *How could I think I could*
> *Live my life like this?*
>
> *Just one of a kind*
> *Was I blind?*
> *And where does it end?*
> *Not one single friend!*
> *I hate being one of a kind!*

GRINCH: It hurts, Max, it hurts! Make it stop, make it cease! I feel *good* toward the Whos, just good will and peace!

MAX: Let it come, Mr. Grinch, you're getting so near!

GRINCH: Is a Who whoever . . . can be of . . . good cheer?

MAX: Arf! Arf arf arf arf arf arf arf!

GRINCH: It couldn't be, could it? Could it really be true? Could I be a— maybe— Am I a Who too?

MAX: Arf arf arf arf arf arf arf!

OLD MAX: What happened then? Well, in Who-Ville they say that the Grinch's small heart grew three sizes that day!

(The GRINCH's small heart grows three sizes right before our eyes.)

GRINCH: You're a wonderful dog, Max— *(The GRINCH kisses MAX, MAX responds.)* —there's just one more thing. I'm Santa—you're Prancer—we've presents to bring! So hitch up this old sleigh and tie up the sack—We've got two or three minutes to bring this stuff back!

MAX: Oh, yes sir! Oh boy! (*Suddenly, the sled on the precipice teeters and threatens to go over—both the* GRINCH *and* MAX *grabbing for it.*) Oh boy. Oh boy. Oh . . . No!

BLACKOUT

ACT FIVE

(OLD MAX *outside the old Grinch cave. He snaps shut the clasps on an old battered suitcase. He adjusts the thick black-rimmed glasses on the end of his nose, picks up a cup of coffee and turns to us. He looks now very like* TED GEISEL.)

OLD MAX: I love telling stories. I like this one the best. And how does it end? I'll let *them* tell you the rest. It's a real wonder, what that singing inspired. As for me, I'm an old dog now. I'm retired. I'd like to stay with you, but I've got to go now. I'll let you kids deck the halls—you've got the know-how.

(OLD MAX *gives us a wave, picks up his suitcase, and disappears.*)

(*Lights rise on the Who-Ville town square: The* WHOS *hand-in-hand singing.*)

WHOS:
> Deck the Halls with Boughs of Holly
> Fa La La La La, La La La La
> Tis the season to be jolly
> Fa La La La La, La La La La

(*We hear a crazy twisted-up horn blast.*)
> Don we now our Gay Apparel
> Fa La La La La, La La La La
> Sing the ancient Yuletide Carol . . .

(*We hear a crazy twisted-up horn blast.*)

ORCHESTRA:
> Fa La La La La, La La La La!

(*Into their midst rides the* GRINCH, *atop a gigantic bag of Christmas presents and trees, blowing a horn, with a no-longer hang-dog* MAX *pushing the sled from behind. The* WHOS *stand stock-still, paralyzed with amazement.*)

GRINCH: Citizens of Who-Ville! I wish you a Merry . . .

MAX: You can do it, Mister Grinch . . .

GRINCH: I wish you a very . . .

MAX: Do it, Mister Grinch.

GRINCH: I wish you . . .

CINDY-LOU: Hi, Mister Grinch.

GRINCH: I wish you a Merry Christmas, Whos one and all!

(*Cheers from the* WHOS, *shouts of Merry Christmas,* MISTER GRINCH! *Merry Merry!*)

GRINCH: I've got presents and wrappings and trappings and toys and I want you to fill Christmas with noise, noise, noise! (*Cheers from the* WHOS.) I've got a wagon for you, my friend, Brother Boo—it's red and it's racy with a stripe colored blue! And presents for Annie and Danny and you, Betty-Lou, and great-tasting food for all of the Whos! And I've got something special for this friend, of course—for my dear Cindy-Lou Who—a red rocking horse!

(*The* GRINCH *and* CINDY-LOU *hug.*)

CINDY-LOU: Thank you, Mister Grinch. There's just one thing you've missed.

GRINCH: Oh no! Really? That's all the gifts on my list.

CINDY-LOU: The presents are great, and we're grateful, it's true. But really the only thing missing was you.

(*"Finale."*)

GRINCH & CINDY-LOU:
> Promise you'll remember me
> Doesn't matter where you'll be
> Specially when the snow is falling
> I'll be calling

ENSEMBLE:
> Even when we're far apart
> You've done something to my heart
> —So this is how you'll always stay
> My Santa for a day. . . .

YOUNG MAX: (*To us.*) So he brought back the toys! And the food for the feast! And he—he himself—The Grinch carved the roast beast!

(*In an instant,* TWO WHOS *have rolled on a table laden with food and a giant roast-beast.*)

ENSEMBLE:
> This will be our song
> You and I belong
> Heart to heart together . . .
> Christmas Day!

(*Lights rise to blinding white.*)

BLACKOUT

(CURTAIN CALL: *The* WHOS, *the* GRINCH *and* MAX *stand on a miraculous horizon, holding hands and singing reprise of "Who Likes Christmas"*)

ALL:
> Who likes Christmas?
> Whos like Christmas!
> Christmas present and Christmas to be!
> Who likes Christmas?

Merry Christmas!
Very Christmas!
Who likes Christmas?

CINDY-LOU WHO: God bless us, every Who!

ALL: *Meee!*

CURTAIN

A LAURA INGALLS WILDER CHRISTMAS

by
Laurie Brooks

A LAURA INGALLS WILDER CHRISTMAS

CHARACTERS

Pa (Charles) Ingalls
Ma (Caroline) Ingalls
Laura Ingalls, ten years old.
Mary Ingalls, twelve years old.
Carrie Ingalls, seven years old.
Johnny Steadman, ten years old, walks with a limp.
Mrs. (Theodora) Starr, forties, wealthiest woman in town.

TIME AND PLACE

Iowa, 1876

Notes: The play operates in various worlds—actual time, Laura's imagination and a distorted, larger than life child's perspective.

The play is done on a bare stage. Much of the action is pantomimed by the actors. A large box is at center around which the action revolves.

Props are kept to a minimum. Lighting and sound play an important role in creating mood and atmosphere.

Ma may use her shawl to create the baby, imagined and real.

For the premiere production, a transformational box was used as the grave, the wagon, a bed and a hope chest that contains the family's belongings.

All songs used in the play can be found in The Laura Ingalls Wilder Song Book.

(Lights. The family is gathered at a grave. They sing an arrangement of "In the Sweet By and By." During the song, MA *takes her china shepherdess and puts it away in the box at center.* PA *takes his fiddle and adds it to the box.* PA *tries to lead* MA *away from the grave. She resists.* PA *takes her by the shoulders and firmly leads her away. One by one the family leaves the grave, each finding separate spaces.)*

INGALLS FAMILY: In the sweet by and by we will meet on that beautiful shore. In the sweet by and by we will meet on that beautiful shore.

*(*LAURA *is left alone at the grave.)*

LAURA: Goodbye, Little Freddie.

*(*LAURA *closes the lid on the box. The elements in the following scene are imagined, the action pantomimed by the actors.)*

(Sounds of rain.)

PA: *(Slapping the reins.)* He-ah. Get up Pip. Get up, Paddy.

(In their own spaces, the family is jostled as they ride, huddled against the rain.)

MARY: If I could feel the sun on my face right this minute I swear I'd never wear my sunbonnet again.

CARRIE: I hate rain!

MARY: Carrie!

CARRIE: Well, I do.

MARY: I dislike rain more than I can say.

CARRIE: Me, too.

(The family is jolted to a stop.)

PA: *(Crack of the whip.)* Get up, Pip. Paddy, git! *(Crack of the whip.)* Caroline!

*(*CAROLINE *is lost in a reverie.)*

PA: *(Cont'd.)* Caroline! Take the reins.

*(*CAROLINE *takes the reins.* PA *gets down to help the ponies.)*

PA: *(Cont'd.)* Come on, Pip. Walk on, Paddy.

(The wagon moves forward out of the mud. PA *realizes* CAROLINE *is crying.)*

PA: *(Cont'd.)* Don't cry, Caroline. We'll be there soon. If only it'd stop raining.

MA: I keep hearing him cry, Charles. He's all alone and . . . it's raining.

PA: Try to think about our new life. The hotel might be the answer to our prayers.

MA: But it's a tavern. What kind of place is that for our girls?

PA: A better place, I hope. *(Crack of the whip.)* He-ah! Git up!

LAURA: I'm worried about Ma. She's gone so quiet.

MARY: She's thinking, is all.

LAURA: I think she's still at Aunt Eliza and Uncle Peter's farm.

CARRIE: But she's right here.

LAURA: I know she is. But it's like she left a part of her behind. She's hardly talked since we left.

CARRIE: Maybe the cat's got her tongue.

LAURA: I think she's too sad to talk.

CARRIE: She misses Little Freddie.

MARY: Hush up about that, Carrie.

CARRIE: Why do I have to hush up? We all miss him.

LAURA: Especially Ma.

CARRIE: Why did he have to die?

MARY: Now see what you've done?

CARRIE: He never even got to have his first birthday.

MARY: Don't be sad, Carrie. Little Freddie's in Heaven now and there's no more beautiful place than Heaven.

CARRIE: Then why don't we all go to Heaven?

LAURA: Because we can't go together. And I wouldn't want to go without you.

CARRIE: Will I go to Heaven when I die and see Little Freddie?

MARY: Yes, Carrie.

LAURA: Maybe Ma wants to die so she can see Little Freddie.

MARY: Hush, Laura. What a thing to say.

PA: Hee-ah! Good boy, Pip. Walk on, Paddy.

(In their separate spaces, the family expresses their individual hopes.)

LAURA: I wish Little Freddie hadn't died.

MA: I wish we had a place to call home.

PA: Wish we'd see the end of this blasted rain.

MARY: I wish I knew what lies ahead.

LAURA: I wish I could make Ma smile.

CARRIE: I wish we were at Bird Oak.

PA: That's Burr Oak, Buttercup.

LAURA: I wish we weren't going to Burr Oak. I don't like living in town.

PA: Well now, since you've never lived in town before, maybe you better wait and see before making up your mind.

LAURA: It's backtracking, Pa. I want to go west.

PA: I know, Half-pint. And we will. In due time. We just need to get back on our feet. Times are hard, and not just for us.

LAURA: Those blasted grasshoppers.

PA: You can say that again.

CARRIE: Those blasted grasshoppers.

PA: Better to backtrack than be beholden to folks. Long as I have a beating heart and two working hands, we'll make it on our own, thank you kindly. Charity's not for this family.

LAURA: *(Pause.)* Are we poor, Pa?

PA: We don't have much and might be headed for even less, but we got each other. *(Pause.)* Git up, boys.

(Lights cross fade.
The family throws off their shawls, coats and hats, and takes up the hustle and bustle of the hotel. Hurrying this way and that they pantomime the work of keeping the hotel running—folding laundry, drying dishes, dusting, stacking wood. This scene is intended to be expressionistic, from a child's larger than life point of view.
Soundscape of the hotel—Honky-tonk piano, banging doors, dishes, front desk bell ringing, shuffling cards, laughing.)

LAURA: Ma, can I go out to the barn now?

MA: Not until you finish your chores.

LAURA: It's so noisy in this hotel.

MARY: Guess we'll just have to get used to it.

LAURA: It's hurting my ears.

MA: Stop complaining and keep working!

LAURA: Pa, can I have a shot of whiskey?

MA AND PA: No!

(Hustle and bustle increases in pace and soundscape increases in volume. LAURA, at center, can't take it another minute.)

LAURA: Wait!

(All freeze.)
(Barn soundscape. Sounds of horses—a nicker, stomping feet, snorts. During the following, LAURA pantomimes currying the horses, feeding them hay, hugging and currying them.)
(During the following, LAURA cannot see the family members or hear their responses as she talks about them.)

LAURA: *(Cont'd.)* Want your supper, Paddy? I've got some bran mash for you. Yes, I've got some for you, too, Pip.

(Playful nickering.)

LAURA: *(Cont'd.)* I'm glad you still remember how to play. Mary forgot how.

MARY: I didn't forget. I just don't have time to play.

LAURA: Her pretty hands are all cracked and chapped.

MARY: Can't be helped. Got laundry to do.

LAURA: Ma hasn't put out her china shepherdess. She always puts out her china shepherdess.

MA: This hotel just doesn't seem like home to me.

LAURA: But it isn't home until Ma puts out the china shepherdess.

MA: Can't be bothered about that now.

LAURA: Pa's put away his fiddle. He hasn't played one single song since we came to this blasted hotel.

PA: Don't have the heart for playing the fiddle just now, I reckon.

LAURA: *(She imitates her Pa.)* "Don't have the heart for playing the fiddle just now, I reckon." That's what he always says, ever since we came to this hotel. I want to hear Pa play the fiddle again. Just one song.

PA: Got chores to do. Better hurry up before it gets dark.

(LAURA speaks directly to her family.)

LAURA: But when will you have the time? When will you bother? When will you have the heart?

(Barn soundscape fades. The family fades. JOHNNY STEADMAN enters the space, walking with a decided limp.)

JOHNNY: Laura Ingalls!

LAURA: What do *you* want, Johnny Steadman?

JOHNNY: I got a horned toad.

LAURA: You do not.

JOHNNY: I surely do. Wanna see it?

LAURA: Your Ma'll whup you if she catches you with that thing in here. No animals allowed in the hotel.

JOHNNY: See if I care. I bring all kinds of sundry creatures to home and never get caught. *(Pause.)* I got it hidden right here in my pocket.

LAURA: Can I hold it?

JOHNNY: Naw. You'll drop it cause it's too squishy.

LAURA: Will not.

JOHNNY: You're afraid of squishy things. All females are.

LAURA: Not this female. I'm not afraid to hold a smelly old toad.

JOHNNY: It's not smelly.

LAURA: Smells like a cow pie.

JOHNNY: That's because I found him in a field.

LAURA: I'll be careful. I won't drop him.

JOHNNY: Cross your heart and hope to die?

LAURA: Stick a pin in my eye.

(LAURA holds out her hands to receive the toad. JOHNNY gives her the "toad." It is a cow pie.)

JOHNNY: *(Cont'd.)* Got ya! Ha! Ha!

LAURA: Ooooo! You liar!

JOHNNY: Fooled you. Fooled you.

(LAURA throws the cow pie at JOHNNY.)

JOHNNY: *(Cont'd.)* Laura's got a cow pie in the house!

LAURA: I hate you, Johnny Steadman. You're the worst boy I ever met!

(JOHNNY fades, laughing.)

MA: What's all this shouting, Laura?

LAURA: It's that awful, mean Johnny Steadman.

MA: Now, Laura, is that a nice way to talk about a friend?

LAURA: He's not my friend.

MA: Why, of course he is. I'm sure he's happy to have someone his own age right here at the hotel. It must have been lonely for him before we came.

LAURA: He's mean and hateful. He pulls my hair and he makes fun of us and . . .

(LAURA *glances in the direction of the cow pie, then thinks better of mentioning it.*)

MA: And what?

LAURA: And everything. He's awful, horrible and dreadful.

MA: Laura, we must be mindful of his infirmity. None of us can know how difficult life is for him, dragging that useless foot.

LAURA: Being crippled is no excuse for being mean.

MA: Nonetheless, you must be extra nice to him, Laura, like a good girl. Do you hear me?

LAURA: Yes, Ma.

MA: Remember the Golden Rule.

LAURA: Do unto others as you would have done unto you. I know, Ma.

(MA *fades.*)

LAURA: But I still hate him.

(*Lights cross fade.*)

(LAURA *and* MARY *sing "The First Noel" in two part harmony.* CARRIE *listens nearby. During the song,* MA's *shawl becomes a baby that* MA *rocks in her arms. At the end of the song,* MA *realizes that her arms are empty.*)

LAURA AND MARY: Noel, noel, noel, noel. Born is the King of Israel.

(PA *and* MA *fade.*)

MARY: That was much better.

LAURA: If we keep practicing every day, we won't even be nervous Christmas Eve.

MARY: I will be. Everyone at church listening and looking at us. I wish I had a good dress to wear instead of this old thing.

LAURA: Me, too. But we'll sing our part so perfectly no one will even notice what we're wearing.

MARY: We'll have to be awful good.

LAURA: We better practice that last part again.

(MARY *leads and the two girls sing the refrain again, a capella.*)

LAURA AND MARY: Noel, noel, noel, noel . . .

(CARRIE *joins on the last line, but sings loudly and off key.*)

LAURA, MARY AND CARRIE: Born is the King of . . .

LAURA: Carrie!

CARRIE: What?

LAURA: You're not supposed to sing.

CARRIE: But I like singing.

LAURA: You sing off key.

CARRIE: No, I don't.

LAURA: You can't even carry a tune.

CARRIE: I don't have to carry it, I'm singing it.

LAURA: Well, don't.

MARY: Laura, you're hurting Carrie's feelings.

LAURA: I don't mean to hurt Carrie's feelings, but Carrie will hurt the Churchgoer's ears.

CARRIE: You don't like my singing.

LAURA: I do. I like your singing.

CARRIE: Then can I sing with you at church on Christmas Eve?

LAURA AND MARY: No!

MARY: I mean maybe you can sing with us next year.

CARRIE: But why can't I sing this year?

LAURA: Because. Ma and Pa will be lonely if they have no one to sit with them.

MARY: Yes, Carrie, you have an important job already.

CARRIE: Okay, but I'd rather sing.

LAURA: Go ahead, Mary, let's practice the reading.

(During the following, JOHNNY sneaks up on the girls. He carries a sled. MARY and LAURA read with high diction or elocution as it was termed in that time.)

MARY: And Mary brought forth her firstborn son, and wrapped him in swaddling clothes and laid him in a manger, because there was no room at the inn.

LAURA: And there were in the same country shepherds abiding in the field, keeping watch over their flock by night. And Lo, the angel of the Lord came upon them . . .

(JOHNNY STEADMAN enters stealthily.)

MARY: Louder, Laura. Project.

LAURA: And Lo, the Angel of the Lord came upon them and the glory of the lord shone round about them, and they were sore afraid . . .

(JOHNNY pulls LAURA's hair.)

LAURA: Ouch!

JOHNNY: (Imitating them.) And they were sore afraid.

LAURA: You skedaddle, Johnny Steadman.

JOHNNY: I live here, too, remember?

LAURA: How could I forget?

CARRIE: Is that your sled?

JOHNNY: Yes. I'm going sledding. Have you ever seen a more beautiful sled? Come all the way from Chicago.

CARRIE: It's the most beautiful sled in the whole wide world. I'd give anything to have a sled like that.

MARY: It is a lovely sled.

LAURA: It's an ugly, old thing.

CARRIE: That's a lie, Laura. It's the most beautiful sled in the world.

LAURA: Pa says beauty is in the eyes of the beholder.

JOHNNY: You're just jealous cause you don't have a sled!

LAURA: I don't want any old sled. I don't even like sledding.

CARRIE: But that's a . . .

(LAURA *puts her hand over* CARRIE's *mouth.*)

JOHNNY: It's fast, too. Fastest sled in town. Take a look at these runners.

LAURA: *(Looks.)* Now I've seen them. You can go.

JOHNNY: You know what? I'm not *going to* let any of you use my sled. Not even one time. Not even once. What do you think about that?

CARRIE: I think that's . . .

(MARY *covers* CARRIE's *mouth again.*)

LAURA: Like I said, I don't like sledding and neither do my sisters.

MARY: That's right. I certainly don't enjoy sledding.

CARRIE: I like . . .

(CARRIE *opens her mouth, but a look from* LAURA *and* MARY *closes it.*)

CARRIE: . . . Christmas.

LAURA: So enjoy your sledding. I hope you don't get hurt.

MARY: Shall we go back to our practicing, Laura?

LAURA: Good idea.

JOHNNY: I'm going out to play and I'll never, never, never let you use any of my things, especially not my sled! Not even if you beg! Because you're just a bunch of females!

(JOHNNY *turns to go and crashes into* MA.)

JOHNNY: Excuse me, Mrs. Ingalls. I wasn't looking where I was going. I was in a hurry. I'm going sledding.

MA: That's a fine sled you have there, Johnny.

JOHNNY: Yes, Ma'am. I'm going sledding.

MA: See that you're careful now.

JOHNNY: *(Suddenly polite.)* Yes, ma'am. Goodbye, Laura. Goodbye, Mary. Goodbye, Carrie. I enjoyed your practicing.

(JOHNNY *fades.*)

LAURA: Good riddance.

MA: Laura!

(*Lights cross fade.*

Barn soundscape. During the following, LAURA *pantomimes currying the horses, feeding them hay and hugging them.* PA *is playing his fiddle in* LAURA'S *imagination.* LAURA *cannot see him.*)

LAURA: Oh, Pip, you're all dirty. Look at you. Did you roll in the dirt? And it's too cold to give you a bath. You'll just have to be a muddy pony until spring. (*A responsive neigh.*) Don't try to sweet talk me. You're just a hairy old mustang pony. And you, Paddy, what are you thinking today? (*Sounds of pawing at the ground.*) Want to go for a ride? Across the river and due west. Far away from Burr Oak.

(PA *stops playing the fiddle and dreams.*)

PA: Out west a man can breathe free. Nothing but the possibilities stretching all the way to the horizon. Who knows what might be waiting for us?

LAURA: When can we move on? Let's pack up the wagon and point the pony's heads west.

PA: Got to keep working. Get us a little money saved up for supplies and such.

LAURA: I wish I had money. I'd buy enough supplies for us to go all the way to Kansas. I'd buy Ma a dress so pretty she'd smile again.

PA: Just gotta be patient. Patient and determined.

LAURA: Guess I just gotta wait and hope for something to happen.

(*Lights cross fade.*)

MRS. STARR: (*Calling.*) Mrs. Ingalls? May I come in?

MA: Who could that be?

(MRS. STARR *appears.*)

MRS. STARR: Good afternoon.

MA: Why, Mrs. Starr. What a surprise.

MRS. STARR: I know I'm not expected, but I took the liberty of arriving unannounced on the chance you might receive me.

MA: Of course, we're happy to see you anytime. Come in. Please, make yourself comfortable.

MRS. STARR: Thank you, dear.

MA: Would you care for coffee? I'm afraid we haven't any tea.

MRS. STARR: Oh, coffee would be fine, Mrs. Ingalls.

MARY: I'll get it, Ma.

MA: Thank you, MARY. How is Doc Starr?

MRS. STARR: Stout as ever and full of vinegar, Heaven be praised.

MA: Glad to hear it.

MRS. STARR: Well. I hardly know where to begin. I had occasion to visit here at the hotel today on some business. But as I arrived, a crowd was gathered in the lobby downstairs, talking quietly but with great excitement. Well, I joined them to ask what all the fuss was about, but was loudly shushed as everyone looked up as if toward heaven. It sounded like two angels had descended from heaven and were singing right here in Burr Oak. It was Mr. Ingalls who told me who it was—Mary and Laura. And when they recited the Christmas story, well, Mrs. Ingalls, it brought tears to these old eyes.

MA: There, there, Mrs. Starr.

MRS. STARR: How fortunate you are to have these two lovely girls.

MA: Three girls, Mrs. Starr. I have Carrie, too.

CARRIE: I didn't know I was an angel.

MRS. STARR: You certainly are and I'm sure it won't be long before you'll join your sisters in the choir.

CARRIE: No, I have to sit with Ma and Pa so they won't be lonely.

MRS. STARR: How charming. Oh, I nearly forgot! I ran across the street to the store to buy these sweets for the girls. I couldn't come calling empty handed now, could I?

(MRS. STARR *holds out the candy and the three girls move toward it, wide-eyed.* MA *steps in between.*)

MA: How thoughtful of you. We'll save it for a treat Christmas morning.

(*The girls stop in their tracks.*)

MRS. STARR: Mrs. Ingalls.

MA: I'd be mighty pleased if you would call me Caroline.

MRS. STARR: Caroline . . . I know this is a bit forward, but do you think I might borrow your girls some afternoons to read to me? I'm so lonely in that big old house now that my own daughters have grown up and gone off to make their own lives, and Dr. Starr, well, you know how busy he is with his patients and all. He's hardly ever home. If you could spare the girls for an hour or two, I'd be so cheered. A house without children, why it's barely a house at all.

MA: What a nice compliment, Laura and Mary.

LAURA AND MARY: Thank you, Mrs. Starr.

MRS. STARR: You're quite welcome. Your singing is a gift. Caroline, I know I'm being presumptuous to even ask, but my girls were such a joy to me and without them, I'm bereft, simply bereft.

MA: Of course you are.

CARRIE: What's bereft?

MA: Well, I . . .

MRS. STARR: It's how you feel when you lose something that you love very much. How I wish I could start all over again with my children as babies. Honestly, Caroline, you can't know what a trial it is to say goodbye to a child.

(MA *turns away in her own grief.*)

MARY: You must miss them terribly, Mrs. Starr.

MRS. STARR: Oh, I do. I do.

MARY: Of course you do.

LAURA: Ma has a beautiful china shepherdess, Mrs. Starr. Would you like to see it?

MRS. STARR: Why, of course I would.

LAURA: Can we show it to Mrs. Starr?

MA: Oh, LAURA, I'm sure Mrs. Starr isn't interested in . . .

MRS. STARR: I'd love to see it. I have quite a collection of china figurines myself.

(LAURA *gets the china shepherdess out of the box and shows it to* MRS. STARR.)

MRS. STARR: This is lovely.

LAURA: Too nice to be shut away, don't you think, Mrs. Starr?

MRS. STARR: Why, yes.

LAURA: Don't you think we should have it out where we can all enjoy it? It's so cheery.

MRS. STARR: (*To the china shepherdess.*) You'll be happier where everyone can see you, won't you? I must show you my collection. Oh, Caroline, may I have the pleasure of your daughters' company now and then?

MA: Well, of course you can.

MRS. STARR: Oh, my dear. You've made me a happy woman!

MA: But I'm afraid I can't spare both of them. There's so much work to be done here at the hotel and they're such a help to me, particularly Mary. But you may have Laura in the afternoons to read to you. After she finishes her chores.

MRS. STARR: Would you like to visit me, dear?

LAURA: Yes, ma'am.

MRS. STARR: You will make a lonely old woman so happy.

MA: Nonsense. You're not an old woman at all.

MRS. STARR: Pshaw, I'm as old as the hills. Shall I look for you tomorrow afternoon, Laura?

LAURA: Yes, ma'am.

MRS. STARR: Do you like cake?

LAURA: Yes, ma'am!

MRS. STARR: Then I have baking to do. Good afternoon, Caroline. Good afternoon, girls. Until tomorrow.

MA: Good day, Mrs. Starr.

(MRS. STARR *fades.*)

LAURA: Yah-hoo! Maybe she'll buy us a sled like Johnny Steadman. All the way from Chicago!

MA: LAURA! For heaven's sake! This is not about what you might receive! It's about what you might give.

LAURA: But Ma, it's not fair. Johnny Steadman is so mean and has such a fine sled and we have to be good all the time and have nothing as nice.

CARRIE: Is it wrong to want a sled like Johnny Steadman's?

MA: It is wrong to think of yourself before others.

LAURA: But, Ma . . .

MA: Laura, there's no money for sleds just now. So you might as well put your mind on something else. I'll hear no more about poor Johnny and his sled.

LAURA: Yes, Ma.

MA: Now you mind, Laura. Be on your best manners at Mrs. Starr's.

MA AND LAURA: No running, quiet voices, hands in your lap. . . .

MA: . . . and only one piece of cake.

LAURA: Yes, Ma.

(MARY *and* CARRIE *fade as lights shift.* LAURA, *at center, watches as* MA *quietly takes the china shepherdess, holds it a moment and puts it back in the box.* PA *enters, reaches out to comfort* MA, *but she turns away.*
Lights cross fade.
LAURA *enters with* JOHNNY STEADMAN's *sled.* CARRIE *follows.*)

LAURA: Shhhh.

CARRIE: Sorry.

LAURA: You have to be quiet or someone will hear us. Then we'll be in a heap of trouble.

CARRIE: But we're just borrowing Johnny's sled, right?

LAURA: That's right. Nothing wrong with borrowing something from a person.

CARRIE: Nope. Nothing wrong in borrowing.

LAURA: Everybody does that now and again.

CARRIE: Laura?

LAURA: What?

CARRIE: Then why are we whispering?

LAURA: Because it's a secret. We don't want anyone to know.

CARRIE: Ohhhh.

(MARY *enters the space.*)

MARY: What are you two whispering about?

CARRIE: It's a secret.

MARY: What is that you have behind your back, Laura?

LAURA: Johnny Steadman's sled.

CARRIE: We're borrowing it.

MARY: What?

LAURA: Oh, Mary, it's so beautiful and Carrie wanted to try it just this once. You know Johnny Steadman will never let us have a turn.

MARY: That's the truth.

LAURA: Please don't tell.

MARY: Ma'll be mighty angry if she catches you. You know better than to take what doesn't belong to you.

CARRIE: We're just borrowing it.

MARY: I think you better put it back right away.

(LAURA *hesitates.*)

MARY: Laura.

LAURA: Okay.

CARRIE: You mean we can't borrow it?

LAURA: I guess not. Come on, Carrie. Let's put it back.

(MA *enters the space.*)

MA: Girls. Don't you have chores to do?

LAURA, MARY AND CARRIE: Yes, Ma.

MA: Then why do you have your coats on?

(*Silence.*)

MA: What is that you're carrying, Laura?

LAURA: A sled.

MA: And just what chore will you be doing with a sled?

LAURA: No chore, Ma'am. I was just putting it away.

MA: Is that the truth, Laura?

LAURA: Well . . . yes.

(*Silence.*)

LAURA: It really is the truth, Ma.

MA: You're sure?

LAURA: Well. It's not exactly the whole truth.

MARY: I think we better start those chores.

CARRIE: Let's all go gather eggs.

LAURA: I took Johnny Steadman's sled without asking so that Carrie could have a turn to sled down the big hill.

CARRIE: Oh, no.

LAURA: But I was putting it back.

MARY: That's true, Ma. She decided to return it. All on her own. She wasn't even going to take her turn.

MA: Laura, you know it's wrong to take something that belongs to someone else without asking. Whatever possessed you to take that sled?

LAURA: I just wanted Carrie to have a turn.

MA: Laura, it won't do to blame this on your little sister. Now I've had just about enough. First you're unkind to that poor little boy and now you steal his sled.

LAURA: I didn't steal it.

MA: What do you call taking something that doesn't belong to you?

(Silence.)

MA: You will return Johnny's sled and make an apology. I'm very disappointed in you, Laura.

(MA fades, with MARY and CARRIE. LAURA is left standing alone. Enter JOHNNY.)

JOHNNY: What are you doing with my sled?

LAURA: You wouldn't share, so I took it. But I changed my mind so you can have it back.

JOHNNY: You stole my sled! Laura Ingalls stole my sled! I'm gonna tell on you.

LAURA: Go ahead. They already know. *(Sighs.)* I'm sorry I took your sled without asking. And I'm sorry I was unkind to you.

JOHNNY: Are you gonna be punished?

LAURA: This is punishment enough.

JOHNNY: I'm sorry, too. I want to be friends. It's so sad I don't have any friends.

LAURA: You'd have friends if you were nicer.

JOHNNY: Would you be my friend, Laura? Please?

LAURA: I guess so.

JOHNNY: You will? Really and truly?

LAURA: Yes. But you have to be nicer.

JOHNNY: I will. I promise. I'll be as nice as can be.

LAURA: And you have to give Carrie a turn on your sled.

JOHNNY: As many as she wants. Want to know a secret?

LAURA: Sure.

JOHNNY: See this? It's a bullet hole.

LAURA: It is not!

JOHNNY: Yes, it is. One time a steady boarder got drunk and chased his wife up and down and all around the hotel, right into this room. He pulled out a pistol and declared, "You better keep running or I'll shoot you full of holes."

LAURA: Why was he so mad?

JOHNNY: Because females make a man crazy, that's why. Well, she ran and he fired, and missed. The bullet hole ended up right here in the floor.

LAURA: Well, I'll be saddled up and rode west!

JOHNNY: The bullet's still in there. You can still feel it. Put your finger in the hole.

(LAURA hesitates.)

JOHNNY: Scared, aren't you? Just like a female.

LAURA: I'm not scared.

(LAURA puts her finger in the hole.)

LAURA: I can't feel it.

JOHNNY: Here, I'll help you.

LAURA: Ow. I don't feel anything in there.

JOHNNY: You don't?

LAURA: No.

JOHNNY: That's because I made it up! Fooled you! Fooled you again!

LAURA: I can't get my finger out!

JOHNNY: You're nothing but a gullible female. It sure is a lot more fun since you came to the hotel!

(JOHNNY *fades, laughing.* LAURA *struggles to get her finger out of the hole but can't.* PA *enters and helps* LAURA *pull her finger out of the hole, gently soothing the hurt finger.*)

LAURA: That Johnny Steadman's the awful-est boy in Iowa.

PA: Boys can be pretty awful.

LAURA: Oh, Pa, I love you.

PA: How much?

LAURA: More than candy.

PA: That's a whole bunch.

LAURA: Even more than Pip and Paddy.

PA: Now that's impressive.

LAURA: More than Christmas!

PA: Don't let Santa hear you say that.

LAURA: Santa would understand.

PA: There's somebody else in this family you love, too.

LAURA: I love Ma, too, but . . .

PA: But?

LAURA: But she doesn't love me.

PA: Now what makes you say that, Half-pint?

LAURA: She's angry with me all the time.

PA: Is that so.

LAURA: She doesn't ever smile special at me anymore or sing or read to me.

PA: Did you ever think that maybe Ma has a powerful lot on her mind besides you?

LAURA: No.

PA: Well, that's the truth. She loves you, just like always. She's feeling poorly right now is all.

LAURA: But she's not sick, is she?

PA: No, it's not like that. She's got a sadness that will take some time to soften its sharp edges.

LAURA: She's sad about Little Freddie, isn't she, Pa.

PA: That's right, Half-pint. But I figure you can help her . . . and me, too.

LAURA: How, Pa?

PA: Trust that Ma loves you, just like always. Be a good girl and do what your Ma says.

LAURA: I try to be good. The best I can. But I'm still bad sometimes. Why is it so hard to be good?

PA: Well now, that's a mighty big question.

LAURA: Do you know the answer?

PA: I'm afraid not, Half-pint.

(Silence.)

LAURA: I think it's easier to be bad than it is to be good.

PA: That's about it, I reckon.

LAURA: There oughta be some rules to make being good easier.

PA: Well, I guess there are a few rules.

LAURA: Always be mindful of others.

PA: That's right. And take a good, long while before making a decision. So you have a chance to ponder the consequences.

LAURA: I'll try, Pa.

PA: I know you will, Half-pint.

LAURA: I just wish being good was more fun.

PA: *(Laughs.)* Fun doesn't last. But you rest easy for the long haul when you're mindful of what's right.

LAURA: But when will the long haul come?

PA: Soon enough, Half-pint. Soon enough.

(Lights cross fade. Home of DOCTOR *and* MRS. STARR.*)*

MRS. STARR: *(Calling.)* Laura! Laura! Continue, dear. I can't wait to hear what's next.

*(*LAURA *joins* MRS. STARR *and reads from a book.)*

LAURA: ". . . and it was always said of Scrooge that he knew how to keep Christmas well, if any man alive possessed the knowledge. May that be truly said of us! And so, as Tiny Tim observed, God bless us, Every One!"

MRS. STARR: *(Wiping her eyes.)* I believe that's my favorite of Mr. Dickens.

LAURA: Mine, too. Course that's the only one I know.

MRS. STARR: And you shall know them all. How happy I am when you're here. Just like when my own girls were at home.

LAURA: Yes, Ma'am. You sure do have a beautiful collection of figurines.

MRS. STARR: I bought them for my daughters. One each year for their birthdays. This one was when Margaret was four. And this one's my favorite . . . Lydia's last Christmas at home. Did I tell you my girls live back East? Philadelphia. Might as well be India, it's so far away.

LAURA: Why didn't they take their figurines with them?

MRS. STARR: Oh, Margaret and Lydia never really cared for them like I do. I don't know why I persisted in buying them year after year. Habit, I suppose. *(Pause.)* They're such good listeners. Goodness how I do go on.

*(*MRS. STARR *pours tea from a china teapot.)*

MRS. STARR: Would you like another piece of cake?

LAURA: *(Hesitates.)* No, Ma'am. Just one piece is all I want.

MRS. STARR: Most children would eat all the cake they could hold.

LAURA: Not me, Ma'am. I never eat more than one piece.

MRS. STARR: Would you like more tea, dear?

LAURA: Yes, please. That's the most beautiful teapot ever.

MRS. STARR: It is lovely, isn't it. I've had it for years. Would you like to have a turn to pour the tea?

LAURA: Yes, ma'am.

(LAURA *carefully pours tea for herself and* MRS. STARR.)

MRS. STARR: Well done. You're a natural, Laura. Now let me see. What shall we read next? *Cricket on the Hearth.* Goodness, we may not have time to get through all the Christmas stories before the big day arrives. My girls used to love to be read to.

LAURA: I guess you miss them.

MRS. STARR: How sad it is to love children. To raise them and love them and have them leave you forever.

LAURA: But you'll visit them.

MRS. STARR: Oh, I'm too old to make such a long journey and my daughters have lives of their own now. The Doctor and I sent them East for their schooling, you know. Why should they return to these God-forsaken western parts? What's here for them?

LAURA: What more could they have back East than you have here? All these books and the china figurines . . . and cake.

MRS. STARR: What a sweet thing to say. Laura, would you like to have one of these figurines?

LAURA: Me?

MRS. STARR: I'd like you to have this one. The schoolgirl. Do you like it?

LAURA: Oh, yes.

MRS. STARR: Well then, it's yours. *(To the figurine.)* You'll have a special home now with Laura.

(MRS. STARR *gives* LAURA *the figurine.*)

LAURA: Thank you, Mrs. Starr. If I was your daughter, I'd never leave a Ma as nice as you.

MRS. STARR: That's the loveliest thing you could say to me.

(MRS. STARR *is overcome with emotion.*)

LAURA: Want my hanky, Mrs. Starr?

MRS. STARR: Pshaw! I'm just a lonely old woman with too much time on my hands.

LAURA: Ma says you're not old.

MRS. STARR: I'm afraid I am quite old. Too old to be alone.

LAURA: But you're not alone. You have Doc Starr.

MRS. STARR: Yes, but he's away all day and sometimes all night with his patients. *(Sighs.)* He has very little time for me.

LAURA: Like Ma.

MRS. STARR: I beg your pardon?

LAURA: Ma doesn't have time for me either.

MRS. STARR: I'm sorry to hear that.

LAURA: It's not polite to complain.

MRS. STARR: You can tell me, dear. It'll be our secret.

LAURA: Well, Ma's tired all the time and sad. All she does is work. And Pa, too. He won't even play his fiddle.

MRS. STARR: Oh, dear.

LAURA: And there's more.

MRS. STARR: Do tell.

LAURA: It's Johnny Steadman.

MRS. STARR: That poor little boy with the crooked foot. All the children are so cruel to him.

LAURA: He's the one who's cruel. He's mean and hateful. (Pause.) Johnny Steadman has a beautiful sled, but he won't let any females use it.

MRS. STARR: I see. And you don't have a sled, is that it?

LAURA: We don't have any money for sleds so we can't have one. And Carrie wants a turn with that sled more than anything in the whole wide world.

MRS. STARR: My goodness. That is sad.

LAURA: Did you ever hear of anything sadder in your whole life?

MRS. STARR: I don't believe I have. There must be something I can do about all this. Just leave it to me, dear. Just leave it to Old Mrs. Starr.

(Lights cross fade.)

MA: Laura! Laura, you're late. It's almost time for supper.

(MRS. STARR *fades.*)

LAURA: I'm sorry, Ma. I lost track of the time.

MA: I have enough to do without worrying about where you are.

LAURA: Look, Ma, Mrs. Starr gave me her schoolgirl figurine. To keep.

MA: Did you say a proper thank you?

LAURA: Yes, Ma. Isn't it beautiful? But that's not all. Mrs. Starr has a china teapot with tiny pink roses all around it and she lets me pour the tea. And I only had one piece of cake, just like you said, even though there were ten pieces cut on the plate. There's lace curtains on the windows and tiny silver spoons for stirring the tea. And a whole collection of china figures, like this one. It would be the best thing in the world to live in a house like that. But the books are the best part. She has hundreds of books. Her own library! Have you read Mr. Dickens, Ma?

MA: Laura, I'm too tired after working all day. Why I can barely keep my eyes open to finish the supper dishes.

LAURA: I miss our reading times together. Remember how you used to sing to us every night before we went to bed?

MA: I'm sorry, Laura. I know I haven't been myself.

LAURA: Remember how Little Freddie would always stop crying when you'd sing?

MA: Laura, please.

LAURA: But only you, Ma. If I sang he'd just wail louder.

MA: Laura! I'm doing the best I can. I just don't feel like singing.

LAURA: Ma? What's the matter?

MA: Nothing.

LAURA: But you're crying.

MA: No, I'm not.

LAURA: Then why are there tears in your eyes?

MA: Call your Pa in for supper. He'll be hungry.

(LAURA *hesitates.*)

MA: Go on, Laura.

LAURA: But, Ma . . .

MA: LAURA, when I ask you to do something I expect it to be done. Now go!

(*Barn soundscape.*)

LAURA: Did you have a Ma, Paddy? Of course you did. Did she get mad at you? Ma's mad at me all the time. And everything I do just makes it worse.

(PA *appears playing the fiddle in* LAURA's *imagination.*
Song: "Where There's a Will There's a Way," sung by MA *and* MRS. STARR.)

MRS. STARR: This life is a difficult riddle.
　　For how many people we see,
　　With faces as long as a fiddle.
　　That ought to be shining with glee.

MA: I am sure in this world there are plenty of good things enough for us all. And yet there's not one out of twenty, But thinks that his share is too small.

MRS. STARR, MA AND LAURA: Then what is the use of repining. For where there's a will there's a way. And tomorrow the sun will be shining. Although it is cloudy today.

(PA *and* MRS. STARR *fade.*)

MA: Laura! Call your Pa in for supper! When I ask you to do something I expect it to be done!

(*Lights cross fade. Hustle and bustle of the hotel with accompanying soundscape. Little by little* LAURA *and* MARY *move more slowly along with the soundscape which becomes more and more distorted.*)

LAURA: I don't feel so good. I feel sick. Really really sick.

MA: Why, you're burning up. Mary, get me some cool water.

(MARY *slowly unfreezes.*)

LAURA: I'm fine, Ma.

MA: We're getting you right to bed.

MARY: Ma . . .

MA: Mary, I thought I told you to get me some cool water.

MARY: I don't think I can . . .

(MARY *faints.*)

MA: Mary!

MARY: I'm sorry, Ma. I think I'm sick, too.

MA: You get right into bed, too. Oh, my dear girls.

CARRIE: Are they gonna die, Ma?

MA: Certainly not, Carrie. We're going to take good care of them until they are well. Run and tell your Pa to fetch Doc Starr.

(CARRIE *runs.*)

CARRIE: Pa! Pa! Get Doc Starr! Laura and Mary are sick and they're gonna die!

MA: Pay no mind, girls. You'll be just fine. I'm not going to lose another child.

(CARRIE *reappears. Climbs onto* MA's *lap.*)

CARRIE: I'm not sick.

MA: Carrie. I thought I told you to find your Pa.

CARRIE: I'm not sick.

(MA *feels* CARRIE's *forehead.*)

CARRIE: I'm not sick!

MA: Oh, my goodness, all three!

(*The box at center becomes a bed, as* MA *tucks the girls in.* MA *fades.* JOHNNY *approaches the sick girls. He pulls* LAURA's *hair.*)

LAURA: Ouch!

JOHNNY: Heard you're sick.

LAURA: Yes, so leave me alone.

JOHNNY: Heard you've got the measles. Too bad. That's awful.

LAURA: What are you doing here, Johnny Steadman?

JOHNNY: Nothing.

LAURA: Go away.

JOHNNY: Can't. Ma says I have to play with you so I'll get the measles.

CARRIE: Your Ma and Pa want you to get sick?

JOHNNY: They want to get it over with.

CARRIE: Why?

MARY: The older you are when you get it the more dangerous it is, especially if you're a grown-up.

JOHNNY: I'm too tough to get the measles. And I don't play with females.

LAURA: I'm too sick to play.

CARRIE: Me, too.

MARY: Me, three.

JOHNNY: Guess I'll have to find something to do then.

(JOHNNY *wanders around the space, looking for something to do.*)

JOHNNY: There's nothing to do here. You don't have anything good to play with.

(JOHNNY *continues looking, making trouble and lots of noise.*)

JOHNNY: Christmas is a bad time to be sick. Almost any time of the year is better than Christmas.

LAURA: What are you talking about?

JOHNNY: Just that Christmas is a bad time to be sick. You won't be able to sing on Christmas Eve. Too weak. So you can't go to church.

CARRIE: But I love church. And I want to hear Laura and Mary sing.

JOHNNY: That's just for starters. You can't eat Christmas dinner. Too feverish. So you'll miss all the good things to eat.

CARRIE: Oh, no.

LAURA: Hush, Johnny Steadman. You're upsetting Carrie.

JOHNNY: You won't even be able to sleep in front of the fire to wait for Santa Claus. Too drafty.

CARRIE: Ma!

LAURA: Hush, Carrie. Pay no attention to him. He's trying to upset you.

JOHNNY: No, I'm not. I'm just thinking out loud how glad I am that I'm not sick.

LAURA: Do you think you could stop thinking out loud? Mary's asleep.

JOHNNY: Sure wish there was something to do around here. Being sick is boring.

(JOHNNY *looks for spots on his body.*)

JOHNNY: No spots. Guess I'm not getting sick. Too bad for you about Santa not coming this year.

CARRIE: What?

JOHNNY: Well, everyone knows that Santa hasn't had the measles. He's not going to come around to where three females are sick with it. Too dangerous.

CARRIE: You mean Santa's not coming this year?

JOHNNY: Not to you.

LAURA: If he's not coming to us then he's not coming to you either, Johnny Steadman.

JOHNNY: I'm not sick. He'll bring me goodies. Presents, too. Maybe he'll come visit you next year.

CARRIE: Ma!

LAURA: Hush, Carrie. Santa will visit this year, just like always. I promise.

JOHNNY: You shouldn't make a promise you can't keep.

LAURA: You shouldn't tease people and hurt their feelings. Ma says I have to be nice to you, Johnny Steadman, but you sure don't make it easy.

JOHNNY: I don't care about any old female being nice to me, that's for sure. You just stay here and be sick!

(JOHNNY *fades.*)

LAURA: I will be nice to him. I will be nice to him. I will be nice . . .

CARRIE: I'm worried about Santa Claus. I don't want Santa to get the measles.

LAURA: He won't, Carrie. I promise.

CARRIE: You promise?

LAURA: Yes, I do.

CARRIE: Laura? I love you.

LAURA: I love you, too.

(CARRIE *snuggles up to* LAURA *and falls asleep. Lights cross fade.*)

MA: How thoughtful of you, Mrs. Starr.

MRS. STARR: I had to come. I've been so worried. How are the darling ones? How's Laura?

MA: Resting comfortably. Rest can be the best cure.

MRS. STARR: Oh, I agree. Now put these herbs in the teapot and bring them to a boil, then fill the sickroom with vapors. It loosens the chest and eases the breath.

MA: I'll put the kettle on right away.

MRS. STARR: Doctor Starr chides me for my home remedies, but I swear by them. Been in my family for generations. They've helped hundreds of his patients, but he won't admit it. Will they be well enough to sing at services Christmas Eve, do you think?

MA: I hope so, Mrs. Starr.

MRS. STARR: So many will be disappointed if they are too ill to take part. But their health is the most important thing. We wouldn't want to put them in any danger.

MA: Oh, they are over any point of danger, I am sure.

(LAURA *overhears voices and creeps closer, listening. She overhears the following.*)

MRS. STARR: Thank Heaven for that. So many young ones are lost. May I tell you how much I have missed Laura these past few days? It is a comfort to have such a lovely companion.

MA: Laura returns home full of talk about your visits. I believe she enjoys them as much as you.

MRS. STARR: Exactly, and that is why I wish to make you a proposal.

MA: A proposal?

MRS. STARR: At first I dismissed it as nonsense, but then after talking to Doctor

Starr and gaining his support . . . I may as well say it right out. Doctor Starr and I are so taken with your Laura, we, well . . . we want to adopt her.

MA: Adopt her!

MRS. STARR: I know your family is hard pressed just now and this would not only ease the burden of so many mouths to feed but would insure Laura's future. We can give her all the best. And when Doctor Starr and I go to our eternal rest, Laura will share equally in the estate, same as our own daughters. Just think of it, Caroline. She'll have the best clothes and books. Perhaps she'll even go to college! I know I'm going on and on but I just can't help myself. To have her with us permanently!

MA: Well, I hardly know what to say.

(MARY *wakes.*)

MRS. STARR: Just say you'll think about it, Caroline. Talk it over with Charles. I know when you've thought it through you'll realize that it's the best thing for Laura.

(*During the following the action moves back and forth between* LAURA *and* MARY, MA *and* MRS. STARR.)

MARY: Laura, what are you doing?

LAURA: Shhhh.

MARY: Are you eavesdropping?

LAURA: Shhh. I can't hear what they're saying.

MARY: Good. You're eavesdropping, Laura Ingalls, and that's a sin.

LAURA: It is not!

MARY: It most certainly is.

LAURA: I just wanted to hear what Ma and Mrs. Starr are saying. They're talking about me!

MARY: If they want you to know, they'll tell you.

LAURA: But, Mary . . . Mrs. Starr wants . . .

MARY: Don't tell me. I don't want to know.

MA: How kind you are. Thank you so much.

MRS. STARR: Thank you, dear. Now I must be off. There is much to do to get ready.

LAURA: Get ready? Oh, no.

MA: I'll see you tomorrow then?

MRS. STARR: Indeed. Until tomorrow.

(MA *and* MRS. STARR *embrace.* PA *enters.*)

MRS. STARR: Charles, just the person I want to see.

PA: Always a pleasure, Mrs. Starr.

MRS. STARR: Come walk with me and we'll have a nice chat.

MA: I'll see you tomorrow then?

MRS. STARR: I can hardly wait!

LAURA: Tomorrow! Tomorrow's Christmas Eve!

(Lights cross fade. Hustle and bustle of the hotel with soundscape. LAURA *hustles faster and harder than the others.)*

LAURA: Ma, I finished milking the cow, bringing in the water and scrubbing the porch. It's real clean.

MA: Thank you, Laura. You're sure you're feeling well enough for all this? Remember, you've got a big evening at church ahead of you.

LAURA: I'm fine, Ma. Fit as a fiddle. Should I scrub up the kitchen floor?

MA: That's Mary's chore, Laura.

LAURA: I don't mind and I finished all my chores.

MA: Don't you want to go out and play?

LAURA: Nope. I want to scrub up the kitchen floor. I want to be real helpful, Ma, as helpful as I can be.

*(*LAURA *scrubs the floor.* MA *fades.* PA *enters.)*

PA: Washing the floor, Half-pint?

LAURA: Yes, Pa. Doesn't it look clean?

PA: Sure does.

LAURA: Aren't you glad you have me around?

PA: Sure am.

LAURA: You wouldn't ever want me to leave, would you?

PA: Well, I expect someday you'll leave your Ma and me to make your own life.

LAURA: But that day will be far, far away, won't it?

PA: Time flies, Half-pint. Might come sooner than you'd expect.

*(*PA *fades.* CARRIE *enters and sees* LAURA *scrubbing and crying.)*

CARRIE: What's the matter, Laura?

LAURA: Oh, Carrie.

CARRIE: What's made you so sad? Is it all this scrubbing?

LAURA: No.

CARRIE: Are you worried Santa won't come? We don't have the measles any more.

LAURA: It's not that, Carrie.

CARRIE: Then what is it?

LAURA: Ma and Pa are giving me away.

CARRIE: You mean like a Christmas present?

LAURA: Doc and Mrs. Starr want to raise me as their little girl.

CARRIE: But you're our little girl.

LAURA: We're poor and they're rich. Ma thinks it would be better if I live with them.

CARRIE: But you can't leave us. You can't.

LAURA: I know.

CARRIE: What are you going to do?

LAURA: I got to ponder on it. Pa says you rest easy for the long haul when you do what's right.

CARRIE: But how do you know what's right?

LAURA: That's what I can't quite figure out. I belong here with all of you, but I got to do what Ma and Pa say. I don't want to be giving them any more trouble than they already had, what with losing the farm to the grasshoppers and Little Freddie and all. But don't you tell about this. Not anyone. It's our secret.

CARRIE: I promise.

LAURA: I don't care about Christmas anymore.

CARRIE: Me, neither. You won't leave me, will you, Laura?

LAURA: I don't know, Carrie. I just don't know.

(MA, PA and MARY burst in.)

PA: Gather round, girls. Your Ma and I have an announcement to make.

MARY: Is it a Christmas surprise, Pa?

PA: I guess you could call it that. Go ahead, Caroline.

MA: Well, we were going to wait for Christmas, but then we decided that now is as good a time as any.

PA: Besides, we couldn't wait to tell you.

LAURA: I already know.

PA: You do?

LAURA: Yes.

CARRIE: Me, too.

PA: You, too, Carrie? News travels fast around here. I'll bet someone has been giving you girls big hints.

MA: I most certainly have not. How did you know?

(LAURA and CARRIE exchange a look.)

MARY: Will somebody tell me? I don't know what you're talking about.

MA: We're expecting.

LAURA: What?

MA: You're going to have a new baby sister or brother. A summer baby.

MARY: Oh, Ma, how wonderful.

CARRIE: A baby? That's the news?

MA: Yes, what did you think it was?

CARRIE: A baby? A real, live baby? Can I hold it?

MA: Of course. You're a big girl now, Carrie. I'll need plenty of help from you when the new baby comes.

PA: Isn't this the best news? And just in time for Christmas.

LAURA: Another mouth to feed.

MA: Laura. What a thing to say.

PA: Don't you worry, Half-pint. Your Ma and I got us some plans, don't we, Ma?

MA: We certainly do. Big plans.

MARY: What plans?

PA: I reckon we've had enough news for one day. Got to save something for Christmas.

(LAURA *runs off but stops to overhear.*)

MA: Laura! What's got into that girl lately?

PA: I have no idea.

CARRIE: She's pondering on the long haul.

(*Lights cross fade.* CARRIE, MARY *and* MA *fade.* PA *in* LAURA's *imagination, plays the fiddle.* LAURA *reprises the chorus of "Where There's a Will, There's a Way."*)

LAURA:

> *Then what is the use of repining*
> *For where there's a will there's a way*
> *And tomorrow the sun will be shining*
> *Although it is cloudy today.*

(*Lights cross fade.* DOCTOR *and* MRS. STARR's *house.* LAURA *and* MRS. STARR *are having tea.*)

LAURA: May I have another piece of cake?

MRS. STARR: But I thought you only eat one piece of cake.

LAURA: I know I said that, but it's not true.

(LAURA *takes and eats the cake as fast as she can.*)

MRS. STARR: I must say it's a surprise to see you today, Laura.

LAURA: Oh, I wanted to come. I didn't feel like doing chores.

MRS. STARR: Well, that's understandable after you've been so sick.

LAURA: I never want to do my chores. Never. Ma and Pa have to force me. I'm lazy and shiftless. Guess you didn't know that about me.

MRS. STARR: As a matter of fact, I didn't.

LAURA: You know what else? I can't learn my multiplication tables. Ma's gone over them and over them with me, but I just can't keep them straight.

MRS. STARR: Well, arithmetic isn't for everyone.

LAURA: May I have another piece of cake?

MRS. STARR: Another one?

LAURA: I love cake.

MRS. STARR: Well, I suppose one more won't hurt.

(LAURA *takes and eats another piece of cake.*)

LAURA: I'm not awful smart.

MRS. STARR: I beg your pardon.

LAURA: I said, I'm not smart.

MRS. STARR: Of course you are, dear. Why, look at the way you read.

LAURA: Oh, I'm good at elocution, but nothing else. I'm mighty useless. Actually.

MRS. STARR: Really.

LAURA: It's true.

MRS. STARR: That's odd. Because your Pa was telling me just the other day how proud he is of you.

LAURA: What did he say?

MRS. STARR: He said he's proud of the fine young woman you're becoming.

LAURA: He said that?

MRS. STARR: He certainly did.

(LAURA *reaches for another piece of cake and stuffs it in her mouth.*)

MRS. STARR: Laura, I think you've had enough cake for one day.

LAURA: But I'm still hungry and it's so good.

MRS. STARR: Nonetheless, dear . . .

LAURA: Can I have more tea, then?

(LAURA *takes the teapot, drops it and it breaks.*)

MRS. STARR: Dear Lord, what's got into you, child?

LAURA: I'm sorry, Mrs. Starr. I'm so sorry.

MRS. STARR: It was an accident, dear.

LAURA: But I broke it. It's broken and it's all my fault.

MRS. STARR: It's nothing to cry about.

LAURA: Yes, it is. It was a beautiful china teapot with flowers all over it. It was special and now it's broken.

MRS. STARR: Oh, Laura. Don't cry, dear.

LAURA: I'm sorry. I'm so sorry. You've been so nice to me and I'm so sorry.

MRS. STARR: I can replace it.

LAURA: No you can't. It can't be replaced. There will never be another one exactly like it. It's lost forever.

(MRS. STARR *embraces* LAURA.)

MRS. STARR: Oh, Laura.

LAURA: It's better you know my faults now rather than later, isn't it? I mean what if you were to find out the worst about me when it's too late?

(LAURA *runs off leaving* MRS. STARR *wondering.*)

MRS. STARR: Oh, my goodness. I understand. (MRS. STARR *lifts her favorite figurine.*) We understand, don't we.

(*Lights cross fade.* MRS. STARR *fades.* PA *plays the fiddle in* LAURA's *imagination throughout the following. Barn soundscape.*)

LAURA: (*Calling.*) Pip, Pip, Pip. Here Pip. I brought you a Christmas Eve treat. There you are. (*Crunching sounds.*) Isn't that good? I knew you'd like it.

Wait your turn, Paddy. I've got one for you, too. (*Crunching again.*) Yes, you like that, don't you. (*Nickering.*) I can't bear to leave. Even if it is what's right for the long haul. Tell you the truth, I don't care about the long haul. I don't want to live in Burr Oak with Doc and Mrs. Starr.

PA: Time to pack up and go. We're moving west again.

LAURA: Oh Pa, take me with you. I want to go away from here and never come back.

PA: Out west a man can be truly free, living on his own, beholden to no one.

LAURA: Nothing more beautiful than the prairie sky. Why, it goes on forever.

PA: Blue as a robin's egg and so high up we can only imagine what's above it. There's better things beyond the horizon.

(*Sounds of* PIP *banging his hoof on his stall door.*)

LAURA: Oh Pip. You want to go west, too.

(*Banging sounds again.*)

LAURA: Stop that, Pip. Even if you want to go more than anything else in the whole world, you have to do as you're told.

PA: Be a good girl and do as your Ma says. You rest easy for the long haul when you do what's right.

(LAURA *makes her decision.*)

LAURA: Good-bye, Pip. Good-bye, Paddy.

(*Lights cross fade. Images of Christmas Eve. Snow, church bells, candles.* MARY *and* LAURA *sing Silent Night.* MA, CARRIE *and* MARY *gather around the fireplace and hang their stockings.* LAURA *quietly packs her few things in a valise.*
   CARRIE *brings* LAURA'S *stocking to her and together they hang it alongside the others.* CARRIE *and* MARY *lie down and go to sleep, leaving* LAURA *alone.*
   Music. Lights indicate night, then Christmas morning. CARRIE *wakes.*)

CARRIE: Wake up, everybody, it's Christmas! Look! Santa was here! There's something in my stocking!

MARY: What did Santa bring you?

CARRIE: It's candy! Look! Ribbons of candy. All colors.

MARY: Me, too. Red and green and yellow.

CARRIE: And there's something else.

(MA *and* PA *enter the space.*)

MA: Merry Christmas, girls.

MARY: Merry Christmas.

PA: Did Santa Claus pay us a visit?

CARRIE: Ohhh. It's a doll. Santa brought me a doll!

MA: Do you like it, Carrie?

CARRIE: Her hair is just like mine!

(MARY *holds up an embroidered apron.*)

MARY: What a beautiful apron. I love it.

PA: You're mighty quiet, Laura. Don't you want to see what's in your stocking?

MRS. STARR: *(Offstage.)* Yoo-hoo. Merry Christmas! Merry Christmas!

(MRS. STARR *enters with packages.*)

MRS. STARR: Goodness! It's a Christmas miracle I made it through all that snow. Doctor Starr has been called away to deliver Mrs. Lindsay's baby. This one will make an even dozen! Merry Christmas everyone.

(LAURA *turns to run from the space but is stopped by* PA.)

PA: Whoa, Half-pint.

LAURA: Oh Pa, can we ride west? I want us to go west again more than anything in the world. Let's go right now. Can we?

MRS. STARR: Certainly not. We have celebrating to do here, Laura.

LAURA: Yes, Ma'am.

(LAURA *takes the schoolgirl figurine out of the valise and hands it to* MA.)

LAURA: Will you keep this for me, Ma? You can put it alongside the china shepherdess so you'll never forget me.

MA: Forget you? I don't understand.

CARRIE: Oh, Ma, don't give Laura to Mrs. Starr for Christmas!

MA: What?

LAURA: I want to do what's right for the long haul, but I don't want to leave you and Ma and Mary and Carrie.

MA: What!

MRS. STARR: Of course you don't. Here I was thinking about all the things I could give you and you've already got the truest, best thing right here.

LAURA: Can I stay with you, Ma? And Pa and Mary and Carrie?

MA: Yes, Laura, forever and ever. Whatever in the world made you think your Pa and I would give you away?

LAURA: I overheard Mrs. Starr ask you if I could come live with her and Doc Starr.

MARY: Eavesdropping. I told you so.

PA: I'm about as confused as a hound dog with a stuffed nose. What are you all talking about?

MA: Laura, I think you missed part of that conversation. I told Mrs. Starr thank you kindly, but your Pa and I could never give you up. Why we'd be sad forever if you weren't our little girl.

LAURA: Like Little Freddie?

MA: Just like Little Freddie.

MA: Oh, Laura, I'm sorry. I've not been mindful of anything but my own sorrow. But don't ever think I don't love you.

LAURA: I'll never leave you, Ma. I belong to all of you. Forever and ever.

(MA *and* LAURA *embrace.*)

MRS. STARR: Well, that puts me in a giving mood. Charles, will you fetch that gift for me?

CHARLES: I'd be glad to, Mrs. Starr.

(PA *exits.*)

LAURA: But if the big plans you were talking about aren't my living with Doc and Mrs. Starr, what are they?

MRS. STARR: Your Ma and Pa have invited me to help with the new baby. Nothing like a baby to lighten the spirit and remind us of what's truly important.

CARRIE: So you won't be bereft?

MRS. STARR: Perhaps not, Carrie.

(PA *enters carrying a sled just like* JOHNNY STEADMAN'S.)

MRS. STARR: Ah, there we are. This is for you, Laura. I was worried that it wouldn't arrive in time but Santa Claus knew that it was an important delivery.

LAURA: Oh, Mrs. Starr.

CARRIE: But if it's Laura's sled, do I get a turn?

LAURA: It's your sled, too, Carrie, and you can have the first turn.

CARRIE: Hooray!

PA: How about me? Can I have a turn?

LAURA: We can all take turns. Thank you, Mrs. Starr. For everything.

MRS. STARR: You're more than welcome.

MA: Allow me to add my appreciation, Mrs. Starr.

MRS. STARR: Will you call me Theodora?

MA: I'd be delighted, Theodora.

(MA *embraces* MRS. STARR.)

LAURA: Oooo. I can't wait to show that Johnny Steadman.

MRS. STARR: I'm afraid that will have to wait for another day. Johnny Steadman has come down with the measles!

(*Everyone laughs.*)

LAURA: Wait! (*All freeze.* LAURA *opens the box at center.*) Ma. (MA *takes out the china shepherdess.*) Pa.

(PA *takes out his fiddle and* LAURA *closes the box.* MA *puts the china shepherdess on it.* PA *plays the fiddle and the family sings,* Deck the Halls. *As the song finishes,* MRS. STARR *fades. The box becomes a wagon and the family climbs aboard,* MA *holding the new baby.*)

PA: Hee-ah! Get up, Pip. Walk on, Paddy.

(*The family is jostled as they ride.*)

MARY: That sun's so bright I guess I better put on my sun bonnet or I'll get a hundred freckles.

CARRIE: Can I have a sun bonnet, too, Ma?

MA: Guess you're about that age now, Carrie.

CARRIE: Can I have a blue one? Blue's my favorite color.

PA: You bet, Buttercup. Soon as we get to Walnut Grove. It sure is a beautiful day.

LAURA: Just about every day's beautiful when we're goin' west, Pa.

PA: That's right, Half-pint. (*Crack of the whip.*) Git up!

(*The family is jostled as they ride. The lights fade.*)

CURTAIN

BRAILLE:
THE EARLY LIFE
OF LOUIS BRAILLE

by
Lola H. and Coleman A. Jennings

BRAILLE: THE EARLY LIFE
OF LOUIS BRAILLE

CHARACTERS

Child Louis ....as a young child
Louis Braille ....age ten to fifteen
Pappa ....Louis' father
Mamma ....Louis' mother
Catherine...Louis' sister
Monsieur Dufau...................................schoolmaster at the Institute
Headmaster Guillie ....director of the Institute for the Blind
Gabriel...student at the Institute
Rene ....student at the Institute
Jean ....student at the Institute
Charles Moreau ....older student at the Institute
Headmaster Pignier ....second director of the Institute
Captain Barbier ....inventor of sonography
Mlles. Morrisot and Colbert ....teachers at the Institute
 Jacques, Marcel, Pierre, Herb Woman, M. Becheret, Parisians,
 Peasant Mother, Blind Beggar

TIME

1812

PLACE

Coupvray, a small town near Paris, France, and later in the Institute for the
Blind in Paris.

(SCENE: *The curtain is up when the* AUDIENCE *enters the auditorium. MUSIC CUE begins as the house lights fade to half.* PAPPA *enters, crosses to his shop area and sings softly as he works at this leather bench.* CHILD LOUIS *can be seen skipping, playing outside. He kneels down, picks up a piece of broken glass and holds it up to the sun. After a few seconds he happily runs to his* PAPPA.)

CHILD LOUIS: Pappa. Pappa! *(End Music Cue)*

PAPPA: Good morning, Louis! *(They embrace and then* PAPPA *lifts* CHILD LOUIS *high above his head amid great laughter.)*

CHILD LOUIS: I want to help you.

PAPPA: *(Heartily.)* Good, good. Here are some leather pieces I saved for you. You may work right here at my side.

CHILD LOUIS: These are just scraps! *(As he takes an awl from the work bench.)* I want to make a real harness.

PAPPA: No, the leather tools are very sharp and very dangerous for little hands. *(PAPPA stares at* CHILD LOUIS *as he,* PAPPA, *holds out his hand. Pause. Slowly* CHILD LOUIS *places the awl in his* PAPPA's *hand.)* Now, see what kind of a picture you can make with your scraps. *(As* CHILD LOUIS *begins arranging the pieces.)* I have a surprise for you—an apron just like mine. Here, let's see if it fits. *(Helping* CHILD LOUIS *put on leather apron.)* I made it.

CHILD LOUIS: Oh, thank you, Pappa! *(Showing off the apron.)* I like it. Some-day . . . I will make things just like you do.

PAPPA: I will teach you everything I know. Before you know it, your hands will be as big as mine. *(PAPPA starts to work.)* You'll make the best har-nesses in France!

MAMMA: *(Off.)* Simon.

(MAMMA enters.)

MAMMA: Simon. A customer is out front.

PAPPA: Come along, Louis. *(CHILD LOUIS follows his* PAPPA *a short way, then stops. After his* PAPPA *is out of sight he moves toward the work block. He hesi-tates. He spots the awl and is once again fascinated by it. He is drawn to the work block and begins imitating the work of his* PAPPA.)

CHILD LOUIS: *(Defiantly.)* I can make a harness now. I'm not too little. *(After two unsuccessful attempts to penetrate the leather with the awl,* CHILD LOUIS *lifts the awl high above his head. His face is close to the leather. His aim is off, and as he stabs the awl down into the leather, he accidentally jabs his right eye with the awl. He screams in pain and terror and continues to cry throughout the fol-lowing scene. Upon hearing the scream* PAPPA *runs to* CHILD LOUIS, *holds him and attempts to comfort him.)*

PAPPA: Monique! Help! Louis has hurt himself with one of my tools! *(As he sees* CHILD LOUIS' *face.)* Oh my God, it's his eye. Louis, my boy.

MAMMA: Oh no, it can't be. *(Taking the bleeding, crying* CHILD LOUIS *from* PAPPA.) How did it happen?

(MAMMA covers CHILD LOUIS' *eye with her shawl as* CATHERINE *enters.)*

CATHERINE: What happened?

PAPPA: *(To* CATHERINE.) Your brother has hurt his eye.

CATHERINE: Oh, no.

MAMMA: Get the herb woman next door—run for her, Catherine. (CATHERINE *leaves.*) What happened, Simon?

PAPPA: (*Clearing the workbench.*) The awl—he was playing with the tool and my harness leather. He jabbed his eye with the awl. Has the bleeding stopped?

MAMMA: (*Carrying* CHILD LOUIS *to the workbench.*) Not yet. What if the herb woman is not at her house?

PAPPA: She will be Monique. She has to be! Wait—I see them. (HERB WOMAN *and* CATHERINE *enter.*) Thank God, you are here. He injured his eye with the awl—it's still bleeding.

HERB WOMAN: (*To* CATHERINE.) I need water and a cloth.

(CATHERINE *exits and returns immediately with bowl and cloth. With mysterious ritual and great urgency,* HERB WOMAN *adds herbs to the bowl. Dips cloth in water and treats eye. As she works she tries to comfort* CHILD LOUIS.)

HERB WOMAN: You are a good boy, Louis, and very brave. Shh, shh. (CHILD LOUIS *gradually becomes quiet.*) I have done all that can be done. The bleeding has stopped, but there may be an infection. We can only wait.

MAMMA: My dear Louis.

CATHERINE: Will he be all right, Mamma?

MAMMA: (*To* HERB WOMAN.) Will he see again?

HERB WOMAN: (*Moving away.*) The wound is very deep. If fever starts tomorrow, that will mean an infection. If it spreads to the other eye, that one could be destroyed, too. It's in God's hands now.

MAMMA: (*Softly crying.*) No, no, no. (*Picking up* CHILD LOUIS *and carrying him away from bench. Sits to hold him.*)

CATHERINE: Look, Mamma. Don't cry. Louis is quiet now.

PAPPA: What can we do?

HERB WOMAN: Wait—and pray! Madame Braille. Madame Braille, come. I must give you instructions.

MAMMA: Simon. (*Hands* CHILD LOUIS *to* PAPPA *who holds him until the* OTHERS *exit.*) You listen, too, Catherine, to help me remember. (HERB WOMAN *instructs* MAMMA *and* CATHERINE *quietly as they exit. Lights and MUSIC CUE indicate a passage of time. After* PAPPA *removes their aprons, they walk together hand in hand. They stop, face front.*)

CHILD LOUIS: Pappa?

PAPPA: Yes, Louis.

CHILD LOUIS: Is there light in the sky yet?

PAPPA: The sun is just coming up.

CHILD LOUIS: When will I see a sunrise?

PAPPA: (*Hesitant.*) My boy . . . (*Pause.*) You won't ever see a sunrise again, Louis.

CHILD LOUIS: Never? I will never see again? Oh Pappa, what will I do? (*Begins to cry as he hugs* PAPPA. PAPPA *kneels in front of* CHILD LOUIS.)

PAPPA: Your Mamma, Catherine and I will help you. The herb woman did all she could.

CHILD LOUIS: Oh, Pappa . . .

PAPPA: It is God's will, but He will guide you, Louis.

(PAPPA *stands. The* ADULT ACTOR *who will henceforth play* TEEN-AGED LOUIS *enters, tapping his home-made cane to find his way to the* CHILD LOUIS. *Facing front* LOUIS *stands with his hand on* CHILD LOUIS' *shoulder.)*

LOUIS: I was never to see again. I was blind. At first I cried a lot. But gradually I forgot what it was like to see. It was as though I'd always been blind.

(PAPPA *exits with* CHILD LOUIS. *With his cane* LOUIS *returns to the past as a child, as three other* CHILDREN *run on calling.)*

JACQUES: Let's play here. Throw me the ball.

MARCEL: Catch. (*Throws small ball.*)

PIERRE: Over here. (JACQUES *throws to* PIERRE.)

LOUIS: Can I play, too? (*Holding stuffed, cloth ball with jingle bells sewn to it.*) I have my own special ball that Mamma made for me.

JACQUES: We're only playing with *my* ball.

PIERRE: Wait, we could play "Keep Away." Louis could be in the middle.

LOUIS: (*Hopefully.*) Can we use my ball?

JACQUES: All right, blindy. If you want to get out of the circle, you'll really have to listen. (BOYS *begin to play.* LOUIS *misses twice, ad libs, "Oh, I missed it. Throw it again."* LOUIS *catches it on third try.*)

LOUIS: I have it! Now you go to the middle.

PIERRE: (*Sarcastically.*) We can see you have it.

JACQUES: Hurry up, Louis. (LOUIS *moves to circle, throws ball right to a* BOY *in center.*)

PIERRE: Too bad. Back in the middle, Louis.

LOUIS: But I just got out.

MARCEL: This is no fun. He can't even throw the ball right once!

PIERRE: Yeah, let's go play by ourselves. (*Giving* LOUIS *the ball with bells and picking up his own.*) Here's your dumb ball, blindy. We don't like baby games.

(BOYS *start to exit, leaving* LOUIS *dejected.* PEASANT MOTHER *enters, observes the* CHILDREN *leaving.*)

PEASANT MOTHER: Come, children. It is time for your lessons.

THREE BOYS: (*Overlapping.*) Now? We just started our game. Can't we do our work later?

PEASANT MOTHER: You must come now while there is light to study by.

(*ALL exit except* LOUIS. MAMMA *enters.*)

MAMMA: Louis, where have you been? (*Sees that* LOUIS *is sad.*) What's wrong?

LOUIS: I wish I could see. I hate being blind. The boys won't play with me and I can't even go to school.

MAMMA: The village school will not take you. (*Taking the ball from* LOUIS.) Your pappa asked, but the master said no.

LOUIS: What am I going to do? (*Crosses to bench and sits.*)

MAMMA: Don't get so upset, Louis. You know you can stay right here at home with your pappa and me. We'll protect you.

LOUIS: I don't *want* to be protected. I want to be treated like everyone else.

MAMMA: When you are blind, you cannot have a life like others.

LOUIS: Why not? I'm not different. I just can't see. I want to go to school, *too.* I already know how to read the alphabet from the board Pappa made for me. See, Mamma, I'll show you. (LOUIS *feels for and finds the board on the bench. Quickly he begins to trace the alphabet created out of nail heads.*) A . . . B . . . C . . .

MAMMA: Tracing letters does not mean you can read.

LOUIS: But it's a start!

MAMMA: Ah Louis, you're never satisfied. (*Crosses away, picks up bucket and taps the side.*) Here, get me some water for supper.

(LOUIS *takes bucket and exits.* PAPPA *enters from work.*)

MAMMA: Simon, what can we do with Louis? All he can think about is going to school.

PAPPA: We could send him to the priest at the church. Last Sunday after Mass, he spoke to me again about Louis. He still wants to teach him about the church and the saints.

MAMMA: (*Sighs.*) Maybe that would satisfy him. I never saw a child so determined to learn. Why would God give us a child like that, and then let him be blind?!

PAPPA: We cannot question God's ways, Monique. Louis is a healthy child. We must be grateful for that.

MAMMA: If the priest told Louis more about the church, that would be like school in a way.

PAPPA: It's worth a try.

(*Scene shifts to* LOUIS *who enters and moves forward, addressing the* AUDIENCE.)

LOUIS: I did learn from the priest. The hours we spent together were filled with his wonderful stories of saints and martyrs who died rather than give up their faith. But I wanted to know more about other subjects, too.

(PAPPA *and* MAMMA *re-entering scene.*)

PAPPA: The priest says you learn quickly, Louis. And you remember everything he tells you.

LOUIS: Couldn't I do that in the village school with the others, Pappa? Ask the master again.

MAMMA: Your pappa and I have never been to school. (*Impatiently.*) Why do you think *you* must go—*you* who can never learn to read or write?

LOUIS: (*Defiant.*) All children go to school. I want to go, too, so I can be like everybody else.

PAPPA: He's right. He needs a chance to be like the other children. We must let him try if the schoolmaster will agree. I'll ask again.

LOUIS: Oh, yes, Pappa (MAMMA *shakes her head sadly.*) Please!

(MAMMA *exits.* LOUIS *moves U, out of scene, sits facing front.* BECHERET *enters, strolling and reading as if on the way home from school.*)

PAPPA: *(Crosses to* BECHERET.*)* Excuse me, sir.

BECHERET: *(Looks up from book, turns to* PAPPA.*)* Yes?

PAPPA: You may remember me. I talked with you before about my son, Louis.

BECHERET: Oh, yes. I do remember you. You're Braille, the harness-maker.

PAPPA: That's right. Well, sir. Louis still wants to come to school. He just wants to listen. He'd be very obedient and give you no trouble.

BECHERET: No, I don't think so . . . *(Crossing away from* PAPPA. PAPPA *follows.*)

PAPPA: It would mean so much to him and to his mamma and me. We were never able to go to school, ourselves.

BECHERET: Well, you *know* he can't ever read . . . or write. *(Starting to leave, stops.)*

PAPPA: *(Quickly.)* I know that. But I think he'd remember what he heard. He can already do sums in his head.

BECHERET: I suppose we could let him try . . .

PAPPA: Oh, if only you would, sir. He could come with Catherine tomorrow.

BECHERET: Well—all right. I'll be expecting him. Good day, Braille. *(Light cue to indicate time change.* PAPPA, *moving to* LOUIS.*)*

PAPPA: Today is the day, Louis.

(MAMMA, CATHERINE *enter.*)

PAPPA: The master can't give you any special attention. You will be on your own, so listen and remember.

LOUIS: I will, Pappa. You will be proud of me, Mamma.

MAMMA: I would be proud of you even if you chose to stay home. Be sure to keep up with your sister, so you will not get lost along the way.

CATHERINE: Come on, Louis. *(Taking his hand.* LOUIS *pulls away.*)

LOUIS: You don't have to hold my hand. I'm not a baby. I'm leaving. *(Rushes away, trips and falls. Slowly picks himself up.* MAMMA *starts to help him, but* PAPPA *stops her.* CATHERINE *follows, then looks at* MAMMA *and* PAPPA *as if asking what to do.)* I wish I could find the way on my own. *(Feeling for help. After a pause* CATHERINE *takes* LOUIS' *hand and helps him up.)*

MAMMA: Catherine, you stay near him.

(MAMMA *and* PAPPA *exit.* CATHERINE *walks with* LOUIS *to the school as the* BOYS *enter noisily.*)

PIERRE: Look, who's coming. *(Pointing toward* LOUIS.*)*

MARCEL: It's Louis Braille. Is *he* coming to school?

PIERRE: He can't do what *we* do, like read and write.

CATHERINE: Hello, Pierre. Louis is going to start school today.

LOUIS: Who's here?

CATHERINE: Pierre, Marcel and Jacques.

JACQUES: Monsieur Becheret won't let him stay. School is for people who see. *(Waves hand before LOUIS' face to show OTHERS he cannot see.)*

PIERRE: Yeah! *(Shoving LOUIS.)* You should stay home where you belong.

CATHERINE: He has as much right to be here as anyone.

MARCEL: *(Chanting, grabbing LOUIS' cane.)* Louis Braille is a blindy.

MARCEL and PIERRE: Louis Braille is a blindy.

MARCEL, PIERRE and JACQUES: Blindy, Blindy.

CATHERINE: *(Snatching cane from MARCEL, returning it to LOUIS.)* Leave him alone.

JACQUES: Blind beggar. The blind are always beggars!

PIERRE: Yeah, go live on the streets where you belong.

CATHERINE: He is not a beggar.

BECHERET: *(Sternly. Hitting the floor of a platform with his disciplining rod.)* Quiet, children. No more of this. Take your places. Louis Braille will be joining us. Sit here, Louis. *(Indicating a place close to him. LOUIS sits.)* Today we will begin with history. The French Revolution began on July 14, 1789, when mobs in Paris stormed the Bastille.

CHILDREN: *(Repeating in unison.)* "The French Revolution began on July 14, 1789, when mobs in Paris stormed the Bastille."

BECHERET: Before that date the king was the absolute authority in France.

CHILDREN: "Before that date the king was the absolute authority in France."

LOUIS: *(Moving forward, addressing the AUDIENCE.)* Gradually the other children got used to my being in school with them. *(OTHERS exit.)* Since much of Monsieur Becheret's teaching was by repetition, I could learn, too. I didn't always know what the words meant, but I memorized them like the rest of the class did. I really envied the rest of the children when they read from books. That's what I wanted to do most. One day Monsieur Becheret told me about a school in Paris for blind boys.

(MAMMA and PAPPA enter.)

LOUIS: I hurried home from school to tell my parents what he said.

PAPPA: Paris is a long day's journey from Coupvray. You would have to live there. We have no money to pay for such a school.

LOUIS: But we don't need money. Monsieur Becheret says that the government gives money to the school. *(Crosses to bench, sits.)* He also says that when the students are finished there, they can support themselves.

MAMMA: How could a blind person support himself? In Paris the blind live in the streets and beg.

LOUIS: Not the ones from this school. Monsieur Becheret says they knit socks and mittens and make house slippers to sell to the people of Paris. Some of them even learn to be musicians. And guess what else?

MAMMA: What?

LOUIS: The students are taught to read from a whole library of special books with raised letters. You can feel the words with your hands—just like the letters on the nail board you made for me, Pappa.

MAMMA: But, Louis, you are only a child. You cannot leave us!

PAPPA: What does Monsieur Becheret think you should do?

LOUIS: He wants me to go—if it's all right with you and Mamma.

PAPPA: Monique?

MAMMA: Well, if he could be taught to earn a living . . .

LOUIS: Monsieur Becheret will write a letter for me, too.

PAPPA: All right. Tell him we give our permission.

(PAPPA, MAMMA *exit.* BECHERET *steps into the spotlight and begins reading.*)

BECHERET: Dear Monsieur Guillie, Headmaster of the Institute for Blind Youth, Paris. A most unusual boy lives in my village of Coupvray. For two years he has been a student in my school, although he is totally blind. I beg you to accept him as a student. He is quick and determined to learn and deserves a chance to make a better life for himself. Your humble servant. Antoine Becheret, Schoolmaster of Coupvray. (*Places letter in envelope and slips it into his pocket.* LOUIS *steps forward.*)

LOUIS: For weeks, we waited for a reply. Finally it came. I was accepted at the school for blind boys in Paris. I was to enter at the beginning of their winter term. I could hardly wait to go.

(LOUIS *steps back into scene. Enter* MAMMA *with package and coat,* CATHERINE *who holds his travel bag, and* PAPPA *who puts on coat.* MAMMA *gives coat to* LOUIS.)

MAMMA: (*Embracing* LOUIS.) We love you, Louis.

PAPPA: We have a long ride ahead of us.

MAMMA: Mind your teachers. (*Pause.*) Say your prayers every day.

LOUIS: I will, Mamma.

CATHERINE: Louis, I've got your things.

LOUIS: Do you have the socks Mamma made for me?

CATHERINE: Yes. I'd be afraid if I were going to Paris. It's so far away.

LOUIS: I am afraid. You know I don't want to leave Coupvray. But I want to go, too.

CATHERINE: I know. (*Hugs him.*)

PAPPA: Are you ready, my boy?

LOUIS: Yes, Pappa.

MAMMA: We will worry, but we know you must go. (*Giving him package.*) Here are some sweets to take with you. Good-bye, Louis. (*They hug good-bye.*) We'll miss you.

LOUIS: Bye, Mamma. I'll miss you, too.

PAPPA: Come, Louis.

CATHERINE: Bye, Louis.

LOUIS: Bye, Catherine. (LOUIS *and* PAPPA *make a counter-clockwise half circle as MUSIC CUE overlaps into next scene. Bench placed DC where* LOUIS *and* PAPPA *sit, facing front as they ride in the "farm cart."* PAPPA *makes a sound for the horse to move. SOUND CUE.)* What does the sky look like now?

PAPPA: It's gray, streaked with blue and peach. The sun will be up soon.

LOUIS: I hope so. The wind is cold. *(SOUND CUE.)*

PAPPA: Listen to the country sounds. What do you hear?

LOUIS: A lark is singing. *(After a brief pause.)* What does Paris sound like?

PAPPA: I'm not sure, Louis. Very different from our little Coupvray.

LOUIS: I'm scared. Pappa. Stop. I don't think I want to go. Take me back home . . . please.

PAPPA: *(Calling to the horse and stopping the carriage.)* Is that what you really want?

LOUIS: I don't know what I want. I don't want to leave home.

PAPPA: But, you do want to go, don't you?

LOUIS: *(Pause.)* Yes, Pappa.

PAPPA: *(Placing his arm around* LOUIS *as he makes a sound for the horse to continue.)* You may be homesick at first, but you'll learn how to be happy there. Who knows, you may like being in Paris more than living in Coupvray.

LOUIS: Maybe—but I don't think so. *(They ride along silently.* LOUIS *sleeps on his* PAPPA's *shoulder. The sounds of the country change to the sounds of the city. SOUND CUE.)*

PAPPA: Louis, we are here and near the school. *(Stops the horse, and gets out of the cart.)* I will ask directions. Wait right here for me. *(*PAPPA *exits.* LOUIS *briefly listens to the new, frightening sounds of Paris.)*

LOUIS: Pappa, wait for me. *(Struggles with his bundle, starts after* PAPPA, *but in the wrong direction.)* Pappa? *(Steps back as he hears the sounds of a passing wagon.)* Pappa!

(Several PEOPLE *rush past* LOUIS, *almost knocking him down. Confused and lost, he stumbles into a seated* BLIND BEGGAR.)

BLIND BEGGAR: Money for the poor, money for the blind. Please help the blind. *(Takes hold of* LOUIS' *coat and pulls him closer to his face. Desperately.)* Please, help the blind.

LOUIS: *(Pulling away, calling.)* Pappa . . . Pappa.

*(*PAPPA *returns, crosses to* LOUIS *and takes him away from the* BLIND BEGGAR.)

PAPPA: Louis, it's all right. I'm here.

LOUIS: Ah, Pappa. I thought you were lost. Everyone is in such a rush in Paris, except for that poor blind beggar. What could I do to help him?

PAPPA: Nothing now, Louis. You have enough to do to help yourself. Come, I've found the school. It's just over here.

(End SOUND CUE. GUILLIE *enters as* LOUIS *and* PAPPA *enter the Institute for the Young Blind.)*

GUILLIE: You are Monsieur Braille?

BRAILLE: Yes, Headmaster Guillie. I bring my son, Louis Braille. We are from Coupvray. He is eager for the chance to learn everything you teach here.

GUILLIE: Good, young man. There is much to be learned here for boys who apply themselves. You will learn to do work with your hands, making things to sell. *(Crosses away.)* The people of Paris will buy these things, but they must be made very well. You will have one outing a week. And church every day. You will have your own uniform, your own bed and a bath once a month. Your uniform will be washed at that time.

PAPPA: *(Crosses to* GUILLIE.) We've heard it said that the boys are taught to read.

GUILLIE: A very few of our older students do learn to read by touch, but that is only for the specially chosen. That is not a concern for Louis now. He will attend classes in grammar, geography, arithmetic and history. How old are you? *(Crossing to* LOUIS.)

LOUIS: Ten years, Monsieur.

GUILLIE: You will be our youngest student. No matter the age all regulations are to be obeyed without questions or exceptions. Those who disobey are punished immediately. Do you wish to be a student here, Louis?

LOUIS: PAPPA? *(Hoping* PAPPA *will answer* GUILLIE. *Pause.)* Yes, Monsieur.

GUILLIE: Then, my advice to you is to be obedient, hard-working and respectful of your teachers. If you do not fit in, you cannot stay for many other blind boys are waiting to take your place.

PAPPA: *(Drawing* LOUIS *aside.)* Obey the teachers, my boy. Show them you belong here. Someday you may even learn to read.

LOUIS: Yes, Pappa. But *when* do you think I'll learn to read?

PAPPA: It will take time.

LOUIS: I wish I could begin today.

PAPPA: Learn to be patient, my boy.

GUILLIE: *(Looking at pocket watch.)* We must be about our business. As we speak Monsieur Dufau is teaching the geography class.

*(*DUFAU *and* CHILDREN *take their place in the classroom.* PAPPA *embraces* LOUIS.)*

PAPPA: Good-bye, my boy. We'll miss you, but you will get to come home in the summer when the Institute is dismissed.

LOUIS: I'm still afraid. Good-bye, Pappa.

GUILLIE: This way, Braille. *(Leads* LOUIS *to classroom.* PAPPA *exits.)* Here's a new pupil, Monsieur Dufau. *(CLASS hears the tapping of* LOUIS' *cane and laughs, immediately interested in the newcomer.* GUILLIE *speaks harshly to them.)* Attend your teacher, class! Immediately! Your job in this classroom is to learn.

DUFAU: *(Crossing toward* LOUIS.) Your name, boy?

LOUIS: Louis Braille.

DUFAU: You'll soon know your way around the school. Sit here and listen carefully to what I say. *(*LOUIS *sits clutching his belongings.)* Class! France is surrounded by five countries: Belgium, Germany, Switzerland, Italy and Spain.

CHILDREN: *(Repeating in unison.)* "France is surrounded by five countries: Belgium, Germany, Switzerland, Italy, and Spain." *(LOUIS falters in the repetition; the others speak out confidently.)*

DUFAU: Of these countries French is spoken only in Belgium and Switzerland.

CHILDREN: "Of these countries, French is spoken only in Belgium and Switzerland."

DUFAU: Braille, name the five countries surrounding France.

LOUIS: Belgium, Switzerland . . . I—I can't.

DUFAU: In which of these five countries is French spoken?

LOUIS: F . . . France? *(Class whispers and softly giggles.)*

DUFAU: *(To Class.)* Silence! *(To LOUIS.)* Braille, you are here to listen and learn. When you are in class, you must pay strict attention to everything I say. We have no room for stupidity and laziness here. We will continue this lesson tomorrow. Class dismissed. *(As DUFAU exits, BOYS gather around LOUIS.)*

JEAN: Hey, Braille, where is your home?

LOUIS: Coupvray. And my name is Louis.

JEAN: A country boy—a farmer! You smell like a farm-boy, all right. *(Shoves LOUIS who falls down.)*

GABRIEL: Let him alone, Jean!

JEAN: We don't get many farmers. He's got a bag and a package. *(Snatches them from LOUIS and feels inside the bag, pulls out a pair of socks.)* Good for cold winters. I can use extra socks. Now what is this? *(Examines parcel.)*

RENE: Maybe he has something worth looking at.

JEAN: He does. *(Sniffs the sweets.)* Home baked and full of cinnamon. *(Takes a bite.)* And butter.

GABRIEL: Stop it, Jean!

JEAN: How nice of you to bring these for us!

LOUIS: Let me have my things back.

JEAN: We don't get much of this here, do we, Rene? *(LOUIS struggles to his feet.)* We'll be thinking of you as we eat them up. *(Laughing, JEAN and RENE begin their exit. GABRIEL remains with LOUIS.)*

RENE: *(Toward LOUIS.)* And if you know what's good for you, you won't tell anybody about this, especially old windbag Dufau. *(Throws the bag to the floor and exits. LOUIS searches the floor for his belongings.)*

GABRIEL: *(Hesitantly.)* Louis . . . ? *(Kneeling, he finds LOUIS' cane.)*

LOUIS: *(Fighting back tears.)* Who is it?

GABRIEL: Gabriel Gauthier. *(Helping LOUIS up, gives him his cane.)* We never get any sweets here, so this always happens when a new boy arrives with food. Jean and Rene aren't so bad once you get to know them.

LOUIS: *(Angry.)* Mamma knitted those socks for me.

GABRIEL: Before long you'll learn to knit socks for yourself. You can make them in your spare time out of scrap yarn from the workshop.

LOUIS: Are the other students like them?

GABRIEL: A few are. It's nearly dinner time. Are you hungry?

LOUIS: Yes, very hungry.

GABRIEL: I'll show you the way. *(Takes* LOUIS' *hand, places it on his own arm, so he can guide him.)* You'll soon know where everything is in the school, and you won't need your cane. *(Starting to exit.)* We'll have porridge and beans.

LOUIS: Ugh! How do you know?

GABRIEL: It's what we have every night. *(Shrugs.)* You get used to it. After dinner I'll show you where we sleep.

*(*LOUIS *and* GABRIEL *exit together.* DUFAU *enters, ringing bell, calling.)*

DUFAU: Five minutes to bedtime!

*(*DUFAU *continues to ring bell as he exits.* GABRIEL *enters with* LOUIS. GABRIEL *carries two blankets and* LOUIS' *uniform jacket which he places on the "cots.")*

GABRIEL: Louis, the housekeeper told me your bed will be the one next to mine. You can store your things underneath.

LOUIS: *(Feeling his "cot.")* What is this? New clothes?

GABRIEL: Yes, it's the uniform. There's a blanket for your bed, but it's too thin to keep you warm. You get used to the cold here. The damp stone walls and floors make it seem even colder.

LOUIS: *(Shivering as he stows away his bag.)* It doesn't seem as warm as home.

GABRIEL: Nothing's like home here—no matter where you come from!

LOUIS: Does everyone teach like Monsieur Dufau? Say and repeat?

GABRIEL: How else could we learn?

LOUIS: By reading in the library here.

GABRIEL: Not many of us use that. It is very difficult. I'd rather learn by repeating after the teacher.

LOUIS: Are there many books in the library? *(Removing his coat.)*

GABRIEL: Hundreds of them.

LOUIS: Then I'm going to learn to read. I don't care how difficult it is.

GABRIEL: You may change your mind when you try it.

DUFAU: *(Off.)* Time for everyone to be in bed and silent. You have one minute!

LOUIS: *(Unfastening, removing his vest and cravat.)* Do we have classes all day long?

GABRIEL: *(Unfastening, removing his jacket.)* Oh no—all morning we make things in the workshop. They want us to do these jobs while we're fresh. Everything we make has to be perfect, so they'll bring a good price from our customers. Afternoons are for classes. Tomorrow afternoon, the first class of the day is music. That's my favorite.

LOUIS: Do you sing?

GABRIEL: Yes. And we play instruments, too. I play the piano. Do you like music?

LOUIS: Oh, yes. Do they teach everyone how to play something?

GABRIEL: Everyone. Two of the older boys even taught themselves how to tune pianos. One night they went to the music room and took the piano completely apart trying to understand how it works. Headmaster Guillie was furious. As punishment he made them stay in the room until they had put it back together. By dinner the next day they had it all finished and in tune. Now they are so good at tuning pianos that they go to people's homes to tune them.

LOUIS: Do you get homesick? (*Crossing away, sits on the floor, hugging his legs.*)

GABRIEL: Not very often. They keep you too busy. Headmaster Guillie says the more we work the less time there is to be homesick.

LOUIS: I know I'll miss my family.

GABRIEL: Sometimes I miss mine, especially when the teachers get very angry with us.

(DUFAU *enters.*)

DUFAU: Boys! Into bed! (GABRIEL *almost falls rushing to his bed.* LOUIS *remains on the floor hoping to be unnoticed.*) Gauthier, you have been keeping our new pupil up after the bedtime call! You know the rules—bread and water only for you tomorrow.

GABRIEL: But, Monsieur . . .

DUFAU: Not another word! Braille, your cot is here. (*Stomps foot to indicate location,* LOUIS *crosses to cot.* DUFAU *stares at them, then exits.*)

GABRIEL: (*In stage whisper.*) Monsieur Dufau is also the dormitory supervisor. He's always very strict.

LOUIS: I was the one who kept asking questions, and I didn't even tell him that! You shouldn't be punished.

GABRIEL: I don't mind. It's only for a day. Good night, Louis.

LOUIS: (*Starts to exit to change costumes, uneasy.*) Good night, Gabriel. I think I'm glad I'm here.

(LOUIS *exits, taking the uniform jacket and his bag with him.* GABRIEL, *moving forward addressing the* AUDIENCE.)

GABRIEL: Louis may not have thought so at first, but it was good to have him at our school. The teachers liked him, because he became a very good student.

(JEAN, GUILLIE *enter.*)

JEAN: At the end of each school year before we were dismissed for the summer, there was an honors program to announce the best students at the Institute. The teachers always chose only the older boys. This year we were in for a surprise.

GUILLIE: This year, we have an unusual circumstance. Two of our younger students have excelled past all expectations. First, it is my pleasure to award Gabriel Gauthier high honors in the study of music. I am also pleased to announce that the youngest boy in our school, Louis Braille, has won highest honors in arithmetic, history and geography. Congratulations to you both.

GABRIEL: (*Moving forward.*) The students liked him, too, because he was kind to everyone.

(GABRIEL *steps back and exits as* LOUIS *enters dressed in the school uniform.* RENE *enters.* LOUIS *touches* RENE.)

LOUIS: Rene, is that you? I have been trying to find you. I made these socks for you.

RENE: Don't you need them?

LOUIS: I can always make another pair.

RENE: *(Taking them, excited.)* Thanks, Louis. I can't seem to learn knitting. Did you hear the workshop foreman scolding me today?

LOUIS: Maybe it would be easier for you to make the house slippers. Why don't you ask if you can change?

RENE: I don't want to ask that mean old Headmaster Guillie for anything!

LOUIS: I'll go with you. We can both ask.

RENE: You will? Thanks, Louis.

(RENE *exits. Benches on top of each other are set to represent piano. Two stools are set.* GABRIEL *enters, moving forward.*)

GABRIEL: Louis always had time to encourage the rest of us. He never wanted to be singled out because of his talents.

(GABRIEL *steps back.* LOUIS *sits and begins to play.* MUSIC CUE. MLLE. MORRISOT *enters and listens.*)

MLLE. MORRISOT: Your lesson has been very good today. How much do you practice?

LOUIS: Whenever I can find an extra thirty minutes.

MLLE. MORRISOT: But you must find more time to practice.

LOUIS: There aren't enough pianos, Mademoiselle. I have to take my turn with everyone else.

MLLE. MORRISOT: Several students from this school have become professional musicians. You could, too. A piano should be available to you first. The others must wait. I will speak to Headmaster Guillie.

LOUIS: No, please don't do that. I'll try to find more time to practice.

MLLE. MORRISOT: If you don't, it will be your loss, Louis. Play the new passage from the Mozart sonata once more and let's see where we are. (LOUIS *plays the beginning.* MUSIC CUE.) Exactly—now here is the last part we will learn today. (MLLE. MORRISOT *plays a short excerpt.* MUSIC CUE. LOUIS *repeats it without error.* MUSIC CUE.) That was very good, Louis. Perhaps you will become a musician without enough practice!

(MLLE. MORRISOT *exits as* LOUIS *continues to play.* MLLE. COLBERT, *rushing in, calling.*)

MLLE. COLBERT: Braille? Where is that boy? Braille? You are making us late. We are ready to leave for the Botanical Gardens. Had you forgotten?

LOUIS: *(Stops playing, crosses to* COLBERT.) No, Mademoiselle . . . I want to go to the library to read a book.

MLLE. COLBERT: You don't even know the alphabet yet!

LOUIS: I do. I learned back in Coupvray.

(CHARLES *enters with guide rope.*)

MLLE. COLBERT: Knowing the alphabet isn't reading. You can't just feel letters. You have to know how to spell words.

CHARLES: Excuse me, Mademoiselle, but he knows words, too. We've been teaching him.

MLLE. COLBERT: When have you had time to do that?

CHARLES: He comes to our reading classroom just after dismissal. One of us older boys stays longer to teach him what we have learned that day.

MLLE. COLBERT: But he's too young to learn to read.

LOUIS: I really want to go to the library. There's never any time.

MLLE. COLBERT: You won't learn to read in one afternoon, no matter how many words the older boys have taught you.

LOUIS: But I could *start* learning.

MLLE. COLBERT: No one can stay with you. You'll be here alone.

LOUIS: I know.

MLLE. COLBERT: All right, Louis. (*To* CHARLES.) Take him to the library. (*Taking the guide rope from* CHARLES.) Then he will understand that he's too young to read. And hurry, Moreau. The others are waiting for us. (*Exits.*)

CHARLES: Louis? (CHARLES *leads* LOUIS *to library. Benches arranged for piano now become table. Bookshelves fly in.*) This is it. (CHARLES *leads* LOUIS *to books on shelves, places his hand on first shelf.*) The books begin here on these shelves. Then, move to your right all the way to the end of this shelf. Then, back to the beginning of the next shelf. (CHARLES *guides* LOUIS.) This table is for holding the books because they're so heavy.

LOUIS: How many books may I read?

CHARLES: As many as you like. But I doubt if you'll want to read very much. The books are not very exciting.

MLLE. COLBERT: (*Offstage.*) Charles!

CHARLES: I must leave now. They are all waiting for me. I'll check on you when I return. (CHARLES *exits.* LOUIS, *carefully removing a book, takes it to the table, sits. He opens it and feels for the words.*)

LOUIS: G-R-A-M-M-A-R, grammar! P-A-R-T, PART 1-5, 15. (*Puzzled as he turns more pages. Again he feels. A bit faster.*) V-E-R-B-S, verbs. (*He stops and thinks. He goes to the shelves, begins reading the spines of the books with his fingers.*) G-R—grammar P-A—part 16. It's still the same book. G—grammar . . . part 128. It must take many volumes of this raised print for each book. What else is here besides a grammar book? (LOUIS *feels to next set of shelves. He reads the spines on the volumes.*) P-R-A-Y-E-R, prayer B-O—book. Prayer Book. P, part 1. (*He quickly feels for last volume, takes it from shelf and holds the book as he reads.*) Prayer Book, Part 175. Is there nothing here but a grammar and a prayer book? Oh no, no. (*He angrily drops book to floor.*) This is no library; this is a lie. Where are the stories? Reading this printing is so hard. Tracing each letter is . . . like . . . trying to find your way around the city alone! I'll never be able to read!

(LOUIS *leaves library. Bookcase flies out as* LOUIS *goes to the dorm and sits on his bed, frustrated and disappointed.* JEAN, RENE, GABRIEL, *and* CHARLES *enter, each holding the guide rope, followed by* MLLE. COLBERT *who is collecting it.*)

MLLE. COLBERT: It was a good trip today. Everybody stayed together and listened carefully I'll ask cook to give everyone an extra helping of porridge for supper tonight. (BOYS' *faces react to prospect of extra portion of awful porridge.*) To your cots, boys, for a short rest before dinner. (COLBERT *exits. The* BOYS *move on to the dormitory.*)

GABRIEL: I wonder if Louis is still in the library.

RENE: Maybe he's finished.

CHARLES: Let's look in the dormitory. If he's not there, I'll go look in the library.

GABRIEL: Are you here, Louis? We're back. (LOUIS *ignores him.* GABRIEL *goes to* LOUIS' *cot and touches him.*) Is something wrong? Why aren't you in the library?

JEAN: (*Rushing to* LOUIS' *cot, trying to tickle him.*) Aaaw—is Louis Braille napping? Wake up—this is no time for sleep. (*Pulling* LOUIS *up.* LOUIS *fights back, furious.*)

LOUIS: Don't ever do that to me again, you bully! I am sick of your pushing everyone around. (*Shoving* JEAN *down on the floor. They begin to fight.* CHARLES *separates the* BOYS.)

CHARLES: Wait, boys. Quiet.

JEAN: (*Astonished.*) I didn't know you knew how to fight.

LOUIS: I can fight as well as anyone, so get out. (JEAN *backs away.* GABRIEL *changes the subject.*)

GABRIEL: Louis—what did you find in the library?

LOUIS: (*Still furious.*) Everyone lied. There are not hundreds of books here. There are only three—a grammar and two prayer books.

CHARLES: The letters have to be so big that only a few words can fit on each page.

RENE: Prayer books! Grammar books! Is that all?

LOUIS: Yes, that's all!

CHARLES: (*To* LOUIS.) It's very expensive to emboss these books in the school press. We can print only a few.

GABRIEL: Will any more be printed?

CHARLES: We are working on the Bible. (*Pause.*) But it won't be finished for ten years. (*The* BOYS *groan.*)

RENE: Ten years?!

CHARLES: We are the only school with *any* books for the blind. Besides it's more important for us to learn a trade than to read books.

JEAN: Could you read the words in the books?

LOUIS: Not very well. No matter how many words you know, you must feel out each one, tracing them letter by letter. How could you read a sentence? You'd forget the beginning before you get to the end. It would take years to read a whole book that way.

JEAN: Maybe the letters can be raised higher.

GABRIEL: Or made smaller.

RENE: I'll never be able to read by feeling letters.

LOUIS: Nobody can read this way, Rene. Somewhere there must be a better way.

GABRIEL: *(Stepping forward.)* Louis was very disappointed, but he kept reading the grammar book, trying to go faster. And then, one day a visitor came to our school with information that changed our lives.

(GABRIEL rejoins BOYS as they sit in dormitory area, motionless, during next scene. BARBIER enters, stepping forward to meet GUILLIE with slate and stylus in hand.)

BARBIER: Good day, Headmaster Guillie. I am Charles Barbier, Artillery Captain, sir. *(Clicks heels, slightly bows to GUILLIE.)* I have come with an invention which will be useful to your blind students.

GUILLIE: And what is that, my good sir?

BARBIER: During the war I invented a system of night-writing for my soldiers. They used it after dark to send short messages during battles. It is also a way for the blind to write and read for it requires no sight. It uses raised dots and dashes made by pinpricks instead of letters. I call it sonography. *(Shows him a sample paper that he takes from slate. GUILLIE, taking paper, looks at it briefly, returns it to BARBIER).*

GUILLIE: What do these bumps say?

BARBIER: *(Feeling stiff paper as he reads slowly.)* Enemy unprepared. Attack at dawn. Here is how to write. *(Putting paper on slate, writes with stylus on paper from right to left. He speaks his name aloud drawn out in syllables as he does so.)* Charles Barbier. *(Removes paper from slate and hands it to GUILLIE. GUILLIE looks at paper.)*

GUILLIE: This is nonsense. No one can read this.

BARBIER: Not with your eyes, sir, but with your fingers after you learn that each set of pinpricks stand for a certain sound. Watch as I read this. *(Demonstrates on the sheet he has written.)* Ch-ar-uhl-z Buh-ar-buh-ee-ay. *(Putting the sounds together.)* Charles Barbier.

GUILLIE: Our teachers are far too busy to learn this. No one would bother to memorize a whole new system just to teach our students to write notes to each other.

BARBIER: The blind would, sir.

GUILLIE: Then they would have a system that only they could use. What about us with sight? They could communicate in secret about us. It would destroy all school authority. You do not understand the blind, sir. Their thoughts are often confused and they are unable to choose what is best for themselves. We sighted must decide that for them. No. We cannot teach them how to communicate secretly.

BARBIER: But they could use my system to make notes about their studies. Surely the blind would be pleased to have a way to write something they could read, themselves, just as we sighted have done for centuries.

GUILLIE: Are you quite through, Captain Barbier?

BARBIER: At least let me leave the explanation of my system along with these writing instruments. It can be easily mastered and taught to the students by anyone who would take the trouble.

GUILLIE: Good day, sir. *(Exits. BARBIER exits in opposite direction still holding slate and stylus. RENE steps forward.)*

RENE: Headmaster Guillie saw no value in the new system from Captain Barbier. Had he not resigned from his job at the school, we might never have heard of sonography. Luckily the next headmaster, Monsieur Pignier, was willing to try new ideas, and he arranged for it to be taught to some of the students. Louis was one of those chosen. Soon he was trying to teach sonography to us. *(Joins BOYS.)*

LOUIS: Try this, Rene. *(Handing him sheet with sonograph.)*

RENE: A-ska-nd it sh-all buh-ee gi-ven yuh-oo. *(Reading slowly, hesitantly as he deciphers each sound.)*

LOUIS: Now put it together.

RENE: I can't.

JEAN: Come on, Rene.

LOUIS: Look—feel here. *(Places his finger on line.)* Ask and it shall be given you. *(Reads aloud as he feels the sets of punctured dots.)*

RENE: You do one. *(Returns paper to LOUIS. LOUIS rises and crosses away from the group.)*

LOUIS: Seek and you shall find. Come here, Rene. Try again. Read here. *(Points to line.)*

RENE: N-ock a-nd it sh-all buh-ee . . . It's no use. I can't do it. *(Frustrated, starting to exit.)*

LOUIS: Wait, Rene. Read down here . . . *(Moves RENE's hand down the page.)* . . . this sentence.

RENE: Er-en-a w-er-k-s huh-ar-duh. *(Uncomprehending, shrugs, throws slate and stylus on floor. Frustrated and angry, runs out. GABRIEL and JEAN follow him.)* I don't know.

LOUIS: *(Calling after him.)* You just read "Rene works hard." *(Picks up slate, stylus. CHARLES, crossing to LOUIS.)*

CHARLES: How long has he been trying?

LOUIS: Several months. Captain Barbier's system is too hard for him. He just can't make words out of the sounds.

CHARLES: But only a *few* of us can read the embossed books in our library.

LOUIS: We need a reading system for everyone—not just a few.

CHARLES: There isn't one and there never will be, Louis.

LOUIS: I think you're wrong. *(Moves out of the scene. CHARLES steps forward.)*

CHARLES: Louis couldn't stop thinking about sonography. All of us were having trouble learning it. Many had given up. That seemed to make Louis work even harder on it. For months he punched out words. One day he asked Headmaster Pignier if he could meet Captain Barbier to ask some questions about his system. The headmaster invited the old captain to the school.

(PIGNIER *enters with* BARBIER.)

PIGNIER: You are very kind to have come today, Captain Barbier. (*Shaking hands.*)

BARBIER: My pleasure, I assure you.

PIGNIER: One of our brightest students has been looking forward to meeting you. Let me introduce him. (*Calls.*) Braille! (LOUIS *moves to* PIGNIER.) Captain Barbier, Louis Braille. (*Taking him to* BARBIER, *they shake hands.*)

LOUIS: I am honored to meet the inventor of sonography.

BARBIER: Ahhh! Then, you have learned my system?

LOUIS: Yes, sir.

BARBIER: And you find it helpful, I'm sure.

LOUIS: (*Hesitantly.*) I think it is a good *beginning*, Captain, but I have some questions.

BARBIER: Questions? (*Crossing to* PIGNIER.) Was I invited here to be cross-examined by a child?

PIGNIER: He knows your system much better than any of our teachers. It is very important to him to talk with you. Go ahead, Braille.

LOUIS: You have done the blind a great service with your invention. But it's very complicated.

BARBIER: What do you mean? (*Pacing back and forth.*)

LOUIS: Each sound is written with too many dots and dashes. It's hard to feel them. And when you write, punching so many dots makes writing very slow.

BARBIER: (*Sarcastically.*) I see. My system is too time consuming. You have so much to do that you must not waste a moment.

LOUIS: (*Frightened but pushing ahead.*) Your system doesn't let us use full sentences, because there is no way to make any punctuation marks.

BARBIER: (*Getting angry.*) This is a note-making system. You don't need periods, commas and question marks when you write short messages.

LOUIS: But sir, we need a system that we can use for books, too.

BARBIER: Since when have the blind needed to read books? (*Crossing to* PIGNIER.) Are these the hopes you encourage in this school, Headmaster Pignier? I thought you were here to teach trades to the blind. (*To* LOUIS.) Is there anything else?

LOUIS: (*Reluctantly.*) I . . . can't find a way to write numbers so we can do arithmetic.

BARBIER: (*Exploding.*) I suppose now you want to be bookkeepers! Foolish child, you do sums in your head. Any number too large for that is not for the blind to be concerned with. Good day, young man! (*Starts to exit.*)

LOUIS: (*Hesitantly, but following after him.*) Also, uh . . . (*Pause.*) Sir?

BARBIER: Well?

LOUIS: We need a way to copy music, so we can read it for ourselves.

BARBIER: You expect too much, young man. I worked long and hard on my invention. My work is complete. If you are so sure there are problems with sonography, you solve them. Good day. (BARBIER *turns on his heel and leaves, insulted and furious.*)

LOUIS: I didn't mean to offend him, sir.

PIGNIER: You have to accept the fact that the blind will never read like the sighted.

LOUIS: I can't do that sir.

PIGNIER: You'll have to. The captain is right, you expect too much for the blind. You may go now, Braille.

LOUIS: Yes, sir.

(LOUIS *exits to join* GABRIEL *and* RENE *as they enter for next scene.* PIGNIER *exits opposite direction.*)

RENE: We've been waiting for you.

GABRIEL: What happened?

LOUIS: He won't change sonography. He says that his work on it is finished. Even Headmaster Pignier thinks we'll never read like people who can see.

GABRIEL: Maybe they are right, Louis.

LOUIS: There has to be a way for us. I'm going to try to find it.

RENE: You're just a boy like us! If a man can't do it, why do you think you can?

LOUIS: I guess because I want to read so much.

GABRIEL: (*Steps forward.* LOUIS *goes to sit on cot, picks up stylus and frame and begins work.*) From that day on, Louis worked every free moment on his own system. Sometimes he sat up all night, punching and punching. By morning he was sound asleep.

(GABRIEL *exits with* RENE. DUFAU *enters.*)

DUFAU: Braille, wake up. (*Pulling him from the bed, shoving him to the floor.*) You've missed breakfast. It's time for your workshops. Aren't you ashamed that you are late? You, a workshop foreman, asleep like a lazy no-good dog! (LOUIS *gets up.*) Headmaster Pignier will hear about this. What do you have to say for yourself?

LOUIS: I couldn't get to sleep last night.

DUFAU: Tomorrow and Friday, you'll have only bread and water. Laziness is not tolerated here.

LOUIS: Yes, sir.

(DUFAU *exits angrily.* LOUIS *moves to next scene.* RENE *enters, stepping forward.*)

RENE: Louis kept on, determined to find a way for us to read and write. (LOUIS *works.*) He missed a lot of fun.

(JEAN *enters hurriedly,* RENE *joins him.*)

JEAN: Louis? Are you in here?

LOUIS: Yes, Jean.

JEAN: *(Finding him.)* We need you right now. The tug-of-wars are about to start. Gabriel is waiting. We aren't enough against the other teams. Come on.

LOUIS: I'm busy, Jean. *(Seated.)*

JEAN: You can't miss this—we'll lose for sure without you. Who cares about reading? (LOUIS *doesn't hear him.*) Louis? *(No answer.)* You are so stubborn. You think of nothing but yourself. What a friend you are! Come on, Rene. (JEAN *exits with* RENE. LOUIS *is seated with his head on his knees, face on the slate which is in his lap. Pause. With face down* LOUIS *begins to speak*).

LOUIS: Ah-Buh- Kuh-Duh, *(Looks up.)* Ah-A, Buh-B, *(Stands up, leaving slate on stage.)* A-B-C-D *(The sonography sounds slowly change into his repeating of alphabet.)* Maybe that is an answer. Instead of sounding out the words, *spell* them with the letters!

(GABRIEL *enters, stepping forward.)*

GABRIEL: He was getting close to a new system. He worked faster. He even walked faster. He missed meals. He didn't sleep, and he stopped playing his music. *(Exits.)*

LOUIS: We don't need Captain Barbier's twelve dots. Six will do it. Six dots to fit under a fingertip. Two, two, two. *(Indicating the three pairs in the air before him.)* The six dots form a shape like a little room that holds the letter. I can't call them a room. *(Thinks. MUSIC CUE.)* I know, I'll call them a cell. Each cell can hold one to six dots. *(Building in intensity.)* One dot *(Indicating the location in front of him in space.)* A; two dots *(Indicating.)* B; move one of the dots *(Indicating.)* C; dot, dot, *(Indicating.)* D; *(Indicating the different locations of the dots.)* Three dots E, F. It's going to work! We will read! And write! What could I spell? *(Crossing to pick up slate, he spells out a word on paper with stylus and slate.)* B-E-A-D. I wrote it. *(Feeling paper.)* Bead! *(Jubilant.)* And I can read it! *(End MUSIC CUE.)* Gabriel!

(GABRIEL *enters with* RENE *and* JEAN.)

GABRIEL: Louis, Louis, are you all right?

LOUIS: I did it. I did it! We're going to read! You don't have to use sounds. You can use the letters of the alphabet.

GABRIEL: Let me see.

LOUIS: Here, feel. *(Punching six dots.)* Six dots. *(Gives slate to* GABRIEL.) Their shape is like a little room . . . so we could call each group of dots a cell.

GABRIEL: I can feel it with only one finger. (LOUIS *retrieves slate.)*

LOUIS: Each letter gets a different pattern of dots. Here's "A." *(Punches it, shares paper with* GABRIEL.)

GABRIEL: Yes. *(Feeling it.)*

LOUIS: Now B—*(Punching and sharing paper with* GABRIEL.)

GABRIEL: B—and A. Yes. Yes. *(Feeling the two cells.)*

JEAN: Let me try, too. *(Feeling the paper.)*

RENE: Me, too. *(Feeling as* LOUIS *guides him.)* A, B. Louis, I can feel the letters in their little rooms.

LOUIS: Cells, Rene. The rooms are cells.

JEAN: What about numbers? Can we use the system for arithmetic?

LOUIS: I don't see why not. Look, Jean. The A cell could become "one," B cell "two," C cell "three." To write twelve you use the A cell first, and then the B cell. One, two—which is twelve!

GABRIEL: And music—would it do for music?

LOUIS: I think I can make it work for music, too. Then we could actually read the music ourselves. We won't have to have someone there playing it for us.

GABRIEL: *(With a great shout of delight.)* Music, too!! Louis, I can't wait!

JEAN: We can be just like those who see. We will write pages and pages and read them back with our fingers.

RENE: I want to keep a diary. I can write my own secrets, and nobody will be able to read them but me!

GABRIEL: We will be free. We can do things by ourselves!

JEAN: But not until we learn how to read, Gabriel. *(Turning to* LOUIS.) When can we start?

LOUIS: We'll have to do it at night after all the others are asleep.

GABRIEL: We can meet at Louis' cot each night after it's quiet. *(LIGHT and MUSIC CUES indicate passage of time.* BOYS *move to* LOUIS' *cot.* LOUIS *whispers.)*

LOUIS: Is everyone here? Jean?

JEAN: *(Whispering.)* Yes.

RENE: *(Aloud.)* I'm here.

GABRIEL: Shhh . . . we must speak softly, Rene. *(BOYS grouped around* LOUIS.) Monsieur Dufau will hear us.

LOUIS: Everyone knows "A" and "B." Remember from yesterday? *(LOUIS gives them paper to feel, which they pass among them.)*

JEAN: I remember.

GABRIEL: Yes.

RENE: This is . . . "A." And this is "B"!

LOUIS: Good. Next is "C." *(Punches C in slate.)* And then D.

(LOUIS punches D and begins to remove paper from slate. CHARLES *enters, stepping forward.)*

CHARLES: Every night for months after everyone else was asleep, Louis secretly taught Gabriel, Jean and Rene his system. They knew they'd be punished if Monsieur Dufau discovered that they were staying up, but that didn't matter because they were so eager to learn to read and write at last. *(Exits.* LOUIS, GABRIEL, JEAN *and* RENE *are still gathered at* LOUIS' *cot. Excitement builds as scene progresses.)*

GABRIEL: *(With papers in hand.)* I took notes today in Monsieur Dufau's geography class. *(Feeling a paper.)* I got most of what he said, too.

LOUIS: Did he see you with the slate?

GABRIEL: I don't know. I sat in the back of the room, hoping he wouldn't.

JEAN: Let me try the cells for arithmetic. *(Picking up slate.)* How do you set up a multiplication problem?

LOUIS: Here. *(Taking his slate and punching the numbers.)* How can we do this? What if we do "8 times 9"? Figure it this way. *(Returns slate to* JEAN. JEAN *writes on the slate.)*

JEAN: I don't know . . . It's hard, Louis.

LOUIS: We'll get it, Jean.

GABRIEL: When can we learn to use your cells for music, Louis?

LOUIS: Soon, I hope.

RENE: *(With paper in hand.)* I want to write a whole letter to my mother! If only she could read it and then write back! *(Slight pause.)* Well, I'll teach her when I go home.

GABRIEL: When are you going to tell Headmaster Pignier about your system?

LOUIS: I don't know. *(Rises. Crosses away from the* BOYS.*)* Would you go with me?

BOYS: *(Ad lib.)* Yes. Of course. Yes.

LOUIS: We'll have to read really well.

GABRIEL: Oh, we will! To convince him that everyone can learn to read this way.

LOUIS: Maybe we'd better practice a little now.

BOYS: Yes. All right.

LOUIS: Come here, Rene. *(RENE crosses to him.)* Here's part of a story I've copied. Can you read it? *(Handing the paper to* RENE, *who feels the dots slowly and hesitates.)* Try it.

RENE: (Text: There once was an old farmer who raised sheep). "There was" . . . I mean . . . There once was a . . . a . . . "Let's see."

(DUFAU enters quietly, unnoticed by BOYS.*)*

JEAN: Come on, Rene.

RENE: "There once was a mold dee . . ." No. "There once was *an* old . . . old . . ." I don't know. It's too hard.

LOUIS: It isn't too hard if you really *try* . . .

DUFAU: *(In a thundering voice.)* What is going on in here? *(All* BOYS, *except* LOUIS, *terrified, move quickly away from* DUFAU.*)* No one is to be out of his cot. Have all of you lost your senses!? I demand an answer.

GABRIEL: We—we are learning to read, Monsieur.

DUFAU: *(Slapping him.)* How dare you be insolent with me, Gauthier! You know lying is not tolerated here. All four of you will report to Headmaster Pignier's office at eight sharp tomorrow morning. I shall recommend a beating for each of you. Tonight you will each sleep on the floor in the hall, since you do not seem to need your beds.

LOUIS: Monsieur—

DUFAU: Not another word from anyone. *(Grabs slate and paper from* LOUIS *as* BOYS *exit.)* Into the hall.

(MUSIC CUE to indicate passage of time. Benches on top of each other are set to represent PIGNIER's *desk.* DUFAU *enters, ushering in* BOYS. PIGNIER *enters.)*

DUFAU: These are the things I confiscated last night. I leave it to you to deal with them. (BOYS *lined up.*)

PIGNIER: Monsieur Dufau has told me what happened. I am so disappointed in you. Why would you defy our rules?

LOUIS: *(Stepping forward.)* It is all my fault, Headmaster Pignier. *(Crossing to* PIGNIER.*)* I worked out a reading system and I was teaching it to them when Monsieur Dufau found us.

PIGNIER: *(Immediately interested.)* A reading system? Do you mean Captain Barbier's sonography?

LOUIS: Not exactly.

GABRIEL: *(Bursting in.)* Oh, no sir, it's much better.

JEAN: It's Louis' own system.

PIGNIER: *(To* LOUIS.*)* Why have you not told me about this?

LOUIS: There hasn't been time. We wanted to see if it was any good before we told anyone, so we were testing it.

PIGNIER: How long has this testing been going on?

LOUIS: Several months.

PIGNIER: *(Angry, pacing about.)* Do you mean that you have been keeping students up far into the night for several months?! How can they possibly keep up with their school assignments and workshops?

LOUIS: Oh, we wanted to learn, sir.

PIGNIER: All the while totally disregarding the dormitory rules of the school.

GABRIEL: We could show you the system, sir.

LOUIS: Oh no, we're not quite ready to show anyone yet. We really need more time to practice.

PIGNIER: *(Sarcastically, crossing to* LOUIS.*)* And when would that be? In the middle of the night? You are an arrogant young man. *(Taking him to the desk.)* You will show me this reading system of yours right now, or you will never use it again.

LOUIS: *(Trying to conquer his fear, picking up the slate.)* If you would read something to me, sir—anything. (PIGNIER *picks up book from desk, leafs through a page or two, finds a passage and stops.*)

PIGNIER: I have found something.

LOUIS: First, Gabriel must leave the room, so he cannot hear the reading. Leave now, Gabriel. (GABRIEL *exits.*)

PIGNIER: Do the others also know your system?

LOUIS: *(Hoping* RENE *will not have to read.)* I think so, sir.

PIGNIER: Then, they must leave also. I want to hear from all three.

RENE: But sir . . . I . . . I would rather just hear the others.

PIGNIER: Are you defying me?

RENE: N-no, sir. *(Exits with* JEAN. LOUIS *holds stylus, ready to write.)*

LOUIS: You may begin reading sir.

PIGNIER: *(Reading slowly, haltingly.)* "I expect to pass through this world but once."

LOUIS: *(Punches out the words.)* You can read faster, sir.

PIGNIER: *(Continues at normal rate.)* "Any good thing, therefore, that I can do, or any kindness that I can show to any fellow creature, let me do it now; let me not defer or neglect it, for I shall not pass this way again."*

LOUIS: *(Calling.)* Gabriel, Jean, Rene.

(LOUIS places slate on desk, holds the paper. BOYS enter. LOUIS gives GABRIEL the paper.)

LOUIS: Read this, please, Gabriel.

PIGNIER: Yes, read it.

GABRIEL: *(Fluently with understanding.)* "I expect to pass through this world but once; any good thing, therefore, that I can do . . ."

LOUIS: Now, Jean.

JEAN: *(GABRIEL passes paper to JEAN who reads but with less assurance.)* ". . . or any kindness that I can show to any fellow creature, let me do it now . . ."

LOUIS: Your turn, Rene. *(RENE, trembling, slowly comes forward, takes the paper. Clearing his throat and running his fingers over the words. Slowly begins.)*

RENE: ". . . let me not . . ." I can't do it, Louis. *(Returns paper to LOUIS. LOUIS pleads.)*

LOUIS: Rene?

RENE: *(Slowly takes paper from LOUIS.)* ". . . let me not defeat . . . defend . . . defer . . . let me not *defer* or neglect it, for I shall not pass this way again!" *(Speeds up last six words gradually into a triumphant end. LOUIS rushes to RENE to embrace him and is joined by JEAN and GABRIEL who pound RENE on the back and give him hugs of congratulation.)*

LOUIS: You did it!

GABRIEL: That's it, Rene.

JEAN: Yes, yes. *(BOYS suddenly become quiet, turn toward PIGNIER.)*

LOUIS: Well, sir?

PIGNIER: *(At first speechless at what he has witnessed.)* I'm not sure I believe what I've heard and seen. What you have done is truly remarkable, Louis Braille. *(As he embraces him.)*

JEAN: His system works for numbers, too. We can even do arithmetic problems.

GABRIEL: And we're going to use it to read music!

RENE: We can take notes and write letters!

PIGNIER: To think that men have been looking for just such a way to read and write for years, and a boy of fifteen, who is blind himself, has found it! I am so proud of you . . . *(Crosses to LOUIS, shakes his hand.)* . . . so very, very proud of you.

LOUIS: May I teach the others during the day, sir?

PIGNIER: I want you to teach us all. I am going to instruct the teachers to begin using your system in their classes as soon as they have learned it from

---

Attributed to Etienne deGrellet (1773–1855).

you. No more middle-of-the-night learning for anyone. The Braille system will change the world for the blind, and it will begin doing that right here in our school—today! (LOUIS *beams. MUSIC CUE.* BOYS *shout their approval, lift him to their shoulders and move about the room.*)

JEAN: We knew you could do it, LOUIS. (CHARLES *joins the* BOYS. LOUIS *is lowered from the* BOYS' *shoulders and crosses D.*)

LOUIS: I was blind. I was never to see again, but my cells gave the blind the freedom to read—and by reading, to see the world.

(MUSIC CUE.)

CURTAIN

BLESS CRICKET, CREST TOOTHPASTE, AND TOMMY TUNE

by
Linda Daugherty

BLESS CRICKET, CREST TOOTHPASTE, AND TOMMY TUNE

CAST OF CHARACTERS

(in order of appearance)

Cricket, young teenage girl
Reese, young teenage boy
Mr./Ms. Bennett, science teacher (may be played by a man or woman)
Tom, Cricket's older brother with Down syndrome
Gran, Cricket's and Tom's grandmother
Tommy, an elegant, imaginary tap dancer in top hat and tails,
Tom's visualization of his inner self

DOUBLING

Young Girl (Prologue) is played by Cricket.
Boy (Prologue) is played by Tom.
Voice of Boy Student is played by Tommy.
Voices in classroom are played by Tom, Gran and Tommy.
Playground Mother is played by Gran or Ms. Bennett.
Playground Child is played by Reese or Tommy.

SETTING

The play moves between a science classroom, the living room and Tom's room in Cricket and Tom's house, playground in Cricket's memory, and Tom's imaginary world. The set must clear quickly for Tom's imaginary world which requires space for Tom and Tommy to dance. In the classroom, an overhead or slide projector is needed.

MUSIC

The musical selections contained in the stage directions are suggestions only.

NOTE

Examples of illustrations referred to in Act One, Scene One, begin on page 152.

ACT ONE

At Rise: *In blackout, a chorus of the song, "Rubber Ducky," from* Sesame Street *plays. Song volume fades but continues to play softly under prologue. Lights rise upstage of a screen upon which shadows will be projected from the rear.* GIRL's *hands appear and cast a large shadow of a duck whose mouth opens and closes, accompanied by* VOICE OF YOUNG GIRL.

VOICE OF YOUNG GIRL: Quack! Quack! See the duck. Quack! Quack! Now you . . . you . . . (*Hands of* BOY *appear, casting quirky shadows without meaning. Enthusiastically.*) Make the duck. Make a duck! You can do it! (GIRL's *hands take the* BOY's *hands and try to mold them to make duck's shadow but it is impossible.*) Look, this one is easy. Really easy. Open your fingers like me. (GIRL's *hands cast shadow of a turkey with her thumb and index fingers making the turkey "speak."*) See the turkey? Gobble, gobble. Gobble, gobble. You do it. Do it! (BOY's *fingers spread and wave wildly. More insistently.*) Hey, we can make a bunny! See how I do it. (GIRL's *hands cast shadow of a hopping bunny.* BOY *laughs at shadow.*)

VOICE OF YOUNG GIRL: It hops. The bunny hops. See? You can do it! *Try.* Try hard! (GIRL's *hands take* BOY's *hands but* BOY's *hands resist. Music volume increases. Angrily.*) Do it! Do it! Why can't you do it?! Why can't you just do it?! (BOY *stands. Dancing wildly and laughing, he moves closer to the screen, casting a giant shadow.*) Do it! Please! Make the bunny, Tom! Please, Tom! Please!!! (*Sound of a needle scratching across record interrupts underscoring song. Blackout.*)

ACT ONE

Setting: *A science classroom.*

At Rise: *In blackout, sounds of noisy class of students before bell rings. Lights up on* CRICKET *who is intently studying before class begins. Students sounds fade.*

CRICKET: (*Reading from her textbook.*) "A cell is the basic unit of life. Each of us is made up of trillions and trillions of cells—each with its own, very special job."

(REESE *enters.*)

REESE: Hey, Cricket!

CRICKET: Hi, Reese! (*She looks up from the textbook, gives him a quick smile and returns to her reading.*) "Simple one cell organisms produce offspring *identical* to the parent through asexual reproduction."

REESE: Come on, you know all of this.

CRICKET: Do you?

REESE: Hey, we made an "A" on the frog.

CRICKET: What do you mean "we"?

REESE: *(Enthusiastically.)* Cricket, you are the best lab partner! You don't get grossed out and you can find all the body parts.

CRICKET: *(Still reading.)* Thanks.

REESE: Hey, Cricket . . . uh . . . would you . . . You want to go to the movie Saturday? My mom'll take us. I already asked her. She'll call your mom.

CRICKET: Reese! Can't you see I'm studying?

REESE: Yeah, I can see that. We could pick you up, see? Where do you live?

CRICKET: No.

REESE: And we could bring you home. No problem. Do you live near school?

(The bell rings as MR./MS. BENNETT *enters. From time to time during following scene,* CRICKET *and* REESE *converse furtively.)*

MR./MS. BENNETT: Reese? *Reese.*

VOICE OF BOY STUDENT: Hel-lo, Reese's Pieces. *Hel-lo!*

*(*VOICES *giggle in background.)*

MR./MS. BENNETT: *(To class.)* We don't need that. Reese, will you please distribute these handouts to those who need them? (REESE *goes to pick up handouts.)* Good morning, class. Before we begin today's lesson, I want to remind you that your science reports on inventors are due tomorrow. No excuses for being late. And I certainly hope no one has waited until tonight to begin. I encourage you to be original and inventive. Surprise me.

REESE: Hey, Cricket, . . . *(He gives* CRICKET *a handout and looks at her notebook which she covers.)*

REESE: *(Cont.)* . . . how about "The Man Who Invented the Peanut Butter Cup"?

MR./MS. BENNETT: Thank you, Reese. Keep digging. This is an opportunity to be creative and *raise* your grade.

REESE: *(Sliding into desk.)* Boy, my average could use another "A." This stuff is way too hard. Was your other school hard?

CRICKET: No.

REESE: Wow. So, have you started it?

CRICKET: The report? Yeah, I'm nearly done.

REESE: You're kidding?! Who's it on?

CRICKET: Marie Curie.

REESE: Who's she?

CRICKET: Ssssh!

MR./MS. BENNETT: Now class, heads up. Someone, please get the lights. *(Lights off as* MR./MS. BENNETT *projects a photograph of students of different races and with different hair and eye colors. The photograph is entitled "Genetics.")* Today we begin our unit on *genetics.* Thank you for helping with the handouts, Reese.

VOICE OF BOY STUDENT: *(Teasing.)* What a sweet boy.

*(*VOICES *giggle again.)*

REESE: Man, I hate my name.

CRICKET: Hey, it could be worse. You could be named after a bug.

MR./MS. BENNETT: Now, class, as you already know, each of you resembles your biological parents in many ways but you have many differences, too. *Genetics* is the branch of biology that tries to explain how this process happens. With advancing technology, the study of genetics becomes more exciting and challenging every day. (MR./MS. BENNETT *projects an illustration of a single human chromosome.*)

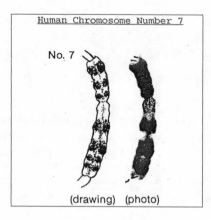

Now, this is a picture of a single human chromosome. How many chromosomes . . . we remember *chromosomes*, don't we? . . . how many chromosomes are in each of our cells?

CRICKET: (*Raising her hand.*) Forty-six.

REESE: (*A beat after* CRICKET.) Yeah, forty-six.

MR./MS. BENNETT: That's right. Forty-six chromosomes. Each tiny chromosome is loaded with genetic information.

CRICKET: Actually, I like your name. (REESE *shrugs, not looking at her.*) And I like the candy, too. (REESE *smiles at* CRICKET.)

MR./MS. BENNETT: Unlike simple organisms, the offspring of humans—and animals—are *not* identical to their parents.

REESE: Do you like *me*?

CRICKET: Ssssh!

REESE: You like me. I know you do.

CRICKET: Yeah, right.

REESE: Admit it.

MR./MS. BENNETT: Now, if we inherit chromosomes from both parents, why don't *our* cells have ninety-two chromosomes? (MR./MS. BENNETT *projects an illustration of the process of meiosis.*) That is because the only cells in our body that have less than forty-six chromosomes are sex cells.

VOICE OF BOY STUDENT: Hey, check out those sex cells!

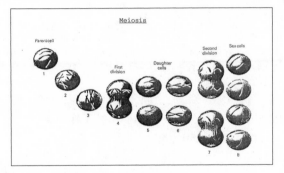

(Embarrassed VOICES *giggle.)*

MR./MS. BENNETT: *(Tapping pointer for quiet.)* I hope most of you are mature enough to take notes on this material and be ready for a *test* next week. Do I make myself clear? I suggest you sketch these illustrations.

*(*CRICKET *and* REESE *sketch, looking up at illustration and down at their sketches.)*

CRICKET: And why do you think I like you . . . I mean, like that?

REESE: 'Cause I *am* so sweet.

CRICKET: Oh, please.

REESE: And because you have hearts and junk and my name written all over the last page of that notebook.

CRICKET: I do not!

MR./MS. BENNETT: Reproductive cells are formed by a special process called meiosis. Spelled how, Reese?

REESE: Uh . . . meiosis? (MR./MS. BENNETT *taps on the wall where word, "meiosis," is projected with illustration.)* Oh, yeah! Meiosis. M, E, I, O, S, I, S.

MR./MS. BENNETT: Trust me. That will be on the test. Meiosis is a type of cell division that produces sex cells with half as many chromosomes as other body cells. This is covered in chapter seven. Please read it before Friday. And read it how?

CRICKET, REESE, and VOICES: Carefully.

MR./MS. BENNETT: Thank you.

(MR./MS. BENNETT *projects an illustration of twenty-three pairs of chromosomes.)*

REESE: *(Teasing.)* Let me see your spiral.

CRICKET: Ssssh!

MR./MS. BENNETT: So each of us receives twenty-three chromosomes from our mother and twenty-three from our father . . . totaling?

CRICKET and REESE: Forty-six.

MR./MS. BENNETT: Yes. *(Pointing to illustration.)* Here, scientists have cut up and paired normal chromosomes from both parents.

REESE: Come on. Show me your notebook.

CRICKET: Ssssh!

(MR./MS. BENNETT *projects an illustration which compares normal and Down syndrome chromosomes each of which is labeled. The twenty-first chromosome in the Down syndrome set is circled.)*

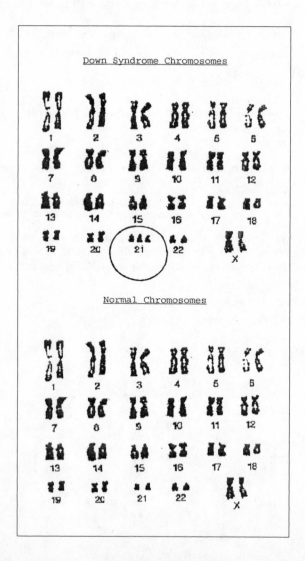

MR./MS. BENNETT: Usually meiosis works perfectly but sometimes a mistake occurs. Take a look at the circled twenty-first set of chromosomes in the illustration on top. There's an extra one. See? An extra one. There are three chromosomes in the twenty-first set. This extra chromosome causes a condition called Down syndrome.

(CRICKET *stops taking notes and stares intently at projected image.*)

REESE: *(Teasing.)* Let me see your notebook.

MR./MS. BENNETT: *(Demanding his attention.)* Reese! See the three?

REESE: Yeah, three chromosomes, right.

MR./MS. BENNETT: Thank you.

REESE: So, Cricket,—

CRICKET: Stop, Reese! I want to hear this!

REESE: Yeah, right, it's so interesting.

MR./MS. BENNETT: Down syndrome is caused by *extra* genetic material. Individuals with Down syndrome have the characteristics of both parents *plus* those of the extra gene.

REESE: Forget the spiral. About the movie, my mom'll pick up.

MR./MS. BENNETT: Individuals with Down syndrome have limited mental abilities—ranging from mild to severe—flattened bridge of the nose, epicanthal folds over the eyes and other physical problems.

REESE: *(Putting his notebook on* CRICKET's *desk.)* Just write down your address. I mean, you're new and I don't know—

CRICKET: *(Harshly pushing notebook away.)* Reese, will you be quiet?!

MR./MS. BENNETT: Down syndrome is the most common serious birth defect in the United States—affecting about one out of every seven hundred children. (MR./MS. BENNETT *continues to lecture as* REESE *tries to talk with* CRICKET.)

MR./MS. BENNETT: There are many other kinds of genetic problems. I'm sure you've heard of Cystic Fibrosis. In 1992, the gene that causes Cystic Fibrosis was identified and scientists are working on ways to correct this defect. Sickle Cell Anemia is another genetic disorder that scientists are working on. It affects one out of every six hundred twenty-five African-Americans in the United States.

REESE: Hey, it was a mistake—looking at your notebook. I didn't mean to see it. I was just giving out Mr./Ms. Bennett's handouts and—

CRICKET: Can't you understand?! Don't talk to me now!

(Embarrassed, REESE *puts his head in his hands.* CRICKET *realizes she has mistreated him but is mesmerized by the information being imparted by* MR./MS. BENNETT.)

REESE: I'm really sorry, Cricket. I'm really sorry about—

CRICKET: *(Distracted.)* . . . the movie . . . maybe . . . maybe . . . I could meet you there . . .

REESE: Yeah? Oh, that would be great!

(CRICKET *slowly moves from her chair to the projection on the wall and stands in front of it.*)

MR./MS. BENNETT: Someday, perhaps many of these genetic problems . . . Is that you, Cricket? Sit down please . . . You're in the way, Cricket. We can't see. (CRICKET *puts her hand on the wall, touching the illustration of the extra chromosome.*) Cricket, are you all right? . . . Cricket? . . . Cricket? (CRICKET *turns around in a daze, barely hearing* MR./MS. BENNETT *call her name. She looks down and sees the chromosomes projected on her body as lights fade.*)

ACT ONE

Scene Two

SETTING: *Living room of* CRICKET's *house. There is a front door, entrances to kitchen and bedrooms, a portable CD player, a desk with books and papers on it and a hat rack.*

AT RISE: *In blackout, recording of Fred Astaire tap dancing to "Begin the Beguine" from* Broadway Melody of 1940. *Lights rise on* TOM *seated on floor center, his back to the audience. He is wearing tails and an oversized top hat which comes down to his ears.* GRAN *calls from the kitchen.*

GRAN: (*Calling offstage.*) Tom, turn that down. (*Music continues.*) Tom! (*No response.*) Thomas! (GRAN *enters from kitchen and turns music off.*) Tom, you are one noisy boy. How about you watch your movie again? (TOM *shakes his head, "no."*)

TOM: Guh movie . . . dancin movie.

GRAN: It was a good dancin' movie, wasn't it? You hungry? You want some popcorn? (TOM *shakes his head, "no."*) You want some cheese and apple? (TOM *shakes his head, "no."*) I think your mom has some goldfish in the cabinet. (TOM *vigorously shakes his head, "no."*) Well, what do you want? (TOM *smiles and holds out his arms. A tap shoe is on each hand. He taps the shoes on the floor. Resigned.*) Uh-huh. I should have known. Well, when you get hungry, Tommy boy, come in the kitchen, okay? (TOM, *sitting on floor, "dances," tapping with his shoes on his hands.*) Okay, Tom? (*No response. She moves closer.*) Okay? (*She moves closer and touches* TOM *on the shoulder. He stops moving and looks up at her with a blank look. She puts her hand under his chin and slowly and gently speaks to him.*) If you get hungry, Tom, Gran'll be in the kitchen. (*She forms a circle "okay" sign with her thumb and index finger.*) O-kay?

TOM: (*Taking a tap shoe off one hand and mimicking* GRAN's *"okay" gesture*) O-kay!

(GRAN *opens her fingers and closes them around* TOM's *circled fingers. They wiggle their intertwined fingers in a familiar routine, obviously shared before.* GRAN *exits to kitchen and* TOM *turns on music [from "Begin the Beguine" from* Broadway Melody of 1940, *sound of Fred Astaire tap dancing without musical accompaniment].* TOM *resumes tapping. Suddenly he takes tap shoes off his hands, crams his feet into shoes and stands. He "taps," making stomping noises with no semblance of tap steps or tap sounds but with great joy. He rushes to the CD player, takes off one tap shoe and taps it on the CD player, his ear to the speaker.*)

GRAN: *(Calling offstage.)* Tom? *(*TOM *continues tapping shoe on CD player.* GRAN *enters.)* Tom, please stop that. If you break Cricket's stereo—*(*TOM *continues tapping.* GRAN *turns off CD player.)* Tom, are you listening to me? If you break Cricket's stereo, you won't have any music to dance to.

TOM: *(Suddenly realizing.)* Where Cricky?

GRAN: It's Thursday, Tom. On Thursday Cricket plays soccer. Remember?

TOM: No.

*(*GRAN *takes tap shoe from* TOM's *hand and puts it on his foot.)*

GRAN: These go on your feet, honey, not your hands. Do you wear shoes on your hands at school, Tom?

TOM: No. I play bayzball at school.

GRAN: That's right. But *shoes* go on *feet.* Tap shoes. Tap . . . *(She points to* TOM's *feet.)* . . . *shoes.* Now, when Cricket gets home from soccer, Tom, she has to study. She has an English test tomorrow and a science report to finish so you have to be real quiet. And shoes go on feet . . . okay?

TOM: O-kay! *(They make their fingers into intertwined circles and repeat ritual. Impulsively,* TOM *begins tapping and spinning.)* O-kay, o-kay! *(Prompting* GRAN *to say, "Maestro, music if you please!")* My! . . . yes! . . . tro! . . . peas!

*(*GRAN *stops him spinning, holding her hands on his shoulders.)*

GRAN: Okay, you whirling dervish. "Maestro, music if you please!"

*(*GRAN *pulls a reluctant* TOM *to her and kisses him on the cheek. She turns on the CD player which plays "Singing in the Rain" sung by Gene Kelly and exits.* TOM *taps joyfully around the room. He turns up the stereo volume and impulsively picks up a stack of lavender colored index cards from desk as he taps by. He pretends to read the cards while singing, turning them around in different directions.)*

TOM: *(Singing while music plays.)* Ol MacDanna hadda farm E-I-E-I-O An onna farm he hadda—

(He tears a strip off the edge of an index card. He stops dancing and focuses on tearing cards into strips and then into smaller pieces. He carefully gathers up the pieces and throws them into the air over his head like confetti. CRICKET, *in her soccer uniform, enters through the front door, carrying her backpack.)*

CRICKET: Hi, I'm home! Whoa! Whoa!!! Too loud, Tom!

*(*CRICKET *turns off music.* TOM *throws his arms around* CRICKET *and they hug affectionately.)*

TOM: Cricky!

CRICKET: Hi, Tom.

TOM: *(Pointing to her soccer shin guards.)* Why you wear tha?

CRICKET: Had my first soccer game today, remember?

TOM: *(Blankly starring at shin guards)* Yep.

CRICKET: *(Playfully mimicking him and pointing at his top hat.)* Why you wear that?

(She pulls brim of hat down over his eyes in a game they have played before. TOM *walks around with arms out as if he can't see, laughing and bumping into* CRICKET *and furniture.)*

TOM: Hey, who turn ow light? Who turn ow lights?

CRICKET: *(Laughing and tapping his hat.)* Very funny, Tom.

*(*GRAN *enters.* TOM *continues to enjoy game, bumping into furniture and walls.)*

GRAN: Cricket, how was your game?

CRICKET: We won.

GRAN: Great. You two want green beans or peas tonight?

CRICKET: Uh . . . peas.

GRAN: Peas okay, Tom?

TOM: Peas . . . and a popsicle!

GRAN: Okay. And, Tom, see all that paper you left on the floor? Please pick it all up. Right now, okay?

TOM: Okay. *(*GRAN *exits.* TOM *gathers up torn cards.* CRICKET *picks up her backpack, ready to go to her room to study.)*
  Cricky, see me! Look! Wain! Wain! *(He throws torn cards in air.)*

CRICKET: *(Uninterested.)* Rain . . . that's right, Tom. *(*TOM *gathers up cards.)*

TOM: Watch gin. Wain! Wain!

CRICKET: I see, Tom. It's rain.

TOM: *(Demanding her attention.)* See me gin. See me! I dancin . . . *(He throws paper in the air again and tap dances.)* . . . in wain.

CRICKET: You're dancing and it's raining. A rain dance! Good, Tom!

TOM: No! No! *Dancin* in wain! You dance wid me, Cricky! Dance in wain!

CRICKET: Not now, Tom.

TOM: It wains, o-kay?

CRICKET: *(Unresponsive.)* Okay, okay.

TOM: Watch! See!

CRICKET: I see, I see.

TOM: It wains on Cricky!

*(*TOM *drops "rain" on* CRICKET *over and over again. She picks up a piece of* Tom *lavender card and realizes that the "rain" is what is left of her science report written on index cards.)*

CRICKET: *(Trying to control her anger.)* Tom . . . Tom . . . your *rain* . . . it's my science report.

*(*TOM *stops throwing paper in air and looks at her intently.)*

TOM: Yes. You wan wain gin, Cricky?

CRICKET: It's not *rain*! It's my science report—my speech. You tore it up. You ruined it! These cards are what I was going to say. *Understand?* Now I have to do it all over and I have an English test tomorrow.

TOM: *(Sympathetically.)* Why cry, Cricky?

CRICKET: I'm not crying! Do you know how long I worked on this? Oh, what's it to you?!

TOM: *(Cheerfully.)* Don cry, Cricky. *(He jumps away and taps.)*
        Sing wid me!
        (Singing)
        Ol MacDanna hadda farm
        E-I-E-I-O
        And onna farm he hadda *wain*—

*(*GRAN *enters unnoticed.)*

CRICKET: *(Frustrated and losing it.)* Why can't you understand anything?! On the farm he had a *cow* or a *horse* or a *chicken*?

TOM: No! Wain!

CRICKET: *(Angrily.)* E-I-E-I-O! Remember?! Then we make the sound of the animal . . . Moo, moo! Cluck, cluck! Why can't you understand?!

TOM: *(Picking up her mood and intensity.)* Wain! *Wain!!* I dancin! I dancin! Wain!!! I dancin!!! *(Angry and frustrated.)*
    In! . . . Wain!!! Wain!!! Wain!!! Wain!!! Wain!!!

*(*TOM *throws himself on the floor, kicking his tap shoes in anger and frustration.* GRAN *goes to him and gently holds his feet still. The tapping stops.* GRAN *rubs his legs and, after a period of silence,* GRAN *speaks softly to* CRICKET.)*

GRAN: I rented "Singing in the Rain" for him. You know . . . Gene Kelly . . . singing and dancing . . . in the rain . . .

TOM: Gene Kelly . . . (Cricket *angrily picks up pieces of index cards.)*

GRAN: I'm sorry, CRICKET, about your report. I should've put it up high—I'm sure your mom always remembers—then he wouldn't have seen it and— *(*TOM *kicks a foot again in frustration.) (Soothingly, patting his legs.)*
    We loved the movie, didn't we, Tom? *(To* CRICKET*)* He was being Gene Kelly, you see.

TOM: *(Overlapping* GRAN.*)* Gene Kelly . . .

GRAN: If you could just see—*(Knock on the front door.* GRAN *flustered)* Oh . . . oh, no, not now. I hope that's not—

CRICKET: What?

*(*TOM *starts to get up to go to door but* GRAN *grabs him.)*

GRAN: Cricket, I think . . . oh, dear, I think I made a mistake.

CRICKET: *(Sarcastically.)* Again?

GRAN: Oh, this is not a good time!

CRICKET: What are you talking about?

GRAN: Reese's mother called—

CRICKET: Oh, no!

GRAN: Get up, Tom! Help me up!

*(*TOM *obeys her.)*
(Nervously.)

Reese wanted to come over . . . well, that seemed nice. You're new, and, oh, his mother said he wanted to come over and study with you for the English test tomorrow, and I thought—

CRICKET: Can't *anybody* think around here?! I'm so sure mom told you I don't ask *anyone* over! I don't want—

(Another knock. TOM, confused, looks at both of them. GRAN and CRICKET look at each other. Resigned, CRICKET crosses to front door. She turns and stares at GRAN who takes the hint and urges TOM to the kitchen.)

GRAN: Come on, Tom. You're hungry.

TOM: I not.

GRAN: Oh, yes, you're hungry . . . for a popsicle, okay?

TOM: Okay, I hungry . . . popsicle! I lie popsicle!

(TOM puts his arm through GRAN's and they exit to kitchen. CRICKET opens door for REESE.)

REESE: *(Excited and smiling.)* Hi!

CRICKET: *(Unemotionally.)* Hi.

REESE: My mom called your grandmother.

CRICKET: Yeah, I know.

REESE: So my mom dropped me off . . .

CRICKET: Yeah, I see.

REESE: *(Confused by CRICKET's reactions and getting nervous.)* So, uh, we could . . . study English. She went to Sack and Save . . . to shop . . . she's got a whole pile of coupons . . . my mom . . . you know, for groceries and junk. I'm gonna walk down and meet her when we're done.

CRICKET: Great.

REESE: So . . . should I come in?

CRICKET: Sure. Come on in.

(REESE comes in and stands awkwardly in middle of room, trying to make conversation.)

REESE: I'm sure glad we have science and English together.

CRICKET: Yeah.

REESE: My mom said your grandmother was real nice on the phone . . . So you live with her?

CRICKET: No. My parents are out of town, on business. My grandmother came to stay while they're gone.

REESE: Oh . . . cool . . . I brought my English book and my old tests.

CRICKET: Great.

REESE: I'm sure your tests have all the right answers anyway. Well, it shouldn't be too hard. Ms. Alcart's tests are pretty easy.

CRICKET: Yeah, should be easy.

REESE: At least for you. I wish I had your brain.

(TOM *bursts through kitchen door, wearing his top hat but not his tails. He has a half-eaten, red popsicle in one hand and another still in the wrapper in the other hand.* GRAN *appears a moment later, trying to keep up with him. She carries* TOM's *tails.*)

TOM: I ga red popsicle!

GRAN: Tom!

TOM: For you, Cricky!

(TOM *hugs and kisses* CRICKET *who pulls away, trying to avoid the sticky popsicle.*)

TOM: *(Cont.) (Noticing* REESE*)* Who he?

(CRICKET *is frozen with embarrassment.*)

GRAN: *(Sensing* CRICKET's *feelings.*)

Oh, that's Cricket's friend, Tom. His name is Reese. (GRAN *takes unopened popsicle from* TOM.) Come on, we better get you cleaned up. Okay, Tom?

TOM: Okay, okay.

(Pointing at REESE.)

He come, too?

GRAN: No. Come on, Tom.

TOM: *(Shoving half-eaten popsicle in* REESE's *hand,* TOM *takes from his pocket a folded picture of a primitive stick figure with top hat along with a yellow squiggly shape.*)

You wan buy pitcher? *(Pointing to figure.)* Tha me. *(Pointing to yellow shape.)* Tha big bird.

GRAN: *(Taking half-eaten popsicle from* REESE.) Tom's having an art show at school. *(Trying to ease* TOM *away.)* I'll buy it, Tom. How about twenty-five cents, okay?

TOM: Okay!

GRAN: *(Firmly.)* Come on, Tom. *Now.* We have to wash that face and brush your teeth. And you'll get your quarter!

(TOM *stares at* REESE.)

TOM: *(Proudly pointing to his teeth.)* I brush teeth Crest too-paste, right?

GRAN: That's right, Crest toothpaste.

(Tapping TOM *on the shoulder.)*

Go on, *right now,* Tom. I'll come checking, okay? Take your pretty picture with you.

TOM: *(Still focused on* REESE.) I pud big bird on fridge wha my mom stick awe my pitchers.

GRAN: That's good.

TOM: My dad say I draw gud.

GRAN: That's right, you do. Now get moving, okay?

TOM: O-kay!

(TOM *runs off.* GRAN *is relieved.*)

GRAN: Hello, Reese. I'm Cricket's grandmother. *(Juggling the two popsicles, she offers her hand to* REESE. *He shakes it politely.)*

REESE: Nice to meet you.

GRAN: I'm so glad . . . *(Eying* CRICKET.) . . . *we're* so glad you could come over and study. We'll try not to disturb you again. *(Hanging* TOM's *tails on the hat rack.)*

I'll just hang this right up. Just let me know if you want some fruit or something.

(GRAN *exits.*)

REESE: *(Nervously thumbing through an old test.)* So . . . uh . . . I guess MRS. Alcart'll ask us to do some diagraming. I always feel like a retard when we have to—*(He looks at* CRICKET, *wishing he hadn't used the word, "retard.")*

I mean—*(Lights rise on flashback of* TOM, PLAYGROUND MOTHER *and* PLAYGROUND CHILD *in silhouette.* TOM *is on his knees, wearing a baseball cap. His head is tilted back with his cupped hand raised in the air as if slowly pouring a stream of sand into his open mouth. Down syndrome chromosomes are projected over flashback. During the following scene, action moves rapidly between* CRICKET *and* REESE *and flashback.)*

PLAYGROUND CHILD: *(Pointing at* TOM.) Mom, look! That big boy is eating sand! Look at him!

PLAYGROUND MOTHER: He's retarded, dear. Something's wrong with him.

CRICKET: So, I guess you'll be telling everyone.

REESE: What?

CRICKET: About my brother.

PLAYGROUND CHILD: Ugh! What's wrong with him?

PLAYGROUND MOTHER: Something's wrong with his mind—his brain.

REESE: *(Nervously.)* Oh, he's your brother? I . . . I didn't know you had a brother.

(Pause.)

CRICKET: Well, go on. Ask.

REESE: *(Innocently.)* What?

CRICKET: Oh, please!

REESE: *(Tentatively.)* So . . . what's wrong with him?

CRICKET: Don't you listen in science?

REESE: Yeah. Actually, no. Not too much.

PLAYGROUND CHILD: There's something wrong with his taster, too! Eating sand?! Ugh!

*(*TOM *spits out the sand, desperately wiping his tongue repeatedly with his hands.)*

CRICKET: My brother has Down syndrome. He's a genetic mistake. Remember, *three chromosomes? Hel-lo?*

REESE: I'm . . . I'm sorry . . . I didn't know.

CRICKET: Well, now you know! You *know*!

TOM: *(Calling and spitting out sand.)* Cricky, Cricky! Help me! Help me!

CRICKET: We had to move so I have to start all over again!

PLAYGROUND CHILD: Mom, I think that little girl's his sister.

PLAYGROUND MOTHER: Sssh. She'll hear you.

CRICKET: And I don't have my stupid science report done because he tore it up!

PLAYGROUND MOTHER: Poor thing. That's too bad.

CRICKET: My brother tore it up to make *rain*!

REESE: Look, I . . . I—

CRICKET: What do you think it's like—trying to study here with his music and tapping all the time?!

REESE: I . . . I—

CRICKET: Can't you think of anything to say?

(Projection of Down syndrome chromosomes spins. TOM *runs off.)*

PLAYGROUND CHILD: *(Reacting as if pelted by sand.)* Hey, she's throwing sand at me! Are you stupid, too?! Stop it, you little moron! Stop it!

CRICKET: You'll have a lot to say at school tomorrow, I bet, Mr. Reese's Pieces! "The new girl's brother is a retard, a moron!" That's what you'll say, right?

*(*REESE *crams tests into his backpack as light fade on flashback.)*

REESE: I . . . I wouldn't do that . . . I wouldn't say—

CRICKET: Oh, yeah?! Why not?! 'Cause you're so sweet?! Don't come over here ever again! Understand?! Don't talk to me! *(Pushing* REESE *out the front door.)*
    And don't ever ask me to any stupid, stupid movie!!!

*(*CRICKET *slams the door. She slides down door and sits there, trying to control herself.* TOM *enters from kitchen doorway with* GRAN *following.)*

TOM: He gone, Cricky?

*(*CRICKET *stands.)*

CRICKET: *(Flatly.)* Yeah. He left. He went to meet his mother at the store.

GRAN: Oh . . . *(*TOM, *dropping his hat on the floor, runs to CD player and looks through his compact discs, choosing by the pictures.* CRICKET *crawls on the floor, collecting pieces of her science report and trying to put it back together. Giving up,* CRICKET *throws pieces of her report in air.)*
    Cricket, your teacher, Mr./Ms. Bennett called this afternoon and—

CRICKET: *(Interrupting.)* And . . .

GRAN: *And* . . . if I may finish . . . he/she said you seemed upset at school.

CRICKET: I'm not upset.

GRAN: He/She wanted to call and check because he/she thought you seemed upset in science class.

CRICKET: *Hello?!* I am not upset!

GRAN: Hello, and I am not deaf . . . at least not yet! (*Hanging* TOM's *hat on hat rack, she continues gently.*) Cricket . . . I'm sorry you have to do your report again and . . . why don't you stay home from school tomorrow?

CRICKET: Right, so they can all talk about me.

GRAN: No, so you don't stay up all night studying. You don't always have to make an "A," Cricket.

CRICKET: I'm going to school tomorrow and I *will* make an "A."

(TOM *rushes to* GRAN, *showing her a CD.*)

TOM: Luk, Gran! Dis gud one!

GRAN: I bet! (TOM *returns to CD player.*) Why don't we call the hotel and try to catch your mom and dad?

CRICKET: They're working, you know.

GRAN: Yes, but wouldn't it be nice to talk to them now?

CRICKET: They'll call Sunday. They're busy. They'll call on Sunday.

TOM: (*Enjoying himself as he looks through his CD's.*) This my favrite! This my favrite one!

GRAN: I know when you look at him, you're not happy with what you see.

TOM: (*Hugging a favorite CD.*) My favrite!

GRAN: But really look at him . . .

TOM: (*Pointing at CD.*) Fred! A! Staire!

GRAN: . . . so happy. Try to see things the way Tom sees them.

CRICKET: (*Sarcastically.*) Oh, I'll try real hard to have an IQ of 53.

(CRICKET *grabs a handful of the torn index cards and her backpack and starts for her bedroom.*)

GRAN: (*Stopping* CRICKET *with her voice.*) Cricket. I'm going to tell you something. The night your brother was born . . . oh, I was so tired from worrying all night in that waiting room. When the doctor told your father and me . . . about Tom, you want to know my first thought? My first selfish thought? (GRAN *waits until* CRICKET *turns and looks at her.*) (*With great difficulty*) I wished he'd never been born.

TOM: (*Blurting out enthusiastically*) Oh, dis one! I play dis one! I dancin! Dance wid me, Cricky! (*He tries to hug* CRICKET.)

CRICKET: (*Pushing him away*) I've got to study. Keep it down, Tom.

(*As* CRICKET *heads to her bedroom with backpack,* TOM *looks after her, startled by her rejection.* CRICKET *pauses in bedroom doorway with her back to* GRAN *and* TOM.)

GRAN: (*Gently*) Not too loud, okay, Tom? Cricket has to study.

TOM: Okay! (*Whispering*) I study, too, Cricky. I study dancin'!

(CRICKET *exits.*)

GRAN: That's right, Tom. You study dancing. You're a good dancer, dear!

TOM: (*Suddenly hugging her with all his being*) Thang yu, Gran!

(TOM *pulls away, goes to CD player and looks through CD's, leaving* GRAN *behind.* GRAN *takes top hat from hat rack, thoughtfully turns it in her hands, looks at* TOM *and proudly places it on his head.*)

GRAN: (*To herself*) What a wonderful grandson you are. (*Crossing to kitchen doorway*) Not too loud, dear. *Please* . . . not too loud.

TOM: (*Whispering and making "okay" sign*) O-kay.

GRAN: (*Making "okay" sign.*) Okay.

(GRAN *exits and* TOM *begins to "tap dance," making loud stomping sounds on floor. He stops dancing, putting his finger to his lips, reminding himself to be quiet with a "sssh." On the third "sssh," the living room disappears, a spinning mirror ball drops from above and from a veil of fog* TOMMY, *an imaginary tap dancer in top hat and tails, appears.* TOM *and* TOMMY *greet one another.* TOMMY *helps* TOM *put on his tails and straightens his top hat. Song, "Let's Face the Music and Dance," sung by Fred Astaire segues into Fred Astaire singing "Top Hat, White Tie and Tails." They bow to one another and begin to dance,* TOMMY *tapping elegantly and* TOM *dancing joyously but awkwardly. As the music ends* TOM *and* TOMMY *bow to recorded enthusiastic applause and in a final pose together gesture "okay!" to the audience. Blackout.*)

ACT TWO

SCENE ONE

SETTING: *Science classroom.*

AT RISE: *In blackout, "French Suites #6 in E: Gigue" by Johann Sebastian Bach plays. Music fades as downlight illuminates* CRICKET *dressed in a home-made 1900's costume as Marie Curie. She holds lavender colored index cards. Projected during following speech are slides such as Young Marie, Map of Poland, Eiffel Tower, Pierre and Marie Curie, their Laboratory, and the Periodic Table of the Elements.*

CRICKET: (*With dramatic flair and in her idea of a Polish accent, obviously rehearsed many times.*) I vas born November 7, 1867, een Varsaw, Poland. Poland at zat time vas controlled by Russia und vomen vere not allowed higher education so I studied secretly vith a tutor. Een 1891, I arrived een Paris to study physics und graduated number vun een my class. Eeen my research of uranium, I soon dizscovered an unknown ray vich I named "radiation." For our remarkable discoveriez, my huzband Pierre und I von the Nobel Prize. To my amazement, I soon found zat radium *X-rays* could take a picture of ze eenside of ze body und destroy diseazed cancer cells. However, our experiments vith radiation vould soon make both Pierre und me sick. Een my desire to use science to "eaze human suffering" I tirelezly studied . . . (*Aside without accent*) Lights, please. (*Blackout as she continues with presentation.*) . . . und I continued my experiments day und night, holding . . . (*She holds up a home-made, glow-in-the-dark rock representing uranium and continues with building enthusiasm.*) . . . ze dangerous rock, uranium, een my handz. Even today, my scientific notebooks are still locked avay. Zey are too radioactive to handle! Who em I?

(Picture of Marie Curie is projected on wall.)

CRICKET: *(Cont.)* I em *Marie Curie!*

(Sound of class applauding. School bell rings.)

REESE: *Lunch!* All right!

(Excited voices and laughter of exiting students.)

MR./MS. BENNETT: *(Talking over noise.)* Reese, will you please get the lights?! Good reports today, everyone! The rest of you, tomorrow!

(Lights up on CRICKET, MR./MS. BENNETT *and* REESE.*)*

Excellent report, Cricket, but I knew yours would be. Better get changed so you don't miss lunch.

*(*MR./MS. BENNETT *exits.* CRICKET *crosses to her desk.* REESE *crosses to his desk and puts his notebook in backpack.)*

REESE: Your report was real good. Really good. The costume and the rock— what was it?

CRICKET: *(Embarrassed by her outburst of the day before.)* Uranium . . . Hey, yours was good, too.

REESE: Ah, Newton's pretty boring. Gravity. No cool X-rays or anything. This apple was all I could think of.

(He offers CRICKET *the apple. She shakes her head "no," and he takes a bite of it.)*

CRICKET: It was interesting. Really. Reese, about yesterday—I'm sorry.

(She takes off costume pieces which are over her school clothes.)

REESE: Forget it.

CRICKET: I just—

REESE: No problem. Listen, I'm really sorry about . . . him . . . your brother.

CRICKET: Yeah . . . real life genetic mistake.

REESE: Well, see, I'm thinking about that—*mistakes,* I mean. Well, sometimes, you know, you can fix mistakes.

CRICKET: *(Giving* REESE *a dismissive shrug.)* What?

REESE: I'm saying, maybe you could fix *Tom.*

CRICKET: *(Incredulously.)* Fix him? Like a *car?*

REESE: Okay, okay, it sounds crazy but, I mean, they give people new hearts and kidneys and junk. I mean, you were standing up there, *Mary* Curie and stuff—

CRICKET: *(Annoyed.)* What are you talking about, Reese?

REESE: Well, somebody's got to figure it out.

CRICKET: Figure what out?

REESE: A cure! For this Down syndrome thing. I mean, they find cures all the time.

CRICKET: Yeah. *Scientists.*

REESE: *(With admiration.)* You are real smart, Cricket. And, standing there in the clothes of Mary Curie, I could imagine you were a real scientist who discovers things . . . who maybe could find cures, maybe even fix some mistakes. You could, Cricket. I think you could.

CRICKET: I don't think so.

REESE: Oh, yeah? What about those *parents* who found a cure for what their kid had in that movie? Remember that old movie, *Leonardo's Oil*?

CRICKET: The movie was called *Lorenzo's Oil*.

REESE: Whatever. Did you see it?

CRICKET: No.

REESE: Well, neither did I but my mom just rented the DVD and they were just a couple of parents with this sick kid and *they* figured out a cure.

CRICKET: It was a *movie*.

REESE: It was based on a real story.

CRICKET: It was?

REESE: Yep. A real, true life story. *(Wetting his finger and making a mark on an imaginary board.)*
Score one for Reese's Pieces. Sweet!

CRICKET: *(Smiling at REESE.)* Okay. You made your point.

REESE: Hey, you're already on your way. You got an "A" in science.

CRICKET: What about you?

REESE: Well, with the frog and . . . *(Holding up half-eaten apple.)*
. . . Mr. Newton, hopefully, I have a "C." My parents would have a heart attack if I brought home a "D." *(Suddenly grabbing his chest.)*
Heart attack! Like on "E.R."! *(Mimicking E.R. doctor.)*
"Clear!" *(He puts his hands on chest, mimicking electro-shock resuscitation.)*
Uhuhuhuh!

CRICKET: *(Amused.)* What are you doing?

REESE: Hold it! Brain wave coming through! *(REESE freaks out "Jim Carrey style.")*
How about a *brain* shock! "Clear!" *(He puts hands on head, mimicking shock.)*
Uhuhuhuh! "Stimulate the cells!" *(He repeats mimicking of shock.)*
Uhuhuhuh!

CRICKET: *(Embarrassed and amused.)* Stop, Reese! You are so weird! Really weird!

CRICKET: *(Slowly realizing.)* No . . . no, wait. Maybe . . . not with electric shock . . . but maybe you could *stimulate* a brain.

REESE: Uh-huh, score two for me.

CRICKET: Maybe you could, like, *exercise* it—*stimulate* the brain by, like, making it do something over and over again.

REESE: No offense but I think you need something faster—like a brain transplant.

CRICKET: Very funny.

REESE: Come on. Tell the truth. You never wished your brother could have a new brain?

CRICKET: Well . . .

REESE: See.

CRICKET: *(Realizing.)* When I was little I *did.* I used to dream about Tom all the time—good stuff . . . *bad* stuff. Anyway, I'd have this dream that Tom's head had this hinge on it—like Monty Python cartoons. And I'd open it and pour stuff in.

REESE: Cool.

CRICKET: Not brain cells. I'd pour in toys and books, "Hello Kitty" stuff—how weird. Hammers, all kind of tools, string, birds' nests—crazy stuff. Every time I dreamed that dream, I'd pour different stuff in his head. I thought it would make him smarter. I thought he needed *more* in his head.

REESE: Ah . . . very cool dream.

CRICKET: No, but then, yesterday in class, when I saw the *picture* of the three chromosomes . . . it's really something *extra* that messed up his brain—*extra stuff.*

REESE: Yeah, like you put too much sugar in iced tea. Wait, but then it's just sweeter, not messed up. Aw, what am I saying? Random. Back to the dream.

CRICKET: Forget the *dream.* The question is how could you take the extra chromosomes from his brain?

REESE: You do brain surgery! Go in and take 'em all out!

CRICKET: But, Reese, *duh.* The chromosomes are so small you'd have to operate with a microscope.

REESE: Uhuhuhuh! *Microscopic . . . brain . . . surgery . . .* dang! How cool is that!

(MR./MS. BENNETT *enters.*)

MR./MS. BENNETT: You're still here? You better get to lunch. You'll both be starving by three o'clock.

CRICKET: We were just talking.

REESE: Yeah, I was telling Cricket how cool her report was.

MR./MS. BENNETT: It was very cool.

(Pointing at rock used in CRICKET's *report.)*
May I?

CRICKET: Sure.

MR./MS. BENNETT: *(Picking up rock and switching it on.)* Very imaginative.

CRICKET: I have a question, Mr./Ms. Bennett.

MR./MS. BENNETT: Yes.

CRICKET: Say somebody wanted to be a scientist—a doctor or do surgery, maybe . . . do research.

REESE: Yeah, and invent stuff, maybe find cures.

CRICKET: Yeah, things like that. How long would it take, I mean, school for that?

MR./MS. BENNETT: Medical school is three or four years. That's after four years of college. And residency—one or more years. Then to specialize—at least one or two more years.

CRICKET: That's like ten years or more.

MR./MS. BENNETT: Yes, it takes a long time.

CRICKET: . . . a long time.

REESE: Well, that's sure not for me! Hey, come on, Cricket. Let's go get lunch!

MR./MS. BENNETT: You better hurry.

(REESE *exits.*)

CRICKET: *(Gathering up backpack, clothes and rock.)* Yeah . . . yeah . . . I need to hurry . . . I need to hurry.

(CRICKET *rushes off as lights fade.*)

ACT TWO

SCENE TWO

SETTING: TOM's *room. There is a bed, a bedside table, a toy basket and a giant Fred Astaire poster.*

AT RISE: TOM *is in bed asleep. His top hat is on the bedside table and his tails are carefully placed on the end of his bed.* CRICKET *comes in with book and CD player. As she puts player on the table,* TOM *stirs.*

CRICKET: Ssssh. It's just me, Tom.

TOM: *(Sleepily.)* I brush teeth—Crest too-paste.

CRICKET: Good, Tom.

TOM: I pud top back on Crest too-paste. *(As* TOM *speaks, he tries to sit up but* CRICKET *gently eases him back down.)*
    I watch "Sesme Street"—Tommy Tune show. He gud dancin.

CRICKET: That's right. Tommy Tune's a good dancer. Now, go back to sleep. I have something to play for you. It'll exercise your brain while you're asleep.

TOM: No, no. Sing. Sing.

CRICKET: This will be good for you, Tom—good for your brain. It's an . . . experiment . . . for school.

TOM: No school now, Crick. Dark time. Sing me, Cricky, okay? Okay?

CRICKET: *(Resigned.)* Okay.

(Singing like a lullaby.)
Old MacDonald had a farm . . .

TOM AND CRICKET: E-I-E-I-O

CRICKET: And on that farm, he had a . . .

(A pause, then TOM *blurts out.)*

TOM: Turkey.

CRICKET: Sssh . . .
 E-I-E-I-O
 With a . . .

TOM: Moo, Moo, he—

CRICKET: No. Gobble, Gobble.

TOM: Gobba, Gobba, he—
 Gobba, Gobba, they
 He Gobba . . . They Gobba . . .

*(*TOM *falls asleep.* CRICKET *pushes button on CD player which plays "Ave verum corpus" [orchestral version] by Wolfgang Amadeus Mozart.)*

TOM: *(Barely awake.)* Wha tha, Cricky?

CRICKET: It's good for you . . . it's by *Mozart*. Sssh . . . *(*CRICKET *pats* TOM *and he relaxes to sleep. With music underscoring,* CRICKET *gently begins math facts, trying to "pour" them into* TOM's *brain.)* Two plus two is four . . . four plus four is eight . . . eight plus eight is sixteen . . . sixteen plus sixteen is thirty-two . . . This'll be good for you, Tom. Every night I'll play different stuff and it'll stimulate your brain activity. You're asleep but you'll still hear it. Like I'm pouring good stuff in your brain. We'll do math and the alphabet. I'll play you *all* the great books. *Tom Sawyer* and *War and Peace* . . . *David Copperfield*. It'll be good for me, too. Good for my education. When I go to college, I'll have already read . . . well, heard . . . so many books. Wouldn't it be great if we could go to the same college and help each other with our book reports? Hey, maybe we could share an apartment and a car and stuff—

*(*TOM *stirs.)*

TOM: "Hadda duck . . . wid moo, moo, he . . . an moo, moo, they . . . ."

(Mozart continues softly as CRICKET *pats* TOM. *She opens book and begins to read, trying to lovingly "pour" story into* TOM.)*

CRICKET: "*The Adventures of Huckleberry Finn.* Chapter I. You don't know about me without you have read a book by the name of *The Adventures of Tom Sawyer*, but that ain't no matter. That book was made by Mr. Mark Twain, and he told the truth, mainly. There were things which he stretched, but mainly he told the truth. That is nothing. I never seen anybody but lied . . . one time or another . . ."

(Looking at TOM *sleeping peacefully, she gently lays her head on his shoulder, quietly crying as lights fade.)*

ACT TWO

SCENE THREE

SETTING: *Science classroom.*

AT RISE: (MR./MS. BENNETT *is seated at desk.* REESE *stands nearby.*)

MR./MS. BENNETT: (*Holding sheet of notebook paper.*) Reese . . .
(*Amused.*)
 . . . about these topics for your research paper . . .

REESE: You liked my list?

MR./MS. BENNETT: (*Sighing.*) In the report you just did, I was looking for orig-
inality but in a *research* paper—(*Reading.*)
 "Topics for Research Paper: Number one, 'Cloning Yourself for Fun and
Profit.' Number two, 'Alien Sightings in *[town where production staged].*'
Number three, 'The Seven Year Digestive Cycle of Swallowed Gum.' "

REESE: Too original?

MR./MS. BENNETT: Uh-huh. These are very funny, Reese, but go home and
come back tomorrow with the real thing.

REESE: Yes, Mr./Ms. Bennett.

(REESE *picks up his backpack and starts to exit as* CRICKET *enters.*)
(*Whispering.*)
 He/She didn't like my topics.

CRICKET: Well, duh!

(REESE *exits.* CRICKET *crosses to* MR./MS. BENNETT'*s desk and puts her backpack
on the floor.*)

MR./MS. BENNETT: Hello, Cricket.

CRICKET: Hi.

MR./MS. BENNETT: How are you?

CRICKET: (*Flatly.*) Fine. (MR./MS. BENNETT *pauses to allow* CRICKET *to continue.*)
 I'm fine.

MR./MS. BENNETT: That's good. I wanted to talk to you, Cricket.

CRICKET: What about?

MR./MS. BENNETT: First, Cricket, I want to say that I'm very proud of your
work in life science. You've made an "A" . . . well, really an "A Plus" on
everything. And your report on Marie Curie was so creative. But the idea
for your research paper . . . well, I just can't approve your topic.

CRICKET: Why not?

MR./MS. BENNETT: I think it's wonderful that you're interested in being a scientist.

CRICKET: I'm *going* to be a scientist.

MR./MS. BENNETT: Well, that's wonderful. I applaud you for knowing what
you want to be at your age.

CRICKET: So what's the problem with my topic?

MR./MS. BENNETT: I encourage students to choose topics that will challenge them. And I'm willing to approve papers on new discoveries and break-throughs in medicine, but your topic, (*Reading* CRICKET's *paper.*)
    "The Future of Medicine—Microscopic Brain Surgery and Trans-plants"—

CRICKET: It's not impossible.

MR./MS. BENNETT: I didn't say it was impossible, but medicine is very far away from—

CRICKET: How do you know?

MR./MS. BENNETT: Cricket, I would appreciate it if you wouldn't interrupt me. You are an excellent student, Cricket, but I'm not able to approve—

CRICKET: (*Desperately trying to change* MR./MS. BENNETT's *mind.*) Mr./Ms. Ben-nett, what if someone wanted to cure something—fix something . . . say, like a genetic mistake. You showed those pictures in class of the chromo-somes. You said people were curing things, trying to fix things like Cystic Fibrosis.

MR./MS. BENNETT: Yes, I did but what—

CRICKET: Well, say someone wanted to cure . . . Down syndrome—cure *some-one* with Down syndrome.

MR./MS. BENNETT: (*Beginning to realize* CRICKET's *personal connection.*) Cure . . . *someone?*

CRICKET: Well, *fix* . . . fix someone. Maybe take out all those tiny extra chro-mosomes . . .

MR./MS. BENNETT: With . . . *microscopic* surgery?

CRICKET: Right, right! Or say someone had this great idea about making someone smarter, like by putting in *more* extra stuff—extra brain cells that could grow—or maybe gene replacement.

MR./MS. BENNETT: (*Sensitively telling the facts.*) Cricket, with some genetic problems, scientists are trying to *replace* a bad gene with a good one. But you can't cure, you can't fix . . . *someone* with Down syndrome.

CRICKET: Why not? Once people thought heart transplants were impossible.

MR./MS. BENNETT: Cricket, with Down syndrome it's a different kind of gene-tic problem. And it's not just brain cells that have an extra chromosome. It's every cell in the body—trillions and trillions of cells. Do you realize that?

CRICKET: Not just brain cells?

MR./MS. BENNETT: That's why people with Down syndrome *look* different—the nose, the eyes, they're shorter—

CRICKET: Every cell . . . *every* . . . cell?

MR./MS. BENNETT: We all begin from *one* cell. That one cell with the extra chromosome divides into two cells with the extra chromosome . . .

CRICKET: No . . .

MR./MS. BENNETT: . . . and those cells divide and those divide and those—

CRICKET: (*Holding her hands over her ears.*) Stop it! Don't! Don't say it!

(CRICKET *runs crying from the classroom.*)

MR./MS. BENNETT: Cricket?! Cricket?!

(Lights down on MR./MS. BENNETT *as* CRICKET *runs out of classroom and into* REESE, *nearly knocking him down and causing both to drop their books and papers.)*

REESE: Cricket, whoa!

CRICKET: *(Angrily.)* What do you want, Reese?

REESE: I want some help with my research paper. I don't know what to write about.

CRICKET: I don't have time, Reese. I don't have a topic either.

REESE: Didn't Mr./Ms. Bennett like—

CRICKET: No, he/she didn't! Face it, Reese. It was a stupid idea—microscopic brain surgery, brain transplants. Please!

REESE: Stupid?

CRICKET: Yeah, stupid. Stupid! Why does everyone around me have to be so stupid?!

*(*REESE *stares at her, dumbfounded.)*

Yeah, why don't you take a long look? I'm used to it. Don't you get it? It's never going to be any different. Tom's never going to be . . . Oh, forget it!

*(*CRICKET *angrily begins collecting her books and papers. Lights up on flashback of* TOM *in silhouette wearing baseball cap. Down syndrome chromosomes are projected over action.)*

TOM: I Cricky big brother—*big* brother.

CRICKET: Do you know what it's like to be with him, like at the park, and everyone's just . . . just staring at you?

TOM: Hi dere. You play? You play wid me?

CRICKET: "What's wrong with him?" they always want to know. "Your brother sure talks funny. He *looks* funny!"

TOM: I go big school with Cricky . . . big school.

CRICKET: "He's your *big* brother? What grade's he in? Minus one?" *(Angrily referring to herself.)*

And you're supposed to be perfect and one day you forget and leave your crayons on the floor and your big brother eats them and has to have his stomach pumped.

(Lights rise on TOM.*)*

| CRICKET: And everybody's mad and scared and he comes back from the hospital and cries and tells you how it hurt and . . . | TOM: Cricky, Cricky! I hurt! It hurt me! It hurt me! |

(Lights down on TOM.*)*

CRICKET: I don't want to tell you this!

REESE: Cricket, I—

CRICKET: So I don't go anywhere with him and I don't have anybody over.

Nobody! Ever! We could've just been friends at school, but you had to mess it up! *(She starts to go.)*

REESE: Mess it up?! Cricket, hey, I . . . I just wanted to hang out with you.

CRICKET: Yeah, right. *(She exits.* REESE *stares after her.)*

ACT TWO

Scene Four

SETTING: *Living room and* TOM'S *room in* CRICKET'S *house.*

AT RISE: *Loud music ("I Can't Be Bothered Now" sung by Fred Astaire) plays as* TOM, *wearing top hat and tails and tap shoes on his hands, is tapping. He "taps" across the floor, up the leg of the desk, across the desk, on the wall, up the wall as high as he can reach and down again.* GRAN *enters from kitchen.*

GRAN: *(Talking over music.)* Be gentle, Tom. Don't scratch anything. Are you listening?

TOM: *(Smiling and tapping.)* I listen. I gentle.

*(*GRAN *turns music down.)*

GRAN: And please don't turn up that music any louder, Tom. Your Gran can't take it. You're already blasting me out of the kitchen.

(Firmly.)

Okay?

TOM: O! O! O! Kay!

(He continues tapping and GRAN *exits to kitchen.* TOM *turns music up.* CRICKET *enters through front door. She drops her backpack on the floor and covers her ears, overcome by the loud music.)*

CRICKET: *(Shouting to him.)* Tom! Tom! Tom!!!

TOM: *(Finally noticing her.)* Cricky!!! *(With tap shoes still on his hands, he taps enthusiastically around her feet.)*

TOM: *(Cont.)* Cricky home! *(Affectionately, he starts to tap on her feet and her legs.)*

CRICKET: Stop tapping! Stop it! Stop, Tom!!! Ugh, this house—I can't stand it! Why do you have to do this crazy tapping all the time? *(*CRICKET *turns off music.)*

I can't think! I can't study! I can't even leave something on the desk! You'll mess it up! You mess up everything! *(*GRAN *appears in kitchen doorway.* TOM *is stunned by* CRICKET'S *outburst.)*

Why can't I just have a normal life?! Why can't you . . . Oh, it's all a stupid mistake! *(*CRICKET *sees* GRAN *and freezes.)*

GRAN: *(Gently.)* Tom . . . come in the kitchen. I have popcorn for you.

*(*TOM, *stunned but not understanding* CRICKET'S *outburst, obeys, dropping his tap shoes on the floor and exiting to kitchen.* GRAN *looks sadly at* CRICKET *and follows* TOM *into kitchen.)*

CRICKET: *(Desperately controlling herself.)* Don't cry. Don't be mad. Don't lose it. Don't put your science report on the desk. Don't be mad you have a mistake for a brother and you can't fix it. Two plus two? I don't think so. *(She sees* TOM's *tap shoes on floor.)*

    I hate these shoes—these stupid, stupid, stupid, *stupid* shoes!!! *(She crams tap shoes in backpack.* GRAN *enters.)*

GRAN: Cricket . . . Won't you come in the kitchen and have some popcorn with us?

CRICKET: I'm going back to school. I've got to start on my science paper. I can't think here!

GRAN: Cricket—

*(*CRICKET *exits out front door.* TOM *enters with bowl of popcorn, hiding a box of salt by his side.)*

TOM: Where Cricky? Where Cricky, Gran?

GRAN: She . . . she went back to school . . . to study, dear. Is your popcorn good?

*(*TOM *nods his head, "yes," and furtively shakes salt on popcorn.)*

(Reaching out to take salt from TOM.*)*

    You don't need any more salt, Tom.

TOM: Okay.

*(*GRAN *puts salt box by the CD player.)*

GRAN: *(Suddenly very tired.)* I'm going to lie down a minute, okay? Why don't you put on some *quiet* music?

TOM: Okay. I dance. *(Pointing to where he left his tap shoes.)*
    Where tap shoe?

GRAN: *(Looking with him for tap shoes.)*
    I don't know, dear.

TOM: Gran, where tap shoe?

GRAN: Let's look in your room, Tom. *(*TOM, *holding bowl of popcorn, follows* GRAN *into his room.)*
    I don't see them. Are they under the bed? *(*TOM *puts popcorn on the bed-side table and looks under bed. He stands, holding bedroom slippers.)* Not under your bed?

TOM: No. No!

GRAN: *(Calmly.)* Why don't you put on your bedroom slippers? When Cricket gets home we'll ask her if she's seen you tap shoes, okay?

TOM: *(Sadly.)* Wan tap shoe.

GRAN: I know.

TOM: Wan tap shoe. Wan Cricky.

GRAN: I know, dear. Me, too. Put on your slippers.

*(*TOM *follows* GRAN *to living room.)*

TOM: Wan tap shoe.

GRAN: *(Gently.)* Sit down, Tom. Put on your slippers. *(*TOM *sits and puts on slip-pers.)* *(Patting his shoulder.)*

I'll be in the bedroom if you need me.

(GRAN *exits.* TOM *begins to dance. The movements are awkward but reflect his melancholy. He tries to make sound with his slippers.*)

TOM: No tap . . . wan tap shoe . . . wan Crick-Crick . . .

(*Dancing without sound frustrates him. He sees the box of salt on the desk and, "putting two and two together," he pours all the salt in the middle of the floor.* TOM *is pleased with the sound his shoes now make. The lights change to blue as* TOM *dances his sad soft shoe, casting his shadow on the wall. Suddenly* TOM'S *shadow is replaced by the elegant dancing shadow of* TOMMY. TOMMY *appears and arranges* TOM'S *top hat and tails. To the music, "Blues in Thirds" by Sidney Bechet Trio, [RCA 80th Anniversary, 1940–1949],* TOM *and* TOMMY *dance, occasionally striking a similar or complimentary pose with* TOM *expressing his raw sadness and* TOMMY *dancing* TOM'S *feelings beautifully and elegantly. As the number is ending they "say goodbye" to each other with the sound of their shuffling feet—one answering the other until* TOMMY *disappears into the darkness and* TOM *returns to his bedroom. He sits on his bed, staring into space. Lights down on* TOM *and up on* CRICKET *who sits exhausted at desk at school. Her backpack is on floor as she flips through her biology book.*)

CRICKET: (*To herself.*) Topics . . . just find a topic. Just do it. (*Reading topic headings.*)
    "Organic Compounds and Energy," "Life Processes in Monerans," "Cell Growth and Division." I don't think so . . .

(*Lights up on flashback of* TOM *in silhouette wearing baseball cap as* CRICKET *remembers.*)

TOM: Look, Cricky! I did it! I fix Barbie! I cut Barbie's hair!

(TOM *holds up several Barbies with hair cut off.* CRICKET *lifts her head, remembering. She resumes reading. Lights down on* TOM.)

CRICKET: (*Reading topic headings.*) "Sponges and Cnidarians," "Echinoderms," "Arthropods," I hate this!

(CRICKET *lays her head on desk. Lights rise on* TOM *in silhouette.*)

TOM: (*Holding something behind his back.*) But this best one, Cricky. This best one I do! For! *You!*

(TOM *happily holds up beautiful Barbie with hair cut off.*)

CRICKET: Tom . . . it's my Scarlett O'Hara . . . (*Unable to stop her tears.*)
    . . . my beautiful Scarlett O'Hara . . .

TOM: Why cry, Cricky? You don like her? You don. I sorry. (*Pulling hair on doll, trying to make it longer.*)
    I sorry, Cricky. I didn mean to . . . (*Lights down on* TOM.)

CRICKET: Oh, Tom . . . (*Reading topic headings.*)
    "Human Body Plan" . . . "Reproductive Systems" . . . "Central Nervous System" . . . "The Senses" . . . (*Lights rise on* TOM.)

TOM: I sorry, Cricky. I sorry I ate cayola.

(He holds up crayon.)
　　I like *red* cayola best! Don cry, Cricky. I didn mean to . . .
　　I didn mean to . . . I didn mean to . . . I didn mean to . . .

(Lights down on TOM.*)*

CRICKET: *(Overlapping* TOM's *"I didn mean to.")*
　　Oh, Tom . . . I meant to . . . I . . . meant . . . to . . . I meant to . . .

*(*CRICKET *lays her head on desk. Lights fade on* CRICKET *and rise on her night-mare. With distorted sound underscoring,* REESE *appears, wearing a surgeon's coat and mask.* MR./MS. BENNETT *enters. She is dressed as a nurse with mask covering her face. They unfurl a white sheet over two school desks, making an operating table.* REESE *and* MR./MS. BENNETT *are cold and impersonal, moving like robots.)*

REESE: Maestro! If you pleaze!

(Music begins [Nr. 1, Introduktion "Zu Hilfe! Zu Hilfe!" from The Magic Flute *by Wolfgang Amadeus Mozart].* TOM *enters in top hat and tap shoes and lies on table.* REESE *covers* TOM *with sheet, leaving only his top hat and tap shoes showing.* MR./MS. BENNETT *removes* TOM's *tap shoes and throws them in trash can.)*

REESE: *(Calling offstage.)* Ve're ready for you, Doctor! *(He holds up a large rolled up paper.)*
　　Und here'z your diploma!

(The light from the projector shines on the wall. CRICKET, *dazed and confused, enters wearing surgeon's coat with mask hanging around her neck. She stands in the projector's light.)*

CRICKET: Doctor . . . doctor?

REESE: Of course. Let uz continue zis historic procedure.

CRICKET: But I don't know how to do it.

REESE: Just vatch ze movie!

(Projection of movie title reading Leonardo's Oil.*)*

CRICKET: Who's the patient?

REESE: Don't you know? Zis iz ze vorld's first brain tranzplant!

(Projection of Down syndrome chromosomes.)

CRICKET: The world's first brain transplant? What will you do with his old brain?

REESE: *(Taking brain from under sheet and holding it in the air as clinical slide of brain is projected.)* Ve throw it avay, of course!

CRICKET: Throw it away?!

REESE: Eet's no good! Can't fix it!

*(*REESE *throws brain in trash can held by* MR./MS. BENNETT.*)*

CRICKET: You threw it away . . . ?!

(MR./MS. BENNETT *picks up plastic trash can and starts to exit as hospital monitor alarm sounds. During remainder of nightmare, projected in succession are slides such as Interior of Brain, DNA Molecules, Phrenology Diagram, "Monty Python" Hinged Head and Distorted Chromosomes.*)

REESE: Oh, no! Ve're losing him! Clear! (REESE *pushes* CRICKET *away with his arm.* REESE, *with* MR./MS. BENNETT's *help, mimics electroshock resuscitation to* TOM's *body under sheet.*) Uhuhuhuh! (*He listens to the "chest," shakes his head and covers* TOM's *top hat with sheet.*)

Ve've lost him.

CRICKET: No! (*Trying desperately to get attention to* MR./MS. BENNETT *and* REESE *who ignore her.*)

I want him back! I want Tom! I want Tom back! (*Standing in the projection of Down syndrome chromosomes.*)

Please . . . please . . . I want him back . . .

(*Lights down on* CRICKET.)

REESE: Sorry, doctor.

MR./MS. BENNETT: Sorry . . .

REESE: Sorry . . .

MR./MS. BENNETT: Sorry . . .

(MR./MS. BENNETT *reaches under sheet, removes top hat and drops it into trash can. Lights down on nightmare and up on* CRICKET *at school with her head on her desk.*)

CRICKET: (*Waking with a start.*)

Tom! (*She takes* TOM's *tap shoes out of her backpack and hugs them tearfully.*) Sorry, Tom . . . sorry . . . sorry . . . sorry . . .

(CRICKET *lays her head on her desk, crying. Lights up on flashback of* TOM *who is playfully hiding something behind his back.*)

TOM: Hey, Crick-Cricki. Watch. Watch me. I had a gud show for you! (CRICKET *looks up, remembering.* TOM *reveals that he has been hiding his top hat.*)

One, two, three! Tada! (*With the flourish of a magician, he pulls a Barbie from his top hat.*)

CRICKET: (*Tearfully.*) That's a good show, Tom.

TOM: You wanna see my show gin?

CRICKET: Sure I do.

(TOM *puts Barbie back in his top hat and repeats sequence.*)

TOM: One, two, three! Tada!

(*He pulls Barbie from hat again.*)

CRICKET: I like your show, Tom.

TOM: I lie *you*, Cricky.

(*Pulling Barbie from top hat again.*)

Tada!

(Lights down on flashback of TOM. *Smiling but with tears in her eyes,* CRICKET *puts* TOM'*s tap shoes on her hands. She holds the shoes up like* TOM *and gently taps them together as the light fades. Lights up on living room.* GRAN *enters and steps in salt.)*

GRAN: Oh, Tom, what were you thinking? What were you— *(*GRAN *hears her feet "crunch" on the salt. She smiles, picks up the empty salt box and shuffles her feet in an imitation of a soft shoe step. Her dance is interrupted by a knock at the door.* GRAN *opens door and* REESE *enters.)*
　　Reese? Come in, come in. I'm sorry, Cricket's not here.

REESE: I didn't come to see Cricket . . . well . . . of course, I'd like to see her but . . . I came to see Tom.

GRAN: Tom? Oh . . . how nice, Reese.

*(*REESE *is puzzled as they cross and "crunch" on the salt.)*

GRAN: *(Explaining.)* Tom couldn't find his tap shoes so . . . well, he had to make noise somehow.

*(*REESE *enjoys stepping on the salt.)*

REESE: Cool. *(He tastes salt with his wet finger.)*
　　Cool! Hey, this is so weird. See, Cricket said it got kind of noisy around here so I thought I'd loan Tom my CD and ear phones, you know, permanently.

GRAN: Oh, Reese—

REESE: Hey, I just mainly watch TV all the time.

GRAN: What a wonderful idea. Thank you, Reese. He'll love it.

*(*GRAN *takes CD from player and gives it to* REESE *who puts it in his player.)*
　　And so will I. Come on. Let's find Tom.

*(*GRAN *and* REESE *cross to* TOM *who is in his bedroom.* GRAN *gives* TOM *the CD player.)*

TOM: Wha this?

GRAN: It's from Reese.

*(*GRAN *puts earphones on* TOM *and* REESE *pushes the "play" button. Delighted,* TOM *listens a moment.)*

TOM: *(Shouting out explosively, startling* GRAN *and* REESE.*)* Gran!!! It ga music!!! It ga music!!!

(To REESE*)*
　　It gud!!! It ga dancin music!!! Thang!!! You!!!

GRAN: That's so generous of you, Reese.

REESE: *(Proudly.)* Yeah.

GRAN: Come in the kitchen. Would you like a popsicle or something?

REESE: A popsicle? Oh, yeah, sure.

GRAN: I need to clean this up. *(*TOM *happily enjoys his music as* GRAN *and* REESE *exit into kitchen.* CRICKET *silently enters the front door, carrying her backpack.*

She stands by door, listening. GRAN *returns with broom and dust pan. They look at each other.)* Cricket . . .

CRICKET: *(Indicating salt on floor.)* What happened?

*(*GRAN *begins sweeping up the salt.)*

GRAN: TOM couldn't find his tap shoes so . . . *(Shuffling her feet in salt.)*
    . . . he put two and two together. Had to make noise while he danced. Have you seen his tap shoes, dear?

CRICKET: Yeah . . . I know where they are.

(Pause.)

    It's so quiet. Where's Tom?

GRAN: In his room.

*(*GRAN *nods to* TOM's *room and continues sweeping.* CRICKET *takes* TOM's *tap shoes from her backpack and crosses to doorway.* TOM, *not seeing her, takes off his earphones.)*

TOM: *(To himself.)* Guh music. Dancin music. *(He reaches for bowl of popcorn on the bedside table. Sitting cross-legged on the bed, he carefully puts bowl between his legs and puts his hands together in prayer.* GRAN *moves unnoticed and stands behind* CRICKET.)*

(Passionately with his eyes closed.)

    Bless Cricky! Crest too-paste! An Tommy Tune! A! Men!

*(*TOM *happily puts earphones on and eats heartily.)*

CRICKET: GRAN . . . *I* took Tom's tap shoes. Why did I—

GRAN: Ssssh . . . You know Tom. He won't remember. He can't add two plus two. He'll never read a book. But don't feel bad, dear. Tom'll never hate . . . or lie . . .

CRICKET: . . . or ever do a mean thing to anyone on purpose. He's the one with something extra. Oh, Gran—

GRAN: *(Gently taking* CRICKET *by the shoulders.)* Just look at him, Cricket. Just *look* at him . . .

*(*GRAN *moves away from* CRICKET, *picks up dust pan and broom in living room and exits to kitchen.* CRICKET *goes into* TOM's *room. She taps him on his shoulder and sits beside him. He smiles and takes off earphones.)*

CRICKET: I'm sorry, Tom.

TOM: Why?

CRICKET: For . . . everything . . .

(Handing TOM *his tap shoes.)*

    . . . and for taking your tap shoes.

TOM: You ga tap shoe?! You find tap shoe!

*(*TOM *excitedly shoves his feet into tap shoes.)*

CRICKET: *(Sarcastically.)* Aren't I a nice sister?

TOM: You bet!

(He impulsively grabs CRICKET *and hugs her.)*
   I lub you, Cricky.

*(*CRICKET *hugs* TOM *back fiercely.)*

CRICKET: I love you, too, Tom.

(The moment is over for TOM *and he wiggles from her hold.)*

TOM: Dance wid me, Crick.

CRICKET: Oh, I don't dance good like you, Tom.

TOM: You guh dance girl, Cricky. Dance wid me.

*(*REESE *and* GRAN *enter from kitchen.* REESE *holds a popsicle.)*
   Look, Cricky, *he* here!

CRICKET: *(Nervously.)* Reese? Hi.

REESE: Hi!

*(*CRICKET *and* REESE *shyly smile at one another.)*

TOM: *(In a sudden outburst.)*
   Reese! *You* dance wid Cricky?!

*(*CRICKET *and* REESE *are embarrassed.)*
(Pointing at REESE.*)*
   You wan wear my tap shoe?!

REESE: Uh . . . uh . . . no, thank you. You go ahead.

(Holding up popsicle.)
   I got a popsicle here.

TOM: Oh, yeah. You ga *popsicle!*

(Trusting and smiling, he holds his arms wide to CRICKET.*)*
   Dance wid me, Cricky. I *Tommy Tune!*

*(*CRICKET *tries to hug* TOM.*)*
   No hug now, Cricky. Sing, sing wid me!

*(*CRICKET *takes* TOM's *hands and they dance and sing.)*

CRICKET and TOM: Old MacDonald had a farm
   E-I-E-I-O
   And on this farm he had a—

TOM: *(Stopping their dance.)* He hadda . . . ah . . . uh . . .

CRICKET: He had a Tommy Tune!

TOM: *(Delighted.)* A Tommy Tune!

CRICKET: With a—

TOM: Widda—

CRICKET: With a . . . ?

(TOM *struggles for an answer.* CRICKET *taps her foot as a clue.*)
   With a . . . ?

TOM: Tap . . . a *tap!!!*

CRICKET AND TOM: (Singing.)
   Wid tap, tap, he
   Tap, tap, they!

CRICKET: Yes!

(CRICKET *and* TOM *"high five."*)

TOM: *(To* GRAN*)* My! . . . yes! . . . tro! . . . peas!

(GRAN *crosses to CD player.* CRICKET *takes* TOM's *hands and they cricle the room, dancing and singing.*)

CRICKET AND TOM: Here a tap, there a tap,
   Everywhere a tap, tap!
   Old MacDonald had a farm—

(GRAN *turns on CD player and* CRICKET *and* TOM *are interrupted by the music ["Changing Partners" sung by Fred Astaire].* CRICKET *takes* TOM's *right hand and puts it around her waist. She takes his left hand in hers as they assume a ballroom dancing position.* GRAN *and* REESE *watch as* CRICKET *and* TOM *begin to dance awkwardly and out of rhythm. The room is transformed as before and they dance in circles from one beautiful pool of light to another. Seemingly from nowhere,* TOMMY *appears.* CRICKET *and* TOM *stop, almost running into* TOMMY. TOMMY *taps* TOM *on the shoulder, indicating that he would like to cut in. With his hands carefully placed in front and back at his waist,* TOM *bows to* TOMMY *and gently pushes* CRICKET *to him. The music segues into "Singing in the Rain," sung by Gene Kelly.* CRICKET *waltzes with* TOMMY *around dance floor as* TOM *watches downstage, his back to the audience. As they twirl and dip and glide, pieces of torn lavender colored index cards "rain" from above while* TOM *joyfully claps together the tap shoes he wears on his hands.*)

CURTAIN

THE GREAT GILLY HOPKINS

by
David Paterson
and Steve Liebman

based on the novel by
Katherine Paterson

THE GREAT GILLY HOPKINS

THE PLAYERS

Gilly Hopkins: an eleven-year-old terror going on thirty
Miss Ellis: Gilly's social worker (role may also be cast as a male)
Maime Trotter: Gilly's new foster mother; very overweight
William Ernest: Trotter's foster son; shy and withdrawn
Mr. Randolph: Trotter's neighbor; an elderly blind black man
Miss Harris: Gilly's new teacher; an attractive young
black woman
Agnes Stokes: Gilly's loud-mouthed classmate
Nonnie: Gilly's grandmother
Courtney: Gilly's mother

THE SETTING

Action takes place in suburban Washington, D.C., in the present.

SCENE 1

(Lights come up on stage, revealing two people sitting as if in a car. MISS ELLIS *is sitting in the front row with her arms in front of her, as if she is holding a steering wheel.* GILLY *is directly behind her.* MISS ELLIS *appears stiff and nervous,* GILLY *appears laid back and in control, chewing a large wad of gum.)*

ELLIS: Gilly, this will be your third home in less than three years. Now I need, we all need, your cooperation. . . . I can't imagine you enjoy all of this moving around. Now this foster mother is very different from Mrs. Nevins. Maime Trotter is very nice, so let's try to get off on the right foot. *(Handing back a tissue.)* Do me a favor, will you? Lose the gum before we get there, okay? (GILLY *takes the tissue and pretends to put the gum away, then sticks the gum under the seat of the car. She hands the crumpled tissue back to* MISS ELLIS. MISS ELLIS *hands* GILLY *a towelette.)* And see what you can do about that guck on your face before we get there. (GILLY *wipes her mouth and tosses the towelette out the car window.)* And Gilly—

GILLY: Galadriel, my name is Galadriel. (GILLY *steps out of the car and approaches the audience.)* Galadriel Hopkins. Gruesome Gilly they call me. I'm famous across the country. Nobody wants to tangle with me. My name strikes fear in the hearts of foster parents everywhere. I am too clever and too hard to manage. And one thing I am particularly proud of is that I am not nice! And movin' home to home is no big deal!

(Song: No Big Deal.)

GILLY:

>Once more I'm aboard
>The shuttle express
>They tried to convince me
>To put on a dress
>Why all fuss, all the bother
>It's no big deal!!!
>
>If I were in charge
>I'd live all alone
>Color TV
>Unlisted phone
>And no phony mother or father
>That's how I feel!!!
>
>Gilly get up!!!
>Gilly's fed up!!!
>Each morning
>Gilly get dressed
>They think they know best
>They don't
>And one day
>
>Galadriel—H
>Will show them who's who
>The world will find out what a hopkins can do
>Autographs please

Be delighted
It's no big deal
All the wrongs I've been wronged will be righted
She's the very first girl to be knighted
It's no—no big deal

(GILLY *steps back into the car, and leans back, hands clasped behind her head.*)

GILLY: Here I come, Maime baby, ready or not.

(*The two exit the car.* GILLY *grabs a suitcase from behind the seats and they approach the front door of the house. The door opens, revealing a large woman,* MAIME TROTTER, *followed by a small frail boy,* WILLIAM ERNEST, *who hides behind* TROTTER.)

TROTTER: Well, I thought I heard ya'll pull up! Welcome to Thompson Park, Gilly, honey.

GILLY: (*Quietly.*) Galadriel. (*Turns away.*) You hippo freak.

TROTTER: (*Not hearing* GILLY.) Oh, I'm sorry, darlin'. You want to meet your new sister, don't you? Gilly, this is William Ernest Teague! (TROTTER *forces* W.E. *in front of her; the boy looks terrified. He quickly disappears behind* TROTTER.) Well come in, come in! I don't mean to leave you standing on the porch like you was trying to sell me something. Let's get ya settled. You belong here now.

(TROTTER, W.E. *and* MISS ELLIS *enter the house.* GILLY *backs away and turns to the audience.*)

GILLY: A wooly mammoth hippo and a goofy coke bottle dweeb. . . . There is no way I'm staying here.

(MISS ELLIS *appears at the door.*)

ELLIS: Gilly . . . Gilly, come inside.

(GILLY *rolls her eyes and follows* MISS ELLIS *into the house and into* TROTTER's *living room.*)

TROTTER: Just sit down and make yourself at home now, or do you want to see your room? William Ernest, honey? You wanna show Gilly where her room is? (W.E. *looks terrified and buries himself behind* TROTTER.) Oh well, we can see that later.

GILLY: This a color TV?

TROTTER: No—we loaned our color TV to the Rockefellers.

(TROTTER *laughs.* GILLY *runs her finger over the TV and looks at the dust on her finger.* MISS ELLIS *glares at* GILLY.)

ELLIS: I've forwarded all of GILLY's medical information to the school and I've taken care of registration and class scheduling. I have all that here in my file.

(*While* MISS ELLIS *talks on,* W.E. *sits up on the back of the couch and stares curiously at* GILLY, *who makes a scary face at* W.E. *He lets out a squeal and falls back off behind the couch.*)

W.E.: AAAhh!

TROTTER: W.E. honey! Are you alright?

(TROTTER *helps a sniffling* W.E. *up as* MISS ELLIS *shoots* GILLY *a mean glance.* GILLY *returns her a "who me?" innocent look.*)

ELLIS: Well, if everything is under control, I need to be getting back to the office. You'll let me know—(MISS ELLIS *glances quickly at* GILLY.) You'll let me know if there are any problems?

TROTTER: Don't you worry none, Miss Ellis. Gilly and William Ernest and me is nearly friends already. My Melvin, God rest him, used to say that I never met a child I couldn't make friends with.

(TROTTER *and* MISS ELLIS *exit, with* TROTTER *babbling on, leaving* W.E. *and* GILLY *in the room.* GILLY *stares at a transfixed* W.E. GILLY *stomps her foot and* W.E. *tears out of the room. She smiles.*)

GILLY: Never met a kid you couldn't make friends with, huh? Good luck Maime Trotter.

(GILLY *climbs the stairs and tosses her suitcase on the bed.* TROTTER *climbs the stairs to see* GILLY *sitting on the edge of her bed, with her suitcase at the foot of the bed.*)

TROTTER: You need anything hon, you just give ole Trotter a holler. . . . TV's downstairs, you're welcome to come on down to watch. This is your home too. . . . It's going to be okay, honey. . . . I know it's been hard to switch around so much—

GILLY: I like moving, it's boring to stay in one place. This way I get to see more of the world.

(GILLY *beings to unpack.*)

TROTTER: Well, you make yourself at home. You hear now?

GILLY: (*Tightly.*) I'm making, okay? (TROTTER *exits and* GILLY *throws herself on the bed.* GILLY *pulls a picture frame from her suitcase and sits back on the bed, staring deeply into the picture, wistfully.*) For my beautiful Galadriel, I will always love you. . . . (*She turns over the frame and reads:*) Courtney Rutherford Hopkins . . . you are a beautiful woman Mommy . . . if you only knew where they've put me . . . if you only knew. . . .

(GILLY *begins to choke up, recovers and kisses the photograph. She places the photograph on the bureau and runs down the stairs. She enters the kitchen where* TROTTER *is busy making a salad.*)

TROTTER: William Ernest is in the living room watching *Sesame Street.* You can go join him if you like.

GILLY: Why in Jesus' name would I watch a retard show like that?

TROTTER: Listen here, Miss Gilly Hopkins. One thing we better get straight right now, *tonight.* I won't have you making fun of that boy. Just 'cause someone isn't quite as smart as you are, don't give you no right to look down on them.

GILLY: Who am I looking down on?

TROTTER: You just said—(*Dropping her tone.*) that William Ernest is retarded.

GILLY: I did not. I don't even know the stupid kid. I never saw him in my life, before today. I just don't wanna watch some stupid kid show.

TROTTER: He's had a rough time of it in this world, but he's with Trotter now, and as long as the Lord keeps him in this house and sees fit that I take care of him . . . ain't nobody on earth gonna hurt him. *In any way!*

GILLY: Good God! All I was trying to say—

TROTTER: One more thing. In this house, we don't take the Lord's name in vain.

GILLY: Alright, alright, already. Forget it.

TROTTER: Gilly . . . is this clear with you?

GILLY: Yeah . . . you are perfectly clear.

TROTTER: Supper's about ready. How about you going next door and getting Mr. Randolph? He eats here at night. I would send William Ernest to fetch him but I think you would be a pleasant surprise. He knew you were coming today.

(GILLY *starts to argue but sees* TROTTER's *eyes.*)

GILLY: Which house?

TROTTER: On the right. He's usually waiting but just in case, knock on the door good and loud so he'll be sure to hear you. Better take your jacket, it's cold out.

GILLY: (*Leaving without her jacket.*) It's cold inside too!

(GILLY *runs out and crosses up to* MR. RANDOLPH's *front porch and knocks. No answer. She knocks harder. The door swings open, revealing an elderly black man.* GILLY *gasps, steps backwards, turns and runs back to* TROTTER's *as fast as she can.* GILLY *enters the kitchen.*)

TROTTER: What's the matter? Where's Mr. Randolph, Gilly?

GILLY: I don't know. . . . He's gone. Some weird little colored man with white eyes came to the door.

TROTTER: Gilly, that was Mr. Randolph. He can't see a thing. You've got to go back and bring him by the hand so he won't fall.

GILLY: I've never touched one of those people in my life.

TROTTER: You've never touched an elderly person before?

GILLY: No . . . black.

TROTTER: (*Tightly.*) Well then. It's about time, ain't it? (*Pause.*) Ain't it? . . . Of course if you can't manage, I can always send William Ernest.

GILLY: I can manage. Don't worry about me.

TROTTER: I should go over and get him. You probably got Mr. Randolph all confused and upset by now.

GILLY: Well, you shoulda warned me.

TROTTER: Warned you? I shoulda warned poor Mr. Randolph. . . . You want me to send over William Ernest?

GILLY: I said I could manage, Good God! (TROTTER *starts to reproach.*) Alright, I didn't say it. Hel . . . heck, a person can't even talk around here.

TROTTER: A nice person like yourself should be able to think of a few regular words to stick in amongst the curses. . . . Well, hurry up if you're going.

(GILLY *rolls her eyes and exits, returning to the front of* MR. RANDOLPH's *porch.* MR. RANDOLPH *is still there.*)

RANDOLPH: William Ernest? Is that you?

GILLY: No . . . me.

RANDOLPH: Oh . . . you must be the new little girl. Welcome to you, welcome. I'm Reginald Randolph, pleased to make your acquaintance.

(He sticks out his hand, GILLY *chooses to take his elbow to guide him.)*

GILLY: Yeah, well, Trotter sent me over here to take you to supper.

RANDOLPH: Well thank you kindly. Thank you.

GILLY: No sweat. *(They step off the porch and begin to walk to* TROTTER's. MR. RANDOLPH *stumbles and* GILLY *throws her arms around him, to catch him from falling.)* Hey, watch it!

*(*MR. RANDOLPH *rights himself and smiles at* GILLY.)*

RANDOLPH: Thank you.

GILLY: No problem . . . you okay?

RANDOLPH: Yes. *(They continue on.)* Now Mrs. Trotter did tell me your name, but I'm ashamed to say I don't recall it.

GILLY: Gilly.

RANDOLPH: Oh yes, it's a pleasure to meet you, Miss Gilly. I feel might close to all Mrs. Trotter's children. Little William Ernest is like a grandson to me. So I feel sure—

GILLY: Watch the door!

RANDOLPH: Yes, yes. I thank you.

(They enter TROTTER's *home.)*

TROTTER: Is that you Mr. Randolph?

RANDOLPH: Yes, indeed Mrs. Trotter, with the sweetest little escort you'd ever hope to see. This little angel kept me from falling on my face. If she hadn't dived before me and caught me on the trip, I'd probably be laying on that chilly cement right now.

GILLY: It wasn't nuthin'.

RANDOLPH: I guess this old house is going to be a bit more lively now, eh Mrs. Trotter?

TROTTER: I wouldn't be surprised. . . . Now why don't you two sit yourselves down? Gilly, you sit here. William Ernest honey, come to supper! *(*W.E. *enters. They all sit.* GILLY *begins to eat.* TROTTER *stares at her and then clears her throat.* GILLY *pauses, looks around the table, sensing something is wrong.)* Would you like to give grace this evening Gilly?

GILLY: *(With her mouth full.)* No.

RANDOLPH: Mrs. Trotter, it would be my pleasure to pass blessing on this most bountiful feast in which we all are about to partake.

TROTTER: Thank you Mr. Randolph.

(Everyone bows their heads to pray, except GILLY, *who steps out towards the audience.)*

GILLY: Little did I know, this was the beginning of a long line of long-winded prayers by ole white-eyes.

(Song: Table for Four.)

RANDOLPH:

> *We humbly thank you for this*
> *Bountiful feast. A-men*
> *May I have the ketchup please?*
> *Oh, and thank you lord for our*
> *New found friend, Amen, again—Now the peas*

TROTTER:

> *Oh Gilly dear*
> *We're glad you're here*
> *Now William Ernest please*
> *Eat your trees*

GILLY: Trotter and nerdo referred to broccoli as little trees. I guess that was supposed to make them more palatable. YUCK. As for W.E., there was only one thing on his mind.

W.E.:

> *I love Sesame Street*
> *It's neat*

TROTTER:

> *I'll cut your meat dear*

W.E.:

> *Cookie monster doesn't eat meat*
> *But boy can he eat on Sesame Street*

GILLY:

> *How can I live with that big tub of lard*
> *And that stupid retard*
> *And that old-lined and black and blind man*
> *Can't say I loved where I was last week*
> *But at least no one there was a freak*

(All together now!)

(GILLY acts as a conductor directing the family as they sing together.)

RANDOLPH:	TROTTER:	W.E:
We humbly thank	*Oh Gilly dear*	*I love Sesame*
You for this	*We're glad*	*Street—It's*
Beautiful feast	*You're here*	*Neat please cut*
Amen—may I	*Now William*	*My meat here*
Have the ketchup	*Ernest please*	*Cookie monster*
Please? Oh and	*Eat your trees*	*Doesn't eat*
Thank you lord		*Meat but boy*
For our new		*Can he eat on*
Found friend		*Sesame Street*
Amen again—		
Now the peas		

(GILLY *now joins in.*)

GILLY:	RANDOLPH:	TROTTER:	W.E:
How can I	*We humbly*	*Oh Gilly*	*I love Sesame*
Live with	*Thank you*	*Dear we're*	*Street*
That big tub	*For this*	*Glad you're*	*It's neat—*
Of Lard and	*Bountiful*	*Here now*	*Please cut*
That stupid	*Feast Amen.*	*William*	*My meat*
Retard and	*May I have*	*Ernest*	*Here cookie*
That old	*The ketchup*	*Please eat*	*Monster*
Lined and	*Please? Oh*	*Your trees*	*Doesn't eat*
Black and	*And thank*		*Meat but*
Blind Man—	*You lord*		*Boy can he*
Can't say I	*For our*		*Eat on Sesame*
Loved	*New found*		*Street*
Where I was	*Friend Amen*		
Last week	*Again—*		
But at	*Now the*		
Least no	*Peas*		
One there			
Was a freak!			

GILLY:

Can't say I loved where I was last week
But at least no one there was a freak!

(*As the lights go out on the dining room,* GILLY *heads up the stairs to her bed and sits.*)

GILLY: What I need to do, what I am gonna do is write my mother. Courtney Rutherford Hopkins would probably sue County Welfare if she knew what kind of place they'd forced her beautiful daughter to live in. Mom wouldn't stand for me to be in a dump like this for one single minute. . . . But how was she to know? Miss Ellis would never admit it. Mother, what kind of lies has Ellis been telling you to keep you from coming and taking me away from all this? I'm gonna find out where you live, somehow, and I'll write you, and tell you to come and take your beautiful Galadriel home!

BLACKOUT

SCENE 2

(*Lights up on* GILLY, *outside* MISS HARRIS' *classroom.*)

GILLY: I was actually looking forward to tackling my newest challenge— school. I had left Hollywood Gardens in a complete wreck and Sherwood Elementary still didn't know what had hit it. So, a new school to crush. But this was even better. At the other schools, I had several teachers to tackle all day. But here, they stick you with one sucker, all day long. Well bring him on!

(*The door opens revealing* MISS HARRIS, *an attractive black woman.* GILLY *takes two steps back.*)

HARRIS: Hello. Welcome to Harris-6. (*Lights up on* HARRIS *classroom.* MISS HARRIS *leads* GILLY *to her desk and picks up a file.*) Galadriel Hopkins. What a beautiful name. From Tolkien, of course.

GILLY: No, Sherwood Elementary.

HARRIS: No, I meant your name. Galadriel is a character from one of Tolkien's books.

GILLY: I would prefer to be called Gilly.

HARRIS: Gilly it is then. Will you take that empty seat next to Monica Bradley? Here, we are on page twenty-seven. (*She hands Gilly a book. Gilly walks over to her seat and plops down, opening her book.*) Now, where were we?

(*The scene freezes as a spot shines on* GILLY.)

GILLY: (*To the audience.*) It ain't fair. None of this crap is fair. I'm smarter than all these jerks, but there's too many of them, and they got a head start. I don't know where I'm at.

HARRIS: (*Who has come over to* GILLY'*s side.*) Did you do division with fractions at your last school?

GILLY: Uh . . . yeah . . . no.

HARRIS: Why don't you bring up your chair to my desk, and we'll work on it?

(GILLY *doesn't know what to say. The bell rings. A relieved* GILLY *steps out of the classroom as the scene changes into the playground.* GILLY *sulks alone in a corner. The sound of children playing is heard.* GILLY *watches the scenario, but doesn't become involved. A smallish, bedraggled girl timidly approaches* GILLY.)

AGNES: I know who you are.

GILLY: Oh yeah? Who am I?

AGNES: You're the new kid. I saw you at the cafeteria. I get free lunch too!

GILLY: Call the *Enquirer.*

AGNES: I'm Agnes.

GILLY: I'm sorry.

AGNES: Well . . . you gonna tell me your name?

GILLY: You gonna get outta my face?

AGNES: Hey, don't push me! What's your problem?

GILLY: My problem? My problem is a whiney little busybody named Agnes, who can't take a hint!

AGNES: I thought since you was new you might want a friend to show you around.

GILLY: You're bothering me! So scram shrimp . . . SCRAM!!!

(GILLY *lunges at* AGNES, *who squeals and runs off.* GILLY *proudly leans against the wall. A basketball rolls in front of her, she grabs it and runs off left. The sound of kids yelling is heard. Someone yells "Fight! Fight!"* MISS HARRIS *enters leading* GILLY *by the arm.* GILLY *wrestles free and leans against the wall.*)

HARRIS: Do you want something for that scratch?

GILLY: (*Glancing at her hand.*) No, it doesn't bother. . . .

HARRIS: Gilly, I would rather have us be friends . . . but if that is not possible, I think we should at least clarify the situation. . . . We are not going to have fighting on the playground . . . or anywhere else around here. You're at a new school now and you have a chance to . . . to make a new start. If you don't want help, there's no way I can make you accept it. But you're not going to be permitted to hurt other people. . . . *(The bell rings.)* I'm going back into class. When you're ready, you can come in and join us, alright?

(MISS HARRIS *goes into class.*)

GILLY: Oh I'm ready! You bet when I walk back in there, there will be at least six boys that know me a little better now than they did twenty minutes ago. The ones that are still standing, that is. . . . Only half a day and already the school is up in arms. The school nurse is still patching up the casualties. Give me a week, and I'll have this whole damn place in an uproar. But today, I'll cool it. Let them worry. Then tomorrow . . . or maybe even the next day . . . WHAM!

(GILLY *dusts off her hands and starts to reenter her class as a school bell rings.* AGNES *dashes off as* GILLY *collects her books, but as* GILLY *crosses* AGNES *reappears.*)

GILLY: *(Without turning around.)* What do you want?

AGNES: Nuthin', I'm just walking home. . . . I thought you and me should get together . . . since you don't know nobody and I've been here a while I could—

GILLY: I don't need no Indian guides, Pocahontas, you got that?

AGNES: I'm Agnes, Agnes Stokes. Not Pocahontas.

GILLY: Go away.

(GILLY *moves on,* AGNES *falls behind.*)

AGNES: You still haven't told me your name.

GILLY: Duh! You're really quick.

AGNES: So, you ain't gonna tell me?

GILLY: *(Spinning towards* AGNES.*)* If I tell you, will you leave me alone? My name is Gilly. Gilly Hopkins! You got that?

AGNES: You don't have to yell. . . . You can call me Ag if you want. . . . Want to come over? My grandma won't mind.

GILLY: Can't. 'Cides, I'm almost home.

AGNES: Can I—

GILLY: You can't come in today!

TROTTER: *(Off stage.)* That you, William Ernest, honey?

GILLY: No, it's me.

TROTTER: Well, how was school today? Make any friends?

GILLY: No.

TROTTER: Oh. (GILLY *starts to go upstairs.*) Wait a minute honey, you got some mail.

GILLY: Ed McMahon got my ten million?

TROTTER: No, no. It's just a postcard, it came this—

(GILLY *snatches the card from* TROTTER'*s hand and runs up to her room. She jumps on the bed, studying the postcard. She reads.*)

COURTNEY: *(Off.)* My Dearest Galadriel. The agency wrote me that you had moved. I wish it were to here. I miss you. All my love, Courtney. . . .

GILLY: All my love . . . and here's an address! California! I could go there. I'll hitchhike across the country! I'll steal some food and maybe some money. People pick up hitchhikers all the time. I'd be in California in a week. People always pick up hitchhikers . . . and beat them up . . . and kill them . . . and toss their bodies into the woods . . . all because I don't have any money for a bus or plane ticket. Oh why does it have to be so hard? Other kids could be with their mothers all the time. Dumb stupid kids who don't even like their mothers . . . or deserve them. It's so unfair! I haven't seen you since I was three . . . and she misses me so much and wishes I was with her.

(TROTTER *appears at the top of the stairs.*)

TROTTER: Anything I can do for you sweetie?

GILLY: Can't anyone have any privacy in this dump?

TROTTER: I just want to make sure that you're alright.

GILLY: I will be as soon as you get your fat self outta here.

TROTTER: Okay. . . . *(Starts downstairs and turns.)* Call me if you want anything. . . . It ain't a shameful thing to need help, you know. Well, alright . . . we'll be downstairs, dinner'll be ready in a little while.

(TROTTER *starts down.*)

GILLY: I don't need help from anybody! . . . except from you . . . (GILLY *picks up the picture from the bureau.*) Oh, Courtney . . . if I write you, if I asked, would you come and get me? I'd be good for you. I'd change into a whole new person. I'd turn from gruesome Gilly into gorgeous, gracious, good, glorious Galadriel.

(GILLY *gently puts the picture away and goes downstairs, joining* TROTTER, W.E. *and* MR. RANDOLPH *sitting at the dining table as the lights come up.*)

RANDOLPH: —and make us truly, truly grateful. Amen.

TROTTER: Amen. My, Mr. Randolph, you do ask a proper blessing.

RANDOLPH: Oh, Mrs. Trotter, when I sit before the spread of your table, I got so much to be thankful for.

GILLY: *(To audience.)* How's a person supposed to eat through this garbage?

RANDOLPH: Well Miss Gilly, how was school for you today?

GILLY: I've seen better.

RANDOLPH: My, you young people have such an opportunity today. Back when I was going to school, oh, thank you Mrs. Trotter, what a delicious smelling plate. And the ketchup please? My oh, my . . . now what was I, oh yes, school. My days—

GILLY: *(Menacingly at* W.E.*)* How do you do sweetums?

(W.E. *coughs up his milk and begins to wheeze.* TROTTER *misses* GILLY'*s face.*)

TROTTER: What's the matter William Ernest, honey?

GILLY: I believe . . . I believe the dear child is choking. It must be something he ate.

TROTTER: Are you alright, baby? (w.e., *still choking, nods.*) Are you sure?

RANDOLPH: Maybe the little boy needs a pat on the back.

GILLY: Yeah. How bout it, W.E. old man? Want me to swat you one?

W.E.: No! Don't let her hit me!

TROTTER: Nobody's gonna hit you honey. Everybody just wants to help. Isn't that right, *Gilly*?

GILLY: Just want to help you little buddy.

TROTTER: He don't always know that. . . . I got an idea. Mr. Randolph, since Gilly is feeling so helpful, maybe she'd like to read for us. We do that on Monday nights. I was told Gilly, that you are some kind of great reader yourself. I know Mr. Randolph would like to hear you read something.

RANDOLPH: Would you do that Miss Gilly? It would be such a pleasure to me.

GILLY: I don't have anything to read.

TROTTER: Mr. Randolph's got enough books to start a public library, haven't you Mr. Randolph?

RANDOLPH: *(Chuckling.)* Well, I do have a few. . . . Course we've got the Bible right here.

GILLY: The Bible? *(Starts to laugh.)* I'll get a book. (GILLY *runs over to* MR. RANDOLPH's *house. After entering, she tries the light switch but nothing happens.* GILLY *goes over and tries a lamp which turns on. She surveys a large wall of books.)* I wonder if he's read all this junk? I bet not. He don't even got these encyclopedias in order. . . . *(She drags a chair over to the bookshelf and stands on it, looking at the book.)* Let's get you back where you belong. (GILLY *pulls out the book and two pieces of paper fall down.* GILLY *steps down and puts the book down. She picks up the two bills.)* Ten bucks!

(GILLY *climbs back up and starts feeling around the back of the books.*)

TROTTER: You alright Gilly, honey? (GILLY *jumps down, pushes the chair away and tries to look nonchalant.*) Mr. Randolph remembered that maybe the bulbs was all burnt out. He tends to forget since they really don't help him much.

GILLY: There's a light here. If there hadn't been, I'd have gone back. I'm not re-tarded.

TROTTER: I believe you mentioned that before. . . . Well, you find anything you wanted to read to Mr. Randolph?

GILLY: Got one here— The Oxford Book of English Verse. . . . I'll give it a whirl.

TROTTER: We best be gettin' back to dinner. C'mon honey. (TROTTER *exits with* GILLY *following, glancing up at the bookshelf. They cross over to* TROTTER's.) I've been trying to get William Ernest to read for Mr. Randolph, but he's still a little on the shy side.

GILLY: No kidding.

TROTTER: It's just a matter of time before he feels ready. Just time and love.

(They enter TROTTER's *home, into the dining room.*)

RANDOLPH: Now, what lovely reading material did you bring us?

GILLY: The Oxford English Book.

RANDOLPH: I beg your pardon?

TROTTER: The poems that we was reading last year, Mr. Randolph.

(GILLY *sits and opens the book.*)

GILLY: Here's one. The Cuckoo Song. (*She frowns.*) Summer is a cumin in, Lhude sing cuckoo. Groweth sed, and bloweth med, (GILLY *slams the book shut.*) You're trying to trick me or something? This ain't English. You're just trying to make me look stupid.

RANDOLPH: No, no Miss Gilly. Nobody's tryin to make a fool of you. The real old English is at the front. Try over a ways.

TROTTER: You want the Wordsworth one, Mr. Randolph, or do you know that one by heart?

RANDOLPH: Both. Page three fifty-seven, William Wordsworth. . . . There was a time when meadow, grove and stream—

GILLY: Found it! There was a time when meadow, grove and stream, The earth, and every common sight, To me did seem, Apparell'd in celestial light, The glory and the freshness of a dream.

(GILLY *stops, drinking in the poem.*)

RANDOLPH: It is not now. . . .

GILLY: It is not now as it hath been of yore: Turn wheresoe'er I may, By night or day.

GILLY and RANDOLPH: The things which I have seen I now can see no more.

RANDOLPH: Go on child.

GILLY: Our birth is but a sleep and a forgetting: The Soul that rises with us, our life's Star, Hath had elsewhere its setting, cometh from afar: Not in entire forgetfulness, and not in utter nakedness.

GILLY and RANDOLPH: But trailing clouds of glory do we come from God, who is our home.

(*Song: Thanks to the Human Heart.*)

GILLY:
>   *Thanks to the human heart by which we live*

RANDOLPH:
>   *Thanks to its tenderness, its joys, its fears*

GILLY and RANDOLPH:
>   *To me the meanest flower that blows can give*

GILLY:
>   *Thoughts that do often lie too deep for tears*

RANDOLPH: Thank you Miss Gilly.

TROTTER: She sure is a handsome reader alright.

(GILLY *is uncomfortable with the sudden warmth.*)

RANDOLPH: Well, what do you think of Mr. Wordsworth, Miss Gilly?

GILLY: Stupid. . . . Like here, right here in the end, "The meanest flower that blows." What the hell, I mean what's that supposed to mean? Whoever heard of a mean flower?

RANDOLPH: The word mean has more than one definition, Miss Gilly. Here the poet is talking about humility, lowliness, not bad nature.

GILLY: I never seen a flower blow, either.

W.E.: Dandelions.

(They all turn, surprised.)

TROTTER: You hear that? Dandelions? Ain't that the smartest thing you ever heard? Ain't it?

RANDOLPH: That is probably exactly the flower that Mr. Wordsworth meant. Surely it is the lowliest flower of all.

TROTTER: Meanest flower there is. And they sure do blow, just like William Ernest says. They blow all over the place.

GILLY: Can I go now?

TROTTER: Sure. . . .

RANDOLPH: Sure do appreciate more than you know—

(GILLY has already left the table and climbed the stairs up to her bedroom. As she sits on the bed, she pulls out the two bills from her pocket. She smoothes them out.)

GILLY: Ten dollars . . . and I bet there's more where that's from. I'll call the bus station . . . find out how much it will cost for one way to San Francisco. . . . I'm coming Courtney . . . trailing clouds of glory as I come. . . .

BLACKOUT

SCENE 3

(Lights up on GILLY walking to school.)

GILLY: My walk to school became pretty routine. The first three blocks I had to myself to plan my latest scheme, but when I got to the corner of Elm and Gardner—

(AGNES appears.)

AGNES: Howdy partner! Funny how we keep running into each other! What's new? See that show last night? How late do you stay up? Sometimes I can—

(GILLY continues to address the audience as AGNES chats away.)

GILLY: The little jerk can't even figure out when she's being ignored! I was soon to find out that this would become ritual. . . .

AGNES: I'll wait for you every day, okay? I don't mind, 'specially with the weather bein' how it is an all—

GILLY: I mean day after day, the moron would fall behind me, blabbing away, mostly nonsense. To and from school. Every day.

AGNES: —if you need help with your homework—

GILLY: *(Stops and turns.)* When are you going to get it through that g-nat brain of yours that I don't want help! *(GILLY starts off, but realizes she's hurt AGNES.)* Of course, every monument has its cracks.

AGNES: Want some bubble gum?

GILLY: Oh, what the heck. The queen had Rumpelstiltskin. Agnes might come in handy some day.

AGNES: I once got six packs of gum in my mouth—golly you should've seen the size of the gob—

GILLY: The trick is knowing how to dispose of people when you're through with them and I've had plenty of practice performing that trick. . . . Besides, motormouth Agnes had the best dirt on the whole neighborhood. But even I could take only so much. *(GILLY stops and faces AGNES.)* I'm gettin' a little sick looking at you. Nothing personal. You're just makin' me sick, that's all. In fact, you probably can't help it. I don't blame you. It's your big fat, flappin' mouth!

AGNES: I ain't got no big mouth.

GILLY: Agnes—

AGNES: I just have a lot of interesting—

GILLY: Agnes—

AGNES: —information that I'm willing to share—

GILLY: AGNES!!!!!

(AGNES clams up.)

(Song: Big Mouth.)

GILLY: *(Singing.)*
You've got a big mouth
A really really big mouth
The entire world can hear you
From east to west
From north to south

It's always going
Your mouth is overflowing
If it ever stops
I'll bet you that
I'll have finished growing

It's yakety yak yak
For words you never lack
An amazing big mouth
A big motormouth

AGNES: *(Speaking.)*
Their house has no heat—
They smell, never bathe—

Avoid that whole block—

And if you ever need—
tests for the next grade—

None of her mom's rings
are real—

AGNES: I ain't got no big mouth—*(Singing.)*
See that kid
Her name is Jane
They say her mother is insane
Disappeared a year ago
Haven't found her even though
She weighs four-hundred pounds

Look at him
He's teacher's pet
Wets his pants when he's upset
Evertime he starts to cry
Clear the way 'cause nothing's dry
Beware the tell-tale sounds

(AGNES *gives* GILLY *an exaggerated cry of a baby and tears off left, leaving an exhausted* GILLY *on stage.*)

GILLY: I managed to avoid Agnes at lunch, but at the end of the day, there she was—

(AGNES *enters crossing to* GILLY.)

AGNES: —And the kid with the funky haircut had lice I heard and blah—

GILLY and AGNES: Blah, blah, blah, blah-BLAH!!!!

GILLY:	AGNES:
You have got a big mouth	*I know all sorts of stuff*
A really really big mouth	*All the dirt, all the fluff*
The entire world	
Can hear you	
From east to west	
From north to south	
It's always going	*Did you hear, did you see?*
Your mouth is overflowing	*Blah, blah, blah blah-blah blah*
If it ever stops	
I'll bet you	
That I'll have finished	*Just between you and me—*
Growing	
It's yakety-yak-yak	
For words you never lack	
A big motormouth	*Their mom dyes her hair—*
A huge motormouth	*They eat cats I swear—*

GILLY: AGNES!!!!!!!

A big astronomically, huge anatomically massively oversized-mouth! (*Speaking.*) You know Agnes you can pass out from lack of oxygen from talking too much. You better rest. You wouldn't want to get an aneurysm or something and have what's left of your brains trickle out! (*To the audience.*) That kept her confused and quiet for the rest of the trip, 'til we got to my house and right before I went in she handed me a note asking me when she could talk again. (AGNES *hands the note and* GILLY *reads.*) Tomorrow. Maybe, we'll see how it goes.

(GILLY *enters house,* AGNES *exits.*)

TROTTER: (*Entering.*) That you, William Ernest, honey?

GILLY: That's me, Maime Trotter baby!

TROTTER: *(Laughing.)* C'mon into the kitchen and get yourself a snack, Gilly, honey. I baked some chocolate chip cookies.

GILLY: *(Tempted.)* Nnnnah. . . . I'm dieting.

(GILLY runs upstairs to her bed and pulls out the two bills from under her mattress, smoothing them out.)

GILLY: I'm too smart to be bought by chocolate chip cookies. Nice try Maime. You're gonna have to try a lot harder to slip ole Gilly up. Ten dollars. . . . There's gotta be more. . . . *(GILLY spins to see W.E. at the top of the stairs, holding a tray with cookies and a glass of milk.)* WHAT!?

W.E.: *(Shaking.)* Tr-tr-tr-Trotter.

GILLY: Well, put 'em down, stupid. Didn't Trotter teach you about knocking before going into a room? *(W.E. nods.)* Well? . . . Get out!!! *(W.E. exits and GILLY crosses to the tray and starts to eat.)* Thank you Maime Trotter and your delicious smelling cookies. My, oh, my . . . um, um. Now, what to do with Agnes. I could use her to help me get Randolph's loot, but with that mouth, it'll be all over school in a sec. . . . I need somebody who won't talk . . . *(Realizes.)* who can't talk! William Ernest! Yeah! Baby-faced Teague. *(Laughs.)* The midget of the Mafia! *(She falls back on the bed, laughing hysterically.)* Well, time to put the plan to work! *(GILLY puts the money away, grabs some paper, and heads downstairs to the living room. W.E. is on the couch, watching* Sesame Street. GILLY *sits on the other end of the couch, folding the paper.)* Where's Trotter?

W.E.: Mista Randolph's.

GILLY: Sorry about yellin' at ya, upstairs. . . . It's just that a lady needs privacy, you know, to freshen up, after school and all. . . .

(W.E. nods as GILLY finishes her paper airplane. She gets up and starts out of the room. W.E.'s eyes follow her; GILLY knows it.)

GILLY: Boy, I hope I can find somebody outside to help me fly this sucker.

(GILLY exits room and enters house porch, flying the plane in her hand. W.E. appears at the door. GILLY sees him.)

GILLY: C'mon out. Say W.E., I just can't get the hang of this airplane tossing stuff. You wanna give it a try?

(His eyes brighten, she hands him the plane. He tosses it and it gently floats down. He is mesmerized.)

W.E.: Pow! *(The plane lands.)* See that? See that?

GILLY: Try it again. *(Hands it to him.)* Here, off the bench!

(W.E. climbs up on the bench and lets the plane sail.)

W.E.: Pow! It sure fly good!

GILLY: Nah, that's you, W.E.! You throw real good! I was just admiring your style. I guess you've had lessons. No? You just taught yourself? No foolin'? Gee, man, you're a real natural! *(TROTTER and MR. RANDOLPH enter the porch.)* Hey, you gotta see this Trotter! William Ernest can do this real good!

TROTTER: *(To* MR. RANDOLPH.*)* Gilly made William Ernest a paper airplane.

W.E.: Watch now!

TROTTER: We're watching William Ernest, honey.

(W.E. *climbs up on the bench and throws.)*

W.E.: Pow!

RANDOLPH: How was it?

TROTTER: I declare, Mr. Randolph, sometimes it's a pity you gotta miss seeing things. I never thought paper airplanes was for anything but to drive teachers crazy, before. (TROTTER *turns to* GILLY.*)* That was really something.

W.E.: That's 'cause I fly it so good, right?

GILLY: Yeah . . . you sure do.

(TROTTER *places her hand on* GILLY's *shoulder.)*

TROTTER: Thank you . . .

GILLY: . . . Sure . . . hey, Mr. Randolph, how 'bout me helping you into the dining room?

(She takes his arm and helps him, followed by W.E.)

RANDOLPH: Thank you, Miss Gilly. I would appreciate that so much.

(As they exit, TROTTER *looks almost overwhelmed, she holds back a tear and enters the house.)*

BLACKOUT

SCENE 4

(Lights up on GILLY, *outside door of Harris-6 classroom.)*

GILLY: By the third week in October, I'd already caught up with my class and passed them. I made sure that everyone knew that I was the smartest in the class. Usually, at this point, I'd pull my time honored trick of stopping all work, just when the teacher was convinced that I was a bloody genius. I would just hand in blank papers. Drives 'em crazy . . . worked like a charm in all the other schools. I knew Harris wasn't gonna crumble at the sight of a blank piece of paper . . . she'd probably just ignore it. . . . I was clueless on how to pull the plug on this machine, until the TV gave me my answer— (GILLY *enters the classroom and goes to her chair, pulls out some paper, a magazine and a pen.)* See, Trotter was watching the news and I wasn't even thinking about Harris. I was scheming on how to get my hands on Randolph's money, but in the background, I heard some politician told a joke about some black guy and people all across the country, black and white, were really ticked off. . . . The news guy didn't repeat the joke, 'cause I coulda used it, but it gave me the idea—a chance to pull the plug on ole Harris-6. (GILLY *selects a page and begins to cut out a figure.)* I looked through a couple of Trotter's magazines until I found just the right picture. It was a black lady, about the same size of Harris, even the clothes were pretty close. Harris was quick, she'd know I meant her. . . . Jokes weren't my strong point, so I settled for a poem. . . . (She thinks, smiles and begins to *write.)* They're saying black is beautiful . . . but the best that I can figger, everyone who's saying that looks mighty like a . . . person with a vested interest in maintaining this point of view. I had to admit it, it was pure genius. My only regret was leaving it anonymous, I would have enjoyed taking credit for it. (GILLY *takes the card over to* MISS HARRIS' *desk and slips it in a book on the desk.)* I snuck into class early that day, baited the trap, and sat back for the snap.

(The school bell rings, the class and MISS HARRIS *enter, and* MISS HARRIS *sits at her desk, pushing the book aside.)*

BLACKOUT

(Lights up on the class, MISS HARRIS *is instructing a student.* GILLY *looks perplexed.)*

GILLY: All day long, I watched excitedly for her to pick up that freakin' book. Even in math—(MISS HARRIS *crosses to her desk reaches for the book, but turns to use a student's book.)* She borrowed some kid's instead of looking in her own! Through lunch . . . nothing. Now, I was getting ticked. I worked hard for this. My brilliant plan was a complete washout, the moron wouldn't open the book!

(The bell rings. GILLY *stars out with the class.)*

HARRIS: Gilly, will you wait a minute, please? . . . You may find this hard to believe, Gilly, but you and I are very much alike. . . . Both of us are smart— and we know it. But the thing that brings us closer than intelligence is anger. . . . You and I are two of the angriest people I know. . . . I was always taught to deny mine, which I did and still do. . . . And that makes me envy you. Your anger is still up here on the surface where you can look it in the face—make friends with it if you want to. But I didn't ask you to stay after school to tell you how intelligent you are or how much I envy you, but to thank you . . . for your card. . . . I took it to the teachers' lounge at noon and cursed creatively for over twenty minutes. I haven't felt so good in years. . . . I'll see you tomorrow . . . *(Smiles.)* and thanks again.

*(*MISS HARRIS *exits. Completely baffled,* GILLY *stares at the audience, then lets off a scream as she tears off stage left, with her hands flailing in the air.* GILLY *reenters, running into the house and up the stairs to her bedroom. She pulls the suitcase out from under the bed and begins to pack haphazardly.)*

GILLY: After the Harris disaster, I decided it was now or never. On my way home from school, I sidetracked to the bus station to find the price of a ticket . . . one hundred, thirty-six, sixty, one way. I was a far cry off from that, with ten bucks. But I had Randolph's shelf for the rest! (GILLY *puts the suitcase under the bed and goes down to where* W.E. *is watching TV.* GILLY *sits down.)* Trotter and Randolph leave yet, for the store?

W.E.: Uh-huh . . . and to Welfare. . . .

GILLY: Well, Mr. Randolph wants me to do him a favor, while they're out.

W.E.: Okay. . . .

GILLY: *(Turning off TV.)* Great! I got Trotter's key to let us in, so let's go! *(They head out of the house and cross to* MR. RANDOLPH'S *house.)* Now Mr. Randolph doesn't want Trotter to know about this, not yet, at least. I think it's kind of a surprise. So, it'll be our secret for now . . . okay?

W.E.: Okay.

(Stepping onto the porch, GILLY *takes a quick look around, and they enter the house, crossing to the shelves.* GILLY *turns on the lamp and pushes a chair against the shelf.)*

GILLY: See, right up there, that big red book on the shelf?

W.E.: I can't reach it.

GILLY: Of course not stup—I can't reach it either. That's why we both have to do it. Just climb up on the chair and I'll be behind you for support, so you won't fall. Then just feel around behind it.

W.E.: I'm scared—

GILLY: Sure you are, but just think, man, how proud everybody's gonna be later. After the surprise can be told and everything. When they found out who was climbing—*(W.E. climbs up on the chair and begins to step up on the shelf.)* Atta boy—uh, W.E. you're tearing out my hair.

W.E.: Oh . . . sorry.

GILLY: Jes!—Please, just feel around, ya ain't got nuthin' to worry about.

(He pulls out a wad of bills.)

W.E.: Pow!

GILLY: Lemme see—

W.E.: Don't let go of my legs!!!

(He drops the roll of bills and grasps her hair again.)

GILLY: Ow! Okay, I got you. Is there any more?

W.E.: No, I don't think so.

GILLY: Okay, here. Let's put the book back in. *(She boosts him up and he slips it in. Then they get down and* GILLY *picks up the money. She pushes the chair back to its original position.* GILLY *ushers* W.E. *out of the house and she locks the door. They cross to* TROTTER's*).* I'll give the money to Mr. Randolph later. Now you can go back to TV, I gotta straighten up my room. And remember, this is our own secret surprise!

W.E.: Okay . . .

(They enter the house and W.E. *goes to the TV, turns it on as* GILLY *runs upstairs to her room. She pulls out the money and as she counts it, her smile disappears.)*

GILLY: Thirty-four . . . thirty-four stinkin' dollars. Forty-four with the other ten I swiped. . . . I get my hair torn out and I can get as far as the Mississippi River. Brilliant Gilly . . . just brilliant. . . .

*(*GILLY *goes over to the bureau and looks at Courtney's picture. She picks up the notepad and pencil on the bureau and lies down on her bed. She thinks and proceeds to write.)*

(Song: Courtney Rutherford Hopkins.)

GILLY:

> Dear Courtney Rutherford Hopkins
> I received your card
> Dear Courtney Rutherford Hopkins
> Life is very hard
>
> My foster mother can hardly read or write
> She's religiously fanatic and her friends aren't even white

(GILLY *crosses out that line and rewrites:*)

> She's religiously fanatic and her friends are . . . weird
> There's a kid here named W.E. who's not completely there

(*Speaking.*) *If you know what I mean*

> And they love him unlike me—that's not fair
>
> Please Courtney Rutherford Hopkins
> I've saved up to go
> Forty-four dollars, not enough I know, I know, I know
> If you send me the rest
> I'll pay you back
> I wont be a pest
> And that's a fact
> I'll get a job, I'm very smart
> I won't be a bother, cross my heart
>
> Dear Courtney Rutherford Hopkins
> Soon you'll know me well
> Love from your daughter

(*She pauses and thinks to herself.*)

> Your one and only daughter

(*She crosses out a line and writes:*)

> Sincerely your daughter
> Galadriel

(GILLY *seals the letter, goes downstairs, out the door and crosses to a mailbox. She posts the letter and reenters the house to see* TROTTER *talking to* W.E.)

TROTTER: Where ya been honey?

GILLY: Out. . . .

TROTTER: I need to talk to you, sit down, Gilly honey. (GILLY *sits on opposite side of couch as* TROTTER *sits.*) I've been meaning to say to you how much I appreciate the way you've been making friends with William Ernest.

GILLY: Sure. . . .

TROTTER: Like Miss Ellis says, you're a special kind of person, Gilly. It makes me praise the Lord to see you so busy helping people instead of hurting them.

GILLY: (*Unheard by* TROTTER.) Shut up, Trotter.

TROTTER: You got so much to give. Mercy, what most of us wouldn't give for half of your brains.

GILLY: Shut up!

TROTTER: Well, I gotta get to fixing up the supper. Mr. Randolph won't be joining us tonight 'cause his son's in town.

GILLY: He's over at the house now?

TROTTER: Yes, he just pulled up.

(TROTTER *starts to exit.*)

GILLY: Trotter? I ain't hungry tonight. I'm gonna go upstairs and do my homework instead.

TROTTER: Maybe I'll bring you something up later.

GILLY: Maybe. . . . (TROTTER *exits.* GILLY *looks panicked. She starts upstairs and spies* TROTTER'S *purse on the table. She cautiously goes over to it, opens it and picks out the wallet. She opens the wallet and gasps. Takes out the cash. She closes the purse and runs upstairs. She takes the money from under her mattress and stuffs the money in her pocket. She pulls the suitcase out and empties the contents of the drawer into it.*) It wasn't supposed to be like this, but with Randolph's son here, I know he'll see that the living room is messed up, and he probably knows about the cash, too. I'll get this welfare money back to Trotter, but there's no time to waste, I gotta fly!

(*She puts the portriat in the suitcase and closes it. She takes a look around the room, takes a breath and starts down the stairs. As she sneaks down the stairs, she sees* W.E.)

W.E.: Where are you going?

GILLY: I uh, just gotta take some stuff over to Agnes'.

W.E.: Don't go.

GILLY: I'm . . . not. Don't tell Trotter—this is part of the secret.

(*She exits off stage right.* W.E. *runs off left.*)

BLACKOUT

SCENE 5

(*Lights up as* GILLY *reenters with her suitcase, followed by* MISS ELLIS. TROTTER *stands at the open door.* GILLY *pauses to see* TROTTER, *then crosses upstage and throws herself on her bed.* TROTTER *and* MISS ELLIS *enter the living room and begin to speak, quietly at first, but an argument builds.* GILLY *lies facedown on her bed, covering her ears with her hands.* TROTTER *is now half-hysterical.*)

TROTTER: Never! Never! Never!

ELLIS: Mrs. Trotter, nobody at the agency looks at it as any indication of failure on your part. I just think we should be grateful the police found her at the bus station, this could have been a lot worse. You can rest assured that this will not affect your record with us. You're too valuable.

TROTTER: I ain't giving her up! Never!

ELLIS: If you won't think of yourself, think of William Ernest. He's come too far in the last year to let—I've seen myself how she upsets him.

TROTTER: It was William Ernest who told me she left—he wanted her back!

ELLIS: Probably because he saw how upset you were. He's a very sensitive child and that is even more reason to remove a damaging influence—

TROTTER: William Ernest has lived with me for over two years. He's gonna make it. I know he is. Sometimes, Ms. Ellis, you gotta walk on your heel and favor your toe even if it makes your heel a little sore. . . . Somebody's got to favor Gilly for a while. She's long overdue.

(GILLY *sits up and crosses to the stairs.*)

ELLIS: I'm quite aware of Gilly's needs. I've been her case worker for nearly five years—five years. And whether you beleive it or not, I really care about her. I *do*. . . . But I don't think it's *her* needs we're talking about right now, is it?

TROTTER: What do you mean?

ELLIS: (*Quietly.*) It's your needs. . . .

TROTTER: Yes, Lord knows. I need her! I like to die when I found her gone.

(GILLY *starts down stairs.*)

ELLIS: You can't do that, Mrs. Trotter. You can't let them tear you to pieces.

TROTTER: Don't try to tell a mother how to feel.

ELLIS: You're a *foster* mother, Mrs. Trotter. You can't afford to forget that— Well, hello Gilly . . . we were just discussing the present situation. . . .

TROTTER: (*Interrupting.*) Ms. Ellis was just saying how it's up to you.

ELLIS: I—

TROTTER: You want to stay on here with William Ernest and me, that's fine. . . . You want Miss Ellis to find you someplace else to live . . . well, that's fine too. . . . You got to be the one to decide.

GILLY: What about my real mother?

ELLIS: I wrote her, Gilly, several months ago, when we decided to move you from the Nevinses. She never answered.

GILLY: She wrote me. She wants me to come out there . . . to California!

ELLIS: If you're referring to the postcard, I'm aware that you received one . . . but Gilly, if . . . if she really wanted you with her, she'd—

GILLY: She does want me! She said so!

ELLIS: Then why hasn't she come to get you? It's been over eight years, Gilly. . . . Even when she lived close by, she never came to see you.

GILLY: It's different now! I know it! She's gonna come! She really wants me!

(GILLY *throws herself on the couch.* TROTTER *comes over and rests her hand on* GILLY's *shoulder.*)

TROTTER: (*Quietly.*) If she knowed you. . . . If she just only knowed what a girl she has . . . she'd be here in a minute.

(GILLY *looks up at* TROTTER, *gets up and walks to the stairs, turning to* MISS ELLIS.)

GILLY: 'Til she comes . . . until Courtney comes for me . . . I guess I'll just stay here.

ELLIS: Officer Rhine told me today at the office that you had well over a hundred dollars with you last night at the bus station. I have trouble believing that was your own money—

GILLY: So.

ELLIS: So, I call taking other people's money *stealing.*

TROTTER: *(Gently grabbing* GILLY's *shoulder.)* So do we, Ms. Ellis. Surely you don't think this is the first time something like this has happened to me over the last twenty years?

ELLIS: No, I know it's not.

TROTTER: Then how about trusting me to handle it? We're gonna do just fine. Don't you worry your pretty little head about us, hear?

ELLIS: I get paid to worry, Mrs. Trotter. . . . I'll see myself out.

(She exits.)

GILLY: Boy, you showed her.

TROTTER: I figure that all that money ain't mine. . . . Where'd you get it?

GILLY: I found it . . . behind some books next door.

TROTTER: You stole from Mr. Randolph?

GILLY: It was just lying there behind the books. . . . He probably didn't even—

TROTTER: *Gilly,* you stole it. Don't put no fancy name on it. It was his, and you took it, right? How much?

GILLY: Forty-four dollars.

TROTTER: Well, you're gonna have to take it back to him.

GILLY: I can't, not all of it. . . . I spent four dollars for food last night.

TROTTER: You did, huh? Well . . . I'll lend you the four to pay Mr. Randolph back and you can work it off. . . . Now I'm gonna give Mr. Randolph a call so we can straighten this out right now. . . .

*(*TROTTER *exits.* GILLY *sits on the couch as lights fade, except a special on* GILLY.)

GILLY: Giving back Mr. Randolph's money was not as bad as it could've been. He actually had no idea that the money was there. He just thanked me, stuck the money in his pocket and as far as he was concerned, the whole situation was history. But Trotter didn't forget. She set up jobs for me to do to make up the money. She obviously never heard of the minimum wage or child labor laws. I could do housework for a measly ten cents an hour. But for twenty-five cents per hour I could help W.E. with his school work. Naturally I started spending a lot of time with W.E. and you know what? He's not as dumb as he looks. But if you'd even look at him cross-eyed, he'd shake like a wet Chihuahua. *(She turns to* W.E. *as lights come up on living room.)* What are ya gonna do when somebody socks you? (W.E. *looks terrified and drops his book off the sofa.)* I'm not gonna hit you. You gonna go through life letting people pick on you? Look, W.E., I'm gonna teach you how to fight. Then when some big punk comes up and tries to start something, you can just let 'em have it. You hear 'bout how I fought six boys at school—all by myself? (W.E. *nods*.) Well, before I get through with you, you're gonna do the same thing! *(She jumps up throwing imaginary punches at an enemy.)* Pow! Pow! Pa-pow! Pow! Pow.

W.E.: *(Mesmerized.)* Wow!

GILLY: First thing, when somebody yells at you, ya gotta stand tall. See, they might not even want to hit you. You stand tall, take a deep breath, and—

(Song: Pow.)

GILLY:

> *Get the hell outta my way*
> *Think you're tough—wanna play?*
> *Pow pow pa-pow pow pow!*
> *Make my day*

GILLY:

> *Now you try it.*

W.E.:

> *. . . Hell's my way!*

GILLY:

> *Ah—no. Just follow me. . . .*

GILLY:

> *Get the hell out of my way*

W.E.:

> *Get the hell out of my way*

GILLY:

> *Think you're tough?*

W.E.:

> *Think you're tough?*

GILLY and W.E.:

> *Wanna play?*
> *Pow pow pa-pow pow*
> *Make my day*

GILLY:

> *Rock 'em, sock 'em, block 'em, clock 'em, bang bam clonkety zonk*

W.E.:

> *Rock 'em, sock 'em, block 'em, clock 'em, bang bam clonkety zonk*

(TROTTER enters.)

GILLY and W.E.:

> *Pow pow pa-pow pow pow*

(W.E. sees TROTTER and leaps at her.)

W.E.:

> *Get the hell outta my way*
> *Think you're tough—wanna play?*
> *Pow pow pa-pow pow pow!*
> *Make my day*

(TROTTER *bursts into tears, hugging* W.E.)

W.E.: *(Meekly.)* I was just practicin' Trotter.

GILLY: Better leave the cussin' out.

TROTTER: Gilly—

GILLY: I'm not gonna teach him to push on people—just how to take care of himself. If he knows how to read and how to stick up for himself, he'll be okay. We'll finish up outside.

(TROTTER *throws her arms around* GILLY *and kisses her on the cheek.*)

TROTTER: I'm sorry, I know you don't allow no kissin', sometimes I just haul off and go crazy.

GILLY: Aw, it's okay. Don't worry about it. C'mon W.E.

(They start to leave.)

GILLY and W.E.:

> Get the (They cover their mouths.) *outta my way*
> *Think you're tough—wanna play?*
> *Pow pow pa-pow pow pow*

(They high five each other.)

TROTTER:

> *Pow pow pa-pow pow pow*

(TROTTER *attempts the high five, missing both kids' hands. They collapse in one big hug, laughing.*)

GILLY, TROTTER and W.E.:

> *Make my day!!!!*

(Lights change as GILLY *crosses down, putting on a bandana and kitchen apron. She begins folding sheets.* MR. RANDOLPH *enters and lays down in a nearby roll-away cot.)*

GILLY: The week before Thanksgiving, old Mr. Randolph got the flu. Trotter made him move on in with us. Didn't seem like a bad idea at the time, but by Thanksgiving Trotter and W.E. were sick too, and Randolph was still babbling about being a bother.

RANDOLPH: I promise not to die in your house. You have my solemn oath.

TROTTER: Gilly, if he looks peaky, we gotta carry him next door as fast as we can. I ain't gonna be sued by his son, the big Virginia lawyer.

GILLY: You're lookin' pretty peaky yourself. It's off to bed with you Trotter, now! No buts, I can hold the fort down.

RANDOLPH: I believe the girl won't be moved, Mrs. Trotter.

TROTTER: Well , alright, I guess.

GILLY: Here, let me help you—

(They exit. MR. RANDOLPH *settles in and drifts off. An elderly woman enters, crosses to the front door and rings the bell.* GILLY *runs to the door.)*

NONNIE: Are you Galadriel? Galadriel Hopkins?

GILLY: Who are you?

NONNIE: I'm . . . I am your grandmother. . . . May I come in?

(NONNIE *and* GILLY *enter the living room.* GILLY *has a pale, expressionless look on her face.*)

TROTTER: *(Off.)* Gilly, honey? Who is it?

GILLY: It's okay, Trotter! I got it! . . . You want to sit down?

NONNIE: Thank you. . . . I'm right aren't I? You are Galadriel? (GILLY *nods.*) I uh . . . *(She opens her purse and produces a letter.)* My daughter left home many years ago. . . . My husband and I never. . . . I'm not doing this well am I? My husband, your grandfather, died nearly twelve years ago—

GILLY: Jeez—that's too bad.

NONNIE: Yes. . . . Yes it was. . . . We . . . I tried to contact Courtney, your mother, at the time, of course. But I was not able to. . . . In fact *(She blows her nose.)* as a matter of fact, this letter, this letter is the first direct word we've . . . I've had from Courtney in thirteen years. . . . . I didn't even know she'd had a baby. . . . Wouldn't you think she'd want her own mother to know she'd had a baby?

GILLY: Yeah—Yes!

W.E.: *(Entering.)* Gilly! I called you and called you. . . . I wet.

GILLY: Excuse me, I'll be right back.

NONNIE: . . . alright.

GILLY: *(To* W.E.*)* It's okay.

W.E.: I couldn't help it.

GILLY: I know. When you're sick, you just can't help it. C'mon, I'll help you change.

(*They exit, leaving* NONNIE *alone in the room. She looks around the room timidly. Suddenly* MR. RANDOLPH *begins to snore, startling* NONNIE, *who thought that she was alone.*)

NONNIE: Oh my goodness!

RANDOLPH: *(Waking.)* What is it? Who is there? Miss Gilly? Miss Gilly?

NONNIE: Who—what? Galadriel? Galadriel?!

GILLY: *(Rushing in.)* What's the matter? Mr. Randolph, just lie down. Just lie down and relax.

RANDOLPH: Who is it Gilly?

GILLY: Don't worry about it, just lie back.

TROTTER: *(Off.)* Gilly, honey? You got company down there?

GILLY: *(Yells off.)* Just playing the TV, that's all!

NONNIE: Bless your heart.

GILLY: Huh?

NONNIE: Courtney didn't exaggerate. I'm just so glad you wrote her, my dear. How could they have put you in such a place? I know I shouldn't have burst in upon you like this, but I felt I had to see for myself before I talked to your case worker.

TROTTER: *(Entering, pale and disorientated.)* Oooh . . . I forgot, I forgot—

GILLY: What did you forget?

TROTTER: The turkey . . . fifteen dollars and thirty-eight cents, and I let it go to rot.

GILLY: *(Going to* TROTTER.*)* Nothing's gone to rot! I got everything in control. Go back to bed Trotter. I'll put the turkey in the oven.

TROTTER: I better sit a minute . . . my head's light. . . . Oh mercy! (TROTTER *collapses, knocking over the end table and pinning* GILLY *underneath her.* TROTTER *begins to giggle.)* Well I done it now, I squished you juicy.

RANDOLPH: What? What is it?

TROTTER: You alright, ain't you Gilly? It's alright Mr. Randolph.

RANDOLPH: But someone fell, I heard someone fall!

TROTTER: Yeah, I feel alright. But it's okay, ain't it, Gilly honey?

GILLY: *(Semi-muffled.)* Just roll Trotter . . . roll over and you'll be off me.

RANDOLPH: What's that? What was that?

TROTTER: It's poor little Gilly . . . here I go. *(With a big groan,* TROTTER *rolls off* GILLY *and rights herself, noticing* NONNIE.*)* You said wasn't nobody here—

NONNIE: I think I'd better go. . . . I don't seem to have come at a very good time.

GILLY: Yeah, you're right. Trotter, get back to bed. I'll be up to check on you.

(TROTTER *exits as* GILLY *leads* NONNIE *out.)*

NONNIE: I'm glad to have met you. I'm sorry to surprise you. . . . I'll get you out of here soon. I'll be in touch.

(NONNIE *exits.)*

GILLY: What have I done?

(GILLY *crosses the room, taking off her bandana to use as a hot pad to pick up a large cooked turkey. As she starts to set up the table for dinner, the ragged bunch of patients gather around the table.* GILLY *presents a small, burned turkey.)*

(Song: Turkey for Four.)

GILLY:

> Turkey for four

W.E.:

> Mashed potatoes galore

GILLY:

> If lumps suit your taste
> Then these won't go to waste

TROTTER:

> Nonsense silly Gilly
> They're smooth and so creamy

W.E.:
What a big . . . meal!

RANDOLPH: I declare Miss Gilly, you're the only person I know who can equal Mrs. Trotter's culinary skill.

TROTTER: I haven't seen such a tasty presentation since the Thanksgiving before my Melvin passed—rest his soul.

W.E.: No trees! No trees!

(GILLY *pulls out a lopsided cake.*)

GILLY:
I've made a cake

TROTTER:
My goodness sake . . . a beauty!

GILLY:
It doesn't look right

RANDOLPH:
It's a glorious sight . . . to me!

GILLY:
You can't see

(GILLY *passes the cake to* TROTTER *who starts to cut it.*)

GILLY: They were all liars . . . and they looked awful, as did the meal . . . but despite everything . . . it really was fun . . . and good. . . . (*A school bell rings.* GILLY *leaves the table with her schoolbooks.*) I was pretty psyched to survive the holiday and actually get back to school. Even ole Harris wasn't rubbing me the wrong way. Still, I was happy to walk W.E. home, since he was still a bit woosy. . . . Of course, with school comes headaches. . . . (*Enter* AGNES *blabbing "blah, blah, blah."*) I just wanted to get home.

AGNES: Or we could go to my house and call people on the phone and breathe weird! It really scares 'em. I've had 'em screaming all over the place at me.

GILLY: It is dumb, Agnes. Dumb, dumb, dumb.

AGNES: C'mon Gilly. Let's do something. You ain't done nothing with me for a long time.

GILLY: My family's been sick.

AGNES: What family? Everybody knows—

GILLY: My brother, my mother and my uncle were sick. I've been taking care of them.

AGNES: Gilly Hopkins, that's the stupidest thing—

GILLY: (*Grabbing* AGNES' *collar.*) You want to discuss this further, sweetheart?

AGNES: (*Backing away.*) It's too dumb to even talk about.

(AGNES *exits as they approach the house.*)

W.E.: Bet I could beat her up.

GILLY: It wouldn't be fair. You against that poor little puny thing. *(She sees* TROTTER *come out the door with a pained look on her face.)* Trotter? What's the matter?

TROTTER: Miss Ellis is here. . . . C'mon inside honey. . . . W.E. c'mon. (W.E. *goes inside.)* C'mon Gilly.

GILLY: No.

TROTTER: Please Gilly . . . come inside—

*(*GILLY *enters the living room to where* MISS ELLIS *is waiting.)*

ELLIS: I got some rather astounding news for you Gilly. Your mother—

GILLY: My mother's coming?

ELLIS: No. Your mother is still in California, but your grandmother, your mother's mother, called the office this morning . . . and then drove up all the way from Virginia to see me. . . . She, and your mother, want you to move in with your grandmother . . . *permanently.*

GILLY: I never said I wanted to live with her! I don't even know her!

ELLIS: Your mother wants you to go to your grandmother's. I talked to her long distance.

GILLY: They can't make me go.

ELLIS: Yes, Gilly, they can.

GILLY: Trotter won't let them take me, will you Trotter? Trotter? Look at me! You said you'd never let me go. I heard you! Never! Never! Never! That's what you said!

W.E.: *(Rushing to* GILLY's *side.)* Don't cry Gilly.

GILLY: I'm not crying! *(She pushes him away.)* I'm yelling. *(She notices how upset* W.E. *is.)* It's gonna be okay, right Trotter?

TROTTER: You tell the child what's got to be done. C'mon W.E., we ain't helping here.

*(*TROTTER *takes* W.E.'s *hand. They exit.)*

ELLIS: You seem to have changed your mind about a lot of things. I'd really like to know why you wrote that letter.

GILLY: You wouldn't understand.

ELLIS: You bet I wouldn't. . . . I don't understand why a smart girl like you goes around booby trapping herself. You could have stayed here indefinitely, you know. They're both crazy about you. . . . Well, it's done now. Your grandmother will come to pick you up at my office tomorrow. I'll come around here tomorrow at nine to pick you up.

GILLY: Tomorrow?

ELLIS: Believe me, it's better this way. Waiting around is no good in these situations.

GILLY: But I got school—

ELLIS: *(Putting on her coat.)* They'll send your records on. . . . I understand from Miss Harris that you've done quite well at Thompson Park Elementary. . . . I must admit that last month when you ran away, I thought, uh oh, here we go again, but I was wrong. You've done well here, Gilly. I'm very pleased.

GILLY: Then let me stay . . . please. . . .

ELLIS: It's out of my hands. I'll see you tomorrow, at nine.

(MISS ELLIS *exits.* GILLY *slowly crosses to the dinner table where* W.E. *is quietly crying.* GILLY *is eating nothing.* MR. RANDOLPH *appears nervous as* TROTTER *surveys the situation.*)

TROTTER: If you all don't start eating this supper, I'm gonna jump up and down on the table, squawking like a two-hundred pound lovesick chicken.

W.E.: Really?

TROTTER: Squawk, squawk, squawk. (MR. RANDOLPH *chuckles,* W.E. *giggles and* GILLY *smiles weakly.*) Now, that's more like it. This was supposed to be a party, not some kind of funeral. We gotta get rid of this turkey, now . . . Gilly's folks are from Louden County, Mr. Randolph.

RANDOLPH: Oh, that's lovely, lovely country, Miss Gilly.

W.E.: We come and see your country, Gilly?

TROTTER: When folks leave, William Ernest, honey, they gotta have a chance to settle in and get used to things. Sometimes it's best not to go visiting, right away.

GILLY: You mean never? . . .

RANDOLPH: Miss Gilly . . . I wasn't quite certain when to give you this . . . but I wanted you to have it—

(MR. RANDOLPH *hands* GILLY *the brown poetry book.*)

TROTTER: We all signed our names in it for ya.

(GILLY *gets up and runs upstairs. Lights fade out on dining room.* GILLY *throws herself on the bed crying. As* TROTTER *slowly climbs the stairs,* GILLY *attempts to pull herself together. She opens the book and reads their inscription.* TROTTER *comes up the stairs to* GILLY's *door, pausing to gather her thoughts.*)

(Song: *Life's Yours.*)

GILLY:

> *What have I done?*
> *Killed all the fun*
> *Before the fun had barely begun*

TROTTER:

> *You are the one*
> *You are the sun*
> *My fearless girl that's second to none*
> *Gilly . . . Gilly . . . my great Gilly Hopkins*
> *How can I let you go?*
>
> *Turn back the clock*
> *Turn back the page*
> *You tried to shock*
> *With all your rage*

The past's your private history
The future is a mystery
Life's yours

TROTTER: Gilly honey? Can I come in? *(Enters.)* You okay baby? . . . I ain't supposed to let on how I feel. . . . I ain't got no blood claim on you . . . but—*(Breaking:)* but it's killing me to see you go.

GILLY: I'll come back and see you all the time.

TROTTER: No, Gilly baby. It don't work that way. Like I tried to tell you at supper. Once the tugboat takes you out to the ocean liner, you got to get all the way on board. You can't straddle both decks.

GILLY: I could.

TROTTER:

Gilly . . . Gilly . . . the great Gilly Hopkins
How can I let you go?

TROTTER and GILLY:

Turn back the clock
Turn back the page

TROTTER:

Open your heart
Let go of the rage

GILLY:

The past's my private history
The future is a mystery

TROTTER:

Life's yours
Sometimes it rains and sometimes it pours
But whatever the weather . . . life's yours

TROTTER: You're gonna make me proud, ya hear? Now, how 'bout you comin' down and having dessert with us.

GILLY: Alright.

(TROTTER stands and goes down stairs to join MR. RANDOLPH and W.E. on the front stoop. GILLY collects her coat and suitcase and comes downstairs. She hugs W.E., stands on her toes to kiss MR. RANDOLPH's cheek and then embraces TROTTER. She crosses to join MISS ELLIS waiting down left. As they exit TROTTER steps out to watch them go.)

TROTTER:

Sometimes it rains
And sometimes it pours
But whatever the weather
Life's yours

BLACKOUT

SCENE 6

(Lights up on NONNIE and GILLY situated as if NONNIE is driving and GILLY is sitting in the front passenger seat.)

NONNIE: Would you like to turn on the radio? I don't really mind, as long as its not too loud. . . . Miss Ellis seems like a nice person.

GILLY: She's okay I guess.

NONNIE: She seems to think I got a rather wrong impression of that foster home she'd put you in.

GILLY: They were all sick last week.

NONNIE: I see. Miss Ellis tried to tell me that you really liked it there, despite everything. From your letter—

GILLY: I lie a lot.

NONNIE: Oh . . . I hoped you'd be glad to come with me. . . . I'm sorry.

GILLY: If you were sorry, you'd turn this old crate around and take me back.

NONNIE: (Not hearing that.) I thought you might like to have Courtney's room. What do you think? It's a big house . . . yes, well . . . you can choose when we get there, would you like for me to help you unpack?

GILLY: Nah! I don't need any help. I can do it.

(GILLY yawns.)

NONNIE: Are you tired, dear?

GILLY: I guess I haven't caught up on all my sleep. I was up a lot last week with everyone sick and all.

NONNIE: Oh my dear. How thoughtless of me. Here I go on and on.

GILLY: No, it's alright. I just need to get some rest. This seat go back?

NONNIE: Yes. . . . And when we get home, you can lie down for a little nap. It's a good idea. I often lie down a little in the afternoon myself.

(GILLY steps out of the car.)

GILLY: In the quiet of the Hopkins home, I sat and tried to figure out my feelings. It really is pretty here. . . . Why had Courtney left? . . . Why should she leave and not look back a single time until now? And why did you leave me? . . . And why did I leave them?

(GILLY produces a pen and a pad and begins writing as a spot lights up on GILLY reciting a letter.)

(Song: Remember My Name.)

GILLY:

> Dear William Ernest I remember you—ha!
> There are horses and servants here—quite La Dee Da!
> We're training a horse, Clouds of Glory's her name
> I miss you, I'm not lying, but it's just not the same

HARRIS:

> Gilly dear Gilly
> It's just not the same without you here

W.E.:

> Gilly dear Gilly I am fine

HARRIS:

> *Enjoy your new school dear*
> *I'm sending you a souvenir*

GILLY:

> *Dear Ms. Harris*
> *Both Tolkien books that you sent me are great*
> *When you showed me love all I showed you was hate*
> *Thank you Ms. Harris now I know about my name*
> *Galadriel never will be quite the same*

TROTTER *and* HARRIS:

> *It's just not the same without you here*

W.E.:

> *Gilly dear Gilly*
> *I wish Clouds of Glory were mine*

RANDOLPH *and* AGNES:

> *Gilly dear Gilly*

AGNES:

> *Remember Jane's mother, the four-hundred pounder?*
> *Well, last week in Las Vegas, they finally found her*
> *She lost tons of weight and so now she's a show girl*
> *And blah blah blah blah*
> *And the men all yell "go girl!"*

GILLY:

> *Agnes oh Agnes*

AGNES:

> *It's just not the same without you here*

TROTTER:

> *Gilly dear Gilly*
> *Guess who got in a fight*

W.E.:

> *Me!*

TROTTER:

> *His nose got all bloody but I guess he's alright*
> *I laughed and I laughed till I thought I had died*
> *Then I sat myself down and I cried and I cried*

GILLY:

> *Wow!*

W.E.:

> *Pow!*

GILLY:

> *Pow!*

GILLY and W.E.:

> *Wow!!*

GILLY:

> *Remember my name*

TROTTER, RANDOLPH and HARRIS:

> *It's just not the same*

W.E.:

> *Lets play a game*

GILLY:

> *Remember My Name*

ALL:

> *It's just not the same*

GILLY: P.S. I just found out my mom's comin' to see me. I know I sometimes lie—but she really is coming . . . to see me!

ALL:

> *Miss you miss you miss you miss you miss you*

(GILLY *crosses down center now wearing a dress.*)

GILLY: The week before Courtney's arrival seemed to go on for ages. I was a nervous wreck, and Nonnie seemed even worse. She went as far as dying her hair for the meeting with mom.

(*Lights up on scene change to airport arrival area.* NONNIE *enters to join* GILLY. COURTNEY *enters.*)

NONNIE: Hello Courtney.

COURTNEY: Hello Nonnie.

NONNIE: This is Galadriel, Courtney.

GILLY: Hi.

COURTNEY: Hey there. (*She clumsily hugs* GILLY.) She's as tall as I am.

NONNIE: She's a lovely girl.

COURTNEY: Well of course she is. She's mine isn't she?

NONNIE: Maybe we should get your luggage.

COURTNEY: I've got it. It's all right here. I'm only here for two days.

NONNIE: Two days? But you said—

COURTNEY: I told you on the phone that I'd come for Christmas and see for myself how the kid was doing—

NONNIE: But when I sent you the money—

COURTNEY: Look, I came, didn't I? Don't start pushing me before I'm hardly off the plane. My God, I've been gone thirteen years, and you still think you can tell me what to do. . . . Can we get out of here?

GILLY: (*To* NONNIE.) I gotta go to the bathroom. (GILLY *starts off but stops, looking back.*) She hadn't come because she wanted to. She came cause Nonnie paid her. Oh, God . . . she ain't gonna take me back. She said she'd always love me . . . it was a lie, I've thrown away my whole life on a stinking lie! (GILLY *sees the pay phone. She picks up the receiver and dials.*) Trotter, it's me.

(*A light goes up in Trotter's living room with* TROTTER *on the phone.*)

TROTTER: Gilly honey, where are you?

GILLY: Nowhere. It doesn't matter. I'm coming home.

TROTTER: What's the matter baby? Your mom didn't show?

GILLY: *(Crying.)* No . . . she came.

TROTTER: Oh, my poor baby.

GILLY: Trotter, it's all wrong. Nothing turned out the way it's supposed to.

TROTTER: How do you mean supposed to? Life ain't supposed to be nothing, 'cept maybe tough.

GILLY: But, I always thought that when my mother came—

TROTTER: My sweet, sweet, baby, ain't no one ever told you yet? I reckon I thought you had that all figured out.

GILLY: What?

TROTTER: That all that stuff 'bout happy endings is lies. The only ending in this world is death. Now that might or might not be happy, but either way, you ain't ready to die are you?

GILLY: Trotter, I'm not talking about dying, I'm talking about coming home.

TROTTER: Sometimes in this world things come easy, and you tend to lean back and say, "Well, finally, a happy ending. This is the way things is supposed to be." Like life owed you good things.

GILLY: Trotter—

TROTTER: And there is lots of good things, baby. Like you comin' to be with us here this fall. That was a mighty good thing for me and William Ernest. But you just fool yourself if you expect good things regular . . . don't nobody owe 'em to you.

GILLY: If life's so bad, how come you're so happy?

TROTTER: Did I say bad? I said it was tough. Nothing to make you happy like doing good on a tough job, now is there?

GILLY: Trotter, stop preaching at me. I want to come home.

TROTTER: You're home, baby. Your grandma is home.

GILLY: I want to be with you and William Ernest and Mr. Randolph.

TROTTER: And leave her all alone? Could you do that?

GILLY: Please Trotter. Don't try to make a stinking Christian out of me.

TROTTER: I wouldn't try to make nothing out of you. . . . Me and William Ernest and Mr. Randolph kinda like you the way you are.

GILLY: Trotter . . . I love you.

TROTTER: I know baby . . . I love you, too.

(GILLY hangs up the phone and tries to compose herself. She takes a big quivering sigh, and takes one step towards the audience.)

GILLY: . . . I'm ready to go home now.

(As her light dims, the cast enters the stage, filling out behind GILLY.)

ALL:

> Thanks to the human heart by which we live
> Thanks to its tenderness, its joys, its fears

(GILLY's spot brightens.)

GILLY:

To me the meanest flower that blows can give

ALL:

Thoughts that do often lie too deep for tears

GILLY:

Remember my name . . . Remember my name . . .
Remember my name

BLACKOUT

CURTAIN

THE WITCHES

by
David Wood

adapted from the novel by
Roald Dahl

THE WITCHES

CAST OF CHARACTERS
WITH SUGGESTED DOUBLING

Companies with more actors available need not use these doubling sugges-tions. It would, however, be difficult to perform the play with less than ten principal actors.

Actor 1 ....Boy
Actor 2 ....Grandmother
Actor 3 ....Display Witch/Witch One/Voice of Maid
Actor 4 ....Lawyer/Hotel Doorman/Head Waiter
Actor 5 ....Sailor/Doctor/Mr. Jenkins/Head Chef
Actor 6 ....Tree-House Witch/Mrs. Jenkins/Witch Two
Actor 7 ....Bruno Jenkins/Frog/Second Chef
Actor 8 ....Grand High Witch
Actor 9 ....Nurse/Waitress
Actor 10 ....Waiter/Puppeteer
Fifteen or so Witches (no individual lines)
Three or Four Diners in the Restaurant (can be doubled by Witches)
A Musician

SYNOPSIS OF SCENES

ACT ONE: Grandmother's Parlour (Norway)
A Ship's Rail
The Tree-House
The Exterior of the Entrance to the Hotel Magnificent
The Hotel Ballroom

ACT TWO: Corner of Ballroom (Giant-Scale)
Two Giant Steps
Grandmother's Hotel Bedroom
Under the Grand High Witch's Bed (Giant-Scale)
The Hotel Restaurant
The Hotel Kitchen
The Hotel Restaurant
Grandmother's Parlour (Norway)

The action of the play takes place in Norway, at sea and in England, in partic-ular at the Hotel Magnificent, Bournemouth

ACT ONE

(As the House Lights go down, the gentle purr of a car engine is heard. The volume increases to an engine roar as the CURTAIN *rises on a darkened stage.*
A sudden screech of brakes. A crash.
A single Light picks out BOY, *downstage.)*

BOY: Christmas holidays. Winter sunshine. Happy. North of Oslo. Papa driving. Mama beside him. Me in the back. Icy road. Skidding, sliding, out of control. Off the road. Tumbling. Into a rocky ravine. *(He calls.)* Mama! Papa! No!

(He turns and runs to GRANDMOTHER's *parlour.*
There is an easy chair, a small table with a lamp. This all creates a cosy atmosphere. GRANDMOTHER *is waiting. She enfolds* BOY *in her arms. She comforts him as he sobs.)*

GRANDMOTHER: Sob your heart out, darling Boy. Grandmamma's here.

BOY: What are we going to do now?

GRANDMOTHER: You will stay here with me. And I will look after you.

BOY: Aren't I going back to England?

GRANDMOTHER: No. I could never do that. Heaven shall take my soul, but Norway shall keep my bones.
    (They continue hugging. GRANDMOTHER *turns to the audience.)* As the days passed, time began to heal the hurt. *(She leads* BOY *to her chair. She sits. He kneels at her feet. A clock ticks.)*
    Each evening I told him stories of summer holidays when I was young. *(To* BOY.*)* We used to row out in a boat and wave to the shrimpboats on their way home. They would stop and give us a handful of shrimps each, still warm from having just been cooked. We peeled them and gobbled them up. The head was the best part.

*(*BOY *looks interested.)*

BOY: The head?

GRANDMOTHER: You squeeze it between your teeth and suck out the inside. *(She demonstrates with relish.)* It's marvelous.

BOY: Ugggggh! It's horrible!

(He is enjoying the horror.)

GRANDMOTHER: *(lighting a thin black cigar.)* Horrible things can be exciting, Boy. Take . . . witches.

BOY: Witches? With silly black hats and black cloaks riding on broomsticks.

GRANDMOTHER: No. They're for fairy-tales. Very tame. I'm talking of *real* witches.

BOY: *Real* witches?

GRANDMOTHER: Real witches dress in ordinary clothes and look very much like ordinary women. That's why they're so hard to catch.

BOY: But why should we want to catch them?

GRANDMOTHER: Because, my darling Boy, they are evil. They hate children. They get the same pleasure from squelching a child as you get from eating a plateful of strawberries and thick cream.

BOY: Squelching?

GRANDMOTHER: She chooses a victim, softly stalks it. Closer and closer, then . . . phwisst! . . . she swoops. Sparks fly. Flames leap. Oil boils. Rats howl. Skin shrivels and the child disappears. Squelched.

BOY: Disappears?

GRANDMOTHER: Not always. Sometimes the child is transformed into something else. Like little Birgit Svenson who lived across the road from us. One day she started growing feathers all over her body. Within a month she had turned into a large white chicken. Her parents kept her for years in a pen in the garden. She even laid eggs.

BOY: What color eggs?

GRANDMOTHER: Brown ones. Biggest eggs I've ever seen. Her mother made omelettes out of them. Delicious they were.

BOY: Are you being truthful, Grandmamma? Really and truly truthful? Not pulling my leg.

GRANDMOTHER: My darling Boy, you won't last long in this world if you don't know how to spot a witch when you see one.

BOY: Then tell me. Please! (GRANDMOTHER *takes a large tome from the table and opens it to show* BOY *a picture. MUSIC. As* GRANDMOTHER *finds the page, the* DISPLAY WITCH *is seen. She is isolated in a pool of light and looks like an ordinary woman. Looking at the book.)* She doesn't look like a witch.

GRANDMOTHER: Of course not. If witches looked like witches, we could round them all up and put them in the meat-grinder. But look, there's a clue. She's wearing gloves.

BOY: Mama used to wear gloves.

GRANDMOTHER: Not in the summer, when it's hot. Not in the house. A witch does.

BOY: Why?

GRANDMOTHER: Because she doesn't have fingernails. (*The* DISPLAY WITCH, *almost in choreographed slow motion, removes a glove.)* She has thin, curvy claws, like a cat.

(*The* DISPLAY WITCH *gestures threateningly with her claws.)*

BOY: Uggggh!

GRANDMOTHER: Second clue. She wears a wig. A real witch is always bald.

(*The* DISPLAY WITCH *removes her wig revealing a bald head.)*

Not a single hair grows on her head.

BOY: Horrid.

GRANDMOTHER: Disgusting.

(*The* DISPLAY WITCH *begins to scratch her bald head.)*

And the wig gives her nasty sores on the head. Wig-rash, it's called. And it doesn't half itch.

BOY: What else, Grandmamma?

GRANDMOTHER: Big nose-holes.

(The DISPLAY WITCH *raises her head and flares her nostrils.)*

BOY: What for?

GRANDMOTHER: To sniff out the stink-waves of children.

BOY: I don't give out stink-waves, do I?

GRANDMOTHER: Not to me, you don't. To me you smell like raspberries and cream. But to a witch you smell—all children smell—like fresh dogs' droppings.

BOY: Dogs' droppings? I don't believe it.

GRANDMOTHER: So, if you see a woman holding her nose as she passes you in the street, that woman could easily be a witch. Now, look at her feet.

BOY: Nothing special about them.

GRANDMOTHER: Wrong. She has no toes.

(The DISPLAY WITCH *takes off a shoe revealing a stockinged stub.)*

BOY: Uggggh!

GRANDMOTHER: And last but not least, a witch has blue spit.

(The DISPLAY WITCH *smiles for the first time, revealing a haze of blue teeth. She cackles menacingly and disappears as the Lights fade on the* DISPLAY WITCH. GRANDMOTHER *closes the book.)*

So, my darling Boy, now you know.

*(*BOY *leaves* GRANDMOTHER *and comes downstage.)*

BOY: Next day talk of witches was forgotten. A man came.

(The LAWYER *enters, with a briefcase, and holding a document.)*

Something to do with my parents' will.

LAWYER: *(To* GRANDMOTHER.*)* They insist the boy continues his education in England. After all, he was born there.

GRANDMOTHER: Very well.

*(*BOY *enters the scene.)*

BOY: Grandmamma, you can't send me away!

GRANDMOTHER: Of course not. I'll come to England, too.

BOY: But you don't want to go. You said so.

GRANDMOTHER: It is important to respect the wishes of the parents. *(To the* LAWYER.*)* Is it not?

LAWYER: I'm sorry, madam.

GRANDMOTHER: Term begins soon. No time to waste.

(The Lights fade as the scene clears. A ship's hooter fills the air, followed by sea-gulls' cries and the sound of the sea.

The Lights come up on a ship's rail. BOY *and* GRANDMOTHER, *wearing topcoats, lean on the rail.)*

BOY: Is that England, Grandmamma?

GRANDMOTHER: The docks of Newcastle, yes. Not the most romantic of land-ing places.

(A SAILOR *enters and passes through the scene.)*

BOY: Grandmamma . . .

GRANDMOTHER: Yes?

BOY: Are there any witches in England?

GRANDMOTHER: Of course. Every country has its own Secret Society of Witches.

BOY: I'm sure I won't meet one.

GRANDMOTHER: I sincerely hope you won't. English witches are probably the most vicious in the whole world.

BOY: What do they do?

GRANDMOTHER: Their favorite ruse is to mix up a powder that turns a child into a creature all the grown-ups hate.

BOY: Such as?

GRANDMOTHER: A slug. Then the grown-ups step on the slug and squish it without knowing it's a child, *their* child maybe.

BOY: That's awful.

GRANDMOTHER: That's English witches for you.

BOY: These . . . Societies of Witches. Do they have meetings? Like our Chess Society at school?

GRANDMOTHER: They have an annual meeting, attended by the Grand High Witch of all the World.

BOY: Grand High Witch? Who's she?

(The SAILOR *passes through again.)*

SAILOR: *(Shouting.)* Prepare for disembarcation if you please.

*(*GRANDMOTHER *ushers* BOY *away.)*

GRANDMOTHER: Come on!

BOY: But, Grandmamma . . .

*(*GRANDMOTHER *exits. As the scene clears,* BOY *steps forward.)*

Soon life was back to sort of normal. We lived in our old house and I went back to school. One Saturday afternoon, when my friend Timmy was in bed with 'flu, I decided to do some work on the tree-house we were building at the bottom of the garden . . .

(The Lights come up on the tree-house. Birdsong. BOY *climbs up and starts nail-ing a plank.*

Sinister music as the TREE-HOUSE WITCH *enters. She sniffs, her nostrils flared. She traces the scent, looking up to* BOY, *who works on, unaware. The birdsong stops.*

Tension mounts as the WITCH *slowly starts to climb the steps to the tree-house.*

BOY *is still hammering the nail. Just as it seems the* TREE-HOUSE WITCH *might reach him, he accidentally drops the hammer with a clatter. The* TREE-HOUSE WITCH *retreats a little.*

BOY *descends to fetch his hammer. He picks it up, turns, and suddenly sees the* WITCH. *He stops.)*

WITCH: *(Waving a gloved hand.)* Hallo, boy.

> *(She smiles a blue smile.)*
>
> Don't be shy. I have a present for you.

> *(*BOY, *nervous, starts to climb the steps.)*
>
> Come down out of that tree, Boy, and I shall give you the most exciting present you've ever had.

> *(Still looking up at* BOY, *she produces, perhaps from her handbag, a thin green snake. It coils itself round her forearm.)*
>
> If you come down here, I shall give him to you.

> *(*BOY, *almost mesmerized by the snake, descends and approaches.)*
>
> It's tame. Come stroke him.

*(*BOY *goes to stroke the snake. Suddenly the* TREE-HOUSE WITCH *grabs* BOY *by the arm. A struggle ensues. Then* BOY *stamps on the* TREE-HOUSE WITCH's *foot. She screams with frustration as* BOY *climbs back up to the tree-house to hide.*

The TREE-HOUSE WITCH *calms herself, then leaves, cackling horribly.*

The Lights fade. Time-passing music. An owl hoots.)

GRANDMOTHER: *(Off.)* Boy!

> *(*GRANDMOTHER *enters with a torch.)*
>
> Boy!

BOY: *(From the tree-house.)* Grandmamma. Up here.

GRANDMOTHER: Come down at once. It's past your suppertime.

BOY: Has that woman gone?

GRANDMOTHER: What woman?

BOY: The woman in the black gloves.

> *(*GRANDMOTHER *is stunned.)*

GRANDMOTHER: Gloves?

BOY: Has she gone?

GRANDMOTHER: Yes, she's gone. I'm here, my darling.

> *(*BOY *descends gingerly. Then, trembling, he falls into* GRANDMOTHER's *arms.)*
>
> There, there. I'll look after you.

BOY: *(With an effort.)* I've seen a witch. *(A cackle echoes through the night as the Lights fade.)*

(The Lights come up in a small area downstage. BOY *steps into the light.)* Just before the end of the summer term, when Grandmamma and I were looking forward to going back to Norway for the holidays, she fell ill. Very ill. *(The Lights come up on another downstage area. A doctor attends* GRANDMOTHER, *slumped in an armchair.)*

Pneumonia. It was touch and go. But Grandmamma was strong. After ten long days she pulled through.

(The DOCTOR *leaves* GRANDMOTHER *and a* NURSE *takes his place.)*

DOCTOR: But she's still weak. Too weak to make the crossing to Norway.

BOY: But our holiday . . .

DOCTOR: Do you want your Grandmother to die?

BOY: Never.

DOCTOR: Then no Norway. But I'll tell you what you can do. Take her to a nice hotel on the south coast of England instead. The sea air would do her good. And stop her smoking those vile black cigars!

(He goes.)

BOY: And that's how we came to stay in Bournemouth. At the Hotel Magnificent.

(MUSIC plays as BOY *exits.*
The scene changes to the imposing front door of the hotel. Steps rise graciously to the entrance. Traffic noises.
As the Lights come up slowly, the hotel DOORMAN *is discovered on duty.*
BRUNO JENKINS *enters and stands near the* DOORMAN *cheekily imitating his stance and making rude faces.*
He laughs at the DOORMAN *who is trying not to react to the rudeness.* BRUNO *then sits on the steps and provocatively starts eating a cream bun.*
A LADY [WITCH] *enters and tries to climb the steps.*
BRUNO *is in her way. She tries to get round him, but he slides himself along the step to block her path.)*

LADY: Excuse me.

BRUNO: *(Rudely.)* Why? What've you done?

LADY: Pardon me?

BRUNO: Granted.

(He laughs.)

LADY: Move, please.

BRUNO: Shan't. So there.

(The DOORMAN *approaches.)*

DOORMAN: Shift yourself, sunshine.

(He pushes BRUNO, *whose face hits the cream bun.)*

BRUNO: *(Spluttering.)* Here!

DOORMAN: Good-day, madam.

LADY: Thank you.

(The door is held open by the DOORMAN. *The* LADY *enters the hotel.)*

BRUNO: *(To the* DOORMAN.*)* I'll set my Dad on you.

DOORMAN: *(Impassively.)* I can't wait. *(Another Lady* [WITCH] *arrives.)* Good-day, madam. Straight through for the meeting.

(He opens the door. Before the LADY *can enter,* MR. JENKINS *squashes rudely through.)*

MR. JENKINS: *(Loudly.)* Bruno.

BRUNO: Yes, Dad.

(The LADY *manages to go in.)*

DOORMAN: *(Long suffering.)* Can I help you, Mr. Jenkins?

MR. JENKINS: No, you can't. You lot only help if there's a tip at the end of it. Beat it, Buttons.

BRUNO: Yes, beat it, Buttons! *(He laughs.)*

DOORMAN: As you please, sir.

(He goes inside.)

MR. JENKINS: Shut your face, Bruno. Where's your Ma?

BRUNO: Gone to buy me a doughnut.

MR. JENKINS: You'll turn into a doughnut, you fat slob.

BRUNO: So?

MR. JENKINS: Tell your Ma I'm in the bar.

(He turns to go.)

BRUNO: Getting drunk time, is it, Pa?

MR. JENKINS: *(stopping by the door.)* What?

BRUNO: I said "Nearly lunchtime, is it, Pa?"

MR. JENKINS: Watch it.

(Another Lady [WITCH] *approaches. The* DOORMAN *opens the door from the inside, knocking it into* MR. JENKINS.*)*

(To the DOORMAN.*)* Watch it.

DOORMAN: *(Sweetly.)* So sorry, Mr. Jenkins.

*(*MR. JENKINS *rudely goes inside ahead of the* LADY.*)*

MR. JENKINS: *(To the* LADY.*)* Watch it.

DOORMAN: Good-day, madam. Straight through.

*(*BRUNO *takes out a magnifying glass and focuses it on a step.* BOY *enters carrying a box.)*

BOY: Hallo, Bruno.

BRUNO: What you got in there? Something to eat? Give us some.

BOY: I've been to the pet shop. Grandmamma gave me some money.

BRUNO: What've you got?

BOY: White mice. I'm going to call them William and Mary.

BRUNO: Boring. Guess what pets I got.

BOY: What?

BRUNO: Chinchillas and mink.

BOY: Oh?

BRUNO: Gonna make me Ma a fur coat, see.

BOY: Oh.

*(Another Lady [*WITCH*] arrives, steps over* BRUNO *and enters the hotel.)*

BRUNO: *(Concentrating on his magnifying glass now.)* Bet my Dad earns more than yours.

BOY: Probably.

BRUNO: How many cars has he got, your dad?

BOY: None.

BRUNO: Mine's got three.

BOY: What are you doing with that magnifying glass?

BRUNO: Roasting ants.

BOY: That's horrible. Stop it.

(He tries to grab the magnifying glass.)

BRUNO: Here. Get away. Shove off.

(A scuffle breaks out
Mrs. Jenkins enters carrying a paper bag.)

MRS. JENKINS: Bruno!

(She tries to pull the boys apart.)

    (To BOY.*)* You great bully. *(She slaps hard an arm which she thinks belongs to* BOY, *but which in fact belongs to* BRUNO.*)* Lay off my little Bruno, do you hear?

BRUNO: *(Wailing.)* Ow! Mum . . .

MRS. JENKINS: *(Going to* BRUNO *and brushing him down.)* Look at you, your shorts are all grubby.

BRUNO: He tried to nick my magnifying glass.

MRS. JENKINS: *(To* BOY.*)* You keep away from my little Bruno, d'you hear? *(To* BRUNO.*)* There's your doughnut, treasure.

BRUNO: *(Taking it greedily.)* Ask him what's in that box, Ma.

MRS. JENKINS: Why? *(To* BOY.*)* Have you nicked that 'n' all?

BOY: No. It's William and Mary.

MRS. JENKINS: What d'you mean, William and Mary? Give us a look.

(She lifts the lid. A mouse's head pops up.)
  Ahhhhhhh! Mice! Aaaaaaaaaaaah!

(She runs up the steps and into the hotel screaming.)

BRUNO: *(Roaring with laughter, calling after her.)* Pa's in the bar, Ma. *(But she has gone.)* Silly old witch.

BOY: *(Alert.)* What did you say?

BRUNO: Nothing.

BOY: I'd better go and see Grandmamma.

(The DOORMAN opens the door for him. He enters the hotel.
Another LADY enters [WITCH]. She is welcomed by the DOORMAN and enters the hotel.
BRUNO sits on the steps and starts eating the doughnut and scooping out jam on his finger.
The DOORMAN descends the steps, pretending not to notice BRUNO. He takes a deep breath or two of fresh air.
Sinister music as another LADY [The GRAND HIGH WITCH] enters.
The DOORMAN turns and sees her.)

DOORMAN: Good-day, madam.

GRAND HIGH WITCH: *(Charming.)* Good-day. Is this the correct hotel for the Annual General Meeting of the Royal Society for the Prevention of Cruelty to Children?

DOORMAN: It is indeed, madam. Welcome.

(He ascends the steps and holds the door open.
The GRAND HIGH WITCH starts to ascend the steps, but suddenly stops. She starts sniffing, as genteelly as possible, and turns to see the source of the stink-waves, which is BRUNO. She approaches him.)

GRAND HIGH WITCH: Vell, hallo, little man.

BRUNO: Eh?

GRAND HIGH WITCH: You are liking your doughnut, yes? *(Bruno nods.)* But vot happens ven it is finished? Vould you like some chocolate?

(She hands him a bar of chocolate.)

BRUNO: *(Enthusiastically.)* Yeah.

(He breaks off a piece and eats it.)

GRAND HIGH WITCH: Good?

BRUNO: Great.

GRAND HIGH WITCH: Vould you like some more?

BRUNO: Yeah.

GRAND HIGH WITCH: I vill give you six more chocolate bars like that if you vill meet me in the ballroom of this hotel at twenty-five-past three.

BRUNO: Six bars! I'll be there.

(The GRAND HIGH WITCH *ascends the steps and enters the hotel, the door held open by the* DOORMAN.*)*

You bet I'll be there!

(The Lights fade on BRUNO, *stuffing his face. Music as the scene changes to the ballroom where there are mirrors and a chandelier, a raised platform, a door and some chairs. There is a folding screen downstage to one side.*

Note: In the original production, the scene changes, in "blue wash" light, was orchestrated by the DOORMAN, *assisted by a* WAITER *and* WAITRESS, *who exited, not through the ballroom door, but offstage as though to a staff area.*

As the Lights come up, BOY, *carrying his box containing* WILLIAM *and* MARY, *enters through the door, impressed by the grand room.)*

BOY: After lunch, Grandmamma had her rest, while I found a secret spot in a colossal empty room called the Ballroom. The perfect place for some mouse circus training.

(Note: At this point, in the original production, the DOORMAN, WAITER *and* WAITRESS *re-entered and set up chairs for the forthcoming meeting. Music accompanied this.* BOY *hid behind the screen as they entered, then re-emerged once the chairs were set and the* DOORMAN, WAITER *and* WAITRESS *had exited.)*

(To the tune of "Entry of the Gladiators") Da da dadelade da da da da, da da dadelade da da da da . . . Ladies and gentlemen, the world famous White Mouse Circus proudly presents William, the wizard of the trightrope! Da da! *(He shows William on a tight rope. He holds a piece of cake in one hand.)* Now then, William, here's a tasty piece of fruitcake, come and get it! Come on, come on, good mouse, good mouse! . . . Yes! *(He gives William a nibble of cake.)* Now back to the centre . . . now Ladies and Gentlemen, William will somersault on the high trapeze! One, two, three, hup! One, two, three, hup! Bravo!!

(Suddenly the Ballroom is flooded with light from the chandelier. BOY *hides downstage of the screen. He reacts with mounting curiosity, watching through a gap in the screen.*

To music, the DOORMAN *enters and ushers in a troupe of ladies [*WITCHES*] who noisily babble and ad-lib the following to each other.)*

WITCHES: *(variously)* Oh hallo, Beatrice. What an adorable dress! . . . Agatha, how lovely to see you. . . . Have you had a good journey? . . . Come and sit next to me, Millie dear. . . . I haven't seen you since the last meeting. *Etc.*

(They arrange themselves, seated facing the platform. As they talk, some scratch their necks with gloved hands.

Eventually the DOORMAN *calls for attention.)*

DOORMAN: Ladies of the Royal Society for the Prevention of Cruelty to Children, pray welcome your President.

(Enthusiastic applause. The GRAND HIGH WITCH *enters in style to a fanfare. She mounts the platform. The* DOORMAN *exits.*

A WITCH *locks the door.*

Note: In the original production WITCH ONE *was presented as an acolyte of the* GRAND HIGH WITCH, *locking the door, helping the* GRAND HIGH WITCH *by receiving her wig and mask on a cushion, holding up the recipe on a scroll etc. This is not essential but helped the* GRAND HIGH WITCH *achieve a regal manner.*

Slowly the GRAND HIGH WITCH *removes her wig and then mask, revealing a wizened, horrible, rotting face. The other* WITCHES *watch in awe.)*

GRAND HIGH WITCH: You may rrree-moof your vigs, and get some fresh air into your spotty scalps. *(With sighs of relief, the* WITCHES *reveal their bald heads.)* Vitches of Inkland. Miserrrable vitches. Useless lazy vitches. You are a heap of idle good-for-nothing vurms! *(A murmur of concern among the* WITCHES.) As I am eating my lunch, I am looking out of the vindow at the beach. And vot am I seeing? I am seeing a rrreevolting sight, which is putting me off my food. Hundreds of rrrotten rrrepulsive children. Playing on the sand. Vye have you not got rrrid of them? Vye? *(No response.)* You vill do better.

WITCHES: We will, your Grandness. We will do better.

GRAND HIGH WITCH: My orders are that every single child in Inkland shall be rrrubbed out, sqvashed, sqvirted, sqvittered and frittered before I come here again in vun year's time.

(A gasp through the audience.)

WITCH TWO: *All* of them? We can't possibly wipe out *all* of them.

GRAND HIGH WITCH: Who said that? Who dares to argue vith me? *(She points dramatically at* WITCH TWO.) It vos you, vos it not?

*(*WITCH TWO *stands, gasping in fright.)*

WITCH TWO: I didn't mean it, your Grandness.

GRAND HIGH WITCH: Come here.

(She beckons. WITCH TWO, *mesmerized, ascends the platform.)*

WITCH TWO: I didn't mean to argue, your Grandness. I was just talking to myself. I swear it.

GRAND HIGH WITCH: A vitch who dares to say I'm wrrrrong

Vill not be vith us very long!

WITCH TWO: Forgive me, your Grandness.

GRAND HIGH WITCH: A stupid vitch who answers back

Must burn until her bones are black!

WITCH TWO: No! No! Spare me!

(Staring at WITCH TWO, *the* GRAND HIGH WITCH *gestures. Sparks fly. Smoke rises.)*

Aaaaaaaaaaah!

*(*WITCH TWO *disappears.*
A great sigh through the audience. BOY *reacts too.)*

GRAND HIGH WITCH: I hope nobody else is going to make me cross today.

(WITCH ONE *finds the smoldering remnants of* WITCH TWO's *clothes and holds them up.*)
Frrrizzled like a frrritter. Cooked like a carrot. You vill never see her again. Now vee can get down to business.

(*A rhythmic pulse conveys an ominous mood. The following sequence grows in intensity.*)

GRAND HIGH WITCH: Down vith children! Do them in!

WITCHES: Boil their bones and fry their skin!

GRAND HIGH WITCH: Bish them, sqvish them, bash them, mash them!

WITCHES: Break them, shake them, slash them, smash them!

GRAND HIGH WITCH: I am having a plan. A giganticus plan!

WITCHES: She is having a plan. A giganticus plan!

GRAND HIGH WITCH: You vill buy sveetshops.

WITCHES: We will buy sweetshops.

GRAND HIGH WITCH: You vill fill them high vith luscious sveets and tasty chocs!

WITCHES: Luscious sweets and tasty chocs!

GRAND HIGH WITCH: You vill have a Great Gala Opening with free sveets and chocs for every child!

WITCHES: Free sweets and chocs for every child!

(WITCH ONE *is carried away with enthusiasm.*)

WITCH ONE: I will *poison* the sweets and *poison* the chocs and wipe out the children like weasels.

(*Silence. The rhythmic pulse stops.*)

GRAND HIGH WITCH: You vill do no such thing. You brainless bogvumper! Poison them and you vill be caught in five minutes flat. No. Vee vitches are vurrrking only vith magic!

WITCHES: (*Building.*) Magic! Magic! Magic!

GRAND HIGH WITCH: You vill be filling every choc and every sveet vith my latest and grrreatest magic formula. (*A sigh of admiration as she produces a potion bottle.*) Formula Eighty-Six Delayed Action Mouse-Maker!
(*Applause. The* GRAND HIGH WITCH *reveals a board or scroll with "Formula Eighty-Six Delayed-Action Mouse-Maker" written on it, followed by the recipe.*) Take down the recipe. (*The* WITCHES *take out pads and pencils.*) You vill notice some unusual ingredients: a grrruntle's egg; the claw of a crrrab-crrruncher; the beak of a blabbersnitch; the snout of a grrrobblesqvirt and the tongue of a catsprrringer. Mix them with forty-five mouses' tails fried in hair-oil till they are crrrisp.

WITCH ONE: What do we do with the mice who have had their tails chopped off, your Grandness?

GRAND HIGH WITCH: You simmer them in frog-juice for vun hour. Then you add two secret ingredients. The wrrrong end of a telescope boiled soft . . .

WITCH ONE: What's that for, O Brainy One?

GRAND HIGH WITCH: To make a child very small you look at him through the wrrrong end of a telescope, do you not?

WITCH ONE: *(To the others.)* She's a wonder. Who else would have thought of that.

GRAND HIGH WITCH: And finally, to cause the delayed action, rrroast in the oven vun alarm-clock set to go off at nine o'clock in the morning.

WITCH ONE: A stroke of genius!

GRAND HIGH WITCH: Inject vun droplet of the formula in each sveet or choc, open your shop, and as the children pour in on their vay home from school . . .

(She chants the following rhyme:)

> Crrram them full of sticky eats,
> Send them home still guzzling sveets,
> And in the morning little fools
> Go marching off to separate schools.

(A WITCH *bangs a gong or a bell rings nine times.)*

> A girl feels sick and goes all pale.
> She yells, "Hey, look! I've grrrown a tail!"
> A boy who's standing next to her
> Screams, "Help! I think I'm grrrowing fur!"
> Another shouts, "Vee look like frrreaks!
> There's viskers growing on our cheeks!"
> A boy who vos extremely tall
> Cries out, "Vot's wrong? I'm grrrowing small!"
> Four tiny legs begin to sprrrout
> From everybody rrround about.
> And all at vunce, all in a trrrice,
> There are no children! Only mice!
> The teachers cry, "Vot's going on?
> Oh, vhere have all the children gone?"
> Then suddenly the mice they spot,
> Fetch mousetrrraps strrrong and kill the lot!
> They sveep the dead mice all away
> And all us vitches shout

ALL: Hooray!

(They rise to a big finish.)

> Down vith children! Do them in!
> Boil their bones and fry their skin!
> Bish them, sqvish them, bash them, mash them!
> Brrreak them, shake them, slash them, smash them!

(The WITCHES, *jumping up, cheer wildly. They sit again. The* GRAND HIGH WITCH *acknowledges their appreciation.*
Suddenly WITCH ONE *leaps up and points to the back of the platform.)*

WITCH ONE: Look! Look! Mice!

(Two white mice are progressing from one side to the other. They stop nervously, looking about.)

BOY: *(Seeing them through the gap in the screen.)* Oh no! William and Mary!

WITCH ONE: Our leader has done it to show us! The Brainy One has turned two children to mice!

(The GRAND HIGH WITCH has seen the mice. The other WITCHES start to applaud.)

GRAND HIGH WITCH: Qviet! *(She approaches the mice, who stop moving. Music for tension.)* These mice are nothing to do with me. These mice are *pet* mice, qvite obviously belonging to some repellent little child in this hotel.

*(She chases the mice, stamping her feet.
The mice scurry away and disappear.)*

WITCH ONE: *(Menacingly.)* A child! A filthy child. We'll sniff him out.

(The WITCHES start sniffing and some move ominously towards the screen. BOY stiffens. The music builds. Then, in the nick of time, there is a knock on the door. The WITCHES react.)

BRUNO: *(Outside the door.)* Hey! Let me in!

(More knocks.)

GRAND HIGH WITCH: Qvick, vitches. Vigs on!

(The WITCHES hurry to make themselves respectable.)

BRUNO: *(Outside the door.)* Hurry up! Twenty-five past three you said.

GRAND HIGH WITCH: Vitches. Vatch this demonstrrration. Earlier today I am giving a chocolate bar vith formula added to a smelly boy.

BRUNO: *(Outside the door.)* Where's them chocolate bars you promised? I'm here to collect! Dish 'em out!

GRAND HIGH WITCH: Not only smelly but grrreedy. The formula is timed for half past three.
(She puts on her wig, but not her face mask.) Let him in. *(WITCH ONE unlocks the door.
BRUNO enters and approaches.
The GRAND HIGH WITCH keeps her back towards him.)*
(Soft and gentle.) Darling little man. I have your chocolate all rrready for you. Do come and say hallo to all these lovely ladies.

(BRUNO ascends the platform. The WITCH re-locks the door.)

BRUNO: OK, where's my chocolate? Six bars you said.

GRAND HIGH WITCH: *(Checking her watch.)* Thirty seconds to go.

BRUNO: What? *(He receives no reply.)* What the heck's going on?

GRAND HIGH WITCH: Twenty seconds!

BRUNO: *(Getting suspicious.)* Gimme the chocolate and let me out of here.

GRAND HIGH WITCH: Fifteen seconds!

BRUNO: *(Looking at the* WITCHES.*)* Will one of you crazy punks kindly tell me what all this is about?

GRAND HIGH WITCH: Ten seconds!

(She turns her face to BRUNO, *who reacts with a terrified scream.)*

WITCHES: Nine . . . eight . . . seven . . . six . . . five . . . four . . . three . . . two . . . one . . . zero!

GRAND HIGH WITCH: Vee have ignition.

(An alarm rings. Strange lighting effects as BRUNO *jumps and yells. He jumps onto a small table, then hops about waving his arms. Then he falls silent and stiffens.)*

(Tension music.)

> This smelly brrrat, this fithy scum
> This horrid little louse
> Vill very soon become
> A lovely little MOUSE!

(A flash. Smoke. Music. BRUNO *appears to shrink; his head darts about like a mouse; his hands, like paws, brush imaginary whiskers.*
He disappears.
In his place on the table-top, a mouse scampers to and fro.)

WITCHES: *(Applauding.)* Bravo! She's done it! It works! It's fantastic! *Etc., etc.*

(The GRAND HIGH WITCH *shoots the mouse, which appears to make a hurried exit through the* WITCHES, *who react.)*

GRAND HIGH WITCH: Vitches, I vill meet you all for dinner at eight. Before dinner, any ancient vuns who can no longer climb high trrrees in search of grrruntles' eggs for the formula may come to my rrroom. I have prrrepared for you *(She shows a tiny bottle.)* a bottle each, containing a limited qvantity. Five hundred doses.

WITCHES: *(Led by* WITCH ONE.*)* Thank you, thank you, your Grandness. How thoughtful.

GRAND HIGH WITCH: Room Four-Five-Four. Any qvestions?

WITCH ONE: One, O Brainy One. What happens if one of the chocolates we are giving away in our shop gets eaten by a grown-up?

GRAND HIGH WITCH: That's just too bad for the grown-up. This meeting is over.

(The WITCHES *start to go.*
Behind the screen BOY *relaxes, relieved. He stands up and stretches. He rubs his aching knees.*
Suddenly . . .)

WITCH ONE: *(Shouting.)* Wait! Hold everything.

(She flares her nostrils, sniffing eagerly. Her face turns towards the screen. Tension music. The WITCHES *freeze and listen.)*

WITCH ONE: *(Following the scent.)* Dogs' droppings. I've got a whiff of fresh dogs' droppings.

GRAND HIGH WITCH: Vot rubbish is this? There are no children in this rrroom!

WITCH ONE: It's getting stronger. Can't the rest of you smell it? Dogs' droppings.

(All the WITCHES *are sniffing now.)*

WITCHES: Dogs' droppings! Yes! Yes! Dogs' droppings! Dogs' droppings! Poo! Poo-oo-oo-oo-oo!

(They head towards the screen.
BOY *is terrified.*
WITCH ONE *looks behind the screen.)*

WITCH ONE: *(With a shriek.)* Boy! Boy! Boy! Boy!

(Pandemonium as a chase ensues. BOY *runs through the* WITCHES, *desperate to escape. He runs anywhere and everywhere. The* WITCHES *chase him. He yells.)*

GRAND HIGH WITCH: *(From the platform.)* Grrrab it! Stop it yelling! Catch it, you idiots! (*BOY is surrounded. Helpless, he submits. He is lifted up.)* Spying little vurm! Bring it to me.

(The WITCHES *carry him to the table and lie him or stand him on it.)*

(To BOY*)* You stinking little carbuncle. You have observed the most secret things. Now you must take your medicine!

BOY: Help! Help! Grandmamma!

GRAND HIGH WITCH: Open his mouth!

(The WITCHES *do so. Dramatically the* GRAND HIGH WITCH *opens a formula bottle and raises it aloft.)*

Five hundred doses! So strrrong vee see INSTANTANEOUS ACTION!

(She pours the potion into BOY's *mouth.*
Strange distorted alarm bells, strobing light.
As the effects end, the WITCHES *step aside, cackling manically.*
On the table there is no sign of BOY. *Just a trembling mouse.)*

CURTAIN

ACT TWO

(The action is still set in the ballroom, but a giant-size section of wall, with skirting board and, perhaps, towering chair legs.
As the Lights come up, a mouse scampers in and sniffs around. It is BOY—*the actor dressed as a mouse. He looks about him.)*

BOY: *(Calling.)* Bruno! Bruno Jenkins! *(No reply.* BOY *frisks around happily.) (To the audience.)* I should be sad. I should feel desperate. I mean, I've never dreamed of being a mouse, like I've dreamed of being, say, a film star. But now that I *am* one, I'm beginning to see the advantages. I know mice sometimes get poisoned or caught in traps but boys sometimes get killed too—run over or get some awful illness. Boys have to go to school. Mice don't. Mice don't have to pass exams. When mice grow up they don't have to go out to work. Mm. It's no bad thing to be a mouse. I'm as free as William and Mary. Hope they're all right. (BRUNO, *dressed as a mouse, enters eating a chunk of bread.*)

(*To* BRUNO.) Hallo, Bruno.

(BRUNO *nods.*)

What have you found?

BRUNO: An ancient fish paste sandwich. Pretty good. Bit pongy.

BOY: Listen, Bruno. Now we're both mice, I think we ought to start thinking about the future.

(BRUNO *stops eating.*)

BRUNO: What do you mean, *we*? The fact that you're a mouse has nothing to do with me.

BOY: But you're a mouse, too, Bruno.

BRUNO: Don't be stupid, I'm not a mouse.

BOY: I'm afraid you are, Bruno.

BRUNO: I most certainly am not. You're lying. I am most definitely not a mouse.

BOY: Look at your paws.

BRUNO: You're barmy! My paws? (*He looks at them.*) Aaaaah! They're all hairy. (*He feels his ears and whiskers.*) Ugh! I *am* a mouse. (*He bursts into tears.*)

BOY: The witches did it.

BRUNO: I don't want to be a mouse! (*He cries more.*)

BOY: Don't be silly, Bruno. There are worse things than being a mouse. You can live in a hole.

BRUNO: I don't want to live in a hole.

BOY: And you can creep into the larder at night and nibble through all the packets of biscuits and cornflakes and stuff. You can stuff yourself silly.

BRUNO: (*Perking up.*) Well, that's a thought. But how can I open the fridge door to get at the cold chicken and leftovers? I do that every evening at home.

BOY: Maybe your rich father will get you a special little mouse-fridge all to yourself. One you can open.

BRUNO: (*Sudden thought.*) My father. What's he going to say? And my Ma. She hates mice.

BOY: I remember.

BRUNO: (*Wailing.*) What are we going to do?

BOY: We'll go and see my grandmother. She'll understand. She knows all about witches.

BRUNO: What's all this about witches? Which witches?

BOY: The witches who turned us into mice. The Grand High Witch gave you the chocolate, remember?

BRUNO: What, her? The miserable old bat.

BOY: Yes, well. Follow me to Grandmother's room. Down the corridor, run like mad.

BRUNO: B . . . b . . . but . . .

BOY: No talking. And don't let anyone see you. Don't forget that anyone who catches you will try to kill you!

BRUNO: *(Terrified.)* Ooooh!

BOY: Come on.

(Music as they scuttle in downstage Light which holds them as the scene changes behind them.

They skirt imaginary walls, occasionally stopping to check the coast is clear. They are frightened by a door slamming, echoing footsteps, and a loud cat miaow.

Then the Lighting comes up on two giant carpeted steps.

Music continues to play as the mice arrive at the steps and consider how to climb them.

First BRUNO helps BOY onto the first step. Then BOY tries to heave up the un-athletic BRUNO. Several false starts, then BOY pulls BRUNO's tail and he finally makes it.

As BOY contemplates the second step, BRUNO notices a giant-scale sweet wrapped in brightly colored paper on the first step. Excited by the thought of food he shows it to BOY. BOY mimes to him to put it down. He does so, and helps BOY up to the second step.

BOY now tries to hoist BRUNO up. Several false starts. BOY ties their tails together to help bring BRUNO up. Eventually BRUNO arrives safely.

BOY exits as though round the corner.

BRUNO goes to follow but can't resist looking down at the sweet and makes his mind up to have it. He carefully goes back down to the first step and grabs the sweet. But now he realizes he has to scale the second step again—single-handed. He throws the sweet to the second step, then tries to haul himself up. Several false starts. He even slips and hangs perilously from the edge. Eventually he manages to get half-way up. He then pulls his own tail to finally succeed in reaching the second step.

He picks up the sweet and exits as the Lights fade.

The scene changes to GRANDMOTHER's hotel bedroom. This is on a "first floor" level above the stage area. There is a bed against the wall, and a dressing table [on which the puppet mice can later act] by the door. The room opens onto a small balcony.

The Lights come up on GRANDMOTHER who is sitting knitting a large sock with three needles.

A female scream from outside her door makes her jump. She puts down her knitting, goes to the door and opens it.)

GRANDMOTHER: What on earth is going on out here?

MAID: *(Off.)* Beg your pardon, madam. I thought I saw a mouse. Aaaaah!

(Her footsteps are heard as she runs away.)

BOY'S VOICE: *(Off.)* Grandmamma! It's me, Boy! Down here. *(Grandmother looks down to the floor outside the door and gasps.)* The witch got me.

GRANDMOTHER: The witch?

(GRANDMOTHER picks up the puppet BOY-MOUSE and brings him into the room. She is shocked and near tears.)

BOY'S VOICE: Don't cry, Grandmamma. Things could be a lot worse. I'm still alive. So's Bruno. The witch got him too. He's in the corridor.

(GRANDMOTHER *bends down outside the door, to pick up* BRUNO-MOUSE. *She enters the room and "puts" both mice on the dressing-table, then sits stunned.*
Note: In the original production the puppet mice were "built into" the dressing-table. Grandmother picked up another Boy-Mouse from outside the door, but, when apparently picking up Bruno-Mouse, left Boy-Mouse outside, and mimed, with her back to the audience, carrying in the two mice. Her body, in front of the dressing-table, masked the arrival of the two puppet mice, who entered from behind the dressing-table mirror.
Suddenly BRUNO *sees a bowl of fruit.*)

BRUNO'S VOICE: Mm. Bananas. I like bananas. Can you peel one for me, please? (*Grandmother, almost in a trance, gets up and peels one.*) Mm! (*He makes eating noises. Pause as Grandmother sits.*)

BOY'S VOICE: Say something, Grandmamma.

GRANDMOTHER: Oh, my darling Boy, my poor sweet darling. What has she done to you?

BOY'S VOICE: It's all right, Grandmamma, really. I'm getting used to it. It's quite fun when you get the hang of it.

GRANDMOTHER: Where did it happen? Where is the witch now? Is she in the hotel?

BOY'S VOICE: Room four-five-four. She's the Grand High Witch of all the World.

GRANDMOTHER: The Grand High Witch, here?

BOY'S VOICE: Yes. And there are masses of other witches in the hotel, too.

GRANDMOTHER: You don't mean they've having their Annual General Meeting here?

BOY'S VOICE: They've had it, Grandmamma. I was there! Hiding. They call themselves the Royal Society for the Prevention of Cruelty to Children.

GRANDMOTHER: Huh! Typical! And how did they catch you, my darling?

BOY'S VOICE: They sniffed me out.

GRANDMOTHER: Mm. Dogs' droppings, was it?

BOY'S VOICE: Yes. And then the Grand High Witch demonstrated her new magic formula. It turns children into mice.

GRANDMOTHER: I can see that, my darling, only too well.

BOY'S VOICE: But Grandmamma, they plan to turn all the children of England into mice.

GRANDMOTHER: The vicious creatures. That's English witches for you.

BOY'S VOICE: We've got to stop them!

GRANDMOTHER: Impossible. Witches are unstoppable. They've got you. Now they'll get the others.

(*Short pause.*)

BRUNO'S VOICE: Can you peel me another banana please?

GRANDMOTHER: *(Peeling one.)* Doesn't he ever stop eating?

BOY'S VOICE: No. *(Suddenly.)* And that's another thing Grandmamma, Bruno's parents. They don't know he's a mouse.

GRANDMOTHER: I can deal with that. But stopping the witches' grand plan is another kettle of fish.

(Suddenly a voice is heard from below. GRANDMOTHER and BOY react.)

GRAND HIGH WITCH'S VOICE:
> Down with children! Do them in!
> Boil their bones and fry their skin!

(She cackles, then chants the rest, her voice getting softer. During the second half of the following chant, BOY and GRANDMOTHER continue their conversation.)
> Bish them, sqvish them, bash them, mash them!
> Brrreak them, shake them, slash them, smash them!

BOY'S VOICE: It's her, Grandmamma, it's her!

GRANDMOTHER: The Grand High Witch?

(She goes out onto her balcony and looks down, then returns.)

(Furious) Would you believe it? The evil woman is in the room below mine!
(We hear a muffled cackle from the GRAND HIGH WITCH.)

It's a disgrace.

BOY'S VOICE: *(After a pause.)* Grandmamma. If she's down there, so is her magic formula.

GRANDMOTHER: Well?

BOY'S VOICE: *(Working out his plan.)* If I could only steal one tiny bottle. Five hundred doses! Works on grown-ups as well as children, she said. So who's to say it wouldn't work on *witches*. Don't you see?

GRANDMOTHER: *(Slowly.)* I do! I do see.

BOY'S VOICE: Witches who are meeting for dinner at eight o'clock tonight!

GRANDMOTHER: Then there's no time to waste. My brilliant, darling, daring Boy.

BOY'S VOICE: Mouse.

GRANDMOTHER: Boy-Mouse, then. *(Declaiming.)* For the salvation of the children of England. Action!

(Exciting music as GRANDMOTHER swings into action. Meanwhile BRUNO continues attacking the fruit bowl. GRANDMOTHER, having had an idea, takes her knitting and places the puppet mouse inside. She has knitted, with three needles, enough for a suitable carrier. She goes out onto the balcony and gently starts to lower the knitting by unravelling the ball of wool. Slowly 'BOY' descends until the knitting disappears from view.)

(She calls.) Out you get! Hurry up!

(Suddenly the sound of the room below's balcony door opening is heard.)

GRAND HIGH WITCH'S VOICE: Vot is this knitting-vool hanging down here?

GRANDMOTHER: *(Innocently.)* Oh, hallo. I just dropped it over the balcony by mistake. So sorry. I've still got hold of one end, so it's all right.

(She starts to pull up the wool.)

GRAND HIGH WITCH'S VOICE: Who vur you talking to just now? Who vur you telling to get out and hurry up?

GRANDMOTHER: *(Retrieving her knitting, now empty.)* My little grandson. He's er . . . been in the bath for ages, reading his book, the little darling. It's time he got out. Do you have any children, my dear?

GRAND HIGH WITCH'S VOICE: Certainly not!

(The sound of the balcony door slamming shut.
GRANDMOTHER *looks concerned.)*

GRANDMOTHER: *(Fervently.)* Good fortune be with you, my darling Boy-Mouse.

(The Lights fade.
In downstage light, BOY-MOUSE *[the actor in mouse-costume] enters, treading gingerly.*
He freezes when suddenly the GRAND HIGH WITCH, *idly chanting, is heard, booming overhead.)*

GRAND HIGH WITCH'S VOICE:

> Down vith children! Do them in!
> Boil their bones and fry their skin!
> Bish them, sqvish them, bash them, mash them!
> Brrreak them, shake them, slash them, smash them!

(In the lull that follows, the BOY-MOUSE *scuttles across, but jumps as he hears a manic cackle from the* GRAND HIGH WITCH.
He exits at speed.
The Lights come up on the giant-scale underneath the GRAND HIGH WITCH'S *bed. This is the space between the mattress and the floor. At the back a bedspread hangs down to the floor.*
BOY-MOUSE *carefully enters under the bedspread, as though to hide. He almost backs his way in.*
The GRAND HIGH WITCH *happily hums a version of her chant. It echoes in sinister fashion. Suddenly, from behind a bedpost jumps a creature. It grabs* BOY-MOUSE, *but not roughly. Nevertheless,* BOY-MOUSE *jumps.)*

BOY-MOUSE: Aaah! *(The creature is a frog. He springs away, trembling.)*
   Hallo. *(He advances. The Frog backs away.)* Hey, Frog, I won't hurt you. *(He stretches out a paw. The Frog huddles up, enjoying the company.)* What are you doing here? Did the Grand High Witch magic you too? *(The Frog nods.)* You were once a child? *(The Frog nods.)* Have you never tried to escape?! *(The Frog shakes its head, fearful.)* You're frightened of her? *(The Frog nods.)* So am I. Listen, Frog, do you know where she keeps her magic formula bottles?

(After a thinking pause the Frog points.
BOY *reaches up and manages to pull down a blue bottle half his size from the bedsprings.*

Note: In the original production, for practical reasons, the bottle was on the floor, in the gloom, to one side. Other bottles were painted on the flown-in flat.)

Thanks, Frog.

(He starts to walk and inadvertently drops the bottle.) Aaah!

GRAND HIGH WITCH'S VOICE: Vot vas that? I heard a noise. *(Musical sting as suddenly a corner of the bedspread lifts and the huge, upside down face of the* GRAND HIGH WITCH *is seen peering under the bed.) (*BOY-MOUSE *manages to drag the bottle into the gloom. The* FROG *is still visible.)* Vas that you, little frrroggy? Making a noise? Are you being good? Guarding my magic bottles? Are you being a good votch-frrrog? *(She cackles.)* Soon I vill be giving my bottles away and you need guard them no longer. *(The* FROG *looks chirpier.)* Then I vill thrrrow you out of the window and the seagulls can have you for suppertime snacks! *(She cackles. The* FROG *trembles. A knock at the bedroom door is heard.)* Aha. The ancient vuns come for their bottles. *(She calls.)* I come. *(Her face goes. The bedspread drops.* BOY, *with the bottle, starts to advance downstage, as though emerging from under the bed. He looks back at the trembling* FROG.) Come on, Frog!

(To music they both escape downstage as the underbed lighting fades, walking on the spot if necessary. In the downstage area lighting covers the escape. After a circuit or two of scuttles and hops, they stop.)

BOY: Off you go, Frog. You're free!

*(*BOY *waves farewell to* FROG. *They exit in different directions.*
The Lights fade. Into a pool of light steps the HEAD WAITER, *banging a gong.)*

HEAD WAITER: Ladies and gentlemen. Dinner is served.

(Music as the Lights come up on the hotel restaurant where a large table [for the WITCHES] *is set upstage centre. We imagine the kitchen is situated off to one side. On the other side is* GRANDMOTHER's *table. Other tables are visible, but do not obscure the* WITCHES' *table.*
HEAD WAITER *enters the scene.*
A WAITER *and a* WAITRESS *hover.* HEAD WAITER *checks all is ready.*
He then exits to deposit his dinner gong offstage.
A group of DINERS *enter.)*

(Note: In the original production, because not all the WITCHES *could be accommodated at the large table, three of them doubled as ordinary diners.)*

(The WAITER *approaches and leads them to a table. The* WAITRESS *begins to take their orders.*
GRANDMOTHER *enters.*
She holds, carefully, her large handbag in which are supposedly the two mice. She waits until the WAITER *approaches.)*

WAITER: Good-evening, madam.

GRANDMOTHER: Good-evening.

WAITER: Your table is this way.

GRANDMOTHER: Thank you.

(He leads her to her table, set with two chairs. She sits on one and carefully places her handbag on the other.

The WAITER *departs to lay plates on the* WITCHES' *table.*
The HEAD WAITER *enters and approaches* GRANDMOTHER *with his notepad and pencil.)*

HEAD WAITER: Good-evening, madam.

GRANDMOTHER: Good-evening.

HEAD WAITER: Where is the young gentleman tonight?

GRANDMOTHER: He's not feeling quite himself. He's staying in his room.

HEAD WAITER: I'm sorry to hear that. Now, this evening, to start with there is green pea soup, and for the main course you have a choice of either grilled fillet of sole or roast lamb.

GRANDMOTHER: Pea soup and lamb for me, please.

HEAD WAITER: Thank you, madam.

GRANDMOTHER: Thank you!

(The Head Waiter leaves, heading for the kitchen.
GRANDMOTHER *surreptitiously speaks into her handbag.)*

GRANDMOTHER: Ready, my darling? Have you got the bottle?

BOY'S VOICE: Yes. Grandmamma, what's the time?

GRANDMOTHER: *(Checking her watch.)* It's five minutes to eight. We're just in time. *(She carefully lowers the handbag to the floor, behind the table.)* Out you get. Stand by. Good luck! *(She brings the handbag up to the table.)*

BRUNO'S VOICE: *(In the handbag.)* I'm starving!

GRANDMOTHER: Quiet, Bruno. Have a bread roll.

(She takes a roll from a side-plate and pops it in the handbag.)

BRUNO'S VOICE: It's got no butter!

GRANDMOTHER: *(Loudly.)* Shut up!

(The WAITRESS *nearby hears and looks round, startled, at* GRANDMOTHER, *who smiles sweetly.*
The WAITRESS *starts to exit.*
GRANDMOTHER *checks the coast is clear, then looks down.)*

　　Go!

(The WAITRESS *freezes as the Lights change.*
A puppet BOY-MOUSE *with a formula bottle scuttles all the way across the stage and exits.*
The Lights change back. The WAITRESS *continues her exit.*
The HEAD WAITER *enters with a bowl. He goes to* GRANDMOTHER.)*

HEAD WAITER: Your green pea soup, madam.

GRANDMOTHER: Thank you. It smells most appetising.

(Eight o'clock chimes, followed by music.
The WITCHES *enter, led by the* GRAND HIGH WITCH *wearing her face mask. They behave very obsequiously.)*

HEAD WAITER: Good-evening, ladies.

GRAND HIGH WITCH: Good-evening.

HEAD WAITER: Your table is this way.

(The HEAD WAITER and the WAITER help them into their chairs. GRANDMOTHER watches. When all are settled the HEAD WAITER speaks.)

Tonight, ladies, there is green pea soup to start with, and for the main course you have a choice of either grilled fillet of sole or roast lamb.

(His words are almost drowned by the rising music. The Lights snap down. Loud kitchen noises as, on the side of the stage opposite GRANDMOTHER's table, a small kitchen set appears. It is pushed on by the HEAD CHEF and the SECOND CHEF. It consists of a dresser with a work-top, pans and kitchen utensils and a counter with an electric hob and saucepans.

The Lights snap up as the two CHEFS burst into activity. The HEAD CHEF stirs the soup and the SECOND CHEF bangs a slice of meat with a rolling pin. Suddenly they freeze, as the focus changes to the top of the dresser.

Music as a puppet BOY-MOUSE appears holding the formula bottle. He negotiates a pot or two. Hiding behind a pot, he peeps round and backs away again.

The Lights come back on the CHEFS. They unfreeze and start stirring and banging again.

The WAITER hurries in.)

WAITER: *(Shouting.)* Two lamb for table four!

HEAD CHEF: Two lamb for table four!

SECOND CHEF: Two lamb for table four!

(Working as a double act, they slap two plates on the counter.)

HEAD CHEF: ⎫
SECOND CHEF: ⎬ *(together)*   Meat!

(They slap a slice on each plate.)

SECOND CHEF: ⎫
HEAD CHEF: ⎬ *(Together, proudly.)*   Meat!

SECOND CHEF: Peas!

HEAD CHEF: Peas!

(They plop a handful of peas on each plate.)

SECOND CHEF: ⎫
HEAD CHEF: ⎬ *(Together, proudly.)*   Peas!

HEAD CHEF: Carrots!

SECOND CHEF: Carrots!

(They chuck a handful of carrots on each plate.)

SECOND CHEF: ⎫
HEAD CHEF: ⎬ *(Together, proudly.)*   Carrots!

SECOND CHEF: Gravy!

HEAD CHEF: Gravy!

(He tips a gravy boat. It is empty.)

No gravy!

SECOND CHEF: No gravy!

HEAD CHEF: *(Idea.)* Do-it-yourself gravy!

SECOND CHEF: Do-it-yourself gravy!

(Each takes a plate and spits on it. Then they plump up the food with their fingers.)

SECOND CHEF: ⎫
HEAD CHEF: ⎭ *(Together, proudly.)*   Two lamb for table four!

SECOND CHEF: ⎫
HEAD CHEF: ⎭ *(Together to the waiter, shouting.)* Two lamb for table four!!

WAITER: *(Taking the plates.)* Two lamb for table four! *(He exits, nearly bumping into the* HEAD WAITER *as he enters.)*

HEAD WAITER: *(Shouting.)* Everyone in the big RSPCC party wants the soup! *(He exits.)*

HEAD CHEF: Soup for the big party!

SECOND CHEF: Soup for the big party!

HEAD CHEF: In the silver soup-tureen!

SECOND CHEF: In the silver soup-tureen!

(They find it under the counter and place it on the work-top right under where the BOY-MOUSE *is hiding.*

As they return to their counter, suddenly the action freezes. The Lights focus on the puppet BOY-MOUSE. *Music as he pushes through the pans on a shelf and pours green liquid from the bottle down into the soup-tureen. The puppet* BOY-MOUSE *retreats.*

The action unfreezes.)

HEAD CHEF: Pour in the soup!

SECOND CHEF: Pour in the soup!

(They take the saucepan and pour soup into the tureen. The soup can be imaginary if the pouring is masked by the saucepan.)

HEAD CHEF: ⎫   ⎰Soup for the big party! *(They shout.)*
SECOND CHEF: ⎭ *(Together.)* ⎱Soup for the big party!

(The HEAD WAITER *enters with a trolley.*

The HEAD CHEF *and the* SECOND CHEF *place the soup-tureen on the trolley.)*

HEAD WAITER: *(As he goes.)* Soup for the big party!

*(*HEAD WAITER *exits pushing the trolley.*

Suddenly an enamel plate or somesuch falls off the top of the dresser, hitting the SECOND CHEF *and revealing the* BOY-MOUSE, *who has inadvertently dislodged it.)*

SECOND CHEF: What was that? *(He looks round and up.)* Hey, look! A mouse! A mouse!

HEAD CHEF: Where, where?

SECOND CHEF: There, there! *(Exciting chase music as the* CHEFS *grab a rolling pin and ladle and try to wallop the* BOY-MOUSE, *who quickly hides behind the pot.)* He's hiding! He's hiding!

HEAD CHEF: There he goes! *(They follow the imaginary progress of the mouse down the side of the dresser, across to behind the counter. Slapstick fun as the* CHEFS *try to whack the mouse but only succeed in whacking each other and bumping into each other.)* Take that!

SECOND CHEF: Ow! Take that!

HEAD CHEF: Ow!

(Suddenly the SECOND CHEF *freezes in horror.)*

SECOND CHEF: Eeeeee!

HEAD CHEF: What is it?

SECOND CHEF: Jeepers creepers! It's gone up my trouser leg! Ah! Ah! Oo! Oo! *(He comes out from behind the counter, jumping up and down, slapping his trouser leg.)* Holy smoke! It's going all the way up! Ah! Oo! Help! *(Now he is jumping up and down as though he is standing on hot bricks.)* Help! Help! *(He stops suddenly.)* It's in my knickers! There's a mouse running around in my flaming knickers! Aaaaah!

HEAD CHEF: Quick! Get 'em off! *(He attacks the* SECOND CHEF, *trying to get his trousers off. The* SECOND CHEF *resists.)*

SECOND CHEF: Stop it! Stop it! You're tickling! *(He giggles hysterically.)*

HEAD CHEF: Off! Off!

(Suddenly the SECOND CHEF's *trousers drop revealing funny underwear.*
Black-out.
Music as the scene clears. The Lights come up on the restaurant as we left it with GRANDMOTHER *at her table and the* WITCHES *awaiting their soup.*
The WAITRESS *enters with rolls for the other diners.)*

BRUNO'S VOICE: Can I have another roll please?

GRANDMOTHER: *(Loudly.)* Quiet, Bruno!

(The WAITRESS *hears and looks, startled, at* GRANDMOTHER *who smiles sweetly.*
The WAITRESS *exits.*
GRANDMOTHER *puts another roll in her handbag.*
The HEAD WAITER *approaches* GRANDMOTHER, *sees her apparently taking the roll, but discreetly ignores it.)*

HEAD WAITER: Have you finished your green pea soup, madam?

GRANDMOTHER: Thank you, it was delicious.

HEAD WAITER: Thank *you*, madam. I'm glad you enjoyed it.

(He starts to exit towards the kitchen, then freezes as the Lights change.
Suddenly the puppet BOY-MOUSE, *without the formula bottle, scuttles from the kitchen side across the stage towards* GRANDMOTHER's *table, apparently arriving behind it.*

The Lights change back. The HEAD WAITER *unfreezes and exits.)*

BOY'S VOICE: Grandmamma, I'm back! Mission accomplished!

GRANDMOTHER: *("Picking him up" and hiding him behind a menu, then revealing him to the audience.)* Well *done,* my darling. Well done, you.

BOY'S VOICE: Have the witches arrived, Grandmamma?

GRANDMOTHER: They're over there, my darling. Look!

(She positions the menu to give BOY-MOUSE *a view.*
Music as the HEAD WAITER, WAITER *and* WAITRESS *enter pushing the soup-tureen on its trolley.)*

HEAD WAITER: Ladies, your green pea soup.

(They arrive at the WITCHES' *table and start to serve it as the focus returns to* GRANDMOTHER's *table.)*

BOY'S VOICE: They're going to drink it, Grandmamma, they're going to drink it!

(The BOY-MOUSE *bobs up and down.)*

GRANDMOTHER: Shhh! Keep still. And cross your fingers.

BOY'S VOICE: I haven't got any fingers to cross.

GRANDMOTHER: Sorry. *(She smiles.)*

*(*MR. *and* MRS. JENKINS *enter, scanning the restaurant. They see* GRANDMOTHER *and head towards her.)*

BOY'S VOICE: Look out, Grandmamma. It's Bruno's parents.

*(*GRANDMOTHER *rearranges the menu to hide the puppet* BOY-MOUSE. *Meanwhile the* WITCHES *start drinking their soup. The* HEAD WAITER, WAITER *and* WAITRESS *hover.)*

MR. JENKINS: Where's that grandson of yours?

MRS. JENKINS: We reckon he's up to something with our . . .

MR. JENKINS: ⎫ *(Together.)* ⎰Bruno.
MRS. JENKINS: ⎭   ⎱

MRS. JENKINS: Some devilment.

MR. JENKINS: The little beggar's not turned up for his supper. Most unlike him.

MRS. JENKINS: Most unlike him.

GRANDMOTHER: I agree. He has a very healthy appetite.

MRS. JENKINS: How do you know? Have you seen him? Where is he?

GRANDMOTHER: I'm afraid I have some rather alarming news for you. He's in my handbag.

(She takes hold of it. MR. *and* MRS. JENKINS *can't believe their ears.)*

MR. JENKINS: What the heck d'you mean he's in your handbag?

MRS. JENKINS: Are you trying to be funny?

GRANDMOTHER: There's nothing funny about it. Your son has been rather drastically altered.

MR. JENKINS: } (*Together.*) {Altered?
MRS. JENKINS: }

MR. JENKINS: What the devil do you mean?

GRANDMOTHER: My own grandson actually saw them doing it to him.

MR. JENKINS: Saw *who* doing *what* to him, for heaven's sake?

GRANDMOTHER: Saw the witches turning him into a mouse.

(*The* JENKINS' *mouths gape.*)

MRS. JENKINS: Call the manager, dear. Have this mad woman thrown out of the hotel.

GRANDMOTHER: (*Calmly.*) Bruno is a mouse.

MR. JENKINS: He most certainly is not a mouse!

(*Suddenly* BRUNO-MOUSE *pops his head out of the handbag.*)

BRUNO'S VOICE: Oh yes I am! Hallo Pa, hallo Ma!

(MRS. JENKINS *nearly screams. She and* MR. JENKINS *back off nervously, horrified.*)

MR. JENKINS: B-b-b-b . . .

BRUNO'S VOICE: Don't worry, Pa. It's not as bad as all that. Just so long as the cat doesn't get me.

MR. JENKINS: But I can't have a mouse for a son!

GRANDMOTHER: You've got one. Be nice to him.

MRS. JENKINS: (*Approaching with difficulty.*) My poor baby! Who did this?

(MRS. JENKINS *picks up* BRUNO *in the handbag, trying to hide her distaste.*)

GRANDMOTHER: That woman over there. (*She points to the* GRAND HIGH WITCH.) Black dress. Finishing her soup.

MR. JENKINS: She's RSPCC. The chairwoman.

GRANDMOTHER: No. She's the Grand High Witch of all the World.

MRS. JENKINS: You mean *she* did it? That skinny woman over there?

MR. JENKINS: What a nerve. I'll make her pay through the nose. I'll have my lawyers on to her for this. (*He turns towards the* GRAND HIGH WITCH.)

GRANDMOTHER: I wouldn't do anything rash. That woman has magic powers. She might turn *you* into something. A cockroach, perhaps.

MR. JENKINS: Turn *me* into a cockroach? I'd like to see her try!

(*He sets off again. But he is stopped in his tracks by a very loud alarm bell. The lighting focuses on the* WITCHES' *table. It should create an eerie atmosphere. It is suggested that all the following action is performed in slow motion against a background of distorted clock and bell sounds.*
The GRAND HIGH WITCH *leaps in the air, onto her chair, then onto the table. She clutches her throat, aware that she has been poisoned. Smoke begins to swirl around*

the WITCHES' *table.* WITCH ONE *and other* WITCHES *start to leap up on the table too, others simply stand. All writhe about waving their arms. The other* DINERS, *the* HEAD WAITER, WAITRESS *and* WAITER, *as well as* GRANDMOTHER *and* MR. *and* MRS. JENKINS *watch the* WITCHES' *behavior in awed amazement. The* GRAND HIGH WITCH *climbs down from the table. She realizes the soup is responsible for her behavior and approaches the tureen in fury. The* HEAD WAITER, *terrified, pushes the tureen trolley toward her in self-defense. The* GRAND HIGH WITCH *avoids the trolley, which collides into* MR. JENKINS. *As the other* WITCHES *start to "shrink," still writhing helplessly, the* GRAND HIGH WITCH *advances downstage. She removes her wig and face mask, revealing her horrid face to the audience, then turns upstage. The other* DINERS, *the* HEAD WAITER, WAITRESS, WAITER, GRANDMOTHER, MR. *and* MRS. JENKINS *react in horror. The* HEAD WAITER *and* MR. JENKINS *advance towards the* GRAND HIGH WITCH, *who evades them, but finds her only escape route is over the trolley. She climbs up on it. The* HEAD WAITER *and* MR. JENKINS *try to reach her, forcing her to step into the tureen.*

Everyone watches as, screaming in a nightmarish echo, the GRAND HIGH WITCH *descends into the tureen and disappears, a desperate hand being the last part of her to go. If a tureen trolley is not possible, the* GRAND HIGH WITCH *could disappear with the other* WITCHES, *but to give her a more horrible end than the others is satisfying to the audience.*

Amazed, the others look on as the HEAD WAITER *picks up the wig and face mask that the* GRAND HIGH WITCH *has dropped, and shows them around.* MR. JENKINS *looks into the tureen and a mouse, covered in green pea soup, slowly appears from the tureen, looking at him and quivering with rage.*

As MR. JENKINS *and the* HEAD WAITER *clear the trolley away, we become aware that all the other* WITCHES *have vanished.*

Then puppet mice appear from behind the table and, if possible, in other places. The WITCHES *have all been turned to mice. As the music rises and the Lights fade,* GRANDMOTHER *holds up the* BOY-MOUSE *puppet in triumph and* MRS. JENKINS *shows* BRUNO-MOUSE *the successful conclusion of the* BOY-MOUSE's *plan.*

After a fade to Black-out, a pool of light reveals GRANDMOTHER *holding the puppet* BOY-MOUSE.*)*

GRANDMOTHER: The Boy-Mouse had saved the children of England. I took him home to Norway where I could best take care of him.

(The Lights come up on GRANDMOTHER's *parlor in Norway. There is now a small ladder stretching from the floor to the tabletop.*

GRANDMOTHER *crosses to her parlor and places the puppet* BOY-MOUSE *on the table, while picking up her embroidery. She sits in her chair.*

If the puppet cannot be operated from under the table, GRANDMOTHER *could simply sit with the puppet* BOY-MOUSE *in her arms.*

The clocks ticks.)

BOY'S VOICE: Grandmamma, has the Grand High Witch really gone forever?

GRANDMOTHER: Yes, my darling. But Grand High Witches are like queen bees. There's always another one to take over. Let's hope there are always people like you brave enough to foil their wicked plans.

BOY'S VOICE: Even if they end up as mice?

GRANDMOTHER: Even if they end up as mice.

(Pause.)

BOY'S VOICE: Can I ask you something, Grandmamma?

GRANDMOTHER: Anything.

BOY'S VOICE: How long does a mouse live?

GRANDMOTHER: Not very long, I'm afraid. Just a few years.

(Pause.)

BOY'S VOICE: And how much longer will you live, Grandmamma?

GRANDMOTHER: Just a few years.

BOY'S VOICE: Good. I'll be a very old mouse and you'll be a very old grand-mother and we'll both die together.

GRANDMOTHER: That would be perfect. *(Pause.)* My darling, are you sure you don't mind being a mouse for the rest of your life?

BOY'S VOICE: I don't mind at all. It doesn't matter who you are or what you look like so long as somebody loves you.

(GRANDMOTHER's *hand and the puppet* BOY-MOUSE's *paw meet. They remain silent and happy together as the music rises and the Lights fade.)*

CURTAIN

MISSISSIPPI PINOCCHIO

book by
Mary Hall Surface

lyrics by
David Maddox and
Mary Hall Surface

music by
David Maddox

MISSISSIPPI PINOCCHIO

ACTOR–CHARACTER LIST*

Man One ....Pinocchio
Woman One...Gepetta
Woman Two ....Townsperson with package/Puppet/
     Speranza (Nurse, Lawyer, Old Woman)/School Teacher
Woman Three ....Cat/Nose/Jury/Pupil 2
Man Two.......................................Fox/Nose/Pole Cat/Jury/Pupil 3
Man Three..................Boatman/Fire-eater/Tree with Night-Birds/
     Dr. Duck/Woodpecker/Pole Cat/Ape Judge/
     Pupil/Dog/Circus Crowd
Man Four ....Lampwick/Puppet/Tree with Night-Birds/
     Dr. Opossum/Woodpecker/Pole Cat/
     Jury/Circus Crowd
Man Five ....Cop/Dime-store Owner/Puppet 1/
     Tree with Night-Birds/Dr. Boll Weevil/Woodpecker/
     Sharecropper/Pupil 1/Ring Master
Woman Four ....Food-Seller/Cricket/Puppet 2/Bird/Jury/
     Pupil 4/Woman in Circus Crowd

The Adventures of Pinocchio *was written by Carlo Collodi as a serial in a children's magazine in Tuscany in 1881. It was wildly popular, but Collodi ended the series after only fifteen episodes with the mischievous puppet left for dead hanging from an oak tree. There was such an outcry from his adoring readers that to continue the series he had to invent the Blue Fairy to bring the puppet back to life. He continued for over twenty more installments, which were together published as a book in 1883. Published in English in 1889, it was equally popular in turn-of-the-century America.*

    A fierce supporter of Italy's new democracy, Collodi believed that the good of the whole is built upon the goodness and right actions of its parts. Pinocchio's journey is, in many ways, a metaphor of what is required of a person to become a good member of the community. Because no community fascinates us more than the American South, our Pinocchio is carved by an Italian immigrant, Gepetta, who arrives in the Mississippi river town of Natchez circa 1910 dreaming of the good life in America. With her comes her guardian angel, Speranza (which means hope in Italian). In Mississippi Pinocchio, *our rogue-hero, the bad good boy, must grow to understand how freedom and opportunity are leavened by compassion and responsibility as he chooses how to live in a world of wild adventures and harsh realities. America, founded on the hope of liberty and equality, is on that same journey from self-absorbed, willfully wooden-headed child to compassionate, responsible and community-minded adult.*

Licensing allows for producers to cast more than nine actors.

Our play's music is in the style of Dixieland and is written for piano, trombone, clarinet/flute double, banjo/guitar double and bass. It is available either as a full score or as a recording (piano only).

—Mary Hall Surface and David Maddox

MISSISSIPPI PINOCCHIO

CHARACTERS

Gepetta: A recently-arrived immigrant from Italy
Boatman: On the steamboat that brings Gepetta to Natchez
Fox: A swindler
Cat: A fancy lady, but a schemer
Food-seller: A poor merchant on the riverfront
Lampwick: The baddest boy in Natchez
Cop: Keeps order in Natchez
Speranza: Gepetta's angel of hope
Pinocchio: Willful little puppet who longs to be real
Cricket: A short-lived advisor to Pinocchio
Dime-Store Owner: Pragmatic businessman on the riverfront
Fire-eater: Empresario of a traveling puppet show
Puppets: Mr. Fire-eater's performers
Dr. Duck: The "quack" doctor who treats Pinocchio
Dr. Opossum: A colleague of Dr. Duck's
Dr. Boll Weevil: A colleague of Dr. Duck's
Sharecropper: Imprisons Pinocchio
Pole Cats: Attempt to lure Pinocchio into mischief
Ape Judge and Jury: Preside over Pinocchio's trial
Schoolteacher: Presides over the classroom
Pupils: Pinocchio's classmates
Police Dog: Pursues and then befriends Pinocchio
Ring Master: Presides over the circus
Woman from the Crowd: Buys the donkey Pinocchio
Actors also used to create the nose transformation, woodpeckers, a bird,
night-bird trees, the river, the catfish and its interior

NOTE

In the acting edition of this script, the cue numbers (i.e. **QA20**) correspond to the cue numbers on the recorded version (piano only) of the score that is available to rent should a producer not be able to use a live band.

These same cue numbers are also listed in the Full Score, which contains all music, text and stage directions. The Vocal Score and Piano-Vocal Score also contain cue numbers and full text.

The placement of the cue number indicates the beginning of the cue. The # sign indicates where the music ends. See the example below:

GEPETTA: Did I make him ears?

QA20

PINOCCHIO:

> *Now that I'm free*
> *And on my own*
> *There's a long list of things*
> *That I'm gonna do*

(PINOCCHIO *runs from* GEPETTA.)

CHORUS:

> *Wide open scenery*
> *Nobody stand in front of me!*
> *No responsibility*
> *The land of the free!*

LAMPWICK: Ain't no puppet gonna out bad me!

#

LAMPWICK: *(cont'd.)* Hey, pine boy. Catch.

QA21

(QA25, cont'd.) indicates that the recorded cue continues to play.

QA7** indicates a track for rehearsal purposes only. In performance, the CD is not stopped at this point.

Note: The music cue numbers as explained here are included in the acting edition of the script.

OVERTURE (OPTIONAL)
OPENING

(Lights up on the bustling river town of Natchez, Mississippi. A big steamboat has just pulled into the dock. The CAT *(a fancy lady), the* FOX *(a swindler),* LAMPWICK *(a troublesome boy), the* BOATMAN, *a* COP, *and* FOOD-SELLER *all welcome the exciting arrival of the steamboat. Goods are unloaded, deals are struck. Riverfront commerce in action!)*

CHORUS:

> Tis a grand day
> America!
> It's my pay day!
> I'm telling ya
> That the band plays
> On America's main street!
> The Mississippi River
> My home!
>
> Living on the river
> I feel so free
> Nobody's going to separate
> My money and me
>
> Big boat big river
> Done sailed right down
> Get away sweat, get away toil
> And make some money in town
> America

*(*GEPETTA, *a poor Italian immigrant, arrives in the New World. She plops her bag down and everything stops.)*

GEPETTA:

> America
> Took a ship across the sea
> Said good-bye to Italy!
> Then a train that took forever
> To a steamboat on this river
> Till I float
> To where I've always dreamed to be

BOATMAN: Natchez, Mississippi!

*(*GEPETTA *gives a delighted shrug, as if to say, "Well, why not?" Town comes to life again.* GEPETTA *moves through the crowd.)*

CHORUS:

> Wide open scenery
> The land of opportunity!
> Nobody stand in front of me
> The land of the free!

GEPETTA:

> *The streets are paved with gold*
> *I'm at the gates of heaven*
> *I don't see any gold yet*
> *But the door to hope is open*
> *To dreams that I'll never stop hoping*
> *Will see me through*

BOATMAN:

> *Hard road*

CHORUS:

> *Gimme some money*

(GEPETTA *shows the* CAT *a letter.*)

FOX AND CAT:

> *Heavy load*

GEPETTA:

> *Oh it's hot and sunny*

(*The cat takes her letter, the fox hands her keys to her new room, lampwick takes her bundle.*)

CHORUS:

> *The steam heat's humming*
> *The water's all a shimmer!*
> *When the boat she lands in Natchez*
> *I'll make my fortune that's a fact!*
> *Tis a grand day*

GEPETTA: Speranza, wish me luck!

(GEPETTA *opens her carpet bag with her statues.*)

CHORUS:

> *I got my dreams to deliver*

GEPETTA:

> *In Italy, Gepetta had learned to carve*
> *beautiful figures of wood.*

CHORUS:

> *The steam heat's humming*

GEPETTA:

> *She sold them in the market of her*
> *village.*

CHORUS:

> *The water's all a shimmer!*

GEPETTA:

> *Gepetta knew the good people of Natchez*
> *would buy all the statues she had to*
> *sell.*

CHORUS:

> *When the boat she lands in Natchez*
> *I'll make my fortune that's a fact!*

GEPETTA:

> Soon she would live in a Southern
> palace on the river with tall white
> columns and a wide front porch!

(GEPETTA *has her carved Statue of Liberty to sell.*)

CHORUS:

> America!
> It's my pay day!
> America!
> The band plays
> On America's main street!
> The Mississippi River
> My home!

(GEPETTA *approaches the* FOOD-SELLER.)

CHORUS:

> I got my baggage in tow
> The motor's she's running

(*The* FOOD-SELLER *has no money to buy a Statue of Liberty.*)

GEPETTA: Gepetta thought everyone in America was rich.

CHORUS:

> That big ole wheel's a turning
> Up the river she'll be churning

(*But the* FRUIT-SELLER *tosses* GEPETTA *a piece of fruit.*)

GEPETTA:

> No more
> Days of hunger, of longing
> No more
> Summers without rain
> Winters without food
> I'm in America, Mississippi!

(GEPETTA *goes out into the town trying to sell her statues, but the townspeople do not buy.*)

CHORUS:

> Hard road
> Gimme some money

GEPETTA:

> Would you like to buy?

CHORUS:

> Heavy load
> Oh it's hot and sunny

GEPETTA: La Statua Liberta!

CHORUS:

> But when the boat she lands in Natchez

GEPETTA: I'll make my fortune that's a fact?

(GEPETTA *tries again and again, but the townspeople ignore her.*)

CHORUS:

> 'Tis a grand day
> America!
> It's my pay day!
> America!
> The band plays
> On America's main street!
> The Mississippi River
> My home!

(GEPETTA *becomes more weary and confused.*)

GEPETTA: Gepetta did not understand. Day after day, week upon week, no one would buy.

CHORUS:

> Living on the river
> I feel so free

GEPETTA: Few people would even speak to her.

CHORUS:

> Nobody's going to separate
> My money from me

GEPETTA: Soon she was as poor as she had ever been in Italy. Gepetta's hope for the good life in America grew dim. Hard road.

CHORUS:

> Gimme some money

GEPETTA:

> Heavy load

CHORUS:

> Oh it's hot and sunny

(LAMPWICK *sneaks up behind* GEPETTA *and steals the Statue of Liberty she is trying to sell.*)

GEPETTA: Auito! Thief! Stop! Stop him!

(*A melee erupts.*)

CHORUS:

> Gimme some money
> Gimme some money
> Gimme some money
> Gimme some money

(*Everyone is grabbing their goods, protecting what is theirs, ignoring* GEPETTA's *pleas for help. The* FOX *points out* LAMPWICK *to the* COP, *then steals the* COP's *wallet.* COP *chases* LAMPWICK *off. The* POLICE DOG *enters and chases her. All exit but* GEPETTA.)

SCENE ONE

(GEPETTA *is alone in the street.*)

GEPETTA:

> *These streets are paved with gold*
> *That's what I was told*
> *And that the door to hope stands open*
> *To dreams that I'll never stop hoping*

(SPERANZA *appears in the sunbeams.*)

GEPETTA:

> *Speranza, can you see me?*
> *My angel of hope*

SPERANZA:

> *Your angel of hope*

GEPETTA:

> *On your wings*
> *You carried me*

SPERANZA:

> *Dear Gepetta*

GEPETTA AND SPERANZA:

> *To America*

SPERANZA:

> *Your new home*

GEPETTA:

> *Hold me in your wings*

SPERANZA:

> *I'll sing you my song*

GEPETTA:

> *Angel of hope*
> *Light my way*

SPERANZA:

> *Light your way*

(*The policeman's billy club rolls into* GEPETTA's *sight.*)

GEPETTA: The stick of the town policeman. This I get in answer to my prayers?

(*When* GEPETTA *reaches for it, the billy club jumps out of her grasp.* SPERANZA *chuckles delightedly.*)

GEPETTA: Che cosa?

(*She stoops and picks it up, but the club jumps wildly in her hand.*)

GEPETTA: A piece of wood with a mind of its own? Come back here!

(*She grabs it, holding it still.*)

GEPETTA: I'll make you jump . . . for *me!*

(SPERANZA, *smiling, disappears as* GEPETTA *rushes to the small room where she lives.*

The actor PINOCCHIO *appears and sits with his back upstage. She begins to carve. With each line of the song, the actor animates his arms and legs as she carves.*)

GEPETTA:

> A perfect little American boy
> With one arm, then two
> I'll give you eyes that shine
> Here's one leg, I'm almost through
> There'll be
> No more
> Days of hunger, of longing
> No more
> Nights without dreams
> Weeks without hope
> How could anyone deny him
> I could live my life beside him

GEPETTA: He'll earn me money

My little American!

(*With a diving somersault, the actor* PINOCCHIO *moves from upstage of* GEPETTA *to sprawling next to her on the floor. He has perfect red circles on his cheeks.*)

GEPETTA: Naughty wooden eyes, why are you looking at me? Ah, you want a mouth to tell everyone to throw money to you!

(*As soon as she carves his mouth,* PINOCCHIO *starts to laugh.*)

GEPETTA: Stop laughing. (*He doesn't.*) I might as well speak to the wall. Stop, you piece of pine. Behave.

(PINOCCHIO *stops laughing, but sticks out his tongue.*
GEPETTA *sees, but pretends not to see, and begins to carve his feet.*
PINOCCHIO *snatches her scarf and puts it on his own neck.*)

GEPETTA: Rascal! Not finished and already you disobey me. Stand up!

(*The billy club becomes the stick from which* PINOCCHIO *is "strung."*)

GEPETTA:

> Piccolo pine seed. Pinocchio!

Do you like that name, puppet?

(GEPETTA *makes him nod his head.*)

GEPETTA: Mississippi Pinocchio! Now do what I say. Walk!

(PINOCCHIO *walks stiffly at first.* GEPETTA *operates him around the room. He gets good at it quickly.*)

GEPETTA: Turn. Dance. Very good! (*He dances as she sings.*)

> The streets are paved with gold
> That's what I came here hoping
> The door to hope stands open— Ahh!

(But PINOCCHIO *breaks free of his "strings" and runs out the door into the town.)*

GEPETTA: Bad puppet! Come back here!!!

SCENE TWO

*(*TOWN *returns.* PINOCCHIO *runs wildly through the town.* GEPETTA *pursues him.)*

CHORUS:

> *Tis a grand day*
> *America*
> *It's my pay day*
> *I'm tellin' ya*

PINOCCHIO:

> *Pinocchio*
> *What d'ya know?!*
> *I'm the king of the world*
> *The red carpet unfurls to me*

LAMPWICK: Hey, look at the puppet!

CHORUS:

> *Living on the river*
> *I feel so free*
> *Nobody's going to separate*
> *My money and me*

GEPETTA: Puppet! I'll pull your naughty ears! Did I make him ears?

PINOCCHIO:

> *Now that I'm free*
> *And on my own*
> *There's a long list of things*
> *That I'm gonna do*

*(*PINOCCHIO *runs from* GEPETTA.*)*

CHORUS:

> *Wide open scenery*
> *Nobody stand in front of me!*
> *No responsibility*
> *The land of the free!*

LAMPWICK: Ain't no puppet gonna out-bad me! Hey, pine boy. Catch.

*(*LAMPWICK *grabs a parcel from a* TOWNSPERSON *and tosses it to* PINOCCHIO *in a game of keep-away.* PINOCCHIO *really enjoys this.)*

GEPETTA: Pinocchio, no!

CHORUS:

> *'Tis a grand day*
> *America!*
> *It's my pay day!*
> *America!*
> *The band plays*
> *On America's main street!*
> *The Mississippi River*

(GEPETTA *intercepts the package, returns it.*)

GEPETTA: (*To* TOWNSPERSON.) Scusi!

CHORUS: My home!

LAMPWICK: Pretty good, pine boy!

PINOCCHIO: It's "Pinocchio!"

LAMPWICK: I'm Lampwick.

                    Wide open scenery

PINOCCHIO:

                    I know who I wanna be

LAMPWICK:

                    Nobody stand in front of me

PINOCCHIO:

                    No responsibilities

LAMPWICK:

                    You've worked it all out?

PINOCCHIO:

                    I've got a philosophy
                    It's summed up in three words
                    And that's me me me.

(LAMPWICK *sneaks up on the* FRUIT SELLER *and steals a piece of fruit. Then* PINOCCHIO *does the same.*)

CHORUS:

                    I got my dreams to deliver
                    The steam heat's humming
                    The water's all a shimmer!
                    When the boat she lands in Natchez
                    I'll make my fortune that's a fact!

(*Then* LAMPWICK *dares* PINOCCHIO *to steal the* CAT's *parasol.*)

CHORUS AND PINOCCHIO:

                    Tis a grand day
                    America!
                    It's my pay day!
                    America!
                    The band plays
                    On America's main street
                    The Mississ—

(PINOCCHIO *snatches the parasol, but the* CAT *snarls at him and the* FOX *leers.*)

CAT: Hiss!

(PINOCCHIO *scrambles to get away from them, just as* GEPETTA *crosses to grab him, both to catch and protect him.*)

GEPETTA: Come here, now!

(GEPETTA *begins to pull on* PINOCCHIO's *ear. He throws himself down in the street and has a screaming tantrum.*)

CHORUS:
> *I got my dreams to deliver*

PINOCCHIO:
> *Let me go!*

CHORUS:
> *The steam heat's humming*

LAMPWICK:
> *Momma's boy!*

CHORUS:
> *The water's all a shimmer!*

GEPETTA:
> *Basta. No crying!*

CHORUS:
> *When the boat she lands in Natchez*

(TOWNSPEOPLE *summon the* COP. LAMPWICK, *hiding, enjoys this.*)

TOWNSPERSON: That's the one!

LAMPWICK: Stole that lady's fruit!

FOX: Ought to know better!

BOATMAN: Urchin!

CAT: (*Referring to immigrants.*) Those people!

(*The* COP *grabs both* GEPETTA *and* PINOCCHIO *by the arm.*)

GEPETTA: Don't arrest him. He's just made.

COP: (*To* GEPETTA.) You're coming with me!

GEPETTA: Me?

(COP *slams handcuffs on* GEPETTA, *reprising the bump of her suitcase on her arrival. She is dragged off.*)

PINOCCHIO:
> *I've worked it all out*

CHORUS AND PINOCCHIO:
> *I've got a philosophy*
> *It's summed up in three words*

PINOCCHIO:
> *And that's me me me!*

(*The* TOWN *exits and* PINOCCHIO *races home.*)

SCENE THREE

(PINOCCHIO *bursts through the door into* GEPPETA's *room, laughing giddily, and locks it behind him.*)

PINOCCHIO: That was fun!! (*A discovery.*) I'm hungry!

CRICKET: Cri-cri-cri.

PINOCCHIO: Who's that?

CRICKET: Cri-cri-cri.

PINOCCHIO: Aw, just an ole cricket on the wall.

CRICKET:

> *I've lived in this room*
> *Nigh on to a hundred years*

PINOCCHIO: Well, it's my room now, Sis Cricket!

CRICKET:

> *I've got a great truth to tell*
> *Only for your ears*

PINOCCHIO: That so? Well, hurry up.

CRICKET:

> *I knew a boy*
> *Who left to see the world*
> *Down the river to the delta*
> *His head all in a whirl*
> *He didn't need no school*

PINOCCHIO: Nobody needs school!

CRICKET: He said: School is just for fools.

PINOCCHIO: I'm doing whatever I want whenever I want it.

CRICKET:

> *Year after year,*
> *Out on a spree*
> *And grew up to be a donkey*

PINOCCHIO: *(Insulted.)* Hey!

CRICKET: Hee-haw!

PINOCCHIO: *I'm* growing up to be king of everything!

CRICKET: Hee-haw!

PINOCCHIO: Let other boys sit in schools and work hard, I'll be—

CRICKET: In the hospital or in jail!

PINOCCHIO: You listen here, Sis Cricket. Take outta here and quick!

CRICKET: You think a wise ole cricket like me is gonna listen to a dumb ole woodenheaded puppet like you??

PINOCCHIO: Yeah!

(PINOCCHIO *picks up a book and smashes the* CRICKET.)

PINOCCHIO: There. Least books are good for something! Now I'm powerful hungry!

(*He looks toward the smashed* CRICKET, *but dismisses the idea of eating it.*)

PINOCCHIO: If that Gepetta lady was here, I wouldn't be dying of hunger.

(PINOCCHIO *sits down on the floor, stamps his feet and cries. He stops. No* GEPETTA. *So he gets up.*)

PINOCCHIO: I'll run me away! Tonight! Who cares! First stop, finding something to eat!

(PINOCCHIO *crosses into the dark town, created by the ensemble. It is night.*)

PINOCCHIO: Why're the houses all shut up tight, dark as death? Aren't even any dogs around. (*Calling up to a window.*) Hey somebody. Can't a puppet get him some bread??!

(DIME-STORE OWNER *pokes his head out of a window.*)

DIME-STORE OWNER: You out ringing doorbells of respectable people in the middle of the night?!

PINOCCHIO: How else am I gonna get me something to eat!

DIME-STORE OWNER: I'll give you something.

(DIME-STORE OWNER *pours a bucket of slop down on* PINOCCHIO.)

PINOCCHIO: Jiminy Criminy! A bucket of slop!

DIME-STORE OWNER: Now get!

(PINOCCHIO *runs home through the night, wet as a chicken. He enters* GEPETTA'*s room and sits by the fire.*)

PINOCCHIO: Least she's got a fire where I can warm my sopping lonely self!

PINOCCHIO:

> Pinocchio
> What do you know?!
> I'm, I'm . . . cold and hungry!!

(*He cries himself to sleep. But* PINOCCHIO'*s feet are too close to the fire. They begin to burn in the fire, until they burn off.*)

SCENE FOUR

(*The next morning,* GEPETTA *struggles to open her door, knocking.*)

GEPETTA: Pinocchio! Pinocchio!

PINOCCHIO: Gepetta!

(PINOCCHIO *tries to run to the door, but he falls flat.*)

PINOCCHIO: Ahh!

GEPETTA: Open the door!

PINOCCHIO: I can't!

GEPETTA: Let me in—!

(GEPETTA *breaks open the door.*)

GEPETTA: You burned off your feet!

PINOCCHIO: Poor me! Walking on my knees the rest of my life!

GEPETTA: Naughty puppet. How did you do that?

PINOCCHIO: I was hungry, then Sis Cricket called me names so I threw a book at her. She died, by accident! Then I asked for bread and got slop instead! Now look at my feet! (PINOCCHIO *cries loudly.*)

GEPETTA: Basta! Don't make a fuss. I can fix you.

PINOCCHIO: Do it now!

GEPETTA: You are lucky if I do it at all! Why should I make you new feet? So you can run away again?

PINOCCHIO: I won't!

GEPETTA: So you can make more trouble for "Gepetta, the Italian peddler," as if I don't have troubles enough.

PINOCCHIO: But—

GEPETTA: I made you!

GEPETTA: And look at the thanks I get. A night in jail!

PINOCCHIO:

I'll be good

GEPETTA: All boys promise to be good when they want something.

PINOCCHIO:

I'll get us a cat

GEPETTA: We can't feed a cat.

PINOCCHIO:

Every day I'll do the shopping

GEPETTA: If we had money for things like that. You'll find more mischief you'll break my heart.

PINOCCHIO:

I'll never do what I shouldn't do.

GEPETTA:

Well that's a start

PINOCCHIO: Fix 'em! Please??!

(*No words are spoken between them for a moment, then* GEPETTA *begins to carve new feet for him.*)

PINOCCHIO: I'll go to school. Soon as I get me a spelling book.

GEPETTA: You have money to buy one?

PINOCCHIO: No.

GEPETTA: Neither do I.

PINOCCHIO: None?

GEPETTA: Not a penny.

PINOCCHIO: Oh.

(*This lands on* PINOCCHIO. *He gets how poor they are.* GEPETTA *finishes his new feet.*)

GEPETTA: But you have feet.

(PINOCCHIO *leaps up, jumps around.*)

PINOCCHIO: Look at me! I'll run me up and down the river front all day—

GEPETTA: (*Scolding him.*) Ahh—!

PINOCCHIO: *After* school, Momma.

GEPETTA: Momma? Did you say "Momma"?

(She's starting to fall for him. He spins her around playfully.)

GEPETTA: *(To her unseen angel.)* Speranza, could a puppet share my dream? *(To* PINOCCHIO.*)* Pinocchio . . .

> *I'm looking for the good life*
> *A good life*
> *One in which I can do*
> *All the things I might*
>
> *Get up in the morning*
> *And work till the dark*
> *In the evening dream of days to come*
> *As my family gets its start*

PINOCCHIO & GEPETTA:

> *In America*

PINOCCHIO:

> *It'll be the good life*
> *All butter and bread*
> *Eat cake till I'm full*
> *And then get out of bed*

GEPETTA:

> *I can sell a small statue*
> *And afford a loaf of bread*
> *It's a good life I can give you*

PINOCCHIO:

> *Maybe I'll conquer the West instead*
> *And then gig me some frogs*
> *And wrestle a snapping turtle*

GEPETTA:

> *This land is so broad*
> *And smells sweet like Crepe Myrtle*

PINOCCHIO & GEPETTA:

> *It's a life like a dream*

PINOCCHIO:

> *Ride down the river in a paddleboat*
> *Money bubbles up like steam*

GEPETTA: Pinocchio!

PINOCCHIO:

> *And decorates my Mardi Gras float*

(She laughs, charmed, that he almost gets it right.)

GEPETTA:

> *I can earn what we need*

PINOCCHIO:

> *I can have what I want*

PINOCCHIO & GEPETTA:

> *We'll be Americans*
> *With the good life*
> *Under endless blue skies*

GEPETTA: Dreams can come true—

PINOCCHIO: I know!

GEPETTA: If you go to school—

PINOCCHIO: Piles of money!

GEPETTA: And work hard.

PINOCCHIO: We'll live in a big house on top of the hill and look down on the dock workers below.

GEPETTA: Pinocchio, we don't look down on anyone.

PINOCCHIO: And I'll fight off all the pirates and the sea monsters!

GEPETTA: *(Laughing.)* I suppose you'd save me from the belly of a whale if one gobbled me up?

PINOCCHIO: I would! Promise!

GEPETTA: Wait here.

PINOCCHIO: But—

GEPETTA: Don't so much as move from that spot.

PINOCCHIO: Yes, Momma.

(GEPETTA *does a false exit, to catch* PINOCCHIO *misbehaving. He has not moved. She exits.* PINOCCHIO *stands perfectly still. He then creeps over to check the spot where he killed the* CRICKET.)

PINOCCHIO: Sis Cricket? Any of you left? *(He checks.)* Ain't. Sorry.

(GEPETTA *returns and* PINOCCHIO *snaps back into his waiting spot. She is not wearing her coat.*)

GEPETTA: *(Handing him a book.)* Take this to school.

PINOCCHIO: This a spelling book?

GEPETTA: That is what the bookseller said. I can't read it. Maybe you'll teach me.

PINOCCHIO: Where's your coat?

GEPETTA: I sold it.

PINOCCHIO: Why?

GEPETTA: Uh . . . it was too hot.

(PINOCCHIO *understands what she has done. He hugs her.*)

PINOCCHIO: Momma! Thank you!

GEPETTA: So like a real boy. Promise me you'll be good and go to school.

PINOCCHIO: *(Lightly, clueless.)* OK.

(*She starts to mess with his clothes, getting ready to send him off. As they sing,* SPERANZA *appears in the sunbeams.*)

GEPETTA: Now off with you.
>   Can you see him grow?
>   Speranza

PINOCCHIO:
>   Today I'll learn to read

GEPETTA:
> One never knows how life will go

SPERANZA AND GEPETTA:
> In America

PINOCCHIO:
> Tomorrow I'll learn to write
> By Friday I'll be rich and smart

GEPETTA:
> My little American!

PINOCCHIO: I'll buy you a new coat, Momma!

GEPETTA AND PINOCCHIO AND SPERANZA:
> Promise!

(PINOCCHIO *happily clutches his book and exits into the world.* GEPETTA *waves good-bye, and* SPERANZA *smiles from the sunbeams.*)

SCENE FIVE

(FOX *and* CAT *enter the town square.*)

FOX:
> What if I were good today?

CAT:
> Good today?

FOX: Sure.

CAT: Why not?

FOX:
> Would it not feel a little strange
> If I stepped out of the mold
> And stretched my range?

CAT: No, better stick with the tried and true.

FOX AND CAT:
> That's what we do

FOX:
> I'm feeling bad

CAT:
> And that feels good

FOX:
> Nothing feels as good as bad

CAT:
> And that's a fact

FOX AND CAT:
> That's why we should
> Relieve somebody now
> Of all their hard earned money
> That makes this being bad feel good!

FOX:
> I'm feeling bad

CAT:
> And that feels good

FOX:
> Nothing feels as good as bad

CAT:
> And that's a fact
> Fox and cat
> That's why we should
> Use someone for our advancement
> Who saw this alley
> But still he chanced it
> And so makes our being bad feel good
>
> Take a stroll and find a dope
> Gullible and hopelessly full of hopeful hope

CAT:
> We'll set him straight on how the world works

FOX:
> It's the clever and ambitious who get all the perks

FOX AND CAT:
> So we should find that rube, we really should,
> That makes this being bad feel good!

CAT: But who?
FOX: Yes, who?

(PINOCCHIO *enters.*)
PINOCCHIO: Wonder which way that schoolhouse is?
FOX AND CAT: *(With delight.)*
> That makes this being bad feel good!

(FOX *and* CAT *lay in wait for* PINOCCHIO *as music of the puppet show is heard.*)
PINOCCHIO: That's showboat music on the river! Shame I gotta go to school . . .

(*The world of the puppet show is revealed to* PINOCCHIO. *It's all color, music, fun.*)
PINOCCHIO: I'm going to school . . . tomorrow!

(PINOCCHIO *races up to the entrance.* FOX *pretends to be the Ticket Taker with the* CAT.)
CAT AND FOX: Ticket, please.
PINOCCHIO: What's a ticket cost?
FOX: How much you got?
PINOCCHIO: Nothing.
CAT: You've got a new speller.
PINOCCHIO: *(Tossing them his speller.)* Here!
FOX AND CAT: In you go!

(PINOCCHIO *enters the puppet theatre, which now comes fully to life.*)

PUPPETS:

> Come paddle along
> Up the river awhile
> Take a load off your feet
> Have a seat and smile
> Laugh your fool head off
> You will, you know
> At Fire-eater's Magnificent
> Travelling Steamboat Puppet Show

PUPPET 1: Come on up, brother!

PINOCCHIO: Me?

PUPPET 2: Course, you.

PINOCCHIO: I'm coming!

PUPPETS: Join right on in!

(PINOCCHIO *jumps happily onto the puppet-stage. He is welcomed joyfully by all the* PUPPETS. *He joins in their dance.*)

PUPPETS AND PINOCCHIO:

> Come on along
> Past the tupelo trees
> Paddle down to Pascagoula
> Then up to Tennessee
> Laugh your fool head off
> You will, you know
> At Fire-eater's Magnificent
> Travelling Steamboat Puppet Show

(GEPETTA *arrives and approaches the* FOX-*ticket taker.*)

GEPETTA: Mi scusi. My Puppet. He is not at school. Is he here?

FOX: Do you have a ticket?

GEPETTA: Che cosa?

FOX: (*Louder and slower.*) Tic-ket! No ticket, no see.

GEPETTA: I must see!

FOX AND CAT: Got any money?

GEPETTA: No.

FOX: Toot-a-loo!

(*Big laugh from* FOX *and* CAT. GEPETTA *is cut off from the world of the* PUPPET *show. She exits sadly.* PINOCCHIO *is being a cut-up.*)

PUPPETS AND PINOCCHIO:

> We dance all night and twist our strings
> No need to worry what the morning brings
> We dance all night and sleep all day
> Singing happy puppets take your troubles away

> Come on along
> Past the tupelo trees
> Paddle down to Pascagoula
> Then up to Tennessee

> *Laugh your fool head off*
> *You will, you know*
> *At Fire-eater's Magnificent*
> *Travelling Steamboat Puppet Show*

(The song gets out of control. FIRE-EATER, *entering from off stage, bellows and the music stops.* FOX *and* CAT *exit quickly.)*

FIRE-EATER:

> *Cease!!!*

FIRE-EATER: What have we here? A trespasser on my stage? A thwarter of my amusement enterprise?? An interloper in Fire-eater's Extraordinary Travelling Steamboat Puppet Show!!

PINOCCHIO: *(To* PUPPET 1.*)* Would that be Mr. Fire-eater?

*(*PUPPET 1 *nods in fright.)*

FIRE-EATER: Ah-ha! A mischief-maker!

PINOCCHIO: Me?

*(*FIRE-EATER, *consummate impresario, kicks into playing the role of a villain in grand declamatory style.)*

FIRE-EATER: You are but a mere piece of wood. Throw him on the boiler fire! Stoke the paddle wheel.

*(*FIRE-EATER *goes for* PINOCCHIO, *who falls on his knees.)*

PINOCCHIO: Please, sir. I don't want to die. I'm just made!

*(*FIRE-EATER *dramatically grabs* PINOCCHIO *and begins to drag him to the boiler.)*

FIRE-EATER: *(To* PINOCCHIO, *sotto voce.)* Keep up the act, Puppet, you're good.

PINOCCHIO: I'm not acting! Help, Momma! Save me!!!

FIRE-EATER:

> *Mother*

PUPPETS:

> *He cries for his mother*

FIRE-EATER: Nothing can save you!

PINOCCHIO: Help!

FIRE-EATER AND PUPPETS:

> *A Puppet who cries for his mother!*

FIRE-EATER: Ha, Ha, Ha! Puppets don't have mothers!

PINOCCHIO: Don't throw me on the fire! I'm not a puppet. I'm real!

FIRE-EATER AND PUPPETS:

> *Real! He says he's real!*

FIRE-EATER:

> *Hey. Great cue for a song!*
> *We've got a Puppet here*
> *Who says he's real.*

> *Are you real as Rockefeller?*
> *That well heeled?*
> *Are you strong as Paul Bunyan*
> *Who conquered the West?*
> *And brave as Davy Crockett*
> *Can you pass the test?*

PINOCCHIO: Yes!

FIRE-EATER: Did you hear what he said?

PUPPETS:
> *He said yes!*

FIRE-EATER:
> *Are you as honest as Abe?*

PINOCCHIO:
> *Well . . .*

FIRE-EATER:
> *Rich as Carnegie?*

PINOCCHIO:
> *No.*

FIRE-EATER:
> *Brainy as Ford who makes the Model-Ts?*

PINOCCHIO:
> *Who?*

FIRE-EATER:
> *Could you rush to Alaska to hunt for Gold?*

PINOCCHIO:
> *Sure!*

FIRE-EATER:
> *There's a paddle wheel leaving next week I'm told*

(PINOCCHIO *starts to take off in excitement, but the* PUPPETS *stop him.*)

FIRE-EATER:
> *Hold up!*

FIRE-EATER AND PUPPETS:
> *You're not ready*

FIRE-EATER:
> *It's not brains, brawn or money*

FIRE-EATER AND PUPPETS:
> *Be honest and true*

FIRE-EATER:
> *You got to hold your head high as Lady Liberty*
> *And do a good turn when it comes round to you.*
> *Can you?*

PUPPETS:
> *Can you?!*

(FIRE-EATER *delivers these like a vaudevillian setting up jokes, but* PINOCCHIO *doesn't know the punch line.* PUPPETS *help set up the scenes.*)

FIRE-EATER:

> Let's say you've got money and are loafing around
> But the hunger inside you is mean
> The baker's left all his bread on the table
> And the baker's nowhere to be seen

PUPPETS: What will you do?

PINOCCHIO: Take the bread!

(PINOCCHIO *reaches over to take the imaginary piece of bread, but is pulled into the next set-up.*)

FIRE-EATER:

> Let's say you got a duty to see through to the end
> Tend the town's two chickens and a sow
> The critters could starve but sure someone else will do it
> 'Cause you want a vacation right now

PUPPETS:

> What will you do?

PINOCCHIO: How come *I* gotta tend 'em?

FIRE-EATER:

> Let's say you're standing on the corner
> A little old lady is crossing the street
> There's a train bearing down on its way through the town
> Now the train and lady are likely to meet

PUPPETS:

> What will you do?

PINOCCHIO: Close my eyes?

FIRE-EATER:

> Let's say that you're down to your last two nickels
> And the guy standing near you has none
> He asks you for help because the cards he's been dealt
> Contain no nickels, not even one.

(PINOCCHIO *looks at the* PUPPET *portraying the poor man. He is drawn to him, but stops short of giving him a nickel.*)

PUPPETS:

> What will you do?
> Can you pass the test?

FIRE-EATER AND PUPPETS:

> Can you pass the test?!

(FIRE-EATER *and the* PUPPETS *do a big bow.* PUPPETS *wave good-bye and exit.*)

FIRE-EATER: *(Over the applause.)* Thank you. See us next week up river! Next year before the crowned heads of Europe!

(*Lights shift to suggest the show is over.* FIRE-EATER *and* PINOCCHIO *are alone.* FIRE-EATER *is now "off stage."*)

FIRE-EATER: Hey little fella, you ought to be in show business!

PINOCCHIO: But I didn't pass the test.

FIRE-EATER: And you never will, long as you're a puppet.

PINOCCHIO: Then I wanna be real.

FIRE-EATER: Can you be honest, responsible, compassionate?

PINOCCHIO: *(Not having the foggiest what those words mean.)* Sure!

FIRE-EATER: Then see if you can pass this test.

(FIRE-EATER *tosses him a bag of coins.*)

PINOCCHIO: You giving me five silver dollars?

FIRE-EATER: Not giving. You earned them. Now see if you can take that money straight home for you and your momma.

PINOCCHIO: That's an easy test! I'm rich! Now I can do whatever I want. I'm free!

FIRE-EATER: Freedom's not something I take for granted. Being free means a whole lot more than just doing what you want. You got to do what's right for yourself and for everybody round you. That's how you live a good life.

PINOCCHIO: My good life's gonna be figurin' how to spend my silver dollars!

FIRE-EATER: Who do you want to be in this world, Pinocchio? A wooden-headed puppet or a good-hearted boy?

PINOCCHIO: A boy!

(FOX *and* CAT *peer in around the corner of the puppet theatre and overhear.*)

FIRE-EATER: Then what you waiting on? Get those silver dollars home and you could be real by dinnertime!

(PINOCCHIO *tucks his money deep down in his pocket and takes off.*)

PINOCCHIO: Thank you, Mr. Fire-eater.

FIRE-EATER: *(Calling after him.)* Remember, every black-eyed susan long the road is watching to see if you do right!

PINOCCHIO: I'm gonna!

FIRE-EATER: *(More to himself.)* Good luck.

SCENE SIX

(PINOCCHIO *re-enters, trailed by the* FOX *and* CAT, *who feign to be lame and blind, one of their many disguises.*)

FOX AND CAT: Good day, Pinocchio.

PINOCCHIO: How do you fancy folks know my name?

FOX: We're friends with your momma, the "Italian."

PINOCCHIO: Ya are?

CAT: We just saw her.

FOX: *I* just saw her shivering in the chill of the evening air—

CAT: Without her coat!

(FOX *and* CAT *shiver dramatically.*)

PINOCCHIO: *(Remembering his bad deed.)* And I traded away my speller! But my momma will never want for nothing again!

FOX: Why's that?

PINOCCHIO: 'Cause I'm rich!

FOX AND CAT: *(Sniggering.)* A puppet!

PINOCCHIO: Am, too! Look!

(The FOX *reaches out his lame hand, and the* CAT *opens her blind eyes to look at the money, but* PINOCCHIO *doesn't notice.)*

FOX: Bet you have big plans for all that money.

PINOCCHIO: I'm getting my Momma a new coat, spun from silver and gold! Then I'll buy me another speller. I'm going to school soon as I get back to town.

FOX: Not that!

FOX: Through my foolish passion for learning I lost a leg.

CAT: And I lost the sight of both my eyes.

PINOCCHIO: At school? Really?

BIRD: *(Appearing.)* Pinocchio, don't be listening to the advice of bad companions. If you do you'll be sor—

*(*CAT *leaps out and eats the* BIRD. *Then shuts her blind eyes again.)*

PINOCCHIO: *(Warily.)* I better get me and my silver dollars on home.

FOX:
> Would you like to double your money?

PINOCCHIO: Sure, but how?

CAT: Easy!

FOX:
> Don't go home

FOX AND CAT:
> Come with us.

PINOCCHIO: I can't.

FOX: Then say good-bye to good fortune and riches.

CAT: Good-bye!

FOX: Why should you turn your measly five silver dollars into five thousand anyway?

CAT: Why indeed.

FOX AND CAT: Bye!

*(*FOX *and* CAT *begin to exit dramatically.)*

PINOCCHIO: Hang on.

PINOCCHIO: How'd you say I could do that?

FOX:
> Can you imagine all the riches
> Of Persian King Salidan?
> Well, I can.

CAT:
> He can.

FOX:
> Can you imagine Vacation Estates
> In the sunny Alaskaland?
> Well, I can

CAT:
> He can

PINOCCHIO:
> And so can I!

FOX AND CAT: Well good!

FOX: Because Pinocchio my boy, I can make your dreams reality!

PINOCCHIO: How?

FOX AND CAT:
> The field of miracles!

FOX:
> All you need to know
> Is a little trick

CAT:
> A sort of gimmick, you see

FOX:
> There's a place where you stick
> Your money in the ground

CAT:
> A magic spot that we've found

FOX:
> And your money like a seed

CAT:
> It grows into a tree

FOX:
> And the fruits are coins

FOX AND CAT:
> That are exactly like these!

PINOCCHIO: You mean money grows on trees??!!

FOX: It's easy to get rich—

FOX AND CAT:
> In America!
> The field of miracles!

PINOCCHIO:
> Can you see me
> Gepetta
> In a fine fancy house
> With servants by the score
> And a gold knocker on the door
> No more thoughts of dreary school
> Or lesson books or teacher's rules

FOX AND CAT AND PINOCCHIO:
> The field of miracles

FOX: How about an ice cream soda to celebrate!

PINOCCHIO: Y'all sure are nice!

FOX AND CAT: Us? Yes.

(FOX and CAT rush PINOCCHIO across to the Dime-store. On the opposite side of the stage, GEPETTA quickly crosses to FIRE-EATER, who is carrying a big trunk.)

FIRE-EATER: Pinocchio? Yes, but I sent him on his way.

GEPETTA: Which way?

FIRE-EATER: Straight home is what he promised.

GEPETTA: But he is not home! I am sure he has run away!

(Focus shifts back to Dime-store. The DIME-STORE OWNER is the slop thrower from earlier. They are toasting with ice-cream sodas.)

FOX AND CAT AND PINOCCHIO:
      The field of miracles

(Focus shifts back to GEPETTA and FIRE-EATER.)

FIRE-EATER: I've never seen a puppet like yours, Ma'am. If business were better, I'd be honored to have you work for me.

GEPETTA: It is I who am honored.

FIRE-EATER: Till I can offer you work, will you accept my help?

(He offers her some money.)

GEPETTA: Thank you, but I will wait and work.

FIRE-EATER: Good luck to you.

GEPETTA: You've been very kind.

(FIRE-EATER gives her a little bow, then exits.)

FOX AND CAT AND PINOCCHIO:
      The field of miracles

(GEPETTA crosses to the Dime-store. She tries to enter, but the DIME-STORE owner stops her.)

DIME-STORE OWNER: Move on along.

GEPETTA: Have you seen my puppet?

DIME-STORE OWNER: I said get!

(GEPETTA begins to leave sadly.)

DIME-STORE OWNER: Unless you're looking for work.

(GEPETTA quickly pulls one of her Statue of Liberties from her pocket. But he offers her a broom.)

DIME-STORE OWNER: Sweep my street.

(GEPETTA takes the broom and sweeps.)

FOX AND CAT AND PINOCCHIO:
>*The field of miracles*

PINOCCHIO:

>*Can you see me?*
>*Gepetta!*
>*In a brand new Model-T*
>*Everybody looks at me*
>*I've got a bag full of money . . .*

(GEPETTA *exits, sadly.*)

FOX: Whoa there, Rockefeller. Best keep it down! There're bad men out in those piney woods waiting to take advantage of a nice puppet like you.

CAT: Bad men!

PINOCCHIO: Ain't a robber alive that can catch me!

FOX AND CAT: Good!

FOX: Gotta go.

CAT: Gotta go.

FOX: Remember—

FOX AND CAT: Watch out for robbers!

(FOX *and* CAT *give him a launching push.* PINOCCHIO *takes off down the road.* FOX *and* CAT *dash off in another direction.* GEPETTA *appears sitting on the dock at the river's edge. She has carved an angel.*)

GEPETTA:

>*Speranza,*
>*Can you see him?*
>*The son born of my dreams*

I have lost my Pinocchio. Find him, my angel of hope. (GEPETTA *sets the angel statue sail upon the river.*) He's a bad little puppet, Speranza. Help him learn to be good. (SPERANZA *appears in the sunbeams.*)

GEPETTA:

>*Find him*

SPERANZA:

>*I'll guide him*

GEPETTA:	SPERANZA:
My angel of hope	*Your Angel of hope*
On this river	*On this river*
That carried me	*That carried you*
To America	*To America*

SPERANZA:

>*I'll hold him in my wings*
>*In a light bright as joy*
>*And show him the road*
>*To be a real boy*

(SPERANZA'S *light grows as she picks up the statue from the water. Lights transform to dark woods.*)

SCENE SEVEN

(PINOCCHIO *appears walking through a dark woods. Night birds fly by—very spooky.*)

PINOCCHIO: This here's the dark piney woods. Now where's that field of miracles? "Watch out for robbers!" I don't believe in robbers! They're just made up by Mommas to frighten adventuring boys into staying home! I ain't scared. If I see me one I'll whup him tooth to toenail!! (PINOCCHIO *sees in the gloom two evil-looking black figures enveloped in charcoal sacks.*)

I wasn't figuring on seeing two! Ahhh!!!

(*The figures leap out and grab him.*)

ROBBERS: Your money or your life!

FOX ROBBER: Give us the money or else.

CAT ROBBER: Or else!

(FOX *and* CAT *go for* PINOCCHIO. *He struggles to escape them. When threatened,* PINOCCHIO *bites the* CAT's *hand.* PINOCCHIO *comes out of the brawl with the* CAT's *paw in his mouth.* PINOCCHIO *spits out the paw.*)

PINOCCHIO: Ain't no outsmarting Pinocchio!!

(PINOCCHIO *runs upstage, but he trips a trap that hangs him in a tree.*)

PINOCCHIO: Ahhh!

FOX ROBBER: Thought you could escape our trap?

CAT ROBBER: But now you're swinging from a hickory tree!

FOX ROBBER: Serves him right—

CAT ROBBER: For taking the advice of bad companions!

(*Big evil laugh.* FOX *cuts one of* PINOCCHIO's *strings, leaving the puppet dangling even more precariously.*)

FOX ROBBER: We'll come back and get your silver dollars.

FOX ROBBER AND CAT ROBBER: When you're dead!

(FOX *cuts another one of* PINOCCHIO's *strings. Another laugh and exit.* PINOCCHIO *swings in the breeze.*)

SCENE EIGHT

(SPERANZA *appears. With the touch of her hand on his cheek,* PINOCCHIO *is released from the tree and magically floats to the ground.* SPERANZA *disappears.*)

(PINOCCHIO *is now surrounded by three wacky* DOCTORS—DR. OPOSSUM, DR. DUCK *and* DR. BOLL WEEVIL. *The* DOCTORS *feel his pulse, his nose, his little toe.*)

DR. DUCK:

> It is my belief
> That the Puppet is quite dead
> Dr. Opossum

> No, no, Doctor Duck
> Should he not be dead
> It is a sign that he is alive!

DR. DUCK: Your opinion, Boll Weevil?

DR. BOLL WEEVIL:

> He needs to be bled!

DRS. DUCK & OPOSSUM:

> Yes, of course
> That's what I said

DR. DUCK:

> That of life he's been deprived

DR. OPOSSUM:

> Is evidence he's not alive!

DOCTORS:

> If he's not alive
> Then he must be dead!

DOCTORS: Excellent diagnosis! Congratulations to you, Dr. Duck! Bravo, brav-o!

(Congratulations all around. PINOCCHIO *sits up. The* DOCTORS *miss it.)*

DR. OPOSSUM: Where is the patient?

DR. DUCK:

> It is now quite clear
> An iron lung is what he needs

DR. OPOSSUM:

> No, no Doctor Duck
> You're a quack indeed
> We need to measure out his brain

DR. DUCK:

> He's hickory, based on grain

DR. BOLL WEEVIL:

> He needs be drained!

DRS. DUCK & OPOSSUM:

> Yes, of course
> As I've maintained

*(*PINOCCHIO, *who has been following this exchange, now faints. This gets the* DOCTORS' *attention.)*

DR. BOLL WEEVIL: Landsake! It's that rascal puppet from Natchez town.

DR. DUCK: Varmint!

DR. OPOSSUM: Ne'er do well!

DR. BOLL WEEVIL: No-count disobedient piece of pine.

DR. OPOSSUM: He'll make his momma die of a broken heart.

PINOCCHIO: *(Revived.)* I won't!

DOCTORS: Ah-HA!

DR. DUCK:

> It is my belief

DR. OPOSSUM:

                That when a dead person cries out

DR. DUCK:

                It is a sign he's getting well

DR. OPOSSUM:

                And will soon be complaining

DR. BOLL WEEVIL:

                He needs therapeutic draining!

DR. DUCK:

                When a dead person cries out

DOCTORS:

                It's a sign that he's sorry to die

PINOCCHIO: I ain't dead yet.

DOCTORS: Nurse!

(SPERANZA enters, disguised as a NURSE.)

PINOCCHIO: *(Looking up at her.)* Purty as an angel!

NURSE SPERANZA: You need medicine, Pinocchio, serious medicine.

PINOCCHIO: Then give it to me, quick!

NURSE SPERANZA: "Give it to me, quick, *please.*" It's pie!

PINOCCHIO & DOCTORS: Pie!

NURSE SPERANZA: Humble pie, for those who need to admit they've done wrong.

DOCTORS: *(Exiting. Grumbling.)* Well, I never. / Indeed. / Got an appointment. / Very important meeting.

(DOCTORS are gone. PINOCCHIO jumps up from the bed.)

PINOCCHIO: No blind varmint doctor's gonna take me off!

NURSE SPERANZA: You ready for that humble pie?

PINOCCHIO: That was a close one with ole man death!

NURSE SPERANZA: About as close as your swinging from that hickory tree. How'd you get yourself up there?

PINOCCHIO: *(Wanting to impress her.)* Well . . . I was fighting off a hundred robbers who wanted my silver dollars that I got from Mr. Fire-eater for being so smart. Hey, my nose feels funny.

NURSE SPERANZA: Does it?

PINOCCHIO: So I jumped up in that hickory tree and swung at them with my sword.

(His nose grows. Ensemble members bring out a pole that actor-PINOCCHIO holds on his face.)

PINOCCHIO: Every one of them ran off quick as greased lightning.

(His nose grows again. Ensemble member exchanges the pole for a longer one.)

NURSE SPERANZA: Then?

PINOCCHIO: I grew me some wings and flew back down??

(His nose grows a third time. Ensemble member exchanges the pole for an even longer one.)

PINOCCHIO: Hey! My nose is so derned long—

(It swoops through the space as he turns.)

That no matter which a-way I turn—*(Ensemble and* SPERANZA *have to duck to avoid his nose.)*

I right near knock out the window panes.

(Big laugh from SPERANZA.)

PINOCCHIO: What you laughing at?

NURSE SPERANZA: Plain as the nose on your face! You're not telling the truth. Woodpeckers!

*(*WOODPECKERS *appear and peck* PINOCCHIO'S *nose back down to size.)*

PINOCCHIO: Ouch! OUCH!!!

*(*WOODPECKERS *exit.* PINOCCHIO'S *nose is back to normal.* ENSEMBLE NOSE-PEOPLE *exit.)*

NURSE SPERANZA: You ready for Humble pie *now*?

PINOCCHIO: *(Taking it.)* Yeah.

NURSE SPERANZA: How's it taste?

PINOCCHIO: Not so good.

NURSE SPERANZA: But good for you. Now, how did you get into such trouble?

PINOCCHIO: I was trying to get my silver dollars home, like I promised, but guess I took me a wrong turn.

NURSE SPERANZA: How'd you get down?

PINOCCHIO: Well . . . Cross my heart—*(He does the motion on the wrong place on his chest.* SPERANZA *shows him the right spot.)* I think it was . . . an angel.

NURSE SPERANZA: *An Angel.* You sure?

PINOCCHIO: *(He's not.)* Well . . .

NURSE SPERANZA: *Did you hear her . . . Sweet Lullaby?*

PINOCCHIO: If it was, I bet she could make me a real boy lickety-split! I'm gonna find her.

*(*PINOCCHIO *is headed out the door.)*

NURSE SPERANZA: Pinocchio, take those silver dollars home to your Momma.

PINOCCHIO: But—

NURSE SPERANZA: If you want to be real, the very first thing you've got to learn is keep your promises.

PINOCCHIO: I ain't gotta worry about things like that, now that he got me an angel!

NURSE SPERANZA: You want more of my medicine?

PINOCCHIO: No ma'am.

NURSE SPERANZA: Then straight home!

PINOCCHIO: Yes ma'am.

NURSE SPERANZA: Might be hope for you yet, little puppet. Now scoot!

(PINOCCHIO exits as the angel light shines on NURSE SPERANZA.)

SCENE NINE

(PINOCCHIO enters and passes LAMPWICK, the prankster, who is readying to drop a melon on the next person who passes by.)

PINOCCHIO: Go straight home, then find your angel; find your angel, then go straight home . . .

LAMPWICK: Where ya been, pine-boy.

PINOCCHIO: Where *you* been, Lampwick.

LAMPWICK: Asked you first.

PINOCCHIO: I been to the tip-top of a hickory tree!

LAMPWICK: Don't believe you!

PINOCCHIO: I climbed up all by myself!

(A NOSE PERSON appears and is moving in on PINOCCHIO.)

PINOCCHIO: No I didn't! I got hung up there by robbers.

(NOSE stops.)

LAMPWICK: How'd you get down?

(NOSE PERSON stands ready to strike.)

PINOCCHIO: An angel!

(The NOSE PERSON retreats. PINOCCHIO takes this as proof.)

PINOCCHIO:
> *Hah! Sure I found me an angel*
> *I wasn't dreaming*
> *Sure I saw her real clear—*

LAMPWICK: What're you talking about. Ain't no such thing!

PINOCCHIO:
> *An angel, sure as shootin'—*

LAMPWICK: What she look like?

PINOCCHIO: I didn't see her exactly.

LAMPWICK: Don't believe in anything you can't see, puppet.

PINOCCHIO: *(a capella)*
> *An angel*

(LAMPWICK laughs at him.)

PINOCCHIO: She can turn me into a real boy!

LAMPWICK: Like me!

PINOCCHIO: I'll be honest and do right—

LAMPWICK: And you'll take what you can get cause nobody gives you nothing. That's what this real boy does.

PINOCCHIO: That don't sound like Mr. Fire-eater's kind of real.

LAMPWICK: Yeah? Well, you go chasing angels, Pinoc. I'm headed downstream. There's a Catfish out in the deepest part of that river. Big as a steam engine. Can swallow you whole. Comes out when it's dark!

PINOCCHIO: *(Scared.)* Really?

LAMPWICK: You scared?

PINOCCHIO: Naw. I'd be protected by my angel— I hope.

LAMPWICK: Hope is for losers. Who you wanna be, Pinoc? A loser or like me?

(Enter SHARECROPPER. LAMPWICK *tosses* PINOCCHIO *a melon.)*

LAMPWICK: Have ya a melon. See ya.

SHARECROPPER: What's this? A melon felon?

PINOCCHIO: I didn't steal no melon!

SHARECROPPER: Bet you been carrying off my chickens, too!

PINOCCHIO: I ain't never seen your chickens!

SHARECROPPER: Ya will now.

(The SHARECROPPER *drags* PINOCCHIO *to his barnyard and puts a dog collar around his neck.)*

PINOCCHIO: Hey! I don't need no dog collar!

SHARECROPPER: Guard my henhouse!

(He pushes PINOCCHIO *to get down like a dog.)*

SHARECROPPER: My watch dog died today. Best ole dog, but never caught him a single chicken-thief. You bark to wake the dead if you see one, hear?

PINOCCHIO: Arf, Arf.

*(*SHARECROPPER *exits.)*

PINOCCHIO: I'm never gonna find no angel or turn real or nothing now that I'm a dog.

*(*PINOCCHIO *howls pitifully.* POLE CATS *slink on.)*

POLE CATS: Hey, wood boy!
        We got a real sweet deal for you to consider.
        Think of it as a steal.

PINOCCHIO: What's that smell?

POLE CATS:
        The old dog that had your job before
        Would wink and take a break from minding the store
        He'd wander off and we'd saunter in
        To take two or three chickens, maybe more

PINOCCHIO: He'd *let* you take the chickens?

POLE CATS: For one in return. *You* hungry?

PINOCCHIO: Sure.

POLE CATS:

> *Then all you got to do is*
> *Look the other way*
> *And we'll steal in*
> *And spirit the chickens away*
> *And for your modest efforts*
> *We'll give you one*

PINOCCHIO: But what about the sharecropper?

POLE CATS:

> *That's part of the fun!*
> *What he doesn't know won't hurt him*
> *We're pretty sure that's certain*
> *So really, there's no harm because . . .*

(POLE CATS head for the chicken house.)

PINOCCHIO: Bark! Bark! Bark!

(The SHARECROPPER appears and the POLE CATS scatter.)

SHARECROPPER: Polecats! I'll be derned. You're a pretty good ole dog after all. Them varmints try to trick ya?

PINOCCHIO: Sure did. But I ain't so woodenheaded that I didn't know they was wrong.

SHARECROPPER: Well, you done right, little puppet. *(Takes the collar off.)*

PINOCCHIO: I did?!

SHARECROPPER: Don't you go ending up a dog again.

PINOCCHIO: I won't! Momma, I'm coming home with my silver dollars!

(SHARECROPPER exits. PINOCCHIO exits happily.)

(End of act one. If performed with intermission.)

SCENE TEN

(GEPETTA enters, just missing PINOCCHIO, carrying a broom.)

GEPETTA:

> *These streets they're not paved with gold*
> *Still I sweep them clean*
> *Here's a penny on the sidewalk*
> *I was never so proud or so mean*
> *To reject a little good fortune (She picks up the penny.)*

> *Life must have something*
> *For me*

> *These streets can be wet and cold*
> *Still I sweep them clean*
> *They lead to the gates of heaven*
> *Though there's no gold to be seen*

It must be just round the corner
Life must have something
For me
Why did I come here? (She is trying hard.)

I heard the door to hope is always open
That these dreams
That I've never stopped hoping
Would see me through
(This memory is too much, and she resumes sweeping.)

Another day
Of hunger, of longing
Another night
With my dreams
My hopes
For Pinocchio

(FOX *and* CAT *enter.*)

FOX: You let him get away!

CAT: You cut his strings.

FOX: He's a puppet!

GEPETTA: *(Overhearing them.)* This puppet you speak. Is it my puppet?

CAT: *(Sotto voce to* FOX.*)* It's the puppet's mother.

FOX: *(Sotto voce to* CAT*)* She's hiding him from us!

GEPETTA: He's hiding?

CAT: Where is he?

GEPETTA: Where!

FOX: You tell us!

GEPETTA: How can I tell what I do not know!

FOX AND CAT: You don't know??

GEPETTA: No!

FOX AND CAT: Oh.

FOX: Keep sweeping.

PINOCCHIO *(from off.)*
              Pinocchio
              What'd ya know? . . .

GEPETTA: Pinocchio!

(CAT, *struggling to put her blind costume back on, signals to the* FOX *to get rid of* GEPETTA.*)*

FOX: His voice is floating down the river from the carnival.

CAT: *(Not following the ruse.)* Carnival?

FOX: I was just there and saw your little fella on the carousel.

CAT: *(Getting it.)* Carousel!

GEPETTA: *(Overjoyed.)* You did?!

CAT: *(Pointing in the opposite direction of* PINOCCHIO.*)* It's that way!

FOX: You'll need a ticket.

GEPETTA: I have only this penny.

FOX: *(Generously.)* It's on me.

GEPETTA: Grazie.

FOX: Toot-a-loo!

(FOX *pick-pockets* GEPETTA *of her penny on her way out.* FOX *spins back around just as the* CAT *whips around with* PINOCCHIO.*)*

FOX: Dearest Pinocchio. What brings you here?

CAT: You here?

PINOCCHIO: I'm lucky to be anywhere. There *were* robbers in those piney woods! They tried to steal my silver dollars, then left me for dead!

(Big gasp from FOX *and* CAT.*)*

FOX: Is it possible to hear of anything more dreadful!

CAT: Where can respectable people—

FOX AND CAT: Like us!

CAT: Find a safe refuge in such a world?

(Great sigh from CAT *and* FOX.*)*

PINOCCHIO: What happened to your paw?

(CAT *whips it behind her back, quickly.)*

FOX: We just met an old gator on the road, faint with hunger, who asked if we might spare some food. (CAT *improvises a re-enactment of the* FOX's *lie, trying to follow along.)* Not having so much as a fish-bone to give him, what did my friend, with the heart of gold, do? She bit off one of her paws and threw it to that poor beast for his lunch.

PINOCCHIO: *(Warily.)* I gotta go.

(PINOCCHIO *starts to leave. They grab him.)*

FOX: Did those villains take your silver dollars?

CAT: Or do you still have them.

PINOCCHIO: I might.

FOX: You haven't forgotten . . .

FOX AND CAT:
                    The field of miracles!

PINOCCHIO: I'm going straight home! Besides, I think you're fooling me about that miracle field any ways.

(FOX *and* CAT *gasp.)*

CAT: You cut us to the quick.

FOX: Would we lie to you?

PINOCCHIO: I figure you are . . . but I'm hoping you ain't.

CAT: See for yourself!

FOX AND CAT:
> It's right over there!

PINOCCHIO: That looks like any ole field.

CAT: Oh, but it's not!

FOX:
> That's the beauty of a simple thing
> That only a connoisseur can tell

CAT:
> The difference between an affair and a fling

FOX:
> Twixt a monkey that spells

CAT:
> And an ape that can sing!

FOX: Look again! You seem like a boy.

PINOCCHIO: Boy!

FOX:
> With a refined sensibility
> One that separates
> The puppets from the boys
> You can see

CAT: Unlike others!

FOX:
> What this field is meant to be:

FOX AND CAT:
> A place for a miracle tree

FOX: Only a real American boy can see the field's potential!

CAT: You look like that real boy to us!

PINOCCHIO: I do?

FOX AND CAT:
> So we know you can see
> What's really true
> That this field has a gift
> That nobody knew
> And this gift
> Can be opened only by you

(The FOX offers PINOCCHIO a spade.)

FOX: Real boys don't dig their hole too deep.

PINOCCHIO: (As if he knows what real boys do.) Right.

FOX AND CAT: Plant!

(PINOCCHIO takes the spade and plants his money.)

FOX AND CAT:
> Now your money like a seed
> It grows into a tree
> And the fruits will be coins

FOX:

> *Thousands!*

CAT:

> *Millions!*

FOX AND CAT AND PINOCCHIO:

> *Just like these!*

CAT: *(Placing him away from where he buried coins.)* Here's a nice place for you to sleep.

FOX: When you wake, you'll be under a magnolia tree dripping with the honey of money.

PINOCCHIO: I'll buy y'all a thank-you present!

FOX: You mustn't!

CAT: Gracious, no!

FOX: We should thank *you* for trusting us.

CAT: Not everybody does.

FOX AND CAT: Arrivederci!

(PINOCCHIO *settles down to sleep.*)

PINOCCHIO:

> *Pinocchio*
> *What do you know*
> *I'll be rich by tomorrow*
> *And home before supper*
> *The star of the show*
> *And a real boy, yessir!*

Wonder if my angel can see? *(He is falling asleep.)* She'll be so proud of me.

(FOX *and* CAT *steal the coins from the hole and exit.*)

SCENE ELEVEN

PINOCCHIO: *(Popping up, awake.)* Wonder how big a money-totin' sack I'm gonna need!

(He looks around.)

There ain't no tree. No coins!

(He digs.)

My silver dollars is gone! Police!

(COP *is already there.*)

COP: Took your money, did they?

PINOCCHIO: Yessir!

COP: Tricked you, did they?

PINOCCHIO: Yessir!!!

COP: Throw him into prison!

PINOCCHIO: What??!!!

(PINOCCHIO *is locked in jail. A courtroom assembles, with an* APE JUDGE *and members of the* MONKEY JURY.)

COP: All rise.

APE JUDGE:

> *We are gathered here to assess the case of Pinocchio*
> *We are gathered here to take complete stock.*
> *Our community at large can make a decision re: Pinocchio*
> *Is his head merely made of a wooden block?*

APE JURY:

> *Here we sit in judgement of a puppet with a problem*
> *Here we sit in judgement with a solemn need to know*
> *This puppet's of an age that he's supposed to use his noggin*
> *But he's a block-headed loser called Pinocchio*

APE JUDGE: Read the charges.

COP: Careless with his money. Tricked out of his five silver dollars. Duped by some clever, good-looking rogues!

APE JURY:

> *Guilty!*

APE JUDGE: Now now, good people of the jury, first things first. What is your verdict?

APE JURY:

> *Guilty!*

(*The* APE JUDGE *smacks the gavel.*)

APE JURY AND COP:

> *Sentence him to life*

APE JUDGE:

> *He should have duped the dupers first!*

APE JURY AND COP:

> *Sentence him to life*

COP:

> *The rogues were bad*
> *The puppet should have been worse!*

APE JURY AND COP:

> *Sentence him to life*

APE JUDGE: Pity the inexperienced puppet! Too good for his own good.

PINOCCHIO: Help!

(SPERANZA *in her lawyer form appears.*)

LAWYER SPERANZA: Your Honor. My client is in need of counsel. Serious counsel.

APE JURY AND COP:

> *The puppet's got a lawyer*

PINOCCHIO: A dern purty one, too!

LAWYER SPERANZA:

> *Pinocchio.*
> *You find yourself in jail*
> *Not because you lost your purse*
> *You must tell bad advice from good*
> *And choose the second not the first*

PINOCCHIO: How do you tell the difference?

LAWYER SPERANZA: Would the court care to enlighten us?

(All the APES scratch their heads. The APE JUDGE smacks the gavel.)

APE JUDGE AND JURY AND COP:

> *Sentence him to life*

APE JUDGE: Adjourned! *(All monkeys exit chattering, congratulating themselves on another successful trial.)*

PINOCCHIO: Wait! Miss Law-lady! Them fox and cat varmints is the ones who did wrong.

LAWYER SPERANZA: Are they now.

PINOCCHIO: They tricked me into thinking I was real!

LAWYER SPERANZA: Don't you have the sense to smell out the skunks of this world?

PINOCCHIO: I did once. But there's bad people out there and monkeys making up the rules!

LAWYER SPERANZA: There're always going to be monkeys, foxes and cats. And good people, too. Tell your lawyer which you are gonna be.

PINOCCHIO: All I'm ever gonna be is a wooden-headed puppet!

LAWYER SPERANZA: Objection! My client will not give up hope for making things better in himself and in the world!

PINOCCHIO: But I failed Mr. Fire-eater's test. I lost my silver dollars. Now I'll never be real.

LAWYER SPERANZA: Make a new test—for yourself. If you pass, you can grow up and fix what's wrong in the world. But first, you gotta fix yourself.

PINOCCHIO: I wish my angel was here!

LAWYER SPERANZA: Angel? What would you promise an angel, Pinocchio?

(LAWYER SPERANZA begins to leave PINOCCHIO.)

PINOCCHIO: Well, I won't take any more bad advice! I'll go straight home. And go to school like I promised my momma. I'll pass that test.

(SPERANZA appears above PINOCCHIO in her angel light. He cannot see her.)

SPERANZA: Might be hope for you yet, little puppet.

(She gestures and PINOCCHIO's prison door opens and he dashes out.)

PINOCCHIO: My angel must have been listening.

(With another magical gesture from SPERANZA, GEPETTA appears on the opposite side of the stage isolated in light.)

GEPETTA: Speranza, can you see him?

PINOCCHIO: Momma!!

(PINOCCHIO *runs to his momma, who is overjoyed to see him.*)

SPERANZA:

Angel of hope

SPERANZA AND GEPETTA:

On your wings

SPERANZA:

I carried him home.

GEPETTA AND PINOCCHIO:

You carried him/me home

PINOCCHIO:

Hold me in your arms

SPERANZA:

I'll sing you my song

GEPETTA:

Angel of hope

PINOCCHIO:

Light my way

GEPETTA AND SPERANZA:

Light his way

(SPERANZA *disappears into the sunbeams.*)

GEPETTA: (*Furious.*) Where have you been! I've been so worried!

PINOCCHIO: It's kind of a long story—

GEPETTA: Do you know how hard I've looked for you?

PINOCCHIO: I'm sorry.

GEPETTA: How many doors have been slammed in my face searching for you!

PINOCCHIO: I—

GEPETTA: How many days I have missed you. I love you!

(*A beat of realizing she's just poured out all this for a puppet.*)

A little puppet.

PINOCCHIO: I won't be a puppet for long. I'm gonna be a real boy who grows up to fix ape courts and catch foxes and cats who do wrong—

GEPETTA: What?

PINOCCHIO: But I gotta start by going to school.

GEPETTA: You have promised that before.

PINOCCHIO: But this time, I promised my angel, too!

GEPETTA: Grazie, Speranza!

PINOCCHIO: We'll have a good life, Momma. I'll help you carve your statues.

GEPETTA: That no one buys? I sweep the streets of Natchez now, Pinocchio. And you know what? They are not made of gold.

PINOCCHIO: I'll make them gold for you, Momma. Promise!

SCENE TWELVE

(Scene breaks as school room is established. SCHOOL TEACHER *and* PUPILS *enter.)*
SCHOOL TEACHER: Sixteen times four is—
PUPILS:
> *Sixty-four.*

SCHOOL TEACHER: Sixty-four times four is—
PUPILS:
> *Two hundred fifty-six . . .*

PINOCCHIO: *(To the other kids.)* I like school.
PUPILS: Puppet!
PINOCCHIO: But y'all don't take too kindly to me.
PUPIL 1: Paint a mustache on his wooden face!
PUPIL 2: See if he's got any splinters!
PINOCCHIO: Yeah, I got one, on my wooden feet!

(He kicks one of the kids, hard as thunder.)
PINOCCHIO: *(Sweetly.)* Anybody else wanna see?
PUPILS: Nice puppet!
PUPILS:
> *Twelve times six is*

PINOCCHIO:
> *Seventy-two.*

PUPILS:
> *Seventy-two times seventy-two is—*

PINOCCHIO: Five thousand one hundred and eighty-four!
PUPIL 2: Egghead.
PUPIL 1: Goody-goody.
PUPIL 3:
> *How come he knows all the answers?*

LAMPWICK: He studies!
PUPIL 1:
> *Makes us look bad*

PUPIL 4: Makes me mad!
PUPIL 3:
> *Let's get him into trouble.*

LAMPWICK: Leave it to me!
ALL:
> *Seven thousand times sixty-two is—*

SCHOOL TEACHER: Recess! Outside on the double! Pinocchio.
PINOCCHIO: Yes ma'am.
SCHOOL TEACHER: Do right.

(PINOCCHIO *does a double-take, thinking this teacher looks familiar, but* SCHOOL TEACHER *leaves.* LAMPWICK *buddies up to* PINOCCHIO *while the others listen just outside.*)

LAMPWICK: Hey, Pinoc!

LAMPWICK:
> *What do you think is the best thing in the world to do?*

PINOCCHIO: Well . . .

LAMPWICK: I'll tell you!
> *When do you think we should do it?*

PINOCCHIO: I think that . . .

LAMPWICK:
> *Can it be years studying Calculus*
> *In a dark dusty nook*
> *All so I can grow up*
> *And balance my checkbook?*
>
> *Can it be years studying History*
> *Knowing where everyone else has been*
> *Maybe I'd rather make my mistakes*
> *So I can be doomed to repeat them!*

PINOCCHIO: I smell trouble comin'.

LAMPWICK:
> *So I've got a plan that any real boy*
> *In the room would jump for*
>
> *It's quite a scheme and I think it seems*
> *That you're the one cut out for*
>
> *Seeing it through*
> *I'm making it plain*
> *We carry this off*
> *And we'll never be the same*
>
> *I'm talking bust loose*
> *Bust out*
> *'Cause freedom's just a word*
> *That this country's all about*
>
> *But we got none!*
> *And I want some!*

(The PUPILS *start to dance.*)
> *But we got none*

PUPILS:
> *And we want some!*

PINOCCHIO: But the teacher—

LAMPWICK: That's my point!
> *She's our jailor don't you see?*
> *That giant scarecrow's got the keys*
> *To the door between us*
> *And the great big world afar*

> *Who holds us down?*

PUPILS:

> *T-E-A-C-H-E-R!*

PINOCCHIO: I promised my momma—

LAMPWICK: I'm not talking about mothers, I'm talking about . . .

PUPILS:

> *Freedom*
> *Freedom*

LAMPWICK AND PUPILS:

> *That's the spirit*
> *The American way*
> *The deum's here*
> *Let's carpe today*
> *The door's ajar*
> *So let me hear it!*

PUPILS:

> *F-R-E-E-D-U-M!*

PINOCCHIO: There's an "o" in "freedom" . . .

PUPIL 2: You wanna broken nose?

> *(A kid takes* PINOCCHIO's *book out of his hand.)*

PUPILS:

> *Freedom*

PINOCCHIO: That's my book.

PUPILS:

> *Freedom*

PINOCCHIO: Give it back.

> *(The book gets thrown in a game of keep-away from* PINOCCHIO.*)*

LAMPWICK AND PUPILS:

> *That's the spirit*
> *The American way*
> *The deum's here*
> *Let's carpe today*
> *The door's ajar*
> *So let's be speedy*
> *F-R-E-D-U-M-B*
> *Freedom*
> *Freedom*

> *(One* PUPIL *is hit by a thrown book. He falls and faints, pale. The* PUPILS, *scared, scatter.)*

PUPILS: Let's get outta here. Beat it!

> *(*LAMPWICK *lingers for a moment, but runs away, too.* PINOCCHIO *crosses to the wounded boy.* COP *enters.)*

PINOCCHIO: We gotta get Eugene to the doctor.

COP: And you to the jailhouse.

PINOCCHIO: What?!

COP: For starting a fight.

POLICE DOG: Woof!

COP: Throwing your books. Injuring a boy.

POLICE DOG: Woof! Woof!

PINOCCHIO: I didn't throw anything. I was trying to help him. Everybody else ran away!

COP: Your book! Your fault!

PINOCCHIO: That ain't fair! I'm sure as shootin' not going back to no jail.

(PINOCCHIO ducks out of reach of the COP and takes off. One KID from the school has pulled GEPETTA to the scene.)

GEPETTA: Pinocchio!

COP: Get him, boy.

(The DOG chases PINOCCHIO off.)

GEPETTA: Pinocchio! You promised!

(GEPETTA runs after PINOCCHIO.)

SCENE THIRTEEN

(PINOCCHIO is running fast towards the river's edge.)

PINOCCHIO: Ahh! That dog's getting closer and closer! He'll chase me right to the river. Ain't nothing else to do but jump on in.

(PINOCCHIO jumps in the river, but the POLICE DOG jumps in after him.)

PINOCCHIO: *(Swimming to get away.)* Ahhh!

POLICE DOG: *(Drowning.)* Awooo. Awooo.

(PINOCCHIO jumps out of the river, but calls back.)

PINOCCHIO: What's wrong, can't you swim?

POLICE DOG: Awooo. Awooo.

PINOCCHIO: I gotta get away!

(PINOCCHIO can't decide. But then he jumps back in and saves the POLICE DOG from drowning.)

PINOCCHIO: There. Don't go chasing me no more.

POLICE DOG:
> What's given is always returned
> We're in this world
> To help one another— Woof!— and learn

(The POLICE DOG runs off.)

PINOCCHIO: *(Wondering.)* Ain't that something for a dog to say.

(SPERANZA *enters disguised as a poor old woman carrying a heavy bucket of water.*)

OLD WOMAN SPERANZA: Please, could you help me tote this back to town?

PINOCCHIO: I can't go back to town.

OLD WOMAN SPERANZA: I'll give you a drink. The water's muddy for boys who're thinking about running off.

PINOCCHIO: How you know what I'm thinking?

OLD WOMAN SPERANZA: But for boys who know that freedom ain't about doing what you want but doing what's right, for them the water's clear.

PINOCCHIO: But at school, I get blamed for doing wrong when I been doing right!

OLD WOMAN SPERANZA: That mean you should stop trying? You did right saving that ole police dog.

PINOCCHIO: I wasn't gonna let him drown.

OLD WOMAN SPERANZA: You even risked your own self to do it. You've got a good heart.

(PINOCCHIO *picks up the bucket from where she placed it down.*)

PINOCCHIO: I'll carry that—least part ways!

SPERANZA: Might be hope for you yet, little puppet.

PINOCCHIO: You sound like that nurse—(SPERANZA's *angel-sunbeams begin to grow.*) And that law-lady! But you couldn't be, could you??

SPERANZA:
> Think I found me

PINOCCHIO AND SPERANZA:
> An angel

SPERANZA:
> Hear a sweet lullaby

PINOCCHIO AND SPERANZA:
> With bright wings she held me

PINOCCHIO:
> Am I just dreaming?
> Sure I found me

PINOCCHIO AND SPERANZA:
> An angel

(SPERANZA *transforms from the old woman into her angel self.*)

SPERANZA:
> Sure I've always been here

PINOCCHIO AND SPERANZA:
> Flying on bright wings

PINOCCHIO:
> Sure you saved me from harm

SPERANZA:
> Sure I saved you from harm

PINOCCHIO AND SPERANZA:
> *Shining like hope*
> *Rocking me in your arms*
> *Sure I found me an angel*

PINOCCHIO:
> *I wasn't dreaming*

SPERANZA:
> *I've always been here.*

PINOCCHIO: I'm ready. Do you use magic dust or a wand or do I just close my eyes?

SPERANZA: What?

PINOCCHIO: I been trying to do right, but I'm still pinewood from top to bottom. I bet you kiss me, don't you. Go ahead.

SPERANZA: You earn being real, Pinocchio. Nobody gives it to you.

PINOCCHIO: Not even you?

SPERANZA: Not even me.

PINOCCHIO: But you're an angel!

SPERANZA: I'm your Momma's hope and yours, too. Don't you understand?

PINOCCHIO: No! Aw, how am I ever gonna be real now?

SPERANZA: Follow your good heart, Pinocchio!

(She gives him a kiss on the cheek.)

SPERANZA: Muddy or clear?

(PINOCCHIO reaches over, cautiously, to ladle up some water for a drink and SPERANZA disappears.)

SCENE FOURTEEN

(Before PINOCCHIO can see what kind of water is for him, LAMPWICK arrives.)

LAMPWICK: Pinoc!

PINOCCHIO: Lampwick! What are you doing out here.

LAMPWICK: Running away! Them policemen couldn't find you so they come after me. Figures.

PINOCCHIO: Guess we outta go back.

LAMPWICK: Why? You think they'll just forgive and forget?! Naw! The teacher's gonna have our hides! And the police, I heard them talking twenty years for hitting Eugene with that book.

PINOCCHIO: But that ain't fair!

LAMPWICK: Never is for kids like us!
> *Kids like us are really quite bad*
> *That's what everyone tells us*
> *So I can't think of many good reasons to stay*
> *Or anyone who'd be very sad.*

PINOCCHIO: My momma would.

LAMPWICK: Not when she's powerful angry at you.

PINOCCHIO: She is?

LAMPWICK: You broke your promise!

(PINOCCHIO *turns away, frustrated, confused.*)

LAMPWICK:

> *So I've got a big proposition*
> *We'll take an interesting trip*
> *Down the river to a place I know*
> *Away from this dreary condition*
> *We'll give all the adults the slip*
>
> *That's Toytown*
> *We can be who we want to be*
> *Nothing but Boys' Town*
> *Fun all day I think you'll agree*
>
> *That nothing beats a town that's*
> *Racing dancing running laughing*
> *Never homework never school*
> *That's because we make all the rules!*

PINOCCHIO: I'd make up easier rules for turning real.

LAMPWICK:

> *Do whatever you want*
> *From morning to night*
> *What did you ever do here*
> *That anyone said was good and right?*
> *But in Toytown we're free*
> *And there's never a scolding in sight*

And it ain't like twenty years in jail neither. That's what you'll get if you go back now.

PINOCCHIO: I ain't going back to jail!

(*Model-T horn sounds.*)

LAMPWICK: Well here comes our ride! (*The* FOX *and* CAT *arrive in disguise, driving a Model-T Ford.*) Whaddya say?

PINOCCHIO:

> *No more monkey judges*
> *Or policemen on my back*
> *Here's my chance for real adventure*

LAMPWICK AND PINOCCHIO:

> *Let's go!*
> *And not come back!*

(PINOCCHIO *and* LAMPWICK *climb aboard the car.*)

PINOCCHIO AND LAMPWICK, FOX AND CAT:

> *That's Toytown*

PINOCCHIO AND LAMPWICK:

> *We can be who we want to be*
> *Nothing but Boys' Town*

FOX AND CAT:
> Fun all day I think you'll agree

PINOCCHIO AND LAMPWICK, FOX AND CAT:
> That nothing beats a town that's
> Racing dancing running laughing
> We got freedom, we're not fools
> That's because we make all the rules!

FOX AND CAT: We're here!

(FOX *and* CAT *exit. The two* BOYS *play and celebrate.*)

PINOCCHIO AND LAMPWICK:
> Oh we're bad bad bad
> And it feels good good good
> To do all the things they said we shouldn't
> Just because they knew we would

LAMPWICK: Was I right or wrong? And you didn't want to come!

PINOCCHIO: Remember how our teacher used to say, "Don't go with Lampwick, he'll lead you astray."

(*Big laugh from the* BOYS. *But as* BOYS *play, they discover they are growing donkey ears.*)

PINOCCHIO AND LAMPWICK:
> Oh we're bad bad bad
> And it feels good good good
> To do all the things they said we shouldn't
> Just because they knew we would

(*Both laugh at each other at first, thinking it is funny.*)

LAMPWICK: Hey, Pinocchio, your ears are as long as shoe brushes.

PINOCCHIO: Maybe we've got donkey fever.

LAMPWICK: I'll be pulling a sharecropper's cart!

PINOCCHIO: I'll be hee-hawing for all to see!

(*Soon they cannot move like boys, but transform more and more into donkeys. It's not so fun now.* FOX *and* CAT *lurk in the shadows.*)

PINOCCHIO: Lampwick. What's happening!! Look . . . at . . . us!

CAT: You got your wish, Pinocchio.

FOX: You're not a puppet anymore.

(*Big evil laugh from the* FOX AND CAT. WOMAN *comes, gives the* COACHMAN (FOX) *a few dollars and puts a halter on* LAMPWICK *and drags him off. The laughing* FOX *and* CAT *fade upstage.*)

PINOCCHIO: Help! Lampwick! Don't take him! Lampwi . . . Hee-haw . . . !!

(PINOCCHIO *has lost his human voice.*)

SCENE FIFTEEN

(A carnival side-show. CHORUS *arrives as carnival audience. A silly clown ruffle is placed around* PINOCCHIO's *neck.)*

RING MASTER:

> Come on down

CHORUS:

> What's the attraction

RING MASTER:

> A carnival

CHORUS:

> Good for a distraction
> Pay my quarter and I wanna see
> Something for my money
> Wanna laugh at something funny

RING MASTER: Step right up! Ladies and Gentlemen! Boys and Girls! Appearing before your very eyes, a beast plucked from the wilds of Mississippi.

*(*RINGMASTER *cracks a big whip.* PINOCCHIO *begins to jump through a large hoop, held by the* CAT *and* FOX.*)*

RING MASTER:

> Look a there

CHORUS:

> Bet he's acrobatic

RING MASTER:

> Watch him jump

CHORUS:

> Or somethin' more dramatic
> Pay my quarter and I wanna see
> Something for my money
> Wanna laugh at something funny

RING MASTER:

> He was a strong-willed little creature
> but no more!
> A lazy beast
> Who understands the whip

CHORUS:

> My gosh, he almost slipped!
> Paid my quarter now I wanna see
> Something for my money

*(*RING MASTER *cracks whip.* CROWD *likes it.)*

CHORUS: Ooooo.

*(*GEPETTA *arrives.* FOX *steps in front of her.)*

FOX: Quarter, please.

GEPETTA: You can't keep me out!

(GEPETTA *pushes past him.* SPERANZA *appears above the crowd, her light is dim.*)

RING MASTER:

> Come on laugh at something crass
> Pinocchio the dancing ass
> For all the world to see

RING MASTER AND CHORUS:

> For all the world to see!
> Look at him, the little donkey!

GEPETTA: Pinocchio! I can do nothing!

(GEPETTA *cries, her head in her hands.* SPERANZA, *too, holds her head in her hands, a mirror of* GEPETTA. PINOCCHIO *reaches longingly for each of them as he is forced to dance.*)

RING MASTER AND CHORUS:

> Watch him turn, see him bow

CHORUS:

> Look at him polka

RING MASTER:

> He just learned how

CHORUS:

> He can rear, stand on his head

RING MASTER:

> Best trick of all, watch him play dead

GEPETTA: No!

(RING MASTER *shoots a gun and a flag saying "BANG" pops out.* PINOCCHIO *falls.* CHORUS *laughs. As* GEPETTA *runs from the carnival,* SPERANZA'S *light slowly goes out.*)

RING MASTER AND CHORUS:

> We want more
> Give us some action
> Look at that whip!
> Need some satisfaction
> Paid my quarter now I wanna see
> Something for my money
> Something for my money
> Something for my money
> Something for my money

(PINOCCHIO *is forced to jump through the hoop a final time but he stumbles and falls, injuring his leg.*)

(*The crowd laughs and applauds.*)

RING MASTER: The donkey's lame! Get him off the stage!

FOX: What'll ya give me for a little lame donkey? Five dollars. Four?

WOMAN FROM CROWD: Four cents!

FOX: Sold!

WOMAN FROM CROWD: I could use me a tough donkey hide to make a drum.

(*She leads* PINOCCHIO *to the river's edge as circus disperses.*)

WOMAN FROM CROWD: Just limp on down to the water's edge, little donkey. I'll tie this here rope round your hooves. Go on. Drown! I'll be back for your hide tomorrow.

(PINOCCHIO *is thrown into the water. The* WOMAN FROM THE CROWD *has tied a rope around his collar and secured the rope to the bank. She exits.*)

SCENE SIXTEEN

(PINOCCHIO *sinks like a stone, but the* POLICE DOG *arrives, and struggles hard to pull him safely out of the water.*)

POLICE DOG:

> What's given is always returned.
> We're in this world
> To help one another and learn

PINOCCHIO: Guess I got me an angel dog now. Thank you.

POLICE DOG: Woof!

PINOCCHIO: I gotta find Lampwick and get back home. Can you help me?

POLICE DOG: Woof!

(*The* DOG *rushes off and* PINOCCHIO *follows him.*)

PINOCCHIO: Wait up!

POLICE DOG: Woof!

(*They arrive at a shed lit by a lantern's pale light.* LAMPWICK *lies there, dying.*)

PINOCCHIO: Friend!

LAMPWICK: I don't deserve that name.

PINOCCHIO: What's happened to you?

POLICE DOG:

> Sick from hunger
> And too much work.

PINOCCHIO: I'll help you. We'll go home.

LAMPWICK: I don't think you can save me. (*Weakly.*)

> Seeing it through
> I'm making it plain
> We carry this off
> And we'll never be . . .

(LAMPWICK *closes his eyes and dies.*)

PINOCCHIO: He's gone.

(*Lights fade on* LAMPWICK.)

PINOCCHIO:

> *Pinocchio, what'd'ya know*

PINOCCHIO AND DOG:

> *About the good life?*

POLICE DOG: Who do you want to be, Pinocchio?

GEPETTA:

> *In America*

(GEPETTA *appears, isolated, as if on the river.* SPERANZA *appears in the distance, tattered, her angel wings lifeless, without her beams of light.*)

GEPETTA:

> *Can you see me?*
> *Hold me with your wings*

PINOCCHIO:

> *Can you see me?*
> *Speranza*

GEPETTA AND SPERANZA AND PINOCCHIO:

> *Can you see me?*

PINOCCHIO: I may never be real, but I know I want to be better than this.

(PINOCCHIO *very deliberately takes off his donkey ears.*)

GEPETTA, PINOCCHIO, SPERANZA AND POLICE DOG:

> *Sure I found me an angel*

POLICE DOG: Today at the shore I saw a woman . . .

GEPETTA, PINOCCHIO, SPERANZA AND POLICE DOG:

> *Heard her sweet lullaby*

POLICE DOG: She was singing of you.

PINOCCHIO: Was it my momma? Have I broken her heart?

GEPETTA AND SPERANZA:

> *Speranza*

POLICE DOG: She is on the river.

GEPETTA:

> *I have lost all hope.*
> *I'm going home.*

PINOCCHIO: She can't lose hope! This is her home!

(*The light begins to shine again from* SPERANZA. *She lifts her head; she is reviving.*)

SPERANZA: Your final test, Pinocchio—

PINOCCHIO: I gotta find her. I have to bring her back!

(PINOCCHIO *lifts his eyes and sees the revived* SPERANZA.)

PINOCCHIO AND SPERANZA:

> *Angel of hope*
> *Light my way*

POLICE DOG: Woof!

PINOCCHIO: Thank you, friend.

(The POLICE DOG *runs off.* PINOCCHIO *sets off for the river.)*

SCENE SEVENTEEN

*(*PINOCCHIO *arrives at the river's edge. There stands the* FOX *and* CAT *in front of a sailboat—the only boat on the shore.)*

FOX: Well, it's the puppet come back to life.

CAT: Back to life.

PINOCCHIO: I need that boat.

FOX: You gonna be a hero now?

CAT: Rescue your momma?

(Big evil laugh.)

PINOCCHIO: Outta my way, devils! You already stole my money. What more do you want!

*(*FOX *whips a sword out of his cane.)*

FOX: It's dangerous out there.

CAT: You don't want to follow your momma.

FOX: Into the jaws of that monster catfish!

PINOCCHIO: What?!!

FOX: He jumped up from the muddy river bottom and swallowed her whole. He was waiting for her.

FOX AND CAT: Just like he's waiting for you.

PINOCCHIO: I'll save her!

FOX AND CAT: Too late!

FOX: Save yourself!

FOX AND CAT: Come with us!

*(*PINOCCHIO *takes a step toward them, but then lunges for the sailboat. By cleverly manipulating the sail, he defeats the* FOX *and* CAT *in an exciting fight, and they fall into the river.)*

PINOCCHIO: Good-bye, devils! You won't be tricking nobody now! Come on, boat.

*(*PINOCCHIO *leaps into the boat and sets sail onto the river. Big mouth of* CATFISH *lunges out of the water.* PINOCCHIO *is very frightened. Then* PINOCCHIO *sees* GEPETTA *on the inside.)*

PINOCCHIO: Momma? Momma!

*(*PINOCCHIO *plunges himself into the mouth of the* CATFISH.*)*

SCENE EIGHTEEN

*(*PINOCCHIO *sees* GEPETTA, *who is near death, without hope.)*

PINOCCHIO: Gepetta! It's me.
                    I'll never do what I shouldn't do

GEPETTA: One last time to look at you . . . I'm cold.

(PINOCCHIO *holds* GEPETTA. *He searches for something to keep her warm. He discovers the* FOX's *tail, cane and coat.*)

PINOCCHIO: Momma, look. That ole fox got what was coming to him. Put this on. Told you I'd get you a new coat.

(*The* CATFISH *growls. When it does, its breath propels them forward.*)

PINOCCHIO: We're getting out of here.

GEPETTA: You go on alone, Pinocchio—

PINOCCHIO: No!

(PINOCCHIO *picks her up, in a fireman's carry. When the* CATFISH *growls, they are propelled forward.*)

PINOCCHIO: Look! It's the light of sunrise shining right through his mouth. Let's keep him growling, Momma.

(PINOCCHIO *holds on to his mother, and using the* FOX's *cane, pokes and pushes his way through the interior, making the* CATFISH *angrier and angrier, until a final huge growl hurls them out of his belly, then on to the shore.*)

FINALE

(*On the shore. It is a new bright day. They embrace.* PINOCCHIO *has lost his red cheeks—he is real.*)

PINOCCHIO: We're home!

GEPETTA: Look at you. You've grown up.

PINOCCHIO: I love you, Momma.

GEPETTA:
> *Can you see him?*

PINOCCHIO:
> *Today I brought you home*

GEPETTA:
> *Speranza*

PINOCCHIO:
> *Tomorrow I'll find us bread*

GEPETTA:
> *My son, my life, my joy.*

PINOCCHIO:
> *All today's a day for you*
> *Tomorrows full of dreams come true*

PINOCCHIO AND GEPETTA:
> *Pinocchio a real boy*

(GEPETTA *pulls something from the pocket of the* FOX's *coat.*)

GEPETTA: Son, what is this?

PINOCCHIO: My silver dollars!!! I promised I'd bring 'em to you and I did!

(TOWN *begins to reassemble.*)

GEPETTA AND PINOCCHIO:
> I got my dreams to deliver

CHORUS:
> The steam heat's humming
> The water's all a shimmer!

FIRE-EATER: (*Entering with his trunk.*) Gepetta?

GEPETTA: Mr. Fire-eater!

FIRE-EATER: I'm hoping to dock my Travelling Steam Boat Puppet show in Natchez for the winter. I can offer you work as a puppet carver if you'll accept. We can make some more Pinocchios.

GEPETTA: Thank you. Yes. This is my good and loving son.

(FIRE-EATER *gives* PINOCCHIO *a delighted smile, then a big hug.*)

FIRE-EATER AND GEPETTA:
> All todays a day for you

PINOCCHIO:
> The door of hope is open

PINOCCHIO, GEPETTA & FIRE-EATER:
> Tomorrows full of dreams come true

PINOCCHIO, GEPETTA & FIRE-EATER & CHORUS:
> Dreams that we never stopped hoping
> Would see us through

(*During this chorus,* PINOCCHIO "*grows up*" *to become Mayor (he is given the red, white and blue ribbon-banner that reads "Mayor" and a boater hat).*

> 'Tis a grand day
> America!
> There's a future
> Stretching out before me
> It's a brand new day!
> America!
> Red white and blue sure
> That all can succeed
> The band plays

(*A new immigrant appears. She is poor, holding her bags, on the threshold of a new life. The carousel stops as it did for* GEPETTA. PINOCCHIO *crosses to the new immigrant. She offers him a carved Statue of Liberty.* PINOCCHIO *takes it in exchange for his bag of gold.* SPERANZA's *light floods* PINOCCHIO, GEPETTA *and the new immigrant—the angel* SPERANZA. PINOCCHIO *takes* SPERANZA's *hand and they join the town.*)

SPERANZA:
> All todays a day for you

PINOCCHIO:
> The door of hope is wide open

PINOCCHIO AND SPERANZA:
> Tomorrows full of dreams come true

CHORUS:

Dreams that we never stopped hoping
Would see us through
Living on the river
I feel so free
Nobody's gonna separate
My hope from me
Big boat big river
We'll settle right down
Away from sweat
Away from toil
In this main street town
America!
America!
On the Mississippi
My home.

CURTAIN

THE WOLF
AND ITS SHADOWS

by
Sandra Fenichel Asher

THE WOLF AND ITS SHADOWS

CHARACTERS

First Actor (female) ....also plays Wolf Maiden
Second Actor (male)..................................also plays Dog, Story Dog,
                                              Young Man/Werewolf, Old Wolf
Third Actor (male) ....also plays Hunter, Puppet Wolf,
                                 Priest, Rival, Shepherd, Story Shepherds,
                                 Puppet Sheep, Voice of Spirit of the Sky

(Actor playing DOG projects a young voice and appearance and the antic, in-decisive manner of a puppy. In contrast, WOLF's voice should be mature and her movements strong and efficient. At first, DOG misinterprets her forceful natural bearing as a personal threat, but it is not. To WOLF, DOG *is* a puppy: amusing, naive. To DOG, WOLF is a mystery, at once both fascinating and dangerous.)

MUSIC

A flute is suggested to highlight certain parts of the action, but other instruments may be used. The effect should be natural, folkloric.

TIME

One night, from dusk until dawn, and imagined times.

PLACE

A forest, and imagined places. The stage may be bare except for tree stumps left and right.

Note: Costumes are simple; masks, puppets, lighting, and language receive emphasis. WOLF *and* DOG *wear masks that are close, at least in spirit, to the actual animals, but puppets and masks of the story characters are highly stylized. There is an obvious difference between the artifice of the stories told by* HUNTER, PRIEST, *and* SHEPHERD *and the stark simplicity of those told by* WOLF.

SOURCES OF THE STORIES

The Fable of the Wolf and the Dog—Aesop
The Foolish Wolf—Russian folktale
The Tired Wolf—Tlingit story
The Caribou and the Wolf—Inuit story paraphrased in NEVER CRY WOLF
by Farley Mowat. Used by permission.
The Old Wolf in Seven Fables—Gotthold Ephraim Lessing
(German, 1729–1781)

(AT RISE: *Flute is heard. As house lights dim, the Milky Way—or Wolf Road— appears above the dark stage. Flute fades out as a chorus of wolf howls begins.* ACTORS, *without masks, enter and take places center, down left, and down right, facing audience. Howls fade. Flute plays softly under the following dialogue.*)

FIRST ACTOR: *(begins a subtle jogging motion with her hands and feet, reminiscent of the wolf's effortless trot. The movement continues throughout this passage creating a mood of ritual rather than realism.)* It is said that the wolf travels easily between the spirit world and our own—

SECOND ACTOR: *(Picking up the rhythmic jog.)* Along the path we now call the Milky Way—

THIRD ACTOR: *(Picking up jog.)* Once known as the Wolf Road.

SECOND ACTOR: Forever moving—

FIRST ACTOR: Moving in shadow—

THIRD ACTOR: Moving in mystery—

FIRST ACTOR: The wolf disappears into the night—

SECOND ACTOR: And returns before the morning sun.

THIRD ACTOR: Knowing what we cannot see—

FIRST ACTOR: Seeing what it cannot say—

SECOND ACTOR: The wolf dies—

THIRD ACTOR: And is reborn—

FIRST ACTOR: Dies—

SECOND ACTOR: And is reborn—

THIRD ACTOR: In both worlds—

SECOND ACTOR: And in the stories people tell.

FIRST ACTOR: *(Stops jogging.)* We tell the stories.

SECOND ACTOR: *(Stops jogging.)* We believe the stories.

THIRD ACTOR: *(Stops jogging.)* We become the stories.

SECOND ACTOR: Be still!

FIRST ACTOR: Listen!

SECOND ACTOR: Understand!

(*Stars and Flute fade.* FIRST *and* SECOND ACTORS *put on masks of* WOLF *and* DOG.)

THIRD ACTOR: *(To audience.)* Early one evening, a wolf and a dog chanced to meet. (THIRD ACTOR *exits. Forest sounds are heard.* WOLF *trots toward* DOG; *circles him at a safe distance.* WOLF *is cautious, but neither aggressive nor afraid. Forest sounds fade under dialogue.*)

WOLF: Good evening, Dog. What brings you into the forest?

DOG: *(Wary, but eager to please.)* Oh, I enjoy a romp in the wilderness now and then, Cousin Wolf. But perhaps I have wandered a bit farther than usual.

WOLF: It is I who have traveled farther than usual. Hunger forced me to leave my pack. *(She growls with the thought of it;* DOG *whimpers and cowers although* WOLF *shows no interest in eating him.*)

DOG: Hu-hunger?

WOLF: We have gone many days without a successful hunt.

DOG: You haven't eaten in *days?* How dreadful!

WOLF: You seem fat and comfortable enough. Tell me, Dog, how do you manage it?

DOG: There's food enough for all at my master's house—if you're willing to work.

WOLF: I do what I must to keep from starving. What is this work you speak of?

DOG: I bark to keep thieves from my master's door. (*Demonstrates with noisy yips and yaps.*) In return, he gives me scraps from his own table, morning, noon, and night. That is the secret of my shiny coat.

WOLF: I could do as much as you and more. (*Emits truly menacing growls and snarls, frightening* DOG *again.*) Is there work for me at your master's house?

DOG: (*More than slightly apprehensive.*) No doubt there is.

WOLF: Good! Show me the way.

(*With a nervous whimper,* DOG *obediently leads the way. Lights, Flute, and Forest sounds indicate a change in time and place as* WOLF *and* DOG *circle stage. Suddenly,* WOLF *stops and sniffs the air suspiciously. Flute and sounds fade. A sharp Whistle is heard offstage, in the distance.*)

WOLF: We must hide! Quickly! (*She searches for a hiding place.*)

DOG: Why? What's wrong? (*Also sniffs air.*)

WOLF: There's a man nearby.

HUNTER: (*Offstage, from a distance.*) Dog! (*Another Whistle.*)

WOLF: (*Not cowardly, but truly concerned.*) Hurry! Hide!

(DOG *hesitates, not sure which way to run.* WOLF *slips away and hides. She may be seen, now and then, watching what follows, but never where the* HUNTER *can see her.*)

DOG: (*Glances off in direction of* HUNTER'S *call.*) It's only a hunter. He won't do *us* any harm.

HUNTER: (*Enters, calling* DOG, *but searching for* WOLF, *shotgun at the ready.*) Dog! Come to me! (*Another second's hesitation and* DOG *trots over, whining apologetically.* HUNTER *lowers gun and pets* DOG.) Why, you're hardly more than a pup! Was it my imagination then? Or did I just see you trotting through the forest with a wolf?

DOG: (*All tail-wagging affection now.*) We're going to my master's house. The wolf intends to ask for work and be given food in return.

HUNTER: You're bringing a wolf to your master's house?

DOG: (*Confiding, in a whisper.*) She'll make a meal of *me* if I don't.

HUNTER: (*Laughs it off.*) She'll have to catch you first.

DOG: She's very quick!

HUNTER: (*Tapping his head.*) But not very clever. The wolf's a fool and that's a fact.

DOG: She didn't seem . . . foolish.

HUNTER: Let me tell you a story. Then you may decide for yourself.

DOG: (*With immediate, childlike eagerness.*) Is there a dog in your story?

HUNTER: There is. (*Puts gun aside and pulls* STORY DOG *mask from his coat or elsewhere on stage. He hands mask to* DOG, *who admires it, "tries it on." Music and*

Lights mark transition into story. Music fades as HUNTER *speaks, but may be used to highlight action.)* A dog that had grown old and weary was of no more use to his master. And so, he was turned out into the forest and left to die.

DOG: How horrible! *(Begins to yip and whine; identifying with the story, he speaks lines in quotation marks as* STORY DOG.)

HUNTER: Bemoaning his fate, the dog made a terrible racket—(DOG *howls mournfully.)* until he attracted the attention of a huge, grey wolf. *(Pulls out* PUPPET WOLF. *At the sight of* PUPPET WOLF, STORY DOG *yips in alarm.* HUNTER *puts* PUPPET WOLF *on his own arm and speaks lines in quotation marks as* PUPPET WOLF.) Greetings, mangy cur. Do you remember me? I was the one you chased from your village when I was driven there by cold and hunger. At last, I will have my revenge!

DOG: What do you intend to do with me, WOLF?

HUNTER: First, I intend to eat your fur—(STORY DOG *whines.)*

HUNTER: —your hide—(STORY DOG *whimpers.)* and your flesh. (STORY DOG *yowls.)* And after I've eaten all that I can, I intend to dance on your miserable bones!

DOG: *(A series of whimpers, then inspiration strikes* STORY DOG.) Foolish wolf! I barely have flesh enough to cover my bones, let alone satisfy your hunger. Why not fatten me up a bit, so you can truly enjoy your feast? Bring me some fresh mare's meat and see the difference it makes.

HUNTER: Hmmm, there's wisdom in your idea, mangy cur. I will slaughter a mare for you. *(With leaps, loud growls, music underscoring and* PUPPET *jaws snapping,* HUNTER *mimes the kill and delivery.)* Here you are!

DOG: Many thanks! *(chomping, slurping, and licking his chops.)* Aaaaah! My first good meal in months. How refreshing!

HUNTER: Well, are you fat enough yet?

DOG: Fatter. Oh, definitely fatter. But not as *tender* as I might be. If you fed me a bit of lamb, you'd be pleased with the difference it would make.

HUNTER: Do you think so?

DOG: Oh, I know so.

HUNTER: Wait here. I'll steal you a lamb from the shepherd's flock.

(Again, much leaping, growling, Music, and snapping.)

DOG: *(To audience.)* Has there ever been a more foolish creature?

HUNTER: *(As "lamb" is delivered,* STORY WOLF *begins to show signs that the effort is taking its toll.)* Your lamb.

DOG: Eternally grateful. *(Chomping and slurping greedily.)* Mmmmmm! With every bite, I feel my old body growing stronger and stronger.

HUNTER: And are you fat enough now?

DOG: Fatter and fatter still. But not as *sweet* as I think you would like. Bring me a wild boar to eat, and my flesh will turn tasty as suckling pig.

HUNTER: Hmmm, yes, I see what you mean.

DOG: I thought you might.

HUNTER: I'll hunt your wild boar. *(More music, leaping about and growling from* PUPPET WOLF *as "boar" is killed with difficulty and delivered.* PUPPET WOLF *is obviously near exhaustion from his efforts; more subtly,* STORY DOG *is gaining strength.)* This is the last of your meals, cur, and the end of my patience as well.

DOG: Won't be a minute! *(Much drooling and chomping, ending in a deeply satis-fied sigh—and a burp.)*

WOLF: I've waited long enough. The time has come for me to kill you and eat you up.

DOG: *(As* PUPPET WOLF *moves toward him.)* Foolish wolf! Thanks to your kind-ness, I've regained my strength and am more than a match for you! *(Much barking, growling, and music, as* STORY DOG *attacks* PUPPET WOLF, *eventually pulling it off* HUNTER's *arm and dashing it to the ground.)* Spend a few days in your den, foolish wolf, licking your wounds and rethinking your plans for me. I suggest you give up all hope of revenge.

(Music and Lights mark transition out of story as DOG *bays triumphantly over fallen* PUPPET WOLF. MUSIC *plays under following exchange until story resumes.)*

HUNTER: *(As himself, to* DOG.) So! You agree with me, then, that the wolf is a foolish creature?

DOG: *(Shaking off the story's spell, puts aside mask and looks at the fallen* PUPPET WOLF.) I suppose you could be right, Hunter. But how could a creature so foolish *survive*?

HUNTER: Ah, well, the story goes on. No dog in this part. Would you mind playing the wolf?

DOG: The wolf?

HUNTER: It's the easiest part.

DOG: *(Uncertainly, as* HUNTER *puts* PUPPET WOLF *on his arm.)* Well, all right.

(Music and Lights mark transition into story as HUNTER *retrieves his gun; mimes placing of meat.)*

HUNTER: No sooner had the wolf decided to be more careful in selecting his prey than he came upon a fine morsel of meat lying in the road right in front of him.

DOG: *(as* PUPPET WOLF, *"happens along" and discovers meat.)* Hmmmmm, no tricks left in that one, I'll wager! Some careless peasant must have dropped it by mistake. His loss is my gain.

*(DOG *moves* PUPPET WOLF *to the meat and begins to devour it noisily.* HUNTER *raises his shotgun and aims it at him.)*

HUNTER: Foolish wolf! It was no careless peasant who left that meat in your path, but a mighty hunter—

*(PUPPET WOLF's *head snaps up and turns toward* HUNTER.)*

DOG: *(As himself, terrified.)* No!

*(GUN *goes off.* PUPPET WOLF *slumps over "dead" as* DOG *cowers, whimpering.)*

HUNTER: And so it was that the foolish wolf met his end. *(Music and Lights mark transition out of story as* HUNTER *grabs* PUPPET WOLF *away from* DOG. *Music fades.)* Oh stop your trembling. It was only a story. But the wolf *is a* fool and not the least bit worthy of your company. Go home to your master. That's where you belong. (HUNTER *strides off, laughing and swinging* PUPPET WOLF *"carcass" carelessly over his shoulder as* WOLF *emerges from hiding and speaks to* DOG.)

WOLF: Are you all right?

DOG: (*His trembling belies his words.*) Oh—yes. It was only a story.

WOLF: This time.

DOG: (*Considering the story as he pulls himself together.*) Tell me something, please. Why would a wolf fatten an old dog with enough meat to feed his own entire pack?

WOLF: He wouldn't.

DOG: I thought not! You're no fool. You were smart enough to hide from that hunter and his gun. And you care for yourself in the wild by your own wit and cunning.

WOLF: I've learned all that from my pack.

DOG: Then why does the hunter tell such a terrible story about you if it isn't true?

WOLF: I don't know. But there are many hunters and many stories.

DOG: Can you tell a different one?

WOLF: I can.

(*Flute plays under the following. Lights create an atmosphere very different from that of* HUNTER's *story.*) One day, men of the Wolf Clan were out fishing when they saw a shadow drifting through the water. They paddled toward it and discovered a wolf, swimming so slowly it barely seemed to move. The poor animal was exhausted.

DOG: (*Full of sympathy and concern.*) Oh! And did the men shoot it?

WOLF: No. They returned with it to their village.

DOG: They brought the wolf home with them!

WOLF: They did. And the wolf remained with the clan. It hunted with the men who had saved its life. Because it knew how to track deer and other wild animals, the clan prospered and never lacked for meat.

DOG: And they all lived happily ever after!

WOLF: (*Patiently.*) And they all lived *well* for many years. But the day came when the wolf lay without moving before the house of the clan chief. Its friends were sad, for they knew it was very old and soon must take the Shadow Trail.

(*Flute fades out.*)

DOG: (*A quiet whimper.*) Oh, my.

WOLF: Just as the sun sank, the wolf died. (*Wolf howls begin, low at first, and then building.*) Then other wolves were heard, singing a death song for it. Their voices rose and fell, filling the forest with sadness. (WOLF *and* DOG *join in plaintive howling, which rises and then slowly fades away.*) From that day on, the song of the wolf was used by the clan as a mourning song, and a figure of the tired wolf was carved and painted on their houseposts. (*Flute plays as*

WOLF *stands or kneels behind seated* DOG, *forming a totem pole.*) "Courageous hunter," the people called the wolf—

DOG: *(Caught up in story.)* Forever moving—

WOLF: Tireless provider—

DOG: Moving in shadow—

WOLF: Loyal companion—

DOG: Moving in mystery.

WOLF: Great Spirit—

DOG and WOLF: —teach me to be like the wolf!

(A pause. Flute fades. WOLF *and* DOG *break up totem pole. Lights return to forest.)*

DOG: *(All puppy enthusiasm again.)* Oh, I like that story, Cousin Wolf! Let's hurry on to my master's house.

*(*DOG *and* WOLF *circle stage in trot, with Lights, Flute, and Forest Sounds indicating change of time and place. Then* WOLF *stops suddenly and sniffs the air as before.)*

WOLF: Wait!

DOG: Another man? *(Sniffs, follows scent to direction of* PRIEST.*)*

WOLF: Yes! Hide!

DOG: It's only the village priest! What harm could he possible do us?

WOLF: Hide, I tell you! *(*WOLF *hides.)*

PRIEST: *(Enters, genuinely alarmed.)* Come here, Dog! *(*DOG *hesitates, then obeys.)* That's it. Come to me. *(Embraces* DOG, *who whimpers, grateful for approval.)* There, there. Nothing to fear now. But what in the name of all that is holy were you doing with that wolf?

DOG: We're going to my master's house. She intends to ask for work and be given food in return.

PRIEST: You're bringing a wolf to your master's house?

DOG: She's not a fool, the wolf. She knows many things—

PRIEST: Indeed she does! *(In a terrified whisper.)* The wolf is the Devil's dog!

DOG: The Devil's dog?

PRIEST: The Devil's *work*—

DOG: *(Getting caught up in* PRIEST'*s insistent chant.)* The Devil's work!

PRIEST: The Devil's *power*—

DOG: The Devil's power!

PRIEST: Beware!

DOG: But there are those who wish to become like the wolf—

PRIEST: *(A fearful whisper again.)* They are the accursed! Men and women who ask the dark forces of the spirit world to give them the wolf's strength and cunning so they may do evil in this world: "Phantom of Darkness, hear me!" they cry. "Send me the shape that freezes men's blood. Spirit of the Night, make me a werewolf!"

(A wolf howl is heard.)

DOG: *(Cowering.)* A werewolf?

PRIEST: You travel the forest at night. Have you never seen such things?

DOG: Never!

PRIEST: Then I must tell you of an innocent like yourself who learned to be more observant.

DOG: *(Concerned, but ever willing to please and be pleased.)* Is there a dog in your story?

PRIEST: No. But if there were, it would send any wolf it met back into the shadows of the night. *(DOG whimpers; PRIEST speaks more gently, takes out YOUNG MAN mask.)* You will play a young man.

DOG: All right. As long as I don't have to play the wolf. Things don't seem to go well for them in stories.

PRIEST: There's good reason for that. Let's begin. *(As SECOND ACTOR exchanges DOG mask for mask of YOUNG MAN, PRIEST takes out mask of RIVAL and shows it to him.)* I will play your rival for the affections of a lovely young maiden.

(Music plays and Lights change to indicate a new time and place as PRIEST points down left, where FIRST ACTOR, in MAIDEN mask, enters.)

MAIDEN: Once there was a maiden beloved of all, both for her goodness and her beauty.

YOUNG MAN: *(Crosses to her.)* Though many a youth came to woo her, there was but one she loved in return.

PRIEST: *(Holds up and points to RIVAL mask.)* But still others loved her and were sore angered that she showed favor to only one—*(Points at YOUNG MAN and speaks disdainfully.)*—and such a one as that!

(As Music plays, MAIDEN sits down left, her back to the OTHERS. PRIEST, playing RIVAL, approaches YOUNG MAN and speaks to him, drawing him away from MAIDEN. PRIEST speaks lines in quotation marks as RIVAL.)

PRIEST: Is it right, do you think, that your old grandfather should come from his grave and claim so young and fair a maiden as his bride?

YOUNG MAN: What do you know of my grandfather that you taunt me?

PRIEST: Ah! There are tales told to us by our own grandfathers that we have not forgot.

YOUNG MAN: *(Moves farther away from MAIDEN, toward his own "home" down right.)* Your bitter words strike at my very soul.

PRIEST: *(Following him, as RIVAL.)* And well they should! Your grandfather was known as a cruel and violent man. Legend says that a curse rested upon him, and that at certain times he was possessed of an evil spirit that wreaked its fury on mankind.

YOUNG MAN: *(Protesting in vain.)* But my grandfather has been dead many years, and there is nothing to remind the world of him except the legend—

PRIEST: And a dagger given to him by a witch! *(As YOUNG MAN surreptitiously takes dagger from its place.)* This dagger, they say, is a marvel among weapons—and it hangs in *your* chamber.

YOUNG MAN: And what of that?

PRIEST: *(Taunting.)* What of that, indeed? *(Strolls away from* YOUNG MAN, *who holds up dagger and speaks to audience.)*

YOUNG MAN: This magical dagger hints at the legend's awful truth: Slumbering a generation, the curse that haunted my grandfather has awakened in my blood. And it is this curse that stands between me and the maiden I adore.

YOUNG MAN: *(Hides dagger in his belt and crosses toward* MAIDEN.) But they say love is stronger than all else, and she is trustful—

MAIDEN: *(Meets* YOUNG MAN *at center and takes his hand.)* My heart rejoices to see you safely returned from your travels.

PRIEST: *(Breaks them apart as he passes between them, speaking as* RIVAL *and leading* MAIDEN *back to her "home area" down left.)* It is strange, is it not, that this gallant lover so often goes away—and to *where* no one knows.

YOUNG MAN: *(To audience, as he returns down right.)* I live in constant terror, suspected by one and loved by another, never knowing in whose presence the curse will seize me—nor how to prevent it.

PRIEST: *(As* RIVAL, *to* MAIDEN.) Have you heard, Lady, that the country round about's been ravaged by a werewolf?

MAIDEN: Aye, the creature's feared by one and all.

PRIEST: By day a man, by night a wolf given to slaughter! They say it leads a charmed life against which no human power prevails.

MAIDEN: Not so. The dream-readers say the earth will be freed of this monster when the most valorous of men offers himself as sacrifice to its rage.

PRIEST: Perhaps. But I have no taste for sacrifice. I prefer a joyous feast—like that in the sacred grove tomorrow night.

MAIDEN: Ah, yes! *(Bypassing* RIVAL, *to his annoyance, she crosses and extends her hand to* YOUNG MAN.)

MAIDEN: Will you come with me to the feast of Saint Alfreda?

YOUNG MAN: I am called away tomorrow.

MAIDEN: Again? By whom? And to where?

YOUNG MAN: Someday, perhaps, I will explain. But now I beg you, on your love for me, do not go to the sacred grove without me.

MAIDEN: My father would be sore displeased were I not there with the other maidens.

YOUNG MAN: Do not go, I beseech you. *(Kneeling.)* See, on my knees I ask it!

MAIDEN: How pale you are, and trembling.

YOUNG MAN: Do not go to the sacred grove tomorrow night.

MAIDEN: *(Coyly.)* Do you doubt my love—or is it the werewolf you fear?

YOUNG MAN: *(Stands, obviously upset.)* It is the werewolf.

MAIDEN: *(Frightened, moves away from him.)* Why do you look at me so strangely?

YOUNG MAN: *(A pause, then—)* Sit beside me and I will tell you why. *(They sit.)* Last night, I dreamed I was the werewolf.

MAIDEN: *(Pulls away from him in alarm.)* You must not speak of such things.

YOUNG MAN: It was only a dream.

MAIDEN: It is evil!

YOUNG MAN: (*Goes on, needing to confess.*) A grizzled old man stood at my bedside. "Thy soul is mine," he said, "and thou shall live out my curse. Go, search, and kill!"

(*There is an anguished howl.* MAIDEN *cries out. Flute sustains eerie note.*)

MAIDEN: (*Backing away from* YOUNG MAN.) How can it be that you dream such terrible dreams?

YOUNG MAN: (*In despair.*) I would tell you—if I could.

PRIEST: (*Approaches them as* RIVAL, *speaking lightheartedly.*) What's this? I think I've never seen a sorrier pair. (*Offers* MAIDEN *his hand, separating the lovers a third time.*) There's nothing to fear, sweet lady. I will escort you to the feast.

MAIDEN: (*Relieved, gives him her hand.*) I thank you, kind sir.

YOUNG MAN: (*Seeing he has no choice.*) Very well, go to the sacred grove if you must. But take this dagger with you. (*Gives dagger to* MAIDEN.)

MAIDEN: You would go on your journey without it?

YOUNG MAN: You may have more need of it than I. If you do, never hesitate to use it.

MAIDEN: But why would I need to—?

YOUNG MAN: (*Avoids her question, kisses her hand.*) Farewell, my beloved. (*To himself, as* RIVAL *leads her away.*) How will you love me when you know my sacrifice? Farewell—forever. (*He exits.*)

PRIEST: (*As himself, to audience, as he and* MAIDEN *circle to center.*) And so without another thought for her young man, the maiden came to the sacred grove the following night.

(*Music plays;* PRIEST, *as* RIVAL, *dances briefly with* MAIDEN.)

MAIDEN: The feast of Saint Alfreda is always so merry. I do love the singing and dancing and games—(*She stops short, alarmed. Music stops abruptly.*)

PRIEST: What is it, my lady?

MAIDEN: (*A howl offstage; she listens, mesmerized, then whispers—*) The werewolf!

(*A scream offstage. Flute sounds a shrill note of alarm. The stage darkens.* SECOND ACTOR, *as* WEREWOLF, *leaps onto stage up right, "bellowing hoarsely, gnashing his fangs, and tossing hither and thither the yellow foam from his snapping jaws."*)

PRIEST: (*Urges* MAIDEN *to cross down left, remains center and speaks to audience as himself.*) Terror seized upon all. Stout hearts were frozen with fear. (PRIEST *holds* RIVAL *mask up, but not in front of his face, and backs away.*) The werewolf sought the MAIDEN straight, as if an evil power drew him to the spot where she stood.

MAIDEN: (*As she and* WEREWOLF *face one another.*) I am not afraid, for my love has given me this dagger—

(*As Flute plays, action proceeds in slow motion.* MAIDEN *raises dagger and begins its arc toward* WEREWOLF, *then hesitates.* WEREWOLF *grabs her wrist, as if to stop her, but actually helps her continue the arc, guiding the dagger and "burying it" above his heart. With a human cry of pain,* WEREWOLF *falls. Struck by the*

WEREWOLF's *human cry,* MAIDEN *remains beside him, transfixed, until, still holding up* RIVAL's *mask,* PRIEST *leads her down left. She leaves* WEREWOLF *reluctantly. Stage goes dark everywhere but down left.)*

PRIEST: *(As* RIVAL, *kneels before* MAIDEN.*)* Why do you seem so troubled, my lady? The people do you homage, for the werewolf is dead, and you alone have slain him.

MAIDEN: *(Still in a daze.)* Bring me my love!

PRIEST: My lady, he is gone and never tells us where!

MAIDEN: I will neither eat nor sleep 'til he is found.

PRIEST: *(Speaks reluctantly, while* YOUNG MAN *rises without* WEREWOLF *mask, staggers "home" and falls.)* There is one among the crowd who swears he saw the young man this very evening, entering his own house—

MAIDEN: I must go to him! *(She rushes across stage as lights come up on* YOUNG MAN. *She mimes pounding on door.)* His chamber door is barred! Answer me, my love!

PRIEST: *(Putting away* RIVAL's *mask; as himself, to audience—)* No answer came. Afraid, the townspeople battered down the door, and when it fell they saw where he lay upon his bed.

MAIDEN: *(Sinks to her knees beside* YOUNG MAN.*)* He sleeps. See, he holds a portrait in his hand—my portrait! How fair he is!

PRIEST: But no, he was not asleep. His face was calm, as if he dreamed of his beloved, but his shirt was red with the blood that streamed from a wound—a dagger wound just above the heart. The Devil's dog—

MAIDEN: *(Aghast,* YOUNG MAN's *blood on her hand.)* The Devil's dog!

PRIEST: The Devil's work!

MAIDEN: *(Stands away from* YOUNG MAN's *body.)* The Devil's work!

PRIEST: The Devil's power!

MAIDEN: The Devil's power!

PRIEST: Beware!

MAIDEN: Beware! *(She runs offstage.)*

PRIEST: *(Quietly, but emphatically.)* Beware! *(Music and Lights indicate end of story.* DOG *replaces his original mask and struggles to lift his weary body from the ground.* PRIEST *picks up* WEREWOLF *mask gingerly. Music fades.)* Do you see now, Dog, why you must watch the company you keep? The wolf is *evil.*

DOG: I have visited the forest often enough, yet I have never witnessed such strange goings-on. But I do see that these stories are hard work—and dangerous.

PRIEST: *(Sternly.)* Take them lightly at your own peril, DOG. *(Dog cowers;* PRIEST *speaks more gently, but with conviction.)* Go home to your master. That's where you belong. *(A last, earnest look and* PRIEST *exits.* FIRST ACTOR *enters as* WOLF, *stands away from* DOG, *unsure of* DOG's *reaction.* DOG *is equally uneasy.)*

DOG: Do you believe you're the Devil's dog?

WOLF: I believe I am wolf, a creature like any other, including the one called "human."

DOG: Then why does the priest tell this story about you?

WOLF: I don't know. But there are many priests and many stories.

DOG: Will you tell me another?

WOLF: *(A pause, as she considers, then—)* I will. *(Flute and Lights indicate a mood change, like that of* WOLF's *earlier story.)* In the beginning there was a Woman—

DOG: *(All puppy enthusiasm again.)* And a dog?

WOLF: *(Patiently.)* Not yet. There was a Woman, and a Man. And nothing else walked or swam or flew in the world—until one day the Woman dug a great hole in the ground and began fishing in it. One by one she pulled out all the animals—

DOG: Now there was a dog!

WOLF: Now there was a dog. And the last animal the Woman pulled out was the caribou. Then the Spirit of the Sky spoke to the Woman—

THIRD ACTOR: *(Unseen, as voice of* SPIRIT OF THE SKY.*)* Caribou will be the sustenance of humankind. Send it out over the land to multiply.

WOLF: In time the land was filled with caribou. The sons of the Woman hunted well. They were fed and clothed and had good skin tents to live in, all from the caribou. But the sons of the Woman hunted only the large, fat caribou, for the weak and the small and the sick were no good to eat—

DOG: I wouldn't mind them!

WOLF: Neither would I. But the people wanted only the fattest and strongest animals, and soon there were fewer of them. When the people saw only sick and weak caribou remaining, they complained to the Woman.

WOLF: Then the Woman made magic—*(Flute and perhaps drum rise and fade under dialogue.)*—and spoke to the Spirit of the Sky: "Your work is no good, for the caribou grow sick and weak, and if we eat them, we must grow sick and weak also."

THIRD ACTOR: *(As* SPIRIT OF THE SKY.*)* My work is good. I shall make the wolf— *(A distant howl rises and fades under dialogue.)*—and he shall tell his children, and they will eat the sick and the weak and the small caribou, so that land will be left for the fat and the strong ones.

DOG: And so the Spirit made the wolf!

WOLF: Yes. And this is why the caribou and the wolf are one; for the caribou feeds the wolf, but the wolf keeps the caribou strong.

(Flute and Lights mark transition out of story.)

DOG: So there is plenty for all!

WOLF: There was—in the beginning.

DOG: *(Undaunted.)* There still *is*—at my master's house. Come and work for him, as we planned. It is almost daylight. We must hurry.

(Once more, WOLF *and* DOG *circle stage as before, accompanied by Flute and Light changes that indicate the approach of dawn. This time, both* DOG *and* WOLF *stop and sniff the air. Music fades.)*

DOG: Sheep.

WOLF: And a man!

DOG: We're close to the edge of the forest. There must be a flock grazing nearby. (*Sniffs the air.*)

WOLF: We must hide!

DOG: But it's only a shepherd. He'll do us no harm.

SHEPHERD: (*Offstage.*) Wolf! Sound the alarm!

WOLF: Hide!

(WOLF *hides, as before.* DOG *hesitates, not sure which way to go.* SHEPHERD *enters; orders* DOG *to his side with the confidence of a master, tapping the ground with his staff.*)

SHEPHERD: Dog! Come! Sit! (*A moment's hesitation, then* DOG *does so, whimpering apologetically.*) What business have we here, you traipsing through the woods with that greedy wolf?

DOG: She didn't seem greedy to me. Only hungry.

SHEPHERD: It begins with hunger, but where does it end?

DOG: At my master's house: She'll be fed well for the work she does—

SHEPHERD: It will end in disaster!

DOG: But she's willing to work—

SHEPHERD: So she says *now*.

DOG: I've no reason to doubt what she says—

SHEPHERD: I'll tell you a story about the wolf and its greed, and that will be reason enough.

DOG: (*Attempting to slip away.*) A story?

SHEPHERD: Sit!

DOG: (*Sits obediently; whimpers meekly*—) Is there a dog in your story?

SHEPHERD: There's talk of dogs, but you will play the wolf. (*Takes out mask of* OLD WOLF *and offers it to* DOG.)

DOG: Oh, I really don't think I would like that.

SHEPHERD: Do as you're told! I will play three shepherds. (*Takes out* PUPPET SHEEP *and puts it on his arm.*) And several sheep.

DOG: All at once?

SHEPHERD: Of course not. One at a time. (*Music, Lights mark transition into* SHEPHERD*'s story.* SHEPHERD *baas once or twice, to "test"* PUPPET SHEEP, *then takes up stance as if tending an entire flock. He baas again, impatiently, at* DOG, *who reluctantly puts* OLD WOLF *mask up in front of his face. Satisfied,* SHEPHERD *begins story. Music fades in and out as needed to underscore the action.*) The wolf had grown old, and decided to mend his ways and live in peace with the neighboring shepherds. So he approached the flock closest to his den. (SHEPHERD *waves* DOG *closer with his staff, while, on the other hand,* SHEEP *baas nervously at* DOG*'s approach.* DOG *speaks lines in quotation marks as* OLD WOLF. SHEPHERD *speaks lines in quotation marks as three different* STORY SHEPHERDS.)

DOG: Shepherd, you consider me a robber and a bloodthirsty one at that.

SHEPHERD: I do, Old Wolf.

DOG: Then you must allow me to make amends. Give me one sheep a year, and I will guard the rest of your flock against all danger—

SHEPHERD: Let me understand, Old Wolf: Are you offering to guard my flock against yourself?

DOG: That is my intention. (SHEPHERD *bursts out laughing;* SHEEP *baas in amusement.*) You laugh? You find my proposal delightful?

SHEPHERD: *(Wipes tears from his eyes.)* I find your proposal ridiculous! But thank you, old fool, for a much needed chuckle. Good day. (SHEPHERD *strolls away with* SHEEP, *chuckling and baaing.*)

DOG: *(Dropping mask, speaks as himself.)* Shepherd?

SHEPHERD: *(As himself.)* What is it, Dog? Why do you interrupt my story?

DOG: I want to know why the shepherd in your story laughed. The old wolf asked for only one sheep a year—

SHEPHERD: One and then two, Dog. Two, and then three. Three, and then four. Four, and then five—

DOG: But how can you be so sure of that?

SHEPHERD: Because, Dog, when I was told this story, *I listened.*

(DOG *whimpers apologetically.*)

SHEPHERD: May I continue now?

DOG: Yes, Shepherd. *(Reluctantly puts on* OLD WOLF *mask again.)*

SHEPHERD: Not long after, a neighboring shepherd's dog *suddenly dropped dead.*

DOG: *(Peeking from behind* OLD WOLF *mask.)* Oh, no!

SHEPHERD: Oh, yes. (SHEPHERD *assumes a new position, in mourning. Sniffling,* PUPPET SHEEP *sympathizes.*) And the old wolf quickly moved in to take advantage of the situation.

DOG: *(Approaching* SHEPHERD.*)* Shepherd! My condolences on the loss of your dog.

SHEPHERD: *(Weeping loudly; blowing his nose, etc.)* Thank you, Old Wolf.

DOG: As it happens, I may be in a position to help you. My fellow wolves and I have had a falling out and are not likely to reconcile. Make me your guard dog and I'll protect your flock from our mutual enemies.

SHEPHERD: You intend to protect me from your own brothers?

DOG: Brothers once, but no kin to me any more.

SHEPHERD: And if I take you in to protect my flock from them, who will protect us from you? (SHEEP *baas in agreement, a congregation of one to the* SHEPHERD'*s preaching.*) What is gained, I ask you, by welcoming a known thief into one's home to guard against the supposed thieves outside? *Baa!* Have we not been warned to fear evil in our midst? *Baa!* Why, down through the ages—*Baa!*

DOG: *(Moving away quickly as the sermon threatens to continue.)* Enough! Spare me your sermons! I'll go! I'm going! I've gone! *(Regaining his composure at a safe distance from* SHEPHERD *and* SHEEP, *he heaves a melancholy sigh.)* Time has sapped all of my strength, and much of my patience, I fear.

SHEPHERD: *(Assuming a new pose in a new place.)* But none of your wit or cunning, greedy wolf.

DOG: Third time's the charm, they say. And I'm desperate now, there's no denying it. *(He sighs and approaches* SHEPHERD *and* SHEEP.*)* Shepherd, what do you think of my fur?

SHEPHERD: *(Mimes stroking* DOG's *back.)* I admire it. It's thick as any I've seen.

DOG: Well, I am old and don't expect to live much longer. So I propose to leave you my fur when I die.

SHEPHERD: And in return?

DOG: You will feed me to death.

SHEPHERD: *(After* SHEEP *baas a warning.)* Another greedy trick, I see! But I, too, have a proposal, Wolf. If your pelt's of no use to you any more, how about making me a present of it *right now*? *(He strikes at* DOG *with his staff;* SHEEP *baas;* DOG *dashes away;* SHEPHERD *freezes with staff raised above his head.* DOG *howls long and mournfully.)*

DOG: *(His pain turning to anger.)* These shepherds have hearts of stone, and my plight will never melt them. Very well, then, I will die their enemy before my hunger kills me, for that's the path *they* have chosen.

(Music plays as with enraged growls, he lunges upstage and mimes his attack, his back to audience.)

SHEPHERD: The Old Wolf went mad. He broke into the shepherds' homes and pulled their children from their beds. *(He pounds the ground furiously with his staff as he speaks—)* There was a terrible struggle, but at last, the shepherds managed to club him to death. *(*DOG *sinks to the ground;* SHEPHERD *stops pounding, calms down. Music fades.)* "Too bad," said one. "Perhaps it was wrong of us to leave the old robber no means to reform." *(*SHEEP *baas dubiously.)* "Oh, why waste our pity?" said another. "He got exactly what he deserved." *(For a moment,* SHEPHERD *looks at* DOG *lying on ground up center, then walks away. Music and Lights mark transition out of story. Music fades.)*

DOG: *(Sitting up, slowly—)* And so they washed the wolf's blood from their hands.

SHEPHERD: *(Puts away* PUPPET SHEEP *and takes* OLD WOLF *mask from* DOG.*)* The wolf was greedy, is greedy, and will always be greedy. Go on home to your master, Dog. That's where you belong. *(*SHEPHERD *exits.* WOLF *enters, hesitantly.)*

DOG: *(Stands up, moaning with the effort, battered and weary from participating in these stories.)* You do kill sheep; you can't deny that.

WOLF: When I have no other choice. I prefer to hunt in the wild.

DOG: I suppose you're going to tell me there are many shepherds—

WOLF: And many stories? No. With the shepherd, it is always the same. He needs land to feed his flock and I need land to hunt. When our paths cross, it is bad for him . . . and worse for me. *(Growls angrily at the thought.)*

DOG: *(As before, backs away at the growl, then stops, reconsiders, confronts* WOLF.*)* But if you are not foolish, not evil, and not greedy, why do you kill?

WOLF: I must kill to live.

DOG: Oh! *(A thoughtful pause, then—)* My master—does the same! *(Another pause, then impulsive and optimistic as always—)* We must hurry. It is almost daylight.

*(*WOLF *and* DOG *trot in circle, as before, with Flute and Light indicating dawn.* WOLF *suddenly stops short in alarm.)*

WOLF: Dog? Why is your neck so red and raw?

DOG: Oh, my collar rubs a little, that's all.

WOLF: Your collar?

DOG: During the day, I wear an iron collar fastened to an iron chain—attached to an iron stake—driven into the ground beside my master's house.

WOLF: You're not free to come and go as you please?

DOG: At night, I'm set free.

WOLF: Chained to a stake in the ground, I would wither and die.

DOG: Not at all! Think of the wonderful food I get!

WOLF: I cannot wear a collar, Dog. I *will* not wear it.

DOG: (*Disappointed, but still eager.*) If you won't be collared, you won't do for guarding my master. (*A moment's thought, then—*) Would you consider offering him some entertainment? I myself have been known to sit up and beg. (*Assumes begging position and pants.*) It's often worth an extra bone or two.

WOLF: I am no fool, and will not play one to amuse him. If you can bear your servitude, Dog, then go your own way. I must go mine.

DOG: But you may starve!

WOLF: I prefer my freedom to a full belly.

DOG: I see. (*A pause, then, wiser than he has ever been—*) That's why terrible stories are told about you, Cousin Wolf. What my master cannot own, he does not understand. And what he does not understand, he fears, he mocks, and he destroys. You pay a high price for your freedom, Wolf.

WOLF: As do you, Dog, for your comfort.

DOG: Perhaps so.

WOLF: You could join me, you know. There's no chain holding you *now*.

DOG: But my master will call for me soon.

WOLF: Must you always go to him when he calls?

DOG: (*Hesitates, considering, and finally says—*) Yes.

WOLF: *Why?*

DOG: (*Quietly, maturely, but not apologetically.*) We are companions, he and I. I am at home in his house.

WOLF: (*Understanding.*) Ah! You belong to his pack.

DOG: I do.

WOLF: (*With regret.*) And I do not.

DOG: (*A pause, then apologetically—*) If you come too close, I'll have to chase you away, you know. He'll expect it of me.

WOLF: I understand. And I prefer to keep my distance.

DOG: Will you find food?

WOLF: If it's there, I'll find it.

DOG: How will I know you're safe?

WOLF: Listen for my song.

DOG: I will. (DOG "*bows*" *to her, respectfully.*) Farewell, Cousin Wolf.

WOLF: (*She returns his "bow."*) Farewell . . . Cousin Dog.

(As WOLF *watches* DOG *exit, Flute plays and continues under following dialogue. Lights dim, stars appear as at beginning.* WOLF *faces audience and begins jogging motion, as* SECOND *and* THIRD ACTORS *enter, without masks, and also face audience down left and right.)*

THIRD ACTOR: *(Taking up jogging rhythm as before.)* It is said that the wolf travels easily between the spirit world and our own—

SECOND ACTOR: *(Picking up the rhythmic jog as he speaks.)* Along the path we now call the Milky Way—

THIRD ACTOR: Once known as the Wolf Road.

SECOND ACTOR: Forever moving—

THIRD ACTOR: Moving in shadow—

SECOND ACTOR: Moving in mystery—

THIRD ACTOR: The wolf disappears into the night—

SECOND ACTOR: And returns before the morning sun.

THIRD ACTOR: Knowing what we cannot see—

SECOND ACTOR: Seeing what it cannot say—

THIRD ACTOR: The wolf dies—

SECOND ACTOR: And is reborn—

THIRD ACTOR: Dies—

SECOND ACTOR: And is reborn—

THIRD ACTOR: In both worlds—

SECOND ACTOR: And in the stories people tell . . .

THIRD ACTOR: *(Stops jogging.)* We tell the stories.

SECOND ACTOR: *(Stops jogging.)* We believe the stories.

THIRD ACTOR: We become the stories.

(Flute fades. WOLF *stops jogging.)*

SECOND ACTOR: Be still!

THIRD ACTOR: Listen!

SECOND ACTOR: Understand!

*(*SECOND *and* THIRD ACTORS *howl in harmony.* WOLF *speaks as howls fade and* ALL *move and speak as if in a pack.)*

WOLF: I am wolf. For a thousand thousand years, I have walked the earth.

THIRD ACTOR: In the first light of dawn, I watch.

SECOND ACTOR: In the gathering of darkness, I wait.

WOLF: I am the shadow that moves in shadow. This is my way.

SECOND and THIRD ACTORS: I am wolf.

WOLF: Destroy me, and your world grows smaller.

SECOND ACTOR: Tame me, and I am no longer wolf.

THIRD ACTOR: Mock me in your stories, but the face behind the mask is your own.

SECOND ACTOR: Be still!

THIRD ACTOR: Listen!

SECOND ACTOR: Understand—

WOLF: I am wonder. I am the wilderness.

ALL: I am wolf.

(Wolf howls begin softly, rise, and fade. Lights fade, leaving stars.)

CURTAIN

EZIGBO,
THE SPIRIT CHILD

by
Max Bush and
Adaora Nzelibe Schmiedl

EZIGBO, THE SPIRIT CHILD

CHARACTERS

Mother..32
Okeke 8
River Spirit
Ezigbo 10
Medicine Woman 45
Ngozi...10
Ogbanje (Three or more) ....They are Forever-Children: child
                             spirits. The literal meaning of *Ogbanje*
                             comes from two roots: "Ogba" means to
                             run away from, "nje" means to run to.
Translator(s)... Any member(s) of the cast.

CASTING NOTES

By doubling Okeke and an Ogbanje, all roles can be played by 7 females and 1 male. If more than three Ogbanje are cast, 50% should be male.

TIME

A long time ago

PLACE

In Nigeria, West Africa: within an Igbo family compound, the bush, and at the riverside.

RUNNING TIME

Approximately one hour.

TAPE

A tape, by Adaora Nzelibe Schmiedl, of all the songs and pronunciations of the Igbo language may be purchased from Anchorage Press Plays.

(AT RISE *we see part of the family compound surrounded by a thatched mud wall about 5 feet high and encircled by the bush. What we see of the compound is the Mother's cooking hut, the family shrine, a tree and a stump.*

The household shrine is off in the corner of the compound. It's a small hut made of wood, with a thatched roof and a small altar that sits in the shrine's opening. Bright cloth, feathers, pots, masks, carved figurines, beads, shells, and a dried skin decorate the shrine. The ground in front of the shrine is hard-packed mud, decorated with geometric chalk drawings.

The cooking-hut is made of bamboo poles that support a square, thatched roof. There are no walls. Within it is a stack of firewood and three rocks that form a tripod and support an iron pot.

The drummer stands and energetically DRUMS the Call to the Play.

DRUMMER(S) finishes, the MOTHER *enters, crosses to foot of stage and addresses the audience directly. She is at once the storyteller and a central character in the play.*

She is followed by the TRANSLATOR(s), *who will also assume a role(s) in the play. She begins animatedly telling the story in Igbo.)*

MOTHER: Oge gara-aga, mgbe ndi mmo na ndi mmadu bi nso, n'ala anyi echefugo, onwe otu nwanyi. Nnanyi a bu nwunye eze.

TRANSLATOR: *(Translating.)* A long time ago, when human beings and spirits were still close, in a land we have forgotten, there lived a woman.

MOTHER: Eze a nuro otutu nwunye, etu eze kwesi e nu, ma nwunye ezizi ya, nke o huru nanya ka-cha cha ndi ozo, a mughi nwa.

TRANSLATOR: Now this woman was the wife of a powerful chief—an Eze. This Eze had many wives, as a powerful chief should have, but his first wife, whom he loved above all others, had no child. (MOTHER *picks up palm broom and slowly drags—sweeps—the compound.)* During feast days, she always took her portion last, because she had no children to share her food. The chores of her house that would have been done by a child, she does alone. (MOTHER *moves upstage, still sweeping.)* This woman could have children, yes, she had given birth, but her womb was possessed by the spirit of an Ogbanje. (OGBANJE *enter playing a version of hide and seek.* MOTHER *doesn't see them, as they seek a place to hide. They wear half-masks and are dressed in a form of brilliantly colorful, traditional Igbo dance attire. The female* OGBANJE *wear a strip of bright fabric around their breasts, while their skirts are flounced and full-petticoat-like. Some wear beads on their ankles and waists. The male* OGBANJE *are bare-chested and wear shorts of the same bright fabric. All of them have drawn geometric designs on their bodies with a soft, dark, pencil-like marker.)* An Ogbanje is an invisible spirit-child that lives among the people. Sometimes this spirit wants to become part of the human world, to do the things that human children do. (EZIGBO, *another* OGBANJE, *enters. She's "it" in the game. She is similarly dressed and marked except she adorns her ankles and wrists with cowrie shells.)* But when the child is born, it longs for the spirit world and the company of its friends. (EZIGBO *moves closer and closer to a spirit.)*

And, if this longing becomes too strong, it will die, and return to the spirit world. *(The* OGBANJE *jump out, yell and* EZIGBO *touches them all. DRUMS; they quickly form a circle around* EZIGBO *and dance around her for a short time. This short dance should reflect and foreshadow the final celebration dance. After dance, the* OGBANJE *dash off, laughing.* EZIGBO *starts off with them, but stops, turns to* MOTHER, *who now kneels in mourning.* EZIGBO *moves near her.)* This particular Ogbanje had visited the Eze's wife five times—five times it was born to this woman as a child—and each time left, leaving grieving parents to mourn. (3RD OGBANJE *re-enters, holds out her hand to* EZIGBO. EZIGBO *runs to her, takes her hand, and they run off.* MOTHER *focuses on shrine. She does not approach it, however. Tending the shrine is the father's responsibility.*)

MOTHER: (*Sings mournfully, without DRUMS.*)

> M na-acho nwa mo

TRANSLATOR: I am looking for my child.

MOTHER: Nwa mu-u nwere obioma eh-eh-eh

TRANSLATOR: My child who had a good heart.

MOTHER: Olemgbe k'm ga-hu anya ozo,

TRANSLATOR: When will I see my child again?

MOTHER: Onwu I me n'aru

TRANSLATOR: Death, you have done me a great wrong.

MOTHER: Mak'o di ba

TRANSLATOR: But I accept.

MOTHER: (*Sings.*)

> M na-acho nwa mo,
> nwa mu-u nwere obioma eh-eh-eh,
> Olemgbe k'm ga-hu anya ozo,
> Onwu i me n'aru.
> Ma k'o di ba.

TRANSLATOR: Time moved on. One morning, the chief's wife went to the banks of the river to wash her clothes. (OKEKE, *8, enters river area, playing enthusiastically with a carved toy—a dug out canoe.* MOTHER *rises, places her clothes basket on her head, moves to the river.* OKEKE *sees* MOTHER *coming, moves away from her, as she begins washing her clothes on a river rock.*) She watched the children playing, then she saw one of her favorite children—

MOTHER: Okeke!

TRANSLATOR: The youngest son of one of her husband's wives. (*Exits.*)

MOTHER: Okeke, come, join me here, while I wash my clothes.

(*He gets a running start and crashes his toy into a rock. He screams and falls as if he were the toy.*)
How is your mother? And what of your sister?

(*He lays dead.*)
Come and show me—if you are still living among us—what you are playing with.

OKEKE: (*Rising, moving coser, but still keeping distance.*)
I need some river-sand to make the bottom smooth. That will make it go faster. It's going to be the fastest canoe in the village.

MOTHER: Okeke, there's some sand over here.

OKEKE: And I found some berries over there that will make red paint. I'm going to paint this like fire.

MOTHER: That will be good. Did you make it?

OKEKE: I made it myself.

MOTHER: *(Stopping washing, moving a step toward him.)*
May I see it?

OKEKE: *(Backing away a step.)*
I made it myself and I'm going to paint it like fire to make it go faster.

(He makes it move fast. EZIGBO dances on. She immediately sees OKEKE and his toy, lays near him, watching closely. She's dying to touch the toy and play with it herself.)

MOTHER: Oh, Okeke, my son, I have something for you.

OKEKE: What is it?

MOTHER: Here, come and see what I have for you.

(From her basket she takes out beancake wrapped in a banana leaf.)
I've made some akara—some beancake,

(EZIGBO jumps up at the sound of akara!)
and I'd love to share it with you. Come closer, come share the akara with me.

(EZIGBO moves to MOTHER's outstretched hand, almost touches the akara.)

OKEKE: *(Moving closer to her.)*
You make good akara.
(EZIGBO clearly agrees with this.)

MOTHER: And this is especially sweet.

(Frustrated, EZIGBO dances away to OKEKE, reaches to touch the toy, then dances by. She stops and watches. 2ND OGBANJE enters, moves to EZIGBO, holds her hand.)

OKEKE: You eat some first.

MOTHER: *(Takes a small bite.)*
Sweet. Okeke, it is sweet. Share it with me; here.

(She holds it out.)
You can have this. I have more.

(He hesitantly moves to her, then begins to reach out to take it. His inner struggle intensifies.)
You can take the akara and then sit down. I have a story to tell you.

(EZIGBO, who loves stories, sits down near MOTHER. 2ND OGBANJE sits next to her.)
You like stories, I know, and I will tell you a new one about Mother Python and her children.

OKEKE: I'm sorry, Oldest Wife. But my mother says I can't take that from you. Because you have an Ogbanje.

(He runs off.)

MOTHER: Okeke! Ah! Okeke . . . you, too . . . don't want what I give . . .

EZIGBO: *(Sadly.)*
No . . .
(1ST, 3RD OGBANJE run on, join the others.)

MOTHER: My child, my Ogbanje, I know you are here. But I can't see you. I can't hold you.

(To river.)
 It would be better to drown than to go back to my empty hut.

EZIGBO: Hah?

(EZIGBO *moves toward her, letting go of* 1ST OGBANJE's *hand. DRUMS for* RIVER SPIRIT. *The moment the* OGBANJE *see her, they withdraw out of respect for her power.)*

RIVER SPIRIT: *(The* RIVER SPIRIT *is played by an unmasked female, with flowing hair, wearing a long blue skirt tightly wrapped around her legs. A long light-blue sash is tied around her chest; the long ends hang down her back. She dances her words, sensuously, beautifully, moving mostly her upper body.)*
 Woman! What can be so wrong?

MOTHER: River Spirit . . .

RIVER SPIRIT: Many children die. Mothers grieve. But even without children, you are a daughter of Igboland . . . Speak.

MOTHER: I have no one to help me wash clothes or take meals to my husband's hut. I sleep alone. And in the evening, when the other women gather their children around to tell their stories, I tell my stories to no one.

RIVER SPIRIT: You know it is an abomination to the earth to cut any human life short. There will be no place to bury you.

MOTHER: You will bury me in your water.

RIVER SPIRIT: I will cast you onto the bank and they will throw you in the Evil Forest.

MOTHER: You would do that?

RIVER SPIRIT: Your life is not just your own. It belongs to your people, your ancestors, to the gods, and to Chukwu, the source of all life.

MOTHER: They have left me; my child has left me. I wish to die in your water.

RIVER SPIRIT: Go, make a sacrifice to Ani, the Earth Spirit, for speaking such things. Then, go to your hut and seven market weeks from now you will have a child.

MOTHER: Mmu?

EZIGBO: *(Indicating herself.)*
 Mmu?

1ST OGBANJE: Sister?

MOTHER: A child . . .

2ND OGBANJE: *(The* OGBANJE *are deeply saddened by this.)*
 Sister . . .

RIVER SPIRIT: But you must never strike your child. Or the child will remember all the friends left in the spirit world and be overcome with longing for the home left behind.

(EZIGBO *looks sadly back at the* OGBANJE.)
 And will leave you alone as you were before.

MOTHER: Oh! I will never strike the child!

(DRUMS change from the sensuous beat of the RIVER SPIRIT *to the celebration rhythm of the birth of a child. Sings and dances.)*

        Eri-meri-na-asu so
        Eri-meri eh-h
        Eri-meri na-asu so
        Eri-meri eh-h

(While she sings, RIVER SPIRIT *exits, the* OGBANJE *move slowly, sadly off.* EZIGBO *moves to* MOTHER, *then dances off in a different direction than the* OGBANJE.*)*

        Onwu egburu nwanyi n'afo ime
        Ka o mutara ya nwa
        K'anyi ta ogboroko
        Nno manya ngwo

(DRUMS continue quietly, MOTHER *begins song again, quietly, to allow translation to be heard.)*

TRANSLATOR:	WOMAN:
Feasting is sweet	*Eri-Meri-Na-Asu so*
(This next is meant to be humorous.)	
Every man, even death, Would like a	*Eri-meri eh-h*
Wife with a pregnant stomach to have	*Eri-meri-na-asu so*
Children for him.	
TRANSLATOR:	MOTHER:
Let us eat dried Fish and drink	*Eri-meri eh-h*
Palm-wine!	

(DRUMS full force. Others enter, join in the song and "Pass the Baby" dance. MEDICINE WOMAN *dances on with baby wrapped in cloth. She presents baby to each child that is dancing, then—if there are no other adults—dances to* MOTHER, *hands her the baby. If there are other adults, the baby is passed between them with the* MOTHER *being passed the baby near the end of the song.)*

MOTHER: *(Joined by others.)*

        Onwu egburu nwanyi n'afo ime
        Ka o mutara ya nwa
        K'anyi ta ogboroko
        Nno manya ngwo.

        Eri-meri na-asu so
        Eri-meri eh-h
        Eri-meri-na-asu so
        Eri-meri-eh-h

(The others dance off, leaving MOTHER *and baby and* TRANSLATOR.*)*

        Onwu egburu nwanyi n'afo ime
        Ka o mutara ya nwa
        K'anyi ta ogboroko
        Nno manya ngwo

TRANSLATOR: And seven market weeks later, she was blessed with a child. And she named the child.

MOTHER: *(Holding the baby high.)*
     Ezigbo, the Good One.

TRANSLATOR: *(Taking baby.)*
    And as she grew, it became obvious to all that Ezigbo's name was fitting. Time moved on. Now she has stayed with her Mother for ten years.

*(*TRANSLATOR *exits as* EZIGBO, *now a thin girl of 10 and dressed as a human girl (unmasked), enters, sweeping the compound.* EZIGBO's *hair is typical of* OGBANJE *children; it has not been cut or combed and she wears isidada, or what we call dreads. Her hair is not unkempt, however, it is oiled and hand combed. Note: It isn't necessary that* EZIGBO *wear dreads, but it is preferred. In contrast to the* MOTHER, EZIGBO *drags broom energetically in large circles.)*

EZIGBO: Mama, can you see how straight the lines are?

MOTHER: Very straight.

EZIGBO: And how perfect the circles?

MOTHER: *(Playfully.)*
    Oh, Ezigbo, people will come from far villages to see your work.

EZIGBO: But I don't know why I have to sweep every day. The sand is so clean. And I don't see any footprints of the spirits.

MOTHER: Don't talk like that when there may be some spirits near—slow ones who have not yet left.

EZIGBO: *(Stopping sweeping, shaking broom at them.)*
    Hurry up, go away. I don't want to do this work over again.

MOTHER: And you shouldn't.

MOTHER and EZIGBO: *(Speaking together.)* Talk about things you don't understand.

EZIGBO: I'm finished. How does it look?

MOTHER: You missed this spot. The spirits walked here last night; I see a footprint.

EZIGBO: *(Looking at that spot. Quietly, to herself.)*
    That is your footprint. Look at how big it is.

MOTHER: They do what they want at night, but we must clean them away in the morning because the day is ours. Now you are finished.

(Embracing EZIGBO.*)*
    And, because you are Ezigbo, the Good One, I have a surprise for you today.

*(*EZIGBO *moves to put broom down near the hut as* NGOZI, *a robust girl about the same age as* EZIGBO, *sneaks on behind her carrying a waterpot under her arm. She puts pot down then moves up behind* EZIGBO *and slaps* EZIGBO's *bottom.)*

NGOZI: Ezigbo!

*(*EZIGBO *starts,* NGOZI *runs.)*

EZIGBO: Ngozi!

(Trying to hit her with the broom, EZIGBO *chases her around* MOTHER.*)*

NGOZI: *(While running away, around* MOTHER.*)*
    I saw you first! I came all the way up to you—

EZIGBO: I'll get you—

NGOZI: —and you did not see me! You didn't see me!

EZIGBO: I do now!

MOTHER: Ezigbo—Ezigbo, you know you should . . .

(NGOZI *squeals, runs off. As* EZIGBO *runs after her,* MOTHER *takes the broom from* EZIGBO. EZIGBO *exits after* NGOZI.)

    . . . not run like that.

(MOTHER *puts broom down, moves to her cooking hut, picks up a flat basket of black-eyed peas and chaff. She picks up another empty basket, moves out of hut, sets down baskets. She picks up a short stool and places it near baskets.* EZIGBO *runs on, into* MOTHER's *arms, followed by* NGOZI.)

EZIGBO: Mama! (NGOZI *runs past, slaps* EZIGBO *on the bottom.*)

    Ah! (EZIGBO *now chases* NGOZI, *catches her, tries to slap her bottom. They wrestle.*)

EZIGBO: I'm going to get you—I'm going to get you—I'm going to get you.

NGOZI: No-no-no-no-Ezigbo—

EZIGBO: Yes, Ngozi, yes, yes!

MOTHER: Eh-eh-eh-eh!

(NGOZI *sits, trying to avoid being hit.*)

EZIGBO: Over! Turn over!

NGOZI: No, no!

(EZIGBO *turns her over and swats her.* NGOZI *screams.*)

EZIGBO: I got you. I told you I would get you.

(EZIGBO *and* NGOZI *collapse into laughter.*)

MOTHER: You had better not let your father see you running and wrestling like a boy.

EZIGBO: We can run faster than boys. Isn't that true, Ngozi?
    (*She coughs.*)

NGOZI: Yes, because we have done it.

EZIGBO: Even older boys.

MOTHER: Which of you girls is older?

NGOZI: I am older.

EZIGBO: No, I am older.

NGOZI: I am older.

MOTHER: If you are older, Ezigbo, you should have more sense. Running is dangerous for you. And if you are older, Ngozi, you should not help her do these things. What would your mother do if she saw you wrestling like a boy?

NGOZI: I would not do that near my mother.

MOTHER: What would she do?

NGOZI: She would make me sit. And then she would say "You will act like a young woman," and then I would laugh and then she would spank me so hard I would feel it for days.

MOTHER: Ah!

EZIGBO: Yes! Yes, that's what she would do. And so would Mama Nkiru, I have seen her.

NGOZI: But Mama Ezigbo, you are much nicer. You never hit Ezigbo and you almost never make her sit so she will laugh at you.

MOTHER: Yes . . . yes, that is true, Ngozi, but . . . Look at what I have.

(MOTHER *picks up flat basket of black-eyed peas.*)

I bought these beans at the market yesterday, and when they are cleaned, I will make akara.

NGOZI and EZIGBO: Akara!

EZIGBO: Should I go to the river and fetch water?

MOTHER: First we must separate the beans from the chaff. Would you like to help me?

NGOZI: I will help you, Mama Ezigbo.

(MOTHER *tosses beans and chaff into the air and catches them on basket. She does this again, then blows on them, blowing the chaff away. She does this rhythmically, gracefully, almost like a dance.*

The CHILDREN *pick up beans in their hands, watch* MOTHER. *They then throw beans up, blow, try to catch them, and most of the handful falls to the ground.*)

MOTHER: Perhaps you should pick out the beans with your fingers.

EZIGBO: I am sorry, Mama.

(*The* CHILDREN *kneel and pick up beans.*
The OGBANJE *run on, move among the people, curious about what they are doing.*
The CHILDREN *will put the cleaned beans in the empty basket throughout the following scene.*)

MOTHER: So, it is time that you two stopped running and pushing.
     You are ten years old.

(*The* OGBANJE *sit together a distance from* EZIGBO, *watching her.*
During the games they move as individuals, but otherwise, the OGBANJE *move as a single unit. When they are standing or sitting, they're in a tight, touching, physically overlapping group.*)

In a year or two you will want to bring home to your family a good bride-price.

(*The* CHILDREN *look at each other.*)

EZIGBO: Bride-price . . .

NGOZI: Ezigbo the bride . . .

EZIGBO: Of a *man.*

(*They fall down laughing.*)

MOTHER: That is right. And a young man and his family do not want a wife who can run faster than him. There is not a race on the wedding day to see who is the fastest. There is . . .

NGOZI: There is what on the wedding day, Mama Ezigbo?

(EZIGBO *struggles to contain her laughter.*)

MOTHER: There is . . .

(*She smiles.*)
     a feast.

EZIGBO: So a young man wants a bride who can eat.

(*They laugh.*)

NGOZI: If that is true, I will bring a big bride-price. I can eat a lot.

(*She eats a raw bean.*)

EZIGBO: You ate that?

NGOZI: It was a bean.

EZIGBO: It was not cooked.

NGOZI: You eat mangos and they are not cooked.

(EZIGBO *puts a bean in her mouth, chews it, finds it tastes bad, then spits it out in her hand.*)

EZIGBO: You will eat anything.

MOTHER: Do not eat those beans. Come, help me.

OGBANJE: (*Singing sadly, quietly, without drums.* EZIGBO *becomes dizzy, faint.*)

M na-acho Ezigbo
Ezigbo mu-u mu-u nwere   1ST OGBANJE:
Obioma eh-eh-eh   *Here, Sister.*
Olemgbe k'm ga-hu anya ozo,
Onwu i me n'aru   3RD OGBANJE:
Ma k'o di ba.   *Come back with us.*

(EZIGBO *rises, feeling faint, moves away from* NGOZI *and* MOTHER *and toward the* OGBANJE.)

MOTHER: (*To* EZIGBO.)
     What is it, Ada? (*A pet, affectionate name.*)

OGBANJE: (*Singing.*)   EZIGBO:
M na-acho Ezigbo,   *I . . . I feel dizzy.*
Ezigbo mu-u nwere
Obioma eh-eh-eh,   2ND OGBANJE:
Olemgbe k'm ga-hu   *Come, Sister, you've*
Anya ozo . . .   *been gone so long.*

(MOTHER *goes to her, takes her hand.*)

                                 MOTHER:
Ogbanje olemgbe k'm ga-hu   Then you should sit down, not stand
                                 up. And you see?
Anya ozo   You should not run like that. It
                                 makes you cough and dizzy.

EZIGBO: (*Distantly.*)
     Yes, Mama.

MOTHER: (OGBANJE *singing trails off.*)
   Ngozi, bring her the other stool.

(NGOZI *gets other stool.* 2ND OGBANJE *rises, moves to* EZIGBO, *stands near her. Warmly to* NGOZI.)
   And you must help her. Ezigbo has fallen in love with her human family—and you—and wishes never to go home again. She has stayed with us ten years and she wants to stay a long, long time. That is right, isn't it, Ezigbo?

EZIGBO: Yes, Mama.

MOTHER: So you must help her stay, Ngozi.

NGOZI: Yes, Mama Ezigbo. (MOTHER *leads* EZIGBO *back to* NGOZI. EZIGBO *sits on the stool;* 2ND OGBANJE *follows her over and sits behind her.* EZIGBO *hums the song the* OGBANJE *were singing.*)

MOTHER: Why do you sing that mourning song?

EZIGBO: I don't know.

MOTHER: There is not a funeral today. There is akara!

EZIGBO: I am sorry. (MOTHER *begins chanting an improvised song to the rhythm of her throwing the beans into the air.*)

MOTHER:

> I went to the market, the market,
> The market.
> I went to the market,

CHILDREN: (*It becomes a song and response.*)

> The market, the market.

MOTHER:

> Looking for some cloth.

CHILDREN: (*Cloth is boring.*)

> Some cloth, some cloth.

MOTHER:

> Did not find the cloth.

CHILDREN: (*Very boring.*)

> The cloth, the cloth.

MOTHER:

> So I looked for some beans.

CHILDREN: (*Much more interesting.*)

> Some beans, some beans!

MOTHER:

> I found some good onions.

CHILDREN: (*Onions make us cry.*)

> Good onions, good onions.

MOTHER:

> With a very big smell.

CHILDREN: (*Smelling the big smell.*)

> Big smell, big smell.

MOTHER:

Then they gave me some pepe.

CHILDREN: *(Pepper, it's hot.)*

Pepe, pepe.

MOTHER:

Then I remembered crayfish.

CHILDREN: *(I love these!)*

Crayfish, crayfish!

MOTHER:

I loaded my basket and carried it home.

CHILDREN: *(Home is also boring.)*

Home, home.

MOTHER:

I began to make akara.

CHILDREN: *(The Best!)*

Akara, akara!

MOTHER:

I pounded the pepe.

CHILDREN: *(They're hot.)*

The pepe, the pepe.

MOTHER:

I added the crayfish.

CHILDREN: *(Love them.)*

Crayfish, crayfish.

MOTHER:

I cut up the onion.

CHILDREN: *(Smelly, tears.)*

Onion, onion.

MOTHER: *(She stops, looks at the girls, then at the basket.)*
But where are the beans?

CHILDREN: *(They chant, frantically picking the beans out.)*
The beans, the beans?

ALL:

Where are the Beans, the Beans, the Beans!

(They laugh as MEDICINE WOMAN *enters, carrying a pot covered with a leaf, and a small bowl.)*

MEDICINE WOMAN: *(Saluting them as they are working.)*

My Daughters, ndeme. *(Ndeme means thank-you. She is thanking them for working. Their working is good for everybody.* OGBANJE *react to* MEDICINE WOMAN*'s entrance, becoming more alert and curious.* 2ND OGBANJE *rises and returns to others.)*

MOTHER and EZIGBO and NGOZI: Oh.

MOTHER: Nno. Welcome, Mama Nkiru.

*(*MOTHER *looks at* EZIGBO, *sees a smudge on her face.)*

MEDICINE WOMAN: Ndugi.
(*Meaning:*)
Life to you, my daughter. Did you wake well from the night?

MOTHER and EZIGBO: Yes.

NGOZI: I did, too.

MOTHER: (*She licks her thumb and wipes smudge off* EZIGBO's *face. She fixes* EZIGBO's *hair.*)
How are you?

MEDICINE WOMAN: Fine.

MOTHER: Have you come to my house, then?

MEDICINE WOMAN: (*Setting down pot and bowl.*)
Yes, I have come.

MOTHER: As yourself or Ani's messenger?

MEDICINE WOMAN: As your Priestess. Are your people well? Is your husband well?

MOTHER: Yes.

MEDICINE WOMAN: Ngozi, how is your mother?

NGOZI: (*Gloomily*)
She is as she always is.

(*Suddenly brightly.*)
She is fine, Mama Nkiru.

MEDICINE WOMAN: Tell her I send my greeting.

(EZIGBO *picks up her stool, offers it to* MEDICINE WOMAN.)
Thank-you.

(*She sits.*)

MOTHER: Since you are here and since it is a good day, let me get some kola nut.

EZIGBO: Should I get the kola?

MOTHER: I will get it.

(MOTHER *exits.* NGOZI *works with beans.*)

NGOZI: Mama Ezigbo is going to make akara.

MEDICINE WOMAN: Akara . . .

NGOZI: My mother never makes it because it takes too many hours and too much work. And she says "I will make it the day you deserve to have it. But on that day, I will probably be long dead." So will I.

(*This amuses* MEDICINE WOMAN.)

OGBANJE: (*Begin singing quietly but passionately. Again,* EZIGBO *becomes dizzy, disoriented, and drifts toward the seated* OGBANJE. PRIESTESS *watches her.*)

M na-acho Ezigbo
Ezigbo mu-u mu-u nwere   3RD OGBANJE: *Here, Sister.*
Obioma eh-eh-eh
Olemgbe k'm ga-hu anya ozo   1ST OGBANJE: *Come home.*
Onwu i me n'aru   2ND OGBANJE: *Come home to us.*
Ma k'o di ba   1ST OGBANJE: *Home. . . .*

MEDICINE WOMAN: Ezigbo, what do you hear?

EZIGBO: I don't hear anything.

OGBANJE: MED WOM:
M na-acho Ezigbo   *Child, why do you stand there?*
Ezigbo mu-u nwere
Obioma eh-eh-eh,   EZIGBO: *I feel dizzy. I want . . .*
Olemgbe k'm ga-hu   *I want . . .*
Anya ozo,
Onwu i me n'aru   2ND OGBANJE: *Sister . . .*
Ma k'o di ba   EZIGBO: *I want . . .*
                                                    (EZIGBO *coughs.*)
                                                . . . . *something.*
                                                NGOZI: *Why aren't you helping me?*
                                                1ST OGBANJE: *Come home.*
                                                NGOZI: *Don't you want akara?*

EZIGBO: Akara!

> (*This breaks* EZIGBO's *reverie and ends the* OGBANJE's *song.*)
> That's what I want! That is my favorite food.

1ST OGBANJE: Sister?

> (MOTHER *enters with kola in a dish made from a gourd.*)

EZIGBO: Mama.

> (*She moves to her, hugs her. The* OGBANJE *move slowly off.*)

MOTHER: What is it, Ezigbo?

EZIGBO: You are making akara.

MOTHER: Yes, but we have a guest now. My Mother?

> (*Holds out kola to* MEDICINE WOMAN.)

MEDICINE WOMAN: (*Passing her horse's tail over gourd.*)
   May the gods bless this kola and bless our conversation. May your husband's god and your household god live in peace. May your child grow taller than all the others. And may Ngozi live healthy and long.

EZIGBO: (*Quietly, to* NGOZI, *while the* MEDICINE WOMAN *breaks the kola.*)
   I will grow taller than you because I am older than you. And I will always will be older than you, so I always will be taller than you.

NGOZI: But I am older than you.

EZIGBO: No, I am older than you.

MEDICINE WOMAN: Ngozi?

NGOZI: But I am older than Ezigbo.

MEDICINE WOMAN: Ngozi, you are the youngest among us. Come.

(As is the tradition, the youngest, NGOZI, takes gourd, offers it to MEDICINE WOMAN, then MOTHER, then, EZIGBO and then takes some herself. She then returns gourd to kitchen hut. The two children sit by the beans and clean them by hand, while MEDICINE WOMAN pulls MOTHER aside.)

Mama Ezigbo, do you watch your child? Do you see how she hears things we cannot hear?

MOTHER: It comes when she is dizzy.

MEDICINE WOMAN: "If you see something dancing on top of the sea, you must know there is another something underneath the waters playing the tune." I know she is ten years old and has stayed this long, but it came to me in the night and again, just now—my heart came out just now as I watched her— the Ogbanje are calling her. And she is listening.

MOTHER: That is why I asked you to come, today.

NGOZI: *(A whisper to EZIGBO.)*
You are older than me. You must behave as if you are older.

(NGOZI throws a bean at EZIGBO; EZIGBO throws a bean at NGOZI. They do this again, then laugh quietly. EZIGBO takes a handful of beans and places them on NGOZI's head. NGOZI shakes her head. They try to stifle their laughing.)

MEDICINE WOMAN: We are warned. "If a chicken crows at dawn, he doesn't crow for nothing."

MOTHER: I want protection from the Ogbanje.

MEDICINE WOMAN: I will give her my blessing.

MOTHER: Thank-you.

MEDICINE WOMAN: Ezigbo, come here.

(EZIGBO rises, crosses to them.)

MOTHER: And I want something more. You understand.

MEDICINE WOMAN: Oh, yes. Ezigbo, go sit down.

(EZIGBO, confused, sits back where she was.)

I have a drink. I have brought it with me. I will give it to her, but then you must pay.

(With real, but small enthusiasm.)

It will be strong. For this I have to have a goat.

MOTHER: A goat? I don't have a goat to give. I have a chicken.

MEDICINE WOMAN: For a chicken I will give her my blessing. For the drink I will need a goat. I went into the bush and found what was necessary; the plants and the tree-bark. This is strong and if you want this you must pay.

MOTHER: I don't have a goat to pay you.

MEDICINE WOMAN: Two chickens and one bag of cowrie shells.

MOTHER: And the cowrie shells? I can give you two chickens but no cowrie shells.

MEDICINE WOMAN: *(Considers a moment.)*

For you, my daughter, and my friend. For my blessing and the drink, two chickens.

MOTHER: Thank-you, Mother. Ezigbo, come here.

(EZIGBO rises, crosses to them.)

MEDICINE WOMAN: Ah, yes.

(Holding up amulet: it is a small leather envelope on a leather string.)

I was hoping to give you this amulet for her to wear; it will always protect her. It is the strongest medicine I have, but you have no goats and no cowrie shells.

MOTHER: Ezigbo, go sit down.

(Confused, she sits back down.)

What must you have for that necklace?

MEDICINE WOMAN: I treated and cured this leather myself. I gathered the charms that are inside. It has the blood of many sacrifices on it. For this you must pay . . . a cow.

MOTHER: A cow?! My husband would not agree to a cow.

MEDICINE WOMAN: And a goat.

MOTHER: And a goat!

MEDICINE WOMAN: And a bag of cowrie shells!

MOTHER: Ah, Mama Nkiru! She will never wear it! And look at her, so thin. Mother, what can I do? She must have this and I can't give it to her.

MEDICINE WOMAN: What can you do?

MOTHER: I will give you a female goat for the amulet.

MEDICINE WOMAN: A female goat, yes, and-a-bag-of-cowrie-shells.

MOTHER: Where will I get them? I have no cowrie shells. A goat and a chicken.

MEDICINE WOMAN: I have chickens! You should know this! You are giving them to me!

MOTHER: A goat and a basket of corn.

MEDICINE WOMAN: A goat and three baskets of fresh corn.

MOTHER: A female goat and one basket of fresh corn.

MEDICINE WOMAN: Two baskets of fresh corn!

MOTHER: One!

MEDICINE WOMAN: Let us not haggle, here, like market women. Look at your daughter. She walks around as if she is in a dream because she is talking with spirits. Two.

MOTHER: Yes, two.

MEDICINE WOMAN: You are a good mother. Ezigbo, come here.

(EZIGBO rises, walks to her, then returns, sits back down where she was.)

Ezigbo, I told you to come here.

(EZIGBO moves to her. MEDICINE WOMAN holds EZIGBO's head.)

I see what is happening to you, Ezigbo; the spirits follow you, they talk to you; they are calling you. But you do not have to listen to them.

(The MEDICINE WOMAN feels the glands in EZIGBO's neck; they are sore and EZIGBO pulls away sharply.)

EZIGBO: Ah! I don't listen to them because I can't hear them.

(MEDICINE WOMAN again feels her neck, but carefully.)

MEDICINE WOMAN: Because they long to play with you, their sister; they want you to leave us. Open your mouth.

(EZIGBO opens her mouth wide, the MEDICINE WOMAN tilts EZIGBO's head and looks in her mouth.)

The spirit world is your home, I know, and it is a joy for you to play there with your friends. But I am a mother myself and understand what the death of a child would mean. Your mother would waste away in grief over you. E na nukwa? *(She pulls EZIGBO's ears.)* Do you hear?

EZIGBO: Ah! Yes, I hear you.

MEDICINE WOMAN: You must keep warm, you must not stay in the water too long, you must be careful what you eat and you must listen to your mother.

(She pulls ears again.)

EZIGBO: *(Pained.)*

But I need my ears if I am to listen to her.

MEDICINE WOMAN: Now . . .

(She takes up the small bowl, uncovers the pot and dips bowl in. She then holds the bowl up to EZIGBO's lips.)

Drink.

EZIGBO: What is that?

MEDICINE WOMAN: Medicine. It will help heal your dizziness and coughing. And the Earth Spirit, Ani, will make your will stronger, to stay with us.

EZIGBO: Does it taste good?

MEDICINE WOMAN: Everything is not akara; it tastes strong, like earth.

EZIGBO: I will drink it if it will help me stay with my mother. And Ngozi. I will do whatever you say.

MEDICINE WOMAN: Drink it all, all at once.

(EZIGBO drinks, starts to pull back as drink is bitter.)

All of it! Yes, all of it, Ezigbo.

(EZIGBO *tries, only it's very bitter. She shivers in disgust.*)
NGOZI: *(With a smile.)*
> Does it taste good, Ezigbo?

(She makes a face that resembles Ezigbo's.)
EZIGBO: It tastes like rotten fish.

(NGOZI *groans.*)
> I think Ngozi should drink some because she is my friend.
NGOZI: No.
EZIGBO: But you will eat anything. You will like it.
NGOZI: Not that. I am not Ogbanje.
MEDICINE WOMAN: *(To* MOTHER.*)*
> You must help her drink a bowl every morning until it is gone.
EZIGBO: All of it?
NGOZI: Look how much there is!
EZIGBO: If I drink all of it, I will die from that.
MEDICINE WOMAN: *(Taking out leather amulet.)*
> And now, Ezigbo—
EZIGBO: Do I have to eat that?
MEDICINE WOMAN: No, you must wear it.
EZIGBO: *(Relieved.)*
> Ah. What's in it?
MEDICINE WOMAN: My most powerful medicine.
EZIGBO: Does it smell bad?
MEDICINE WOMAN: It smells like earth.
EZIGBO: *(She smells it expecting the worst. Pleasantly surprised.)*
> No . . . Like . . . the trees after rain.
MEDICINE WOMAN: *(Putting amulet on* EZIGBO; EZIGBO *sits on her lap.)*
> In it I have put symbols of our love for you. You must never take this off so you know, and the Ogbanje know that we want you with us. So, when you hear the Ogbanje and you feel their hands on you, you can touch this and remember how many people in the village want you here. Touch this and you will remember how much your mother loves you.
EZIGBO: Thank you. Ngozi. . . .

(She holds it up to NGOZI *to see;* NGOZI *begins to reach to touch it.)*
MEDICINE WOMAN: I have heard that one touch of that can kill someone.

(NGOZI *snaps her hand back.*)
> No one else may touch it.

(NGOZI *sniffs it and smiles.* MEDICINE WOMAN *rises, faces the shrine, raises her hands.*)
> Ogbanje.

(*DRUMS: forceful and insistent.*)

Ogbanje!

(*The* OGBANJE *run on. DRUMS continue under following.*)

See what we have done! The sacrifices have been made! Hear what the voice of Ani says! And when Ani speaks, what Ogbanje dares not listen?

(*To* EZIGBO.)

Walk about and show these Ogbanje how powerful you are, now. Let them know your will to stay is strong.

(EZIGBO *walks around compound, holding the amulet.*)

EZIGBO: I am staying. With my mother and my family. And Ngozi.

(*The* OGBANJE *move toward her. One reaches toward the amulet, pulls hand back as if shocked. They back away.*)

I am getting well. I am getting stronger. I will stay strong. I am staying.

MOTHER: Now you are protected. Now you will stay with me.

(MOTHER *and* EZIGBO *embrace.*)

MEDICINE WOMAN: (*To* EZIGBO.)

And now you can be first wife, like your mother. And have many children.

(*To the* OGBANJE.)

Leave this child to her mother. Leave this family. Go. Go!

(*A flourish of DRUMS, as* OGBANJE *exit. End DRUMS.*)

And like this, my work is done.

EZIGBO: Ndeme: Thank you, Mama Nkiru.

(MEDICINE WOMAN *exits.*)

Mother, the Priestess said that I would be a first wife. Have you been thinking of someone for me?

MOTHER: Oh, yes.

EZIGBO: Who?

(NGOZI *cleans up the beans and replaces stools in cooking hut.*)

MOTHER: (*Fixing* EZIGBO's *hair.*)

Whatever boy or young man we choose will be wonderful.

EZIGBO: Who are you thinking of?

MOTHER: Someone who will be a good farmer, kind to the land, and kind to you.

EZIGBO: It is not Okoli, is it?

NGOZI: Okoli!

MOTHER: You know I cannot tell you. Now, Ezigbo, I need more water to soak the beans for akara and to cook the meal. Take one of our pots and go to the river.

NGOZI: I have to get water for my mother, too.

(Getting her pot.)

MOTHER: *(She gets a pot, gives it to* EZIGBO.*)*
I want you to be sure to come back before dark. Because bad things go walking in the bush at night.

EZIGBO: Yes, Mama.

MOTHER: Go; and do not run so much.

*(*MOTHER *exits. Both girls place a rolled cloth on their heads and put the pots on their heads.* EZIGBO *and* NGOZI *walk the path toward the river.)*

NGOZI: I am glad you are staying. Even though you are older.

EZIGBO: I think I will like you more than my husband.

NGOZI: Who do you think they are thinking of for you?

EZIGBO: I hope it is not Okoli.

NGOZI: *(The demon himself.)*
Okoli!

EZIGBO: He teases me all the time. "Oh, come here," he calls."Come here, my little wife."

NGOZI: *(They stop walking.)*
He says that to you?

EZIGBO: Whenever there's anyone else around, he does. "Come here, my little wife. Let me untie your waist beads."

NGOZI: Ugh! Never.

EZIGBO: He smells bad.

NGOZI: Yes he does. And he spits a lot.

(That is disgusting.)

EZIGBO: All the time.

(She shows how he does it, pretending to spit.)
Ugh. And he laughs like a pig.

(She laughs like a pig. NGOZI *laughs at this, then laughs like a pig as well.* EZIGBO *laughs for real, then snorts again.)*
I will ask the River Spirit to not let it be Okoli.

(They walk. EZIGBO *begins to sway her hips.)*

NGOZI: How are you walking?

EZIGBO: *(Exaggerating her swaying.)*
You would not understand. I am older. I understand.

NGOZI: You are walking like Nkiru when she walks in front of boys.

EZIGBO: Yes! Nkiru walks like this, but only when boys are watching!

NGOZI: That is because she is much older—2 years.

EZIGBO: *(Even more exaggeration.)*
"I am Nkiru. Look at me. See how I walk? I am beautiful."

NGOZI: I can walk like that.

(They walk and sway together, exaggerating their hip movements. They float down the path.)

Do boys like this?

EZIGBO: No, they think it is funny.

NGOZI: Why don't they laugh, then?
(They stop.)

EZIGBO: They do laugh. After Nkiru has passed by, they look at each other and laugh.

NGOZI: I think they like it.

EZIGBO: Why?

NGOZI: Because they like Nkiru. And I know this because when they see her coming, they jump on each other and wrestle so when she walks by, she will see how strong they are.

(They walk on.)
"I am Nkiru."

EZIGBO: "Nnnkiiirruu."

NGOZI: "I am beautiful. Oh, you are such a good wrestler. You are so strong.

(EZIGBO *picks up on this, takes pot off her head, and begins to walk like a man.)*
Won't you talk to my father?"

EZIGBO: *(As a man.)*

My father and your father will talk.

(She pretends to spit, wipes her mouth.)
NGOZI: Oh, Okoli, it is you! I love the way you spit!

(They gag in disgust.)
EZIGBO: You come over here, my little wife. I'll fix those waist beads.

(NGOZI *screams in fear,* EZIGBO *laughs imitating* OKOLI.)
NGOZI: I love the way you laugh.

(They laugh like him.)
And we will have such wonderful children.

(They become the small children, laughing like little pigs. Dropping game.)
We should marry brothers. Then we would be friends and sisters too.

EZIGBO: Yes! I will tell my mother and father to look for two brothers for us.

(They proceed to the river. EZIGBO *puts her pot down, kneels, tests the water.)*
The water is warmer, today. Let's bathe.

NGOZI: You know you should not bathe; you were coughing, today.

EZIGBO: But the water is warmer. Come bathe with me.

NGOZI: But it is not warm enough. You shouldn't walk back wet.

EZIGBO: It was the River Spirit who first told my mother I was going to be born. When I am bathing, I think I hear her talking to me.

NGOZI: (NGOZI *and* EZIGBO *kneel to put water in their pots.* NGOZI *wipes away the top of the water, dips and fills her pot, but* EZIGBO *loses momentum and sits back on her heels, staring at the water.*)
Ezigbo?

EZIGBO: I'm going to stay here a while.

NGOZI: I cannot. I have to bring my mother the water or she'll have a *good* reason to spank me, again.

EZIGBO: You can go on.

NGOZI: (*No one ever does this.*)
You want to stay here alone? Why?

EZIGBO: Will you tell my mother I stayed by the river and I'll come back soon?

NGOZI: You're not going in the water, are you?

EZIGBO: I promise I won't go in the water.

NGOZI: How will you get your pot on your head?

(*She takes* NGOZI's *pot,* NGOZI *kneels,* EZIGBO *helps her place the pot on* NGOZI's *head.* NGOZI *rises.*)

EZIGBO: I have done that before.

NGOZI: (*Heading out.*)
Don't stay too long. Your mother needs the water to soak the beans for akara.

EZIGBO: Don't forget to tell her I am here.

NGOZI: (*As she goes off.*)
"I am Nkiiirruuu. I am sooo beautiful. And you are sooo strong."

EZIGBO: (EZIGBO *turns to the river, sighs. She sits on a rock, looks down one way, then the other. To river.*)
Will I have children?

(*DRUMS the sensuous beat of the* RIVER SPIRIT. *She appears.* EZIGBO *does not see her, yet.*)
Will I grow older and have children?

RIVER SPIRIT: (*As before, dancing the words.*)
Child, every day you come to me with questions.

EZIGBO: (*Seeing her, jumping up, but looking down in reverence.*)
I am sorry.

RIVER SPIRIT: Speak.

EZIGBO: You talked to my mother and you told her what would happen to her—seven market weeks later, you said, and I was born.

RIVER SPIRIT: I spoke to comfort her, and you.

EZIGBO: Will I have children?

RIVER SPIRIT: You long to stay in life, and you long to return home to the spirit world.

EZIGBO: But what is the answer?

(RIVER *does not answer.*)

Have I made you angry?
(*No answer.*)

Biko? Please?

RIVER SPIRIT: (*Moving to her.*)
What more can I give you?

EZIGBO: I do not understand your answers. Will I marry well? Will I have children?

RIVER SPIRIT: Sacrifices have been made. Promises will be kept. All laws will be respected with you.

(*She sees* EZIGBO *is still not satisfied.*)

Every day the earth is growing and dying; the water flows through Igboland and the people drink and bathe; every day, the water flows to the sea.

EZIGBO: Yes?

RIVER SPIRIT: What more can I say to you? You are Ogbanje.

(*She moves away from* EZIGBO, *and exits.*)
EZIGBO: (*She turns away in frustration. She turns back to* RIVER, *but no longer sees her.*)

River Spirit? . . . But what does your answer . . . ? Thank you for speaking to me.

(*She sighs.*)   .

Ogbanje . . .
(*She again looks up and down the river. Then she sings quietly to herself, slowly and absentmindedly. She sings both the refrain and response.*)
                    Onye ga-agba egwu?
                    E-yow-yow-yow . . .

(*She drifts off. Then she begins again.*)
                    Onye ga-agba egwu. E-yow . . .

(*She trails off, then stands and walks to the river's edge. She begins song again, setting a rhythmic step.*)
                    Who will dance with me?
                    E-yow-yow-yow. E-yow-yow. E-yow!

(DRUMS. *The* OGBANJE *run on, and, once facing* EZIGBO *in a semi-circle, they "twirl" and become visible. This "twirl" is something that recurs and should be done with the same DRUM theme and movements throughout the play.*
    EZIGBO *does not see them as she is looking down river.* OGBANJE *DRUMS end.*)
                    Will no one dance with me?

EZIGBO AND OGBANJE: (DRUMS *for song. All sing and dance.* EZIGBO *dances differently to this song than the* OGBANJE, *who, as usual, move as a group.*)

                    E-yow-yow-yow. E-yow-yow.
                    E-yow!

(EZIGBO *turns and sees them. She does not recognize them or know who they are, nor is she startled.*

Rather, she's somewhat delighted. OGBANJE *form a circle around* EZIGBO *and they all sing and dance.*)

EZIGBO:
>Will no one dance with me?

OGBANJE:
>E-yow-yow-yow. E-yow-yow.
>E-yow!

EZIGBO: *(Fairly seriously.)*
>Is there something wrong with me?
>Is my hair too messy,
>Are my knees way too big?

OGBANJE:
>E-yow-yow-yow. E-yow-yow.
>E-yow!

1ST OGBANJE: (1ST OGBANJE *moves into middle,* EZIGBO *joins the circle and they dance the song again.*)
>Who will dance with me?

EZIGBO AND OGBANJE:
>E-yow-yow-yow. E-yow-yow.
>E-yow!

1ST OGBANJE:
>Will no one dance with me?

EZIGBO AND OGBANJE:
>E-yow-yow-yow. E-yow-yow.
>E-yow!

1ST OGBANJE: (*In contrast to* EZIGBO's *seriousness during this verse,* 1ST OGBANJE's *rendering is much more comical.*)
>Is there something wrong with me?
>Is my hair too messy,
>Are my knees way too big?

EZIGBO AND OGBANJE:
>E-yow-yow-yow. E-yow-yow.
>E-yow!

(*They sing and dance one more time, as* 2ND *and* 3RD OGBANJE *move to middle, dance as before;* EZIGBO *tries to follow their movements.*)

2ND AND 3RD OGBANJE:
>Who will dance with me?

ALL:
>E-yow-yow-yow. E-yow-yow.
>E-yow!

2ND AND 3RD OGBANJE:
>Will no one dance with me?

ALL:
>E-yow-yow-yow. E-yow-yow.
>E-yow!

2ND AND 3RD OGBANJE:
> *Is there something wrong with me?*
> *Is my hair too messy,*
> *Are my knees way too big?*

ALL:
> *E-yow-yow-yow. E-yow-yow.*
> *E-yow!*

(Song ends; DRUMS are quiet.)

EZIGBO: *Who are you?*

OGBANJE: *(DRUMS; singing and dancing refrain.)*
> *E-yow-yow-yow. E-yow-yow.*
> *E-yow! (They laugh. DRUMS end.)*

EZIGBO: I am Ezigbo, daughter of a chief. What village are you from and who is your family?

2ND OGBANJE: A village close to here.

(The OGBANJE find this tricky answer amusing.)

EZIGBO: You knew the song. But I haven't seen dancing like that before.

1ST OGBANJE: We make our own dances. And we make our own games.

(Reaching out, touching EZIGBO's face.)
> And we can teach you many new songs, sister.

(They all move to EZIGBO, touch her. Their interest is so intense, she backs up until she sits on a rock and they surround her. They are especially curious about her clothes, adornnments and hair, but avoid her amulet.)
> We will play a long time.

3RD OGBANJE: Tell me, Ezigbo, do you like fetching water?

EZIGBO: I must do it. Do you like to fetch water?

2ND OGBANJE: That looks like fun, carrying the pot on your head.

EZIGBO: Don't you carry your pots on your head?

3RD OGBANJE: We don't work. We only play.

2ND OGBANJE: Do you like to sweep the compound?

3RD OGBANJE: Do you like sweeping more or gathering firewood?

EZIGBO: I don't like sweeping, I would rather go to the farm with the older girls. But I like getting firewood.

2ND OGBANJE: What is it like to eat your mother's akara?

EZIGBO: Oh, she makes the best akara in the village.

2ND OGBANJE: What is it like?

EZIGBO: Do you mean the taste? It tastes like . . . akara—the best akara. She is making some today and that is why I have to be careful with the water, so there is enough to soak the beans.

1ST OGBANJE: Who would like to do these chores, eh? We'd rather play!

(Pulling EZIGBO off rock.)
> And so would you, sister. We all want to play!

3RD OGBANJE: What is that?

EZIGBO: My amulet.

(3RD OGBANJE *reaches out, thinks better of it, withdraws her hand.*)
   Do you want to smell it? It smells good.

3RD OGBANJE: *(Holding out hand.)*
   May I hold it?

EZIGBO: Oh, I can't take it off.

3RD OGBANJE: Yes you can. It will come off over your head. May I hold it?

EZIGBO: I won't take it off. It protects me.

(3RD OGBANJE *reaches out to take it.*)
   I have heard that one touch of this may kill someone.

(3RD OGBANJE's *hand snaps back in pain.*)
   No one may touch it but me. But you can smell it.

(1ST *and* 2ND OGBANJE *lean, smell it. Seriously repelled, they choke, trying to vacate what they have inhaled; back away repulsed.*)

1ST AND 2ND OGBANJE: Ah!

EZIGBO: *(Assuming they are playing.)*
   Oh, I see you like it. So do I.

(*She smells it, reacts like they did, coughing and shaking; then she laughs.*)
   You said you make your own games. Will you teach me one?

3RD OGBANJE: Watch and when you understand, join us.

1ST OGBANJE: Animal game!

3RD OGBANJE: Animal game!

1ST OGBANJE: First!

2ND & 3RD OGBANJE: First! First!

1ST OGBANJE: I am first this time!

2ND OGBANJE: Second!

(*They form a semi-circle, facing audience.* EZIGBO, *intrigued, watches them, as the Animal Game begins. DRUMS may accompany game. See additional description at end of text.*

*The character on stage-right of the semi-circle—*1ST OGBANJE*—moves out from the group and becomes an animal, both physically and vocally (an eagle). Once he has fully assumed the animal and expressed it as well as he can, the person who is now stage-right in the semi-circle moves out, becomes an animal (a tiger) and challenges the first player.*

The two animals challenge each other, attempting to be fiercer, stronger, more powerful and frightening than the other. They do not physically engage each other; it is a show of force.

The watching players make comments on the struggle, cheering and voicing support for excellent representations of an animal, and of particularly dynamic moves.

Soon, one or the other of the animals backs down (the eagle). Once he has turned and moved away, he returns to human form, returns to the end of the line and the winner of the face-off celebrates (in the style of the animal she is playing, a tiger).

Then the next player comes out of group as a monkey and challenges the winner of the first confrontation (the tiger). During that confrontation, the monkey appears stronger than the tiger, the tiger turns and runs. Then the player drops the tiger (comments on the struggle), and moves to the end of the line, while the monkey celebrates by leaping about, screeching like a monkey.

EZIGBO *joins the game after the first two or three players have gone. As soon as she does, the* OGBANJE *move her to first in line.*

MOTHER *enters, carrying wooden bowls and a long wooden spoon.* TRANSLATOR *enters. The game continues under narration.)*

MOTHER: Ezigbo we soro ndi Ogbanje gwuba-eguu, anwu we nna.

TRANSLATOR: Ezigbo followed the children and played until the sun left the sky.

*(*TRANSLATOR *exits.* MOTHER *moves to cooking hut and works on preparing the evening meal. She stirs the soup with the long wooden spoon.*

EZIGBO *goes out as a lion and challenges. We should see that she is adept at the game. During the challenge, when* EZIGBO *isn't looking,* 2ND OGBANJE *takes* EZIGBO's *pot off.*

EZIGBO *wins her challenge and when she turns to celebrate, the* OGBANJE *run off.* DRUMS *end. She is suddenly alone, growling and rearing like a lion, celebrating her victory. She sees she's alone, stops playing.)*

EZIGBO: Where . . . where did you . . . I won! I scared you all and you ran home! I won! Home—

(She notices darkness descending on her. Sounds of the night begin to be heard.)
Oh! Water . . .

(She goes to get her pot.)
Where . . . ? Where did I . . . ? Our pot!

(She searches.)
I put it there. I put it here . . . Our pot . . . Where . . . ?

*(*EZIGBO *looks up, sees how dark it is. She looks for pot one more time, then begins to walk the path to the compound.)*

MOTHER: *(Moving from fire, looking out into the night.)*
Ezigbo . . .

*(*MOTHER *sets out the two low stools, a large bowl of fou-fou and two soup bowls, one for her and one for* EZIGBO. EZIGBO *emerges from the bush.)*

MOTHER: *(Greatly relieved.)*
Ezigbo!

EZIGBO: Mama.

*(*MOTHER *runs to her.)*

MOTHER: Are you hurt?

EZIGBO: No.

MOTHER: Where have you been?

EZIGBO: I was playing with some new friends by the river and we played a game and it was getting dark—

MOTHER: You must come home before dark, otherwise I worry too much.

EZIGBO: Yes, Mama, I know, but—

MOTHER: Because you do not stay away like this. You always do what I ask. How do you feel?

EZIGBO: Fine.

MOTHER: You weren't sick?

EZIGBO: No, I was playing.

MOTHER: Ah, you are here. Not hurt and not sick. You are here. Ah. Where is the water?

EZIGBO: I lost the pot.

MOTHER: What?

EZIGBO: I looked and looked for it but I couldn't find it.

MOTHER: You lost it?

EZIGBO: Yes, Mama.

MOTHER: You are one of the best children, Ezigbo, but you are the first child to lose a pot in any village, anywhere.

EZIGBO: I am?

MOTHER: You will find it, tomorrow. Come, I borrowed some water from Mama Okeke and made the meal.

(They move to stools.)

EZIGBO: Is it ready?

MOTHER: I set it out. Sit down.

EZIGBO: I have to bring food to Father.

MOTHER: I had to take food to your father.

EZIGBO: I will take it!

MOTHER: You were gone too long.

EZIGBO: No.

MOTHER: He asked me where you were. I had to make up a story. Do not make me do this again.

EZIGBO: I am sorry.

MOTHER: Sit *(Both sit on short stools. There is one bowl of fou-fou and two bowls of soup placed between them. They eat only with their right hands. Each picks up fou-fou, delicately roll it in her fingertips. Mother dips hers in the soup and eats.* EZIGBO *dips hers, but stops before she eats, holds her food.)*

EZIGBO: Will I have children?

(The question catches MOTHER *off-guard; she hesitates.)*

　　Will I grow older and have children?

MOTHER: Yes.

EZIGBO: I asked the River Spirit but She wouldn't answer me. She has never answered me.

MOTHER: She appeared to you, again?

EZIGBO: Yes. Have I made Her angry, too?

MOTHER: She honors you by speaking to you.

EZIGBO: Then why does She not answer me?

MOTHER: Maybe She does not know. But I know. You will be first wife and have many children.

EZIGBO: Will they . . . will they be Ogbanje?

MOTHER: No one can know that.

EZIGBO: (After a moment.)
I hope they are like Ngozi. Not like me.

(EZIGBO stands, looks into the night, lost in thought.)

MOTHER: What are you thinking, Ada?

EZIGBO: About Ngozi's sister Nkechi. Why didn't you let me go to her funeral? And Okafo's funeral and Uche's funeral and—

MOTHER: Many children die; there are too many funerals for children in Igboland.

EZIGBO: Ngozi was allowed to go. Nkiru went. Why couldn't I go?

MOTHER: I do not want you to think so much of death.

(Short silence.)

EZIGBO: Do you?

MOTHER: Death is for me to think of, Ada. Not you.

EZIGBO: I do not know how to not think of it. I have always thought of it. It is always around me. I must think of it or it will come.

MOTHER: Think of how much there is here for you.

(Short silence.)

EZIGBO: I want to stay. I want to stay.

(She sits, eats.)

MOTHER: Yes, you think of staying.

(They eat in silence. They dip the fou-fou into the soup and swallow without chewing. They delicately lick their fingertips. EZIGBO looks at MOTHER's bowl.)
You may have that.

EZIGBO: What?

MOTHER: I see you looking at that piece of meat.

EZIGBO: I wasn't looking at that piece of meat.

MOTHER: You know what happens to children who eat too much meat?
They grow up to be thieves.

EZIGBO: I know, but I wasn't looking at it. I was looking at that big piece of okra under it.

MOTHER: (Picking meat out, putting it in EZIGBO's mouth.)
Eat. It will keep you strong. But do not tell Ngozi I gave that to you. Or her mother will be over here again, complaining how I spoil you.

EZIGBO: I won't tell Ngozi, if you won't tell her I lost my pot. Because then her mother will be over here again, complaining how strange I am.

MOTHER: I won't tell her.

EZIGBO: Then, when her mother comes here to complain, she can complain about something else, like Ngozi eating all the food in the hut, again. (*She dips her fou-fou, eats. Her* MOTHER *smiles at her.*)

MOTHER: (*Turns to audience.* EZIGBO *rises, takes food and bowls to cooking hut.*)
    Mgbe chi furo, Mama Ezigbo zi nna-gu ozi; echu-mmiri; ha ga-anu, na mmiri ha ya-esi nri.

TRANSLATOR: When morning came, Mama Ezigbo called her daughter.

MOTHER: Ezigbo.

EZIGBO: Yes, Mama.

MOTHER: Here is your medicine. Drink.

(*She hands* EZIGBO *a cup of medicine.*)

    There is no drinking water in the hut. Please go to the river and return as fast as you can, so that we may prepare the meal.

EZIGBO: Yes, Mama.

(EZIGBO *drinks, finds it very difficult to swallow the bitter liquid.* NGOZI *sneaks on, carrying her pot.*)

MOTHER: And look for our other pot by the river.

(*She moves to get the other pot.*)

EZIGBO: I see you, Ngozi!

NGOZI: I saw you first, Ezigbo!

(EZIGBO *finishes the drink.*)

MOTHER: (*Quietly, so the approaching* NGOZI *can't hear.*)
    This is the last one we have.

(*Putting pot on* EZIGBO's *head.*)

EZIGBO: (*Quietly.*)
    Nothing will happen to this pot.

NGOZI: Good morning, Mama Ezigbo. How are the beans?

MOTHER: They are soaking.

NGOZI: When will the akara be finished?

MOTHER: Tomorrow.

NGOZI: Tomorrow? Tomorrow . . .

(*While* NGOZI *is suffering,* EZIGBO *starts down path to the river.* NGOZI, *pot on her head, hurries to follow her.*)

MOTHER: Stay on the path—and come right back!

EZIGBO: (*To herself, as she hurries down path.*)
    I will go and be back so fast Mama will forget about last night.

NGOZI: Wait. Wait!

(EZIGBO *speeds up.*)

Oh, I see. But it isn't a fair race because I didn't know we were racing and you did. And you started ahead of me . . . like a boy.

(*To herself.*)

I will still be first to the river.

(*She speeds up; they race.* EZIGBO *sees her getting closer, squeals and speeds up more.*)

1ST OGBANJE: (*Off.*)

Ezigbo . . .

2ND OGBANJE: (*Off.*)

Ezigbo . . .

(EZIGBO *slows down, suddenly dizzy and out of breath.*)

3RD OGBANJE: (*Off.*)

Sister . . .

2ND OGBANJE: (*Off.*)

Come play with us . . .

NGOZI: (NGOZI *moves ahead.*)

Ah!

(*They come into the river clearing;* NGOZI *jumps on rock.*)

I won! Even though you started first, I won!

EZIGBO: You won. You were faster.

(EZIGBO *quickly puts pot down, sits on rock, pulls her knees up and puts her head down.*)

NGOZI: Even though you are older, I won!

(*Sees* EZIGBO *is distressed, moves off rock.*)

But you slowed down. Why? Were you dizzy?

(*No answer.*)

You were dizzy.

EZIGBO: I am all right, now. I always feel better by the river.

(*She looks around for her new friends.*)

NGOZI: It was not a fair race so it was not a race. No one won. We will walk back slowly.

(*She kneels. The* OGBANJE *run on, invisible to everyone.* EZIGBO *senses their presence.*)

Ezigbo, what do you hear?

EZIGBO: Nothing.

2ND OGBANJE: (*Whispered.*) Sister . . . (EZIGBO *coughs.*)

NGOZI: You are still dizzy.

EZIGBO: No.

NGOZI: Then fill your pot.

(NGOZI fills her pot. The OGBANJE wait in the background.)

EZIGBO: You can go, Ngozi, I will come soon.

NGOZI: You shouldn't be here alone when you are sick.

EZIGBO: But I feel better, now.

NGOZI: What do you do here alone?

EZIGBO: Talk to the river.

NGOZI: Yesterday you stayed here until after dark. I know this because your mother came looking for you.

EZIGBO: Ngozi, go on.

NGOZI: There are bad things that walk about at night. They will find you.

EZIGBO: The sun is still high in the sky.

NGOZI: *(Standing.)*
Your mother will be angry. I heard her say come right back. She will ask where you are.

EZIGBO: Tell her where I am.

NGOZI: Then she will be angry at me. She does not hit you but she will hit me if I leave you here alone and you come home after dark, again.

EZIGBO: *(Standing.)*
She will not hit you! She has never hit you!

NGOZI: You know you should come with me! Fill your pot and come back!

EZIGBO: I want to be alone!

NGOZI: Stop acting like an Ogbanje!

EZIGBO: I am an Ogbanje!

(Silence. Quieter.)
I am an Ogbanje.

NGOZI: *(Much softer.)*
Then you should come with me so you are all right. And not act so strange.

EZIGBO: I have an amulet to protect me. I am safe.

(She takes NGOZI's pot, NGOZI kneels, EZIGBO helps her place the pot on NGOZI's head. NGOZI rises, starts off.)

NGOZI: Ogbanje.

(She exits. Ezigbo looks for her friends, doesn't see them. She turns to the river bank. DRUMS. The OGBANJE "twirl" and become visible. DRUMS end.)

EZIGBO: Our other pot . . . I put it right here, I know I did. But . . .

(She looks for the other pot. OGBANJE charge her.)

OGBANJE: Ezigbo, Ezigbo, play with us! Play with us! We love playing with you!

EZIGBO: No—

OGBANJE: The animal game! Play the animal game!

EZIGBO: Not the animal game, again, I won that game yesterday. You ran away.

(Next 3 speeches said simultaneously.)

3RD OGBANJE: Dance with us!

1ST OGBANJE: Oh, yes, dance, dance.

2ND OGBANJE: Dance. You haven't danced with us.

EZIGBO: No—No. I must go back and give my mother her water. My mother was angry at me because I played too long yesterday.

1ST OGBANJE: Angry?

EZIGBO: Yes.

1ST OGBANJE: What did she say?

3RD OGBANJE: What did she do?

EZIGBO: She said I was the only child in any village anywhere to lose a pot. And she had to take my father his food. After I have given her the water, I will come back and play with you.

2ND OGBANJE: Oh, but Ezigbo, look, we have a new dancing game!

3RD OGBANJE: We know you love dancing games.

1ST OGBANJE: Look at this one.

OGBANJE: Dancing game! Dancing game!

EZIGBO: I have to go home with water so—

3RD OGBANJE: The sun is still high in the sky. There's plenty of time.

2ND OGBANJE: Play with us for a small, small time, and then you can go back.

1ST OGBANJE: Remember how much fun we had when we played the animal game?

EZIGBO: Yes, but—

1ST OGBANJE: This is more fun. It's a dancing game. We know you love to dance.

OGBANJE: Dancing game! Dancing game! *(They break into the dancing game. EZIGBO moves to river, kneels to fill her pot with water but stops, watches the game.*

They play the dancing game accompanied by drums. More description at the end of text.)

SINGER: *(Dancing.)*

> Nobody Can Dance Like This.

(She holds out her arms, falls back, is caught by others.)

CHORUS:

> Ay A—Like This!

(On "This," the others throw DANCER back up and on her feet and she dances and sings.)

SINGER:

> Nobody Can Dance Like Me.

(She holds out her arms, falls back, is caught by OTHERS.)

CHORUS:

> *Ay, A—Like Me!*

(On "ME," the OTHERS throw DANCER back up and on her feet and she dances and sings.)

SINGER:

> *Like A Man, Like A Woman!*

(She holds out her arms, falls back, is caught by OTHERS.)

CHORUS:

> *Ay, A—Like A Woman!*

(On "Woman," the OTHERS throw DANCER back up and on her feet and she dances like a woman then a man and sings.)

SINGER:

> *Like A Woman, Like A Man,*

(She holds out her arms, falls back, is caught by OTHERS.)

CHORUS:

> *Ay, A—Like A Man!*

(On "Man," the OTHERS throw DANCER back up and on her feet and she dances back into group. Everyone dances during the following. The next PLAYER dances to the front becoming the SINGER, the first SINGER dances back into OTHERS.)

> *Ta Mbo Mbo, Mbo Mbo Ta.*
> *Mbo Mbo, Mbo Mbo Ta.*
> *Mbo Mbo, Mbo Mbo Ta.*

2ND SINGER: *(Dancing.)*

> *Nobody Can Dance Like This (Falls.)*

CHORUS:

> *Ay, A—Like This! (Throw.)*

2ND SINGER: *(Dancing.)*

> *Nobody Can Dance Like Me. (Falls.)*

CHORUS:

> *Ay, A—Like Me! (Throw.)*

2ND SINGER: *(Dancing.)*

> *Like A Man, Like A Woman (Falls.)*

CHORUS:

> *Ay, A—Like A Woman! (Throw.)*

2ND SINGER: *(Dancing.)*

> *Like A Woman, Like A Man (Falls.)*

CHORUS:

> *Ay, A—Like A Man! (Throw.)*
> *(Dancing, moving into next position.)*

ALL:

> *Ta Mbo Mbo, Mbo Mbo Ta.*
> *Mbo Mbo, Mbo Mbo Ta.*
> *Mbo Mbo, Mbo Mbo Ta.*

(EZIGBO *joins the game after the second* SINGER *finishes.* EZIGBO *is fourth or fifth to be the* SINGER. *She is an adept player of this game as well. Lights fade during the latter part of the game.* DRUMS, *twirl theme. While* EZIGBO *sings, after her turn, the* OGBANJE *"twirl" the opposite direction they used to appear, and they disappear to* EZIGBO.)

EZIGBO:

> Mbo Mbo, Mbo Mbo Ta.
> Mbo Mbo, Mbo Mbo Ta.

(*The* OGBANJE *withdraw into the night, but not out of sight of the audience.* DRUMS *are suddenly silent. We hear the night-sounds of the bush.*)

> Mbo Mbo, Mbo Mbo Ta.

Where . . . where did—Why do you do that? . . . Our pot!

(*She runs to it, picks it up.*)

Here!

(*Relieved.*)

Mother, it is here.

(*She looks skyward.*)

Oh.

(*She moves to the river, kneels, wipes top of water, dips her pot. She places the cloth on her head, then struggles to put pot on her head, then starts off down the path home.*)

There is still light. I can still see.

(*The* OGBANJE *dance after her, making quiet sounds of the night. They move in surging waves, then fall back, only to move up on her again. When they're near her,* EZIGBO *tries to hurry.*

Down the path, 1ST OGBANJE *lays on its back and puts out its arm.* EZIGBO *approaches, trips, the pot begins to fall.* 2ND OGBANJE *catches it, carries it off.*)

EZIGBO: No! No, no!

(EZIGBO *frantically tries to find the pot by feeling with her hands.* 1ST *and* 3RD OGBANJE *remain, continuing to make quiet sounds of the night.*)

It didn't break. I didn't hear it break. Where is it? It must be here! . . . Not our second pot . . .

(MOTHER, NGOZI *and* MEDICINE WOMAN *enter variously and move to the cooking hut.*)

MEDICINE WOMAN: I could not find her. Have you seen her?

NGOZI: No one has seen her.

MOTHER: She said she would come home before dark.

NGOZI: Maybe she is just late.

MEDICINE WOMAN: And she plays just as a disobedient child plays.

(EZIGBO *gives up feeling for the pot, rises and walks toward home.* OGBANJE *follow her.*)

MOTHER: She always does what she says.

MEDICINE WOMAN: Some children change and that is all it is.

MOTHER: Then I do not like this change.

1ST OGBANJE: *(Whisper.)*
Sister, stay with us.

3RD OGBANJE: Come home.

(3RD OGBANJE *tries to hold* EZIGBO's *hand;* EZIGBO *pulls away and runs into compound.)*

EZIGBO: Mama!

MOTHER: Ezigbo!

EZIGBO: They were following me—

MOTHER: Who was following you?

(While MOTHER *tries to calm her,* MEDICINE WOMAN *looks into the night to see if there is anything there. Frightened,* NGOZI *stays next to* MEDICINE WOMAN.)

EZIGBO: They were calling me—

MOTHER: Who?

EZIGBO: I couldn't see—

3RD OGBANJE: *(Calling out, longing for Ezigbo.)*
Sister!

EZIGBO: Aaahh!

MOTHER: What? Why are you screaming?

EZIGBO: They're out there!

MOTHER: Who? What happened!

EZIGBO: I don't know! There are noises—

MOTHER: Yes, there are noises. If you came back before dark, there would be no noises. Where were you?

EZIGBO: Playing at the river, but—

MOTHER: Ezigbo, what is it! You have never given me any trouble before. Why now?

EZIGBO: I met some new children, and they were teaching me dancing games, and I forgot to see what time it is, and then I forgot . . .

MOTHER: You have so many friends here in the compound. When I send you on an errand to fetch the water, come back with it and then go play.

EZIGBO: That is what I said, but they wanted me to play.

MOTHER: Where is our pot?

EZIGBO: I heard noises, and I started to run, and it fell off my head, and I couldn't find it in the dark.

MOTHER: *(She glances at* MEDICINE WOMAN. *Strongly.)*
When I tell you to do something, I don't want to hear any excuses! You will do it and come back with it finished!

EZIGBO: Yes, Mama.

MOTHER: And you will not tell me one thing and then do another! You said you would be back before dark and you were not!

EZIGBO: Yes, Mama.

MOTHER: Now we will have to eat our food without water. And tonight, again, you cannot bring food to your father.

MEDICINE WOMAN: Ezigbo, come here.

(EZIGBO *moves to her.*)

When you were born, I was sorry for your mother; I was angry at you.

EZIGBO: Angry at me?

MEDICINE WOMAN: Yes, for coming back *again*. Nothing good will come of this child, I said. She is Ogbanje, she will find a way to leave her mother. But I was wrong. You have stayed. You are Ezigbo, the Good One. Your mother's joy. Do you know this?

EZIGBO: Yes, My Mother.

MEDICINE WOMAN: Now, what noises did you hear in the bush?

EZIGBO: Animal noises; and some like children.

MEDICINE WOMAN: And did they call your name?

EZIGBO: I think so.

MEDICINE WOMAN: (*Takes* EZIGBO's *head, feels the glands in her neck.* EZIGBO *exhibits no pain.*)
Were you dizzy?

EZIGBO: No.

NGOZI: She was dizzy by the river.

EZIGBO: But that was a long time ago.

MEDICINE WOMAN: Did you take your amulet off?

EZIGBO: No, never.

(MEDICINE WOMAN *holds out* EZIGBO's *hair in her hands. She lets it fall, holds it out again, examining it.*)

MEDICINE WOMAN: What were you playing by the river?

EZIGBO: Dancing games.

MEDICINE WOMAN: And did you know these children?

EZIGBO: I met them yesterday. They are from another village.

MEDICINE WOMAN: Were there others from our village who saw these children?

EZIGBO: No.

MEDICINE WOMAN: Show me your hands.

(*She holds out her hands.* MEDICINE WOMAN *feels* EZIGBO's *hands, paying special attention to her nails.*)

Show me your feet.

(EZIGBO *sits down, lifts her feet.* MEDICINE WOMAN *looks at the bottoms of each of them.*)

MOTHER: What is it?

MEDICINE WOMAN: *(Holding foot.)*
> What is this?

(She rubs the bottom of EZIGBO*'s foot with her finger,* EZIGBO *squirms, laughs.)*
> Ezigbo, I can find nothing wrong with you. You are healthy and strong. And you have big feet.
> *(She throws foot.)*

EZIGBO: *(*EZIGBO *stands.)*
> That is why I can run faster than boys.

(She runs around the campground, ending up next to NGOZI*.)*

MEDICINE WOMAN: If these children come to you again, you must use your big feet and run home fast to your mother.

EZIGBO: I will.
> *(Upset,* NGOZI *moves away from her.)*
> Ngozi?

MOTHER: *(Pulling* MEDICINE WOMAN *aside.)*
> So you believe it was the Ogbanje she played with by the river?

MEDICINE WOMAN: Ogbanje? Hah. I don't know why Ani or the River Spirit would allow it. Probably they were children from another village and she played too long and came home late.

MOTHER: Thank-you, Mother.

MEDICINE WOMAN: *(To all.)*
> It is time for food. Let us eat well.

(To EZIGBO*.)*
> Ka chi fo, may the morning come.

(She exits. NGOZI *begins to move off.* MOTHER *sees and hears the following.)*

EZIGBO: Ngozi?

NGOZI: *(Turning back to* EZIGBO. *Genuinely hurt.)*
> You told me you would be back before dark, and you were not. I asked you what you were doing by the river, and you said talking to the River Spirit. You did not tell me you were playing with friends from another village. You played with them all day yesterday and today.

EZIGBO: You said you could not stay.

NGOZI: I would have stayed if you had told me you had new friends to play with.

EZIGBO: But you said your mother would hit you.

NGOZI: Yes, she would hit me, but you knew I would have stayed with you, anyway. You chose not to tell me, because you did not want me to play with you.

(She exits.)

EZIGBO: *(Calling after her.)*
> Ngozi? I want to play with you. I will go with you to the river tomorrow and stay with you! Ngozi!

(Silence, as EZIGBO *tries to understand what just happened.)*

MOTHER: *(After a moment.)*
   Come eat . . . even though we must fight with our food to go down without water.

EZIGBO: I'm sorry.

MOTHER: *(Much softer.)* I know, I know. Ezigbo. *(They walk toward hut.* TRANSLATOR *enters.* MOTHER *turns to audience.)*
   N'ubosi sorp anyasi ahu, Mama Ezigbo gboro nwa ya, si ya bia-nso.

TRANSLATOR: On the day that followed that night, the Mother called her daughter close.

MOTHER: Ezigbo.

EZIGBO: Yes, Mama.

MOTHER: Drink your medicine.

(She hands EZIGBO *cup of medicine, she drinks.)*
   How is your cough?

EZIGBO: Better.

MOTHER: And were you dizzy this morning?

EZIGBO: No; the medicine is working.

MOTHER: We need water to drink and to cook. Should I fetch the water myself?

EZIGBO: No, no. Everyone will laugh at me if you go, because they will think I cannot even get water for my mother.

MOTHER: I will go, then I know it will be done.

EZIGBO: No; no one will call me The Good One again. It is my chore. I will go.

MOTHER: *(Getting a painted, highly decorative pot.)*
   I borrowed a pot from one of the other wives, because we have no more waterpots in the hut. Now this belongs to Mama Okeka, it is their favorite pot, so please, bring it back in one piece, eh?

EZIGBO: Yes, Mama.

MOTHER: We've had a peaceful life, here, with no troubles with the other wives. As First Wife it is our responsibility we live in peace.

EZIGBO: I know.

MOTHER: Wait for Ngozi, then go.

(She exits.)

EZIGBO: I'm not going to wait for the other girls. I'll go now and I will get back so fast Mama will not even know I am gone.

*(*EZIGBO *takes up the pot and walks down the path with grim determination.*
Drums. 1ST OGBANJE *appears behind* EZIGBO, *dancing to* DRUMS, *twirls, making itself visible to* EZIGBO. EZIGBO *turns back, sees the* OGBANJE *following her, then walks on with determination.*
   2ND OGBANJE *dances on ahead of* EZIGBO, *twirls and appears to her, dancing.*
   3RD OGBANJE *dances on ahead of her, twirls, appears to* EZIGBO. *As the* OGBANJE *dance down the path in synchronized movements,* EZIGBO *tries to pass them, but they block her way.*

The group enters the river clearing. The DRUM *finishes the song, the* OGBANJE *jump towards* EZIGBO, *cutting her off and* 3RD OGBANJE *quickly takes pot from* EZIGBO's *head.)*

(Simultaneously exploding.)

EZIGBO: No, no, give that back, no, no, no, give me Mama Okeke's pot!

OGBANJE: Play with us, dancing game, dancing game!

EZIGBO: Can't you see I am fetching water for my mother? I have to bring it back now.

(She takes pot back from the OGBANJE.*)*

I have to bring her the water, now.

3RD OGBANJE: How is your mother?

EZIGBO: *(She goes to the river, dips the pot.)*

Angry. I did not bring any food to my father again last night. And we had to fight with our food to go down without water. She was going to fetch the water herself, that is how angry she is.

*(*OGBANJE *react at this.* EZIGBO *carefully places pot on her head.)*

I am not playing with you. I am going back, now.

(She starts off. The OGBANJE *circle her, speak in her ear.* EZIGBO *walks determinedly, but they turn her around, confuse her.)*

1ST OGBANJE: Ezigbo, there is plenty of time before the sun goes down.

2ND OGBANJE: See? The sun is still high in the sky.

1ST OGBANJE: We want to play with you. We miss you.

EZIGBO: You always run away.

3RD OGBANJE: Stay with us.

1ST OGBANJE: *(Carefully pulling her.)*

Play with us.

EZIGBO: *(Afraid her pot will fall.)*

Don't! No! The pot will break!

(She holds it with both hands. They gently pull her farther off the path.)

3RD OGBANJE: We have new games—

2ND OGBANJE: New dancing games, new clapping games.

OGBANJE: Clapping games! Do you like clapping games?

(They let her go and begin a clapping rhythm. EZIGBO *walks farther off the path. Lights begin a long fade into evening.)*

AI-EH-AI-EH! (Clap-clap) AI-EH-AI-EH! (Clap-clap)

AI-EH-AI-EH! (Clap-clap) AI-EH-AI—

EZIGBO: No, no, I can't play with you!

2ND OGBANJE: There is plenty of time.

EZIGBO: We have to prepare the evening meal.

2ND OGBANJE: You don't have to eat. You can stay and play.

EZIGBO: No, Mama—My Mother is waiting for me.

(They each pull her in a different direction.)
3RD OGBANJE: This way—
1ST OGBANJE: This way—
2ND OGBANJE: This way.
1ST OGBANJE: No, this way.

(DRUMS, twirl theme. As each OGBANJE says her name, they "twirl," disappear to EZIGBO.)
1ST OGBANJE: Ezigbo—
2ND OGBANJE: Ezigbo—
3RD OGBANJE: Ezigbo—
OGBANJE: *(Whispered.)*
    Sister . . .

(They crouch together. In the quiet, EZIGBO regains her balance.)
EZIGBO: Gone. Good.

(She looks for path, doesn't see it.)
    Where . . . where is the path?

(Night-noise begins to be heard. She moves one way, then the other.)
    Where's the path? . . . This way?

(She walks one way, stops.)
    No. There?

(She walks another way.)
    No.

(She looks up.)
    Darker . . .

(She clenches her amulet, then smells it.)
    Medicine Woman and Mother and Ngozi, all the people of Igboland and Ani, the Earth Spirit are here with me.

(She smells it, again, clenches it.)
    Sacrifices have been made! I am protected! I am staying!

(To the bush.)
    I am staying.

(She begins to walk.)
    Just walk and you will find the way.

(She sees the path.)

    Ah! The path. You see? This way!

(She moves quickly down the path. OGBANJE let her go a distance, then move to her in a wave.)

(Next 3 speeches delivered simultaneously.)

1ST OGBANJE: Sister come home. Come home.

2ND OGBANJE: We miss you, sister.

3RD OGBANJE: Sister, stay with us. Stay with us.

(DRUM sound effects of the night-bush. In the darkening night, the OGBANJE circle her, put their hands on her affectionately. She reacts, pulls away, holding onto her pot.
They release EZIGBO and she moves down the path, then they surge at her again.)

(Next 3 speeches delivered simultaneously.)

3RD OGBANJE: Sister come home. Come home.

1ST OGBANJE: We miss you, sister.

2ND OGBANJE: Sister, stay with us. Stay with us.

(1ST OGBANJE takes pot, passes it to 3RD OGBANJE who passes it to 2ND OGBANJE.)

EZIGBO: No! My pot, my pot, no—

(2ND OGBANJE throws the pot down and it smashes. DRUMS end.)

    Ah!

(EZIGBO sits near smashed pot, picks up some large pieces, begins to cry.)

    Mama . . .

2ND OGBANJE: *(Touched by EZIGBO's sadness.)*
    Sister . . .

1ST OGBANJE: *(Quietly)*
    Amulet . . .

3RD OGBANJE: *(Quietly.)*
    Amulet . . .

(3RD OGBANJE comes up behind her, tries to take hold of the leather string on the back of EZIGBO's neck, but is burned.
1ST OGBANJE tries to take off amulet, but is burned.
EZIGBO slowly rises, starts off down the path in sadness, carrying pieces of the pot. The OGBANJE follow her.
MOTHER appears near hut, waiting angrily for EZIGBO. She's followed by MEDICINE WOMAN and NGOZI.
EZIGBO enters compound.)

MOTHER: *(Angrily.)*
    Ezigbo.

EZIGBO: Mama.

MOTHER: Were is Mama Okeke's pot?

EZIGBO: It broke.

MOTHER: What did I tell you?

EZIGBO: But I didn't play with my friends. I got lost and I couldn't find the path—

MOTHER: You know the way! You go to the river every day! How many times do I have to tell you the same thing! I told you to come home before dark. And you said you would.

EZIGBO: I tried but they wouldn't let me. I didn't play and I filled the pot with water and—

MOTHER: And you have broken Mama Okeke's favorite pot after I promised her you wouldn't.

EZIGBO: The pot got caught on something and broke.

(The next two speeches are delivered simultaneously.)

MOTHER: And still we have no water. Three times! Ezigbo—don't you—listen to me. Listen to me, Ezigbo—no, no—

EZIGBO: Mama, it felt like somebody took it off my head—Mama, no, listen to me, no, no—

(MOTHER lightly slaps EZIGBO. MEDICINE WOMAN and OGBANJE react. River DRUMS; lights up on River. MOTHER, in horror, starts to go to EZIGBO, who pulls away, holding her face.)

MOTHER: Ezigbo . . .

EZIGBO: No (RIVER SPIRIT dances, "drawing" EZIGBO's spirit toward her through the following. DRUMS continue.)

MOTHER: *(Horrified.)* But I didn't mean . . . *(Again the MOTHER goes for her, again EZIGBO backs away.)* Ezigbo?

EZIGBO: I thought you would never . . .
(She coughs.)

MOTHER: I am sorry, Ezigbo. I am sorry.

1ST OGBANJE: Sister . . .

EZIGBO: *(She begins to faint.)*
Oh . . .

MOTHER: Ada?

(MOTHER moves to her.)

EZIGBO: I cannot . . . Mama.

(EZIGBO collapses into MOTHER's arms. RIVER SPIRIT moves into a repetitive, flowing movement.)

MOTHER: Ezigbo! Mother, help her. I will give you anything you ask.

(She lays EZIGBO down, EZIGBO's head on her knee.)

MEDICINE WOMAN: What can I do?

MOTHER: Keep her with us. Make her will stronger to stay. Call on the spirits to heal her!

MEDICINE WOMAN: I cannot insult the River Spirit by asking her to change her laws. She has spoken.

MOTHER: But I did not mean to strike her.

MEDICINE WOMAN: You should know it is much more than that, my Daughter. The spirits have called her, and she has listened. She was dancing with the Ogbanje at the riverside. Now they are calling her home.

MOTHER: River Spirit, please, do not take her from me! I will—

RIVER SPIRIT: *(Moving sharply in anger toward the MOTHER.)*
     Woman!

MEDICINE WOMAN: Do not dare to call the River Spirit yourself! She will strike you in anger!

1ST OGBANJE: Sister . . .

(EZIGBO hears this, stirs.)

MOTHER: *(Suddenly hopeful.)*
     (Ezigbo?)

(RIVER SPIRIT calms. DRUMS end. Light slowly fades out on River.)

OGBANJE: Sister?

(EZIGBO slowly sits up.)

MOTHER: She is still here. Ezigbo? How do you feel? Can you—Ezigbo?

(EZIGBO rises.)

2ND OGBANJE: *(The OGBANJE begin to come into focus.)*
     Sister?

EZIGBO: Sister?

(EZIGBO now sees the OGBANJE, moves to them. She reaches for them, touches them.)
     Sister.

MOTHER: No, no, no. Mother, please!

MEDICINE WOMAN: She was with you ten wonderful years. You are more of a family with the other wives and children, now. And no one can say you did not have a child. We will still call you Mama Ezigbo.

MOTHER: Ngozi, speak to her. *(i.e. to EZIGBO.)*

NGOZI: *(To EZIGBO.)*
     I would have helped you. Why didn't you let me help you? You sent me away. You do not have to go. You can stay and we will marry brothers so we can be friends and sisters.

EZIGBO: *(Standing among the OGBANJE.)*
     Ngozi . . . strong and healthy . . . you will live long.

NGOZI: You can, too.

MEDICINE WOMAN: Take comfort, Mama Ezigbo, she is Ogbanje. She will always be around you, playing. And for her, there is joy.

MOTHER: Joy!

MEDICINE WOMAN: Yes, *joy.* She is going home. They will welcome her with a celebration.

MOTHER: *(EZIGBO backs away from OGBANJE, turns to MOTHER.)*

Stay, you can stay, I know you can stay, Ada. Please. You are the Good One.

EZIGBO: Mama . . . *You* are The Good One.

(EZIGBO *stands alone, sings, without DRUMS, directly to her* MOTHER. MOTHER *groans and cries.*)

Ewo Nne Me O	MOTHER:
Udu'm A Lapu Kwam O.	*No, no, no, no, no . . .*
OGBANJE: *(Singing.)*	
Udu	
EZIGBO:	MOTHER:
Ewo Nna Ma O	*Ezigbo . . .*
Udu'm A Lapu Kwam O.	*(She sinks to the ground)*

OGBANJE:

    Udu

EZIGBO:

    Udu M Ji Echube Mmiri
    Ma M'egbu Ya Nata

OGBANJE:

    Udu

EZIGBO:

    Udu M Ji Echube Mmiri
    Ma M'egbu Ya Nata

OGBANJE:

    Udu

EZIGBO:

    O M Na-Agba O?

OGBANJE:

    Udu

EZIGBO:

    O M Na-Agba O?

OGBANJE:

    Udu

EZIGBO: *(Repeats. She walks toward* MOTHER *who rises.*
    EZIGBO *takes off her amulet.)*
    Ewo Nne Me O
    Udu'm A Lapu Kwam O

OGBANJE:

    Udu

EZIGBO:

    Ewo Nna Ma O
    Udu'm A Lapu Kwam O.

OGBANJE:

    Udu

EZIGBO: *(She lets amulet fall to the ground. Sadly, she touches* MOTHER'S *face, then kisses her mother.* MOTHER *desperately embraces her.)*

> *Udu M Ji Echube Mmiri*
> *Ma M'egbu Ya Nata.*

(EZIGBO *pulls away from* MOTHER.)

OGBANJE:

> *Udu*

EZIGBO:

> *Udu M Ji Echube Mmiri*
> *Ma M'egbu Ya Nata.*

(EZIGBO *moves to* OGBANJE *and they enfold her. She turns and continues singing directly to her* MOTHER.)

OGBANJE:
Udu

EZIGBO:
O M Na-Agba O?

OGBANJE:
Udu

EZIGBO:
O M Na-Agba O?

OGBANJE:
Udu

EZIGBO AND OGBANJE:

> *Anyi Ga-Agba Na-Agba Ewo*
> *Anyi Ga-Agba Na-Agba Ah-Ah*
> *Anyi Ga-Agba Na-Agba Ewo*
> *Anyi Ga-Agba Na-Agba Ah-Ah*

TRANSLATOR: (*As* OGBANJE *repeat this last part of the song quietly.*)
We will run to leave.
All of us must leave in haste.
Oh, my father,
Oh, my mother,
Farewell.

(OGBANJE *lead her center.*)

OGBANJE:	EZIGBO: (*Sings over them.*)
Anyi Ga-Agba Na-Agba Ewo	*Ewo, Ewo, Ewo, Ewo,*
Anyi Ga-Agba Na-Agba Ah-Ah	*Ewo Nna M O*
Anyi Ga-Agba Na-Agba Ewo	*Ewo Nna M O*
Anyi Ga-Agba Na-Agba Ah-Ah	*Ewo Nna M O*
Anyi Ga-Agba Na-Agba Ewo	*Ewo Nna M O*
Udu	*Ah Ah Ah Ewo*
	Ah Ah Ah Ewo

(*Song ends. DRUMS.* OGBANJE *form a circle around* EZIGBO. *The* OGBANJE *do a Celebration Dance around* EZIGBO. *DRUMS are energetic, the dance is exuberant; full of color and joy. The* OGBANJE *welcome* EZIGBO, *invite her to join them.*

Halfway through the dance, EZIGBO *begins to join in their movements. By three quarters she is dancing ecstatically and in complete synchronization with them.*

In the end, the OGBANJE, *one after another, dance off.* EZIGBO *dances after them without looking back.* DRUMS *end.* MOTHER *turns to audience.)*

MOTHER: *(Narrates.)*

Etua ka akwukwo m si we kwusi.

TRANSLATOR: And this is how my story ends.

(Lights dim out.)

CURTAIN

INUK AND THE SUN

by
Henry Beissel

INUK AND THE SUN

CAST

NOTE

The play can be performed by as few as five actors (plus masks).

Inuk *is not an Inuit or Eskimo play—any more than* Romeo and Juliet *is an Italian play. It is a fantasy which explores on an archetypal level the fundamental human experience of life and death, and of the need to understand and accept our place in nature in order to survive. The figure of Inuk ("human being") represents humanity, and he learns through his adventures to regard death not as a punishment or misfortune, not as an enemy, but as the knot that ties all life together. You cannot celebrate the one without celebrating the other. In this realization the play reflects and pays tribute to the profound spirituality of the Inuit. It was for this reason, and because the North is a challenge that demands of humans the utmost in courage, endurance, and wisdom, that I chose an Inuit setting, Inuit characters and their mythology, to tell a story which is my own fiction. At this level the play celebrates the triumph of the spirit of the Inuit over the vast and icy silences of the North.*

Inuk *was written for all ages, and is meant to be performed by masks, marionettes, and actors, so that the audience may viscerally experience different levels of reality. But it is theatrically flexible and has been presented solely by actors, by marionettes alone, and by all possible combinations of the two plus masks.*

—Henry Beissel

PROLOGUE

(A stark flat landscape. A few igloos at the edge of an Inuit village. The sun is setting; its warm orange glow fades slowly and is replaced by the silvery ice-blue light of the rising moon. The music evokes the bleak harshness of the land. A flock of wild geese departs noisily as the blustering wind increases in intensity. Wolves howl at close distance.

With a sinister cackle, a jet-black RAVEN *appears and circles the stage, chanting in a cracked voice.)*

RAVEN:

> White is black, and black is white—
> Arctic winter, arctic night.
> Snow wind, ice wind, wolves at bay:
> Man and beast are winter's prey.
>
> Gull and goose have followed the sun,
> Moose and caribou have gone,
> Whitefish, flatfish, whale and shark—
> All have fled the howling dark.
>
> Snow wind, ice wind, wolves at bay:
> Man and beast are winter's prey.
> White is black, and black is white—
> Arctic winter, arctic night.

(The RAVEN *settles on an igloo.)*

EPISODE ONE

(A light goes on inside the igloo—yellow glow in the sombre polar night. The wind howls. When INUK *and his* FATHER *emerge from the igloo, dogs bark and yelp wildly.)*

INUK: Quiet!! . . . Down!!! . . . *(Ad. lib.)*

FATHER: The dogs are frantic to be off on the hunt. They're hungry.

INUK: I'm hungry, too. *(The dogs yelp again.)* Quiet! . . . Down! . . . *(Ad. lib.)* We're all hungry! *(Wolves howl; the dogs fall silent.)*

FATHER: Even the wolves are hungry.

INUK: We must find game.

FATHER: It won't be easy. Most of the animals have followed the sun.

INUK: We'll track down those that stayed behind.

FATHER: A killer wind is blowing. It jumps on the backs of animals and forces them to the ground. Then it covers them with a thick fur of snow. We should wait till the wind is out of breath and grows tired.

INUK: The wind has a long breath, and we need food. For seven days we've waited out the blizzard. I cannot wait any longer. I want to prove myself a man, Father, and a man is a hunter.

FATHER: A hunter knows how to wait.

INUK: Wait? What for? A hunter stalks and kills his prey.

FATHER: *Ayorama*. Everything happens as the spirits have decreed. That is why we must know how to wait. Wait for the right moment to shoot the arrow. Wait with the harpoon over the ice-hole for the seal. Wait in the igloo for the storm to pass. Wait for the return of the caribou and the sun. Winter is the season of waiting.

INUK: Where does the sun go, Father, when she leaves us?

FATHER: No one knows for sure. She leaps over the edge of the world. Some say, into the sea to warm the fish. Others say she goes to shine for the spirits of the dead. There are even rumors that she is under the curse of an evil spirit. But no one knows.

INUK: Has no one ever followed the sun to see where she goes?

FATHER: We must let the secrets of the world be. It's as the Spirits have decreed. *Ayorama*.

INUK: Can the spirits be trusted, Father?

FATHER: There are good spirits and bad ones.

INUK: I think most of them are bad. That's why we go hungry in winter. They make us suffer. Sometimes they even kill us.

FATHER: But the good ones help us, and with their help we can overcome all difficulties.

INUK: Then I want to go and find the sun and ask her to help us.

FATHER: You're too impatient, Inuk, and reckless.

INUK: But the good spirits will help us travel right to the edge of the world and show us the way to the sun.

FATHER: There's no return from beyond the edge of the world.

INUK: The animals follow the sun there every year and they return.

FATHER: And it's animals we must hunt, not the sun. We need food and clothing.

INUK: But if we hunt the sun and capture her and bring her back here, then all the geese and hares and caribou and seals will come back too, and we'll have lots of food.

SPIRIT OF THE MOON: *(Shaking with laughter.)* He wants to hunt the sun!

(The RAVEN *starts up and circles the stage with his sinister cackle.)*

INUK: *(Frightened.)* Who's that?

SPIRIT OF THE MOON: You're bold, little one. What's your name?

INUK: I'm Inuk. And I'm not little anymore.

SPIRIT OF THE MOON: You bear a proud name, Inuk, but you still have a lot to learn.

INUK: That's true, but that doesn't make me little.

SPIRIT OF THE MOON: So you're human. D'you know who I am?

INUK: You're the Spirit of the Moon.

SPIRIT OF THE MOON: That's right. And don't you forget it. I'm the Moon. I rule this land of the long night. The black sky is my dominion, and the stars are spirits in my service. I make a glittering feast of the night.

INUK: But you're so cold, Moon, so bitter cold.

SPIRIT OF THE MOON: Is that why you want to bring back the sun and drive me out of my land?

FATHER: Inuk is young and foolish.

SPIRIT OF THE MOON: Teach him then that all things have their season. I paint your igloos and your hunting-grounds as white as my face so that you should find your way in the long winter night. What more d'you want?

INUK: The sun is brighter and warmer.

SPIRIT OF THE MOON: Yes, of course, my sister, the sun. Everybody loves her. Foolish creatures! Don't you know that her love is deadly? Go ahead, love her and let her burn you up! But me, me you must respect and admire because I shall outlast her. She consumes herself with fiery passion, I am immutable and at peace.

INUK: You're nothing without her. You wax and wane because—

SPIRIT OF THE MOON: Silence! . . . I tell you, I am who I am. I never change.

INUK: Then why do all the animals follow the sun?

SPIRIT OF THE MOON: They too will be consumed. And so will you! (*Laughs uproariously.*) A boy hunting the sun to banish me! What impudence!

(*The* RAVEN *circles with cackling laughter and flies off.*)

FATHER: Inuk is hungry. He doesn't know what he's saying.

SPIRIT OF THE MOON: You know the ancient customs. If you need food, call the spirits for the hunt! (*To* INUK.) And you must learn that music and dance triumph where conceit comes to a bad end. Remember that, Inuk, remember that. (*Withdraws.*)

FATHER: See what you've done. He's gone.

INUK: Where?

FATHER: Back into the igloo of his clouds.

INUK: Let's go after the sun, Father.

FATHER: We'll do no such thing. Get such foolish and dangerous notions out of your head! We shall go on a hunt alright, but we shall hunt for food. Let's call the Spirit of the Caribou to help us. Start the drums, Inuk!

EPISODE TWO

(*Music. The* MOTHER *emerges from the igloo.* INUK *and his parents perform a ritual dance enacting the stalking and killing of the caribou.* INUK *is the caribou and wears an antlered headgear. He imitates the movements and the sounds of a caribou. His* FATHER *is the hunter, the* MOTHER *and other Inuit villagers assist. Drums, rattles, and clappers. Authentic Inuit rhythms. The climax is reached with the mock killing of* INUK, *the caribou, and by the others dancing around the "dead body," chanting.*)

FATHER:

> Great Spirit of the Caribou,
> The Inuit are calling you.

MOTHER:

> When we're by snow and wind pursued
> You give us fur and oil and food.

FATHER:

> We Inuit must hunt to live
> And owe our lives to what you give.

MOTHER:

> Great Spirit of the Caribou,
> We sing and dance in praise of you.

ALL: (Chorus.)

> The Inuit are calling you,
> Great Spirit of the Caribou,
> Please come and visit our igloo.

(A bone rattle accompanies the appearance of the SPIRIT OF THE CARIBOU. All other music stops. INUK leaps up and withdraws into the igloo.)

SPIRIT OF THE CARIBOU: You called me.

FATHER: Great Spirit of the Caribou!

MOTHER: Help us! We're hungry.

FATHER: A blizzard trapped us in our igloos.

MOTHER: We haven't eaten for many days. The wind brings us nothing but snow.

FATHER: And it strangles the bark in the throat of our dogs.

MOTHER: The flame burns low in our blubber lamps.

FATHER: Our days are nights now, and we cannot find game. We need your help, Great Spirit.

MOTHER: Help us, Great Spirit! We are cold and hungry.

FATHER: We're setting out on a hunt. Help us find game!

SPIRIT OF THE CARIBOU: I'm the protector of the caribou. Why should I help you who kill many caribou each year?!

FATHER: We honor the caribou and help you against foxes and wolves. We never kill more than we need to live. That's the law of the North.

MOTHER: We celebrate the grace and courage of the caribou in our songs and dances. Who'll praise you when we die?

SPIRIT OF THE CARIBOU: That's true. But how can I help? My herds are grazing in the sun. They go south when the Ice Spirit returns. Here, under the moon, the cold wind holds sway. Nothing moves without his consent while he rides the hounds of snow.

FATHER: Speak for us to the wind.

SPIRIT OF THE CARIBOU: The wind never listens. When he's awake he raises his voice so that nothing else can be heard. And when he's asleep he's deaf.

(Unnoticed by the others, INUK has emerged from the igloo with bow and arrow.)

INUK: (Shouts.) You don't want to help us!

SPIRIT OF THE CARIBOU: I cannot help you. Not until the sun retu-u-u-r-r-r-n-sss. . . . (He is struck by the arrow INUK has shot in anger and disappears with a scream in a flash of light. The RAVEN returns with his sinister cackle.)

FATHER: (Choking with laughter.) Inuk, you fool! You tried to kill a spirit! Don't you know the spirits are immortal?

MOTHER: Beware! A spirit never forgets insult or injury until he's revenged.

RAVEN: *(Circling throughout the following song.)*

> White is black and black is white—
> Arctic winter, arctic night.

MOTHER:

> Gull and goose have followed the sun,
> Moose and caribou are gone.

FATHER:

> Whitefish, flatfish, whale and shark—
> All have fled the freezing dark.

RAVEN:

> Snow wind, ice wind, wolves at bay,
> Man and beast are winter's prey.

EPISODE THREE

(Arctic winter. Arctic night. There is no moon. The wind is howling. We hear the barking dog team offstage.)

FATHER: *(Offstage.)* Ho-o-oh! . . . Quiet! . . . *(Ad. lib.)*

INUK: *(Offstage.)* Down! . . . Quiet! . . . *(Ad. lib.)*

(INUK and his FATHER emerge from the dark.)

FATHER: It's too dark to read the map the wind has drawn in the snow.

INUK: Have we lost our way?

FATHER: The moon will tell us—if you harness your tongue to patience!

INUK: I see no sign of the moon.

FATHER: Wait and see. We'll build a shelter here and rest.

(They pull the sled into view and set it up as a shelter against the wind. The dogs start to bark again.)

INUK: Quiet! Or the wind'll give you a whipping!

FATHER: The dogs are hungry.

INUK: So am I.

FATHER: Lie down and sleep. You need no food while you sleep.

INUK: I'm too hungry to sleep. *(Addresses the night as though in prayer.)*

> Animals of the long night,
> Where are you?
> Animals of the long night,
> Why do you flee from us?
> We're your friends.
> We need you.
> Animals of the long night,
> Come, bring us your flesh.

FATHER: They cannot hear you in this wind. Lie down and sleep. We must wait for the moon.

(There is a spectacular display of Northern Lights.)

INUK: Look, Father! Northern Lights! How beautiful they are! They look like many-colored waves. The sky is a big black igloo decorated for a happy dance. Maybe that's the glittering feast the moon was talking about.

FATHER: No, Inuk. It's giant spirits playing with the skulls of our ancestors. The souls of our fathers and mothers have returned to earth, but their bodies are up in the sky or down in the sea, and sometimes the spirits play games with their skulls to while away the time.

INUK: I wish I could join them. It'd be one way to keep warm.

FATHER: You're too reckless, Inuk. One day the spirits'll punish you.

INUK: I'm not scared.

FATHER: Sleep now. The moon'll soon be rising. (*Lies down to sleep.*)

INUK: (*Gets up stealthily and talks to the Northern Lights in the sky.*)

> *Help me, O Spirits!*
> *I'm a shadow*
> *in a land of shadows.*
> *The wind plays with me,*
> *the moon plays with me.*
> *I'm fair game for the dark.*
> *Help me become a man.*
>
> *Help me conquer my fear*
> *of the moon, of the wind.*
> *Give me the strength*
> *of the polar bear,*
> *the foxes' speed,*
> *and the skill of wolves.*
> *For I want to hunt the sun.*
>
> *Help me, Good Spirits.*
> *I'm a shadow*
> *in a land of shadows.*
> *I'm a boy*
> *at the mercy of the wind,*
> *at the mercy of the moon.*
> *Help me become a man.*

(*The wind now howls at full force. Abruptly the* SPIRIT OF THE WIND *swoops down from the sky and suddenly—all is still.*)

SPIRIT OF THE WIND: So you're afraid of me, are you, Inuk? I'm the Spirit of the Wind.

INUK: Yes, I'm afraid of you—but I stand up to you all the same.

SPIRIT OF THE WIND: Bravo! Only the brave stand up to me, and I favor the brave.

INUK: Will you help me then?

SPIRIT OF THE WIND: Perhaps. If you're willing to follow me.

INUK: Follow you? Where?

SPIRIT OF THE WIND: I'll show you the way to the sun. You're looking for her, aren't you?

INUK: This isn't some trick you're playing, is it?

SPIRIT OF THE WIND: Why d'you say that? My directions are always true.

INUK: You've led us astray too often. I don't trust you.

SPIRIT OF THE WIND: Suit yourself. But I don't see how else you're going to get to the sun unless you follow me.

INUK: I can't leave my father alone here.

SPIRIT OF THE WIND: You'll have to—sooner or later. You want to become a man, don't you?

INUK: Yes, but—

SPIRIT OF THE WIND: All you have to do is follow me, follow the wind. When the moon rises, everything will be arranged. Now, lie down and sleep. It'll be a long journey to the sun.

INUK: (Lies down.) I wish you'd lie down too, Spirit of the Wind, so that we can find some game. My father and I are hungry. Our dogs are hungry, too.

SPIRIT OF THE WIND: Leave it to me, Inuk, leave it to the wind. (Disappears in a swoop that brings back the Wind's howl full force.)

(INUK and his FATHER are sleeping.)

EPISODE FOUR

(When the SPIRIT OF THE DREAM appears, the wind falls silent. The story she tells is accompanied by an appropriate play of shadow puppets.)

SPIRIT OF THE DREAM: Sleep, Inuk, sleep. You'll need all your strength when you wake. I'm the Spirit of the Dream and I can see into the future. You're still a boy, but you'll be a man soon. In between lies a dangerous journey. There! That's the giant Sea Monster. He is blind and ferocious. All the fish, even the whale and the shark, are afraid of him. He's so powerful that once upon a time he climbed out of the sea to break a large piece out of the sky. He wanted to have it for a ceiling in his underwater cave. But the sun blinded him, and he fell back into the sea. Now, in revenge, he snatches the beautiful sun from the sky every year. The wild geese always try to stop him, but he makes an arrow of them and shoots them way . . . way into the air until they disappear in the clouds. He wants to keep the sun imprisoned in his cave until she gives him back his sight—but you'll soon find out what happens. (INUK's shadow appears in the shadow play.) Beware, Inuk! The giant Sea Monster knows no mercy. He cannot see you, but he feels and senses you with his tentacles from the slightest movement in the water. Watch out, Inuk! If he catches you, he'll tear you apart and the sharks will have a feast.

(In the shadow play INUK confronts the SEA MONSTER. Sharks are closing in. INUK throws his harpoon, but the SEA MONSTER snaps it like a twig, and his silent, sinister laughter changes into the wild barking of the dogs. The SPIRIT OF THE DREAM vanishes.)

EPISODE FIVE

(INUK wakes up to find himself face to face with a POLAR BEAR beset by the dogs who have surrounded and are attacking him.)

INUK: Father! A polar bear!

(In a flash Inuk's FATHER *is up and ready, harpoon in hand, to meet the* BEAR *who has begun to kill the dogs one by one.)*

FATHER: Stay behind me, Inuk! *(To the* BEAR.*)* Come on, pride of beasts—it's your life or mine. *(The* BEAR *turns on the* FATHER *who keeps him at bay with his harpoon.* INUK *circles and attacks him from behind. He is about to throw his harpoon—)* Don't throw it! You lose it and you're lost. . . . It takes more than a harpoon to kill a bear. . . . Use your snow knife! *(In the ensuing life-and-death struggle, the* BEAR *kills* INUK'S FATHER *but is himself killed by* INUK.*) (Dying.)* I'm proud of you, Inuk. You've killed your first bear. You're a man now.

INUK: O good Spirits, don't let my father die.

FATHER: Don't grieve, Inuk . . . *Ayorama* . . . All is decreed.

INUK: Listen, Father! You'll be alright!

FATHER: I'm not sorry to leave this world of struggling. . . . I'm tired.

INUK: I'll build you an igloo and go back to the village to get help.

FATHER: In the Land of the Dead I'll find peace. . . . Perhaps the sun shines there forever.

INUK: You'll be alright! You hear me?

FATHER: The Spirits . . . give warmth . . . and peace. *(Dies.)*

INUK: Father! Father—come back!!! *(Shakes him, then breaks down crying.)*

(The SPIRIT OF THE MOON *appears and harshly lights the scene.)*

SPIRIT OF THE MOON: *(Laughing.)* Your father is dead. (INUK *cries.)* Yes, weep, Inuk. A man must know to weep. And you're a man now—albeit a little man. Tears are the price of living. There's much weeping in the mutable world. Every snowflake is a frozen tear.

(The SPIRIT OF THE WIND *swoops down from the sky.)*

SPIRIT OF THE WIND: *(Angrily.)* Don't listen to him, Inuk. Look, he's laughing while he tells you to weep! That's how he deceives the living. He hates them because he's dead. But you're alive. Your sorrow will pass. Life is full of joy.

SPIRIT OF THE MOON: Listen to him talk, Inuk! His heart is full of air. You, Wind, envy me because you're condemned to be forever on the move and I'm at peace. You roam the world without rest. Joy, Inuk, passes quickly . . . like your father, like you!

SPIRIT OF THE WIND: Don't delude yourself, Moon! You're forever on the move, too, except that you're locked into the monotony of your prescribed circles. I pity you. And you, you're jealous of my freedom to come and go as I please. Life means change, Inuk, and change brings joy.

SPIRIT OF THE MOON: Some joy—your father's death! Weep for him, Inuk. And weep for yourself. Because he's at peace now.

SPIRIT OF THE WIND: Bury your father, Inuk, and move on. There's laughter over the horizon.

INUK: *(Screams.)* Shut up! *(Then, frightened by his audacity, softer.)* Must you quarrel at my father's grave?!

SPIRIT OF THE WIND: Your father's spirit lives on. It lives on in the Land of the Dead and in your children.

SPIRIT OF THE MOON: That's something we can agree on. The spirit lives on forever.

INUK: Yes, that's right, isn't it. What I bury is only his body. But where has his spirit gone? Where is the Land of the Dead? I want to go there and speak with him. Will you help me go there, Great Spirits? Please.

SPIRIT OF THE WIND: To get there you must travel beyond the edge of the world.

SPIRIT OF THE MOON: Ha! And when you get there you're done for! *(To the* SPIRIT OF THE WIND.*)* Besides, how do you propose that he travel? His dog-team is dead. Will you blow his sled across the ice?

INUK: I can pull my own sled. I'm young and the bear has given me his flesh to eat. I have his strength now.

SPIRIT OF THE MOON: Don't be a fool, Inuk. The Land of the Dead is a long way away for you.

INUK: I don't care. I'll go over the edge of the world. My father said the sun was there too. Will you show me the way?

SPIRIT OF THE MOON: I can't. I won't.

SPIRIT OF THE WIND: I know where you can find the sun. I'll show you the way there.

(The following song is accompanied by a wind instrument.)

> *Follow the wind, follow me.*
> *Though heaven is my place of birth*
> *I know every corner of the earth*
> *from the mountains across the tundra to the sea.*
>
> *I blow from the east*
> *I blow from the west*
> *I breathe and whisper*
> *and howl without rest.*
>
> *I blow from the west*
> *I blow from the east*
> *I can comfort or kill*
> *both man and beast.*
>
> *I blow from the north*
> *I blow from the south*
> *I blow the very words*
> *right out of your mouth.*
>
> *I blow from the south*
> *I blow from the north*
> *and if I don't have my way*
> *I have my will by force.*
>
> *Follow the wind, follow me.*
> *Though heaven is my place on earth,*
> *I know every corner of the earth*
> *from the mountains across the tundra to the sea.*

SPIRIT OF THE MOON: Empty boasts! Empty promises! You listen to the wind and you're lost.

INUK: *(To the* SPIRIT OF THE WIND.*)* Will I find the spirit of my father where you take me? And the sun?

SPIRIT OF THE WIND: You ask too many questions. Just follow me. Follow the wind!

SPIRIT OF THE MOON: You're a fool to trust the wind, Inuk. He's gentle as a summer breeze now to hide that he's a killer at heart.

INUK: I'm a man now. I trust my own strength.

SPIRIT OF THE MOON: I'll light up the whole length of my long night to watch the wind lead you astray. *(Laughs uproariously.)*

(The MOON's *laughter is taken up by the* RAVEN *who returns with his sinister cackle and circles* INUK, *who begins to pile stones over his* FATHER's *body. The* SPIRIT OF THE MOON *and then the* SPIRIT OF THE WIND *withdraw.)*

SPIRIT OF THE WIND: Follow me! I'm the breath of the spirits. Follow the wind! *(Exits.)*

RAVEN:

> White is black and black is white—
> Arctic winter, arctic night.
> Man kills beast and beast kills man—
> thus it was since time began.
> Snow wind, ice wind, wolves at bay—
> man and beast are winter's prey.

EPISODE SIX

(Three days later. INUK *is stumbling across the icy wasteland. His feet are sore and he is approaching exhaustion.)*

INUK: How much farther is it to the Land of the Sun? *(Silence.)* Can you hear me, Great Spirit of the Wind? *(Silence.)* I've walked three days now. The knife-edged ice has cut my boots, and my feet are cold and sore. I've eaten the last of the bear meat. And the end of the world is as far away as ever. *(Silence.)* What shall I do, Great Spirit of the Wind? *(Silence.)* Why don't you answer me? I followed you. Now what? *(Silence.)*

> I'm a shadow
> in a land of shadows.
> The wind plays with me,
> the moon plays with me.
> I'm fair game for the dark.
> Help me, spirits in the sea and in the sky!
> I didn't come this far to die.

(The MOON *breaks into prolonged, uproarious laughter.)*

SPIRIT OF THE MOON: You see, Inuk, the Wind has abandoned you. I warned you. You wouldn't listen. You should've gone home to your igloo.

INUK: I couldn't return to the village, to my mother, empty-handed. And my father dead.

SPIRIT OF THE MOON: You're lost now, aren't you? You don't know where to go. *(Laughs.)*

INUK: I know the direction. There—where the light is the color of blood! *(Points to the horizon where a faint glow of sunlight stains the darkness.)*

SPIRIT OF THE MOON: Well, you don't need my help then. Why don't you go on?

INUK: My feet are sore. I have little strength left. And it seems still so far to go.

SPIRIT OF THE MOON: You foolish boy—to run after my dazzling sister! Don't you know it's I who rule the Land of the Long Night?!

(With a menacing air:)

> *Ice-light brittle*
> *shadows crunch*
> *moonbeam skittle*
> *back and hunch.*
>
> *Skull-faced silence*
> *crack-crazed loon*
> *snow-crust islands*
> *knife the moon.*
>
> *Black blood river*
> *sickle-starred*
> *glaciers shiver*
> *bonebite-scarred.*
>
> *Ice-clot spittle*
> *frost harpoon*
> *snow-night brittle:*
> *Hail the moon!*

INUK: I'm not afraid of you. You're just jealous of the sun, because she's more beautiful than you.

SPIRIT OF THE MOON: Oh, you find her beautiful, do you? *(Laughs.)* Don't you know that her fire is fatal. Her light blinds you. Her scarlet rays are nothing but a net of fire in which to trap you and burn you up.

INUK: All I know is that without her we have no food. Her fire is the fire of life. When she comes the ice runs away, the animals return, and the rocks burst into flowers.

SPIRIT OF THE MOON: Time will tell, my boy. I have no more to say. Speak to the musk-oxen. Perhaps they'll help you. But remember to hail me, hail the Moon!

(While the MOON *withdraws laughing, a group of* MUSK-OXEN *appears.)*

MUSK-OXEN: *(Pick up the* MOON's *last line.)*

> *Hail the moon!*
> *Bone-face spirit*
> *ice-crack horn*
> *silver hoof-print*
> *shadow born.*
>
> *Flaming snow torch*
> *night beast eye*
> *shag-fur frost-scorch—*
> *praise the sky!*

(During this speech a group, of MUSK-OXEN *enter to the rhythm of a dark, slow drum.* INUK *waits till their dance is finished before he approaches them. The bull comes forward menacingly.)*

INUK: Peace, mighty Musk-ox! I'm hungry, but I don't want to kill you.

MUSK-OX: Kill me? You . . . little man . . . kill me? (*Laughs; the other* MUSK-OXEN *join in.*)

INUK: Don't laugh! I've killed my first polar bear. I'm a big hunter now.

MUSK-OX: (*Amused.*) My respects, my respects. . . . But you're still little to me. We can run you into the ground quicker than a blizzard.

INUK: I don't want to fight you. I need help.

MUSK-OX: Lay down your harpoon then. (INUK *does so.*) Now we can talk in peace.

INUK: I'm hungry. I need food.

MUSK-OX: What d'you want us to do about it? Food is scarce for us, too. We have to scratch through ice and snow for scraps of grass. Not much of a meal.

INUK: I'm hunting the sun. The wind promised to show me the way, but he has abandoned me. I've traveled for three days and I'm lost. Help me find the sun, please. It'll make your life brighter, too.

MUSK-OX: Why should I? What d'you want of the sun anyway?

INUK: I need to bring her back to the Land of the Inuit. My people are hungry.

MUSK-OX: She's going to return in her own good time.

INUK: Winter is long and cruel to us. Often we Inuit suffer from the cold, the bitter cold. Our bodies don't grow the shaggy furs that keep you warm.

MUSK-OX: I know. You hunt and kill us for our skin.

INUK: The moon says that's the law of the North.

MUSK-OX: He can talk.

INUK: He says we all have to live by the law of the North—my people, your herds, all living creatures. But I prefer to live under the rule of the sun. Under the sun the land is bright and happy, and there's plenty of food for us all. And everybody is nice and warm.

MUSK-OX: Well, for us Musk-oxen, it does get a little too warm under our thick fur in the summer. But you're right, it is a happier time all 'round.

INUK: That's why I want to find the sun and bring her back here.

MUSK-OX: She'll come back. You'll just have to wait.

INUK: If we must wait any longer, we'll all be dead.

MUSK-OX: She always comes back. Every year.

INUK: There's no game, and my people are starving.

MUSK-OX: Everything has its season.

INUK: Winter is long and cruel.

MUSK-OX: The seasons measure our patience as well as our courage.

INUK: Besides, I'm looking for the spirit of my father. A polar bear killed him, and I want to find his spirit to know when and where he returns to the world.

MUSK-OX: I understand, but I cannot help. We don't know exactly where the Land of the Sun lies. We see her roll along the horizon till she falls over the rim of darkness and disappears. Our ancestors tell us that's where the Land of the Dead is, but how to get there. . . . (*Shakes his head slowly.*) Sorry. Why don't you ask the Arctic Fox over there? He has relatives in the Land of the

Sun. He should know. But beware! He's sly. He doesn't like to give away his secrets.

(An ARCTIC FOX *is discovered sleeping curled up in the snow.* INUK *bows to the* MUSK-OXEN *who depart gravely.* INUK *picks up his harpoon and jumps the* ARCTIC FOX, *holding the harpoon to his throat.)*

INUK: Don't move and I won't hurt you!! . . . Listen! I'm in search of the sun. You must show me the quickest way there—or else!

ARCTIC FOX: *(Sly.)* Or else what?

INUK: Else I'll kill you!!!

ARCTIC FOX: What good would that do you?

INUK: That's true, but I can't afford to argue. You tell me where I can find the sun. I count to three!

ARCTIC FOX: But I don't know the way there.

INUK: You're lying. You have relatives in the Land of the Sun.

ARCTIC FOX: Well . . . sort of.

INUK: Alright. Then you must know how to get there. ONE!

ARCTIC FOX: But I don't know—honest!

INUK: There's no such thing as an honest fox. TWO!!

ARCTIC FOX: I've never been there. I've only heard talk about it.

INUK: This is your last chance, liar. THREE!!!

ARCTIC FOX: Wait! I know who can show you the way—the whistling swan! He flies there every year. He knows. Look! There's one up there. *(He points over* INUK's *head into the sky behind him. As* INUK *turns to look, the* ARCTIC FOX *slips away.)* Happy hunting, Inuk—in the Land of the Dead! *(Exits.)*

(The SPIRIT OF THE MOON *reappears, convulsed with laughter.)*

SPIRIT OF THE MOON: Ha-ha-ha! He tricked you! A little Arctic Fox tricked big man Inuk! A whistling swan indeed! *(Laughs.)* Don't you know there's not a whistling swan left in all the arctic lands. They've all gone south with the sun before the long night took over.

INUK: It's easy for you to mock me, Moon. You're not hungry and tired as I am. . . . But I deserve your mockery. It's shameful for a hunter to be cheated by a fox.

SPIRIT OF THE MOON: You're not a hunter yet, my boy. You still have a lot to learn about the world. So . . . what are you going to do now? You're not only tired and hungry, you're also lost. Maybe you'll reach the Land of the Dead sooner than you think.

(The SPIRIT OF THE WIND *swoops down from the sky.)*

SPIRIT OF THE WIND: Don't listen to him! His light is the color of the cruel polar bear, and his heart is a chip of ice. Follow me, follow the wind!

INUK: Follow you where? Where've you been, Spirit of the Wind?

SPIRIT OF THE WIND: I'm busy raising huskies of snow and driving them southward across the tundra toward the sun.

INUK: And you leave me here helpless—without food or shelter. I called you and you didn't come.

SPIRIT OF THE MOON: That's the Wind for you—nothing but noise!

SPIRIT OF THE WIND: Listen who's talking! You've nothing to do but lie around in the black sky sunning yourself and scoffing at those of us who've got work to do.

INUK: Would you please stop quarreling, both of you. Spirit of the Wind, you promised to show me the way to the sun.

SPIRIT OF THE WIND: Right. And I've taken a short break to do just that. Now look over there! See the seal-hole in the ice?

INUK: Yes.

SPIRIT OF THE WIND: That's a breathing-hole for the seals.

INUK: I know that.

SPIRIT OF THE WIND: Of course you do. Now stand there with your harpoon at the ready. The moment a seal comes up, throw your harpoon. If you hit it, the seal will show you the way to the sun.

INUK: And if I miss?

SPIRIT OF THE WIND: Then you'll have to wait for it to come back. Or for another seal to come up.

SPIRIT OF THE MOON: If you're still alive by then.

SPIRIT OF THE WIND: There's no other way. Good luck! I must be off again. Don't lose heart, Inuk! The world belongs to the brave. And I'll protect you. I have a long and strong arm. *(Departs.)*

(INUK *stands over the seal-hole, poised with his harpoon, waiting for a seal to appear.)*

SPIRIT OF THE MOON: I have to admire your courage, Inuk. You, a little boy, defying me, the illustrious ruler of the night. I like that. Perhaps you'll grow up to be a man after all. But so long as you put your trust in the wind, you're asking for trouble.

(Just before the end of the SPIRIT OF THE MOON's *speech, a* SEAL *comes up for air.* INUK *hurls his harpoon and strikes it. The* SEAL *dives quickly and pulls the struggling* INUK *into the sea and under the ice.)*

SPIRIT OF THE MOON: For you, Inuk, the way to the fire leads through the water. But I remain behind—immutable and at peace.

EPISODE SEVEN

(The action continues from the previous episode, but it now takes place underwater as INUK *is dragged by the* SEAL *to an underwater cave where he is quickly surrounded by other* SEALS *who tie him up in his harpoon line and perform a ritual dance around him.)*

SEALS: *(Chorus)*

> We are the seals,
> the cheerful seals.
> We sleep on ice.
> and eat codfish and eels.
>
> All winter we live
> under the sea

under the ice—
flipper-de-lee.

We are the seals
with flippers and tail.
We're hunted by man
by shark and by whale.

We're nowhere safe,
so we live with fear,
but all the same
we're full of cheer.

We caught a little man
from the Land of the Moon
and pulled him down
by his own harpoon.

We are the seals,
the cheerful seals—
shall we try and see
if the little man squeals?

(SEDNA, *Goddess of the Sea, appears and the* SEALS *scatter. She is ugly and imperious.*)

SEDNA: What's going on here? (*To* INUK.) Who're you? What are you doing here?

INUK: I'm Inuk. I think I've drowned.

SEDNA: Have you ever heard a drowned man talk?

INUK: Well, no . . . but—

SEDNA: Don't talk nonsense then! . . . Well then, have you lost your tongue? What are you doing here?

INUK: I don't really know. . . . I mean I don't know where I am.

SEDNA: You're out to capture the sun. That's a serious matter.

INUK: (*Startled.*) How d'you know about that?

SEDNA: I ask the questions here, you answer them.

INUK: But who are you?

SEDNA: That's the first riddle you must solve.

INUK: I don't understand.

SEDNA: You don't seem to know or understand very much, do you.

INUK: What riddles are you talking about?

SEDNA: Listen. As a special favor to the Spirit of the Wind, and because he specifically asked me to, I'm prepared to help you find the sun—on three conditions! First, you must discover who I am.

INUK: You must be one of the sea witches.

SEDNA: Are you trying to insult me?!

(*The* SEALS *are giggling in the background.*)

INUK: No, but you're so ugly.

SEDNA: Think before you speak, Inuk! Or I shall feed you to the sharks.

INUK: No, please, don't do that. I'll try my best. I promise.

SEDNA: Alright then. Listen to the second riddle:

> *Wind or Moon—*
> *who is the groom,*
> *who is the bride*
> *crying in the tide?*

INUK: *(Repeats, dumbfounded.)*

> *Wind or Moon—*
> *who is the groom,*
> *who is the bride*
> *crying in the tide?*

That's too difficult. It doesn't make any sense. How d'you expect me to know the answer to something that doesn't make any sense.

SEDNA: The Sea Monster knows the answer.

INUK: The Sea Monster? I can't ask him. I don't even know where to find him.

SEDNA: He will find you. The Seals will take you to his cave.

INUK: But the Sea Monster is a terrible giant. I dreamt of him. He'll kill me.

SEDNA: A man is known by his trials, and I heard you boasted that you were a man, Inuk.

INUK: Anyway, he isn't going to tell me anything.

SEDNA: It's up to you to make him tell you the secret.

INUK: How am I to do that? He'll tear me to pieces before I can open my mouth. *(Outburst.)* Oh why didn't I listen to my father! It was foolish to go hunting for the sun.

SEDNA: Aahhh—you're learning.

INUK: Yes, the hard way.

SEDNA: Don't you want to know your third and final task?

INUK: Not if it's as difficult as the first two. I'd sooner go back to my village.

SEDNA: And never see your father again?

INUK: Well, no . . . I mean, yes, I want to find him. But make it something easy.

SEDNA: All it takes is a little courage. Two ferocious sharks guard the entrance to the Great Hall of the Iceberg. Your task is to get past them and enter the Great Hall.

INUK: *(Desperately.)*

> *O Good Spirits!*
> *You have forsaken me.*
> *I am a shadow amongst shadows*
> *at the bottom of the sea*
>
> *at the mercy of a monster*
> *at the mercy of the shark—*
> *Oh why is the world*
> *so cold and so dark?*

SEDNA: Take heart, Inuk. There's no darkness in the Iceberg. Once you're inside the Great Hall, everything will be bright and clear. Because you'll find the sun there.

INUK: Will the spirit of my father be there too?

SEDNA: I told you, I ask the questions here, you answer them. Now tell me: who am I?

INUK: Please, can I have a little time to think?

SEDNA: The length of three waves, no more.

(INUK *furtively exchanges signs and gestures with the* SEALS *until he realizes what they're telling him.*)

SEALS: (*Chorus*)

> We are the seals,
> the cheerful seals,
> we sleep on ice
> and eat codfish and eels.
>
> We're happy in winter,
> we're happy in summer.
> Are we sad? No!
> Because we serve
> the Goddess Sedna . . .
> The Goddess Sedna . . .
> Sedna, Goddess of the Sea.
> Happy—yes! Sad—no!
> Because we serve Sedna,
> Goddess of the Sea . . .

(*The* SEALS *carry on till* INUK *comprehends.*)

INUK: I'm ready.

SEDNA: Answer me then. Who am I?

INUK: (*Play-acting.*) You are . . . you are . . .

SEDNA: Yes, I am . . .

INUK: You're not a sea witch.

SEDNA: I'm not.

INUK: You are . . . you are . . .

SEDNA: Yes, yes—who?

INUK: You are . . . you are . . . not a sea fairy.

SEDNA: (*Increasingly impatient.*) I don't want to know who I'm not but who I am!

INUK: Then you are . . . you must be . . .

SEDNA: Yes, I must be . . .

INUK: Sedna, the Goddess of the Sea!

SEDNA: (*Furious.*) Earthquake and tidal wave!!! How did you guess? Someone must've betrayed me.

(*The* SEALS *are half giggly, half fearful, in the background.*)

INUK: Betrayed you? There's no one here to betray you. No. I'm Inuk, and Inuk knows how to use his head.

SEDNA: Alright then. I am Sedna, Goddess of the Sea. You have solved the first riddle. Now let's see if your head is a match for the Sea.

> *Monster! Remember:*
> *Wind or Moon—*
> *who is the groom,*
> *who is the bride*
> *crying in the tide?*

INUK:

> *Wind or Moon—*
> *who is the groom,*
> *who is the bride*
> *crying in the tide?*

How can I find the answer to such a strange and difficult puzzle?

SEDNA: *(To the* SEALS.*)* Take him to the Monster's cave! . . . *(To* INUK.*)* If you pass all your tests, we'll meet again. If not *(Gestures ominously.)* the more the pity.

INUK: Can't you give me a clue?

SEDNA: Farewell, Inuk. And good luck! *(Exits.)*

INUK: *(Calls after her.)* If the Monster doesn't kill me and the sharks don't eat me, we'll meet again. Farewell. *(The* SEALS *beckon.)* I'm coming, I'm coming. *(To himself.)* How I wish I were back on firm land. It's better to be hungry than to be eaten. *(Exits with Seals.)*

EPISODE EIGHT

*(*INUK *arrives in the cave of the* SEA MONSTER. *He is terrified by the huge octopus-like creature.)*

SEA MONSTER: *(Full of menace.)* I sense a presence . . . *(Probes the air with his tentacles, but* INUK *eludes him.)* . . . an alien presence. . . . I do not tolerate uninvited visitors in my cave.

> *(Incantation)*
> *I'm the Monster of the Sea.*
> *With my many tentacles*
> *I choke my enemy.*
> *I choke the whale*
> *and I choke the shark—*
> *I'm as mean as can be*
> *because I live in the dark*
> *and I cannot see.*
>
> *But I can sense and I can feel*
> *every movement in the water*
> *whether it's creature or ship's keel.*
> *Someone's entered my cave,*
> *someone too bold and too brave.*
> *It isn't seal or whale or shark*
> *because I know them in the dark,*
> *I know their song, their whistle and their bark.*

(The SEA MONSTER *has been trying to capture* INUK *with his tentacles, but so far* INUK *has eluded him. He is now exasperated.)*

Who or what thing are you? Are you a giant crab? . . . A sea urchin . . . Are you a stingray? . . . *(Each time he waits for an answer, but* INUK *is busy evading the* SEA MONSTER's *attempts to catch him.*) No, I can sense it. You're an alien creature plucked from the air. . . . I warn you! No one enters my cave uninvited and lives. . . . My tentacles will catch you. Beware! . . . There! I've got you!! . . . No, you got away again!

INUK: (*Trying to put a brave face on a losing situation.*) I'm Inuk, the mighty hunter!

SEA MONSTER: When I catch you, I'll suck the life out of you. (*Charges with increasing fury; in self-defense* INUK *strikes off one of the* SEA MONSTER's *tentacles.*) Ouch!!! You've cut off one of my tentacles. You must die!

INUK: You watch that you don't die! I've killed a polar bear with my harpoon.

SEA MONSTER: (*Laugh.*) Are you trying to frighten me? I have polar bear for breakfast.

> (incantation)
> I'm the Monster of the Sea.
> With my many tentacles
> I choke my enemy.
> I choke the whale,
> and I choke the shark.
> I'm as mean as can be
> because I live in the dark
> and I cannot see.

INUK: You've told me that before. But I'll cut off your tentacles one by one till you've none left.

SEA MONSTER: You insolent creature! For every tentacle you cut off I grow two new ones. (*The struggle between them intensifies.* INUK *cuts off another tentacle and the* SEA MONSTER *immediately sprouts two new ones to replace it. Eventually* INUK *is caught.*) Ha!—I've caught you!! . . . Now you must die.

INUK: (*In desperation, a shot in the dark.*)

> Wind or Moon—
> who's the groom,
> who's the bride
> crying in the tide?

SEA MONSTER: (*Startled.*) Who told you that?

INUK: Sedna.

SEA MONSTER: You know her name?!

INUK: The Goddess of the Sea.

SEA MONSTER: Did she send you?

INUK: Yes, she did.

SEA MONSTER: What does she want?

INUK: The answer, the answer to the riddle.

SEA MONSTER: (*Very agitated.*) Never . . . never! I hate the Goddess of the Sea. It's she who banished me to this black cave. Every year I snatch the sun from the sky, but Sedna takes her away from me and gives her to the Spirit of the Ice, her own son, who keeps her in the Great Hall of the Iceberg. . . . I hate Sedna . . . and since you're one of her band all the more reason for you to die.

INUK: Hold it! I'm not one of her band. I'm Inuk, an Inuit boy. I'm looking for the sun.

SEA MONSTER: You're looking for the sun?

INUK: Yes. To be quite honest, the Goddess of the Sea is ugly and mean. I don't like her any more than you do.

SEA MONSTER: You're just saying that to curry favor with me.

INUK: No, honest! She's set me three difficult and dangerous tasks before I get inside the Iceberg. That's where I hope to find the sun. And my father. A polar bear killed my father.

SEA MONSTER: I'm sorry to hear that. But what do you want of the sun?

INUK: I want to take her back to the Land of the Inuit.

SEA MONSTER: Where is this Land of the Inuit?

INUK: It's the land of my people up above the ice and by the edge of the sea. Our land is cold and barren without the sun.

SEA MONSTER: And you want to take the sun there?

INUK: Yes. Because when the sun comes to us, our land is full of color and life and beauty. . . . But I can't get to the sun without knowing the answer to the riddle:

> *Wind or Moon—*
> *who is the groom,*
> *who is the bride*
> *crying in the tide?*

SEA MONSTER: That's my secret.

INUK: I tell you what I'll do. You give me the answer to the riddle, and I promise you a special gift from the sun.

SEA MONSTER: What kind of gift?

INUK: Well, for instance, a chunk of sunlight to stick in your ceiling.

SEA MONSTER: *(Considering this.)* Ye-es.

INUK: Then you'll be able to see again. Because you're not really blind. It's because of the darkness in your cave that you can't see.

SEA MONSTER: And what guarantee do I have that you'll keep your promise once I let you go?

INUK: Cross my heart!

SEA MONSTER: I shall come and tear out your heart if you deceive me!

INUK: I won't deceive you, believe me.

SEA MONSTER:
> *I warn you. I'll know where to find you!*
> *I'm the Monster of the Sea.*
> *With my many tentacles*
> *I choke my enemy.*
> *I choke the whale*
> *and I choke the shark.*
> *I'm as mean as can be*
> *because I live in the dark*
> *and I cannot see.*

INUK: Don't worry, you won't be in the dark anymore. All you need is a chunk of sunlight. I'll keep my promise.

SEA MONSTER: Alright then. Here's the story. (*Whispers at length in* INUK's *ear and then lets him go.*)

INUK: What a sad story!

SEA MONSTER: Not really. But that's all I can tell you. That's all you need to know for now.

INUK: Thank you, you kind Monster. You'll have your sunlight yet . . . provided I survive the sharks that guard the entrance to the Iceberg! (*Departs.*)

SEA MONSTER: I shall tear him limb from limb if he has tricked me!

EPISODE NINE

(*Accompanied by the* SEALS, INUK *arrives outside the entrance to the Great Hall of the Iceberg which is guarded by two fierce sharks.*)

INUK: There is the entrance to the Iceberg. But how will I ever get in? How will I get past those fierce sharks? They'll tear me to pieces.

> Oh Good Spirits!
> I'm a shadow
> in a sea of shadows
> at the mercy of the sea
> at the mercy of the dark.
> Help me, please,
> conquer these shark.

SEALS: (*Chorus*)

> Listen to the seals,
> the cheerful seals.
> No need to conquer the shark.
> Just accept the light with the dark.

INUK: I don't know what you mean. I'm only a boy. I can't fight these ferocious sharks.

SEAL: Oho! You're only a boy, are you? I thought you were a man—(*Sarcastic in a good-natured way.*) Inuk, the mighty Inuit hunter!

INUK: Well, yes . . . but they're so much bigger than I . . .

SEAL: We'll see what we can do.

SEALS: (*Chorus*)

> Listen to the seals,
> the cheerful seals,
> with flippers and tail.
> We'll get you past the sharks
> disguised as a whale, a humpback whale.

INUK: Disguised as a whale, a humpback whale? . . . Yes, that's a good idea. They're big enough to scare even the sharks. But how can I disguise myself as a humpback whale? They're a hundred times bigger than me.

SEAL: Exactly. A silly idea! It can't be done. I have a much better idea. We'll trick them.

INUK: Trick them? But how? Sharks are no fools.

SEAL: Maybe not, but we'll outsmart them. You watch. *(Whispers to* INUK.)
INUK: This I've got to see. I just hope I won't end up a meal for them.

(The SEALS *now move close to the* SHARKS, *displaying themselves in order to lure them into pursuit and away from the entrance to the Iceberg. This gives* INUK *an opportunity to sneak around their backs.)*
SEALS: *(Chorus)*

> We are the seals,
> the cheerful seals,
> we sleep on ice
> and eat codfish and eels.
>
> We are the seals
> with flippers and tail,
> we're hunted by man.
> By shark and by whale.
>
> We're nowhere safe,
> so we live with fear
> but all the same
> we're full of cheer.

INUK: *(Just before he enters the Iceberg.)* Thank you, good Seals, thank you. I'll always be your friend. *(Exits.)*

(Too late the SHARKS *realize they've been tricked. As they swim furiously back and forth in front of the entrance to the Iceberg, the* SEALS *depart, laughing at them.)*
SEALS: *(Chorus)*

> You were tricked by a boy,
> you silly shark—
> your teeth are bright
> but your brains are dark.
>
> You were tricked by a boy
> and by the cheerful seals
> who sleep on ice
> and eat codfish and eels. (exit)

EPISODE TEN

(A startling, dazzling change of light! We're in the Great Hall of the Iceberg. Everything glistens and sparkles in white, silver and soft turquoise. The SPIRIT OF THE ICE *sits in a frozen position on a block of ice which glitters golden because the* SUN *is evidently locked in it; what movements he makes must be slow and stiff. Inuk's* FATHER *lies frozen inside another block of ice.* INUK *enters and stares in awe and amazement at the radiant magnificence of the Great Hall.)*

INUK: Where am I? . . . The light is so bright I can't see! Like summer snow. . . . And yet it's so cold! . . . As if I'd fallen into the Moon. . . . How did I get here? . . . I've never seen anything so sparkling, so glittering, so beautiful. . . . Now I remember—the Seals! This must be the Great Hall of the Iceberg. . . . Oh, Good Spirits, don't let me freeze to death here!

> Spirits of the Sea and of the Sky!
> You've pulled me down
> over the edge of the world

> *without telling me why.*
> *I'm a shadow now*
> *in this crystal hall of light:*
> *don't let me die!*

(He discovers his FATHER *in a block of ice.)*

There's my father! ... *(Runs over to him.)* ... Father, Father! I've found you ... *(The* FATHER *is rigid in the ice.)* It's me, Inuk! Wake up! ... *(Hammers with his fist on the ice-block.)* Can you hear me? Wake up, Father! ... Come on!! Shake off the ice!!! It's me, Inuk, your son! *(The* FATHER *doesn't move.* INUK *looks about distraught and discovers the Sun in another ice-block. He rushes over to it and shakes it wildly.)* This must be the sun. Get up, Sun! Rise! I've been looking for you all over the Land of the North.... *(The Sun doesn't stir; to himself.)* If I chipped off a piece, just a little piece—off the sun, I mean, I could use it to melt the ice that holds my father and free him.

> *O Spirits Good and Bad!*
> *I know now that in your hands*
> *I'm nothing but a toy,*
> *you play your games with me*
> *and give me time to enjoy*
> *the warmth and radiance of the sun*
> *until you've had your fun and tire,*
> *then you throw me like a harpoon*
> *back into the winter world of the moon.*

(He raises his harpoon and prepares to throw it at the frozen Sun.)

> *But when you play with me*
> *you play with fire.*
> *I defy you, Spirits!*
> *While I have life*
> *I must have the sun!*

SPIRIT OF THE ICE: *(Sharp, loud—like ice cracking.)* You're undone!!! *(Startled,* INUK *looks about and only now discovers the* SPIRIT OF THE ICE.*)* You dare raise your harpoon against me, the Spirit of the Ice, in my own Great Hall?! *(*INUK *is frightened and lowers his harpoon.)* What impudent creature are you?!!

INUK: I am—

SPIRIT OF THE ICE: *(Thundering.)* Silence!!! Do you think I don't know who you are??

INUK: *(Timidly.)* You asked.

SPIRIT OF THE ICE: You're human. You belong to a race of creatures that thinks the world was made for them alone! That's why you must die. I shall turn you into a block of ice!

INUK: No, no, Great Spirit of the Ice. You've got it all wrong. I'm Inuk. I belong to the people of the North. We think of all creatures as our brothers and sisters. Nanuk the bear, the wolf, the fox, the whale, the wild geese— they all are our brothers and sisters.

SPIRIT OF THE ICE: Then why do you raise your harpoon against me? I too have my place in the order of things.

INUK: I didn't raise my harpoon against you, Great Spirit of the Ice. I was aiming at the sun.

SPIRIT OF THE ICE: You were aiming at the sun? You were going to throw a harpoon at the sun?? That, little human, is even worse than aiming your weapon against me!

(Unnoticed by either INUK *or the* SPIRIT OF THE ICE, *the* SPIRIT OF THE SUN *enters and listens to their exchange.)*

INUK: I've traveled the whole length of the winter earth to find the sun. My people are starving. The caribou herds have long gone and the sea is frozen. Our land is dark and cold, and we have nothing to eat. We need the sun to survive.

SPIRIT OF THE ICE: You need the sun to survive and yet you raise your harpoon against her. You're mad.

INUK: I meant no harm. I just wanted to take a chip of the sun to melt the ice and free my father.

SPIRIT OF THE ICE: *(In disbelief.)* You wanted to take a chip out of the sun??

INUK: Or maybe capture her and take her back to the Land of the Inuit.

SPIRIT OF THE ICE: Capture the sun?? The supreme ruler of everything—capture her and take her away??? These are grave offences punishable by death.

INUK: But I wanted to capture her because I love and admire her—her warmth, her radiance, her—

SPIRIT OF THE ICE: *(Interrupts him.)* Flattery will get you nowhere! You've forfeited your life. Prepare to die!

SPIRIT OF THE SUN: *(Steps forward and tells the* SPIRIT OF THE ICE.*)* I pardon him. *(Turns to* INUK.*)* I am the Spirit of the Sun. And I like your spirit, Inuk. I like the fire in your eyes.

INUK:

> *It's your fire*
> *that burns in my eyes,*
> *as it's your light*
> *that flushes our skies.*
>
> *O Great Spirit of the Sun,*
> *I didn't know*
> *you were so beautiful*
> *—and still so young.*
> *Now I understand*
> *why the animals follow you*
> *and joy colors the land*
> *wherever you go.*
>
> *Come back with me,*
> *drive the long night away,*
> *break the ice-crust off the sea*
> *and wake the lavish day!*
> *Scatter your flowers,*
> *bring back the beasts*
> *so that in your honor*

we may tell our stories
and sing and dance and feast.

SPIRIT OF THE ICE: Enough wheedling and fawning!! How dare you, you impudent little boy—how dare you try to flatter the Sun with empty words!

INUK: They're not empty words.

SPIRIT OF THE SUN: And he's not a little boy—not any longer. Only a man would have the courage and the knowledge to enter here.

SPIRIT OF THE ICE: *(Put in his place.)* That's true, that's quite true. I have two ferocious sharks guarding the entrance. . . . *(To INUK.)* How did you manage to get past them?

INUK: Sedna, the Goddess of the Sea, sent me here.

SPIRIT OF THE SUN & SPIRIT OF THE ICE: *(In chorus.)* Sedna?!

INUK: Yes, Sedna. She showed me the way.

SEDNA: *(Bursting in.)* On three conditions! Two you've fulfilled. You discovered my identity, and you've got past the sharks. The third condition shall determine whether you'll be turned to ice or returned to earth.

SPIRIT OF THE ICE: *(Aside.)* Good! There's a chance yet that I may keep him.

SEDNA:

Wind or Moon—
who is the groom,
who is the bride
crying in the tide?

SPIRIT OF THE ICE: Ha, Inuk. Now unriddle us that riddle!

INUK: That's very difficult.

SPIRIT OF THE ICE: You bet it is.

SPIRIT OF THE SUN: Sedna, you're asking too much of him.

SEDNA: He must solve the riddle or he is lost.

INUK: Well then, I say the Moon is the groom.

SEDNA: And who is the bride?

INUK: I wonder if it is . . . *(Hesitates playfully.)*

SEDNA: Yes, you wonder if it is . . .

INUK: *(Quickly.)* You, Goddess of the Sea! You're the Moon's bride.

SEDNA: *(Taken aback.)* And why am I crying in the tide?

INUK: Because you're betrothed to the Moon. But month after month the Moon puts off the wedding. You cry in the tide because you fear you'll never be married to him. You cradle the Moon on your waves but he can never be yours. *(To the accompaniment of bone rattles, SEDNA quickly changes from an ugly hag to a beautiful young woman. The SPIRIT OF THE ICE puts his hands over his eyes as though he were blinded. INUK watches SEDNA's transformation in amazement.)* I don't believe my eyes. . . . How you've changed!

SEDNA: It's you who has changed, Inuk.

INUK: Just a moment ago you looked like an old hag—

SPIRIT OF THE ICE: Watch your language!

INUK: I mean you looked . . . not so good—now you're a beautiful woman. How can you change like that?

SEDNA: It's you who has changed, not I. Understanding has changed you, and courage. The better you understand and the braver you are, the more beautiful I and all things shall be.

INUK: I'm afraid I don't understand that.

SEDNA: Some day you will—if you think enough about it. . . . Now go! You may return to your people. And leave the Moon's courtship to me.

SPIRIT OF THE SUN: And I'll go with you as your bride—if you want me.

INUK: Want you? Want you?? I love you, I admire you, Sun. Just imagine— Inuk, the mighty Inuit hunter, married to the Sun!

SPIRIT OF THE SUN: No, not Inuk, the mighty hunter—I go with Inuk, the understanding and loving human.

SEDNA: And let me warn you. The Sun is betrothed to the Spirit of the Ice in the same way that I, Goddess of the Sea, am betrothed to her brother, the Moon. She'll never be wholly yours.

INUK: But why not?

SEDNA: Every year she must return for a time here to the Great Hall of the Iceberg.

INUK: But why?

SEDNA: That's the law. And all things must live by the law, even the Sun.

INUK: It's a cruel law that separates what belongs together.

SEDNA: Some day you'll understand.

SPIRIT OF THE SUN: All things have their season—remember, Inuk?

INUK: All things have their season. . . . Yes, I remember now. . . . A long time ago. When we started out on our hunt. My father said that. *(Remembers his FATHER.)* My father! What about my father? Can he come with me?

SPIRIT OF THE ICE: *(Categorical.)* No, he stays! He's locked forever in the eternal ice.

FATHER: *(From within the ice-block.)* I'm proud of you, Inuk. You've become a mighty hunter and a man.

INUK: You must come back with me to our people, Father.

FATHER: No, Inuk. My season is done. Leave me to the peace I've found.

INUK: But we need you, Father. I need you, Mother needs you.

FATHER: The living need each other in their struggles. You look after your mother now as she has looked after you before.

INUK: I can't return to the village without you, Father.

FATHER: It's decreed that my struggles are over.

SPIRIT OF THE SUN: He cannot return, but his spirit will be reborn in our first son so that in time he can become the father of your grandchildren when you've gone to rest.

SEDNA: No earthly shape or creature can last forever.

SPIRIT OF THE SUN: But everything returns forever and ever in a different shape.

SEDNA: Everything must forever change and go on changing, Inuk. That's the law.

SPIRIT OF THE ICE: Even I must melt and return in new forms. That's the law.

INUK: Yes, but can't he live just a little longer, please.

FATHER: My time is up, Inuk. *Ayorama.*

INUK: No, no, no!!! You can't leave me alone!!!

FATHER: Don't grieve, Inuk. You're a man now. My spirit will return to your children. That is the law. . . . Farewell, Inuk, and take my greetings to our people. *(Dies.)*

INUK: Farewell, Father.

SEDNA: You may go now, Inuk. And take the Sun with you.

INUK: I almost forgot. I made a promise—

SPIRIT OF THE SUN: —to the Sea Monster. I know. You shall keep your promise. When we rise above the sea, I'll throw a handful of sun-rays into his cave to light it up as bright as a summer morning, but whether it'll cure his blindness . . . *(Shrugs her shoulders.)*

INUK: He'll feel the light if he can't see it.

SPIRIT OF THE SUN: Yes. He'll know the season has come round again.

INUK:

> O beautiful Spirit of the Sun,
> your fire makes me stronger
> than whale, musk-ox and polar bear,
> your light makes me happier
> than seal or arctic hare.
> I'm a shadow in a land of shadows no more.
> I'm Inuk, a man now in his stride,
> I bring to my people the Sun as my bride.

SPIRIT OF THE ICE: For one short season only!

SEDNA: For a long season!

SPIRIT OF THE SUN: And every year!

(Music. Drums. The SPIRIT OF THE SUN *and* SEDNA *slowly dance in a circle with* INUK. *The* SPIRIT OF THE ICE *stealthily gets hold of* INUK's *harpoon and suddenly hurls it at him. The harpoon misses* INUK *and instead strikes the Sun still imprisoned in a block of ice. There is a flash and a thunder clap, and slowly the Sun rises in a blaze of light. Quick scene change without break.)*

EPILOGUE

(Same set as in Prologue; but now the moon is setting and the sun is rising. The wind is softer, and the howling of the wolves more distant. The RAVEN *flies in and circles the scene.)*

RAVEN:

> Summer comes, winter must fly,
> the sun is climbing into the sky.
> Snow wind, ice wind, pass away,
> night must now make way for day.
>
> Gull and goose come back with the sun,
> char and salmon start their run.

Herds of caribou return
along with arctic shrew and tern.

Summer comes and winter goes,
winter comes and summer goes,
man kills beast and beast kills man—
thus it was since time began.

(The RAVEN *completes his song when the sun has flushed the scene with her burning light and flies off with a sinister cackle. Cut lights quickly.)*

CURTAIN

A VILLAGE FABLE

by
James Still

a play adaptation of *In the Suicide Mountains* by
John Gardner

music by
Michael Keck

A VILLAGE FABLE

The 60-minute version
For an ensemble cast (minimum 7 if doubled)

CHARACTERS

Chudu
Prince Christopher
Armida
The King
A Child
Armida's Mother
Armida's Father
Armida's Stepmother
Clarella
The Six-Fingered Man
Suitors, Advisors, Villagers, Storytellers

(An empty space. From the darkness we hear several voices, and people appear.)

VOICES: *(Sing.)*

> This is a song about some stories that you've never been told
> Stories kept secret from the young by the old
> There's a Village in a Valley next to mountains in the sky
> A Village in a Valley Where a River Ran Dry.

(They assume the roles of people and animals of the village, singing.)

ALL:

> The children always listen
> The dogs always howl

MEN:

> The women always gossip

WOMEN:

> And the men always growl

ALL:

> The sun comes out
> The world goes 'round
> A nail sticking up will be hit. Back. Down.

VILLAGER: Always stir the batter in the same direction!

ANOTHER VILLAGER: Combing your hair after dark makes you lose your memory!

AND ANOTHER VILLAGER: Rats will leave you alone . . . if you write them a letter—

CHILD VILLAGER: And seal it with butter.

VILLAGERS: *(Sing.)*

> Don't pull a kitten's tail on Thursday
> Never give a chicken away on a Monday
> Only change a horse's name on Friday
> It's bad luck to kill a deer on Sunday
>
> Walk on the right, all the houses are white
> Counting the stars will bring trouble from Mars
> Wear black socks! Just blend in!
> Lock all doors! So . . . when:
>
> The sun comes out
> The world goes 'round
> A nail sticking up will be hit. Back. Down.

(The village marketplace. People sell food, goods. The atmosphere is lively, energetic, social, specific.)

VILLAGER #1: Get your pine cones!

VILLAGER #2: Snake skins!

VILLAGER #3: Dandelions here!

VILLAGER #4: Bird nests!

VILLAGE STORYTELLER: In the Village in the Valley Where the River Ran Dry— there was one thing people wished for more than jewels—

ANOTHER VILLAGE STORYTELLER: One thing they wished for more than kisses—

AND ANOTHER VILLAGE STORYTELLER: Even more than gold!

CHILD: Mama! I'm thirsty!

VILLAGE STORYTELLER: They wished—for water.

ANOTHER VILLAGE STORYTELLER: But the river had long ago run dry, and the hearts of the people grew as thirsty and brittle as the grass that had dried up all around the village.

AND ANOTHER VILLAGE STORYTELLER: High in the mountains in the sky— there lived a monster—

CHILD: *(Correcting him.)* A terrible monster.

AND ANOTHER VILLAGE STORYTELLER: A terrible monster who had made the river run dry.

ANOTHER VILLAGE STORYTELLER: No one had ever seen him—

CHILD: *(Correcting him.)* No one had ever seen him AND lived to *tell* about it.

ANOTHER VILLAGE STORYTELLER: But everyone had heard of—the Six-Fingered Man.

CHILD: *(Correcting him.)* The notorious Six-Fingered Man.

AND ANOTHER VILLAGE STORYTELLER: But since it was impossible to defeat the notorious Six-Fingered Man, they did their best to forget him. And looked for other monsters to blame for all their troubles.

(In the village marketplace:)

VILLAGER #1: Get your pine cones!

VILLAGER #2: Snake skins!

VILLAGER #3: Dandelions here!

VILLAGER #4: Bird nests!

A VILLAGE STORYTELLER: In the Village in the Valley Where the River Ran Dry—there lived an UGLY humpbacked dwarf—who went by the name— "Chudu" . . .

(The sound of whistling. Someone approaching. Everyone in the market stops, listening to the whistling.)

VILLAGER #1: Is it—?

VILLAGER #2: Could it—?

VILLAGER #3: Would it—?

ALL VILLAGERS: SHHHHHH!

(The VILLAGERS freeze, listen. The whistling gets closer. Everyone in the market is tense, cautious.)

VILLAGER #1: *(Whispering.)* It's him!

VILLAGER #2: *(Panicking.)* Oh dear!

VILLAGER #3: *(Fainting.)* Oh, God!

ALL VILLAGERS: He's near!!!

(Everyone in the market tries to resume his or her normal activities.)

VILLAGER #1: Pine cones! *(Gossiping with other VILLAGERS.)* Chudu can turn a child into a wish!

VILLAGER #2: Snake skins! *(Hissing.)* His mother was a goat . . . his father a fish!

(The other VILLAGERS *whisper "*CHUDU, CHUDU, CHUDU*" rhythmically in agreement.)*

VILLAGER #3: Dandelions! *(Nodding.)* Chudu has weeds growing out of his chin!

VILLAGER #4: Bird nests! *(Warning.)* Chudu can shake you right out of your skin!

(A funny-looking man—bearded, hunchbacked, half-man and half-goat—enters the marketplace. He whistles and is full of hope.)

CHUDU: *(To anyone who will listen.)* What a beautiful day! *(The* VILLAGERS *turn away.)* A beautiful day for a walk! (CHILDREN *hide in their mothers' skirts.)* Hello!

VILLAGER #1: *(Startled by* CHUDU.*)* Chudu makes your heart flop!

CHUDU: *(Tries to make contact with another* VILLAGER *who moves away.)* Hello!

VILLAGER #2: *(Turning away.)* Chudu makes your ears pop!

CHUDU: Hello . . .

VILLAGER #3: *(Looking away.)* Chudu makes your temperature drop!

CHUDU: *(Trying to get someone to look at him.)* Hello?

CHILD: Did Chudu make the river stop?

CHUDU: No, I—

(The CHILD's MOTHER *grabs the* CHILD *and pulls her away. The* MOTHER *begins the chant and the other* VILLAGERS *join in tensely, to one another, out of the sides of their mouths.)*

MOTHER VILLAGER:
> *Don't touch Chudu*
> *Never look him in the eye!*

ANOTHER VILLAGER:
> *He's a dwarf!*

AND ANOTHER VILLAGER:
> *He's a freak!*

TWO VILLAGERS:
> *If you touch him, you will die!*

THREE VILLAGERS:
> *Don't touch Chudu*
> *Never look him in the eye!*

ANOTHER VILLAGER:
> *He's a goat!*

AND ANOTHER VILLAGER:
> *He's a fish!*

ALL VILLAGERS:
> *If you touch him, you will die!*

(One by one, the VILLAGERS *pull their hats down over their eyes to avoid meeting* CHUDU's *gaze. They chant with bodies turned away, hats over their faces.* CHUDU

goes to each of them, one at a time, trying to find something to buy. The crowd whispers, chants, screams:)

ONE VILLAGER: CHUDU: *(Sings.)*
Chudu is different!   *I need some food . . .*
Never look him in the eye!
Chudu is evil!
. . . A blizzard in July!   *I need to eat*

TWO VILLAGERS:
Chudu is different!
Never look him in the eye!
Chudu is evil!
. . . A blizzard in July!

THREE VILLAGERS:
Chudu is different!   *How much is that?*
Never look him in the eye!
Chudu is evil!
. . . A blizzard in July!

ALL VILLAGERS:
Chudu is different!   *I'll take the beets . . .*
Never look him in the eye!
Chudu is evil!
. . . A blizzard in July!

(CHUDU *reaches for a beet and the* MERCHANT *pulls it away before he can touch it. Pause, breath. Then acceleration:)*

VILLAGERS
#1: He has teeth just like a saw blade!   *A bit*
#2: And his skin is like a mushroom!
#3: And his legs are short and crooked!   *A beet*
#4: And his ears are big and hairy!
#5: And his nose looks like a cherry!   *Some food*
#6: Both his eyes are strange and scary!
#7: He is very-very-very-very . . .   *To eat?*

(They can't think what else to call him.)

ALL: Ugly!!!!!!

CHUDU: *(Looking at them.)* But you don't know me, I'm really not that strange. *(He tries to make contact.)* Let me show you—(VILLAGERS *look away.)* If I could, I'd probably change who I am—but I am Chudu . . .

CHILD: *(Correcting him.)* Chudu . . . the Goat-Man!

(The VILLAGERS *pull away and disappear. But the curious* CHILD *sneaks back out and moves toward* CHUDU *to get a closer look.* CHUDU *lights up when he sees the* CHILD *approaching. He tries to charm the* CHILD*, whistles, the* CHILD *whistles back. Delighted,* CHUDU *magically produces a cup of precious water out of his shirtsleeve. The* CHILD *gratefully accepts the water and just as she is about to take a sip, her* MOTHER *violently yanks the* CHILD *away.)*

MOTHER: *(Chanting: warning, to the* CHILD*.)*
                    Don't touch Chudu
                    Never look him in the eye!

CHILD: But I'm thirsty!

ANOTHER VILLAGER:
>He's a demon who knows magic
>If you touch him you will die!

(The VILLAGERS *shrink from* CHUDU, *whispering to one another. The* CHILD *looks at all the frightened adults. He moves toward* CHUDU *and looks back at the adults who stare and cower. The* CHILD *looks back at* CHUDU *and suddenly throws the water in* CHUDU's *face. Satisfied, the* VILLAGERS *disappear. The market disappears. The* CHILD *runs off. Adding insult to injury, the* CHILD *runs back on, throws the empty cup at* CHUDU *and runs away.* CHUDU *is stunned.)*

CHUDU: *(Sings.)*
>They never look me in the eye
>Looking deeper, deep inside
>
>Am I everything they say?
>If I am I must be mad
>
>They won't even shake my hand
>I am Chudu . . .

(Spoken.)
Chudu, the Goat-Man. *(He exits, alone.)*

VILLAGE STORYTELLER: The Village in the Valley Where the River Ran Dry— was ruled by a king who was so powerful he didn't need a name—people just called him "the King."

ANOTHER STORYTELLER: The King was famous for never losing a war and as his riches grew—it seemed the King had everything a man could want.

AND ANOTHER STORYTELLER: Everything except a son. He had nineteen daughters, each of them strong and smart—but the King wanted a son.

KING: I want a son!

VILLAGE STORYTELLER: He wanted an heir to the Royal Throne.

KING: I want an heir to the Royal Throne!

ANOTHER STORYTELLER: And finally, the King got everything he wanted.

KING: Finally! I have everything I want! *(Holding the baby up to the crowd, triumphant.)* A son! The Heir to the Royal Throne! Prince . . . Christopher!

CROWD: *(Cheers.)* Hail to Prince Christopher!!!

(The KING *proudly holds the infant* PRINCE *in his arms.)*

KING: *(Sings.)*
>He'll slay dragons, ride horses, win battles in war
>He'll love politics, government, power and more, he'll—

(The baby PRINCE *suddenly lets out a blood-curdling scream. The* KING *is horrified and exits holding the baby like a piece of rotten fruit.)*

VILLAGE STORYTELLER: It was the beginning of a very—complicated— relationship.

(The KING *returns with* PRINCE CHRISTOPHER *as a little boy.)*

ANOTHER STORYTELLER: Hundreds of gifts poured into the Royal Castle for Prince Christopher.

KING: *(Looking over the gifts, pleased.)* Solid suits of armor. Prized horses. The best swords. *(Holds up a violin.)* What's this??? *(The* KING *tosses the violin aside. The* BABY *reaches for the violin.)*

AND ANOTHER STORYTELLER: From the first moment Prince Christopher laid eyes on that violin, something stirred deep inside him.

(The BABY *begins to play the violin. A crowd watches.)*

VILLAGER: How can such a tiny baby make such a beautiful sound?

(More people from the village gather around the BABY *playing the violin. The* KING *watches, amused but alarmed by his son's gift.)*

KING: *(Explaining to people watching the* PRINCE.*)* It's a phase.

VILLAGE STORYTELLER: Five, six, seven years old and the prince couldn't stop playing.

*(*CHRISTOPHER *finishes playing and the crowd applauds. The* KING *goes to* CHRISTOPHER *and shares the crowd's accolades. He grabs the violin but* CHRISTOPHER *holds on tightly. The two of them grip the violin—smiling at the crowd. The* KING *whispers tensely so only* CHRISTOPHER *can hear:)*

KING: This WILL stop. *(Tense.)* Right?

(The PRINCE *begins to play the violin again.)*

ANOTHER STORYELLER: Eight, nine, ten years old and the music didn't stop.

(Twelve-year-old CHRISTOPHER *plays his violin in the village square for an enthusiastic audience who dance to* CHRISTOPHER's *wild music. Suddenly* SEVERAL GUARDS *pick* CHRISTOPHER *up and carry him off to the* KING. *He continues to play. The* KING *thrusts his sword toward* CHRISTOPHER. *Though he is playful, there is an edge, he means business.)*

KING: You're twelve years old, Christopher!

(Out of desperation, CHRISTOPHER *awkwardly uses his violin bow as a sword and playfully tries to spar with his father. There is something likable and charming about* CHRISTOPHER's *clumsy attempt to play his father's game.)*

PRINCE CHRISTOPHER: I'm not very good at fencing . . .

KING: Nonsense! *(Pinning* CHRISTOPHER *with his sword.)* I was quite impressive with a sword when I was twelve years old.

PRINCE CHRISTOPHER: I know, Father. *(Escaping from his father.)* I said I'm not very good at fencing.

KING: *(Pursuing his son.)* You disappoint me. *(*CHRISTOPHER *backs away, the* KING *thrusts again.)* You disgrace me. *(*CHRISTOPHER *darts away, the* KING *thrusts again.)* You dishonor me.

PRINCE CHRISTOPHER: But I have something beautiful I want you to hear—

KING: You will learn to use a sword and you will love it. *(Backing him up.)* You will learn to ride a horse and you will love it. *(Holding the sword to* CHRISTO-PHER's *chest.)* You will learn about the history of wars and you will love it.

PRINCE CHRISTOPHER: But what about my music?

KING: Starting tomorrow there will be no music! NONE! From sunup to sundown, all of your days will be spent learning to be a man.

PRINCE CHRISTOPHER: A man?

KING: And you will love it.

PRINCE CHRISTOPHER: But—

(The KING *pushes* CHRISTOPHER *through his "manhood paces":)*

KING: *(Sings.)*

> Spar! Defend! Leap! Attack!
> Thrust! Protect! Gallop! Whack!
> Charge! Sneak! Sprint! Jab!
> Slice! Advance! Crawl! Stab!

(The KING *chases* CHRISTOPHER *offstage.)*

A VILLAGE STORYTELLER: Beyond the Village in the Valley Where the River Ran Dry—across the empty river and through the trees, there lived a blacksmith, his wife and their daughter named Armida.

ANOTHER STORYTELLER: The people in the village thought Armida's family was—a bit strange.

CHILD: Sometimes—they build giant bonfires—

SECOND CHILD: —and Dance!

CHILD: Barefoot!

SECOND CHILD: —until the sun comes up!

CHILD: *(Disgust.)* They're . . . gypsies!

SECOND CHILD: Gypsies!

(The two CHILDREN *do a fast, secret hand gesture to ward off the evil spirits.* ARMIDA, ARMIDA'S MOTHER *and* ARMIDA'S FATHER *dance around a bonfire.)*

ARMIDA'S MOTHER & FATHER: *(Sing.)*

> Around and 'round and 'round the fire
> Never give up and never get tired
> 'Round and 'round and 'round all night
> Up to the moon and take a bite
> Up to the moon!
> Up to the moon!
> Up to the moon and take a bite.
>
> A bit of moon to drink at night
> The moon is bright and such a sight

MOTHER:

> It's there!

FATHER:

> It's yours!

BOTH:

> So sing the tune:
> The moon, the moon, the moon, the moon!

ALL:
> Up to the moon!
> Up to the moon!
> Up to the moon and take a bite!

(They laugh, continue to dance playfully, without inhibition.)

CHILD: *(Commenting on the dancing.)* They're not from around here.

SECOND CHILD: Once I saw the mother and father wrestling in the mud. *(Fascinated.)* And they were laughing!

CHILD: They're definitely not from around here.

SECOND CHILD: The little girl is as strong as twelve men!

CHILD: Once I saw the little girl carrying a cow—on her shoulders!

SECOND CHILD: The mother isn't wearing shoes!

CHILD: The mother NEVER wears shoes!

(ARMIDA sees the CHILDREN watching them. ARMIDA's MOTHER assures her, sings playfully, taunts the CHILDREN:)

ARMIDA'S MOTHER: *(Sings.)*
> No shoes! No shoes! I refuse to wear shoes!
> I never wear shoes!
> No shoes! No shoes! I refuse to wear shoes!
> No shoes, no shoes!
> I never wear shoes! And what about you?

ARMIDA: What about the snow, Mama? It's cold!

ARMIDA'S MOTHER: Walk in the sun, Armida. Walk in the sun!

(ARMIDA cautiously tries out the cold on her feet. Her MOTHER encourages her, nodding, coaxing.)

ARMIDA: *(Sings.)*
> No shoes?
> No shoes . . .
> I—refuse—to wear shoes . . .
> *(Looking to her MOTHER.)*
> I'll never wear shoes.

ARMIDA & ARMIDA'S MOTHER:
> No shoes! No shoes! I refuse to wear shoes!
> I never wear shoes!

(ARMIDA and her MOTHER sing/dance together.)

ARMIDA & ARMIDA'S MOTHER:
> No shoes! No shoes! I refuse to wear shoes!
> I never wear shoes!
> No shoes! (MOTHER: *Run wild*)
> No shoes! (MOTHER: *My child*)
> I refuse to wear shoes
> No shoes! (MOTHER: *The sky*)
> No shoes! (MOTHER: *You'll fly!*)
> I refuse to wear shoes

ARMIDA:	ARMIDA'S MOTHER:
Up to the moon!	*Up to the moon and take a bite*
Up to the moon!	*No shoes run wild, my child, you'll fly:*

ARMIDA & ARMIDA'S MOTHER:
> *Up to the moon and take a bite!*

ARMIDA: The moon, the moon, the moon, the moon!!!

A VILLAGE STORYTELLER: Suddenly Armida reached up and grabbed the handle of the Big Dipper, swinging from star to star until she grabbed the full moon—

ANOTHER STORYTELLER: And then she took a bite right out of it!

AND ANOTHER STORYTELLER: Moon juice dripped down her face.

ARMIDA'S MOTHER: *(Looking up at* ARMIDA *in the sky.)* What does the moon taste like?

ARMIDA: *(Sings.)*
> *It tastes like*
> *I don't know how to describe it.*

A VILLAGE STORYTELLER: Armida took another bite.

ARMIDA: *(Sings.)*
> *It tastes like—*
> *I want to stay here inside it*

(Looking down at her MOTHER *and* FATHER.)
> *It tastes like being strong*
> *It tastes like breaking free*
> *It tastes like being loved*
> *It tastes like family*
> *But most of all: It tastes like me!*

FATHER: *(Toasting her with moon juice.)* To Armida! Wherever your heart takes you!

MOTHER: *(Toasting her with moon juice.)* To Armida! Let your dreams awake you!

(They begin to dance again. Mother teaching daughter. The MOTHER *throws the scarf up in the air, and slowly moves out of the dance.)*

ARMIDA: Mama? Mama!!! *(*ARMIDA *watches the scarf slowly float into her own hands. She looks around. The* MOTHER *is gone.* ARMIDA *screams:)* Mama, no! Noooooooooo!

VILLAGE GOSSIP #1: Did you hear?

VILLAGE GOSSIP #2: What I said?

VILLAGE GOSSIP #3: Is it true?

VILLAGE GOSSIP #4: Is she dead?

VILLAGE GOSSIP #1: What a shame!

VILLAGE GOSSIP #2: What a shock!

VILLAGE GOSSIP #3: The mother's dead?

SECOND CHILD: *(Entering.)* What's the talk???

CHILD: The mother's dead!

(The VILLAGE GOSSIPS *and* CHILDREN *exit whispering to one another like chickens.* ARMIDA *looks around, lost.)*

A VILLAGE STORYTELLER: All through the village, the ground shook and tears fell from the moon like shooting stars. It was the sound of Armida's heart breaking.

(Far away, we hear ARMIDA'S MOTHER *humming "No Shoes." It's like a presence that hangs in the air.* ARMIDA'S FATHER *sits frozen, removed.* ARMIDA *approaches, puts on her best face.)*

ARMIDA: I've done all the work in the shop, Father. *(Her* FATHER *grunts.)* All the horses have shoes—*(She stops on the word, her* FATHER *looks away.)* Maybe we could build a bonfire tonight. *(He doesn't answer.)* We could dance.

ARMIDA'S FATHER: I don't think so, Armida.

ARMIDA: *(Looking up at the moon.)* I could go to the moon and bring back some moon juice.

ARMIDA'S FATHER: *(Distant.)* I'm not thirsty.

ARMIDA: The moon seems so far away.
(Singing to herself:)

> It tastes like being strong
> It tastes like breaking free
> It tastes like being loved
> It tastes like family—

ARMIDA'S FATHER: Stop it, Armida!

ARMIDA: I miss Mama. *(Her* FATHER *doesn't respond.)* I miss—you. *(Beat.)* I better get back to work. *(She starts to go.)*

ARMIDA'S FATHER: Armida—

ARMIDA: *(Turning quickly to him.)* Yes, Father?

(He can't think of what to say, how to put it in words. He looks away. And ARMIDA *runs off.)*

A VILLAGE STORYTELLER: The world rolled on and things went from bad to worse for poor Chudu the Goat-Man.

*(*CHUDU'S NEIGHBORS *chant tensely, urgently under* CHUDU'S *protests:)*

CHUDU:	VILLAGERS:
(Trying to stop them from leaving.)	*Don't touch Chudu*
I was NOT *to blame for the*	*Never look him in the eye!*
wine going sour in the church,	*He's a dwarf! He's a freak!*
or for last year's poor cabbage crop.	*If you touch him, you will die!*
	Don't touch Chudu
	Never look him in the eye!
	He's a goat! He's a fish!
	If you touch him, you will die!

CHILD: Chudu the Goat-Man is hiding under my bed!

CHUDU: I didn't even KNOW the woman who fell down the coal chute.

ANOTHER CHILD: It's not my fault! Chudu the Goat-Man made me do it!

CHUDU: I didn't make the river run dry! The Six-Fingered Man did that!

(CHUDU *comes face to face with the* CHILD *from the earlier water scene. The* CHILD *turns away in fear.*) Not you, too! You don't have to be afraid! Haven't I been a good neighbor? Haven't I always said "Good morning"? Haven't I always walked close to the curb so I could easily step off into the gutter if any of you wanted to pass? (*He tries not to lose his temper.*) 1-2-3-4-5-6-7-8-9-10! All right! (*Threatening the crowd.*) If you don't stop, I'm going to go under that bridge—and—and—I'll just go right under there—and—I'll—never come out again. (*The* VILLAGERS *stare blankly at* CHUDU.) I'm warning you! Don't try and stop me! Don't even try it! (*No one does.*) Because if I go down there—I won't come out! (*They don't move.*) Do you hear me? You'll never hear from me again! (*They don't move.*) I'm going—right now. I'm going down. (*They don't move.*) You'll never see me again. (*Almost breaking down.*) You'll never hear from old Chudu the Goat-Man ever again! (*Defeated.*) Ever. (CHUDU *looks at all of the* VILLAGERS; *they do not look at his eyes. He stands on the bridge.*) Then. (*He disappears under the bridge. No one moves.* CHUDU *pops up, sheepishly.*) Goodbye.

(*He disappears. There is a moment of silence. The* VILLAGERS *wait cautiously to see if* CHUDU *will keep his word. Somebody beats once on a pan. They wait. Somebody else makes a noise. Another beat. More sound. The sound builds and suddenly they break into celebration. Pots and pans become musical instruments. The* VILLAGERS *dance off with joy. Alone, the* CHILD *dances on the bridge—like dancing on a grave. She catches herself whistling and runs away. The* KING *drives* CHRISTOPHER *onstage with his sword, putting him through more manhood paces.* CHRISTOPHER *is exhausted but the* KING *persists.*)

KING: (*Sings.*)

> Guard! Proceed! Strike! Race!
> Force! Propel! Drive! Chase!
> Fight! Support! Jump! Lunge!
> Shield! Maintain! Invade! Plunge!

(*The* KING *chases* CHRISTOPHER *off.* ARMIDA'S FATHER *enters with a* WOMAN *and her* DAUGHTER.)

ARMIDA'S FATHER: (*Calling out.*) Armida?

STEPMOTHER: Armida, dear?

VILLAGE GOSSIP #1: Did you hear?

VILLAGE GOSSIP #2: What I said?

VILLAGE GOSSIP #3: Is it true?

VILLAGE GOSSIP #4: Are they wed?

VILLAGE GOSSIP #1: Is it true?

VILLAGE GOSSIP #2: What you said?

VILLAGE GOSSIP #3: Are they wed???

VILLAGE GOSSIP #4: Are they wed???

ARMIDA'S FATHER: Armida?

(ARMIDA *enters wearing baggy blacksmith overalls and no shoes.*)

ARMIDA'S FATHER: This is your new stepmother.

(*The* STEPMOTHER *curtsies,* ARMIDA *shakes her hand with a firm grip. The* STEPMOTHER *pulls her hand away in pain, wipes off the dirt and grime.*)

STEPMOTHER: And this is your new stepsister, Clarella.

(ARMIDA *looks at the mindless* STEPSISTER *who is dressed in a lacy dress and ribbons. She tries to shake her hand but the* STEPMOTHER *steps between them and takes over. She suddenly puts lipstick on* ARMIDA's *lips.*)

STEPMOTHER: We'll have you fixed up in no time! (*She puts a book on* ARMIDA's *head and* ARMIDA *plods across stage—like a bull in a china shop.* CLARELLA *has a book on her head and walks perfectly, balancing the book.*) Don't stagger! Walk! Try to be more like Clarella!

ARMIDA: (*Wiping the lipstick off.*) This can't be happening! I'm a blacksmith, not some—tell her, Father!

STEPMOTHER: (*To* ARMIDA's FATHER, *jumping in.*) Do you want people to laugh at her because all she knows how to do is shoe a horse?

ARMIDA: (*As if trying to wake her* FATHER *from a deep sleep.*) Father! What about bonfires and dancing?

STEPMOTHER: No, no, no!

ARMIDA: (*To her* FATHER.) What about my heart? My dreams?

STEPMOTHER: Think flimsy but graceful—

ARMIDA: What about the moon? "It tastes like family"—

STEPMOTHER: Helpless—but fluttery!

ARMIDA: (*Pulls the book off her head and throws it to the floor.*) What about Mama!

STEPMOTHER: (*To* ARMIDA.) Hopeless. (*To* CLARELLA.) Hopeless! (*To* ARMIDA's FATHER.) Hopeless! (ARMIDA's FATHER *starts to say something but the* STEPMOTHER *interrupts.*) Her hands are always dirty, she knows nothing about the kitchen, and she's headstrong and powerful as an ox in May. No one but the beastly Six-Fingered Man would want to marry such a creature! (*Calling out sweetly:*) Armida! I have a present for you! (ARMIDA *is suspicious; the* STEPMOTHER *holds out a box.*) Go ahead! It's for you!

(ARMIDA *opens the box.*)

ARMIDA: (*Stricken.*) Shoes. (ARMIDA *looks at her* FATHER. *The* STEPMOTHER *and* CLARELLA *look at the* FATHER. *He caves in.*)

ARMIDA'S FATHER: Put them on, Armida. (ARMIDA *reluctantly puts on the shoes. She can barely stand up, she looks as if she might fall over.*)

STEPMOTHER: Now maybe you'll learn how to walk like a real woman!

(*The* STEPMOTHER *and* CLARELLA *exit, victorious. The* FATHER *can't bear to look at* ARMIDA *and he exits, too.* ARMIDA *is left alone, staring at her feet. She sings slowly. Her* MOTHER *sings in counterpoint, in the distance from a long time ago:*)

ARMIDA: (*Sings.*)	MOTHER: (*Sings.*)
Hello, shoes . . . Hello	No shoes . . . No shoes . . .
Hello, shoes . . . Hello	I refuse to wear shoes . . .
(*Looking up at the sky.*)	I never wear shoes
Hello, Moon	And neither do you . . .
Good-bye	No shoes . . . No shoes . . .
Good-bye.	

(ARMIDA *limps off, barely able to walk in the shoes.*)

A VILLAGE STORYTELLER: By day, Christopher did his best to please his father.

(From another direction, CHRISTOPHER enters pursuing the KING with a heavy sword. CHRISTOPHER tries very hard to do everything his father has taught him.)

PRINCE CHRISTOPHER: *(Sings.)*

> Guard . . . Proceed . . . Strike! Race!
> Force . . . Propel . . . Drive . . . Chase!
> Fight! Support . . . Jump . . . Lunge!
> Shield . . . Maintain . . . Invade . . . Plunge!

(CHRISTOPHER does a big finish then waits anxiously for his father's approval.)

KING: Better. *(Exits.)*

PRINCE CHRISTOPHER: *(Alone.)* Better? . . . *(CHRISTOPHER pulls his violin out of hiding and sneaks into the village streets.)*

ANOTHER STORYTELLER: But at night, Christopher roamed the streets of the village. He didn't sleep for several years.

(Night. The village square. We hear violin music approaching.)

VILLAGER #1: *(Raising his window, calling back inside to his family, excited.)* It's him!

VILLAGER #2: *(Coming out to the street still dressed in nightclothes.)* He's near!

VILLAGER #3: *(Running to the street.)* I hope—

VILLAGER #4: *(Calling to everyone, banging on doors.)* He's Here!!! He's Here! He's Here! He's Here!!!

(PRINCE CHRISTOPHER strolls on playing the violin and people spill out of their houses dressed in their nightclothes. People greet the PRINCE affectionately and he plays and plays and plays. The VILLAGERS dance, young lovers rendezvous, an OLD MAN dances a jig. The KING watches from the shadows.)

OLD MAN: *(Dancing.)* Faster! Faster!

(The dance ends with applause and the KING walking through the crowd, applauding rhythmically, evenly, he doesn't stop. CHRISTOPHER looks at his father, frightened yet hopeful.)

PRINCE CHRISTOPHER: You liked it!

KING: *(Still applauding.)* You mock me.

PRINCE CHRISTOPHER: No—

KING: You defy me.

PRINCE CHRISTOPHER: No, I—

KING: You play me for a fool?!?

PRINCE CHRISTOPHER: No!

KING: *(To the crowd of people who watch, unsure what to do.)* There will be no music tonight! *(The crowd groans.)*

PRINCE CHRISTOPHER: *(Reassuring the crowd.)* Tomorrow night! *(The crowd brightens.)*

KING: There will be no music tomorrow night. *(The crowd groans.)*

PRINCE CHRISTOPHER: *(To the crowd.)* The next night! *(The crowd brightens.)*

KING: There will be no music. Any night. Ever! *(The crowd is silent.)*

PRINCE CHRISTOPHER: You can't stop me! *(The crowd gasps.)*

KING: *(To* CHRISTOPHER.*)* If they listen, they will die. (CHRISTOPHER *defiantly begins to play his violin. The* KING *addresses the crowd.)* If you listen, you will die.

(The crowd understands. No one protests. Slowly one by one they turn away and disappear inside their houses.)

PRINCE CHRISTOPHER: NO! No, wait! wait!!! (CHRISTOPHER *continues to frantically play his violin. Slowly a* VILLAGER *turns his back.* CHRISTOPHER *plays even more passionately. Another* VILLAGER *turns her back. Another. More. All of the people in the village turn and walk away leaving* CHRISTOPHER *alone with the* KING. *Silence.* CHRISTOPHER *is stunned by the abandonment. The* KING *is all business.)*

KING: Now that that is over, you will do my bidding.

(The KING *claps his hands twice and his* ROYAL ADVISORS *sweep onto the scene carrying a suit of armor and weapons. They quickly surround* CHRISTOPHER *and begin to dress him from head to toe in the armor.)*

KING: For centuries the mountains have been plagued by that fiend who has caused the river to run dry—

PRINCE CHRISTOPHER: What?!?

KING: The notorious . . . Six-Fingered Man.

PRINCE CHRISTOPHER: *(Looks as though he will faint.)* You're sending me—your own son—to fight the Six-Fingered Man???

KING: Stop waving your hands around like some princess! All your life we have known this moment would come.

PRINCE CHRISTOPHER: Do you want me to die???

KING: From the time you were a small boy, I have tried to prepare you for this day. *(Direct.)* It hasn't been easy.

PRINCE CHRISTOPHER: *(Insisting, stuck on the idea.)* Do you want me to die?

KING: You're sixteen years old, Christopher. You're a MAN! It's time you started acting like one!

PRINCE CHRISTOPHER: What did I do wrong? Tell me! I want to know! I play the violin. That's what I do. That's what I'm good at. Why can't you see that?

KING: I've put up with this for sixteen years! No more! You will fight the Six-Fingered Man.

PRINCE CHRISTOPHER: I can't.

KING: You will do this or you will never be king.

PRINCE CHRISTOPHER: I can't.

KING: You will do this or you will leave this village.

PRINCE CHRISTOPHER: I can't.

KING: You will do this or you will leave this family.

PRINCE CHRISTOPHER: I can't.

(The decision has been made. The KING *makes his.)*

KING: You will do this or you are not my son.

PRINCE CHRISTOPHER: Not your son? Why? Because I hate fighting? Because I hate politics? Because I hate horses??? Because I hate—I am not you!

KING: I do not know you.

PRINCE CHRISTOPHER: *(Holding out the violin.)* It's just wood, some string, it makes—a beautiful sound. *(The* KING *turns to exit.)* You don't hate this violin, Father! *(The* KING *looks back at his son.)* You. Hate. Me. Me! (CHRISTOPHER *suddenly smashes the violin on the ground. Stunned by his action and lost in his rage, he smashes the violin again and again and again:)* You hate Me! Me! Me! Me! Me! Me! Me! *(He smashes the violin until there is nothing left but bits of splintered wood.)*

KING: *(Kicking a piece of the violin aside.)* I'm proud of you, son. Good luck. *(The* KING *exits followed by the* ROYAL ADVISORS. CHRISTOPHER *drops to the ground, raw, exhausted, defeated, empty. There is a long silence. He picks up every piece of the violin, looks toward the mountain and exits.)*

A VILLAGE STORYTELLER: *(To the audience.)* For one hundred years, Chudu stayed all alone under the bridge at the edge of the Village in the Valley Where the River Ran Dry.

ANOTHER STORYTELLER: Chudu got through the long days and nights as best he could. He tried to whistle.

*(*CHUDU *tries to whistle.)*

VILLAGE STORYTELLER: He read the dictionary from beginning to end thirty-seven times:

CHUDU: Zebra . . . zenith . . . zero . . .

ANOTHER STORYTELLER: He counted aloud as far as he knew how:

CHUDU: . . . nine-hundred and ninety-nine trillion-zillion—

VILLAGE STORYTELLER: And when he ran out of numbers, he made up new ones:

CHUDU: *(Rambling in a made-up language.)* . . . trenky-tato sashin moo, trenky-tato sashin faj, trenky-tato sashin—Well. *(Sad.)* Tomorrow is a new day.

ANOTHER STORYTELLER: One morning Chudu woke up to the strangest, sweetest sound.

(We hear CHUDU *whistling.)*

VILLAGE STORYTELLER: It was something he hadn't heard for a long, long time.

VILLAGE GOSSIP #1: *(Suspicious.)* Did you hear?

VILLAGE GOSSIP #2: What I heard?

VILLAGE GOSSIP #3: *(Frightened.)* Was it him???

VILLAGE GOSSIP #4: No no no! Not a word!

(The GOSSIPS *hold their breath.* CHUDU's *whistling gets louder, more confident.)*

VILLAGE GOSSIP #1: *(Suspicious.)* Did you hear?

VILLAGE GOSSIP #2: What I heard?

VILLAGE GOSSIP #3: *(Frightened.)* Was it him???

VILLAGE GOSSIP #4: No no no! Just a bird.

(CHUDU pops out from under the bridge and squints at the sunlight. The GOSSIPS run away in fear.)

CHUDU: *(Tender.)* Oh, Mr. Sun . . . One-hundred years. I've missed you. *(CHUDU closes his eyes, feels the warmth of the sun. He opens his eyes and sees a CHILD skipping toward him.)* Maybe my luck has changed! Maybe he'll talk to me. Maybe we'll be friends and—and—we could—whistle together.

(CHUDU puts a cup of water where the CHILD will see it. The CHILD sees it, looks around, looks closer at the water.)

CHILD: Water! *(The CHILD guzzles some water. She hears CHUDU whistling, looks over and sees him looking at her.)*

CHUDU: Morning! What a beautiful day! What a beautiful day for a walk! *(The CHILD nods, continues to drink.)* I've been saving that water for hundreds of years. Drink up! *(Extending a hand to the CHILD.)* My name's Chudu—

CHILD: *(Chokes on the water.)* Chudu—the Goat-Man? *(The CHILD's eyes bulge, her lips purse, she looks cautiously to the left and right. She backs away, disappears down the road calling out to all the VILLAGERS.)* Chudu the Goat-Man! He's here! Chudu the Goat-Man!

CHUDU: *(Sings.)*

> What's the use, why do I try?
> And try and try and try . . .
> Years and years without a friend,
> Does my story ever end?
> Looking deeper, deep inside
> Deeper, deep inside . . .
> *(Makes difficult realization.)*

I want to die . . . *(CHUDU seems startled by his deep pain, his true feelings. He thinks about what he has said, repeats it softly.)* I want to die. *(He looks toward the mountains and slowly sets off, his burdens weighing him down to half his original small size.)*

A VILLAGE STORYTELLER: As if things couldn't get worse for Armida, her father suddenly died.

ANOTHER STORYTELLER: And if Armida's life had been terrible before, it was now ten times more terrible.

AND ANOTHER STORYTELLER: The same girl who had taken a bite out of the moon hardly recognized herself anymore.

(ARMIDA enters dressed identically to CLARELLA. A YOUNG SUITOR presents her with flowers.)

ARMIDA: *(Using a fake, breathy voice.)* My. What lovely, delicate flowers. How many are there?

YOUNG SUITOR: Three. *(Counting the flowers, as if to a child.)* One-two-three . . .

ARMIDA: *(Laughing in a high-mannered pitch.)* Silly me! I'm so terrible at math.

YOUNG SUITOR: That reminds me of a story—

ARMIDA: *(Laughing suddenly.)* That's such a wonderful, funny story!

YOUNG SUITOR: I haven't told it yet.

ARMIDA: *(Breathy.)* Of course. Silly me.

YOUNG SUITOR: Perhaps we can ride horses together.

ARMIDA: *(Old self.)* Horses! *(Breathy, weak.)* Oh I couldn't! I'm so afraid of horses!

YOUNG SUITOR: In the moonlight . . .

ARMIDA: *(Saying the word, recognizing something.)* The Moon . . . ? (ARMIDA *exits on the* YOUNG SUITOR's *capable arm.)*

VILLAGE STORYTELLER: And the more she pretended—the more men would parade to her door like ants at a picnic.

ANOTHER STORYTELLER: It was like possessing some awful, secret scent that could wake the dreamer from his deepest sleep.

(ARMIDA staggers on as if running from wild animals. She is out of breath, her dress is ripped in a few places, her hair a mess. She sneaks quietly, looking back from where she came. She searches for herself in a hand-mirror. Her painted smile is smeared and crooked. There is real fatigue in her face, her spirit seems worn. SUITORS *seem to spring from the woodwork. Every direction* ARMIDA *turns, a* SUITOR *is waiting. Their affection is ghoulish, demanding, faceless, creepy.* ARMIDA *cannot escape them. They sing her name over and over like an opera gone out of control:)*

SUITORS: *(Sing.)*

> Armida!!!! Armida! Armida! Armida! Ar-mi-da!
> Armida! Armida!
> Armida! Armida! Armida! Armida! Armida!
> Armida!

(The SUITORS *simultaneously try to woo* ARMIDA, *faster/faster/faster.* ARMIDA *tries to keep the rehearsed, pasted smile but she is exhausted, unhappy, false. She tries to sneak away and they swarm her, she runs for her life. She escapes.)*

ARMIDA: Nooooooo!!!

(CLARELLA runs on, primping for the attention of all the SUITORS. *They take one look at* CLARELLA, *groan in disgust, and run after* ARMIDA. CLARELLA, *alone, wails in humiliation, then exits. From another direction,* ARMIDA *floats on, like a ghost of her former self. She sings through a teeth-clenched smile.)*

ARMIDA: *(Sings.)*

> I'm going crazy!
> I'm lost inside this dress.
> I'm going crazy, crazy . . .
> I'm going crazy!
> I hate ribbons, I confess
> I'm going crazy!
> I can flutter, bat my eyes, act silly as a duck
> I pretend that I'm helpless—and so with any luck
> I'll just go crazy . . . crazy, crazy!
>
> I'm going crazy!
> And no one has a clue.
> I'm going crazy, crazy . . .

I'm going crazy!
Can a heart be black and blue?
I'm going crazy!

I can flutter, bat my eyes, act silly as a duck
I pretend that I'm helpless—and so with any luck
I'll just go crazy . . . crazy, crazy!

(ARMIDA *floats off, frozen smile and all.* CLARELLA *re-enters—still crying, very loudly. The* STEPMOTHER *comforts her jealous, heartbroken daughter.* ARMIDA *sneaks back out and pretends to peek through a keyhole and listen to their conversation.*)

STEPMOTHER: Hush, hush, Clarella, dear. Dry your tears! Mama knows . . . Armida thinks she's so smart—every man in town has eyes for no one but her! Tonight—sleep on the side of the bed against the wall. Let Armida sleep on the edge. When she's gone to sleep, I'll sneak into the room and— (*The* STEPMOTHER *whispers into* CLARELLA's *ear and* CLARELLA *lights up.* ARMIDA *frantically tries to hear what's being said.*) Do as I say and by morning all of our troubles will be over once and for all.

A VILLAGE STORYTELLER: (*To the audience, quiet, like a ghost story.*) That night Armida lay awake at the edge of the bed until she heard her stepsister snoring, and then she got over on the side against the wall and pushed Clarella to the edge and lay perfectly still, waiting.

ANOTHER STORYTELLER: She heard her coming. Up the steps. Creak. Creak. Creak. Her stepmother snuck in the room, groped about in the dark until she found Clarella's neck, and then *down* came an ax with all her might.

AND ANOTHER STORYTELLER: Thinking it was Armida, she chopped off her own daughter's head. (CLARELLA's *head tumbles to the ground.*) Then she snuck back downstairs and went back to bed.

(*An owl hoots.*)

VILLAGE GOSSIP #1: Did you hear?

VILLAGE GOSSIP #2: What I said?

VILLAGE GOSSIP #3: Is it true?

VILLAGE GOSSIP #4: Is she dead?

VILLAGE GOSSIP #1: Is it true?

VILLAGE GOSSIP #2: What you said?

VILLAGE GOSSIP #3: Is she dead?

VILLAGE GOSSIP #4: Is she dead?

A VILLAGE STORYTELLER: Armida jumped out of bed.

ARMIDA: Am I mad? Am I dead?

ANOTHER STORYTELLER: Blood was everywhere.

ARMIDA: On my shoes, in my hair.

(*We hear the blood-curdling scream of* ARMIDA's STEPMOTHER. *She has discovered* CLARELLA's *dead body.*)

STEPMOTHER: (*Off.*) Armida!!!!!!!

VILLAGE STORYTELLER: She had to escape!

ANOTHER STORYTELLER: There was only one place left where Armida felt safe.

(ARMIDA *begins to run. She is still wearing the shoes. She runs until she gets to the graves of her parents. She throws herself on the ground. She is exhausted, frightened, alone.*)

ARMIDA: (*Sings.*)

> Do you know me?
> I used to be Armida
> Do you know me?
> You used to hold me tight
>
> Do you know me?
> I used to be your daughter
> Do you know me?
> You used to be my light.
>
> The more I pretend, the more they pursue,
> I can't go on, I hate myself
> I don't know what to do.
>
> I don't know me
> So this must be goodbye
> If I'm not me
> I'd rather die.
> I'd rather die . . .

(*Exhausted and stunned by her admission,* ARMIDA *looks out at the distance. She takes her first steps toward the mountains.*)

ARMIDA: I'd rather die.

VILLAGE GOSSIP #1: Did you hear?

VILLAGE GOSSIP #2: Do you know?

VILLAGE GOSSIP #3: Is it true?

VILLAGE GOSSIP #4: Where'd he go?

VILLAGE GOSSIP #1: Up the mountain!

VILLAGE GOSSIP #2: To the cliff!

VILLAGE GOSSIP #3: He won't do it.

VILLAGE GOSSIP #4: But what if . . . he jumps?

VILLAGE GOSSIP #1: Chudu!

VILLAGE GOSSIP #2: Chudu!

VILLAGE GOSSIP #3: Chudu!

VILLAGE GOSSIP #4: Chudu!

VILLAGE GOSSIP #1: (*Pointing to the mountains.*) There he is!

VILLAGE GOSSIP #2: (*Pointing to the mountains.*) There he is!

VILLAGE GOSSIP #3: (*Pointing to the mountains.*) There he is!

VILLAGE GOSSIP #4: (*Pointing to the mountains.*) There he is!

(*A road. The wind blows. Darkness. Shadows fall like long, bony fingers across the road.* CHUDU *runs on, looks around, frightened, haunted, angry. Note: The journey up the mountain is not sung, it is a musical, rhythmic rant.*)

CHUDU:
> On a road, up a hill, getting there, going where?
> Up, up, up, up the mountains,
> Up, up, up, up the mountains
> Got to got to got to got to got to get there fast
> Got to got to got to got to got to try to last . . .

(The VILLAGERS begin a rhythmic breath sound on "hhu hhu hhu hhu" that underscores CHUDU's rant. Established, then CHUDU comes back in with his rant:)

> Nobody likes me!
> 1-2-3-4-5-6-7-8-9-10!
> What could I do?
> Stay in my house?
> Forever?
> 1-2-3-4-6-8-9-10!
> I'll show them!
> 1-5-9-6-8-2-10-10!
> No more Chudu! No more Chudu! No more Chudu!

(Sound of "hhu hhu hhu hhu" ends.)

VILLAGE GOSSIP #1:
> Did you hear?

VILLAGE GOSSIP #2:
> Do you know?

VILLAGE GOSSIP #3:
> Is it true?

VILLAGE GOSSIP #4:
> Where'd he go?

VILLAGE GOSSIP #1:
> Up the mountain!

VILLAGE GOSSIP #2:
> To the cliff!

VILLAGE GOSSIP #3:
> He won't do it.

VILLAGE GOSSIP #4:
> But what if . . . (Sharp inhale.) He jumps? (Another sharp inhale.)

VILLAGE GOSSIP #1: The prince!

VILLAGE GOSSIP #2: The prince!

VILLAGE GOSSIP #3: The prince!

VILLAGE GOSSIP #4: The prince!

VILLAGE GOSSIP #1: (Pointing to the mountains.) There he is!

VILLAGE GOSSIP #2: (Pointing to the mountains.) There he is!

VILLAGE GOSSIP #3: (Pointing to the mountains.) There he is!

VILLAGE GOSSIP #4: (Pointing to the mountains.) There he is!

(Rhythmic breath on "hhu hhu hhu hhu" resumes. Then CHRISTOPHER dressed in armor appears on the road alongside CHUDU.)

PRINCE CHRISTOPHER:

> *Left, over rock, toward the tree*
> *Watch the branches, oh! The road is hard to—*
> *See see see see see the mountains,*
> *See see see see see the mountains!*
> *Look look look look! A star in the sky!*
> *I wish I wish I wish I wish I wish that I could—*

(He stops, shocked by his wish, panting rhythmically.)

> *Hhu hhu hhu hhu . . .*
> *Why can't he love me?*
> *I'm nobody's son!*
> *Why can't he love me?*
> *He thinks that he's won!*
>
> *I'll show him!*

CHUDU:
I'll show them!

No more Christopher!

No more Chudu!

No more Christopher!

No more Chudu!

No more Christopher!

(Sound of "hhu hhu hhu hhu" stops.)

VILLAGE GOSSIP #1: Did you hear?

VILLAGE GOSSIP #2: Do you know?

VILLAGE GOSSIP #3: Is it true?

VILLAGE GOSSIP #4: Where'd she go?

VILLAGE GOSSIP #1: Up the mountain!

VILLAGE GOSSIP #2: To the cliff!

VILLAGE GOSSIP #3: She won't do it.

VILLAGE GOSSIP #4: But what if . . . *(Sharp inhale.)* She jumps? *(Another sharp inhale.)*

VILLAGE GOSSIP #1: Armida!

VILLAGE GOSSIP #2: Armida!

VILLAGE GOSSIP #3: Armida!

VILLAGE GOSSIP #4: Armida!

VILLAGE GOSSIP #1: *(Pointing to the mountains.)* There she is!

VILLAGE GOSSIP #2: *(Pointing to the mountains.)* There she is!

VILLAGE GOSSIP #3: *(Pointing to the mountains.)* There she is!

VILLAGE GOSSIP #4: *(Pointing to the mountains.)* There she is!

(Rhythmic breath on "hhu hhu hhu hhu" resumes. ARMIDA *dressed in night-clothes and the shoes, wrapped in a blanket, appears on the road alongside* CHUDU *and* CHRISTOPHER.)*

ARMIDA:

> Turn, on a road, in the night
> 'Round the river bed that's—
> Dry I I I I see the mountains
> I I I I I see the mountains!
> Go! I can't run, it's the shoes—
> Cannot stop, have to prove,
> Have to move and move and move and move and—

(She stops to catch her breath.)

> Hhu hhu hhu hhu . . .
> I changed how I walked
> I changed how I talked
> I changed every part
> But I can't change my heart!

> I'll show her!

PRINCE CHRISTOPHER:
> I'll show him!

CHUDU:
> I'll show them!

No more Armida!

PRINCE CHRISTOPHER:
> No more Christopher!

No more Armida!

CHUDU:

No more Armida!   No more Chudu!

ARMIDA/CHUDU/PRINCE CHRISTOPHER.
> No more me! Me! Me!

(They begin to breathe rhythmically on "hhu hhu hhu hhu"; VILLAGERS continue breath under:)

CHUDU:	CHRISTOPHER:	ARMIDA:
Faster—	Let me—	First—
Let me	Go—	Let me—
Jump!	Jump!	Jump!
Let me—	Ow—	In my way
'Round the—	Back—	Up the—
Hey!	Wait for me!	This is right,
This is left,	This is wrong!	I don't feel the bottoms of my—
Feet—	Over trees	Falling down,
Getting up	Keep on going,	Cannot stop.
The air is getting thin.	The clouds are rolling in.	The shadows burn my skin.
(Pause.)		
Just go— >	And run— >	And move— >
And stop.	Heart beat.	Beat-beat.
Beat-beat.	Beat-beat.	The sky is crying bittersweet
Sweet-sweet.	Sweet-sweet.	Sweet-sweet.

CHUDU:	CHRISTOPHER:	ARMIDA:
It's cold	*And hot*	*And cold*
And dark and	*Hot and*	*And and*
I.	*Want.*	*To.*
I.	*Don't.*	*Feel.*

(Breathing sounds stop. Thunderclap. Lightning.)

Beat-beat.	*Beat-beat.*	*Beat-beat.*
I am tired.	*I am so tired!*	*I am so so tired!*
Why can't just one person—	*One teeny person—*	*One teeny-tiny person*
See my pain . . .	*Feel my pain . . .*	*Know my pain . . .*
They'll never know.	*Never ever know.*	*Never ever never*
No!	*No!*	*No!*
Not in a million years . . .	*A billion years . . .*	*A zillion years . . .*
Ba-gillion—	*Ga-pillion—*	*Pa-jillion!*

(Each one suddenly discovers the truth:)

Oh—	*My—*	*God!*
I hate Chudu the Goat-Man!	*I hate Prince Christopher!*	*I hate Armida!*
I—	*I—*	*I—*

(They look at one another. Blank. Introduce themselves:)

My name's Chudu.	*My name's Prince Christopher.*	*My name's Armida.*

(Pause.)

Yes.	*Well.*	*Hm.*

(They look back out at the road. Up the mountain. The wind blows in their faces.)

So I'm—	*That's where—*	*It's not—*
Can I?	*Will I?*	*Should I?*

(The rhythmic breath on "hhu hhu hhu hhu" comes back in. The trio hits the road again, renewed purpose.)

Out of my way—	*I want to go—*	*Don't want to know you!*
You don't know	*What it's like*	*How it feels*
Nobody likes me—	*He doesn't love me—*	*She wants to kill me.*
I'll show them!	*I'll show him!*	*I'll show her!*
I'm soaked.	*It's cold.*	*The wind.*
Is mean.	*The wind—*	*The dark—*
The wind—	*The dark—*	*The moon—*
The fog—	*Mountains high,*	*Far away.*
Which way?	*Which way?*	*Which way?*

(Village rhythmic breathing out on big exhale.)

(All three simultaneously:)

CHUDU:	CHRISTOPHER:	ARMIDA:
Don't look Chudu in the eye!	*You're a man, Christopher!*	*Hopeless! Hopeless! Hopeless!*
Don't let Chudu turn you into a wart!	*It's time you started acting like one!*	*Armida! I have a present for you!*
I WANT TO DIE	I WANT TO DIE!	I WANT TO DIE!

(They look at one another as if for the first time.)

What did you say?	*What did you say?*	*What did you say?*

(Pause.)

	Tried to be what he said.	*She wanted me dead.*

(Beat.)

Have a piece of bread?

(CHUDU *holds out the bread.* ARMIDA *and* CHRISTOPHER *look at the bread. It looks like a mirage to them. They lick their lips. Suddenly* ARMIDA *and* CHRISTOPHER *reach for the bread at the same time. The three of them fight ferociously over the bread. It is a free-for-all, wild animals fighting to the death.)*

ARMIDA: Give it to me!

PRINCE CHRISTOPHER: I command you to give me the bread!

CHUDU: *(Mocking.)* I command you to give me the bread!

ARMIDA: *(To* CHUDU.) Give him the bread, dwarf!

PRINCE CHRISTOPHER: *(Defensive.)* Who are you calling a dwarf?

ARMIDA: *(About* CHUDU.) Him!

CHUDU: *(To* ARMIDA.) Why are you on his side?

ARMIDA: I'm not on his side! (ARMIDA *swipes the bread from* CHUDU *and begins to munch as* CHUDU *and* CHRISTOPHER *continue fighting:)*

PRINCE CHRISTOPHER: She called me a dwarf!

CHUDU: She didn't call you a dwarf! She called me a dwarf! I'm the dwarf! I suppose you want to take that away from me, too . . . What do you know about being a dwarf anyway? You're just a stupid Prince!

PRINCE CHRISTOPHER: Oh! And you think it's so easy being the stupid prince? *You* should try being the stupid prince—

CHUDU: I'd like to see you be poor Chudu the Goat-Man! For one day!

PRINCE CHRISTOPHER: Fine!

CHUDU: For one hour!

PRINCE CHRISTOPHER: Good!

CHUDU: For one minute!

PRINCE CHRISTOPHER: It would be a pleasure!

(Suddenly they look at ARMIDA. *She chews, swallows the last bite, licks her fingers. The bread is gone.)*

CHUDU: Where's my bread?

ARMIDA: I ate it.

PRINCE CHRISTOPHER: You can't just eat someone else's bread!

ARMIDA: I was hungry.

CHUDU: So was I!

PRINCE CHRISTOPHER: So am I!

CHUDU: I've never been this hungry in my life!

PRINCE CHRISTOPHER: I've never been this hungry in my life ever, ever, ever!
(The wind howls.)

ARMIDA: I'm cold.

CHUDU: I'm thirsty.

PRINCE CHRISTOPHER: I'm hungry.

ARMIDA: No one in the world has ever been this cold—

CHUDU: This thirsty—

PRINCE CHRISTOPHER: This hungry . . .

(They huddle together under ARMIDA's *blanket. They peer out at the road. Their eyes dart from side to side.)*

ARMIDA: Stop looking at me!

PRINCE CHRISTOPHER: Stop listening to me!

CHUDU: Stop breathing on me!

(They struggle to separate and the blanket rips into three small, pathetic pieces. They wrap themselves in their tiny pieces and split away from each other.)

ARMIDA: I'm all alone.

CHUDU: I'm all alone.

PRINCE CHRISTOPHER: I'm all alone.

CHUDU:	CHRISTOPHER:	ARMIDA:
Beat-beat.	*Beat-beat.*	*Beat-beat.*
I hear a bird!	*I hear nothing.*	*I see the moon!*

(Trying to whistle.)

I don't remember	*There's no music*	*Moon juice.*
how . . .	*now . . .*	*I remember*
		moon juice!

(All three begin to cry, loudly, violently, nonstop.)

I used to be	*I used to play music*	*I used to be strong*
hopeful . . .		*and smart . . .*
And sure of my—	*God!*	*What has happened*
To me!	*To me!*	*To me!*

(Beat. We hear the rhythmic breath begin again: hhu hhu hhu hhu . . .)

And go!	*And run!*	*And move!*
And pain!	*Shooting through my*	*Legs!*

CHUDU:	CHRISTOPHER:	ARMIDA:
What's that noise?	*Saw some eyes*	*They saw me*
Keep on the road	*It's hard to see*	*Hhu hhu hhu*

(All three simultaneously.)

Hhu hhu hhu hhu	*Hhu hhu hhu hhu*	*Hhu hhu hhu hhu*
They spit at—	*Me fight the Six-*	*And ran and ran*
	fingered Man???	*and ran!*
Are we there?	*Are we there?*	*Are we there?*
Have to get there—	*Want to be there—*	*I'll be free there.*
There it is!	*There it is!*	*There it is!*

(Sound of rhythmic breathing stops.)

I am there.	*I am there.*	*I am there.*
Beat-beat.	*Beat-beat.*	*Beat-beat.*
Beat-beat.	*Beat-beat.*	*Beat-beat.*

(The trio balances on the edge of the highest cliff, overlooking the valley. Standing there in the cold and wind, exhausted and raw from the journey, reality stings. They pull away from one another. They can barely speak. They are trying not to give up. Determined:)

CHUDU: So.

PRINCE CHRISTOPHER: So.

ARMIDA: So.

(They turn their backs on the cliff and slowly begin to walk away. It is as if they have changed their minds. Then suddenly from deep inside—they erupt!)

CHUDU/PRINCE CHRISTOPHER/ARMIDA: Noooooooooooooooo!

(Screaming at the top of their lungs, language no longer compares to the full expression of their primal screams. They fight to get back to the cliff, pushing one another out of the way, clawing, trying to be first to jump off the cliff.)

CHUDU: Let go of me!

PRINCE CHRISTOPHER: Get out of my way, dwarf!

ARMIDA: I was here first!

(In the mad scramble to be first to the cliff's edge, one of them accidentally kicks a rock into the cavern below. They precariously balance on the cliff's edge. Holding their breath, looking down, they watch the rock fall. Silence. It takes a long time but the rock finally hits bottom with a very theatrical BANG. They wince. Sobering. Beat.)

CHUDU: Oh. *(Beat.)*

PRINCE CHRISTOPHER: Oh. *(Beat.)*

ARMIDA: Oh.

(They peek over the edge, cautiously now.)

CHUDU:	CHRISTOPHER:	ARMIDA:
It's a long, long	*It's a long, long,*	*It's a long, long,*
way down.	*LONG way down.*	*long, LONG way down.*

(One by one, slowly, they back away from the edge of the cliff, suddenly fright-ened by how close they came to killing themselves. They are each talking to them-selves, talking themselves out of doing it.)

CHUDU:	CHRISTOPHER:	ARMIDA:
No need to rush . . .	*What if I change my mind?*	*In mid-air?*
What then?	*But when?*	*What now?*
And how?	*Where to?*	*With who?*

(They stop and eye one another suspiciously. It's the first time they've really LOOKED *at one another. Then the moment passes and they go back to themselves, looking over the edge of the cliff.)*

Down there.	*That's all.*	*That's it.*

(They each make their own version of the sound of falling/landing:)

(Sound of falling/ landing.)	*(Sound of falling/ landing.)*	*(Sound of falling/ landing.)*
Finished.	*Forever.*	*The end.*

(Beat. Softening.)

No more Chudu?	*No more Christopher?*	*No more Armida?*

(They back away from the edge of the cliff.)

I don't know.	*I don't know.*	*I don't know.*

(They turn their backs on the cliff and start to walk away. They are lost, disoriented—they have no idea where to go, what to do.)

SIX-FINGERED MAN: *(A voice from beneath the cliff.)* Hurry up and get it over with!!!

(Suddenly, a hand holding a human bone claws its way up over the cliff. An old man collapses on the cliff and nibbles on the bone. His eyes are dark, his head is hooded, his hands hidden in the long sleeves of his tattered robe.)

SIX-FINGERED MAN: Speedily a tale is spun, with much less speed a deed is done. I've never seen such indecisive idiots in my life. *(Ferocious, a wild man.)* I'm hungry! You came to—

CHUDU:	CHRISTOPHER:	ARMIDA:
Jump.	*Jump.*	*Jump.*

SIX-FINGERED MAN: Good! Good! Good! *(He stares at them, waiting.)* So why don't you—jump? Jump? Jump???

(The trio is quick to answer.)

CHUDU:	CHRISTOPHER:	ARMIDA:
Well—	*I—*	*Don't—*
No.	*No.*	*No.*

SIX-FINGERED MAN: Jumping off the cliff is the ultimate love affair. *(Relishing the invitation.)* Imagine the beating of the heart! *Bam-Bam-Bam!* The gasping for air! *Guh-Guh-Guh!* Hurtling down thousands of feet and landing on your head. Over in an *instant* but imagine that ONE instant! Or landing on your feet! That's a beautiful thing—*Smash! (Carried away with the images.)* In a split second your feet and legs shatter like glass. Your back breaks—*wang!* Your organs crash downward, upward, inward . . .

CHUDU:	CHRISTOPHER:	ARMIDA:
Downward?	*Upward?*	*Inward?*

(They back away. The SIX-FINGERED MAN *pursues them relentlessly.)*

SIX-FINGERED MAN: Perhaps you should consider drowning! *(Enthusiastic.)* The lungs wail for air and water starts ringing and thundering in the drowning man's ears!

CHUDU/PRINCE CHRISTOPHER/ARMIDA: *(Looking horrified.)* No.

SIX-FINGERED MAN: *(A brilliant idea.)* Poison!

CHUDU/PRINCE CHRISTOPHER/ARMIDA: No!

SIX-FINGERED MAN: Yes! The stomach knots! The spine twists and turns until it shapes itself into a pretzel. The poison travels through the bloodstream on a pirate's ship setting up tiny ports of suffering at each joint. *(The trio tries to get away but the* SIX-FINGERED MAN *won't let them. He clutches, grabs, claws.)* Or perhaps you'll go mad instead! *(With zeal.)* All of the voices crashing in your head like the waves at highest tide. Chopping your life into tiny dead pieces . . . silence that cries out for sunrise, for the starting line, for page one . . .

CHUDU/PRINCE CHRISTOPHER/ARMIDA: *(Overlapping.)* I don't want to die! *(This is the first time in a long time that they've been passionate about living. It registers.)*

SIX-FINGERED MAN: Come on, come on, come on! *(Loses all patience.)* I'm hungry!

CHUDU: *(Trying to find a crumb of bread in his pockets.)* I might have a crumb of bread in my—

SIX-FINGERED MAN: I don't eat bread! I eat misery and pain and loneliness! I even eat ugly little runts like you.

(CHUDU looks as though he might faint.)

ARMIDA: *(Defending him without thinking.)* He's not ugly!

CHUDU: *(Shocked by* ARMIDA's *gesture.)* Thank you.

PRINCE CHRISTOPHER: *(To* ARMIDA.*)* He's kind of ugly.

ARMIDA: *(To* CHRISTOPHER, *reverting to her fake, breathy self.)* Well he's not that ugly.

SIX-FINGERED MAN: *(To* ARMIDA.*)* And *you!* Stupid girl who flutters around— your head probably tastes like air! Rotting, stinking air!

CHUDU: *(Sticking up for* ARMIDA.*)* She's very smart.

PRINCE CHRISTOPHER: *(Re* CHUDU.*)* Smarter than him.

CHUDU: *(To* CHRISTOPHER.*)* Stronger than *you!*

SIX-FINGERED MAN: *(To* CHRISTOPHER.*)* I believe it. You sniveling little weakling. Is there a real man under all that armor?

PRINCE CHRISTOPHER: *(Insulted.)* Do you know who I am?

SIX-FINGERED MAN: *(Reckless, waving his hands around like a mad scientist.)* Do you know who I am???

PRINCE CHRISTOPHER: I am Prince Christopher!

SIX-FINGERED MAN: *(Lighting up.)* Ahhhhhh! Royal . . . blood!

PRINCE CHRISTOPHER: *(Defending himself, blurting out.)* I came to fight the Six-Fingered Man who caused the river to run dry!

SIX-FINGERED MAN: Well, Prince, this is your lucky day. You're looking for the notorious Six-Fingered Man. *(Dramatic pause as he stretches out his hands for them to see.)* Here he stands!

(The SIX-FINGERED MAN *draws a sword with lightning-quick motion. The trio gasps and takes a step back—closer to the ledge of Suicide Leap. He grabs at* CHUDU.*)*

PRINCE CHRISTOPHER: You can't do that!

ARMIDA: He's defenseless!

SIX-FINGERED MAN: *(Laughing.)* How thoughtless of him.

CHUDU: Wait! Please! I don't want to die!

SIX-FINGERED MAN: Too late, dwarf! It's dinnertime.

*(*ARMIDA *and* CHRISTOPHER *watch in horror as the* SIX-FINGERED MAN *prepares to quarter* CHUDU *with his sword.* CHUDU *is no match, doesn't stand a chance against the powers of the* SIX-FINGERED MAN.*)*

SIX-FINGERED MAN: *(Sings.)*
> Let's see . . . to start:
> I'll have the broken heart
> Sautéed in sadness
> And deep-fried in madness
> And then:

CHUDU: *(Calling out to* CHRISTOPHER *and* ARMIDA *who watch helplessly.)* Help me! Please! Don't touch Chudu, never look him in the eye! *(Crying.)* He's a dwarf, he's a freak . . .

SIX-FINGERED MAN: *(Sings.)*
> Now then:
> I'll take the greasy chin!
> A foot that is lonely,
> Two knees that are only a snack:
>
> How delicious is the back!
> Shoulders au gratin
> And teeth that are rotten—

PRINCE CHRISTOPHER: *(To* ARMIDA, *watching helplessly.)* We have to do something!

ARMIDA: *(Breathy, stuck, trying to find her old self.)* I—don't know—what—to do . . .

SIX-FINGERED MAN: *(Sings.)*
> The nose!
>
> Teeny-tiny toes
> Lunching on agony is
> Not what it used to be . . .
> The hips!

> *Tender little lips,*
> *Two eyes and one ear*
> *That are pickled in fear—*

(CHUDU *suddenly, finally, makes a whistling noise. It startles the* SIX-FINGERED MAN *for an instant. Without thinking,* CHRISTOPHER *makes a dash for the* SIX-FINGERED MAN. *Without looking, the* SIX-FINGERED MAN *decks* CHRISTOPHER. *Wearing the armor,* CHRISTOPHER *bounces on the ground, landing in a heap. The* SIX-FINGERED MAN *laughs. He turns back to* CHUDU.)

SIX-FINGERED MAN: Now. Where was I?

CHUDU: (*Without thinking, in a tiny, frightened voice he sings back the last line to the* SIX-FINGERED MAN.)
> *. . . Two eyes and one ear that are pickled in fear . . .*

SIX-FINGERED MAN: Oh, yes!
(*Sings.*)
> *Thanks for the meat:*
> *Let's eat!*

(ARMIDA *struggles to find some part of her old self—maybe her old arm, her knee—from deep inside. The* SIX-FINGERED MAN *is distracted by* ARMIDA. *Piece by piece, it's as if her body breaks through her lacy dress. She struggles to pull the shoes off her feet.*)

ARMIDA: No shoes! No shoes! I refuse to wear shoes! (*She pulls off the shoes and suddenly seems taller. Renewed and free,* ARMIDA *faces the* SIX-FINGERED MAN.)

SIX-FINGERED MAN: (*Laughing at* ARMIDA.) You think you're man enough to destroy the Six-Fingered Man?

ARMIDA: (*Holds up both shoes like weapons on her hands, referring to* CHUDU.) Let him go.

SIX-FINGERED MAN: Well. Filet of young girl. How delicious.

(CHUDU *scrambles away to where* CHRISTOPHER *lies in a heap of armor.* ARMIDA *and the* SIX-FINGERED MAN *begin to do battle. The* SIX-FINGERED MAN *has the initial advantage,* ARMIDA *seems without weapon.* CHUDU *yells warnings to* ARMIDA *as he tries to get* CHRISTOPHER *to wake up. Back and forth, each one of them almost getting the best of the other. Then,* ARMIDA *unzips her "Clarella dress" and steps out of it—swinging it around her head like a slingshot, taking the* SIX-FINGERED MAN *by surprise.* CHRISTOPHER *finally regains consciousness and sits up to see the* SIX-FINGERED MAN *driving* ARMIDA *back to the edge of the cliff.*)

CHUDU: (*Screaming to* CHRISTOPHER.) We have to do something! We have to help her! Don't you know how to do anything? (CHRISTOPHER *doesn't know what to do. He rips off the armor. He cuts some of* CHUDU's *beard.*) Ow! That's my beard!

(CHRISTOPHER *attaches the strands of beard to part of his abandoned armor and makes a very unusual violin. He uses his sword as a bow and begins to play his new "violin." The* SIX-FINGERED MAN *stops fighting. He looks at* CHRISTOPHER, *mystified, tender.*)

SIX-FINGERED MAN: (*Gentle, surprised.*) What are you doing? (*Disoriented.*) What's happening to me? (*Panics.*) What are you doing to me!?! (*He's feeling something inside, it scares him.*) Stop it! (*Backing away.*) I don't like this!

I'm a monster—I can't—I don't—feel—this—Stop it! (CHRISTOPHER *continues to play the violin. The* SIX-FINGERED MAN *struggles.*) Look around you! Behind you! Inside you! Monsters are never hard to come by . . . (*He staggers, weeping.*) Stop it! Stop it! Stop it . . . (*The* SIX-FINGERED MAN *weeps uncontrollably.*)

A VILLAGE STORYTELLER: The Six-Fingered Man hadn't cried for thousands of years . . .

(*The* SIX-FINGERED MAN *cries and cries, disintegrating into the water of his own tears.*)

ANOTHER STORYTELLER: But that day he cried so hard and so long that he disappeared into the water of his own tears.

(CHRISTOPHER *stops playing the violin. The three of them look down at the puddle of water that used to be the* SIX-FINGERED MAN.)

CHUDU: That's—

PRINCE CHRISTOPHER: Him.

ARMIDA: Was.

(*Suddenly they realize they're standing in water. Discovery. It is the sweetest gift.*)

CHUDU: Water?

PRINCE CHRISTOPHER: Water.

ARMIDA: Water!

(*They look out over the valley.*)

CHUDU: The river's filling up!

PRINCE CHRISTOPHER: The valley's turning green!

(*In the distance—in the valley below—we hear* VILLAGERS *selling new goods:* "Beeswax! Hot Pies! Corn Meal! Wild Flowers!")

ARMIDA: (*Looking up at the sky.*) The sun!

CHUDU: (*Amazed.*) We did it!

PRINCE CHRISTOPHER: We destroyed the Six-Fingered Man!

ARMIDA: We're alive!

(*They spontaneously embrace. Then they become self-conscious, pull away. They look at one another.*)

CHUDU: Thank you—

PRINCE CHRISTOPHER: Well, she—

ARMIDA: We—

CHUDU: All.

PRINCE CHRISTOPHER: Three. (*Beat.*)

CHUDU: Yes.

PRINCE CHRISTOPHER: Yes.

ARMIDA: Yes.

CHUDU: *(To* ARMIDA.*)* You're really strong.

*(*ARMIDA *nods. She's back.)*

PRINCE CHRISTOPHER: *(To* CHUDU.*)* You whistled again!

*(*CHUDU *smiles, whistles.)*

ARMIDA: *(To* CHRISTOPHER.*)* I never heard such beautiful music in all my life.

PRINCE CHRISTOPHER: *(Touched.)* Really?

ARMIDA: Well, it didn't make me cry a river. *(Admission.)* But I cried. *(They look out at the village in the valley below. Tentative:)* Do we ... have to—go—

(They stare out at the village, not sure they'll be able to face where they came from.)

CHUDU:	CHRISTOPHER:	ARMIDA:
Home.	*Home.*	*Home.*

PRINCE CHRISTOPHER: I'm scared.

CHUDU: I'll go with you. *(They nod.)* What if we get tired?

ARMIDA: I'll carry you. *(*ARMIDA *and* CHUDU *splash in the water as* CHRISTOPHER *begins to play the violin again.* ARMIDA *begins to move to the music.)* Oh, that music! *(To* CHUDU.*)* Let's dance!

CHUDU: *(Shocked.)* You're asking ME—to dance?

ARMIDA: *(Dancing.)* Yes or no. *(*CHUDU *hesitates.)* Come on!

CHUDU: *(Ashamed.)* I don't know how.

ARMIDA: First, you have to take off your shoes!

*(*CHUDU *takes off his shoes and throws them far away. We hear two loud splashes.* ARMIDA *and* CHUDU *awkwardly dance,* CHRISTOPHER *plays the violin.* PEOPLE *from the village follow the* KING *up the mountain.* CHRISTOPHER *stops playing his new violin.* CHUDU *and* ARMIDA *stop dancing. They face the* VILLAGERS *and the* KING.*)*

KING: Which one of you did this? Which one of you destroyed the Six-Fingered Man and restored water to our village?

(The trio look at one another. It's a difficult question to answer.)

CHUDU/ARMIDA/PRINCE CHRISTOPHER: Well . . .

CHUDU: She—

ARMIDA: He—

PRINCE CHRISTOPHER: We.

CHUDU: All—

ARMIDA: Three.

*(*CHRISTOPHER *takes* ARMIDA'*s hand, he takes* CHUDU'*s hand. The* VILLAGERS *are shocked.)*

PRINCE CHRISTOPHER: Us.

(The CHILD *emerges from the crowd, fills up her cup with water from the flowing river and holds it out—to* CHUDU. CHUDU *drinks from the cup and passes it to* ARMIDA *who drinks and passes it to* CHRISTOPHER *who drinks, and passes it to the* KING. *The* KING *drinks and passes it to a* VILLAGER *and it continues, as: The* KING *moves toward* CHRISTOPHER. CHRISTOPHER *assumes the worst. He looks down, away, shrinks.)*

KING: Prince Christopher—Battler of the Six-Fingered Man—Restorer of Water—Violin-playing . . . Son. And . . . whatever.

PRINCE CHRISTOPHER: Musician.

(The KING *takes off his crown and puts it on* CHRISTOPHER'S *head.)*

KING: Royal Musician. *(He embraces his surprised son and the* VILLAGERS *cheer.)*

PRINCE CHRISTOPHER: I hereby decree that *music* not only be allowed—but be *celebrated!* *(The crowd cheers again as* CHRISTOPHER *puts the crown on* ARMIDA'S *head.)* Armida! The Royal Blacksmith!

ARMIDA: Wherever your heart takes you, let your dreams awake you! And take off your shoes! *(The crowd throws their shoes up in the air. Everyone cheers.* ARMIDA *puts the crown on* CHUDU'S *head.)* From this day on, Chudu the Goat-Man becomes just plain "Chudu"—a good friend to many people.

*(*CHUDU *whistles and everyone whistles in imitation.)*

OLD VILLAGER: Wait a minute! Wait a minute! That's not exactly how I remember it happening—

THE OLDEST VILLAGER: Never mind the details. *(Simple.)* Sometimes—life follows art.

(The music and dancing starts again.)

VILLAGERS: *(Sing.)*
> Dance through the night, the moon shining bright
> A river runs free—but not without a fight
> Strong and wild!
> Tender and mild!
> The sun comes out
> The world goes 'round
> Today may be lost but tomorrow may be found

A VILLAGE STORYTELLER: The world rolled on and the Village in the Valley eventually disappeared.

ANOTHER STORYTELLER: The only thing that remains are its stories.

AND ANOTHER STORYTELLER: And the river.

AND ANOTHER STORYTELLER: It's the only salt-water river in the world . . .

(Among the VILLAGERS *we see someone who looks remarkably like the* SIX-FINGERED MAN. *He smiles and seems to fit right in.)*

SIX-FINGERED MAN: *(Sings.)*
> Monsters are never hard to come by . . .

VILLAGERS: *(Sing.)*
> The sun comes out
> The world goes 'round

Today may be lost but tomorrow may be found . . .
The sun comes out
The world goes 'round
Today may be lost but tomorrow may be found!

(The VILLAGERS *continue to chant the song softly as they disappear into darkness.)*

CURTAIN

THE WITCH OF BLACKBIRD POND

by
Y York

from the novel by
Elizabeth George Speare

THE WITCH OF BLACKBIRD POND

CAST OF CHARACTERS

Kit "Katherine" Tyler—female, seventeen: confident, intelligent, witty, kind, homely; makes mistakes because of cultural ignorance, not meanness or insensitivity

Nat Eaton—male, twenty: thoughtful, respectful, independent traveler, distrustful of the Puritan ways

Reverend Gideon Gish—male, forties: religious, formal, narrow, powerful within the town; resentful of those who do not agree/follow his ideals; cares for his family

Rebecca Gish—female, forties: desperate to please, do the right thing, follow the rules; loves her child; harshness comes from fear, not meanness

Prudence Gish—female, ten: on the way to becoming a beaten-down soul; responds with energy and curiosity when shown affection and interest

John Holcomb—male, nineteen: a divinity student; optimistic, open, boyish, innocent, religious

Matthew Wood—male, forties: proud, religious, cares for his family; a man of growing contradictions; his rationalism conflicts increasingly with his religion

Rachel Wood—female, forties: a deeply loving and generous woman, but fear and superstition inhibit those good instincts

Mercy Wood—female, nineteen: badly crippled by childhood disease, it's amazing that she lived; kind, generous, loving, expansive, imaginative

Judith Wood—female, seventeen: haughty, beautiful, narrow, confident until her plan begins to erode; deeply frightened of the unexplained and supernatural; actions against her cousin fueled by fear, not jealousy

William Ashby—male, twenty: wealthy, confident, conservative

Hannah Tupper—female, seventy: independent, strong, generous; believing that the worst has already befallen her, she has no fear

Miss Cat—female: a cranky, but kind feline, played with the help of a completely visible human puppeteer of either sex [Note: Miss Cat's English translations are not spoken]

Magistrate Talbot—male, forties: an officer of the church; absolutely convinced of the existence of witches and evil; confident and thorough.

Note to actors/directors: No English accents. No ending sentences or phrases with upward inflections unless a question mark appears as the punctuation.

SETTINGS

ACT ONE: Scene One: 1687, river on Connecticut shore
Scene Two: Wood House, outside and inside
Scene Three: Meeting House
Scene Four: Blackbird Pond
Scene Five: Wood House, outside and inside

ACT TWO: Scene One: Next morning. Blackbird Pond
Scene Two: Wood House
Scene Three: One week later. Wood House
Scene Four: Dusk. Blackbird Pond
Scene Five: Meeting House, outside
Scene Six: One week later. Meeting House, inside and outside

The action of the play is continuous. There are no blackouts between scenes.

SCENE ONE

(1687, A river on the Connecticut shore, a splash. A soaked KIT *drags* NAT *from the water. They are wet, cold and out of breath.* KIT *carries a pathetic carved wooden doll.)*

NAT: That was, that was—

KIT: I'm freezing. I'm numb to the bone.

NAT: The stupidest—

KIT: *(Agreeing.)* And the *meanest.*

NAT: What?!

KIT: What a cruel woman.

NAT: Who's a cruel woman?

KIT: Goody Gish. She's so mean to Prudence. Mean *and* stupid.

NAT: I'm talking about *you*! You're stupid.

KIT: I didn't know the water was this cold. How do people swim in this icy river?

NAT: They don't! . . . I can't believe it. *(Calling off.)* She's all right!

KIT: *I'm* all right? *(Calling off.)* He's all right!

NAT: I jumped in to save you.

KIT: Learn to swim before you start saving people.

NAT: People in Connecticut *don't* swim. This isn't *Barbados,* Miss.

KIT: Well, I didn't notice *you* rushing in to save the doll.

NAT: . . . This fuss is over a doll?!

KIT: Prudence's only toy!

NAT: I warn you, Kit, you mustn't swim here for *any* reason.

KIT: . . . So you do know my name.

NAT: Of course I know your name. We were at sea eight weeks.

KIT: You never used it. You didn't once say "Good morning, Miss Kit. Howdedo, Kit?"

NAT: You never said my name, either.

KIT: How could I say *your* name before you said *my* name?

NAT: You didn't need my company. You spent every daylight hour with John Holcomb.

(Enter PRUDENCE *who runs to* KIT.*)*

PRUDENCE: Kit! Oh Kit, you saved her, you saved her.

KIT: Precious little thing. Hold tight, never let her go.

(Enter GIDEON, REBECCA, JOHN.*)*

REBECCA: Come away, Prudence.

*(*GIDEON, REBECCA, PRUDENCE *stand apart.* JOHN *gives his coat to* KIT.*)*

REBECCA: Gideon, did you see, did you see her float?

GIDEON: I saw. Now quiet, please, Rebecca.

JOHN: Put this on, Kit.

KIT: Thank you, John.

REBECCA: She floated as if—

GIDEON: I saw, gentle wife. Please. Is that how you take charge of a longboat, Nat, by abandoning it?

NAT: *(Firm, but respectful.)* You were in no danger, Reverend. The oarsmen secured the boat.

GIDEON: What do you suppose *the captain* will say about this?

NAT: My father will agree with me, Sir.

PRUDENCE: Can I have my doll, Ma?

REBECCA: You'll have your doll when you can take care of it.

KIT: It wasn't her fault, Goody Gish. It was almost herself went in the water and not the doll.

PRUDENCE: Yes, Ma. It was almost myself—

REBECCA: Prudence, be still.

GIDEON: Where's Matthew Wood, girl?

NAT: I signaled before dawn. He should be here.

GIDEON: He's not at the landing.

KIT: Well, clearly, Reverend, my uncle has been delayed.

GIDEON: Your uncle will not tolerate insolence.

KIT: Tell me the way, and I'll save him the trip.

JOHN: But you have so many trunks.

KIT: I'm sure they'll be safe among all these Puritans.

GIDEON: You'll not win friends by mocking us.

KIT: I didn't mean—

GIDEON: That's enough now. Rebecca, I'm going to accompany Miss Tyler to her uncle. John will see you and Prudence home safely.

JOHN: *(Worried.)* Kit. You *will* come to meeting today.

KIT: I don't go to church. Grandfather said God is everywhere.

GIDEON: It would be good if people see you pray.

KIT: Why should anyone need to see me pray?

GIDEON: Because they've seen you float.

Scene Two

(The Wood house, outside. MATTHEW, MERCY, *who limps,* JUDITH, NAT, GIDEON, KIT, *her trunks.)*

MATTHEW: I have a niece named Katherine Tyler, but I've never met her, and I'm certainly not expecting her.

NAT: She calls herself Kit.

GIDEON: Not expecting her?

MATTHEW: Not at all.

GIDEON: Didn't you send word that you were coming?

(They look at KIT.*)*

KIT: It takes *months* for a reply.

GIDEON: You take a lot on faith, Miss.

KIT: There was no time. I had to leave Barbados.

GIDEON: Why? Why did you have to leave Barbados?

KIT: I was desperate. I—

MATTHEW: Enough, now. Katherine, that's *enough*. Judith, get your mother.

*(*JUDITH *exits.* MATTHEW *changes the subject.*)*

MATTHEW: Thank you, Gideon. I'm sorry your return has been spoiled by my niece.

GIDEON: No need to apologize, Man.

MATTHEW: We're anxious to meet your new pupil.

GIDEON: He's an enthusiastic student.

KIT: *(Handing him the coat.)* Thank John for the loan of his coat, Reverend.

GIDEON: I shall. You will be at meeting today, Kit.

MATTHEW: She'll be there.

GIDEON: Your niece is headstrong, Matthew. Ask her how she got so wet.

NAT: Stay dry, Kit.

GIDEON: You and your parents are welcome at meeting, too, Nat.

NAT: We know, Reverend. Goodbye Goodman Wood, Mercy Wood.

MATTHEW: Don't forget your trunks.

GIDEON: The trunks belong to her.

*(*NAT, GIDEON *exit.*)*

MATTHEW: Are you traveling with everything you own?

KIT: I am.

MATTHEW: Take what you need inside. The rest we'll store in the barn.

KIT: My trunks will be in a barn?

MATTHEW: If there's room.

KIT: What about my books?

MATTHEW: We *have* a Bible. . . . How *did you* get so wet?

MERCY: Did you fall in the river, Cousin Kit?

KIT: I didn't—I— . . . I was knocked about. Somebody fell into me, and—as you see—soaked to the skin.

MATTHEW: Put on something more seemly when you change.

KIT: Seemly, Uncle?

MATTHEW: You can't go to meeting in prideful dress.

(Enter JUDITH *and* RACHEL.*)*

RACHEL: Judith is full of mystery; what is it, Matthew? *(Sees* KIT, *stunned.)* Margaret, God in heaven, Margaret!

KIT: Aunt Rachel—

RACHEL: It cannot be . . .

MATTHEW: Rachel, what is it?

RACHEL: She's dead, I know she is—

KIT: Aunt Rachel, I'm not Margaret, I'm her daughter. (*Pause.*) I'm your niece, Kit.

RACHEL: Kit . . . Margaret's little girl . . . You're the image of your mother.

JUDITH: I'm sorry, Ma. I should have said.

RACHEL: Look at you. Judith, Mercy, this is exactly how my sister looked the last time we saw each other.

JUDITH: Did she dress like that, Ma?

RACHEL: Both of us, in beautiful satin gowns. But not wet ones. What happened, Kit?

MERCY: She fell in the river, Ma, off the longboat.

RACHEL: You might have been killed.

KIT: Oh, no . . . I was never in danger. None at all. Really.

RACHEL: You must write and tell your grandfather you're safe.

KIT: Grandfather's dead, Aunt Rachel.

RACHEL: When . . . ?

KIT: He died from smallpox four months ago.

RACHEL: You poor girl. You've seen so much death.

MATTHEW: Who's looking after your farm?

KIT: It's gone. It was sold to pay our debts.

MATTHEW: Is that why you were "desperate" to leave Barbados?

KIT: Yes, and . . . yes.

MATTHEW: Good. I feared something more sordid. What are your plans, Katherine?

RACHEL: She'll live here. Safe under God's watch now.

KIT: I was afraid you wouldn't let me stay.

RACHEL: Nonsense. You belong with us. Isn't that right, Matthew?

MATTHEW: (*Brief pause.*) All right now. There's work to be done before meeting. Remember what I said about your dress, Katherine.

KIT: Please, Uncle. Call me Kit.

MATTHEW: As you wish. (*Kisses* MERCY *on forehead.*) Work well today, Mercy.

KIT: Uncle . . . I have no plain clothes.

RACHEL: Do the best you can, Kit.

MATTHEW: (*Kisses her forehead.*) Don't be late for meeting, Judith.

JUDITH: Yes, Father.

KIT: Thank you, Uncle, for letting me stay.

(MATTHEW *exits, carrying off one of the heavy trunks.*)

RACHEL: I have to get back to Goody Hamilton.

JUDITH: How is she?

RACHEL: Too sick to look after the baby. See you make your cousin welcome. (RACHEL *exits.*)

MERCY: Come inside, Kit.

KIT: Is there someone can carry a trunk?

MERCY: I'll help you.

JUDITH: No! I'll do it, Mercy.

(JUDITH *and* KIT *carry a trunk inside; they talk as they go.*)

JUDITH: We'll have to find a place for you to sleep.

MERCY: She'll sleep with me. My bed's plenty big enough.

JUDITH: But what if I get cold?

MERCY: (*Getting her spinning wheel.*) Then you'll sneak in like you always do. Put the trunk there. We'll carry it up before dinner, Kit.

KIT: Up where?

MERCY: Up there, where we sleep.

KIT: There are rooms up there?

JUDITH: Two rooms.

KIT: They can't be very big rooms.

JUDITH: They are completely adequate rooms.

KIT: I'm sorry, I—I'm sorry.

MERCY: . . . Tell us about Barbados, Cousin.

(JUDITH *shreds wool on her carding board.*)

JUDITH: Mercy, no idle chatter.

MERCY: Only when Father's here.

JUDITH: You'll give Cousin Kit the wrong impression of us.

MERCY: Judy, sweet Judy, this *isn't* idle chatter. It's Kit's *history,* and Father says history's important.

JUDITH: All right. Tell us your history, cousin.

KIT: (*As she changes out of her wet dress.*) My history. Well, Mother said Aunt Rachel was the most beautiful girl in their town; she could have married anybody, but she fell in love with the Puritan firebrand Matthew Wood and followed him across the ocean to Connecticut.

JUDITH: Father a firebrand!

MERCY: And *your* mother falls in love with the handsome boy from Barbados and goes to live on his magnificent farm.

JUDITH: Yes. The beautiful sister ends up poor in Connecticut, while the ugly sister ends up rich in Barbados—

MERCY: Judith!

JUDITH: 'm sorry, cousin.

KIT: . . . Mother *wasn't* beautiful, but she had friends and filled our house with laughter. I'm like that a little—to make up for my own plain face.

MERCY: (*Tries to put the conversation on safe ground.*) Was Nat your great admirer during the journey?

KIT: Nat never even said my name until today. I didn't think he knew it.

MERCY: (*Spinning a tale.*) But today, when he realized you were gone from his ship, he said your name.

KIT: Not exactly.

MERCY: Admiring you from afar until the last possible moment.

JUDITH: Mercy can make a fanciful adventure from the most dreary history.

MERCY: Kit sails the Atlantic with Nat secretly watching her every move from the mast. The sea breeze giving her cheeks a ruddy healthy glow.

KIT: (*Laughs.*) I didn't notice a ruddy glow, but I did love the sea.

MERCY: (*Grand invention.*) Cousin Kit ties herself to the mast so she can watch the captain's son as he guides the ship safely through the storm.

KIT: It wasn't romantic in the least, certainly not between me and Nat. Or me and John Holcomb.

MERCY: Is that the minister's new pupil?

KIT: Yes. John and the Reverend's family boarded *The Dolphin* two weeks ago in Saybrook.

MERCY: John the minister boy and Nat the captain's son come to blows, dueling for the affection of the young maiden Kit.

KIT: Mercy, you sound like a play I have. (*Looking in her trunk.*) Do you know it?

MERCY: I don't know a play.

KIT: (*Hands her book.*) You speak just like this wonderful play.

JUDITH: Mercy, put it down.

KIT: No, she must read it; it's about two very young people who fall in love and *die.*

JUDITH: Mercy, you *can't*—It's simply not allowed, Cousin.

KIT: I'm sorry. I only thought of it because Mercy spoke of dueling.

(*Brief pause.*)

MERCY: (*Quietly.*) Who do you want to win the duel?

KIT: Boys don't duel over me; boys don't even notice me— . . . except . . .

MERCY: (*Concerned.*) What is it, Kit?

KIT: I wasn't going to speak of it—there was somebody in Barbados—a man.

MERCY: Oh dear.

KIT: Nothing bad, nothing *sordid.* A wealthy friend of Grandfather's. He wanted to marry me and pay all the debts, but I couldn't do it. He was *forty.*

JUDITH: Is this why you were desperate to leave Barbados?

KIT: I was afraid I'd have to marry him if I stayed.

(JUDITH *finds a beautiful dress in the trunk.*)

JUDITH: That's not what you said to Father.

MERCY: It's not possible to talk to Father about boys.

KIT: That's what I thought.

MERCY: Kit flees the embrace of the ancient and shriveled suitor to find a young, true love in Connecticut.

JUDITH: *(With dress, happy.)* Look at me, Mercy.

MERCY: Oh! Put it on, the color makes you sparkle!

JUDITH: Can I try it? Just over my dress.

KIT: Of course. . . . Mercy, you spin so easily.

(JUDITH *pulls the dress on.)*

MERCY: I've always been the spinner in our family.

JUDITH: Do you spin, Kit?

KIT: Goodness, no.

JUDITH: Weave?

KIT: I don't.

JUDITH: Do you cook?

KIT: I hate a hot kettle.

MERCY: What do you do all day?

KIT: I read. I swim. I am me. I am Kit.

JUDITH: How do I look, Mercy?

MERCY: The most beautiful thing I've ever seen.

JUDITH: I wish I could wear it to meeting so William could see.

MERCY: He would be filled with rapture at the sight.

KIT: Wear it. I don't mind.

JUDITH: Father will not allow it.

MERCY: If we change the neckline, he might.

JUDITH: Oh, Mercy, can you change it? Now, before meeting?!

MERCY: I can try.

KIT: Wait. I meant as a loan. To borrow. Not to cut it.

(Pause.)

MERCY: Of course.

KIT: Maybe Uncle will let you wear it like it is.

JUDITH: He won't. . . . Never mind. It was wrong of me to try it on. It was wrong to want to have it.

MERCY: Judy, sweet Judy. William doesn't need to see you in finery. He is driven to distraction by the mere sight of you.

JUDITH: Then why doesn't he ask Father's permission to court me?

MERCY: He takes you on walks.

JUDITH: Those are unofficial walks, until he gets permission.

MERCY: He will, and then you will marry and live on Blackbird Pond in a fine, fine house.

JUDITH: William doesn't need our land. He already has too much.

KIT: Grandfather said a man *can't* have too much land.

MERCY: No, it goes to waste.

JUDITH: They have slaves to work the extra land.

KIT: We didn't. Grandfather only kept bonded servants.

JUDITH: It's the same.

KIT: It's not. Slavery is forever. A bonded servant is free at the end of the term.

JUDITH: Fourteen years. They die before they're free.

KIT: They don't if the master is kind. My Serena, my bondwoman, I loved her like a sister.

MERCY: Did you bring her with you?

KIT: No, I had to sell her to the governor for passage money.

MERCY: Will *he* be kind?

KIT: I don't know—Of course! I wouldn't have sold her otherwise.

JUDITH: You loved her like a sister and you sold her for passage money?

KIT: It broke my heart.

JUDITH: Father says bonding is immoral.

MERCY: He and Reverend Gish had a big . . . well, they . . . disagreed about it.

JUDITH: Loudly.

MERCY: . . . Lay your dress by the fire, Kit.

JUDITH: Why didn't you sell your fine dresses for passage money?

KIT: I . . . didn't think to.

JUDITH: You dragged your trunks across an ocean for no reason.

KIT: My trunks aren't filled only with dresses. I have paper, books.

JUDITH: Reading is for meeting, and then only the Bible.

KIT: How do you fill your days if you don't read plays or poetry?

JUDITH: We pray. And we work. And then it's time to go to bed.

(MERCY *spins,* JUDITH *cards, brief pause.*)

KIT: Let me try the wheel, Mercy.

MERCY: You won't like it.

JUDITH: No, Mercy. She should learn how.

(KIT *fumbles, the wheel is heavy.*)

MERCY: Your foot pumps the wheel, and your fingers guide the wool into thread.

(KIT *turns the wheel.*)

KIT: Oh! My fingers.

MERCY: Oh! no. (MERCY *binds* KIT's *fingers in a cloth.*) Here, cousin. Hold it tight.

JUDITH: Perhaps you'd like to try this.

KIT: What is it?

JUDITH: (*Showing carding board.*) Wool comes tangled from the lamb. I have to straighten it before Mercy can spin it into thread. First carding, then spinning, then weaving cloth, all to make a new seemly garment for you.

KIT: I'll learn to do it myself. Nobody has to do it for me.

MERCY: Don't worry. Nobody learns in one sitting, Kit. . . . It's time to go, Judith.

JUDITH: Come on, cousin, or we'll be late. We've four miles to cover.

KIT: Mercy. Are you coming?

JUDITH: She can't make the walk. Mercy stays home and spins.

KIT: Spins thread . . . and beautiful stories.

SCENE THREE

(The meeting house, outside are standing stocks; GIDEON, REBECCA, PRUDENCE. *Music over as the* REVEREND *introduces* JOHN *to* WILLIAM, MATTHEW, RACHEL, *then the arriving* JUDITH. REBECCA *shuns* KIT, *and pulls* PRUDENCE *away. Male and female separated. Everyone faces the* REVEREND.*)*

GIDEON: Today we will express our gratitude for our safe journey and the safe delivery of our new pupil, John Holcomb. Turn to page. . . .

*(*GIDEON's *mouth continues to move, he continues to be animated, but no sound comes out for several beats.* KIT *shifts in her seat.* WILLIAM *stares at her.)*

GIDEON: . . . and our gratitude for our prosperity, peace, and the good health of our parishioners. Amen.

ALL: Amen.

*(*KIT *starts to rise.* RACHEL *pulls her down.)*

GIDEON: In the next hour, we will focus on the outsider who comes from a far away land.

*(*GIDEON's *mouth continues to move, but no sound comes out.* KIT *squirms in her seat.)*

GIDEON: . . . not only important to avoid evil, but the appearance of evil as well . . . For the next half of our meeting—

*(*GIDEON's *mouth continues to move, but no sound comes out.* KIT *whispers something to* RACHEL *and goes outside.* KIT *rubs her numb behind.* NAT *enters. He carries a miniature portrait on a ribbon.)*

NAT: *(Amused.)* Hello, Kit.

KIT: *(Startled.)* Nat!

NAT: Is something wrong with your—your—

KIT: Nothing's wrong with my anything. Why isn't there a cushion or some small pillow? Look at this dreary place. Why don't they paint it some happy *color*?

NAT: They think color is frivolous. It distracts from prayer.

KIT: Are *you* here for prayer?

NAT: No.

KIT: Then shouldn't you be sailing to some place or other in the world?

NAT: We should be and will be. You dropped your picture in the longboat. *(Hands it to her.)*

KIT: I forgot, I completely forgot. I threw it off before I dove in the water. It's for my Aunt Rachel.

NAT: I almost kept it to remind me of our swim.

KIT: . . . It isn't me. You thought it was me?

NAT: It looks like you.

KIT: It's my mother. You thought I hugged and talked to my own face?

NAT: Why not? It's a pleasant enough face.

KIT: Then why didn't you keep it?

NAT: What you did was, well, it was stupid, but it was also brave. You shouldn't lose the picture for being brave.

KIT: . . . Thank you. Was your father angry that you swam?

NAT: No, it was as I said, and my mother was below deck, so she didn't see . . . I better go. We sail upriver as soon as there's wind.

KIT: Wait. Um—(*To keep him there.*) What's this thing? Some silly kind of hitching post?

NAT: It's the stocks. It's to shame you if you disobey or misbehave.

KIT: How does it do that?

NAT: Your head goes here, your hands go here, closed and locked. After a day or two, the devil himself will repent.

KIT: A day or two? You can't mean it.

NAT: This is tame compared to what they do with a hot branding iron.

KIT: (*Thinks it's a joke.*) What would they do with a—

GIDEON: Amen.

ALL: Amen.

(*The crowd stands, shake the* REVEREND's *hand.*)

NAT: I have to go. . . . Be careful, Kit.

(NAT *exits.* JOHN *comes outside.*)

JOHN: Kit, what were you thinking of, to leave like that?

KIT: My behind went numb.

JOHN: Don't say behind.

KIT: Everybody in Connecticut is determined to correct my behavior.

JOHN: You can't say or do everything that comes to mind. It doesn't look right.

KIT: They saw me pray; isn't that sufficient?

JOHN: You must pray, you must mean it when you pray.

KIT: John, you're just a boy. Don't act so stuffy . . . Look. Nat brought me the portrait of my mother.

JOHN: He should have come inside to hear the reverend.

KIT: Yes, he needs some wind.

JOHN: Really, Kit, that won't do.

KIT: But we've been serious for hours. When do we laugh again?

JOHN: You may laugh, but you must also pray and work.

KIT: John, you really do sound like some stuffy old person.

JOHN: I'm trying to sound old. Reverend Gish says I should think of myself as grown. (*Beat, shy.*) He says I should marry.

KIT: *(Disbelief.)* Really?

JOHN: I should marry so that I am not . . . distracted.

KIT: John! My cousin Mercy.

JOHN: *(Annoyed.)* Oh, Kit!

KIT: No, it's perfect. I'm sure of it. Her mind is a canvas and she paints the most beautiful pictures.

(WILLIAM *approaches.* KIT *pulls* JOHN *away.*)

KIT: That boy won't stop staring at me.

JOHN: It's an admiring stare.

KIT: I don't want it.

(JUDITH *joins them.*)

JUDITH: *(To* JOHN.*)* Hello. I'm Judith Wood, Kit's cousin.

JOHN: It's good to have you at meeting, Judith. John Holcomb.

(They shake hands. The others approach.)

WILLIAM: Judith, introduce me.

JUDITH: William Ashby, this is my cousin, Katherine Tyler.

WILLIAM: How do you do, Miss Katherine?

KIT: It's *Kit*. And I'm fine. *(Runs to* RACHEL.*)* Aunt Rachel. Look, this is for you; it's Mother.

RACHEL: Thank you. *(Looking.)* You are so like her.

GIDEON: Come, John. You have reading to do before dark.

JOHN: It was my pleasure. To meet you all.

RACHEL: Reverend, bring your pupil to dinner, if he likes.

PRUDENCE: Me, too?

REBECCA: Don't speak out, Prudence.

PRUDENCE: Sorry, Ma.

RACHEL: We'll be pleased to see you and Prudence, too, Rebecca.

GIDEON: Thank you, Rachel. Goodbye.

(JOHN, GIDEON, REBECCA, PRUDENCE *exit.* PRUDENCE *sneaks a wave to* KIT.*)*

WILLIAM: Goodman Wood.

MATTHEW: Yes, William.

WILLIAM: I would like to ask. If I might be so bold. To call on your household.

JUDITH: *(Gasps in anticipation.)*

WILLIAM: To greet your niece, Kit Tyler.

JUDITH: *(Blurts.)* But—

RACHEL: *(Gently.)* Judith. Be still.

JUDITH: But Ma—

RACHEL: *(Gently.)* Still.

MATTHEW: You may visit if Kit welcomes your company. Come along, Rachel. *(Gently.)* Judith, come with us.

JUDITH: Yes, Father.

MATTHEW: Kit, you may stay for a moment.

KIT: Don't leave me, Judith, please stay.

JUDITH: *(Trying to save face.)* I will stay if you wish.

MATTHEW: Are you sure, Child?

JUDITH: Certainly Father, if cousin needs me, I shall stay.

MATTHEW: *(Kisses* JUDITH *on forehead.)* All right, Judith.

(MATTHEW *and* RACHEL *exit.*)

WILLIAM: Kit, is it?

KIT: Kit, yes, I prefer Kit to Katherine.

WILLIAM: May I call on you, Kit?

KIT: *(Confused and mortified.)* I don't know. I suppose.

WILLIAM: Well, that's all then, goodbye. Goodbye Judith. *(Exits.)*

KIT: Why did he notice me? Boys never notice me.

JUDITH: It's your dress. We never see a nice dress like that in Connecticut.

KIT: He likes me for my dress?

JUDITH: William has . . . many good qualities to recommend him.

KIT: William. William?! Is this *your* William?

JUDITH: He's his own William. He seems to like you very much. Why not? William's family owns servants, as did yours. His family has great influence and wealth. I'm sure with so much in common you'll be very happy together.

KIT: I just met him!

JUDITH: You needn't worry about learning to spin or sew or cook. When you marry William, your life of leisure will return. You will be able to be read, to be *you,* to be *Kit.*

KIT: I didn't make him notice me.

JUDITH: Well, he noticed you, nonetheless. Tell me about your handsome friend John.

KIT: John isn't handsome!

JUDITH: Well, I think he is! I think . . . I think this John will make a good husband for me.

KIT: . . . You want John to marry you?

JUDITH: *(Growing anger.)* Why not? I'm a pious girl. I'll be a good wife for a minister.

KIT: I can't imagine John as your husband.

JUDITH: So now you tell us who we shall marry?

KIT: No, I didn't mean to. I just don't think so.

JUDITH: First take our bed, then take our food, take up our very space with your useless trunks—

KIT: I don't take anything.

JUDITH: Where will you sleep?

KIT: I—I'll sleep on the floor.

JUDITH: Yes? And where will your food come from?

KIT: I don't know.

JUDITH: Then let me tell you. It will come from our plates. If we give you a blanket, there's one less for us. You will take plenty, Kit, and what will you give in return? You who can't spin or weave, you who hates a hot kettle.

KIT: I didn't mean any harm.

JUDITH: No, you were just being Kit.

KIT: (Hurt.) I have no home, I have nothing.

JUDITH: And you have nothing to give. Is it any wonder Father didn't welcome you?

KIT: I—

(KIT runs off.)

SCENE FOUR

(Blackbird Pond, HANNAH and her CAT. HANNAH's forehead is branded; she carries a basket, gathers greens. CAT only meows; translations in parentheses are subtext only.)

CAT: Meow. (I'm tired!)

HANNAH: I'm tired, too, thee selfish old feline. Let me gather my dinner.

CAT: Meow. (I brought you a mouse.)

HANNAH: Yesss, thee did offer to share, but truth be told, Miss Cat, I can't stomach a dinner of fresh field mouse.

(KIT enters, sits, sobs. MISS CAT approaches carefully.)

CAT: Meow! (Stops crying.)

KIT: . . . Come here you pretty. Pretty round thing.

CAT: Meow. (I am not round!)

(The widow approaches. Her hood hides her brand.)

HANNAH: She likes to hear that she is pretty—

KIT: (Gasps.)

HANNAH: —but not that she is round.

KIT: (Stands.) I'm sorry. I didn't know anyone was here.

HANNAH: I live here.

KIT: I'm sorry. I'll go.

HANNAH: There is no need to go.

KIT: I didn't mean any harm. I'm sorry.

HANNAH: Stop apologizing for a moment and tell me thy name, friend.

KIT: I'm sorry. I mean— . . . Kit. My name is Kit. . . . You don't talk like the other Puritans I've met.

HANNAH: I'm not a Puritan.

KIT: (Relieved.) You're not?! Kit Tyler. My whole name is Kit Tyler. How do you do?

HANNAH: I am pleased to meet thee Kit Tyler. I am Hannah Tupper.

KIT: *(Looking around.)* What is this *beautiful place*?

HANNAH: It's called Blackbird Pond, though the birds that come here be of many colors.

KIT: My cousins spoke of Blackbird Pond, but they didn't say somebody lives on it.

HANNAH: I live just there.

CAT: Meow! (What about me?)

HANNAH: I mean, *we* live just there.

KIT: *(Looks, disbelieving.)* That's a house?

HANNAH: Just big enough for me and my cat. Unless *thee* needs shelter, friend?

KIT: I—? No. *(Touched.)* I don't, but thank you. You live all alone way out here?

HANNAH: We don't live alone. We live together.

KIT: The cat won't be any help if you fall or get sick.

HANNAH: If there is no one to help me, there is also no one to harm me.

KIT: Who would harm you? The Puritans are harmless, silly people.

HANNAH: . . . Where does thee come from, Kit?

KIT: Barbados.

HANNAH: I have a friend tells me of Barbados. A very different place from Connecticut. *(Gathers greens; bending is difficult.)*

KIT: Here, I'll do that.

(KIT takes the basket and gathers greens. HANNAH sits apart, and in so doing reveals her brand.)

KIT: Barbados is very different. As different as night and day. But I thought people would be the same everywhere. I hoped my aunt and uncle would love me; I wanted my cousins to be like sisters, the three of us reading to each other from books and plays. Like Serena. They all think I'm insolent and thoughtless. You should have seen the fuss when I dove into the river.

HANNAH: Thee dove—?

KIT: Yes, I dove! I dive, and I swim and I laugh, just like I always did. And it made people love me, Grandfather and Serena loved me, and I loved them, but maybe I didn't love them enough, but that shouldn't mean I have to spend the rest of my life with these *silly Puritans. (Takes the basket to HANNAH.)*

HANNAH: Thee wearies me with thy muddled speech, girl.

KIT: *(Gasps.)* Your face—

HANNAH: It doesn't hurt. It's from long ago.

KIT: Is it—is that a brand?

(THE WIDOW is without bitterness. MISS CAT climbs in her lap.)

HANNAH: Yes.

KIT: Who—who did it?

HANNAH: "Harmless, silly Puritans" did it.

KIT: . . . Why?

HANNAH: I will not worship at their meetings. The brand is to warn others that I don't believe as they.

KIT: Reverend Gish did that?

HANNAH: No. It was in Massachusetts. Tom and me ran there from England. We thought it would be safe, but the Puritans hated us as much as the English did.

KIT: Why do the Puritans hate *you*?

HANNAH: I'm a Quaker. I can't worship at a Puritan meeting. It would be a lie.

KIT: I would lie a thousand times to save myself that pain.

HANNAH: After a time, a lie hurts more than a brand.

KIT: It's *not* a lie; God is everywhere. If they come again, go into their meeting house and look for God inside.

HANNAH: That is thy advice?

KIT: Yes. Is this Tom?

CAT: Meow! (No!)

HANNAH: No. This is Miss Cat. Tom was my husband. He died in Massachusetts proving he was no witch.

KIT: How did he prove *that*?

HANNAH: They tossed him on the water. They say the guilty ones float.

KIT: The guilty ones—? . . . You mean, they think I'm a witch?

HANNAH: If thee floated, they think it.

KIT: I'll not believe it.

HANNAH: My poor Tom sank like a stone. When that proved him innocent of witchery, they were content to brand me and send me away.

CAT: Meow. *(You met me.)*

HANNAH: Yes, I was fortunate to *meet thee*, Miss Cat.

KIT: You understand the cat?

HANNAH: I like to think I do.

CAT: Meow. *(I do, too.)*

HANNAH: And she likes to think she understands me.

KIT: Here. What are you going to do with all these weeds?

HANNAH: Eat them.

KIT: No!

HANNAH: What has thee done to thy fingers, Kit?

KIT: I cut them spinning.

HANNAH: See that bush just there. Pluck a few of the small new leaves. We'll go inside and I'll show thee the trick to protect thy soft fingers from the thread.

SCENE FIVE

(Wood house, MERCY *and* RACHEL *outside;* JUDITH *inside.)*

MERCY: Kit's a bold, smart girl. If she's lost, she'll find her way soon enough.

RACHEL: She knows the tropics. She knows nothing of the forest. Did Judith say something to make Kit run away? . . . I know Judith is disappointed about William.

MERCY: Oh, Ma, Judith's a beauty. She'll get another boy.

(Enter KIT *running.)*

MERCY: See! I told you she was fine; you are fine, aren't you, Kit?

KIT: I'm sorry. It got dark so early.

MERCY: You and Judith didn't fight. You just decided to take a walk, didn't you?

KIT: *(Brief pause, then getting it.)* Yes, I went walking, and I saw a beautiful place. A beautiful meadow.

MERCY: *(To distract.)* I mended something for you, Kit.

RACHEL: Mercy, go in the house.

MERCY: Yes, Ma.

*(*MERCY *goes in,* RACHEL *is both relieved and angry.)*

KIT: Aunt Rachel, I—

RACHEL: Don't make excuses, Kit. You can't wander through the dark. There are terrible dangers here.

KIT: I didn't mean for you to worry.

RACHEL: Good intentions will be no comfort to me if you disappear into the forest. Come here. *(Hugs her.)* I just found you; I don't want to lose you. Go inside now. I'm going to the barn. Your uncle never knows what to say to the Gishes.

KIT: The Gishes are in the barn?

RACHEL: Yes. Go help your cousins with dinner.

*(*RACHEL *exits,* PRUDENCE *comes out from hiding and runs to* KIT.*)*

PRUDENCE: Psst, Kit!

KIT: Sweet thing.

PRUDENCE: Kit, I miss you so. We'll never get to talk like we did when Ma and Pa were seasick.

KIT: I miss you, too.

PRUDENCE: I have to sneak back before they notice. Look at this. *(Hands her a page.)* Can you make it out?

KIT: Is this your *name*, Prudence?

PRUDENCE: Yes! Written by me. That's my name, just as you showed me.

KIT: *(Smiles.)* It's . . . almost readable. *(Unfolding paper.)* But what is it you've written your name *on*?

PRUDENCE: *(Defensive.)* There is no other paper! I had to.

KIT: All right, Prudence. This will be our secret. But don't tear any more pages out of your Pa's Bible, or both of us will be in big trouble. *(*KIT *puts the bible page in her carrying pocket.)*

PRUDENCE: How will I write my name? And other names. And remembrances?

KIT: You can have my slate.

PRUDENCE: Pa won't let me. He says girls can't learn.

KIT: . . . Well, they can't learn if they don't study. I know a place we can study, if you will meet me there.

PRUDENCE: You will meet me at a place?

KIT: Yes. Do you know where Hannah Tupper lives?

PRUDENCE: The evil woman.

KIT: *(Surprised.)* She's not a bit evil.

PRUDENCE: They say so.

KIT: She's as generous and good as my own mother. If you meet me, I will give you a slate. You can practice writing and no one will tell. Can you meet me in the morning?

(WILLIAM *enters.*)

WILLIAM: Hello, Kit.

KIT: What—?

PRUDENCE: I have to get back. (PRUDENCE *exits.*)

WILLIAM: . . . I've come to call. Will you walk with me?

KIT: No.

WILLIAM: No?

KIT: It's dinnertime and it's getting dark.

WILLIAM: We can still see.

KIT: I'm exhausted, William. Connecticut is very tiring so far.

WILLIAM: Then may I sit with you?

KIT: I suppose.

(*They sit. He stares at her with unabashed adoration. A silence.*)

KIT: Well, this has been—

WILLIAM: *(Same time.)* Are you—?

KIT: Pardon.

WILLIAM: No, you go ahead.

KIT: No, please.

WILLIAM: I forgot what I was going to ask.

KIT: You said "are you—?"

WILLIAM: Oh, yes. Are you warm enough?

KIT: Yes, I'm fine.

(*Another silence.* WILLIAM *stares at* KIT *as she squirms.*)

KIT: *(Stands.)* Well, William. This has been very nice.

WILLIAM: *(Confused.)* What—?

KIT: Yes, we should do it again very soon. Bye bye, now.

WILLIAM: Well, good-bye then.

(*Enter* JOHN.)

JOHN: Kit, there you are. I'm going to see if I can be of any help inside. I don't know a thing about loft construction.

WILLIAM: That's no surprise.

JOHN: Pardon?

WILLIAM: You bookish boys are all the same. Useless when it comes to anything practical. What do you need to know? I know all about loft construction.

JOHN: Then you should go to the barn. Reverend Gish is advising Kit's uncle on the construction of a new chicken loft.

WILLIAM: That would suit your purposes just fine, if I went to the barn and left you alone with Kit.

JOHN: I beg your pardon.

WILLIAM: I suppose you've come to stake your claim.

JOHN: What claim?

WILLIAM: On Kit. I won't stop you, but I'll prove that I'm the better man.

KIT: William, you can't just claim—

WILLIAM: I am now speaking, Kit.

(MERCY *and* JUDITH *come outside with buckets.*)

MERCY: *(Startled to see them.)* Oh.

JUDITH: Look how our Cousin Kit entertains two gentlemen all by herself.

KIT: I'm not entertaining anybody—

JUDITH: John, you haven't met my sister Mercy.

MERCY: . . . I'm going in.

JUDITH: Mercy, don't be silly.

MERCY: I don't know what to say to them.

JUDITH: Say whatever comes to mind.

MERCY: William, you aren't expected.

JUDITH: Mercy!

MERCY: There isn't enough food.

JUDITH: I'm sorry, William. Mercy isn't used to company.

MERCY: Boys eat more than girls.

WILLIAM: I came to take Kit for a walk in the moonlight, Mercy, not for dinner.

MERCY: Moonlight to turn the heart of any normal human man into a raging beast . . . It came to mind.

(JOHN *laughs.*)

JUDITH: Mercy, please don't get fanciful now.

JOHN: Miss Mercy, you speak like the Bible.

MERCY: What part?

JOHN: . . . Revelation.

JUDITH: Don't let us keep you from your walk, William.

KIT: We can't walk in the dark.

MERCY: No, you can. Judith always did when William was courting her—

JUDITH: Mercy!

MERCY: What?!

JUDITH: *(Recovering.)* William and I were never *courting*. We are the best of *friends* and will be to the day we die. Nothing else. Isn't that right, William?

WILLIAM: . . . Yes! That's exactly right.

JUDITH: William! Now you can start! The grand house for your wife.

WILLIAM: Oh, Judith, I *have* started. Today, right after meeting. I staked out the foundation. I ordered the windows. Eight-foot leaded glass windows all through the house.

(KIT *watches* WILLIAM *and* JUDITH *talk.*)

JUDITH: There will be so much light.

WILLIAM: Yes, even in winter.

JUDITH: Where will it be?

WILLIAM: On my land near yours on Blackbird Pond. I saw your Hannah Tupper have some visitor.

JUDITH: Don't call her ours. We have nothing to do with her.

KIT: Have you ever spoken with her?

MERCY: We aren't allowed to.

JUDITH: *(Afraid.)* I wouldn't speak to her. A witch can make your hair turn white or twist your thoughts.

KIT: . . . I don't *believe* in witches.

WILLIAM: You will when you see a herd of cattle die for no reason.

JUDITH: Or a cloud of beetles swarm down from the sky.

JOHN: We should pray for her soul.

WILLIAM: We should pray she leaves our town.

JOHN: A lost soul is lost no matter what town it lives in, William.

WILLIAM: . . . I don't need to be reminded of charity, thank you. Good night. Kit, I'll call again, if I may?

(Brief pause.)

JUDITH: Don't just stand there, girl, answer the man!

KIT: Yes! As you wish.

(WILLIAM *exits.*)

JUDITH: How nice that William will be a regular visitor.

KIT: *(To* JUDITH.*)* I think this William is not meant for me.

JUDITH: Well, he thinks he is. *(To change the subject.)* We have to fetch the water, Mercy.

KIT: *(Taking bucket.)* I'll fetch water.

MERCY: They're heavy when they're full.

KIT: I can manage. Take John inside. Get him to read something to you, Mercy.

(As they go inside, KIT *fills buckets.)*

MERCY: Oh, John, will you read something?

JUDITH: Do, John. Mercy doesn't get to go to meeting.

JOHN: I think I can do that.

(KIT *tries to pick up buckets and falls from the weight.*)

KIT: Oh. Oh dear.

(*Enter* MATTHEW, RACHEL, REBECCA, GIDEON *and* PRUDENCE.)

MATTHEW: Take the pails inside, Kit.

(KIT *tries again, fumbles,* MATTHEW *grabs the buckets, all head inside. Join* JU-DITH *and* MERCY *and* JOHN.)

JOHN: "And he shall be like a tree planted by the rivers of water, that bringeth forth his fruit in his season; his leaf also shall not wither; and whatsoever he doeth shall prosper."

MERCY: Oh, don't stop, don't stop!

JUDITH: Mercy—

MERCY: (*Same time.*) So beautiful.

JUDITH: Let him rest.

JOHN: Yes, you must have some mercy, Mercy.

(*Laughing,* MERCY *retrieves an ugly jacket.*)

MERCY: Look Kit. I mended this so you can wear it.

KIT: It . . . it was kind of you.

REBECCA: Finally, a modest garment.

KIT: I didn't mean to offend—

RACHEL: Now she has the jacket, she'll be modest. How's our supper, Mercy?

MERCY: I hope it's as good as you make it.

JUDITH: Ma was gone all morning.

GIDEON: I must thank you, Rachel, for looking after my sister. That was very kind.

RACHEL: I pray she recovers.

GIDEON: So do we all.

MERCY: John read to me from the Bible, Ma.

RACHEL: Mercy, you're flushed. Let me feel your forehead.

MERCY: (*Pleads.*) No, Ma, I'm not sick. Let me stay with the company.

RACHEL: All right, girl. Rebecca, sit nearer the fire. You, too, Reverend.

MERCY: We have suet pudding for dessert. (MERCY *shows off the dessert which is under a particular cloth.*)

PRUDENCE: A pudding!

GIDEON: Wife—(*Make her be quiet.*)

REBECCA: Prudence, be still.

PRUDENCE: Yes, ma'am.

REBECCA: Stand up, child. Stand behind me.

KIT: But there's plenty of room—

REBECCA: I say she stands.

GIDEON: When her mother says she stands, she stands. The child has to learn discipline. The ways of the tropics are not the ways of Connecticut. We must be tough and strong, or we don't survive.

(Brief pause.)

RACHEL: Come girls.

(JUDITH and MERCY help RACHEL prepare plates.)

PRUDENCE: Can I help them, Ma?

REBECCA: *(Pleased.)* That's a good girl. Rachel, do you need more help?

RACHEL: No, but thank you Prudence. More help and we'll be stepping on each other's feet.

KIT: *(Stands.)* Mercy, take my chair. I'll serve.

(RACHEL puts food on plates, JUDITH and KIT deliver it.)

RACHEL: Mercy says you tried spinning, Kit.

KIT: It was a complete failure; my fingers bled.

RACHEL: They'll toughen up.

KIT: I know; I know the trick now.

(KIT proudly shows the leaves from HANNAH, thinking that everybody knows this remedy.)

RACHEL: What will you do with leaves?

KIT: Spit on them, and rub my fingers until the skin gets tough.

REBECCA: I don't know this remedy.

GIDEON: Did you bring the leaves from Barbados?

(KIT realizes she's made a blunder.)

KIT: . . . Yes.

GIDEON: Let me see them. *(Handles them.)* They're green and soft. I think these leaves have been plucked recently.

MATTHEW: Kit? What of the leaves?

KIT: . . . I don't know.

MATTHEW: Where did you get the leaves? *(Silence.)* Say!

KIT: I learned the trick today from Hannah Tupper.

JUDITH: *(Fearful.)* It was you William saw.

REBECCA: This girl will damn us all. First she dives into water and now finds magic in leaves.

RACHEL: She fell.

GIDEON: She didn't fall.

JUDITH: She told us she fell.

GIDEON: She dove, floated for a moment, then swam as if possessed by a fish.

RACHEL: *(Fearful.)* She floated—?

REBECCA: *(To RACHEL.)* You don't know this girl. You don't know her at all.

RACHEL: *(Unsure.)* But she's my sister's child. She's her very image. *(Looking at the miniature portrait.)*

REBECCA: A witch can change her image. *(Re portrait.)* Or leave a token to twist your thoughts.

KIT: That's ridiculous.

REBECCA: You mock like the devil.

(RACHEL *takes off the portrait.*)

GIDEON: We would all feel safer, Matthew, if you made the Widow Tupper leave your land.

MATTHEW: She has nowhere to go. She's branded like a criminal.

GIDEON: Because she will not worship.

KIT: She worships quietly in her own fashion.

MATTHEW: You stay out of this, girl.

REBECCA: She works spells on those who are not cautious.

MATTHEW: There are no spells on us. We prosper, we live in peace and health.

GIDEON: But we must be vigilant in our faith.

MATTHEW: Don't question my faith. I crossed an ocean to worship in this way.

GIDEON: A good reason to protect yourself from a heretic.

MATTHEW: I say she is no witch. Stubborn and strange, but no danger.

GIDEON: *(Sincere.)* Perhaps you are under a spell.

MATTHEW: Are you accusing me of something, Gideon?

GIDEON: *(Quietly.)* Come, wife. Prudence, John—

PRUDENCE: But Pa, there's pudding—

REBECCA: Hush.

GIDEON: Enough, child. *(To* MATTHEW, *sincere.)* Be careful, Matthew. You give charity to a woman who is a non-believer and suspected of worse. Men have been dismissed from the church for less.

REBECCA: They've been hanged for less.

(JOHN *hands his plate to* MERCY.)

JOHN: Thank you, and . . . thank you.

(*The* GISHES *and* JOHN *exit.*)

MATTHEW: You didn't fall? You dove into the water?

KIT: . . . To save Prudence's doll.

MATTHEW: Why were you at Blackbird Pond?

KIT: By accident.

MATTHEW: You will not go there again.

KIT: Uncle I know you pity her—

MATTHEW: Say you will not go.

KIT: Let me pity her, too.

MATTHEW: You will obey while you live under my roof.

KIT: She has nothing. Her house is empty of any comfort.

RACHEL: She went in that house.

MATTHEW: You can't go in that house.

KIT: She has no food, she eats weeds.

MATTHEW: You can't be seen in that house.

KIT: She's so lonely she talks to a cat.

RACHEL: Oh, no!

KIT: She's a helpless old woman.

MATTHEW: I will not debate with this girl!

(MATTHEW *goes outside*, RACHEL *follows, then* KIT, *who overhears*.)

RACHEL: Matthew—

MATTHEW: I don't want her going there.

RACHEL: (*Worried, carrying the portrait.*) Matthew? Do you think Kit is—she is our niece, isn't she?

MATTHEW: (*Reassuring, replaces portrait around her neck.*) Yes, Rachel, *she is* our niece. Our *headstrong and willful* niece.

RACHEL: You're sure?

MATTHEW: I'm sure.

RACHEL: All right. Even so, you shouldn't fight with the Reverend.

MATTHEW: He has no right to say who can live on my land.

RACHEL: He believes Hannah is a danger.

MATTHEW: And I disagree with him!

RACHEL: . . . I *do not* disagree with him.

MATTHEW: (*Gentler.*) . . . Then I disagree with you as well.

RACHEL: I'm not worried about *our* disagreements. These arguments with Gideon are more and more frequent.

MATTHEW: We disagree about this one thing only.

RACHEL: You taught the girls to read—

MATTHEW: Girls should read.

RACHEL: Bonded servants—

MATTHEW: Having bonded servants is evil. I'll not bend on that either.

RACHEL: Isn't it you who says a tree that will not bend breaks in the storm?

MATTHEW: What are you saying?

RACHEL: . . . I think you are becoming an unbending sort of man.

MATTHEW: (*Pause, relenting.*) What would you have me do?

RACHEL: I would have you make up with Gideon. If we hurry, we can catch up to them.

MATTHEW: All right, Rachel. We shall tell the Reverend that Kit needs only to learn our ways. He shouldn't go to sleep thinking we harbor a witch in our house. (RACHEL *and* MATTHEW *exit*. KIT *steps forward*.)

KIT: (*Quietly.*) A witch?

(*End of* ACT ONE.)

INTERMISSION

ACT TWO

SCENE ONE

(The next morning. Blackbird Pond. CAT *and* PRUDENCE, *with her doll.)*
PRUDENCE: Meow.

CAT: Meow. *(Scratch my head.)*

PRUDENCE: Meow.

CAT: Meow. *(Just a little scratch.)*

(Enter HANNAH *with a cup and bread.)*
HANNAH: She wants thee to scratch her head.

PRUDENCE: I'm not talking to you. I'm waiting for my Kit.

HANNAH: Thy Kit may be delayed or unable, friend. Here's tea and a piece of
bread in the meanwhile.

*(*PRUDENCE *longs for bread and tea. Dares not. Turns away.)*
HANNAH: I'll put it here. This is not for thee, Miss Cat.

*(*HANNAH *exits.* KIT, *wearing the seemly jacket over her dress, out of breath, enters with the suet pudding and the slate.)*
KIT: *(Relieved.)* I feared you wouldn't come.

PRUDENCE: Ma's taking extra rest this morning.

KIT: You're a brave girl.

PRUDENCE: I'll probably turn into a goat if I eat her bread.

CAT: Meow! *(No!)*

KIT: Hannah's a good and generous person, not a witch.

(They eye the bread. KIT *takes a piece to show that it is safe.* PRUDENCE *eats the rest.)*
CAT: Meow? *(Can I have some?)*

PRUDENCE: *(Gives* CAT *bread.)* Bread could be a trick. To make us love the devil.

KIT: I brought suet pudding. Does that make *me* the devil?

PRUDENCE: Is it for me?

KIT: *This* is for you. *(*KIT *gives* PRUDENCE *the slate.)*

PRUDENCE: It's beautiful beyond belief. *(*PRUDENCE *writes.)*

KIT: Grandfather made it for my tenth birthday.

PRUDENCE: Is my name perfect?

KIT: Well, the *P* is very beautiful.

PRUDENCE: The *P* is perfect. Where should we keep it?

KIT: You decide. It's yours.

PRUDENCE: Mine? To keep?

KIT: For always.

PRUDENCE: Thanks.

KIT: Welcome.

(HANNAH, *who has overheard, enters.*)

HANNAH: Thee can keep the slate here if thee wants.

PRUDENCE: *(Cautious.)* Want to see my name?

HANNAH: I do. *(Looks.)* My. What a perfect *P*.

PRUDENCE: *(Beaming.)* This is my slate. My own for always.

HANNAH: And a fine one it is.

(*Enter* NAT *with a bundle.*)

NAT: Hello.

KIT: *(Happy, surprised.)* Nat!

HANNAH: It's the boy captain. Welcome, lad.

NAT: I see you've met Kit.

KIT: What are you doing here?

NAT: Hannah and I are old friends. I usually have her all to myself. *(Worried.)* Why is Prudence here?

PRUDENCE: I'm writing. Look at my name, Nat.

NAT: That's a very nice *P*.

PRUDENCE: It's a perfect p.

HANNAH: What a happy surprise. I saw thy ship pass yesterday. I thought I wouldn't see thee.

NAT: We're becalmed upriver. I brought you flour.

KIT: *(Oneupsmanship.)* I brought you suet pudding.

HANNAH: I thank thee both.

KIT: *(To NAT.)* I thought you left yesterday.

NAT: I'll oblige you as soon as there's wind.

KIT: I didn't mean—You don't oblige me by leaving. I just thought I wouldn't see you again.

NAT: What's that you're wearing?

KIT: It's part of my new seemly attire.

NAT: *(Sarcasm.)* Fitting right in, are you?

KIT: I'm fitting in perfectly well, thank you.

NAT: *(Skeptical.)* Uh-huh. How's the roof, Hannah?

HANNAH: It's a good roof.

NAT: Does it still leak?

HANNAH: It does.

NAT: Then it's a roof in need of thatching.

PRUDENCE: Should I get straw?

NAT: You practice writing your name.

KIT: Here. I'll write it so you can copy it.

NAT: Then we'll teach you to write all our names.

KIT: I'm sure one teacher is plenty.

NAT: *(Gentle sarcasm.)* Well, Kit, it's nice to see you again, too.

PRUDENCE: Can I have more bread? I have a terrible hunger; we got no dinner from Rachel Wood last night.

NAT: Rachel Wood sent you home without dinner?

PRUDENCE: No. We left because Ma and Pa think Kit's a witch.

HANNAH: What more has happened?

KIT: It's all nonsense.

NAT: Don't challenge them, Kit.

KIT: I say my thoughts. That's no crime.

PRUDENCE: I never say my thoughts.

KIT: *(Sad.)* Oh, girl. You can say your thoughts to me.

PRUDENCE: No, it's better not to. I see thoughts cross Ma's face, she never says them. It's better not to say them, so you don't get hit.

NAT: So you don't get put in the stocks.

KIT: . . . What do you need, Nat? To fix this roof.

NAT: Straw. The pile is just there.

HANNAH: Am I to *watch* while others work?!

NAT: You can help Prudence practice her letters.

HANNAH: A mighty job, that. Come Prudence, we'll go inside and slice up this pudding.

(PRUDENCE, HANNAH, CAT *exit.* KIT *and* NAT *thatch roof.*)

KIT: You might have told me about this *Connecticut.*

NAT: You wouldn't have listened.

KIT: A few men with a few tools could steady this house in one afternoon. Why doesn't somebody help her?

NAT: Good Puritans don't help old Quaker women. Even your uncle.

KIT: He does more than the others!

NAT: Yes, but still he won't come, or allow his family to. He won't approve of you coming here, either.

KIT: I don't intend to tell him.

NAT: Good. But what about Prudence? Is she so able to dissemble as yourself?

KIT: I—I don't know.

NAT: It will be bad for her if someone sees her here. They wouldn't pause, Kit, they'd put her an hour or two in the stocks.

KIT: I don't believe it.

NAT: Believe it. They did it to me when I was no more than eight. Half a day. And it's a punishment you don't soon forget. Other children will tease her, her parents will threaten her with it every time she misbehaves.

KIT: Did your parents threaten?

NAT: No. After that, my father decided we would *all* travel on *The Dolphin.* Wethersfield wasn't safe, if they could put a little boy in the stocks.

KIT: What had you done?

NAT: Someone saw me here. Hannah found me crying by the pond.

KIT: She found *you* crying?

NAT: I was lost!

KIT: I didn't mean—I just meant—She found me crying, too.

NAT: You said you were fitting right in.

KIT: I'm fine now!

NAT: I'm sure you are.

KIT: I'll tell Prudence she's not to come anymore. . . . What did Hannah do, that they hate her so?

NAT: Nothing. They need somebody to blame when the crops fail or their children die.

KIT: She should leave. You should take her with you.

NAT: The sea is no place for an old woman.

KIT: She'd love it. I loved it.

NAT: You did?

KIT: Well, yes. *(Embarrassed.)* I mean, your mother loves it, doesn't she? Sailing with your father?

(Enter PRUDENCE, HANNAH, with the sliced pudding, CAT.)

PRUDENCE: Kit, do you know the words inside my name?

KIT: What words are those?

(PRUDENCE shows the slate to KIT and NAT on the roof.)

KIT: That's quite a list.

NAT: Read it, Prudence.

(HANNAH whispers the words to PRUDENCE.)

PRUDENCE: Rude, crude, rend, rue, nude, prune.

NAT: There aren't any words in my name.

KIT: *Tan* and . . . *at* are in your name.

NAT: *(Annoyed.)* No words of *note* are in my name. Your roof is fixed, Hannah.

HANNAH: I thank thee, Lad. That's enough work now. Let's have this pudding for breakfast.

PRUDENCE: Breakfast?! Here, keep this for me. *(Hands slate to HANNAH.)*

NAT: We want to talk to you—

PRUDENCE: I can't. *(Exiting.)* I'll see you tomorrow, Kit.

(PRUDENCE runs off.)

KIT: Prudence, wait—. . . . I'm late, too, Hannah.

NAT: We'll have breakfast together next time. I'm going to see Kit home.

KIT: That's not necessary.

NAT: But it's going to happen, nonetheless.

Scene Two

(The Wood house. MERCY *sewing,* RACHEL, JUDITH, WILLIAM, *outside.)*

WILLIAM: Did no one see her go?

JUDITH: She was gone when we woke up.

MERCY: Vanished.

RACHEL: *(Covering.)* I'm sure she's merely gone for a walk. She seems to have a fondness for walking.

JUDITH: And for *reading,* and for "just being Kit."

*(*NAT *and* KIT *enter.)*

MERCY: There, no danger, Ma; she's with Nat Eaton, the captain's son.

WILLIAM: Well!

NAT: Not only a captain's son, Mercy, but soon to be a captain with a ship of my own.

KIT: *(Surprised.)* You might have told me—

RACHEL: Kit, we feared you— . . . We didn't know where you'd gone.

JUDITH: Our disappearing cousin.

MERCY: It's a disappearing kind of day. The pudding's gone.

NAT: *(To tease* KIT.*)* Maybe it was taken by elves.

WILLIAM: Don't think it, lad. This is a righteous house.

NAT: I'm sure it is. Lad.

KIT: I—I took it. I ate it.

WILLIAM: The whole pudding?

MERCY: *(To excuse.)* We had no dinner, William.

WILLIAM: But still, a whole pudding—

MERCY: I'm weak this morning, myself.

WILLIAM: I've been waiting for you, Kit.

KIT: I didn't know you were coming.

WILLIAM: I said I was.

KIT: You didn't.

JUDITH: He did. Where were you all this time?

RACHEL: No matter! She's here, she's safe.

WILLIAM: I placed a purchasing order with your father, Nat.

NAT: For lead windows. I know.

WILLIAM: The sooner the better. *(Stands next to* KIT.*)* We can't marry until I finish my house.

NAT: *(Brief pause.)* You'll have no cause to delay your marriage on my account. I'll see to your windows myself. I extend my very best wishes to the bride. Good day, all.

MERCY: Bye, Nat. Father should know Kit is safe. *(*MERCY *starts off.)*

RACHEL: I'll go.

MERCY: No, Ma. It's just to the barn. *(Exits.)*

JUDITH: It's not far, Ma.

RACHEL: *(Worried.)* She has fever.

WILLIAM: Kit, gluttony is a sin.

KIT: What do you mean?

JUDITH: He means you single-handedly gobbled a pudding meant for eight people.

RACHEL: We'll hear no more about this pudding.

WILLIAM: But Goody Wood, surely you don't think—

RACHEL: Whatever I think, William, is no concern of yours.

WILLIAM: No, really, when it comes to *food sins,* we must be just as vigilant—

RACHEL: Enough! We will hear no more about it.

WILLIAM: . . . As you will. I'm off to select lumber for the house. I'll call again tonight, Kit. If I may.

KIT: Tonight—?

RACHEL: No, William. There's been too much excitement. Give us a day to recover.

WILLIAM: As you will. Good-bye, my Kit. *(Exits.)*

RACHEL: *(Sits.)* Skipping dinner has made *me* weak, too.

KIT: Would you like me to get you something, Aunt Rachel?

RACHEL: You, Miss, will tell me where you were all morning—

(Enter MATTHEW and MERCY, who immediately sits.)

MATTHEW: *(Mad.)* You will not leave the house before we rise; you will not run off from meeting; you will stay with us, or we will know where you are. Do you understand me?

KIT: I'm sorry, Uncle Matthew. Please don't be mad at me—

(Enter JOHN. Nervous.)

JOHN: Good morning. Good. The whole family. My. No, it's good, good.

MATTHEW: Has no one any work in this colony?!

JOHN: I've come on the Reverend's suggestion. Actually, he doesn't know *where* I've come, but it was his idea, and he said I should act *quickly!*

MATTHEW: *(Brief pause.)* Lad, you're speaking in riddles. What do you want?

JOHN: Oh! I didn't say! I, um, a minister should marry, and as I'm not, *married*, or a minister either, yet, I suppose . . .

JUDITH: Father, he wants to call! To court.

JOHN: Yes! That's it exactly.

MATTHEW: Get on with it.

JOHN: Well. Goodness. I, um—

JUDITH: Have some pity, Father; he's bursting with shyness.

MATTHEW: *(Sigh.)* If the girl will receive you, you may call. I will not force marriage on my daughters.

JUDITH: Yes, I'll receive you, yes, you may court me, yes!

(A silence.)

JOHN: But—

JUDITH: I say yes, what now, you silly boy?

KIT: No—

JUDITH: Do you mean to have all the boys to yourself, Kit?

KIT: No, I—

MERCY: Kit, be still . . . Sit down and court Judith, John. Welcome to our family. I'll get you tea.

(MERCY stands and faints. MATTHEW lifts her.)

JOHN: Please. Let me help.

(They take MERCY inside and lay her down.)

RACHEL: *(Near tears.)* What's wrong, what's wrong with her?

JUDITH: She's all right. She'll be all right, Ma. *(Feeling RACHEL's forehead.)* Ma, you're burning up.

RACHEL: I can't rise.

JUDITH: Father! Father hurry. It's Ma.

MATTHEW: *(Re-entering.)* Rachel—?

RACHEL: I can't rise.

MATTHEW: You're on fire.

RACHEL: What's happening; my thoughts are tangled—

JUDITH: Let me help.

MATTHEW: *(Touches JUDITH's face.)* Go to bed, while you can still walk. You're sick, too, Judith.

(They go inside. KIT picks up MERCY's sewing, sees that it is the unfinished seemly skirt. JOHN comes outside.)

KIT: John. It's Mercy that you love. Why didn't you say something?

JOHN: I made a terrible blunder. And now, if I hurt Judith, Mercy will not love me.

KIT: *(Worried.)* What is making them so sick?

JOHN: They're hot and Mercy has red marks on her face—

KIT: No—

JOHN: It may be smallpox.

KIT: Oh, please no.

(MATTHEW comes outside. He is shaken.)

MATTHEW: Kit, go inside. I'm going to ask Rebecca Gish if she will nurse them.

KIT: I can do it, Uncle. I can nurse them.

MATTHEW: You?

KIT: I can. If it's smallpox, I've seen it. I know it. Please let me.

MATTHEW: They're very sick.

JOHN: Goodman Wood, Rebecca Gish is frail. I don't think she will be able to care for two households.

KIT: I nursed Grandfather! I can do it!

MATTHEW: *(Reluctantly.)* All right. Fetch water. They're burning with fever.

SCENE THREE

(A week later. The Wood house. Inside, MERCY sleeps fitfully. JUDITH is weak. KIT goes from one to the other, fusses and wipes, stirs the cooking pot. KIT is exhausted. JOHN enters and crosses to MERCY. KIT tries to feed JUDITH.)

KIT: *(Relieved.)* John.

JOHN: She's so pale.

JUDITH: John—

KIT: You must eat, Judith.

JUDITH: *(Weak.)* Give me water.

KIT: A little food first.

(MERCY kicks off her cover.)

MERCY: *(Delirious.)* Fire.

JOHN: *(Wipes her head.)* Be still, be still. Shhh. Shhh.

JUDITH: Mercy . . .

KIT: Save your strength, Judith. *(About JUDITH.)* Her fever is gone, but she is still so weak.

(JUDITH lies down, but stays awake. MERCY trembles and reaches for the cover in her delirium. JOHN covers her.)

KIT: One minute she's burning, the next she's quaking from cold. *(KIT takes JUDITH's dish to the pot. JOHN joins her.)*

JOHN: Are you getting any rest, Kit?

KIT: Rest. I long to read a poem. Or take a walk with William even. . . . Are many sick?

JOHN: Almost every household. Six are dead. Last week, Goody Hamilton.

KIT: The Reverend's sister?

JOHN: Yes, and this morning her baby. Two days ago, four children.

KIT: Not Prudence!

JOHN: Prudence is fine; our household is blessed.

KIT: . . . And the others are *cursed*? For all their *sins*? John, this isn't a sinful household.

JOHN: We pray every hour. None of us are ill.

KIT: It's a *sickness*! Prayer has nothing to do with it.

MERCY: John!

(KIT and JOHN go to MERCY.)

JOHN: Yes, Mercy, I'm here.

MERCY: Where is John?

KIT: He's here, Mercy.

MERCY: *(Fearful.)* Is it a dream?

JOHN: Mercy, sweet Mercy, I'm here, sweet love, see me, please see me.

MERCY: *(Quieting.)* John, John.

JOHN: I'm right here.

MERCY: *(Relieved.)* I saw John. I saw him.

JOHN: I'm here, right by your side.

    (MERCY sleeps.)

JOHN: Right here. Forever.

KIT: *(Brief pause.)* I think she looks a little better.

JOHN: My sweet, sweet Mercy.

KIT: I must go up and tell Aunt Rachel—

JUDITH: Say it's a lie.

KIT: . . . Judy, dear cousin—

JUDITH: Say it's a lie, John. You say this so she will live. You love *me*.

JOHN: *(Cannot speak.)*

JUDITH: No.

KIT: *(Gently.)* He didn't mean to be cruel. It was a mistake.

JUDITH: How can you love Mercy instead of me? She's a crooked silly girl.

KIT: . . . Don't make yourself sick again.

JUDITH: *(Growing fear.)* . . . You bewitch him. You want him to love Mercy, and you make it happen.

KIT: What are you saying?

JUDITH: First you steal William, then make John love Mercy.

JOHN: No one *made* me . . .

JUDITH: You have twisted my thoughts.

KIT: Judith, save your strength.

JUDITH: *(Crying.)* Why? So I *live*? What do I care if I live? Get away from me.

    (MATTHEW enters house. MATTHEW goes to MERCY.)

MATTHEW: She seems almost peaceful. And not so hot.

MERCY: Kit—

MATTHEW: It's Father, Mercy.

KIT: *(Grabbing bucket.)* We need more water.

MATTHEW: Kit—

KIT: What is it, Uncle?

MATTHEW: *(MATTHEW kisses her forehead.)* Good Kit.

KIT: *(Moved.)* Oh, Uncle. *(Goes to well.)*

JUDITH: *(Weakly.)* No.

MATTHEW: *(Crosses to her.)* Judith, girl, you weep so.

JUDITH: Last. I am always last.

MATTHEW: *(To* JOHN.*)* She was *better*. What happened?

JUDITH: I fear her. I fear this Kit.

MATTHEW: Judith, child. Kit fed you when you couldn't lift a spoon. We'll not think badly of her again.

JUDITH: Father, help me. She's twisting my thoughts, my mind—

MATTHEW: Dear child—be still.

(Enter GIDEON *with a musket,* REBECCA.*)*

GIDEON: Matthew Wood.

*(*MATTHEW *comes outside.* KIT *watches unnoticed, though not spying.)*

MATTHEW: Rebecca—Gideon. We've no time for company.

REBECCA: This is not a visit.

MATTHEW: Then let me look to my family.

GIDEON: We're going on your land, Matthew.

MATTHEW: *(Confused.)* You ask permission to go on my land?

GIDEON: No. We're going on your land.

*(*MATTHEW *waits.)*

GIDEON: To speak to Hannah Tupper.

MATTHEW: We settled this Gideon. She leaves us alone, we leave her alone.

GIDEON: She's killing us, Matthew.

MATTHEW: She's no witch, Gideon.

GIDEON: My sister is dead. Her son is dead.

MATTHEW: From smallpox, Man.

GIDEON: Get rid of that old woman and this "smallpox" will leave with her.

*(*KIT *quietly puts down the bucket and exits.* JOHN *comes outside.)*

MATTHEW: Why would she witch us after all these years?

GIDEON: It's their way. To live quietly until we cease our vigilance. Come, John.

JOHN: I'm needed here.

GIDEON: Nursing the sick is useless until we rid ourselves of this witch. Come on, lad. We do God's work now.

*(*JOHN *exits with* REBECCA *and* GIDEON.*)*

SCENE FOUR

(Blackbird Pond. Dusk. HANNAH *and* CAT.*)*

CAT: Meow. *(Something's wrong.)*

HANNAH: Nothing's wrong, thee silly thing. Come inside and we'll go back to sleep.

CAT: Meow! *(It isn't safe.)*

HANNAH: It *is* safe, now stop thy howling. If I wanted howling, I'd have a dog for a friend.

(KIT *enters out of breath.*)

HANNAH: Look Miss Cat, friend Kit has returned at long last. Prudence misses thee.

KIT: Prudence—

HANNAH: We read together every day.

KIT: Hannah, you must leave here. It isn't safe.

HANNAH: Is this about the smallpox?

KIT: Yes! They want to blame it on you.

CAT: Meow! (*Look!*)

KIT: They're coming; please hide. (*As they hide.*)

HANNAH: It will do no good.

KIT: Be still.

(*Enter* REBECCA, GIDEON, JOHN.)

GIDEON: Hannah Tupper! Hannah Tupper, come outside. (*To* JOHN.) Check she's not hiding on the other side of the pond.

(JOHN *exits.*)

GIDEON: Wait here, Rebecca. I'm going inside.

REBECCA: Take me with you.

GIDEON: It might be dangerous.

REBECCA: If there's danger, I want to help.

GIDEON: All right. Stay behind me though. (*As they go inside the house,* KIT, HANNAH, *and* CAT *emerge.*)

HANNAH: Too bad Nat can't see us.

KIT: Nat? Where is *Nat*?

HANNAH: (*Points.*) *The Dolphin* waits there, on its way out to sea tomorrow.

(KIT *takes off her dress.*)

HANNAH: Planning a midnight swim, Kit?

KIT: If I can pull Nat to shore, I can pull you to *The Dolphin*. Please Hannah, don't be afraid.

CAT: (*Pushing* HANNAH.) Meow. (*Go with her.*)

HANNAH: What about Miss Cat?

KIT: I'll take her home with me. Please.

HANNAH: Miss Cat, don't let them see thee.

CAT: Meow. (*Go.*)

(HANNAH *and* KIT *exit, as* GIDEON *and* REBECCA *reenter;* GIDEON *has* HANNAH'S *Bible and the slate.*)

GIDEON: Look, there.

REBECCA: Yes, in the water.

(*As they approach the water,* MISS CAT *steps in front of them and runs off.*)

CAT: Meoooow! (*Boo!*)

REBECCA: (*Gasps.*)

GIDEON: It's alright, Rebecca, it's only a cat.

REBECCA: . . . Gideon—it's her! It's Hannah Tupper.

GIDEON: Catch it. Catch the cat.

(*An elegant chase, during which* JOHN *reenters and pets* CAT, *hears the* REVEREND *and* GOODY GISH—)

JOHN: What is it? What's wrong?

GIDEON: It's a witch. Catch it!

(JOHN *gasps.* MISS CAT *runs off;* JOHN *goes after her.* GIDEON *comforts* REBECCA, *who is very afraid, near tears.*)

GIDEON: It's alright, Rebecca.

REBECCA: At least there's proof now.

GIDEON: Yes. Only a witch can change herself into a cat.

(REBECCA *sees* KIT's *dress.*)

REBECCA: She left her human garment behind.

GIDEON: No; that's Kit Tyler's prideful dress.

(REVEREND *hands slate and Bible to* REBECCA *and picks up* KIT's *pocket, looks inside.*)

GIDEON: What's this? (*Takes Bible page from pocket.*)

REBECCA: Tell me.

GIDEON: It's a page torn from a Bible, defiled with magic writing.

REBECCA: Burn it!

GIDEON: No. It's evidence.

REBECCA: There's writing on the slate. What does it say?

GIDEON: (*Taking it.*) Oh, no. It can't be . . .

REBECCA: What?

GIDEON: (*Shows her.*) Do you see this word? It is the name of our daughter.

REBECCA: (*Gasps.*)

GIDEON: (*Carefully.*) Tell me, Rebecca. Is Prudence always in your care?

REBECCA: She is.

GIDEON: Even those mornings when you require extra rest?

REBECCA: She is always in my care!

GIDEON: All right, then. Make sure she doesn't wander.

REBECCA: What's out there? Something—what is it?

GIDEON: Quiet.

(*They lay in wait for* KIT *who crawls from the water.*)

KIT: (*Calling, out of breath.*) Miss Cat? Where are you? Meow—?

REBECCA: (*Gasps at what she assumes is witch behavior.*)

KIT: Who's there?

REBECCA: I fear her.

KIT: Goody Gish? Reverend? Don't shoot! It's Kit.

GIDEON: Stand there. Don't run.

KIT: I'm too tired to run.

REBECCA: Don't let her speak. She'll witch us.

GIDEON: Cover yourself, girl. Do not speak.

(KIT *dresses.* JOHN, *reenters running.*)

JOHN: It made itself invisible. Kit! What are you doing in this foul place?

GIDEON: Practicing foul deeds.

KIT: John, I haven't—

GIDEON: Silence. John, run to Matthew Wood. Tell him his niece is arrested.

KIT: I haven't done anything.

GIDEON: Not one word more. Tell him to come to the meeting house. Go!

SCENE FIVE

(*Outside meeting house.* GIDEON, KIT, REBECCA. *Stocks.*)

KIT: God in heaven, no. Reverend, I will not flee, I beg you a thousand times, please.

GIDEON: Do not say the name of God.

KIT: Please, I'm sorry—

GIDEON: Lay in your hands and head . . . I swear, I can shoot you if you choose.

KIT: No! No, I will—(KIT *puts her head and hands in the stock.* REBECCA *closes the stocks and* GIDEON *locks them.*)

GIDEON: Come help me prepare the storing closet, Rebecca.

(REBECCA *and* GIDEON *exit.* KIT *begins to panic, struggle, and babble.*)

KIT: Come back. It's a mistake, all a mistake. I'm no witch, not a witch, a thoughtless, silly girl. Just a silly, silly girl.
(CAT *enters. Paws the edge of the stocks.*)

KIT: Who's there?

CAT: Meow. (*Me.*)

KIT: (*Relieved.*) Miss Cat. Oh, Miss Cat.

CAT: Meow. (*Don't be scared.*)

KIT: Hannah didn't abandon you, sweet Cat, I promised her I'd take you home with me. She's going on a long trip with Nat, where she'll be safe from people who would hang her. Nat wanted me to go, too. I wish I had. Maybe he'll take Hannah to Barbados. (*Crying.*) I would to God I'd never left it. I would to God I'd never abandoned Serena. I would to God I'd never stepped on these cruel shores.

CAT: Meow. (*You met me here.*)

KIT: But then I'd never have met you, or Hannah, or Mercy, or Prudence. God, keep Prudence safe. Don't let her get caught at Blackbird Pond. Miss Cat! Someone's coming. Hide. Scat!

(CAT *hides. Enter* RACHEL *and* MATTHEW.)

RACHEL: (*Afraid.*) It's some horrible dream.

KIT: Aunt Rachel, let me out, please let me out.

MATTHEW: It's no dream. You poor girl, where is that man?

KIT: Uncle Matthew, hold my hand. I'm so afraid.

MATTHEW: It's all right, Kit. I'll find him and his wretched key.

RACHEL: No—

(MATTHEW *realizes that* RACHEL *is afraid of* KIT.)

MATTHEW: Rachel? Oh, Rachel. Look at her. She's a pitiful girl. She is no witch.

RACHEL: I'm sick.

KIT: Aunt Rachel, I'm no witch. A pitiful stupid girl.

RACHEL: I cannot think—

KIT: I promise to be good. Please, please—

(*Enter* GIDEON *and* REBECCA. RACHEL *walks away from* KIT.)

GIDEON: Matthew, stand away, she's a prisoner.

MATTHEW: Take her out of the stocks. They're for punishment, not confinement.

GIDEON: (*Unlocking* KIT.) I know the law, Matthew. I have a jailing place ready now.

(*Free,* KIT *throws herself at* RACHEL's *feet.*)

KIT: Aunt Rachel, let me come home, please. I'll be good. I swear.

RACHEL: (*Torn.*) Oh, child.

REBECCA: Rachel. The devil makes tears to weaken us.

(RACHEL *pulls away.*)

MATTHEW: Let us take her home, Gideon. We can bring her back tomorrow if you need to talk to her.

GIDEON: She is arrested, Matthew. She will not go with you.

KIT: (*Crying.*) No, please, please let me go home.

GIDEON: I'll send to Saybrook for the magistrate. He will decide if she goes free.

SCENE SIX

(*A week later, inside the meeting room. One of* KIT's *trunks is there and open; the books beside it.* MATTHEW, RACHEL, JUDITH, MERCY, JOHN, REBECCA, WILLIAM, MAGISTRATE TALBOT. MATTHEW *watches at the door.*)

RACHEL: Matthew, come sit.

MATTHEW: He's bringing her now.

(*Enter* GIDEON *with* KIT *who is dirty and tired; her hands are tired.* GIDEON *puts her in a seat and stands behind her.*)

MATTHEW: Kit—Look how pitiful she is. We'll clean you up when we get you home, Kit.

GIDEON: She may not go home.

MATTHEW: Did you even feed her? She looks like she hasn't eaten all week.

(MERCY *rises and crosses to* KIT.)

RACHEL: Mercy, sit down.

MERCY: Yes, Ma. (*She continues toward* KIT.)

RACHEL: Mercy?

MERCY: Yes, I will sit in a moment. (*She wipes* KIT's *face.*)

KIT: (*Happy.*) How did you get here?

MERCY: John helped me.

KIT: You're almost pink again.

MERCY: And you are so pale. Oh, Kit, don't be afraid. We're here to tell how you saved us from death.

GIDEON: To turn you into witches.

TALBOT: Mercy Wood, take your seat.

MERCY: Her wrists are bleeding. May I loosen the rope?

TALBOT: This is not a game. She is bound so that she cannot do us evil. Show some respect for this hearing and take your seat.

MATTHEW: (*Hesitant.*) It isn't justice, Reverend Talbot, if Kit is harmed before she is tried.

TALBOT: Don't lecture me on what is justice, Goodman Wood. Mercy Wood, sit down!

(MERCY *sits.*)

TALBOT: . . . The security of a community depends on its piety, its righteousness. Our Piety is a great wall that keeps out witchery and evil. When our wall cracks, evil drifts in like a poisonous smoke, spreading over everything, killing, corrupting the minds of the good people, who for the briefest moment allowed their piety to drop. This community is suffering from a terrible blight; the only way to save those still sick and dying is to identify and eliminate the cause. . . . Katherine Tyler, called Kit, is accused of consorting with a known witch—

MATTHEW: Pardon, your honor, but Hannah Tupper is *suspected*, not *proven* a witch.

(When TALBOT *calls their name, individuals stand.*)

TALBOT: If you are so anxious to speak, we will begin testimony with you, Matthew Wood. (MATTHEW *stands.* TALBOT *refers to his notes.*) You didn't welcome your niece kindly into your home.

MATTHEW: How can this be known?

TALBOT: Is it true?

MATTHEW: (*Uncomfortable.*) It is. A pampered child, I feared she would perish or drain us. I was wrong. Kit saved my girls from death.

TALBOT: Did you know she visited Hannah Tupper?

MATTHEW: I knew.

TALBOT: Did she have your permission?

MATTHEW: She did not.

TALBOT: *(Brief pause.)* Elaborate, Man!

MATTHEW: Ask me your questions and I will answer!

TALBOT: *Did you* forbid Kit Tyler to visit Hannah Tupper?

MATTHEW: When I knew of it, I forbade it.

TALBOT: Did she obey?

MATTHEW: She didn't obey, but it was for charity—

TALBOT: She didn't obey. . . . Do you know that when Kit arrived she dove into the water.

MATTHEW: I know of it.

TALBOT: Who told you?

MATTHEW: She arrived *wet*.

TALBOT: And told you, did she not, that she fell?

MATTHEW: It was to avoid my wrath.

TALBOT: She lied. Sit down. . . . Rachel Wood—

RACHEL: Please Your Honor, I am confused. I can be of no help.

GIDEON: I will speak.

TALBOT: In good time, Reverend. Goody Wood. *(She stands.)* Kit Tyler lived in your house; you will speak. What do you know of this girl?

RACHEL: . . . When I look at her—I—I don't know.

TALBOT: . . . Look at her.

RACHEL: *(Doesn't.)* I—

TALBOT: Do as I ask.

(RACHEL *looks at* KIT.)

TALBOT: What do you see?

RACHEL: She is so like my sister.

TALBOT: You're saying she resembles her mother?

RACHEL: It isn't a *resemblance*. It is Margaret's same image.

MATTHEW: Rachel—

RACHEL: She is identical.

MATTHEW: Our own daughters carry *our* image. It is not witchery.

TALBOT: Goodman Wood, has your association with Hannah Tupper made you an expert on witchery?

MATTHEW: I have no association—I meant only . . . many carry the stamp of family on their face. I mean no disrespect.

TALBOT: Sit down, both of you. Rebecca Gish. What do you know of this girl?

(REBECCA *looks to* GIDEON *who nods for her to speak.)*

REBECCA: She is arrogant and irreverent. I saw her fly into the air, then dive into water. She floats like no mortal.

GIDEON: We know she learned spells with leaves from Hannah Tupper.

KIT: Not a spell. A trick, to toughen my fingers.

TALBOT: Interrupt this hearing, and we will bind your mouth shut. *(To GIDEON.)* Go on, Reverend Gish.

GIDEON: We know she was at Blackbird Pond when Hannah Tupper turned herself into a cat. We know how many have died since Kit Tyler landed on our shores.

REBECCA: I know that I fear her.

TALBOT: Sit down, Goody Gish. John Holcomb. Tell of the incident where Kit knew your mind before you knew it yourself.

KIT: John, please.

TALBOT: Silence, girl.

MATTHEW: How do you know this?

TALBOT: I've made interviews.

MATTHEW: But who told you these things?

TALBOT: Quiet! John Holcomb, tell of this incident.

JOHN: It was recommended that I marry. When I told Kit Tyler, she spoke of her cousin Mercy Wood as a wife for me.

TALBOT: Did you know Mercy?

JOHN: I hadn't met her yet.

TALBOT: What did you discover when you met her?

JOHN: That I found her sweet. That I soon thought of her as a wife.

KIT: It was an innocent idea.

TALBOT: To know the future is not innocent.

KIT: John, tell him I never witched you.

TALBOT: John?

JOHN: *(Hesitates.)* It feels like true affection, Your Honor, but as I have never felt it before, I can't be sure.

TALBOT: Sit. Judith Wood.

MATTHEW: Your Honor, my daughter has been sick—

TALBOT: This community has been ravaged by sickness, and I will get to the bottom of it. Judith Wood, say what you know of Kit Tyler.

JUDITH: *(Very quiet.)* She is . . .

TALBOT: Louder.

JUDITH: *(Crying.)* She is a witch she is a witch she is a witch.

(Commotion.)

MERCY: Judy, no—

MATTHEW: *(Same time.)* Judith, sit down.

KIT: *(Same time.)* How can you say it?

GIDEON: *(Same time.)* There, you see.

TALBOT: Order. Silence! Be silent! Explain, Judith.

JUDITH: She has bewitched me; my thoughts are not my own, I am bewitched.

TALBOT: You are safe, girl. Tell what you told me before.

MATTHEW: *(Shocked.)* Judith—

(TALBOT *holds up his hand to silence* MATTHEW.)

JUDITH: She tempted me with her beautiful dress, and once I lusted for it, she took it away. She beguiled my long-time friend William Ashby, then forced me to watch as he wooed her.

KIT: I never did.

TALBOT: William Ashby. Did you ever think of Judith as a wife?

WILLIAM: We had never spoken of it, Your Honor.

TALBOT: I ask of your heart and mind, not what was spoken.

WILLIAM: In my heart and mind . . . I had thought of it.

KIT: *(To* WILLIAM.*)* I didn't *make you* notice me.

TALBOT: Quiet, girl. Go on, Judith.

JUDITH: When it was clear that John Holcomb would become my husband, she bewitched him so that he would love Mercy.

TALBOT: John, did you ever think of Judith for a wife?

JOHN: When I met Judith . . . I had just been told to find a wife, so I was thinking about it. And, of course, Judith is so lovely—

JUDITH: It was witchery.

MATTHEW: Reverend Talbot, my daughter had a raging fever and so much disappointment—

TALBOT: She is not sick now.

JUDITH: She has beguiled us all. She has made me jealous of Mercy who I love more than my life.

MERCY: Judy, sweet Judy—

JUDITH: It's not my fault, Mercy. It's her. She makes anger and hate pour from me.

TALBOT: *(Brief pause.)* You may sit.

MATTHEW: It's not evidence.

TALBOT: I am the judge of what is evidence, Goodman Wood.

KIT: William! Speak for me. Tell him I am no witch. I didn't make him notice me, I don't know why he noticed me, I don't know I don't know I don't know . . .

TALBOT: William Ashby, do you have testimony to add?

WILLIAM: . . . No, Your Honor. I have nothing to add.

MATTHEW: None of this is true evidence. Where is evidence we can see and touch?

TALBOT: Reverend—(TALBOT *gestures to* GIDEON, *who crosses to* REBECCA *who gives him the evidence: slate,* HANNAH's *Bible, torn page from Bible.)*

MATTHEW: What is it? What do you have there.

TALBOT: It is evidence we can "see and touch."

(Enter HANNAH *and* NAT. *A commotion when* HANNAH *is seen.)*

NAT: Your Honor, sir—

REBECCA: *(Same time, afraid.)* Husband—

JUDITH: Oh, no! Ma—

KIT: *(Same time.)* Hannah, run away, please run away—

JUDITH: I must escape.

TALBOT: Silence, all of you, silence.

(HANNAH *enters calmly.*)

TALBOT: Are you Hannah Tupper?

HANNAH: Yes.

TALBOT: Who are you?

NAT: Nat Eaton, Your Honor. My father is captain of *The Dolphin.*

TALBOT: Stand there, next to the accused, both of you.

KIT: He will hang us all.

NAT: Kit—

TALBOT: Where have you been hiding, Hannah Tupper?

NAT: She's been with my family.

TALBOT: I've heard of your family, lad. Non-believers all of you.

NAT: We believe in *God,* Your Honor.

TALBOT: You are not Puritans. Hannah Tupper, why do you not—

MERCY: Let her sit.

TALBOT: What now?!

MERCY: Pardon, Your Honor. She is *old.* Can we please let her sit?

HANNAH: Thee is kind, friend.

TALBOT: If you make another outburst, Mercy Wood, you will go in the stocks.

MATTHEW: She does not know how to behave in court—

TALBOT: That goes for you, as well, Goodman Wood. *(To* HANNAH*)* Why will you not attend meeting, Hannah Tupper?

HANNAH: I am a Quaker. I don't worship as thee, but my belief in God and God's goodness is great. I wish no evil on Wethersfield or any of its inhabitants.

GIDEON: They, neither of them, got the sickness!

MATTHEW: You didn't get it either, Gideon.

GIDEON: What are you saying, Man?!

MATTHEW: It should also be noted Your Honor, that in her absence the illness *continued.* That proves she is not the cause.

TALBOT: . . . I take your point. If you were safely away, why did you return?

HANNAH: To hide . . . to fear, made me a prisoner.

TALBOT: Are you saying you came back from conscience?

HANNAH: No, friend. I am saying that I would rather be dead than live in fear. Of thee or any other who would do me harm.

TALBOT: . . . Show your evidence, Reverend Gish.

GIDEON: This slate filled with lewd words we found in Hannah Tupper's house. *(Holds up page.)* This page torn from a Bible, I found in Kit Tyler's carrying pocket. It is defiled with magic writing.

KIT: *(Mirthless laugh.)* It's hopeless.

GIDEON: You see how she mocks us! *(Holds up slate.)* The name at the top of the list of words is my daughter's name. My Prudence. Kit Tyler and Hannah Tupper tried to bewitch my own daughter to harm me. Going after the innocent is a witch's way.

(PRUDENCE *with her doll, unnoticed, appears.*)

TALBOT: *(Taking the slate.)* Here is the name Prudence and below it an evil incantation. Lewd words written in a jagged hand: crude, nude, prune, rend.

MATTHEW: Is Prudence harmed? Let the child speak.

GIDEON: She was the innocent target of their spells. She was never at Blackbird Pond.

MATTHEW: You can't mean to find Kit guilty on this evidence—

TALBOT: On this evidence and the testimony.

GIDEON: We can give them the water test.

KIT: I shall float and be hanged, and Hannah and sweet Nat will drown.

PRUDENCE: Kit, don't cry.

KIT: Prudence, run away!

REBECCA: *(Same time.)* Prudence—

GIDEON: I told you to stay home!

PRUDENCE: I'm sorry, Pa!

TALBOT: Send the child away, Gideon!

GIDEON: Yes, Your Honor—

PRUDENCE: I am evidence.

TALBOT: What evidence?

GIDEON: Your Honor—

TALBOT: Quiet. What evidence do you have, Child?

PRUDENCE: *(Takes page.)* This is mine, not Kit's. There wasn't any other paper, and I needed to write my name.

REBECCA: She can't write.

TALBOT: What did you do when you wanted to write your name?

PRUDENCE: I tore the page from Pa's Bible. But not a page he reads much.

(TALBOT *studies the page.*)

TALBOT: This is a *name*?

PRUDENCE: I write it better now. That's a P.

TALBOT: This *is* a P. The other letters are not readable.

PRUDENCE: I'm improved. I practice in the dirt with a stick.

TALBOT: Do you know this slate?

PRUDENCE: Kit gave it to me. She said it was my own forever.

TALBOT: What are these words beneath your name? Crude, rude—

PRUDENCE: Words that come from inside my name.

GIDEON: She can't write. She has no learning.

PRUDENCE: I have learning.

TALBOT: Where did you get learning?

PRUDENCE: At Blackbird Pond.

GIDEON: Your Honor, the child is lying. She is never out of our sight.

REBECCA: Gideon, no—

GIDEON: What?

REBECCA: . . . Prudence doesn't lie.

GIDEON: What then? She is always in your sight. You said so.

REBECCA: She—she was not always in my sight.

TALBOT: *(Pause.)* Alright, then. *(To PRUDENCE.)* Why did you go to Blackbird Pond?

PRUDENCE: To learn.

TALBOT: Weren't you afraid?

PRUDENCE: At first. But Hannah called me friend and recited with me.

TALBOT: What did you *recite*?

PRUDENCE: *(She looks at HANNAH.)* "Keep me as the apple of Thy eye, hide me under the shadow of Thy wings. From the wicked that oppress me, from my deadly enemies who—, who—"

HANNAH: *(Quietly coaches.)* "Who compass . . ."

PRUDENCE: "—who compass me about."

(The room is subdued, relieved.)

GIDEON: It is a lie. She cannot write.

(TALBOT wipes slate, hands it to PRUDENCE.)

TALBOT: Show us.

(PRUDENCE writes her name, GIDEON and REBECCA approach and look over PRUDENCE's shoulder as she writes.)

REBECCA: Your name is lovely.

PRUDENCE: Are you angry with me, Ma?

REBECCA: No. I'm proud you can write your name.

GIDEON: The child is bewitched.

REBECCA: *(Amazed.)* She can write. *(Quietly, but firm.)* You said a girl couldn't learn. You said I couldn't learn.

TALBOT: . . . Unbind the girl.

(MATTHEW and NAT untie KIT.)

GIDEON: I saw Hannah Tupper change herself into a cat.

HANNAH: I had a cat. Perhaps thee saw her when thee came to my house.

GIDEON: Then where is it? Produce this cat, if you can!

TALBOT: Let it go, Reverend.

GIDEON: I will not—

TALBOT: No. *(Holding page and slate up.)* This evidence has unraveled.

GIDEON: There is more evidence, Your Honor. . . . A cow in our herd has stopped giving milk.

TALBOT: Let it go, Man.

GIDEON: Last night I dreamt of the devil.

TALBOT: I say, let it go. The sickness continued, even though Kit Tyler was closeted and Hannah Tupper was away. . . . Let it go.

JUDITH: What about me? What about what she has done to my mind?

TALBOT: *(Kind.)* . . . Perhaps your mind . . . is not completely over your fever, Judith Wood.

(RACHEL *comforts* JUDITH.)

TALBOT: Katherine Tyler, you can have your trunks and your vain dresses, but your books I will destroy.

KIT: But—

MATTHEW: Be still, Kit.

TALBOT: Goodman Wood, this confusion is your fault. Be warned who you let live on your land. Hannah Tupper. Your presence upsets the peace of this community. You will leave, and you will not return.

HANNAH: Is that my Bible?

TALBOT: Yes. Reverend Gish took it from your house.

HANNAH: May I have it?

(TALBOT *returns the Bible to* HANNAH.)

HANNAH: *(Sincere.)* I thank thee, Friend.

MATTHEW: Is there to be no apology?

RACHEL: Matthew—

TALBOT: I don't apologize for protecting our faith. Reverend Gish, walk with me; we will discuss ways to protect our parishes from heretics and these devil dreams you are currently having. (TALBOT *exits with* KIT's *books.* GIDEON *follows.)*

REBECCA: Come, Prudence.

PRUDENCE: May I take the slate, Ma?

REBECCA: You may. . . . You may say goodbye to Kit.

PRUDENCE: Bye, Kit.

(REBECCA, PRUDENCE *exit.)*

RACHEL: *(Hesitant.)* You're free to come home, Kit.

MATTHEW: We'll be a family again.

JUDITH: *(Quietly.)* She bewitched my mind.

MATTHEW: *(Gently.)* That's enough now, Judith.

MERCY: Judy, it will be good again.

JUDITH: *(To herself, exiting.)* It will never be good again.

(RACHEL *wants to follow.*)

RACHEL: Matthew—

MATTHEW: Will you come, Kit?

KIT: Go to Judith, Uncle. She needs you.

MATTHEW: (*Exiting.*) We'll put this behind us, you'll see.

KIT: Uncle? Thank you.

(RACHEL *and* MATTHEW *exit.*)

KIT: (*Quietly.*) How can we put it behind us? How can we ever put it behind us?

WILLIAM: We'll put it behind us.

KIT: (*Disbelief.*) What do you say?

WILLIAM: With good food, long walks and prayer. Let me take you home, Kit.

KIT: Stay away from me.

WILLIAM: But, Kit—

KIT: No. You stay away from me.

WILLIAM: I said nothing against you.

KIT: You said nothing. Nothing *for* me, *to* me. You would have let them hang me.

WILLIAM: I was only—it was a very serious charge.

KIT: Yes. It was. Stay away from me, William. Forever.

(WILLIAM *exits.*)

MERCY: Oh, Kit. Poor Kit.

KIT: No, don't cry. It doesn't matter; none of it. You're well and that's all that matters . . . You wear my mother's portrait.

MERCY: Ma doesn't—Yes. I wear it to remind me of you.

JOHN: Kit, it was the truth, I spoke. I never meant to harm you. It sounded so awful as it came out of my mouth.

KIT: (*Unforgiving.*) Yes. It did sound awful.

MERCY: Don't hate Judith, Kit; she's confused that I will have a husband and she won't.

KIT: Yes, that would "confuse" her. (*In trunk, finds the dress* JUDITH *had on in Act One.*) Here. Fix it, Mercy, make it *seemly*, and make sure that William sees Judith wearing it.

MERCY: Oh Kit, I knew you'd forgive her!

JOHN: (*Anxious to leave.*) Come away, Mercy, you should rest.

MERCY: We'll see you at home, Kit.

JOHN: Goodbye, Kit. Nat. (JOHN *glances fearfully at* HANNAH *as he and* MERCY *exit.*)

HANNAH: (*Sad.*) That boy thinks I'm a witch.

NAT: Let's get out of this meeting room.

HANNAH: Yes. It's ugly and mean in here.

(KIT *takes* HANNAH'*s hand.* NAT *follows. They speak as they go.*)

KIT: Come on. Why did you come back, Hannah?! They might have hanged you!

HANNAH: Because they might have hanged thee. Thee tried to protect me. Thee was brave and silly.

(KIT *takes off and tosses away the seemly jacket.* MISS CAT *approaches.*)

KIT: I will never go in there again.

CAT: Meow? (*Is it safe?*)

HANNAH: Miss Cat! The magistrate almost tossed me in the river because he thought I was thee.

CAT: Meow! (*You don't look a thing like me.*)

KIT: Where will you go, Hannah?

HANNAH: I don't know. Miss Cat, we have no home.

CAT: Meow! (*We'll live in the woods.*)

HANNAH: No, we *can't* live in the *woods.* (*Exiting.*) Come on, you silly feline, I'll show you Nat's fine new ship, and we'll discuss our future.

CAT: Meow! (*Stay on the ship.*)

HANNAH: Well, only if we're *invited* can we stay on the ship.

NAT: (*Surprised.*) Hannah? Do you want to sail with me?

CAT: Meow! (*Yes.*)

NAT: It's a hard life, but I suppose no harder than the one you've been leading.

HANNAH: We thank thee, Nat; we'd like that very much. (*Exiting.*) Come, Miss Cat. There's a mouse on board who can't wait to meet thee.

NAT: *Do you* forgive Judith?

KIT: I don't know if I can.

NAT: Why did you give her your dress?

KIT: So she can get a husband. If Judith has no marriage, she'll destroy Mercy's.

NAT: You have to forgive them, if you're going to live among them.

KIT: I can't *live among them.* Did you not see them? My poor Aunt Rachel? John? They still half believe I'm a witch.

NAT: Where will you live?

KIT: I'm going back. I'll sell my dresses for passage money.

NAT: There's nothing for you in Barbados anymore.

KIT: No, I want to go back. I left a mess back there.

NAT: What mess?

KIT: I'll convince the governor to let me take on Serena's bond so she can be free.

NAT: A *bond servant* has a hard life, Kit.

KIT: She should have a hard life instead of me?!

NAT: You could get married.

KIT: No! I'm not going to marry some rich old man just to avoid work.

NAT: I wasn't going to suggest you marry a rich old man. You should marry me.

KIT: Marry you? *(Laughs.)*

NAT: You won't have to pay for passage, so you can use the dress money to pay off this bond.

KIT: You can't ask me to marry you.

NAT: Why not?

KIT: Because—you didn't court me. And I won't be rushed!

NAT: Set sail with me on Friday, and I'll court you the whole way to Barbados.

KIT: With no female companion? This is not seemly.

NAT: My mother and Hannah should be seemly enough. Hannah will stand up for you when we marry in Barbados.

KIT: If I say yes.

NAT: When you say yes, yes, she will. Come on. Let me show you *The Witch of Blackbird Pond*.

KIT: Who?!

NAT: That's my ship.

KIT: Nat! Hannah's not a witch.

NAT: I know. I didn't name her for Hannah. *(Very sincere.)* I named her for you.

(As they exit, lights fade.)

KIT: For me? Then . . . why didn't you call her something like . . . *Kit? The Kit?*

NAT: She's my ship; I'll call her what I want.

KIT: Or *Katherine,* you could call her *The Katherine* . . . that's a wonderful name for a ship . . .

CURTAIN